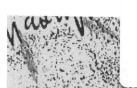

The Complete Works of Friedrich Nietzsche

EDITED BY ALAN D. SCHRIFT, DUNCAN LARGE,

AND ADRIAN DEL CARO

Friedrich Nietzsche

The Joyful Science

Idylls from Messina

Unpublished Fragments
from the Period of *The Joyful Science*
(Spring 1881–Summer 1882)

Translated, with an Afterword,
by Adrian Del Caro

STANFORD UNIVERSITY PRESS

STANFORD, CALIFORNIA

Stanford University Press
Stanford, California

Translated from Friedrich Nietzsche, *Sämtliche Werke: Kritische Studienausgabe*, ed. Giorgio Colli and Mazzino Montinari, in 15 vols. This book corresponds to Vol. 3, pp. 333–663, Vol. 9, pp. 441–687, and Vol. 14, pp. 229–77 and 644–59.

Critical edition of Friedrich Nietzsche's *Sämtliche Werke* and unpublished writings based on the original manuscripts.

"'Jokes, Cunning and Revenge': Prelude in German Rhymes" and "Appendix: Songs of Prince Vogelfrei" were originally published in Friedrich Nietzsche, *The Gay Science: With a Prelude in German Rhymes and an Appendix of Songs*, edited by Bernard Williams, © 2001 Cambridge University Press. Reproduced with permission of Cambridge University Press through PLSClear.

Printed in the United States of America on acid-free, archival-quality paper.

CIP data appears at the end of the book.

Contents

Unpublished Fragments
(Spring 1881–Summer 1882)

Reference Matter

A Note
on This Edition

This is the first English translation of all of Nietzsche's writings, including his unpublished fragments, with annotation, afterwords concerning the individual texts, and indexes, in nineteen volumes. The aim of this collaborative work is to produce a critical edition for scholarly use. Volume 1 also includes an introduction to the entire edition, and Volume 19 will include a detailed chronology of Nietzsche's life. While the goal is to establish a readable text in contemporary English, the translation follows the original as closely as possible. All texts have been translated anew by a group of scholars, and particular attention has been given to maintaining a consistent terminology throughout the volumes. The translation is based on *Friedrich Nietzsche: Sämtliche Werke. Kritische Studienausgabe in 15 Bänden* (1980), edited by Giorgio Colli and Mazzino Montinari. The still-progressing *Nietzsche Werke: Kritische Gesamtausgabe,* which Colli and Montinari began in 1963, has also been consulted. The Colli-Montinari edition is of particular importance for the unpublished fragments, comprising more than half of Nietzsche's writings and published there for the first time in their entirety. Besides listing textual variants, the annotation to this English edition provides succinct information on the text and identifies events, names (except those in the Index of Persons), titles, quotes, and biographical facts of Nietzsche's own life. The notes are numbered in the text and are keyed by phrase. The Afterword presents the main facts about the origin of the text, the stages of its composition, and the main events of its reception. The Index of Persons includes mythological figures and lists the dates of birth and death as well as prominent personal characteristics. Since the first three volumes appeared, important corrections to the 1980 edition of the *Kritische Studienausgabe* have been noted, and these corrections have been incorporated into the translation that appears here.

ERNST BEHLER AND ALAN D. SCHRIFT

The Joyful Science.
("la gaya scienza")

"To the poet and sage all things are friendly and sacred, all experiences useful, all days holy, all human beings divine."

Emerson[1]
[motto of the 1882 edition]

This house is my own and here I dwell,
I've never aped nothing from no one
And — laugh at each master, mark me well,
Who at himself has not poked fun.

Over the door to my house.
[motto of the 1887 edition]

Preface
to the Second Edition.[1]

I.

Perhaps this book needs more than only one preface; and ultimately the doubt would still remain whether anyone could be brought closer to the *experience* of this book through prefaces without having experienced something similar. It seems to be written in the language of the thaw wind: it contains exuberance, unrest, contradiction, April weather, so that one is constantly reminded as much of the proximity of winter as of the *triumph* over the winter that comes, must come, perhaps has already come . . . Gratitude pours out continuously, as if the most unexpected thing had just happened, the gratitude of a convalescent — for *convalescence* was this most unexpected thing. "Joyful science": this means the saturnalia of a spirit that has patiently resisted a terrible, long pressure — patiently, rigorously, coldly, without giving up, but without hope — and that now all at once is seized by hope, by hope for health, by the *drunkenness* of convalescence. Small wonder that in the process, much that is unreasonable and foolish comes to light, much willful tenderness wasted even on problems that have a prickly hide and are not accustomed to being fondled and lured.[2] This entire book is but nothing more than an amusement after long renunciation and impotence, the jubilation of returning strength, of the newly awakened belief in a tomorrow and a day after tomorrow, of the sudden sense and foretaste of a future, of adventures close at hand, of seas that are open again, of goals that are allowed again and avowed again. And what at this point did not lie behind me! This stretch of desert, exhaustion, unbelief, icing up in the middle of my youth, this dotage inserted in the wrong place, this tyranny of pain surpassed even by the tyranny of pride, which rejected the *conclusions* of pain — and consequences are consolations — this radical isolation as self-defense against a contempt for human beings that had become pathologically clairvoyant, this fundamental restriction to the bitter, sour, hurtful aspects of knowledge as they were prescribed by *nausea,* which had gradually arisen from a careless spiritual diet and overindulgence — it is called romanticism[3] — oh if only someone could feel this as I did! But anyone who could would surely pardon me for even more than a bit of foolishness, frolicking, "joyful science" — for instance the handful of songs added to the book this time — songs in which a poet pokes fun at all poets in a manner that is scarcely pardonable. — Oh, it is not only upon the poets and their beautiful "lyrical feelings" that this revenant must unleash his malice: who knows what kind of victim he seeks, what kind of monster of parodic material will soon charm him? "*Incipit tragoedia*"[4] — is what it says at the conclusion of this seriously unserious book: take heed! Something extraordinarily wicked and malicious is being announced: *incipit parodia,*[5] there is no doubt . . .

2.

— But let us leave Mr. Nietzsche: what does it concern us that Mr. Nietzsche regained his health? . . . A psychologist knows few questions as alluring as those dealing with the relationship between health and philosophy, and in the event that he himself becomes ill, he will bring along his entire scientific curiosity into his illness. For a person, assuming that one is a person, also necessarily has the philosophy of his person: but here there is a considerable difference. In one it is the flaws that philosophize, in the other it is the riches and the strengths. The former *needs* his philosophy, whether as support, sedative, medication, redemption, elevation, self-alienation; for the latter it is only a beautiful luxury, in the best case the voluptuousness of a triumphing gratitude that in the end has to inscribe itself into the heaven of concepts in cosmic majuscules. In other more ordinary cases, however, when the state of distress does philosophy, as in all sick thinkers — and perhaps the sick thinkers are preponderant in the history of philosophy — : what becomes of the thought itself that is brought forth under the *pressure* of illness? This is the question that concerns psychologists: and here an experiment is possible. Just like a traveler who resolves to wake up at a certain hour and then calmly entrusts himself to slumber, so too we philosophers, assuming that we become ill, temporarily surrender with body and soul to illness — we close our eyes to ourselves, as it were. And just as the traveler knows that something is *not* sleeping, something is counting the hours and will awaken him, so we also know that the decisive moment will find us awake — that something then will jump out and catch the mind *in the act,* I mean in its weakness or reversal or surrender or hardening or gloominess or whatever else all the pathological states of the mind are called, which in healthy days have the *pride* of the mind against them (for it is as the old rhyme says, "the proud mind, the peacock, and the horse are the three proudest animals on earth" —).[6] After a self-interrogation, self-temptation of this kind, one learns to look with a subtler eye at everything that has ever been philosophized; better than before, one guesses the involuntary detours, side streets, resting places, *sunny* places of thought to which suffering thinkers are led and misled[7] precisely as sufferers, one knows henceforth where the sick *body* and its neediness unconsciously press, push, lure the mind — toward sun, calm, mildness, patience, medication, refreshment in some sense. Every philosophy that places peace higher than war, every ethic with a negative version of the concept of happiness, every metaphysics and physics that knows a finale, a final state of any kind, every predominantly aesthetic

or religious longing for an apart, beyond, outside, above permits the question whether it was not illness that inspired the
philosopher. The unconscious cloaking of physiological needs
beneath the mantles of the objective, ideal, purely spiritual
goes horrifyingly far — and often enough I have asked myself
whether on the whole philosophy to date might only have
been an interpretation of the body and a *misunderstanding of
the body*. Behind the highest valuations by which the history
of thought has been guided to date, misunderstandings of
bodily constitution lie concealed, be it on the part of individuals or classes or entire races. One may always regard all
those bold inanities of metaphysics, especially its answers to
the question of the *value* of existence, chiefly as symptoms of
certain bodies; and even if such world-affirmations and world-
negations do not contain a grain of significance, measured scientifically and on the whole, still they give the historian and
psychologist all the more valuable tips as the aforementioned
symptoms of the body, of its successes and failures, its fullness,
might, self-glorification in history, or on the other hand its
inhibitions, exhaustions, impoverishments, its foretaste of the
end, its will to the end. I am still expecting that a philosophical
physician in the exceptional sense of the word — someone who
sees his task as investigating the problem of the overall health of
a people, a period, a race, humankind — will one day have the
courage to bring my suspicion to its conclusion and venture
the proposition: in all philosophizing to date it was not at all a
matter of "truth" but instead something else, let us say health,
future, growth, power, life . . .

3.[8]

— One surmises that it is not without gratitude that I wish
to take leave of that period of severe infirmity whose benefit I
have not exhausted even today: just as I am well enough aware
of what advantage I have from my on-and-off health over all
foursquare minds. A philosopher who has made the passage
through many healths and repeatedly does so has also gone

through just as many philosophies: he *can* simply not do otherwise than to translate his state each time into the most spiritual form and distance — this art of transfiguration simply *is* philosophy. We philosophers do not have the choice to distinguish between body and soul as the common people do, and even less do we have a choice to distinguish between soul and mind. We are no thinking frogs, no objectifying and registering devices with chilled bowels — we must constantly give birth to our thoughts from our pain and maternally provide them with everything we have in ourselves by way of[9] blood, heart, fire, desire, passion, agony, conscience, destiny, doom.[10] Living — for us that means constantly transforming everything that we are into light and flame, even everything that hurts us, we simply *cannot* do otherwise at all. And as concerns illness: are we not almost tempted to ask whether we could even dispense with it? Only great pain is the ultimate liberator of the spirit, as the schoolmaster of the *great suspicion* that makes an X out of every U,[11] a real proper X, that is, the penultimate letter before the final one . . . Only great pain, that long slow pain that takes its time, in which so to speak we are burned as if on green wood, compels us philosophers to descend into our ultimate depth and rid ourselves of all trust, all that is good-natured, cloaking, mild, mediating in which perhaps we had formerly placed our humanity. I doubt whether such pain "improves" us — ; but I know that it *deepens* us. Now whether it is because we learn to counter it with our pride, our scorn, our will power, as does the American Indian who repays his torturer with the malice of his tongue, no matter how badly he is tortured;[12] whether we withdraw from pain into that oriental nothing — we call it Nirvana — into that mute, rigid, deaf self-surrender, self-forgetting, self-extinguishing: one emerges from such long dangerous exercises of mastery over oneself as a different human being, with a few more question marks, above all with the *will* henceforth to question more, more deeply, more rigorously, more harshly, more evilly and more quietly than one had questioned before. The trust in life is gone: life

itself became a *problem.* — But we should not believe for a
second that this necessarily turns one into a gloom monger!
Even the love for life is still possible — only one loves differently. It is the love for a woman who makes us have doubts . . .
But the lure of everything problematic, the joy of X in such
more spiritual, more spiritualized human beings is too great
for this joy not to smolder again and again like a bright ember
over all the adversity of the problematic, over all danger of
uncertainty, even over the jealousy of the lover. We know a
new happiness . . .

4.

Finally, to ensure that the most essential point does not go
unsaid:[13] one returns from such abysses, from such severe infirmity, even from the infirmity of severe suspicion *newborn,* having shed one's skin, more ticklish, more malicious, with a more
refined taste for joy, with a tenderer tongue for all good things,
with keener senses, with a second more dangerous innocence
in joy, simultaneously more childlike and a hundred times
more cunning than one had ever been. Oh how repulsed one
is now by pleasure, crude, dull, brown pleasure as it is otherwise understood by our pleasure seekers, our "educated," our
rich and rulers! How maliciously we now listen to the great
fairground boom-boom with which the "educated person" and
metropolitan let themselves be raped nowadays by art, books
and music for "spiritual pleasures," with the aid of alcoholic
spirits! How the theater-cry of passion now hurts in our ears,
how foreign to our taste has become the whole romantic uproar
and sensual confusion loved by the educated rabble, along with
its aspirations for the sublime, elevated, deviated![14] No, if we
convalescents still need an art at all, then it is a *different* art — a
mocking, light, fleeting, divinely undisturbed, divinely artificial
art that blazes like a bright flame into a cloudless sky! Above all:
an art for artists, for artists only! In retrospect we have a better
understanding of what is chiefly necessary *for this,* cheerfulness,
any cheerfulness, my friends! also as artists — : I would like to

prove it. We know some things too well, we knowers: oh how from now on we are learning to forget well, to *not* know well, as artists! And as concerns our future: one will scarcely find us again on the paths of those Egyptian youths who make temples unsafe at night, embrace statues and want to unveil, uncover, shed bright light on absolutely everything that with good reason should remain concealed.[15] No, this bad taste, this will to truth, to "truth at any cost," this youth's insanity in the love for truth — are spoiled for us: for this we are too experienced, too earnest, too fun-loving, too burned, too deep . . . We no longer believe that truth still remains truth after one has lifted her veil; we've lived too much to believe this. Today we regard it as a matter of decency that one would not want to see everything naked, be present for everything, understand and "know" everything. "Is it true that dear God is present everywhere?" a little girl asked her mother: "but I find that indecent" — a hint for philosophers! One should better honor the *modesty* with which nature has hidden herself behind riddles and colorful uncertainties. Perhaps truth is a woman who has grounds for not letting her grounds be seen?[16] Perhaps her name, to speak Greek, is Baubo?[17] . . . Oh these Greeks! They knew how to *live:* this requires stopping bravely at the surface, the fold, the skin, worshipping appearance, believing in forms, tones, words, in the entire Olympus of appearance![18] These Greeks were superficial — *out of profundity*! And are we not just now coming back to this, we daredevils of the spirit, we who have climbed the highest and most dangerous peak of present-day thought and have looked around from up there, we who have *looked down* from up there? Are we not in this point precisely — Greeks? Worshippers of forms, tones, words? And therefore — artists?

Ruta, near Genoa
in autumn[19] 1886.

"Jokes, Cunning and Revenge":[1]
Prelude in German Rhymes.

1. *Einladung.*
Wagt's mit meiner Kost, ihr Esser!
Morgen schmeckt sie euch schon besser
Und schon übermorgen gut!
Wollt ihr dann noch mehr, — so machen
Meine alten sieben Sachen
Mir zu sieben neuen Muth.

2. *Mein Glück.*
Seit ich des Suchens müde ward,
Erlernte ich das Finden.
Seit mir ein Wind hielt Widerpart,
Segl' ich mit allen Winden.

3. *Unverzagt.*
Wo du stehst, grab tief hinein!
Drunten ist die Quelle!
Lass die dunklen Männer schrein:
"Stets ist drunten — Hölle!"

4. *Zwiegespräch.*
A. War ich krank? Bin ich genesen?
   Und wer ist mein Arzt gewesen?
   Wie vergass ich alles Das!

1. *Invitation*[2]

Dare to taste my fare, dear diner!
Come tomorrow it tastes finer
And day after even good!
If you still want more — I'll make it,
From past inspiration take it,
Turning food for thought to food.

2. *My Happiness*

Since I grew weary of the search
I taught myself to find instead
Since cross winds caused my ship to lurch
I sail with all winds straight ahead.

3. *Undaunted*[3]

Where you stand, there dig deep!
Below you lies the well!
Let obscurantists[4] wail and weep:
"Below is always — hell!"

4. *Dialogue*[5]

A. Was I ill? Have I recovered?
   Has my doctor been discovered?
   How have I forgotten all?

B. Jetzt erst glaub ich dich genesen:
   Denn gesund ist, wer vergass.

5. *An die Tugendsamen.*

Unseren Tugenden auch soll'n leicht die Füsse sich heben:
Gleich den Versen Homer's müssen sie kommen *und gehn*!

6. *Welt-Klugheit.*

Bleib nicht auf ebnem Feld!
Steig nicht zu hoch hinaus!
Am schönsten sieht die Welt
Von halber Höhe aus.

7. *Vademecum — Vadetecum.*

Es lockt dich meine Art und Sprach,
Du folgest mir, du gehst mir nach?
Geh nur dir selber treulich nach: —
So folgst du mir — gemach! gemach!

8. *Bei der dritten Häutung.*

Schon krümmt und bricht sich mir die Haut,
Schon giert mit neuem Drange,
So viel sie Erde schon verdaut,
Nach Erd' in mir die Schlange.
Schon kriech' ich zwischen Stein und Gras
Hungrig auf krummer Fährte,
Zu essen Das, was stets ich ass,
Dich, Schlangenkost, dich, Erde!

9. *Meine Rosen.*

Ja! Mein Glück — es will beglücken — ,
Alles Glück will ja beglücken!
Wollt ihr meine Rosen pflücken?

B. Now I know you have recovered:
    Healthy is who can't recall.

5. *To the Virtuous*[6]
Our virtues too should step lively to and fro:
Like the verses of Homer, they have to come *and go*!

6. *Worldly Wisdom*[7,8]
Stay not where the lowlands are!
Climb not into the sky!
The world looks best by far
When viewed from halfway high.

7. *Vademecum — Vadetecum*[9,10]
My way and language speak to you,
You follow me, pursue me too?
To thine own self and way be true:
Thus follow me, but gently do!

8. *On the Third Shedding*[11]
Already cracks and breaks my skin,
My appetite unslaking
Is fueled by earth I've taken in:
This snake for earth is aching.
Among the stones and grass I wear
A path from fen to firth,
To eat what's[12] always been my fare
You, my snake food, you my earth.

9. *My Roses*
Yes! My joy — it wants to gladden —
Every joy wants so to gladden!
Would you pluck my rose and sadden?

Müsst euch bücken und verstecken
Zwischen Fels und Dornenhecken,
Oft die Fingerchen euch lecken!

Denn mein Glück — es liebt das Necken!
Denn mein Glück — es liebt die Tücken! —
Wollt ihr meine Rosen pflücken?

10. *Der Verächter.*

Vieles lass ich fall'n und rollen,
Und ihr nennt mich drum Verächter.
Wer da trinkt aus allzuvollen
Bechern, lässt viel fall'n und rollen — ,
Denkt vom Weine drum nicht schlechter.

11. *Das Sprüchwort spricht.*

Scharf und milde, grob und fein,
Vertraut und seltsam, schmutzig und rein,
Der Narren und Weisen Stelldichein:
Diess Alles bin ich, will ich sein,
Taube zugleich, Schlange und Schwein!

12. *An einen Lichtfreund.*

Willst du nicht Aug' und Sinn ermatten,
Lauf' auch der Sonne nach im Schatten!

13. *Für Tänzer.*

Glattes Eis
Ein Paradeis
Für Den, der gut zu tanzen weiss.

14. *Der Brave.*

Lieber aus ganzem Holz eine Feindschaft,
Als eine geleimte Freundschaft!

You must crouch on narrow ledges,
Prop yourself on ropes and wedges,
Prick yourself on thorny hedges!

For my joy — it loves to madden!
For my joy — is malice laden!
Would you pluck my rose and sadden?

10. *The Scornful One*

Much do I let fall and spill,
Thus I'm scornful, you malign.
One who drinks from cups too full will
Often let much fall and spill —
Yet never think to blame the wine.

11. *The Proverb Speaks*[13]

Sharp and mild, dull and keen,
Well known and strange, dirty and clean,
Where both the fool and wise are seen:
All this am I, have ever been —
In me dove, snake and swine convene!

12. *To a Friend of Light*[14,15]

If you want to spare your eyes and your mind,
Follow the sun from the shadows behind!

13. *For Dancers*[16]

Slipp'ry ice
Is paradise
As long as dancing will suffice.

14. *The Good Man*[17,18]

Better an enmity cut from one block
Than friendship held together by glue!

15. *Rost.*

Auch Rost thut Noth: Scharfsein ist nicht genung!
Sonst sagt man stets von dir: "er ist zu jung!"

16. *Aufwärts.*

"Wie komm ich am besten den Berg hinan?"
Steig nur hinauf und denk nicht dran!

17. *Spruch des Gewaltmenschen.*

Bitte nie! Lass diess Gewimmer!
Nimm, ich bitte dich, nimm immer!

18. *Schmale Seelen.*

Schmale Seelen sind mir verhasst;
Da steht nichts Gutes, nichts Böses fast.

19. *Der unfreiwillige Verführer.*

Er schoss ein leeres Wort zum Zeitvertreib
In's Blaue — und doch fiel darob ein Weib.

20. *Zur Erwägung.*

Zwiefacher Schmerz ist leichter zu tragen,
Als Ein Schmerz: willst du darauf es wagen?

21. *Gegen die Hoffahrt.*

Blas dich nicht auf: sonst bringet dich
Zum Platzen schon ein kleiner Stich.

22. *Mann und Weib.*

"Raub dir das Weib, für das dein Herze fühlt!" —
So denkt der Mann; das Weib raubt nicht, es stiehlt.

23. *Interpretation.*

Leg ich mich aus, so leg ich mich hinein:
Ich kann nicht selbst mein Interprete sein.
Doch wer nur steigt auf seiner eignen Bahn,
Trägt auch mein Bild zu hellerm Licht hinan.

15. *Rust*[19]

Rust must be added: sharpness goes unsung!
Else they will always say: "he is too young!"

16. *Upward*[20]

"How do I best get to the top of this hill?"
Climb it, don't think it, and maybe you will!

17. *Motto of a Brute*[21,22]

Never beg! It's whining I dread!
Take, I beg you, just take instead!

18. *Narrow Souls*[23]

It's narrow souls that I despise;
Not good, not evil, not my size.

19. *The Involuntary Seducer*

He shot an empty word into the blue
To pass the time — and downed a woman too.

20. *Consider This*[24,25]

A twofold pain is easier to bear
Than one pain: care to take a dare?

21. *Against Arrogance*

Don't let your ego swell too much,
A bubble bursts with just a touch.

22. *Man and Woman*[26]

"Rob yourself the woman, who to your heart appeals" —
So thinks a man; the woman does not rob, she steals.

23. *Interpretation*[27]

If I read me, then I read into me:
I can't construe myself objectively.
But he who climbs consuming his own might
Bears me with him unto the bright light.

24. *Pessimisten-Arznei.*

Du klagst, dass Nichts dir schmackhaft sei?
Noch immer, Freund, die alten Mucken?
Ich hör dich lästern, lärmen, spucken —
Geduld und Herz bricht mir dabei.
Folg mir, mein Freund! Entschliess dich frei,
Ein fettes Krötchen zu verschlucken,
Geschwind und ohne hinzugucken! —
Das hilft dir von der Dyspepsei!

25. *Bitte.*

Ich kenne mancher Menschen Sinn
Und weiss nicht, wer ich selber bin!
Mein Auge ist mir viel zu nah —
Ich bin nicht, was ich seh und sah.
Ich wollte mir schon besser nützen,
Könnt' ich mir selber ferner sitzen.
Zwar nicht so ferne wie mein Feind!
Zu fern sitzt schon der nächste Freund —
Doch zwischen dem und mir die Mitte!
Errathet ihr, um was ich bitte?

26. *Meine Härte.*

Ich muss weg über hundert Stufen,
Ich muss empor und hör euch rufen:
"Hart bist du; Sind wir denn von Stein?" —
Ich muss weg über hundert Stufen,
Und Niemand möchte Stufe sein.

27. *Der Wandrer.*

"Kein Pfad mehr! Abgrund rings und Todtenstille!" —
So wolltest du's! Vom Pfade wich dein Wille!
Nun, Wandrer, gilt's! Nun blicke kalt und klar!
Verloren bist du, glaubst du — an Gefahr.

24. *Medication for Pessimists*[28,29]

You whine that nothing pleases you?
Still pouting, friend, and must you mutter?
I hear you curse, and shout and sputter —
It breaks my heart and patience too.
Come[30] with me, friend! A nice fat toad,
If swallowed voluntarily
With eyes closed and summarily —
Might lessen your dyspeptic load.

25. *Request*

I know another person's thought
And who I am, I know that not.
My vision is too close to me —
I am not what I saw and see.
I'd help myself more perfectly
If I could move away from me.
Yet not so distant as my foe!
My closest friend's too far off, no —
Give me instead the middle ground!
Do you surmise what I propound?

26. *My Hardness*[31]

I must leave by a hundred stairs,
I must ascend though I hear your cares:
"You are hard: Are we made of stone?"
I must leave by a hundred stairs,
And being a stair appeals to none.

27. *The Wanderer*[32]

"The path ends! Abyss and deathly silence loom!"
You wanted this! Your will strayed to its doom!
Now wanderer, stand! Be keen and cool as frost!
Believe in danger now and you — are lost.

28. *Trost für Anfänger.*

Seht das Kind umgrunzt von Schweinen,
Hülflos, mit verkrümmten Zeh'n!
Weinen kann es, Nichts als weinen —
Lernt es jemals stehn und gehn?
Unverzagt! Bald, sollt' ich meinen,
Könnt das Kind ihr tanzen sehn!
Steht es erst auf beiden Beinen,
Wird's auch auf dem Kopfe stehn.

29. *Sternen-Egoismus.*

Rollt' ich mich rundes Rollefass
Nicht um mich selbst ohn' Unterlass,
Wie hielt' ich's aus, ohne anzubrennen,
Der heissen Sonne nachzurennen?

30. *Der Nächste.*

Nah hab den Nächsten ich nicht gerne:
Fort mit ihm in die Höh und Ferne!
Wie würd' er sonst zu meinem Sterne? —

31. *Der verkappte Heilige.*

Dass dein Glück uns nicht bedrücke,
Legst du um dich Teufelstücke,
Teufelswitz und Teufelskleid.
Doch umsonst! Aus deinem Blicke
Blickt hervor die Heiligkeit!

32. *Der Unfreie.*

A. Er steht und horcht: was konnt ihn irren?
   Was hört er vor den Ohren schwirren?
   Was war's, das ihn darniederschlug?
B. Wie Jeder, der einst Ketten trug,
   Hört überall er — Kettenklirren.

28. *Consolation for Beginners*[33]

See the child, with pigs she's lying,
Helpless, face as white as chalk!
Crying only, only crying —
Will she ever learn to walk?
Don't give up! Stop your sighing,
Soon she's dancing 'round the clock!
Once her own two legs are trying,
She'll stand on her head and mock!

29. *Stellar Egoism*[34]

If I, round barrel that I am,
Did not roll 'round me like a cam,
How could I bear, and not catch fire,
To chase the sun as I desire.

30. *The Closest One*

The closest one from me I bar:
Away and up with him, and far!
How else could he become my star?

31. *The Disguised Saint*

Joy too great you are concealing,[35]
You engage in dev'lish dealing,
Devil's wit and devil's dress.[36]
But no use! Your eye's revealing
Piety and holiness!

32. *The Bound Man*[37]

A. He stands and hears: what's wrong, he's thinking?
  What sound provokes his heart to sinking?
  What was it hurled him to the ground?
B. Like all who once in chains were bound,
  He hears around him — iron clinking.

33. *Der Einsame.*

Verhasst ist mir das Folgen und das Führen.
Gehorchen? Nein! Und aber nein — Regieren!
Wer *sich* nicht schrecklich ist, macht Niemand Schrecken:
Und nur wer Schrecken macht, kann Andre führen.
Verhasst ist mir's schon, selber mich zu führen!
Ich liebe es, gleich Wald- und Meeresthieren,
Mich für ein gutes Weilchen zu verlieren,
In holder Irrniss grüblerisch zu hocken,
Von ferne her mich endlich heimzulocken,
Mich selber zu mir selber — zu verführen.

34. *Seneca et hoc genus omne.*

Das schreibt und schreibt sein unaussteh-
lich weises Larifari,
Als gält es primum scribere,
Deinde philosophari.

35. *Eis.*

Ja! Mitunter mach' ich Eis:
Nützlich ist Eis zum Verdauen!
Hättet ihr viel zu verdauen,
Oh wie liebtet ihr mein Eis!

36. *Jugendschriften.*

Meiner Weisheit A und O
Klang mir hier: was hört' ich doch!
Jetzo klingt mir's nicht mehr so,
Nur das ew'ge Ah! und Oh!
Meiner Jugend hör ich noch.

37. *Vorsicht.*

In jener Gegend reist man jetzt nicht gut;
Und hast du Geist, sei doppelt auf der Hut!
Man lockt und liebt dich, bis man dich zerreisst:
Schwarmgeister sind's — : da fehlt es stets an Geist!

33. *The Solitary One*[38]

Despised by me are following and leading.
Commanding? Even worse to me than heeding!
Who does not scare *himself* can frighten no one:
The one who causes fear can lead another.
But just to lead myself is too much bother!
I love, as do the sea and forest creatures,
To lose myself a while[39] in nature's features,
To hide away and brood in[40] secret places
Until, lured home at last from distant traces,
My self-seduction lets me see — my features.[41]

34. *Seneca et hoc genus omne*[42,43]

They write and write their desiccat-
ing learned la-di-da-di,
as if *primum scribere,
deinde philosophari.*[44]

35. *Ice*

Yes! At times I do make ice:
Useful is ice for digesting!
If you had much for digesting,
Oh how you would love my ice!

36. *Juvenilia*[45]

My old wisdom's A and O[46]
Sounded here: what did I hear?
Now it does not strike me so,
Just the tired Ah! and Oh!
That youth inspired fills my ear.

37. *Caution*

Into that region trav'lers must not go;
And if you're smart, be cautious even so!
They lure and love you till you're torn apart:
They're half-wit zealots — : witless from the heart!

38. *Der Fromme spricht.*

Gott liebt uns, *weil* er uns erschuf! —
"Der Mensch schuf Gott!" — sagt drauf ihr Feinen.
Und soll nicht lieben, was er schuf?
Soll's gar, *weil* er es schuf, verneinen?
Das hinkt, das trägt des Teufels Huf.

39. *Im Sommer.*

Im Schweisse unsres Angesichts
Soll'n unser Brod wir essen?
Im Schweisse isst man lieber Nichts,
Nach weiser Aerzte Ermessen.
Der Hundsstern winkt: woran gebricht's?
Was will sein feurig Winken?
Im Schweisse unsres Angesichts
Soll'n unsren Wein wir trinken!

40. *Ohne Neid.*

Ja, neidlos blickt er: und ihr ehrt ihn drum?
Er blickt sich nicht nach euren Ehren um;
Er hat des Adlers Auge für die Ferne,
Er sieht euch nicht! — er sieht nur Sterne, Sterne.

41. *Heraklitismus.*

Alles Glück auf Erden,
Freunde, giebt der Kampf!
Ja, um Freund zu werden,
Braucht es Pulverdampf!
Eins in Drei'n sind Freunde:
Brüder vor der Noth,
Gleiche vor dem Feinde,
Freie — vor dem Tod!

42. *Grundsatz der Allzufeinen.*

Lieber auf den Zehen noch,
Als auf allen Vieren!

38. *The Pious One Speaks*[47]

God loves us *because* he created us! —
"Man created God!" — respond the jaded.
And yet should not love what he created?
Should even deny it *because* he made it?
Such cloven logic is limping and baited.

39. *In Summer*[48]

Beneath the sweat of our brow
We have to eat our bread?[49]
If you sweat, eat nothing now,
The wise physician said.
The dog star winks: what does it know?
What says its fiery winking?
Beneath the sweat of our own brow
Our wine we should be drinking!

40. *Without Envy*

His gaze is envyless: and him you praise?
No thirst for your esteem perturbs his gaze;
He has the eagle's vision for the long view,
It's stars he sees, just stars — he looks beyond you!

41. *Heracliteanism*[50]

Happiness on earth, friends,
Only stems from war!
Powder smoke, in fact, mends
Friendship even more!
One in three all friends are:
Brothers in distress,
Equals facing rivals,
Free men — facing death!

42. *Principle of the All Too Refined*[51]

Rather on your tiptoes stand
Than crawling on all fours!

Lieber durch ein Schlüsselloch,
Als durch offne Thüren!

43. *Zuspruch.*

Auf Ruhm hast du den Sinn gericht?
Dann acht' der Lehre:
Bei Zeiten leiste frei Verzicht
Auf Ehre!

44. *Der Gründliche.*

Ein Forscher ich? Oh spart diess Wort! —
Ich bin nur *schwer* — so manche Pfund'!
Ich falle, falle immerfort
Und endlich auf den Grund!

45. *Für immer.*

"Heut komm' ich, weil mir's heute frommt" —
Denkt Jeder, der für immer kommt.
Was ficht ihn an der Welt Gered':
"Du kommst zu früh! Du kommst zu spät!"

46. *Urtheile der Müden.*

Der Sonne fluchen alle Matten;
Der Bäume Werth ist ihnen — Schatten!

47. *Niedergang.*

"Er sinkt, er fällt jetzt" — höhnt ihr hin und wieder;
Die Wahrheit ist: er steigt zu euch hernieder!

Sein Ueberglück ward ihm zum Ungemach,
Sein Ueberlicht geht eurem Dunkel nach.

48. *Gegen die Gesetze.*

Von heut an hängt an härner Schnur
Um meinen Hals die Stunden-Uhr:
Von heut an hört der Sterne Lauf,

Rather through the keyhole scanned
Than gazed through open doors!

43. *Admonition*[52]
It's fame on which your mind is set?
Then heed what I say:
Before too long prepare to let
Honor slip away.

44. *The Well-Grounded One*[53,54]
A scholar I? I've no such skill! —
I'm merely *grave* — just heavy set!
I fall and fall and fall until
I to the bottom get.

45. *Forever*[55]
"Today I come, I choose today" —
Think all who come and mean to stay.
Though all the world may speculate:
"You come too early! Come too late!"

46. *Judgments of the Weary*[56]
The sun is cursed by all men jaded;
To them the worth of trees is — shaded!

47. *Going Down*[57,58]
"He sinks, he falls now" — thus resumes your mocking;
In truth, look closely: Down to you he's walking![59]

His superjoy became too much to bear,
His superlight dispels your gloomy air.[60]

48. *Against the Laws*[61]
From now on time hangs by a hair
Around my neck, suspended there:
From now on stars shine randomly,

Sonn', Hahnenschrei und Schatten auf,
Und was mir je die Zeit verkünd't,
Das ist jetzt stumm und taub und blind: —
Es schweigt mir jegliche Natur
Beim Tiktak von Gesetz und Uhr.

49. *Der Weise spricht.*

Dem Volke fremd und nützlich doch dem Volke,
Zieh ich des Weges, Sonne bald, bald Wolke —
Und immer über diesem Volke!

50. *Den Kopf verloren.*

Sie hat jetzt Geist — wie kam's, dass sie ihn fand?
Ein Mann verlor durch sie jüngst den Verstand,
Sein Kopf war reich vor diesem Zeitvertreibe:
Zum Teufel gieng sein Kopf — nein! nein! zum Weibe!

51. *Fromme Wünsche.*

"Mögen alle Schlüssel doch
Flugs verloren gehen,
Und in jedem Schlüsselloch
Sich der Dietrich drehen!"
Also denkt zu jeder Frist
Jeder, der — ein Dietrich ist.

52. *Mit dem Fusse schreiben.*

Ich schreib nicht mit der Hand allein:
Der Fuss will stets mit Schreiber sein.
Fest, frei und tapfer läuft er mir
Bald durch das Feld, bald durchs Papier.

53. „*Menschliches, Allzumenschliches.*"
Ein Buch.

Schwermüthig scheu, solang du rückwärts schaust,
Der Zukunft trauend, wo du selbst dir traust:
Oh Vogel, rechn' ich dich den Adlern zu?
Bist du Minerva's Liebling U-hu-hu?

Sun, rooster crow, and shadow flee,
Whatever brought time to my mind
That now is mute and deaf and blind: —
All nature's still in me, it balks
At ticking laws and ticking clocks.

49. *The Wise Man Speaks*[62]
Unknown to folks, yet useful to the crowd,
I drift along my way, now sun, now cloud
And always I'm above this crowd!

50. *Lost His Head*[63]
Now she has wit — what led her to this find?
Because of her a man had lost his mind.
His head was rich before this misadventure:
His head went straight to hell — no! no! to her!

51. *Pious Wishes*[64]
"Keys should all just disappear,
Lost from stem to stern,
And in keyholes far and near
Skeletons[65] should turn!"
Thus thinks when the day is done
Each who is — a skeleton.

52. *Writing with One's Foot*[66]
I do not write with hand alone:
My foot does writing of its own.
Firm, free, and bold my feet engage
In running over field and page.

53. *"Human, All Too Human"*
A Book[67]
When looking back you're sad and not robust,
You trust the future when yourself you trust:
Oh bird, do you belong to eagle's brood?
Are you Minerva's[68] favorite hoot hoot?[69]

54. *Meinem Leser.*

Ein gut Gebiss und einen guten Magen —
Diess wünsch' ich dir!
Und hast du erst mein Buch vertragen,
Verträgst du dich gewiss mit mir!

55. *Der realistische Maler.*

"Treu die Natur und ganz!" — Wie fängt er's an:
Wann wäre je Natur im Bilde *abgethan?*
Unendlich ist das kleinste Stück der Welt! —
Er malt zuletzt davon, was ihm *gefällt.*
Und was gefällt ihm? Was er malen *kann!*

56. *Dichter-Eitelkeit.*

Gebt mir Leim nur: denn zum Leime
Find' ich selber mir schon Holz!
Sinn in vier unsinn'ge Reime
Legen — ist kein kleiner Stolz!

57. *Wählerischer Geschmack.*

Wenn man frei mich wählen liesse,
Wählt' ich gern ein Plätzchen mir
Mitten drin im Paradiese:
Gerner noch — vor seiner Thür!

58. *Die krumme Nase.*

Die Nase schauet trutziglich
In's Land, der Nüster blähet sich —
Drum fällst du, Nashorn ohne Horn,
Mein stolzes Menschlein, stets nach vorn!
Und stets beisammen find't sich das:
Gerader Stolz, gekrümmte Nas.

59. *Die Feder kritzelt.*

Die Feder kritzelt: Hölle das!
Bin ich verdammt zum Kritzeln-Müssen? —

54. *To My Reader*[70,71]

Strong teeth and good digestion too —
This I wish thee!
And once my book's agreed with you,
Then surely you'll agree with me!

55. *The Realistic Painter*[72]

"To all of nature true!" — How does he plan?
Would nature fit an image *made by man*?
The smallest piece of world is infinite! —
He ends up painting that which he *sees fit*.
And what does he see fit? Paint what he *can*!

56. *Poet's Vanity*

I'll find wood, just give me substance
Strong enough to bind like glue!
Cramming sense in rhyme is nonsense
Worthy of a boast — or two![73]

57. *Choosy Taste*[74]

Were it my choice to exercise,
I know that I would opt for
A cozy place in Paradise:
Better still — outside the door!

58. *The Crooked Nose*[75]

Your nose projects, so grand and plump,
Into the land, its nostrils pump —
Thus hornless rhino,[76] lacking grace
You fall, proud mortal, on your face!
And that's the way it always goes:
Straight pride alongside crooked nose.

59. *The Pen Scribbles*[77]

My pen, it scribbles: this is hell!
Have I been damned to have to scribble? —

So greif' ich kühn zum Tintenfass
Und schreib' mit dicken Tintenflüssen.
Wie läuft das hin, so voll, so breit!
Wie glückt mir Alles, wie ich's treibe!
Zwar fehlt der Schrift die Deutlichkeit —
Was thut's? Wer liest denn, was ich schreibe?

60. *Höhere Menschen.*

Der steigt empor — ihn soll man loben!
Doch Jener kommt allzeit von Oben!
Der lebt dem Lobe selbst enthoben,
Der *ist* von Droben!

61. *Der Skeptiker spricht.*

Halb ist dein Leben um,
Der Zeiger rückt, die Seele schaudert dir!
Lang schweift sie schon herum
Und sucht und fand nicht — und sie zaudert hier?
Halb ist dein Leben um:
Schmerz war's und Irrthum, Stund' um Stund' dahier!
Was suchst du noch? *Warum?* — —
Diess eben such' ich — Grund um Grund dafür!

62. *Ecce homo.*

Ja! Ich weiss, woher ich stamme!
Ungesättigt gleich der Flamme
Glühe und verzehr' ich mich.
Licht wird Alles, was ich fasse,
Kohle Alles, was ich lasse:
Flamme bin ich sicherlich.

63. *Sternen-Moral.*

Vorausbestimmt zur Sternenbahn,
Was geht dich, Stern, das Dunkel an?

I dip it boldly in the well
And write broad streams of inky drivel.
See how it flows, so full, so pure!
See how each thing I try succeeds!
The text's not lucid, to be sure —
So what? What I write no one reads.

60. *Superior Humans*[78]

He climbs on high — him we should praise!
But that one comes from high up always!
Immune to praise he lives his days,
He *is* the sun's rays!

61. *The Skeptic Speaks*[79,80]

Your life is halfway spent,
The clock hand moves, your soul quakes with fear!
Long roaming forth it went
And searched but nothing found — and wavers here?
Your life is halfway spent:
In pain and error how the hours did crawl!
Why can you not relent? —
Just this I seek — some reason for it all!

62. *Ecce Homo*[81]

Yes! I know now whence I came!
Unsatiated like a flame
My glowing ember squanders me.
Light to all on which I seize,
Ashen everything I leave:
Flame am I most certainly!

63. *Stellar Morality*

Ordained to move as planets do,
What matters, star, the dark to you?

Roll' selig hin durch diese Zeit!
Ihr Elend sei dir fremd und weit!

Der fernsten Welt gehört dein Schein:
Mitleid soll Sünde für dich sein!

Nur Ein Gebot gilt dir: sei rein!

Roll blithely through our human time!
Beyond its wretched mis'ry climb!

The furthest world deserves[82] your shine:
For you compassion is a crime!

One law applies to you: be thine!

Book One

The teachers of the purpose of existence. — Now whether I look at people with a kind eye or an evil eye, I always find them involved in a single task, all of them and each individual in particular: To do what promotes the preservation of the human species.[2] And to be sure not out of a feeling of love for this species, but simply because nothing in them is older, stronger, more inexorable, more unconquerable than that instinct — because this instinct is simply *the essence* of our species[3] and herd. While one tends quickly enough, with the usual myopia at five paces, to neatly separate one's neighbors into useful and harmful, good and evil, in a large-scale calculation and upon longer reflection of the whole, one becomes suspicious of this neatness and separation and ultimately lets it go. Even the most harmful human being is perhaps still the most useful with respect to the preservation of the species; for in himself or through his effect on others he maintains drives without which humankind would have long ago fatigued or rotted. Hatred, schadenfreude, the lust to rob and rule and whatever else is called evil: it belongs to the amazing economy of species preservation, on the whole a most foolish, wasteful and costly economy, to be sure: — but which *has proven* to have preserved our race thus far. I no longer know whether you, my dear fellow human being and neighbor, *can* even live to the detriment of the species, in other words[4] "unreasonably" and "badly"; that which could have harmed the species perhaps became extinct

already many millennia ago and⁵ now belongs among the
things that are no longer possible even in God. Indulge your
best or your worst desires and above all: perish! — in both cases
you are probably still somehow the promoter and benefactor
of humankind and are therefore allowed to have your eulogists
— and likewise your mockers! But you will never find anyone
who knows entirely how to mock you, the individual, even
at your best; who could sufficiently bring home to you your
boundless fly- and frog-wretchedness, as truth would demand!
To laugh at oneself as one must laugh in order to laugh *from
out of the whole truth* — for this even the best so far did not
have enough sense of truth and the most talented had far too
little genius! Perhaps even laughter still has a future! — namely
when the proposition "the species is everything, one is always
none" has been incorporated by humankind and everyone has
open access at any time to this ultimate liberation and irrespon-
sibility. Perhaps then laughter will have united with wisdom,
perhaps then there will henceforth be only "joyful science."
For the time being things are still quite different, for the time
being the comedy of existence has not yet "become aware" of
itself, for the time being it is still the age of tragedy, the age
of moralities and religions. What is the meaning of the ever
newly emerging founders of moralities and religions, those authors
of the struggle for ethical valuations, those teachers of the stings of
conscience and the wars of religion? What do these heroes mean
on this stage? For up till now they have been the heroes of all
this, and everything else that at times was visible and all too
near only served as preparation for these heroes, whether as
machinery and coulisse or in the role of confidants and valets.
(The poets for instance were always the valets of some morality.) — It is self-evident that these tragedians also work in
the interest of the *species,* even if they like to believe they are
working in the interest of God and as God's emissaries. They
too promote the life of the species *in that they promote faith in
life.* "It is worth it to live" — thus cries each one of them —
"there is something to this life, life has something behind it,

beneath it, beware!" That drive that reigns equally in the highest and crudest human beings, the drive of species preservation, breaks forth from time to time as reason and passion of the spirit; it then has a brilliant retinue of grounds around it and wants with all its might to make us forget that in its ground it is drive, instinct, folly, groundlessness. Life *shall* be loved, *for*! A human being *shall* promote himself and his neighbor, *for*! And so on with whatever all these Shalls and Fors are called and might be called in the future! In order for that which happens necessarily and always, on its own and without any purpose, to appear from now on as if done for a purpose that occurs to us humans as reason and ultimate commandment — enter the ethical teacher as the teacher of the purpose of existence; for this he invents a second, different existence and by means of his new mechanism he lifts this old ordinary existence off its old ordinary hinges. Indeed, he by no means wants us to *laugh* about existence, nor about ourselves — nor about him; for him One is always One, something first and final and monstrous; for him there is no species, no sums, no zeros. However foolish and fanatical his inventions and valuations may be, however much he misjudges the course of nature and denies its conditions: — and all ethical systems from time immemorial have been foolish and antinatural to the degree that humanity would have perished from any of them had they gained power over humanity — nonetheless: each time "the hero" stepped onto the stage something new was achieved, the horrific counterpart of laughter, that deep convulsion of many individuals at the thought: "yes, it is worthwhile to live! yes, I am worthy of living!" — life and I and you and all of us again became *interesting* to ourselves for a time. — It cannot be denied that laughter and nature and reason triumphed *in the long run* over every single one of these great teachers of purpose to date: the brief tragedy in the end always faded back into the eternal comedy of existence, and the "waves of uncountable laughter"[6] — as Aeschylus says — must ultimately crash over even the greatest of these tragedians. But even with all this corrective laughter, human nature on the whole has really been changed by this ever-new appearance of those teachers of the purpose of existence — now it has one more need, namely the need for the ever-new appearance of such teachers and teachings of "purpose." The human being has gradually become a fantastic animal that has one more condition of existence to fulfill than every other animal: the human being *must* believe from time to time that it knows *why* it exists, its[7] species cannot thrive without a periodic trust in life! Without faith in *reason in life*! And again and again from time to time the human race will decree: "there is something at which we are absolutely not allowed to laugh any more!" And the most careful philanthrope will add: "not only laughter and joyful wisdom, but also the tragic with all its sublime unreason belongs among the means and necessities of species preservation!" — And consequently! Consequently! Consequently! Oh do you understand me, my brothers? Do you understand this new law of ebb and flow?[8] We too have our time![9]

2.

The intellectual conscience. — I repeatedly have the same experience and likewise repeatedly resist it anew, I don't want to believe it, even if it is immediately palpable: *most people lack intellectual conscience*; indeed, it has often seemed to me that by demanding such a thing, even in the most populous of cities one is as lonely as in a desert. Everyone looks at you with strange eyes and fumbles with their scale, calling this good and that evil; no one blushes with shame when you point out that these weights are not full weight — nor does it evoke any outrage toward you: perhaps they laugh at your doubts. I mean: *most people by far* do not find it contemptible to believe this or that and to live according to it, *without* first becoming aware of the final and most certain reasons for and against and without even concerning themselves with such reasons afterward — the most talented men and the noblest women still belong to this "most people." But what are good-heartedness, refinement and genius[10] to me when the human being who possesses these virtues tolerates in himself slack feelings in faith and judgment, when *the demand for certainty* does not constitute his innermost desire and deepest need — as that which separates the superior humans from the lower! In certain pious people I found a hatred of reason, and I liked them for it: at least this way their bad intellectual conscience was revealed! But to stand amidst this *rerum concordia discors*[11] and the whole wonderful uncertainty and ambiguity of existence *and not question,* not tremble with the desire and joy of questioning, not even hate the questioner, perhaps even find him slightly amusing — this is what I feel as *contemptible,* and it is this feeling that I seek first in everyone: — some kind of folly persuades me time after time that every human being has this feeling, as a human being. It is my brand of injustice.

3.[12]

Noble and common. — To common natures all noble, magnanimous feelings seem to be inexpedient and therefore chiefly implausible: they wink when they hear about these, and seem to want to say "there is surely some good advantage there, one can't see through every wall": — they are suspicious of the noble one, as if he sought his advantage surreptitiously. If they become all too clearly convinced of the absence of selfish intentions and gains, then they regard the noble one as a kind of fool: they despise him in his joy and laugh at the sparkle in his eye. "How can someone be glad to be disadvantaged, how can someone with open eyes want to end up disadvantaged! A sickness of reason must be connected with the noble affection" — thus they think while looking down their noses: just as they belittle the joy that the madman derives from his fixed idea. The common nature is distinguished by the fact that it unwaveringly keeps its eye on its advantage and that this thinking about purpose and advantage is even stronger than the strongest drives in it: not allowing itself to be misled into inexpedient actions by those[13] drives — this is its wisdom and sense of self.

Compared to it the higher nature is *more unreasonable:*[14] — for the noble, magnanimous, self-sacrificing one in fact succumbs to his drives, and in his best moments his reason *pauses.* An animal that risks its life to protect its young or follows its female even into death during the mating season does not think about danger and death, its reason likewise pauses, because it is totally dominated by the pleasure in its brood or in its female and the fear of being robbed of this pleasure; it becomes more stupid than it otherwise is, like the noble and magnanimous person. The latter possesses some feelings of pleasure and displeasure of such strength that the intellect must remain silent against them or surrender to their service: at such times they lose their head to their heart and now one speaks of "passion." (Here and there the opposite of this, the "reversal of passion" as it were, also occurs, for example when someone once put his hand on Fontenelle's heart saying: "What you have here, my dearest fellow, is also a brain.") It is the unreason or antireason[15] of passion that the common despise in the noble, especially when it is directed at objects whose value seems to him wholly fantastic and arbitrary. He is angered by someone who succumbs to the passion of the belly, but he indeed comprehends the attraction that here constitutes the tyrant; but he does not comprehend, for instance, how someone could risk health and honor for the sake of a passion for knowledge. The taste of the superior nature is directed at exceptions, at things that usually leave us cold and seem to have no sweetness; the higher nature has a singular standard of value. In addition, it believes mostly that it does *not* have a singular standard of value in its idiosyncrasy of taste, but rather posits its values and unvalues[16] as generally valid, thereby becoming incomprehensible and impractical. It is very rare that a higher nature has enough reason left over to understand and treat everyday people as such: for the most part it believes in its own passion as the passion of all others that they keep concealed, and precisely in this belief it is full of ardor and eloquence. Now when such exceptional human beings do not feel themselves to be exceptions, how could they ever understand the common natures and fairly evaluate the rule! — and so they too speak of the foolishness, inexpediency and phantasms of humankind, full of marvel at the madness of world events and why it will not admit to what "it needs." — This is the eternal injustice of the noble.

4.[17]

What preserves the species. — The strongest and evilest minds have so far carried humankind forward the most: again and again they ignited the sleeping passions — all orderly society lulls the passions to sleep — they again and again awakened the sense of comparison, of contradiction, of pleasure in innovation, daring, the untried; they forced humans to set opinions against opinions and model against model. Mostly with weapons, by toppling the boundary markers, through violating pieties: but also through new religions and moralities! The same "malice" is in every teacher and preacher of the *new* — which makes a conqueror notorious even if it expresses itself more subtly, does not immediately put its muscles in motion and for that simple reason also does not immediately make someone so notorious! The new, however, is under all circumstances the *evil*, as that which wants to conquer, to throw down the old boundary markers and the old pieties; and only the old is the good! The good human beings of every period are those who dig the old thoughts deep into the ground and bear fruit with them, the plowmen of the spirit. But all land eventually becomes exhausted, and again and again the plowshare of evil must come. — Now there is a fundamentally erroneous teaching of morality that is celebrated especially in England: according to it, the judgments "good" and "evil" are the accumulation of the experiences concerning "expedient" and "inexpedient"; according to it, what is called good is what preserves the species, but what is called evil is what is harmful to the species. In truth however the evil drives are expedient, species-preserving and indispensable to exactly the same degree as the good: — only their function is different.

5.[18]

Unconditional duties. — All people who feel that they need the strongest words and sounds, the most eloquent gestures and postures to be *at all* effective, revolutionary politicians, socialists, repentance preachers with and without Christianity, all of whom do not allow for only partial successes: they all speak of "duties" and to be sure of duties whose character is unconditional — without these they would have no right to their great pathos: this they know very well! Hence they reach for philosophies of morality that preach some kind of categorical imperative, or they take a good portion of religion upon themselves, as Mazzini for example has done. Because they want to be trusted unconditionally, they first need to trust themselves unconditionally, on the basis of some ultimate indisputable and in itself sublime command whose servants and instruments they feel themselves to be and wish to pass for. Here we have the most natural and usually very influential opponents of moral enlightenment and skepticism: but they are rare. On the other hand, there is a very comprehensive class of these opponents wherever the prevailing interest teaches submission, while fame and honor seem to prohibit submission. Whoever feels degraded by the thought of being the *instrument* of a prince or a party and sect or even of a monetary power, for instance as the descendant of an old proud family, but wants to be or has to be this instrument before himself and before the public, requires pathetic principles that one can mouth at any time: — principles of an unconditional ought, to which one may submit without shame and show it. All subtler servility clings firmly to the categorical imperative and is the mortal enemy of those who wish to deprive duty of its unconditional character: decency demands this of them, and not only decency.

6.

Loss of dignity. — Reflection has lost all its dignity of form, the ceremony and the solemn gesture of reflection have become

a laughingstock, and a wise man of the old style would no longer be tolerated. We think too hastily, and on the move, and in
the midst of walking, in the midst of all kinds of activities, even
when we are thinking about the most serious things; we need
little preparation, even little silence: — it is as if we were carrying an unstoppable, rolling machine around in our heads, one
that keeps working even under the most unfavorable circumstances. Formerly one could tell if someone wanted to think
— it was probably the exception! — that he now wanted to
become wiser and was preparing himself for a thought: his facial
expression changed, as if praying, and he stopped in his tracks;
indeed, one stood still for hours in the road when the thought
"came" — on one leg or two legs. Thus the "dignity of the matter" demanded!

7.[19]

Something for the industrious. — Whoever wishes to conduct
a study of moral things now opens up a tremendous field of
work for himself. All kinds of passions must be individually
thought through, individually traced through periods, peoples,
great and small individuals; their entire reason and all their valuations and elucidations of things have to be brought to light!
Up till now, everything that has imparted color to existence
still has had no history: or where would we find a history of
love, of avarice, of envy, of conscience, of piety, of cruelty? Even
a comparative history of law, or merely of punishment, has
been completely lacking so far. Has anyone yet made the various divisions of the day, the consequences of a regular sched-
ule of work, festival and rest the subject of research? Does one
know the moral effects of types of food? Is there a philosophy
of nutrition? (The clamor that breaks out repeatedly for and
against vegetarianism already proves that there is still no such
philosophy!) Have the experiences of cohabitation, for instance
those of the monasteries, been collected yet? Has the dialectic
between marriage and friendship been portrayed yet? The customs of scholars, of merchants, artists, artisans — have they

found their thinkers yet? There is so much to think about in them! Everything that human beings have so far regarded as their "conditions of existence," and all the reason, passion and superstition in this regard — has this ever been researched at length? Just observing the different growth that human drives have had and still could have depending on different moral climates already causes too much work for the most industrious individual; entire generations, and generations of scholars collaborating according to plan, would be required to exhaust the viewpoints and the material here. The same holds true for proving the reasons for the diversity of the moral climate ("*why* does the sun of this particular basic moral judgment and major value standard shine here — and another there?"). And it is a new labor again to establish what is the erroneousness of all these reasons and the whole nature of moral judgment to date. Assuming all these labors to be done, then the trickiest question of all would come to the fore, whether science is capable of *providing* goals of behavior after it has proven that it can take and annihilate such goals — and then an experimentation would be in order, in which every manner of heroism could satisfy itself, a centuries-long experimentation that could eclipse all the great labors and sacrifices of history to date. So far science has not built its cyclopic buildings;[20] the time will come for that too.

8.

Unconscious virtues. — All qualities of a human being of which he is conscious — and especially when he also presupposes they are visible and evident for his environment — are subject to completely different laws of development than those qualities that are unknown or badly known to him, which through their subtlety conceal themselves even from the eyes of the subtler observer and know how to hide as if behind nothing. This is the case with those fine sculptures on the scales of reptiles: it would be an error to presume them to be ornament or weapon — for they are visible only under a microscope, hence with the kind of artificially sharpened vision that similar animals, to whom they might signify ornament or weapon, do not possess! Our visible moral qualities, and especially those we *believe* to be visible, go their way — and the invisible, completely homonymous ones that are neither ornament nor weapon with respect to other people *also go their way:* probably a quite different way, and with lines and subtleties and sculptures that might be a pleasure to a god with a divine microscope. For example we have our industriousness, our ambition, our acuteness: the whole world knows about it — and in addition we probably also have *our* industriousness, *our* ambition, *our* acuteness; but the microscope has not yet been invented for these reptile scales of ours! — And here the friends of instinctive morality will say: "Bravo! At least he considers unconscious virtues possible — we're satisfied with that!" — Oh you easily satisfied ones!

9.[21]

Our eruptions. — Countless things that humankind acquired in earlier stages, but so feebly and embryonically that no one was able to perceive them as acquired, suddenly burst into the light much later, perhaps after centuries: meanwhile they have become strong and ripe. Some ages seem to be lacking this or that talent, this or that virtue entirely, some people as well: but just wait until the grandchildren and great-grandchildren, if you have time to wait — they will bring to light the inside of their grandfathers, that inside of which not even the grandfathers knew anything. Often the son is already the betrayer of his father: the latter understands himself better after having his son. All of us have hidden gardens and plantings in us; and, to take a different metaphor, we are all growing volcanoes that will have their hour of eruption: — but of course how near or how distant this is nobody knows, not even the dear Lord.

10.[22]

A kind of atavism. — I prefer to understand the rare human beings of an age as abruptly surfacing aftergrowths of past cultures and their powers: as the atavism so to speak of a people and its civilization: — in this manner we can actually *understand* something about them! Now they appear strange, rare, extraordinary: and whoever feels these powers in himself has to nurse, defend, honor and cultivate them against an opposing different world: and thus he will either become a great human being or a crazy and odd one, to the extent that he simply does not perish early. Formerly these same qualities were ordinary and therefore considered common: they were not distinguishing. Perhaps they were demanded, required; it was impossible to become great with them and for the simple reason that the danger was also lacking of becoming insane and isolated with them. — The *preserving* generations and castes of a people are primarily the ones in which such relapses of old drives appear, whereas there is no probability of such atavism where races, habits, valuations change too rapidly. Tempo after all means just as much among the powers of development of peoples as it does in music; for our case an andante of development is absolutely necessary, as the tempo of a passionate and slow spirit: — and such indeed is the spirit of conservative generations.

11.

Consciousness. — Consciousness[23] is the final and latest development of the organic and consequently also what is most unfinished and most impotent in it. From consciousness arise countless mistakes that cause an animal, a human being to perish earlier than would be necessary, "beyond fate," as Homer says.[24] If the preserving nexus of instincts were not so exceedingly more powerful, if it did not serve on the whole as a regulator: humankind would have to perish from its skewed judgments and its fantasizing with open eyes, from its lack of thoroughness and its gullibility, in brief from its very being conscious: or rather, without the former, the latter would have long ago ceased to exist! Before a function is developed and mature, it is a danger to the organism: all the better if it is properly tyrannized for a long time! Thus consciousness is properly tyrannized — and not least by the pride we have in it! One thinks, here we have *the kernel* of human being, its enduring, eternal, ultimate, most original element! One takes consciousness to be a fixed, given magnitude! Denies its growth, its intermittences! Takes it to be a "unity of the organism"! — This ridiculous over-estimation and misjudgment of consciousness results in a great utility, for it has *hindered* its all too rapid development. Because humans have believed themselves to already have consciousness, they have expended little effort to acquire it — and even now the situation is no different! The task is still an entirely new one, just now dawning on human eyes and still barely discernible, *the task of incorporating knowledge* and making it instinctive — a task that can only be seen by those who have grasped that heretofore only our *errors* have been incorporated and that all our consciousness refers to errors!

12.[25]

On the goal of science. — What? The ultimate goal of science is supposed to be to bring human beings as much pleasure and as little displeasure as possible? Now what if[26] pleasure and displeasure were so knotted together with a single rope that[27] whoever *wants* to have as much as possible of the one also *must* have as much as possible of the other — that whoever wants to learn to "jubilate to high heaven" must also stay prepared for being "depressed to death"?[28] And maybe this is how things are! At least the Stoics believed things were like this,[29] and they were consistent when they desired as little as possible in order to have as little displeasure as possible from life (when they kept repeating the proverb "The virtuous person is the happiest person," for them it served both as a shop-sign of the school for the great masses, and a casuistic subtlety for the subtle). Even today you still have the choice: either *as little displeasure as possible,* in brief painlessness — and at bottom socialists and politicians of all parties could not honestly promise their people anything more — or *as much displeasure as possible* as the price for the growth of a profusion of subtle and heretofore rarely savored pleasures and joys! If you opt for the former, if therefore you want to suppress and diminish the painfulness of humanity, well then, you must also suppress and diminish its *capacity for joy*. Indeed, with *science* we can promote one goal as well as the other! Today perhaps it is better known for its power to deprive human beings of their joys, and to make them colder, more statuesque, more stoic. But it could yet be discovered as the *great bringer of pain*! — And then maybe its counterforce would be discovered at the same time, its tremendous faculty to light up new galaxies of joy!

13.

On the teaching of the feeling of power. — With beneficence and doing harm one exercises one's power over others — one desires nothing more here! With *doing harm* it is over those who must first learn to feel our power; for pain is a much more sensitive means for this than pleasure: — pain always asks for its cause, whereas pleasure is inclined to stop with itself and not look back. With *beneficence* and benevolence it is over those who already depend on us somehow (that is, those who are accustomed to think of us as their causes); we want to increase their power because in this manner we increase our own, or we want to show them the advantage of being in our power — then they will be more satisfied with their situation and more hostile and ready to fight against the enemies of *our* power. Whether we make sacrifices in our beneficence or harm-doing does not change the ultimate value of our actions; even when we risk our lives, like the martyr for the sake of his church, it is a sacrifice made to *our* longing for power, or for the purpose of preserving our feeling of power. Someone senses "I possess the truth," but how many possessions does he not abandon in order to save this sensation! What does he not throw overboard in order to stay "on top" — that is *above* the others who are lacking "truth"! Of course the state in which we do harm is rarely as pleasant, as straightforwardly pleasant as the one in which we do good — it is a sign that we are still lacking power, or it betrays annoyance over this poverty, it entails new dangers and insecurities for our existing possession of power and it clouds our horizon with the prospect of revenge, scorn, punishment, failure. Only for the most irritable and greedy who partake of the feeling of power might it be more pleasurable to impress the stamp of power on those who resist; for those to whom the sight of the already subjugated (who are the object of benevolence) is a burden and a boredom. It depends on how one is accustomed to *spicing* one's life; it is a matter of taste whether one would prefer to have the slow or the sudden, the safe or the dangerous and daring growth of power — one seeks this or that spice always according to one's temperament. An easy prey is something contemptible to proud natures, they perceive a feeling of well-being only at the sight of unbroken human beings who could become their enemy, and likewise at the sight of all possessions that are hard to access; they are often harsh toward the suffering one, because he is not worth their effort and pride — but they are all the more obliging to their *equals,* with whom a fight and struggle would at least be honorable, *if* such an opportunity were ever to present itself. Under the feeling of well-being of *this* perspective, the people of the knightly caste accustomed themselves to an exquisite courtesy toward one another. — Compassion is the most pleasant feeling among those who have little pride and no prospect of great conquests: for them the easy prey — and that means everyone who suffers — is something delightful.[30] Compassion is celebrated as the virtue of prostitutes.[31]

14.[32]

What gets called love. — Avarice and love: how differently we perceive with each of these words! — and yet it could be the same drive named twice, disparaged one time from the standpoint of those who already have, in whom the drive has quieted down somewhat and who now fear for their "havings"; another time from the standpoint of the dissatisfied and thirsty, and therefore glorified as "good." Our love of one's neighbor — is it not a craving for new *property?* And likewise our love for knowledge, for truth and generally all that craving for new things? We eventually become tired of the old things we securely possess and we again reach out our hands; even the most beautiful landscape in which we have lived for three months is no longer certain of our love, and some more distant coast lures our avarice: ownership usually becomes diminished through owning. Our pleasure in ourselves wants to maintain itself in such a manner that it repeatedly transforms something new *into ourselves* — precisely that is called owning. To become tired of owning something means: to become tired of ourselves. (One can also suffer from excess — even the desire to throw away, to distribute can adorn itself with the honorable name of "love.") When we see someone suffering, we gladly use the opportunity offered here to take possession of him; this is done for example by the benevolent and compassionate person, he too gives the name "love" to the desire kindled in him for new possessions, and he takes his pleasure in it as if in a new beckoning conquest. But it is love between the sexes that most clearly betrays itself as a craving for property: the lover wants unconditional sole ownership of the person he longs for, he wants as unconditional a power over her soul as over her body, he alone wants to be loved and to live and rule in the other's soul as the supreme and most desirable thing. If one imagines that this means nothing other than *barring* the whole world from a precious good, happiness and pleasure; if one imagines that the lover is bent on the impoverishment and renunciation of all other suitors and wishes to become the dragon of his golden hoard, as the most ruthless and selfish of all "conquerors" and exploiters: if one imagines, finally, that to the lover the entire other world seems indifferent, pale, and worthless, that he is prepared to make any sacrifice, disrupt any order, subordinate any interest: then one is amazed indeed that this savage avarice and injustice of sexual love has been glorified and deified to such an extent as it has been at all times, indeed that one has derived from this love the concept of love as the opposite of egoism, while it is actually perhaps the most unabashed expression of egoism. Here apparently the non-owners and the wishful influenced linguistic usage — there have probably always been too many of them. Those who were favored in this area with much ownership and satiety may have hinted occasionally at a "raging demon," like that most gracious and beloved of all Athenians, Sophocles:[33] but Eros laughed every time at such blasphemers — they were always his greatest favorites,[34] after all. — There is probably here and there on earth a kind of continuation of love in which that avaricious longing of two persons for each other has yielded to a new desire and avarice, to a *shared* higher thirst for an ideal that stands above them: but who knows this love? Who has experienced it? Its proper name is *friendship*.[35]

15.[36]

From a distance. — This mountain makes the entire region that it dominates charming and significant in every way: after we have said this to ourselves for the hundredth time, we are so unreasonably and so gratefully disposed toward it that we believe it, the provider of this charm, must itself be the most charming thing in the region — and so we climb up it and are disappointed. Suddenly the mountain itself and the whole landscape around us, beneath us, are as if disenchanted; we had forgotten that some greatness, like some goodness, only wants to be viewed from a certain distance, and absolutely from below, not from above — *its effect* depends on this. Perhaps you know people in your vicinity who ought to look at themselves only from a certain distance, in order to find themselves even tolerable or attractive and bracing; self-knowledge is ill-advised for them.

16.[37]

Across the footbridge. — When interacting with persons who are bashful about their feelings, one has to be capable of dissembling; they sense a sudden hatred of anyone who catches them in a tender or zealous and elevated feeling, as if he had seen their secrets. If one wants to do them any good in such moments, then one should make them laugh or say something cold and jokingly sarcastic: — this will freeze their feeling, and they regain their control. But I am giving away the moral before the story. — At one point we were so close in life that nothing seemed to inhibit our friendship and brotherhood anymore, and only a small footbridge lay between us. As you were just about to set foot on it, I asked you: "Do you want to cross the footbridge to me?" — But then you no longer wanted to; and when I asked again, you were silent. Since then mountains and roaring streams, and whatever separates and estranges have been thrown between us, and even if we wanted to reach each other, we could no longer do it! If you think back now to that little footbridge, you no longer have words — only sobbing and bewilderment.

17.

Motivating one's poverty. — Of course we are not able through any trick to make a rich, richly flowing virtue out of a poor one, but surely we can reinterpret its poverty beautifully into a necessity, so that the sight of it no longer hurts us and we cease on its account to glare reproachfully at fate. This is what the wise gardener does, who places the poor little trickle of his garden into the arms of a fountain nymph and thereby motivates its poverty: — and who wouldn't need nymphs just as he does!

18.[38]

The pride of antiquity. — We are lacking antiquity's coloration of nobility because our feeling is lacking antiquity's slave. A Greek of noble lineage found such tremendous intermediate stages and such a distance between his elevation and that ultimate baseness, that he could scarcely even see the slave clearly: Plato himself did not quite see him anymore. It is different with us, accustomed as we are to the *teaching* of equality among human beings, though not to equality itself. A being that cannot dispose over itself and that lacks idleness — in our eyes this is still by no means regarded as contemptible; perhaps there is too much of this slavishness in each of us, according to the conditions of our social order and activity, which are fundamentally different from those of the ancients. — The Greek philosopher went through life with the secret feeling that there were many more slaves than people thought — namely, that everyone was a slave who was not a philosopher; his pride overflowed when he considered that even the mightiest of the earth were among these his slaves. This pride, too, is foreign and impossible to us; not even as a metaphor does the word "slave" have its full power for us.

19.

Evil. — Examine the life of the best and most fruitful people and peoples and ask yourself whether a tree that is supposed to grow proudly into the heights could dispense with bad weather and storms: whether external adversity and resistance, whether various kinds of hatred, envy, stubbornness, mistrust, harshness, avarice and violence do not belong among the *advancing* conditions without which a major growth even in virtue is scarcely possible? The poison from which a weaker nature perishes is strengthening to the strong human — and he doesn't call it poison either.

20.

Dignity of folly. — A few more millennia on the course of the last century! — and in everything that people do the highest cleverness will be visible: but that is precisely why prudence will have lost all its dignity. Then it will be necessary to be prudent, of course, but it will also be so ordinary and so vulgar that a more disgusted[39] taste will perceive this necessity as a *vulgarity.* And just as a tyranny of truth and science would be capable of causing a steep rise in the price of a lie, so too a tyranny of cleverness could usher in a new kind of noble sensibility. Being noble — maybe then it would mean: to have follies on the brain.

21.[40]

To the teachers of selflessness. — One calls the virtues of a person *good* not with respect to the effects they have for him personally, but rather with respect to the effects that we presuppose from them for ourselves and society: — from time immemorial in their praise of virtues, people have been "selfless" only very little, "unegoistic" only very little! For otherwise one would have to have noticed that the virtues (like industriousness, obedience, chastity, piety, justice) are mostly *harmful* to their owners, as drives that reign all too ardently and greedily in them, and do not allow themselves to be kept in balance by reason with the other drives. If you have a virtue, a real, whole virtue (and not only a tiny drive for a virtue!) — then you are its *victim*! But your neighbor praises your virtue for that very reason! One praises the industrious, even though they harm the acuity of their eyesight or the originality and freshness of their spirit with this industriousness; one honors and pities the youth who "has worked himself to death," because one reasons: "For the great whole of society even the loss of our best individual is only a small sacrifice! Too bad that the sacrifice is necessary! But much worse to be sure if the individual were to think differently and to take his preservation and development more seriously than his work in the service of society!" And so this youth is pitied not for his own sake, but because a devoted *instrument* who was ruthless toward himself — a so-called "decent human being" — has been lost to society by this death. Perhaps one considers whether it would have been more useful in the interest of society if he had worked less ruthlessly against himself and had preserved himself longer — indeed, one probably admits to an advantage in this regard, but deems that other advantage to be higher and more enduring, namely that a *sacrifice* was made and the mentality of the sacrificial animal once more *visibly* confirmed itself. Therefore, it is the instrumental nature that is really praised first in virtues when virtues are praised, then the blind drive that dominates in every virtue, which does not allow itself to be curtailed by the overall advantage of the individual, in short: the unreason in virtue, by dint of which the individual being allows itself to be transformed into a function of the whole. The praise of virtue is the praise of something privately harmful — the praise of drives that rob a human being of his noblest selfishness and his strength for the highest stewardship of himself. — To be sure: for the purpose of education and for incorporating virtuous habits one parades a series of virtuous effects that make it seem as though virtue and private advantage are sisters — and there exists in fact such a sisterhood! Blindly raging industriousness, for example, this typical virtue of an instrument, is portrayed as the path to wealth and honor and as the most wholesome poison against boredom and the passions: but one remains silent about its danger, its gravest danger. Education proceeds in this manner without exception: it seeks to condition the individual through a series of stimuli and advantages into a way of thinking and acting that, once it has become habit, drive and passion, reigns in and over him, *contrary to his ultimate advantage,* but "for the general good." How often do I see that blindly raging industriousness indeed creates riches and honor, but at the same time deprives those organs of subtlety by dint of which there could be an enjoyment of wealth and honors, likewise that the chief means of thwarting boredom and the passions simultaneously dulls the senses and makes the intellect resistant to new stimuli. (The[41] most industrious of all ages — our age — knows nothing better to do with all its industriousness and money than make ever more industriousness and ever more money: after all it takes more genius to spend than to earn! — Well, we will have our "grandchildren"!) If education is successful, then each virtue of the individual is a public utility and a private disadvantage in the context of the higher private goal — probably some kind of intellectual-sensual atrophy or even premature decline: from this standpoint one should consider in turn the virtue of obedience, of chastity, of piety, or justice. The praise of the selfless, the self-sacrificing, the virtuous — hence of the one who does not spend his entire strength and reason on *his* preservation, development, elevation, promotion, expansion of power but instead lives modestly and thoughtlessly, perhaps even indifferently or ironically with regard to himself — this praise in any case has not sprung from the spirit of selflessness! Our "neighbor" praises selflessness because *he has his advantage in it*! If the neighbor himself were to think "selflessly," then he would reject this impairment of strength, this damage for *his* benefit, work against the development of such inclinations and above all exhibit his selflessness precisely by *not* calling it *good*! — With this we touch upon the basic contradiction of that morality that is held very much in honor right now: the *motives* of this morality stand opposed to its *principle*! What this morality wants to prove itself with, it[42] refutes out of its criterion of what is moral! In order not to countermand its own morality, the proposition "you shall renounce yourself and sacrifice yourself" could only be decreed by a being that thereby renounced its own advantage and perhaps contributed to its own demise in the demanded sacrifice of individuals.[43] As soon as the neighbor (or society) recommends altruism *for the sake of utility,* though, the exact opposite proposition is applied, "you shall seek your advantage even at the expense of everything else," ergo in a single breath a "thou shalt" and a "thou shalt not" gets preached![44]

22.

L'ordre du jour pour le roi.[45,46] — The day begins: let us begin to arrange for this day the business and festivities of our most merciful master, who deigns still to slumber. His majesty has bad weather today: we will be wary of calling it bad; we will not speak of the weather — but today we will conduct business somewhat more solemnly and the festivities somewhat more festively than would otherwise be necessary. Perhaps his majesty may even be ill: for breakfast we will present the latest good news from the evening, the arrival of Mr. Montaigne, who knows how to joke so pleasantly about his illness — he

suffers from a stone. We will receive a few persons (persons!
— what would that old puffed up frog, who will be among
them, say when he hears this word! "I am no person," he would
say, "but rather always the matter itself") — and this reception
will last longer than anybody finds pleasant: reason enough to
tell about the poet who wrote on his door: "whoever enters
here does me an honor; whoever does not, a favor."[47] —This is
verily what it means to utter a discourtesy in a courteous manner! And perhaps this poet has every right for his part to be
so discourteous: it is said that his verses are better than the
verse-smith. Well, let him make many more and withdraw as
much as possible from the world: and that is indeed the meaning of his well-mannered bad manners! Conversely, a prince is
always worth more than his "verse," even if — but what are
we doing? We are chatting, and the entire court thinks we
are already working and racking our brains: no light is visible earlier than the one that burns in our window. — Listen!
Wasn't that the bell? To hell with it! The day and the dance are
beginning, and we don't know the plan! So we have to impro-
vise — the whole world improvises its day. Today let's just do
as the whole world! — And with that, my odd morning dream
vanished, probably retreating before the harsh strokes of the
tower clock that just proclaimed the fifth hour with all of its
typical importance. It seems to me that this time, the god of
dreams wanted to ridicule my habits — it is my habit to begin
the day so that I can organize and make it bearable *for myself,*
and it may be that sometimes I've done this too formally and
too much like a prince.

23.[48]

The signs of corruption. — One should pay attention to the
following signs of those conditions that are necessary from
time to time in a society and are characterized with the word
"corruption." As soon as corruption sets in anywhere, a colorful *superstition*[49] takes over and the previous overall faith[50] of
a people becomes pale and impotent against it: superstition,

after all, is second-rate free-spiritedness — whoever yields to it selects certain forms and formulas that appeal to him and allows himself the right of choice. The superstitious person, compared with the religious person, is always much more a "person" than the latter, and a superstitious society will be the kind in which there are already many individuals and delight in individuality. Seen from this standpoint, superstition always appears as *progress* against faith and as a sign that the intellect is becoming more independent and wants to have its rights. Then the venerators of the old religion and religiosity complain about corruption — up till now they had also determined linguistic usage and had given superstition a bad reputation even among the freest of spirits. Let us learn that it is a symptom of *enlightenment.*[51] — Secondly, a society in which corruption gains a foothold is accused of *exhaustion:* and clearly the esteem for war and the delight in war diminish in it, and the comforts of life are now just as ardently coveted as previously the warlike and athletic honors. But one tends to overlook that the old popular energy and popular passion that got their magnificent visibility through war and war games have now transposed themselves into countless private passions and have merely grown less visible; indeed, it is probably in states of "corruption" that the power and force of the now expended energy of a people are greater than ever, and the individual wastes them as extravagantly as he could not before — he was not yet rich enough for it at the time! And so it is precisely in times of "exhaustion" when tragedy runs through the houses and streets, when great love and great hate are born, and the flame of knowledge blazes up to the sky. — Thirdly, one tends to say regarding such times of corruption, to compensate as it were for the reproach of superstition and exhaustion, that they are gentler and that now cruelty diminishes considerably when contrasted with the older more faith-oriented and stronger time. But I can no more agree with this praise than with that reproach: I will admit only this much, that now cruelty refines itself, and from now on its older forms run counter to taste;

but injury and torture through word and gaze reach their highest development in times of corruption — only now is *malice*
created and the delight in malice. The people of corruption are
witty and slanderous; they know there are other kinds of murder in addition to dagger and assault — they also know that
whatever *is well said* will be believed. — Fourthly: when "morals decline," then those beings surface for the first time whom
we call tyrants: they are the forerunners and so to speak the
premature *firstborn of individuals*. Just a while longer: and this
fruit of fruits[52] will hang ripe and yellow on the tree of a people
— and this tree existed only for the sake of these fruits! When
the decline reaches its apex and likewise the battle among all the
different kinds of tyrants, then the Caesar always comes along,
the final tyrant, who puts an end to the weary struggle for absolute rule by letting weariness work for himself. During his time
the individual is usually ripest and consequently "culture" is at
its highest and most fruitful, but not on his account and not
through him: although the highest cultural individuals love to
flatter their Caesar by making themselves out to be *his* work.
But the truth is that they need to have external peace because
they have their unrest and work inside themselves. In these
times bribery and treason are greatest: for the love of the newly
discovered ego is now much mightier than the love for the old,
used-up, talked-to-death "fatherland"; and the need to secure
oneself somehow against the terrible fluctuations of fortune
pries open even nobler hands as soon as someone powerful and
wealthy shows he is ready to pour gold into them. There is now
so little secure future; so one lives for today: a state of the soul
whereby all seducers play an easy game — after all, one lets
oneself be seduced and bribed just "for today," and preserves
one's future and virtue! Individuals, these genuine "in and of
themselves," are known to care more about the moment than
their antipodes, the herd people, because they regard themselves to be just as unpredictable as the future; they likewise
prefer to attach themselves to violent men because they know
themselves to be capable of actions and information that could

neither be understood nor pardoned by the masses — but the tyrant or Caesar understands the rights of the individual even in his transgressions and has an interest in advocating for and even extending a hand to a bolder private morality.[53] For he thinks of himself and wants others to think of him what Napoleon once articulated in his classical way: "I have the right to respond to everything that I am accused of with an eternal 'That's me.' I am apart from the whole world, I accept conditions from no one. I want people also to subject themselves to my fantasies and to find it quite natural that I devote myself to this or that diversion."[54] Thus Napoleon once spoke to his wife when she had occasion to question the marital fidelity of her spouse. — The times of corruption are those in which the apples fall from the tree: I mean the individuals, the seed-bearers of the future, the authors of spiritual colonization and of the reshaping of states and societies. Corruption is only a pejorative for the *autumn times* of a people.

24.

Different types of dissatisfaction. — The weak and as it were feminine type of the dissatisfied are inventive in the beautification and deepening of life; the strong type — the manly ones, to keep to the metaphor — in the improvement and securing of life. The former reveal their weakness and femininity in that they like to let themselves be deceived at times and tend to settle for a bit of intoxication and fanaticism, but on the whole they can never be satisfied and they suffer from the incurability of their dissatisfaction; moreover they are the promoters of all those who know how to provide opiates and narcotic consolations, and are therefore[55] ill-disposed toward those who esteem the physician more highly than the priest — this way they maintain the *continuation* of real distress! If there hadn't been a majority of the dissatisfied of this type since the time of the Middle Ages in Europe, then perhaps the famous European capacity for constant *transformation* would have never originated: for the demands of the strong dissatisfied type are too crude and at bottom too undemanding not to be finally put to rest at some point. China is the example of a country where dissatisfaction on a large scale and the capacity for transformation died out many centuries ago; and the socialists and idolaters of the state in Europe could easily bring about Chinese conditions and a Chinese "happiness" in Europe too, with their measures for the improvement and securing of life, assuming they could first exterminate the sicklier, more delicate, more effeminate dissatisfaction and romanticism that for the time being are still superabundantly in existence here. Europe is a sick person who owes supreme gratitude to its incurability and the eternal transformation of its suffering; these constantly new conditions, these just as constantly new dangers, pains and means of information have ultimately produced an intellectual irritability that nearly amounts to genius, and is in any case the mother of all genius.

25.

Not predestined for knowledge. — There is a stupid humility which is not at all rare and, when contracted, once and for all disqualifies someone from being a disciple of knowledge.[56] Namely: the minute this kind of person perceives anything conspicuous, he turns on his heel, so to speak, and says to himself: "You made a mistake! Where were your senses? This can't be the truth!" — and now, instead of just looking or listening more closely a second time, he runs away as if intimidated by the conspicuous thing and tries to get it out of his head as soon as possible. For his inner canon says: "I don't want to see anything that contradicts the usual opinion of things! Am *I* cut out to discover new truths? There are already too many of the old ones."

26.[57]

What does life mean? — Life — that means: incessantly fending off something that wants to die; life — that means: to be cruel and implacable toward everything that becomes weak and old in us, and not only in us. Life — so that means: to be without piety toward the dying, the wretched and the aged? To continually be a murderer? — And yet old Moses said: "Thou shalt not kill!"[58]

27.[59]

The renouncer. — What does the renouncer do? He strives for a higher world, he wants to fly further in all directions than all[60] affirming people — *he throws away much* that would burden his flight, and much of it not worthless to him, not unloved by him: he sacrifices it to his desire for the heights. This sacrificing, this throwing away is now precisely the only thing that remains visible in him: accordingly he is given the name renouncer, and this is how he stands before us, cloaked in his monk's cowl and as if he were the soul of a hair shirt. But he is probably satisfied with this effect that he has on us: he wants to conceal from us his desire, his pride, his intention to fly out *beyond* us. — Yes! He is cleverer than we thought, and so polite to us — this affirmer! For he is that, just like us, even while he renounces.[61]

28.[62]

To injure with one's best. — Our strengths at times drive us so far ahead that we can no longer tolerate our weaknesses and we perish of them: we may even foresee this outcome and yet want it just the same. Then we become harsh toward that in us that wants to be spared, and our greatness is also our mercilessness. — Such an experience, for which we must ultimately pay with our lives, is a metaphor for the overall effect of great human beings on others and on their time: — precisely with their best, with that which only they can do, they destroy many weak, insecure, developing, aspiring people, and in this they are harmful. Indeed, it can be the case, all things considered, that they only injure because their best is accepted and as it were imbibed only by those who lose their mind and their sense of self to it, as if to a drink that is too strong: they become so

intoxicated that they will have to break their limbs on all the
false paths to which intoxication drives them.

29.[63]

Those who add lies. — When in France they began to con-
test the Aristotelian unities[64] and consequently also to defend
them, then we got to see something again that can be seen so
often, but is seen with such aversion: — *they lied reasons into
existence* for why these laws should remain, simply so as not
to have to admit to themselves that they had become *accustomed* to the rule of these laws and no longer wanted it otherwise. And this is how it is done within every ruling morality
and religion and how it has been done from the beginning:
the reasons and the intentions behind the habit are always lied
into it only when a few begin to dispute the habit and to *ask*
for reasons and intentions. Herein lies the great dishonesty of
conservatives of all times: — they are the ones who add lies.

30.[65]

Comedy of the famous. — Famous men who *need* their fame,
like for example all politicians, never choose their allies and
friends anymore without ulterior motives: from this one they
want a piece of luster and the reflected luster of his virtue, from
that one the fear induced by certain dubious qualities that
everyone sees in him, from another they steal the reputation of
an idler, his lying in the sun, because it suits their purpose on
occasion to be regarded as inattentive and sluggish: — it conceals the fact that they lie in wait; at their side, alternatingly,
they need the visionary, the knower, the ponderer, the pedant,
and as their actual self so to speak, but then just as quickly they
no longer need them! And so their surroundings and exteriors
are constantly dying off, while everything seems to crowd into
this one vicinity and want to form itself into their "character": in this manner they resemble big cities. Their reputation
is constantly in flux just like their character, for their changing
methods demand this change, and will push now this, now

that real or fictional quality to the fore and *onto* the stage: their friends and allies belong, as noted, to these stage qualities. On the other hand, what they want must remain standing all the more firmly and brazenly and gleaming from afar — and this, too, occasionally requires its comedy and its stage play.

31.[66]

Trade and nobility. — Buying and selling are now regarded as base, like the art of reading and writing; everyone is practiced in it now, even if they are not merchants, and the technique gets more practice every day: exactly as formerly, in the age of a more savage humankind, everyone was a hunter and practiced the technique of hunting day after day. Back then hunting was base: but just as hunting finally became a privilege of the mighty and the noble and thus lost its character of everydayness and baseness — due to the fact that it ceased to be necessary and became a matter of mood and luxury: — so too this could happen at some point with buying and selling. There are conceivable societal conditions in which there is no buying or selling, and in which the necessity of this technique will eventually be lost entirely: perhaps then individuals who are less subject to the laws of the general condition will indulge themselves in buying and selling as if in a *luxury of the senses.* Only then would trade acquire nobility, and nobles would then perhaps occupy themselves with trade just as they did formerly with war and politics: whereas, conversely, their estimation of politics could have changed completely. Already now politics ceases to be the handiwork of a nobleman: and it would be possible that some day one would find it so base as to place it, like all literature devoted to party and daily news, under the rubric of "prostitution of the spirit."

32.[67]

Undesired disciples. — What am I to do with these two youths! cried an annoyed philosopher, who "corrupted" youths just as Socrates once corrupted them — these are unwelcome pupils. That one over there cannot say No and the other says "half and half" to everything. Assuming they grasped my teaching, then the former would *suffer* too much, for my way of thinking demands a warlike soul, a desire to harm, a lust for No-saying, a hard skin — he would languish away from open and inner wounds. And the other one would contrive a mediocrity to suit himself out of every cause that he represents, and thereby reduce it to a mediocrity — such a disciple I wish for my enemy.

33.[68]

Outside the lecture hall. — "In order to prove to you that the human being at bottom belongs among the good-natured animals, I would remind you of how gullible he has been for so long. Only now, quite late and after enormous self-overcoming, has he become a *mistrustful* animal — indeed! The human being is now more evil than ever." — I don't understand this: why should the human being be more mistrustful and more evil now? — "Because now he has a science — needs to have one!" —

34.[69]

Historia abscondita.[70] — Every great human being has a retroactive force: all history gets placed on the scale again for his sake, and a thousand secrets of the past crawl out of the woodwork — out into *his* sunshine. There is no way at all of knowing what kinds of things may yet become history. Perhaps the past is essentially still undiscovered! So many retroactive forces are still needed!

35.[71]

Heresy and witchcraft. — Thinking differently than is customary — this is much less the effect of a better intellect, than it is the effect of stronger, more evil inclinations, more detaching, isolating, defiant, gloating and spiteful inclinations. Heresy is the counterpart of witchcraft and certainly neither less harmless nor inherently worthy of veneration. Heretics and witches are two species of evil human beings: what they have in common is that they also feel themselves to be evil, but their unconquerable desire is to lash out harmfully against whatever dominates (people or opinions). The Reformation, a kind of doubling of the medieval spirit at a time when it already no longer possessed a good conscience, produced both of these in the greatest abundance.

36.

Last words. — It will be recalled that Emperor Augustus, that terrifying human being who was as self-controlled and as able to keep silent as any wise Socrates, incriminated himself with an indiscretion in his last words: he let his mask fall for the first time when he divulged that he had worn a mask and played a comedy — he had played the father of the fatherland and the wisdom on the throne, played them well and to the point of illusion! *Plaudite amici, comoedia finite est!*[72] — The thought of the dying Nero: *qualis artifex pereo!*[73] was also the thought of the dying Augustus: a histrionic's vanity! a histrionic's loquacity! And the very opposite of the dying Socrates! — But Tiberius died in silence, this most tortured of all self-torturers — *he* was genuine and no actor! What might have been the last thing to come to his mind? Perhaps this: "Life — that is a long death. Fool that I am, for shortening the lives of so many! Was *I* cut out to be a benefactor? I should have given them eternal life: then I could have *watched* them *die* eternally. *That's why* I had such good eyes after all: *qualis spectator pereo!*"[74] When after a long struggle with death he seemed to be regaining his strength, they considered it advisable to suffocate him with bed pillows — he died a double death.

37.

Because of three errors. — In recent centuries science has been promoted, in part because with it and through it one hoped best to understand God's goodness and wisdom — the main motive in the soul of the great Englishmen (like Newton) — in part because one believed in the absolute utility of knowledge,[75] namely in the innermost bond of morality, knowledge[76] and happiness — the main motive in the soul of the great Frenchmen (like Voltaire) — in part because one believed[77] that one had and loved in science something selfless, harmless, self-sufficient, truly innocent, in which the evil drives of human beings did not participate at all — the main motive in the soul of Spinoza, who as a knower felt himself to be divine: — hence because of three errors.

38.[78]

The explosive ones. — When one considers how explosion-needy are the powers of young men, then one is not surprised to see them so unrefined and so unselective in deciding for this or that cause: What lures them is the sight of the zeal that attaches to a cause, and the sight of the smoldering fuse, as it were — not the cause itself. The subtler seducers therefore know how to present them with the prospect of an explosion while diverting their gaze from the reasoning behind the cause: these powder kegs are not won over with reasons![79]

39.

Changed taste. — The change of general taste is more important[80] than that of opinions; opinions with all their proofs, refutations and the whole intellectual masquerade are only symptoms of changed taste and quite certainly *not* what they are still so frequently considered to be, its causes. How does the general taste change? Through the fact that individuals, powerful and influential ones, unabashedly proclaim and tyrannically assert *their* own *hoc est ridiculum, hoc est absurdum,*[81] hence the judgment of their taste and disgust: — this is how they impose pressure on many, from which eventually a habit of still more and ultimately a *need of all* develops. But that these individuals perceive and "taste" differently, usually has its reason in a peculiarity of their lifestyle, nourishment, digestion, perhaps in a plus or minus of inorganic salts in their blood and brain, in short, in their *physis*:[82] but they have the courage to acknowledge their *physis* and to dignify its demands even down to the subtlest tones: their aesthetic and moral judgments are these "subtlest tones" of *physis*.

40.[83]

On the lack of noble form.[84] — Soldiers and leaders still have a much higher relationship with one another than workers and employers. For the time being, at least, all militarily grounded culture stands high above all so-called industrial culture: the latter in its current shape is in fact the basest form of existence to date. Here quite simply the law of need is in effect: one wants to live and must sell oneself, but one despises the person who exploits this need and *buys* the worker. It is odd that subjugation to powerful, fear-inducing, even terrible persons, to tyrants and generals, is perceived as far less painful than this subjugation to unknown and uninteresting persons, as are all captains of industry: workers usually see in the employer only a cunning, voraciously sucking dog of a human who speculates on every plight, whose name, stature, customs and reputation are completely indifferent to them. Till now the manufacturers and magnates of commerce have probably been lacking too much in all those forms and indicators of a *higher race* that allow *persons* to become interesting in the first place; if they had the nobility of birth in their look and their gestures, perhaps there wouldn't be any socialism of the masses. For at bottom the masses are prepared for *slavery* of any kind, assuming that the superiors over them constantly legitimize themselves as higher, as *born* to command — through the use of noble form! The basest man feels that nobility cannot be improvised and that he must honor in it the fruits of the ages — but the absence of higher form and the notorious vulgarity of manufacturers with their red, fat hands give him the impression that only accident and luck elevated one over the other here: well then, he privately concludes, let *us* try accident and luck for once! Let us toss the dice! — and socialism begins.

41.

Against remorse. — In his own actions the thinker sees experiments and questions for providing some kind of information: success and failure are for him primarily *answers.* However, to be angry or even to feel remorse over something that doesn't work out — this he leaves to those who act because they are ordered to, and who can expect a beating if his lordship is dissatisfied with the result.

42.[85]

Work and boredom. — Seeking work for the sake of pay — in the civilized countries now almost all human beings are the same in this respect; work is a means for all of them, and not the goal itself; which is why they are hardly subtle in their choice of work, as long as it generates an ample reward. Then there are those rarer human beings who would rather perish than work without *pleasure* in their work: those choosy, hard to satisfy types whose needs are not met by an ample reward if the work itself is not the reward of all rewards. To this rare type of human being belong the artists and contemplators of all kinds, but also those idlers who spend their lives hunting, traveling or in love affairs and adventures. All of these want work and adversity, to the extent they are connected with pleasure, and even the hardest, harshest work if need be. Otherwise, though, they exhibit a resolute indolence, even if impoverishment, dishonor, danger to health and life should be linked to this indolence. They do not fear boredom so much as work without pleasure: indeed, they need a lot of boredom if *their* work is to succeed. For the thinker and for all inventive spirits boredom is that unpleasant "doldrums" of the soul, which precede the happy voyage and the cheerful winds; he has to tolerate them, has to *wait for* their effect on him: — *this* is precisely what lesser natures are thoroughly incapable of achieving! It is base to repel boredom in every way: just as working without pleasure is base. Perhaps Asians are distinguished above Europeans in that they are capable of a longer, deeper calm than Europeans; even their narcotics take effect slowly and demand patience, in contrast to the repulsive abruptness of the European poison, alcohol.

43.[86]

What the laws betray. — One is seriously mistaken if one studies the penal code of a people as if it were the expression of its character; laws do not reveal what a people is, rather what seems foreign, odd, outrageous, outlandish to it. Laws relate to the exceptions of the morality of customs;[87] and the harshest penalties target whatever is consonant with the customs of the neighboring people. Thus among the Wahhabis[88] there are only two mortal sins: to have a different god than the Wahhabi god and — smoking (among them it is described as "the disgraceful way of drinking"). "And what about murder and adultery?" — asked the incredulous Englishman[89] upon learning this. "Well now, God is gracious and merciful!" — said the old chieftain.[90] — Similarly, among the ancient Romans there was the idea that a woman could mortally sin in only two ways: on the one hand by adultery, then — by drinking wine. Old Cato thought that kissing among relatives was made into a custom only in order to keep women under control in this context; a kiss meant: does she smell of wine?[91] Women who were caught drinking wine were actually put to death: and certainly not only because women occasionally lose their ability to say no under the influence of wine; above all the Romans feared the orgiastic and Dionysian essence that from time to time afflicted the women of southern Europe back then, when wine was still new in Europe; feared it like a monstrous foreign presence that overturned the foundation of Roman sensibility; to them it was like a betrayal of Rome, like the incorporation of the foreign.

44.[92]

The motives people believe. — As important as it may be to know the real motives on which humankind has acted to date: perhaps the *belief* in certain motives, what humankind itself has so far alleged and imagined as the actual lever of its actions, is something more essential for the knower. For the inner happiness and misery of human beings are granted them according to their belief in this or that motive — *not* however by what was the real motive! All of the latter are of second-order interest.

45.

Epicurus. — Yes, I am proud to perceive the character of Epicurus differently than perhaps anyone, and to enjoy the happiness of the afternoon of antiquity in everything I hear and read of him: — I see his eyes gaze upon a broad whitish sea, across shoreline boulders bathed by the sun, while animals large and small play in its light, secure and calm as this light and these very eyes. Such happiness could only have been invented by a constant sufferer, the happiness of an eye before which the sea of existence has become calm and that now cannot see enough of the surface and the multihued, tender, trembling skin of the sea: never before has such a modesty of voluptuousness existed.[93,94]

46.[95]

Our amazement. — There is profound and thorough good fortune in the fact that science discovers things that *withstand* and again and again furnish the basis of new discoveries: — it could indeed be otherwise! In fact, we are so very convinced of the uncertainty and fancifulness of our judgments and of the eternal change of all human laws and concepts that it actually amazes us *how much* the results of science withstand! Earlier nothing was known of this mutability of all things human, the customs of morality preserved the belief that the entire inner life of humans was joined to iron necessity[96] by eternal clamps: perhaps back then one felt a similar voluptuousness of amazement when people told folk and fairy tales. The miraculous did a lot of good for those who occasionally must have grown tired of rules and eternity. To lose the ground for once! To soar! To err! To be crazy! — that belonged to the paradise and debauchery of earlier ages: whereas our bliss resembles that of the shipwrecked survivor who has climbed onto land and planted both feet on the old solid earth — amazed that it does not teeter.

47.

On the repression of the passions. — If one constantly forbids oneself expression of the passions, as if this were something to leave to the "base," the cruder, bourgeois, peasant-like natures — hence not wanting to repress the passions themselves, but only their language and gestures: then one nonetheless ends up *also* achieving precisely what one doesn't want: the repression of the passions themselves, at least their weakening and alteration: — as was experienced in the most instructive example by the court of Louis XIV and everything that depended on it. The age that *followed*, trained in the repression of expression, no longer had passions themselves and in their place a graceful, shallow, playful nature — an age that was afflicted with the inability to be ill-mannered: so that even an insult was accepted and returned in nothing less than obliging words. Perhaps our present age serves as the most remarkable counterpart: I see everywhere, in life and in the theater, and not least in all that gets written,[97] enjoyment of the *cruder* outbursts and gestures of passion: now a certain convention of passionateness is demanded — but no longer passion itself! Nevertheless *passion* will be reached this way ultimately, and our descendants will possess a *genuine savagery* and not just a savagery and unruliness of forms.

48.[98]

Knowledge of distress. — Perhaps human beings and ages differ from one another through nothing so much as through the different degree of the knowledge of distress that they have: distress of the soul as well as the body. With respect to the latter, we moderns are all perhaps bunglers and visionaries, despite our frailties and fragilities, due to a lack of abundant self-experience: compared to an age of fear — to the longest of all ages — where the individual had to protect himself against violence and for the sake of this goal had to be violent himself. Back then, a man was richly schooled in bodily torments and deprivations and he understood that even a certain cruelty against himself, a voluntary exercise of pain, was an essential means to his own preservation; back then, one trained his entourage to tolerate pain; back then, people liked to inflict pain and they watched the most terrible things of this kind unleashed upon others with no feeling other than that of their own safety. But as concerns the distress of the soul, I now look at every human being with an eye toward whether he knows it from experience or from description; whether he still considers it necessary to fake this knowledge, perhaps as a sign of more refined cultivation, or whether at the bottom of his soul he does not even believe in great pains of the soul and when they are mentioned, he responds similarly to when great bodily tribulations are mentioned: in which case his own toothaches and stomachaches come to mind. But this is how it stands with most people today, it seems to me. Now from the general unfamiliarity with pain of both types, and from a certain rareness of the sight of suffering people, an important consequence appears: people hate pain now much more than earlier human beings did, and malign it much more than ever before, indeed, they find even the presence of pain *as an idea* scarcely tolerable, and they make it into a matter of conscience and a reproach for the whole of existence. The emergence of pessimistic philosophies is absolutely not the sign of greater, more terrible conditions of distress; rather, these question marks regarding the value of all life are made in times when the refinement and alleviation of existence already consider the inevitable mosquito bites of the soul and body to be far too bloody and malicious, and in the absence of real pain experiences, would prefer to allow even *tormenting general ideas* to appear as suffering of the highest order. — There[99] would of course be a recipe against pessimistic philosophies and supersensitivity, which to me seems like the real "distress of the present age": — but this recipe probably sounds too cruel and would itself be attributed to the symptoms that inform today's judgment: "Existence is something evil." Well then! The recipe against "distress" reads: *distress.*

49.

Magnanimity and related matters. — Those paradoxical phenomena, such as the sudden chill in the behavior of a warm-hearted person, such as the humor of a melancholic, above all *magnanimity* as a sudden renunciation of revenge or satisfaction of envy[100] — these show up in people in whom there is a powerful inner centrifugal force, in people of sudden satiety and sudden disgust. Their satisfactions are so rapid and so strong that they are immediately followed by weariness and revulsion and a flight to the opposite taste: in these opposites, the spasm of sensation is dissolved in one person by a sudden chill, in another by laughter, in a third by tears and self-sacrifice. To me the magnanimous — as least that type among them who has always made the strongest impression — seems to be a human being of the most extreme thirst for revenge, for which a satisfaction is close at hand, and who drinks it so copiously, thoroughly and to the last drop *already in his imagination,* that a tremendously rapid disgust follows this rapid dissipation — he now rises "above himself," as they say, and forgives his enemy, indeed blesses and honors him. With this rape of himself, with this mockery of his drive for revenge that was so powerful just moments ago, he merely succumbs to the new drive that now suddenly became powerful in him (disgust), and does this just as impatiently and dissipatively as moments ago when he *anticipated* the pleasure of revenge in his mind, and, as it were, drained it. In magnanimity there is the same degree of egoism as in revenge, but a different quality of egoism.

50.[101]

The argument of isolation. — The reproach of conscience even in the most conscientious person is weak against this feeling: "This and that is counter to the good customs *of your* society." A cold glance, a sneer on the part of those among whom and for whom one has been raised, is still *feared* by even the strongest. What is actually feared here? Isolation! As the argument that vanquishes even the best arguments for a person or a cause! — Thus the herd instinct speaks through us.

51.[102]

Sense of truth. — I commend every kind of skepticism to which I am permitted to respond: "Let's try it!" But I do not want to hear anything more about all the things and all the questions that are not subject to experimentation. This is the boundary of my "sense of truth": for this is where courage lost its rights.

52.

What others know about us. — What we know and store in our memory about ourselves is not as decisive for the happiness of our lives as one thinks. Someday what *others* know (or think they know) about us crashes down on us — and now we recognize that it is more powerful. One has an easier time getting over a bad conscience than a bad reputation.

53.[103]

Where the good begins. — Where our meager eyesight is no longer capable of seeing the evil drive as such because of its continued refinement, there humans posit the realm of goodness, and the sense of having crossed over now into the realm of goodness excites all those drives that were threatened and curtailed by the evil drives, such as the feeling of security, of comfort, of benevolence. Therefore: the duller our eyesight, the further goodness extends! This explains the eternal cheerfulness of the common people and children! This explains the gloominess and the sorrow, akin to bad conscience, of great thinkers!

54.[104]

The consciousness of appearance. — How wondrous and new and at the same time how horrific and ironic I feel with my knowledge in relation to the whole of existence! I *discovered* for myself that the old human- and animal-kind, indeed the whole primordiality and past of all sentient being continues to invent, love, hate, and infer in me — I suddenly woke up in the middle of this dream, but only to the consciousness that I am simply dreaming and that I *must* dream on in order not to perish: as the sleepwalker must dream on in order not to fall down. What is "appearance" to me now! Truly not the opposite of some essence — what can I assert about any kind of essence besides just the predicates of its appearance! Truly not a dead mask that one could put on an unknown X and just as surely take off it! Appearance for me is what is itself effective and living; it goes so far in its self-mockery as to make me feel that here there are appearance and will o' the wisp and spirit dance and nothing else — that among all these dreamers I, too, the "knower," dance my dance, that the knower is a means of prolonging the earthly dance and therefore belongs to the stewards of existence, and that perhaps the sublime consistency and connectedness of all knowledge is and will be the highest means of *preserving* the universality of dreaming and the perfect comprehension[105] shared by all these dreamers, and likewise as well *the duration of the dream.*

55.[106]

The ultimate sense of nobility. — So what is it that makes "noble"? Certainly not that one makes sacrifices; even the frenzied lecher makes sacrifices. Certainly not that one pursues some kind of passion; there are contemptible passions. Certainly not that one does something for others and without selfishness: the consistency of selfishness is perhaps greatest precisely in the noblest individual.[107] — Rather, the passion that befalls the noble is something special, without his knowing about this specialness; the use of a rare and singular standard and nearly a craziness; the feeling of heat in things that feel cold to all others; figuring out values for which the scale has not yet been invented; making sacrifices on altars consecrated to an unknown god; bravery without the will to honor; a self-sufficiency that overflows and shares itself with people and things. Till now, therefore, it was rarity and the ignorance of this being rare that made someone noble. But here one should consider that by means of this yardstick, everything ordinary, closest and indispensable, in short, that which most preserves the species and in general was the *rule* in humankind up till now, has been unfairly judged and on the whole slandered for the sake of exceptions. To become the advocate of the rule — that could perhaps be the ultimate form and subtlety in which the sense of nobility manifests itself on earth.

56.[108]

The craving for suffering. — When I think of the craving to do something, as it constantly tickles and pricks millions of young Europeans, all of whom can't endure boredom and themselves — then I grasp that in them there must be a craving to suffer something, in order to extract from their suffering a probable grounds for action, for a deed. Neediness is needed! Hence the shouting of politicians, hence the many false, made-up, exaggerated "states of emergency"[109] of all possible classes and the blind readiness to believe in them. This youthful world demands that what should come or become visible *from outside* is — not happiness, for example — but unhappiness instead; and their imagination is busy in advance shaping a monster from it, so that later they can fight a monster. If these distress addicts felt the power in themselves to benefit themselves internally, to do something to themselves, then they would also understand how to create their own, genuine distress for themselves, internally. Then their inventions could be subtler and their satisfactions could sound like good music: whereas now they fill the world with their cries of distress and consequently far too often with *feelings of distress*! They don't know what to do with themselves — and so they paint the unhappiness of others on the wall: they always need others! And time and again other others! — Pardon me, my friends, I have dared to paint my *happiness* on the wall.

Book Two

57.[1]

To the realists. — You sober people, who feel armed against passion and fancifulness and would gladly make a point of pride and an adornment out of your emptiness, you call yourselves realists and imply that the world really is as it seems to you: before you alone reality stands unveiled, and you yourselves would probably be the best part of it — oh you beloved images of Sais![2] But aren't you, too, in your most unveiled state, still supremely passionate and obscure beings, compared to fish, and still all too similar to an artist in love? — and what is "reality" to an artist in love! You are still carrying around with you the valuations of things that have their origin in the passions and infatuations of earlier centuries! Your sobriety still has a secret and ineradicable drunkenness incorporated in it! Your love for "reality," for instance — oh that is an ancient "love"! In every sensation, in every sensual impression there is a piece of this old love: and likewise it was worked on and woven by some fancifulness, a prejudice, an unreason, an ignorance, a fear and who knows what else! That mountain there! That cloud there! What's "real" about them? Try to deduct from them, for once, the phantasms and whole human *added ingredient,* you sober ones! Yes, if only you could do *that*! If you could forget your descent, past, early training — your entire humankind and animalkind! For us there is no "reality" — and not for you either, you sober ones —[3] we are by no means as foreign to one another as you think, and maybe our good will to get beyond drunkenness is just as respectable as your belief that you are *incapable* of drunkenness.[4]

58.[5]

Only as creators! — This has cost me the greatest effort and continues to cost me the greatest effort: recognizing that there is unspeakably more at stake in *what things are called* than in what they are. Reputation, name and appearance, validity, the usual measure and weight of a thing — mostly error and arbitrariness originally, thrown over things like a dress and completely foreign to their nature and even their skin — have gradually grown onto things and become their body, so to speak, through faith in them and its continued growth from generation to generation: from the start, appearance almost always ends up becoming essence and *has the effect* of essence! What kind of fool would believe it suffices to point to this origin and this misty shroud of delusion to *annihilate* the world that passes for essential, so-called "*reality*"! Only as creators can we annihilate! — But let us not forget this either: it suffices to create new names and valuations and probabilities in the long run, in order to create new "things."

59.[6]

We artists! — When we love a woman, we easily develop a hatred for nature, mindful of all the repulsive natural things to which every woman is subject; we would prefer not even to think about it, but once our soul touches these things, it winces impatiently, as mentioned, and gazes with contempt upon nature: — we are offended, nature seems to intrude on our possession and does so with the profanest of hands. Then we refuse to listen to all physiology and secretly decree to ourselves: "I don't want to hear any more about how human beings consist of anything but *soul and form*!" "The human being beneath the skin" is an abomination and a monstrous thought to all lovers, a blasphemy against God and love. — Well, just as the lover still feels vis-à-vis nature and naturalness, formerly every worshipper felt about God and his "holy omnipotence": in everything that was said about nature by astronomers, geologists, physiologists, physicians, he saw an intrusion and therefore an attack on his most precious possession — and on top of that a shamelessness in the attacker! "Law of nature" even sounded to him like a slandering of God; at bottom, he would have all too gladly seen the whole of mechanics traced back to moral acts of will and acts of arbitrariness: — but because no one could provide him this service, he *concealed* nature and mechanics from himself as best he could, and lived in a dream. Oh these human beings of yore knew how to *dream* and didn't even need to fall asleep first! — and also we people of today still know it much too well, even with all our good will for being awake and for the day! It suffices to love, to hate, to desire, to feel anything at all — *immediately* the spirit and the power of dream come over us and we climb on the most dangerous paths, open-eyed and cold to all danger, up onto the rooftops and towers of fancifulness, and without the least bit of dizziness, as if born to climb — we sleepwalkers of the day! We artists! We concealers of naturalness! We moon- and God-addicts![7] We deathly silent inexhaustible wanderers on heights that we do not even see as heights, but instead as our plains, as our security!

60.[8]

Women and their action at a distance. — Do I still have ears? Am I only ears now and nothing more? Here I stand in the midst of the blaze of the surf,[9] whose white flames are licking at my feet: — from all sides it is howling, threatening, screaming, shrilling at me, while in the deepest depths the ancient earth-shaker sings his aria, rumbling like a bellowing bull: he stamps a beat to it, such an earth-shaking beat that the hearts of even these weathered boulder monsters here tremble in their bodies. Then, suddenly, as if born out of nothing, there appears before the gate of this hellish labyrinth, only a few fathoms away — a great sailing ship gliding up silently as a ghost. Oh this ghostly beauty! With what magic does it touch me! What? Has all the calm and taciturnity of the world boarded this ship? Does my very happiness sit in this quiet place, my happier self, my second, departed self? Not being dead and yet no longer living either? As a ghostly, quiet, watching, gliding, hovering middle being? Resembling the ship that with its white sails skips over the dark sea like an enormous butterfly! Yes! Skipping *over* existence! That's it! That would be it! — — It seems the noise here has turned me into a visionary? All great noise causes us to place our happiness in the quiet and the distance. When a man stands amidst *his* noise, amidst his surf of projectiles and projects:[10] then he, too, likely sees quiet magical beings gliding past him, whose happiness and seclusion he longs for — *they are women.* He almost thinks that his better self dwells there among the women: in these quiet places even the loudest surf could become deathly silence and life itself a dream about life. And yet! And yet! My noble fanatic, even on the most beautiful sailing ship there is so much sound and noise and unfortunately so much petty pitiful noise! The magic and the mightiest effect of women is, to speak the language of philosophers, an effect at a distance, an *actio in distans:* but this requires, first and foremost — *distance*!

61.

In honor of friendship. — That the feeling of friendship was reckoned by antiquity as the highest feeling, even higher than the most celebrated pride of the self-sufficient and wise man, indeed in a way as this pride's only and even holier sibling: this is expressed very nicely in the story of that Macedonian king who gave a gift of a talent[11] to an Athenian philosopher who despised the world, only to have it returned to him. "What?" said the king, "doesn't he have a friend?" By this he meant: "I honor the pride of this wise and independent man, but I would honor his humanity still more highly if the friend in him had won out over his pride. In my eyes this philosopher has lowered himself by

showing that he does not know one of the two highest feelings
— and the higher one at that!"

62.

Love. — Love forgives the lover even his desire.

63.

Woman in music. — Why is it that warm and rainy winds
also bring a musical mood and the inventive pleasure of melody? Aren't these the same winds that fill the churches and give
women amorous thoughts?[12]

64.[13]

Skeptics. — I fear that women who have grown old are more
skeptical in their most secret heart of hearts than all men: they
believe in the superficiality of existence as its essence, and all
virtue and profundity is to them only a veiling of this "truth,"
the very desirable veiling of a pudendum — hence a matter of
decency and shame, and nothing more!

65.

Devotion. — There are noble women with a certain poverty
of spirit[14] who, in order to *express* their deepest devotion,
know of no better way than to offer up their virtue and shame:
to them it is their highest. And often this gift is accepted without obligating oneself as deeply as the givers assume — a very
melancholy story!

66.

The strength of the weak. — All women are subtle about
exaggerating their weakness, indeed they are inventive in their
weaknesses, in order to appear completely as fragile ornaments
who are harmed by even a speck of dust: their existence is supposed to make a man aware of his clumsiness and pin it on
his conscience. In this way they defend themselves against the
strong and all "might makes right."

67.

To feign oneself. — She loves him now and ever since she has just beamed with such peaceful confidence, like a cow: but alas! Precisely this was what bewitched him, that she seemed completely changeable and unfathomable! He already had too much steady weather of his own! Wouldn't she do well to feign her old character? To feign lovelessness? Do you not therefore counsel — love? *Vivat comoedia!*[15]

68.

Will and willingness. — They took a youth to a wise man and said: "See, this is someone who is being corrupted by women!" The wise man[16] shook his head and smiled. "It's the men," he cried, "who corrupt the women: and everything that's wrong with women should be atoned for and improved by men — for a man makes himself an image of woman, and the woman shapes herself in this image."[17] — "You are too lenient toward women," said one of the bystanders, "you don't know them!" The wise man[18] answered: "A man's way is the will, a woman's way is willingness — thus it is the law of the sexes, truly, a harsh law for the woman! All human beings are innocent of their existence,[19] but women are innocent to the second degree: who could have enough balm and lenience for them." — What do you mean balm! What do you mean lenience!" cried another from the crowd; the women have to be raised better!" — "The men have to be raised better," said the wise man[20] and he beckoned for the youth to follow him. — But the youth did not follow him.[21]

69.

Capacity for revenge. — That someone cannot defend himself and consequently does not want to, does not make him a disgrace in our eyes: but we hold in low esteem someone who has neither the ability nor the good will for revenge — regardless whether man or woman. Would a woman be able to hold on to us (or as they say "captivate" us), if we did not trust her to know under certain circumstances how to skillfully wield the dagger (any kind of dagger) *against* us? Or against herself: which in a certain case would be the more grievous revenge (Chinese revenge).

70.[22]

The mistresses of masters.[23] — A deep powerful alto voice, the kind one occasionally hears in the theater, suddenly raises the curtain for us on possibilities that we usually do not believe in: we suddenly believe that somewhere in the world there can be women with lofty, heroic, royal souls, capable of and prepared for grandiose responses, resolutions and sacrifices, capable of and prepared for mastery over men, because in them the best of man has become their incarnate ideal, beyond gender. To be sure, according to the intention of theater such voices are precisely *not* supposed to provide this notion of woman: usually they are supposed to portray the ideal male lover, for instance a Romeo; but judging by my experience, the theater and the musician who expect such effects from such voices quite routinely miscalculate. One doesn't believe in *this* lover: these voices still harbor a coloring of the maternal and the housewifely, and precisely for the most part when love is in their tone.

71.[24]

On female chastity. — There is something quite astonishing and outrageous in the upbringing of noble[25] women, indeed there is perhaps nothing more paradoxical. The whole world agrees on bringing them up as ignorant as possible *in eroticis,*[26] and on instilling in their soul a deep shame of such things and the most extreme impatience and flight at the mere suggestion of these things. All the "honor" of woman is at risk basically here only: what would we not forgive them otherwise! But here they are supposed to remain ignorant to their heart of hearts: — they are supposed to have neither eyes nor ears nor words nor thoughts for this their "evil": indeed just knowing is already evil here. And now! To be hurled as if by a horrific stroke of lightning into reality and knowledge, by marriage — and what's more by the one they love and esteem most: to catch love and shame in contradiction,[27] indeed, to have to sense thrills, surrender, duty, sympathy and terror over the unexpected proximity of God and beast and whatever else! all in one! — Here, in fact, we have tied ourselves a psychic knot that has no equal! Even the pitying curiosity of the wisest connoisseur of human nature does not suffice to guess how this or that woman comes to terms with the solution of this riddle and this riddle of a solution, and what kind of horrifying, far-reaching suspicions must be stirring here in this poor unhinged soul, indeed how the ultimate philosophy and skepticism of woman at this point drops anchor! — Afterward the same deep silence as before: and often a silence before oneself, a closing of one's eyes before oneself. — Young women make a great effort to appear superficial and thoughtless; the subtlest among them feign a kind of impudence. — Women easily perceive their husbands as a question mark against their honor and their children as an apology or a penance[28] — they need children and wish for them in an entirely different sense than a man wishes for children. — In brief, one cannot be lenient enough toward women![29,30]

72.

The mothers. — Animals think differently about females than humans do; for them the female is considered the productive being. Paternal love does not exist among them, but something like love for the children of a lover and habituation to them. In their children females have a satisfaction of their lust to rule, a possession, an occupation, something entirely comprehensible to them with which they can chatter: all of this together is maternal love — it can be compared to the love of an artist for his work. Pregnancy has made women milder, more patient, more fearful, more eager to submit; and likewise spiritual pregnancy produces the character of the contemplative ones, which is related to the female character: — these are the male mothers. — Among animals the male sex is considered the beautiful one.

73.

Holy cruelty. — A man who held a newborn child in his hands approached a saint. "What am I supposed to do with this child?" he asked, "it is miserable, misshapen and doesn't have enough life to even die." "Kill it," cried the saint in a terrifying voice, "kill it and then hold it for three days and three nights in your arms, so that you make yourself a memory of it: — then you will never again beget a child when it is not time for you to beget." — When the man heard this he walked away disappointed; and many reproached the saint because he had counseled cruelty, for he had counseled the man to kill the child. "But is it not more cruel to let it live?" said the saint.

74.

The unsuccessful. — Those poor women who become restless and insecure and talk too much in the presence of the one they love are always lacking success: for men are most firmly seduced by a certain mysterious and phlegmatic tenderness.

75.[31]

The third sex. — "A small man is a paradox, but still a man — but the small women seem to me, compared to tall women, to be of a different sex" — said an old dance master. A small woman is never beautiful — said old Aristotle.[32]

76.

The greatest danger. —If there had not been at all times a majority of human beings who felt the discipline of their mind — their "rationality" — as their pride, their obligation, their virtue, who were offended or embarrassed by all fantasizing and dissipation of thought, as friends "of healthy common sense": then humankind would have long ago perished! Over it the eruption of *insanity* hovered and hovers constantly as its greatest danger — this means simply the erupting of arbitrariness in perceiving, seeing and hearing, the pleasure of lack of discipline of the mind, joy in human unreason. Not truth and certainty are the opposite of the world of the insane, but the universality and the all-connectedness of a faith, in sum, the nonarbitrary in judging. And the greatest work of humans so far was agreeing with one another on very many things and imposing on themselves a *law of agreement* — regardless of whether these things are true or false. This is the discipline of mind that has preserved humankind — but the counterdrives are still so powerful that at bottom one may speak with little confidence about the future of humankind. The image of things is still continually shoving and shifting, and perhaps from now on more and faster than ever; precisely the choicest spirits continually bristle at this all-connectedness — the explorers of *truth* in the vanguard! Continually, that faith as the faith of the whole world produces a disgust and a new lust among subtler minds: and already the slow tempo that it demands for all spiritual processes, that imitation of the turtle that is here recognized as the norm, makes artists and poets into deserters: — it is these impatient spirits in whom a veritable joy of insanity erupts, because insanity has such a cheerful tempo! So what's needed are virtuous intellects — oh! I want to use the most unambiguous word — what's needed is *virtuous stupidity,* what's needed are unflappable beat-keepers for the *slow* spirit, so that the faithful of the overall-faith stay together and continue to dance their dance: it is a necessity of the first degree that commands and demands here. *We others are the exception and the danger* — we need eternal defense! — Well, something really can be said in favor of the exception, *assuming that it never wants to become the rule.*[33]

77.[34]

The animal with a good conscience. — The vulgarity in everything that is liked in southern Europe — be it Italian opera (for

example Rossini's and Bellini's) or the Spanish adventure novel
(most readily accessible to us in the French guise of Gil Blas[35])
— is not lost on me, but it does not offend me, any more so than
the vulgarity one encounters on a walk through Pompeii and at
bottom even in reading any ancient book: why is this? Is it that
here modesty is lacking and that all vulgarity appears with the
same assuredness and self-confidence as anything noble, lovely
and passionate in the same kind of music or novel? "The animal
has its rights like the human being: so it is free to run around,
and you, my dear fellow human, are still this animal too, despite
everything!" — that seems to me to be the moral of the story
and the peculiarity of southern European humanity. Bad taste
has the same rights as good taste, and even a prior right in cases
where it is the great need, the assured satisfaction and a universal language, so to speak, an absolutely intelligible mask and
gesture: good, discerning taste, on the other hand, always has
something searching, rehearsed, not fully certain of its intel-
ligibility — it never is and never was popular![36] What is and
remains popular is the *mask*! So let all this masquerading flow
into the melodies and cadenzas, into the leaps and merriments
of the rhythm of these operas! And as for the life of antiquity!
What does one understand of it if one does not understand the
pleasure of the mask, the good conscience of all masquerading!
Here we have the baths and the recreation of the antique spirit:
— and perhaps these baths were even more necessary to the rare
and sublime natures of the ancient world than to the vulgar. —
On the other hand, I am offended by a vulgar turn in northern
works, for example in German music, unspeakably offended.
Here *shame* is present, the artist has lowered himself in his own
eyes and in the process could not even avoid blushing: we are
ashamed along with him and are so offended because we intuit
that he believed he had to lower himself for our sake.[37]

78.

What we should be grateful for. — Only artists, and especially
those of the theater, have provided humans with eyes and ears

in order to hear and see, with a bit of enjoyment, what everyone himself is, himself experiences, himself wants; only they
have taught us to esteem the hero who is hidden in each of all
these ordinary human beings, and the art of seeing oneself as
a hero, from a distance and simplified and transfigured, as it
were — the art of "staging" oneself before oneself. It is only in
this way that we get over certain lowly details about ourselves!
Without this art, we would be nothing but foreground and we
would live entirely under the tyranny of that perspective that
makes the closest and the basest things tremendously large
and makes them seem like reality itself. — Perhaps there is a
similar merit in the religion that exhorted us to view the sinful-
ness of every individual human being with a magnifying glass,
and made a great, immortal criminal out of the sinner: insofar as it described eternal perspectives around them, it taught
human beings to see themselves from a distance and as something past, something whole.

79.[38]

The attraction of imperfection. — Here I see a poet who,
like so many human beings, exerts a higher attraction through
his imperfections than through everything that emerges from his
hands developed and perfectly shaped — indeed, his advantage
and his fame rest much more on his ultimate incapacity than on
his rich powers. His work never quite expresses what he really
wishes to express, what he *wishes to have seen:* it seems he had
a foretaste of a vision and never the vision itself: — but a tremendous craving for this vision has remained in his soul, and
from it he takes his likewise tremendous eloquence of longing and ravenousness. With this, he lifts up his listener, over
and beyond his work and all "works" and gives him wings to
climb higher than listeners ever otherwise climb: and so, having become poets and seers themselves, they lavish the author
of their happiness with such admiration as if he had initiated
them directly into the spectacle of his most holy and ultimate,
as if he had reached his goal and actually *seen* and imparted his

vision. It benefits his fame that he did not actually arrive at his goal.

80.[39]

Art and nature. — The Greeks (or at least the Athenians) liked to hear good speaking: indeed they had a greedy penchant for it, that distinguishes them more than anything else from non-Greeks. And so they demanded even of passion on the stage that it speak well, and they let the unnaturalness of the dramatic verse wash over them with bliss: — in nature, after all, passion is so tongue-tied! so mute and embarrassed! Or when it finds words, so confused and irrational and so ashamed of itself! Now all of us, thanks to the Greeks, have accustomed ourselves to this unnaturalness on the stage, just as we tolerate that other unnaturalness, *singing* passion, and gladly tolerate it, thanks to the Italians. — It has become a need of ours, one that we cannot satisfy from everyday reality: to hear human beings in the most difficult situations speaking well and at length: now it delights us when the tragic hero is able to find words, reasons, eloquent gestures and on the whole a bright intellectuality where life approaches the abyss, and real human beings usually lose their heads and certainly beautiful speech. This kind of *deviation from nature* is perhaps the most welcome repast for the pride of humans; for its sake generally we love art, as the expression of a lofty, heroic unnaturalness and convention. One is justified in reproaching the dramatic poet if he does not transform everything into reason and word, but instead always remains holding a remnant of *silence*.[40] — just as one is dissatisfied with the musician of opera who doesn't know how to find a melody for the highest affect, but instead only an affect-laden "natural" stammering and screaming. Here nature simply *must* be contradicted! Here the base attraction of illusion simply *must* yield to a higher attraction! The Greeks went far in this direction, far and — terrifyingly far! Just as they constructed the stage as narrowly as possible and forbade themselves all deep background effect, just as they made it impossible for the actor to have facial expressions and easy movement and transformed him into a solemn, stiff, masklike bogey man, so too they stripped even passion of its deep background and dictated a law of beautiful speech to it, indeed they generally did everything to counteract the elementary effect of fear- and pity-inducing images: *they simply did not want fear and pity* — no dishonor, indeed highest honors to Aristotle! but he certainly did not hit the nail, let alone the nail's head, when he spoke of the ultimate purpose of Greek tragedy![41] One should scrutinize the Greek tragic poets on the basis of *what* most incited their industry, their ingenuity, their competitive spirit — certainly not the intent of overwhelming the spectators through affects! The Athenian went to the theater *in order to hear beautiful speeches*! And beautiful speeches are what Sophocles was interested in — forgive me this heresy! — Matters are very different with *serious opera:* all of its masters make a point of preventing their characters from being understood. An occasional snatched-up word might come to the aid of the inattentive listener: on the whole the situation has to explain itself — the speeches have nothing to do with it! — that is how they all think and that is why they all played their pranks with the words. Perhaps they only lacked the courage fully to express their ultimate contempt for words: a bit more impudence in Rossini, and he would have just made them sing la-la-la-la throughout — and that would have been perfectly reasonable! The characters in opera are simply not supposed to be taken "at their word," rather by sound! That is the difference, that is the beautiful *unnaturalness* for whose sake one attends the opera! Even the *recitativo secco*[42] is not really supposed to be heard as word and text: rather, this kind of half-music is mainly supposed to give the musical ear a small pause (a pause from the *melody,* as the most sublime and therefore also strenuous enjoyment of this art) — but very soon something different: namely a growing impatience, a growing resistance, a new desire for *whole* music, for melody. — Seen from this point of view, how do things stand with the art of Richard Wagner?[43] Perhaps differently? It often seemed to me as if one had to have learned the words *and* music of his creations by heart before the performance: for without this — so it seemed to me — one could *hear* neither the words nor the music itself.[44]

81.

Greek taste. — "What's beautiful about that?" — said that surveyor following a performance of *Iphigenia*[45] — "nothing is proved in it!"[46] Were the Greeks so far from this in their own taste? At least in Sophocles "everything is proven."

82.[47]

Esprit is un-Greek. — In all their thinking the Greeks are indescribably logical and plain; this they did not tire of, at least for their long good period, as the French so often do: who all too gladly make a small leap into the opposite and really only tolerate the spirit of logic when, through numerous small leaps of this kind into its opposite, it betrays its *sociable* grace, its sociable self-denial. Logic seems necessary to them, like bread and water, but like these it also seems a kind of prisoner's fare as soon as it is supposed to be eaten alone and on its own. In good society one must never want to be completely and solely right, the way pure logic wants it: hence the small dose of unreason in all French *esprit*. — The social sensibility of the Greeks was far less developed than that of the French is and was: this is why there is so little *esprit* in their most intelligent men, and so little wit even in their wittiest jokers, this is why — alas! One will already fail to believe these sentences of mine, and how many more of the same kind I still have on my mind! — *Est res magna tacere*[48] — says Martial, along with all who are loquacious.

83.[49]

Translations. — One can estimate the degree of historical sense an age possesses according to how this age makes *translations* and seeks to incorporate past ages and books. The French of Corneille and also those of the Revolution appropriated

Roman antiquity in a manner to which we would no longer have the courage — thanks to our higher historical sense. And Roman antiquity itself: how brutally and simultaneously naïvely it laid hands on all that was good and elevated in the more ancient Greek antiquity! How they translated things into the Roman present! How they deliberately and callously brushed off the dust from the wings of the butterfly moment! Thus Horace here and there translated Alcaeus or Archilochus, thus Propertius likewise translated Callimachus and Philetas (poets of the same rank as Theocritus, if we are *permitted* to judge): what did they care that the actual creator had experienced this and that and had inscribed the signs of it into his poem! — as poets they were averse to the antiquarian detective spirit that precedes the historical sense, as poets they did not validate these entirely personal things and names and everything that was unique to a city, a coast, a century as its costume and mask, rather, they swiftly instated the present and the Roman in its place. They seem to be asking us: "Shouldn't we make the old new for us, and make *ourselves* comfortable in it? Shouldn't we be allowed to breathe our soul into this dead body? for it is dead, after all: how ugly is everything dead!" — They did not know the pleasure of the historical sense; the past and the foreign were awkward to them, and as Romans they took it as an incentive for a Roman conquest. In fact, back then one conquered when one translated — not only by leaving out the historical: no, one added allusions to the present, and above all, one deleted the name of the poet and instated one's own in its place — not with a feeling of thieving, but instead with the very best conscience of the *imperium Romanum*.[50]

84.

On the origin of poetry. — The lovers of the fantastic in humans, who at the same time represent the teaching that morality is instinctive, reason thus: "assuming that for all time utility has been honored as the supreme deity, where then in the whole wide world did poetry come from? — this rhythmicizing of speech that sooner counteracts the clarity of communication than aids it, and that nevertheless shot up and continues to shoot up everywhere on earth like a mockery of all useful expediency! The savagely beautiful irrationality of poetry refutes you, utilitarians! Precisely in wanting to *escape* for once from utility — this elevated humans, this inspired them to morality and art!" Now in this matter I must concur for once with the utilitarians — they are so seldom right, after all, that it's pitiful! In those ancient times that called poetry into existence, utility was indeed the goal and a very great utility — back then when rhythm was allowed to penetrate speech, that force that rearranges all the atoms of a sentence, commands that words be selected and adds new coloration to thoughts and makes them darker, stranger, more remote: a *superstitious utility* to be sure! By virtue of rhythm a human concern was supposed to be more deeply impressed on the gods, after it was noticed that humans retain a verse in their memory[51] better than unbound speech; likewise people believed that through a rhythmic tick-tock they could make themselves audible across greater distances; rhythmicized prayer seemed to get closer to the ears of the gods. Above all, however, they wanted to have the utility of that elementary overpowering that humans experience when listening to music: rhythm is a compulsion; it produces an irresistible urge to give in, to chime in; not just the steps of the feet, even the soul itself follows the beat — and probably, so they reasoned, the souls of the gods too! One attempted therefore to *compel* them through rhythm and to exert a power over them: one cast poetry over them like a magic snare. There was an even stranger idea: and precisely this one probably contributed most powerfully to the origin of poetry. Among the Pythagoreans it appears as a philosophical doctrine and as a strategy in education: but long before there were philosophers, people conferred on music the power to discharge affects, to purify the soul, to temper the *ferocia animi*[52] — and moreover precisely through music's rhythm. When the proper tension and harmony of the soul was lost, then one had to *dance* to

the beat of the poet[53] — that was the prescription of this ther-
apy. Terpander used it to calm a riot, Empedocles to sooth a
maniac, Damon to cleanse a lovesick youth; one also used it
to treat the gods who had gone wild with vengefulness. Initially this was done by driving the giddiness and boisterousness
of their affects to the extreme, therefore driving the insane into a
rage, and making the vengeful drunk with revenge: — all the
orgiastic cults wanted to discharge the *ferocia* of a divinity all at
once and turn it into an orgy, so that afterward it would feel
freer and calmer and leave humans in peace. According to its
root meaning *melos*[54] is a tranquilizer not because it is tranquil itself, rather because its effect renders tranquil. — And
not only in the cult song, but also in worldly songs of most
ancient times lies the assumption that the rhythmic exerts a
magic power; for example in drawing water or in rowing, the
song casts a spell on the demons thought to be active here,
making them pliant, unfree and into tools for humans. And
whenever one takes action, one has occasion to sing — *every*
action is connected to the assistance of spirits: magic song and
incantation appear to be the primeval form of poetry. When
verse was used even in oracles — the Greeks said that hexame-
ters were invented at Delphi — rhythm was supposed to exert a
compulsion here as well. To have something prophesied — this
originally meant (according to the derivation of the Greek word
that seems probable to me): to have something determined; one
believed one could compel the future by winning over Apollo
for oneself: he who according to the most ancient conception
is much more than a seer god. Just as the formula is spoken,
literally and rhythmically precise, so too it binds the future: but
the formula is the invention of Apollo, who as god of rhythms
can even bind the goddesses of destiny. — Viewed and asked
on the whole: was there anything more *useful* generally than
rhythm for the ancient superstitious type of human? One
could do everything with it: magically advance a task; compel a
god to appear, to be near, to listen; shape the future to comply
with one's will; discharge one's own soul of some excess (of

fear, of mania, of compassion, of vengefulness), and not only one's own soul, but that of the most evil demon — without verses one was nothing, through verses one nearly became a god. Such a fundamental feeling can no longer be fully eradicated — and even now, after millennia of long work in combating such superstition, even the wisest among us occasionally becomes a fool of rhythm, be it only in the fact that he *senses* a thought to be *truer* if it has a metrical form and approaches with a divine hop, skip and a jump. Isn't it a very comical affair that the most serious philosophers still invoke *poetic proverbs,* as rigorous as they otherwise are in all matters of certainty, in order to lend force and credibility to their thoughts? — and yet it is more dangerous for a truth if the poet approves of it, than if he contradicts it! For as Homer said: "Much indeed do the poets lie!"[55]

85.

The good and the beautiful. — Artists *glorify* constantly — they do nothing else — : and in particular all those states and things whose reputation suggests that with them and in them, humans can for once feel good or great, or drunk, or joyful, or well and wise. These *selected* things and states, whose value for human *happiness* is considered certain and calculated, are the objects of the artists: they always lie in wait to discover such things and to pull them into the sphere of art. I mean to say: they themselves are not the appraisers of happiness and the happy ones, but they always push their way close to these appraisers, with the greatest curiosity and eagerness to immediately make use of their appraisals. And so, because in addition to their impatience they also have the big lungs of heralds and the feet of runners, they will always also be among the first to glorify the *new* good, and will often *seem* to be those who first name it good and appraise it as good. But this, as mentioned, is an error: they are merely faster and louder than the real appraisers. — And who, then, are the real ones? — They are the wealthy and the idle.

86.[56]

On theater. — This day provided me again with strong and elevated feelings, and if in the evening I could have music and art, then I well know which music and art I would *not* like to have, namely, whatever wants to intoxicate its listeners and *drive them up to the heights* of a moment of strong and elevated feeling — those same humans of the everyday soul, who in the evening do not resemble victors in triumphal chariots but instead exhausted mules on whom life has wielded its whip a bit too often. What would those people know anyway about "more elevated moods," if not for intoxicating substances and idealistic lashes of the whip! — and so they have their inspirers in the same way they have their wines. But what is their drink and their drunkenness *to me*! What does the inspired one need with wine! On the contrary, he gazes with a kind of disgust at the means and mediators who are supposed to produce an effect here without a sufficient reason — an aping of the soul's high tide! — What? We put wings and proud conceits on a mole — before bedtime, before he crawls into his hole? We send him to the theater and put big glasses on his blind and weary eyes? Humans whose life is not a "plot" but a business deal, sit in front of a stage and watch strange creatures for whom life is more than a deal? "That's just decency," you say, "that's entertaining, that's how culture would have it!" — Well then! All too often I am lacking culture: for all too often the sight of this makes me nauseous. Whoever has enough tragedy and comedy in himself will probably prefer to avoid the theater; or, in the exceptional case, the whole event — theater and public and poet included — turns into an actual tragic and comic spectacle for him, so that by comparison the play that is being performed means only little to him. Whoever is something of a Faust or a Manfred, what does he care about the Fausts and Manfreds of the theater! — whereas it certainly gives him pause *that* such characters are even depicted in theaters. The *strongest* thoughts and passions displayed before those who are not capable of thinking and passion — but of *intoxication*! And *those* as a means to intoxication! And theater and music as the hashish-smoking and betel-chewing of Europeans! Oh, who can tell us the entire history of narcotics! — It is nearly the history of "culture," of so-called higher culture![57,58]

87.[59,60]

On the vanity of artists. — I believe artists often do not know what they do best, because they are too vain and have trained their minds on something prouder than these little plants seem to be, that are new, rare and beautiful, and capable of growing to real perfection in their soil. What is actually good in their own garden and vineyard is casually dismissed by them, and their love and their insight are not of equal rank. There is a musician[61] who more than any other musician has his expertise in finding sounds from the realm of suffering, oppressed, tortured souls and giving voice even to dumb animals. No one is his equal in the colorings of late autumn, the indescribably stirring happiness of a last, very last, very briefest enjoyment, he has a sound for those mysterious-uncanny[62] midnights of the soul, where cause and effect seem to have come unhinged and in any moment something can arise "out of nothing"; he draws most successfully of all artists from the deepest bottom of human happiness and from its drained cup, so to speak, where the bitterest and most repulsive drops have mingled for better or worse with the sweetest; he knows that weariness of the soul that has to push itself, that can no longer leap and fly, indeed can no longer walk; he has the shy look of concealed pain, of understanding without comfort, of taking leave without confessing; indeed, as the Orpheus of all secret misery he is greater than anyone, and only through him some things have been added to art generally that previously seemed inexpressible and even unworthy of art, things for instance that could only be scared off by words, not grasped by them — some very small and microscopic things of the soul: yes, he is the master of the miniature. But he does not *want* to be! His *character* loves great walls and daring frescoes! It escapes him that his *spirit* has a different taste and inclination and prefers to sit quietly in the nooks of collapsed buildings: — here, hidden, hidden from himself, he paints his real masterpieces, which are all very brief, often only a single bar in length — only here does he become entirely good, great and perfect, perhaps here alone. — But he doesn't know it! He is too vain to know it.

88.

Seriousness about truth. — Seriousness about truth! How many different things people understand by these words! Precisely the same views and types of evidence and testing that a thinker perceives as carelessness in himself, to which he succumbed in this or that hour to his shame — just these very same views can give an artist who encounters and lives with them for a while the impression that now the profoundest seriousness about truth has him in its grip, and it is admirable that he, although an artist, yet at the same time displays this most serious desire for the opposite of appearance. Thus it is possible that precisely with his pathos of seriousness, someone betrays how superficially and modestly his spirit has played so far in the realm of knowledge. — And is not everything that we consider *weighty*[63] our betrayer? It shows where our weights lie as well as where we have no weights.

89.[64]

Now and formerly. — What does all our art of artworks matter if that higher art, the art of festivals, is lost to us! Formerly all artworks were exhibited along the great festival road of humankind, as commemorations and memorials of elevated and blissful moments. Now we use artworks to lure aside, for a tiny lascivious moment, the wretched exhausted and sick from humankind's great road of suffering; we offer them a small intoxication and madness.

90.[65]

Lights and shadows. — Books and writings represent different things for different thinkers: one of them brought together in his book the lights that he was able to hastily snatch up and carry home from the rays of knowledge that dawned on him; another reproduces only shadows, afterimages in gray and black of what built up in his soul the day before.

91.

Caution. — Alfieri, as is known, lied a lot in telling his astonished contemporaries his life's story. He lied out of that despotism toward himself that he demonstrated for example in the manner in which he created his own language and tyrannized himself into becoming a poet: — in the end he had found an austere form of the sublime into which he *impressed* his life and his memory: he must have suffered great agony in doing so. — I would also not believe a life's story of Plato written by himself: any more than Rousseau's, or Dante's *Vita Nuova.*[66]

92.[67]

Prose and poetry. — It is certainly noteworthy that the great masters of prose have almost always also been poets, be it publicly or even only in secret and in the "closet"; and truly, one only writes good prose *in the face of poetry*! For prose is an uninterrupted well-mannered war with poetry: all of its charms consist in the fact that poetry is constantly being avoided and contradicted; every *abstractum*[68] wants to be recited as a prank on poetry and as if with a mocking voice; everything dry and cool is supposed to drive the lovely goddess to lovely despair; often there are approaches, momentary reconciliations and then a sudden leaping back and malicious laughter; often the curtain is raised and harsh light is admitted, while the goddess was just enjoying her twilights and muted colors; often the words are taken out of her mouth and sung to a melody that makes her put her dainty hands over her dainty little ears

— and so there are a thousand pleasures of war, the defeats included, of which the unpoetic, the so-called prose people, know absolutely nothing: — and so they also speak and write only bad prose! *War is the father of all good things,*[69] war is also the father of good prose! — There were four very unusual and truly poetic human beings in this century who achieved mastery in prose, for which this century is otherwise not suited — from a lack of poetry, as indicated. Not including Goethe, who is claimed fairly by the century that produced him: I see only Giacomo Leopardi, Prosper Mérimée, Ralph Waldo Emerson and Walter Savage Landor, the author of *Imaginary Conversations,* as worthy of being called masters of prose.

93.[70]

But why then do you write? — A: I am not one of those who *thinks* with a wet quill in his hand; still less am I one of those who abandon themselves to their passions in front of an ink-well, sitting on their chair and staring at the page. All writing makes me angry or ashamed; writing for me is a basic necessity — to speak of it even metaphorically is repugnant to me. B: But why then do you write? A: Yes, my good man, if I may confide: so far I have found no other means of getting *rid* of my thoughts. B: And why do you want to get rid of them? A: Why do I want to? Do I even want to? I must. — B: Enough! Enough!

94.

Growth after death. — Those little audacious words about moral things that Fontenelle threw out in his immortal *Dialogues of the Dead*[71] were regarded in his day as paradoxes and games of a not insignificant wit; even the highest judges of taste and intellect saw nothing more in them — indeed, perhaps Fontenelle himself did not. Now something incredible happens: these thoughts become truths! Science is proving them! The game becomes serious! And we read those dialogues with a different feeling than Voltaire and Helvetius when they read them, and we involuntarily lift their author into a different and *much higher* classification of intellects than they did — justly? Unjustly?

95.[72]

Chamfort. —That such a connoisseur of human beings and the masses as Chamfort actually joined the masses and did not stand off to the side in philosophical resignation — this I can only explain to myself as follows: One instinct in him was stronger than his wisdom and had never been satisfied, his hatred for all nobility of blood: perhaps the old and only too explicable hatred felt by his mother,[73] which he sanctified in himself through his love for this mother — an instinct for revenge going back to his boyhood years, that just waited for the hour to avenge his mother. And now life and his own genius and, alas! probably the paternal blood in his veins most of all seduced him into joining the ranks of this nobility as their peer — for many many years! In the end however he no longer endured the sight of himself, the sight of the "old world man" under the old regime; he fell into a violent passion of repentance, and *in it* he donned the cloak of the rabble as *his* kind of hair shirt! His bad conscience stemmed from his failure to avenge. — Assuming Chamfort had remained more the philosopher by a single degree back then, the Revolution would not have acquired its tragic wit and its sharpest sting: it would be regarded as a much more stupid event and would not be such a seduction of intellects. But the hatred and revenge of Chamfort educated an entire generation: and the most illustrious human beings passed through this school. Bear in mind that Mirabeau looked up to Chamfort as if to his higher and older self, from whom he expected and tolerated inspiration, warnings and verdicts — Mirabeau, who as a human being belongs in an entirely different order of greatness than even the foremost of statesmen-luminaries of yesterday and today. — It is odd that despite such a friend and advocate — we have after all the letters of Mirabeau to Chamfort[74] — this

wittiest of all moralists has remained a stranger to the French,
no differently than Stendhal, who among all the French of
this century probably had the most thoughtful eyes and ears.
Is it because the latter at bottom had too much of a German
and an Englishman in him, to be still bearable to the Pari-
sians? — whereas Chamfort, a human being rich in depths
and backgrounds of the soul, gloomy, suffering, smoldering
— a thinker who found laughter necessary as a remedy against
life, and who nearly counted himself lost on any day when he
had not laughed[75] — seems much more like an Italian and a
blood relative of Dante and Leopardi than a Frenchman! We
know Chamfort's last words: "*Ah! Mon ami,*" he said to Sieyès,
"*je m'en vais enfin de ce monde, où il faut que le coeur se brise ou
se bronze —.*"[76] Those are certainly not the words of a dying
Frenchman.

96.[77]

Two orators. — Of these two orators, one only achieves the
complete rationality of his cause when he abandons himself
to passion: only this pumps enough blood and heat into his
brain to compel his superior intelligence to revelation. The
other from time to time attempts pretty much the same: to
present his case in fulsome tones, emphatically and stirringly
with the help of passion — but usually with a negative result.
Very soon thereafter he speaks obscurely and confusedly, he
exaggerates, makes omissions and arouses mistrust toward the
rationality of his cause: indeed, he himself senses this mistrust, and this explains his sudden leaps into the coldest and
most repulsive tones, prompting doubt in the listener as to
whether his entire passionateness was even genuine. In him passion floods the intellect every time; perhaps because it is stronger than in the first orator. But he is at the peak of his power
when he resists the onrushing storm of his sensations and mocks
them, so to speak: only then does his intellect step forth from
its hiding place, a logical, mocking, playful and yet terrible
intellect.

97.

On the loquaciousness of writers. — There is a loquaciousness of wrath — frequent in Luther, also in Schopenhauer. A loquaciousness from an overabundant supply of conceptual formulations, as in Kant. A loquaciousness from joy in ever-novel expressions of the same thing: we find this in Montaigne. A loquaciousness of spiteful natures: whoever reads writings of the current era will recall two writers.[78] A loquaciousness from delight in good words and forms of speech: not rare in the prose of Goethe. A loquaciousness from inner[79] delight in noise and confusion of sensations: for example in Carlyle.

98.[80]

In praise of Shakespeare. — The most beautiful thing I could say in praise of Shakespeare *the human being* is this: he believed in Brutus and he did not cast a speck of suspicion on this kind of virtue! He dedicated his best tragedy to him — it is still called by the wrong name today — to him and the most terrific epitome of high morals. Independence of the soul! — that's at stake here! No sacrifice can be too great here: one must be able to sacrifice even one's dearest friend to it, even if he is the most magnificent human being, the ornament of the world, a genius without peer — if in fact one loves freedom as the freedom of great souls, and *this* freedom is threatened by him: — this is how Shakespeare must have felt! The heights upon which he placed Caesar are the finest honor he could confer on Brutus: only thus does he enormously elevate his inner problem and likewise the psychic strength that is able to cut asunder *this knot*! — And was it really political freedom that drove this poet to sympathize with Brutus — that turned him into Brutus's accomplice? Or was political freedom only a symbol for something inexpressible? Do we perhaps stand before some unknown, dark event and adventure of the poet's own soul, of which he wanted to speak only in signs? What is all Hamlet-melancholy compared to the melancholy of Brutus! — and perhaps Shakespeare knows[81] the latter just as he knew the former, from experience! Perhaps he too had his gloomy hour and his evil angel, like Brutus![82] — But whatever similarities and secret relationships of this kind there may have been: Shakespeare threw himself to the ground before the whole stature and virtue of Brutus and felt himself unworthy and distant: — he wrote the proof of this into his tragedy. Twice he introduced a poet in it and twice he piled on him such impatient and ultimate contempt that it sounds like a scream — like the scream of self-contempt.[83] Brutus, even Brutus loses his patience when the poet enters, conceited, pathetic, obtrusive as poets tend to be, a being who seems to brim with possibilities of greatness, also of moral greatness, yet who in the philosophy of deed and life rarely even achieves ordinary integrity. "*I'll know his humor*[84] when he knows his time — away with the jiggling fool!"[85,86] — cries Brutus. This should be translated back into the soul of the poet who created it.

99.[87]

The followers of Schopenhauer. — What one is able to see when cultured peoples and barbarians come into contact: that the lower culture regularly adopts from the higher first its vices, weaknesses and excesses, from there it feels an attraction, and finally by means of the adopted vices and weaknesses it lets some of the valuable force of the higher culture flow over to it: — this can also be seen up close and without traveling to barbaric peoples, though of course in a somewhat refined and spiritualized and not so easily palpable manner. Yet what do the followers of *Schopenhauer* in Germany tend to adopt first from their master? — compared to his superior culture, they must seem barbarous enough in their own eyes, in order to be barbarously fascinated and seduced by him in the first place. Is it his sense for hard facts, his good will to brightness and reason that often makes him seem so English and so slightly German? Or the strength of his intellectual conscience, that *endured* a lifelong contradiction between being and willing and compelled him to contradict himself constantly even in his writings and on almost every point? Or his cleanliness in matters of the Church and of the Christian God? — for in this he was clean like no German philosopher to date, so that he lived and died "as a Voltairean." Or his immortal doctrines of the intellectuality of intuition, of the apriority of the law of causation, of the instrument-nature of the intellect and the unfreedom of the will? No, all this does not enchant them and is not felt as enchanting: but Schopenhauer's mystical embarrassments and evasions in those passages where the thinker of facts allowed himself to be seduced and ruined by the vain urge to be the unriddler of the world, the unprovable doctrine of *a single will* ("all causes are only occasional causes for the appearance of the will at this time in this place,"[88] "the will to life is present in every being, even the slightest, wholly and undivided, as completely as in all beings that ever were, are and will be taken together"[89]), his *denial of the individual* ("all lions are at bottom only a single lion,"[90] "the multiplicity of individuals is an illusion"[91]); just as *development* is only an illusion: — he calls Lamarck's idea "an ingenious, absurd error,"[92] the fanaticism about *genius* ("in aesthetic intuition the individual is no longer individual, but pure, will-less, painless, timeless subject of knowledge";[93] "so the subject also, being entirely absorbed into the intuited object, has become this object itself"[94]), the nonsense about *compassion* and the breaking through of the *principium individuationis* enabled by it as the source of all morality, including such assertions as "dying is actually the purpose of existence,"[95] "the possibility cannot outright be denied a priori that a magical effect might not also come from somebody already dead":[96] these and similar *excesses* and vices of the philosopher are always accepted first and made into an article of faith: — vices and excesses after all are always easiest to imitate and do not require long training. But let's speak of the most famous of the living Schopenhauerians, of Richard Wagner. — He experienced what many an artist has already experienced: he made a mistake in interpreting the characters he created, and he misunderstood the unspoken philosophy of his own art. Richard Wagner let himself be led astray by Hegel until the middle of his life; he did the same again when later he read Schopenhauer's doctrine into his characters and began to use formulations like "will," "genius" and "compassion." Nevertheless, it will remain true: nothing is more contrary to the spirit of Schopenhauer than precisely this genuinely Wagnerian dimension of Wagner's heroes: I mean the innocence of the highest selfishness, the faith in great passion as the good in itself, in a word, the Siegfried-like features in the faces of his heroes. "All that smells more of Spinoza than of me" — perhaps Schopenhauer would say. Therefore as good as Wagner's reasons were to look around for other philosophers than Schopenhauer: the enchantment he was under in relation to this thinker blinded him not only against all other philosophers, but even against science itself; increasingly his entire art wants to pose as a companion piece and complement to Schopenhauerian philosophy and with increasing explicitness it renounces the loftier ambition of becoming[97] the companion piece and complement to human knowledge and science. And what attracts him to this is not only the whole mysterious pomp of this philosophy, which would have attracted even a Cagliostro: the individual gestures and affects of the philosophers were also constantly seducers![98] Schopenhauerian, for instance, is Wagner's vehemence about the corruption of the German language; and even if here one should sanction this imitation, then it surely must not be withheld that Wagner's very style suffers in no small way from all the ulcers and tumors whose sight made Schopenhauer so furious, and that regarding the Wagnerians writing in German, Wagnerianism is beginning to prove itself as dangerous as any kind of Hegelianism has proven to be. Schopenhauerian is Wagner's hatred of the Jews, to whom he is incapable of being fair even regarding their greatest deed: the Jews after all are the inventors of Christianity. Schopenhauerian is Wagner's attempt to construe Christianity as a wind-blown seed of Buddhism and to prepare a Buddhist age for Europe, using a temporary reconciliation with Catholic-Christian formulas and sensibilities. Schopenhauerian is Wagner's preaching on behalf of mercy in our dealings with animals; Schopenhauer's predecessor in this, it is well known, was Voltaire, who perhaps already understood how to disguise his hatred for certain things and human beings as mercy toward animals, like his successors. At least Wagner's hatred of science, as can be heard in his preaching, is certainly not from the spirit of charitableness and kindness — nor is it, self-evidently, from any *spirit* at all. — In the end, the philosophy of an artist is of little consequence if it is merely an afterthought philosophy and does no damage to his art itself. One cannot guard enough against begrudging an artist his occasional masquerade, however unfortunate and presumptuous it might be; let us not forget, after all, that our dear artists one and all are and must be a bit of the actor, and without acting they would have difficulty lasting very long. Let us be loyal to Wagner for what is *true* and original in him — and specifically for us disciples, by remaining loyal to what is true and original in ourselves. Let's allow him to have his intellectual moods and cramps, and let us in fairness weigh instead what peculiar nourishment and basic needs an art like his *must* have in order to live and grow! It is of no consequence that he is so often wrong as a thinker; justice and patience are not *his* affair. It is enough that his life is and remains justified before itself: — this life to whom each of us cries out: "Be a man and do not follow me — but yourself instead! Yourself instead!"[99] *Our* life too should remain justified before us! We too shall grow and blossom out of ourselves in innocent selfishness, freely and fearlessly! And so even today, in reflecting on such a human being, these sentences resound in my ears as before: "that passion is better than Stoicism and hypocrisy, that being honest, even where evil is concerned, is better than losing oneself in traditional morality, that the free human being can be both good and evil, but that the unfree human being is a disgrace to nature and shares neither in any heavenly nor in any earthly consolation; finally that *any person who wants to become free must accomplish this through himself,* and that freedom does not fall like a surprise gift into anyone's lap." (*Richard Wagner in Bayreuth* p. 94)[100,101]

100.[102]

Learning to pay homage. — Human beings must learn to pay homage just as they learn how to despise. Anyone who walks on new paths and has led many along new paths discovers with astonishment how clumsy and poor these many are in expressing their gratitude, indeed how seldom gratitude *can* even express itself at all. It is as if something were to get stuck in its throat each time it wanted to speak, so that it merely clears its throat and then falls silent in clearing its throat. The manner in which a thinker grows aware of the effect of his thoughts and their reshaping and devastating power is nearly a comedy; at times, it looks as if those who have been affected felt offended at bottom and could only express their threatened self-reliance, as they perceived it, in all kinds of churlishness. It takes entire generations to invent even a single courteous convention of gratitude: and only very late does that point in time arrive when a kind of spirit and genius is infused into gratitude itself: then usually there is also someone on hand who is the great recipient of thanks, not only for the good that he himself did but mostly for what had been gradually accumulated by his predecessors as a treasure of the highest and best.

101.[103]

Voltaire. — Wherever there was a court, it provided the law for good speech and therewith also the law of style for all who wrote. But courtly speech is the language of courtiers, *who have no specialization* and even in conversations about scientific matters forbid themselves all convenient technical expressions, because they smack of specialization; therefore, technical expression and everything that betrays the specialist is a *blemish on style* in countries with a courtly culture. One is astonished today, now that all courts have become caricatures of past and present, to find Voltaire himself unspeakably stiff and precise on this point (for instance in his judgment about such stylists as Fontenelle and Montesquieu) — we are all simply emancipated from courtly taste, whereas Voltaire *perfected* it!

102.

A word for the philologists. — That there are books, such valuable and royal ones that entire generations of scholars are well engaged if by their efforts these books are maintained in a pure and intelligible state — philology exists to fortify this faith again and again. It presupposes that there is no lack of those rare human beings (whether or not one sees them) who really know how to use such valuable books: — they will surely be those who create or could create such books themselves. I mean that philology presupposes a noble faith — that for the benefit of a few who always "will come" and are not here, a very great amount of painstaking, even unclean labor must be done first: it is all labor *in usum Delphinorum.*[104]

103.[105]

On German music. — German music today is already, more than any other, European music, because in it alone the transformation that Europe experienced through the Revolution has found expression: only German composers are skilled in the expression of impassioned masses of people, in that tremendous artificial din that needn't even be very loud — whereas for example Italian opera knows only choruses of servants or soldiers, but no "people."[106] In addition, from all German music a profound bourgeois jealousy of the nobility can be heard, in particular of *esprit* and *élégance* as the expression of a courtly, knightly, ancient, self-assured society. This is no music like that of Goethe's singer before the gate,[107] that is also pleasing "in the great hall" and in particular to the king; here we do not read: "the knights gazed on bravely / And the ladies at their laps."[108] Even grace does not appear in German music without being visited by the sting of conscience; only with charm, the provincial sister of grace, does the German begin to feel completely moral — and from here onward and ever-higher upward to his fanatical, scholarly, often gruff "sublimity," the sublimity of Beethoven. If one wishes to imagine the human being to *this* music, well, just imagine Beethoven as he appears next to Goethe, perhaps during that encounter in Teplitz: as semi-barbarism next to culture, as folk next to nobility, as the good-natured human being next to the good and even more than merely "good" human being, as the visionary next to the artist, as the consolation-seeker next to the consoled one, as the exaggerator and suspicious one next to the fair-minded, as the moody one and self-tormentor, as the foolishly ecstatic, the blissfully unhappy, the guilelessly boundless, as the presumptuous and clumsy — and all in all as the "untamed human being":[109] thus Goethe himself perceived and characterized him, Goethe the exceptional German for whom a music of equal rank has not yet been found! — Finally, one should consider whether that now ever-spreading[110] contempt for melody and atrophy of the melodic sense in Germans can be understood as a democratic churlishness and an aftereffect of the Revolution. For melody has such an open joy in lawfulness and such an aversion to everything becoming, unformed, arbitrary, that it sounds like an echo from the *old* order of European things and like a seduction and return to it.

104.[III]

On the sound of the German language. — One knows where the German comes from that has been the standard literary German for a couple of centuries. With their respect for everything that comes from the *court,* the Germans have studiously adopted the chanceries as a model for everything they had to *write,* hence in particular for their correspondence, records, wills and so on. Writing in the chancery style, that was writing according to the court and the government — that was something noble compared to the German of the city in which one happened to live. Eventually one drew the consequences and also began to speak as one wrote — thus one became even nobler, in the form of the words, in the selection of words and expressions and ultimately also in the sound: one affected a courtly tone when one spoke, and eventually the affectation became natural. Perhaps nothing quite like this has happened anywhere else: the triumph of literary style over speech, with an entire people's affectation and pretensions to nobility as the foundation of a common and no longer dialect-driven language. I believe the sound of the German language in the Middle Ages, and especially after the Middle Ages, was deeply rustic and vulgar: in recent centuries it has ennobled itself somewhat, mainly insofar as one found it necessary to imitate so many French, Italian and Spanish sounds and specifically on the part of German (and Austrian) nobility, which absolutely could not make do with the mother tongue. But for Montaigne or even Racine, German must have sounded unbearably vulgar despite this practice: and still today, on the lips of travelers in the midst of the Italian rabble, it sounds very coarse, woodsy, hoarse, as if emanating from smoky rooms and impolite regions. — Now I notice that once again a similar craving for nobility of tone is spreading among the former admirers of the chanceries, and that the Germans are beginning to comply with a quite peculiar "tonal charm" that in the long run could become a real danger to the German language — indeed one would seek in vain for more abominable sounds in Europe. Something scornful, cold, indifferent, negligent in the voice: this today sounds "noble" to the Germans — and I hear the good will for this nobility in the voices of the young officials, teachers, women, merchants; indeed, even the little girls already imitate this officer's German. For the officer, and specifically the Prussian officer, is the inventor of these sounds: this same officer who as soldier and specialist possesses that admirable tact of modesty from which Germans as a whole could learn something (the German professors and composers included!). But as soon as he speaks and makes a move, he is the most immodest and distasteful character in old Europe — unbeknownst to himself, without any doubt! And also unbeknownst to the good Germans who gape at him as their man of the foremost and noblest society and gladly let him "set the tone" for them. And this he certainly does! — first it's the sergeants and the noncommissioned officers who imitate and coarsen his tone. Just listen to the shouted commands that virtually encircle German cities with bellowing, now that drills take place before all the gates: what presumption, what raging authoritarian emotions, what scornful coldness resound from all this bellowing! Are Germans really supposed to be a musical people? — What is certain is that the Germans are now militarizing themselves to the sound of their language: it is probable that once trained to speak militarily, they will also write militarily in the end. For the habit of certain sounds burrows deep into one's character: — soon one has the words and expressions and finally even the thoughts that match this very sound! Perhaps we're already writing in officer style; perhaps I read only too little of what gets written in Germany today. But one thing I know with all the more certainty: the public German proclamations that also make their way abroad are not inspired by German music, but rather by precisely these new sounds of a distasteful presumptuousness. In almost every speech of the foremost German statesman and even when he makes himself heard through his imperial mouthpiece, there is an accent that the ear of a foreigner[112] rejects with revulsion: but the Germans[113] tolerate it — they tolerate themselves.

105.

The Germans as artists. — When a German really works himself into a passion for once (and not only as usual into a good will toward a passion!), then he behaves in it as he simply must, and doesn't give any further thought to his behavior. But the truth is that he then behaves very clumsily and ugly and as if without tact and melody, so that the spectators are embarrassed or touched by this and nothing more: — *unless* he raises himself into the sublime and the rapturous of which some passions are capable. Then even the German becomes *beautiful*! The inkling they have of *what heights* it takes for beauty to pour its magic over even Germans drives German artists into the heights and superheights, and into excesses of passion: a really profound longing, then, to get beyond ugliness and clumsiness, at least to see beyond it — over to a better, lighter, more southerly, sunnier world. And so their spasms are often only signs that they want to *dance:* these poor bears in whom hidden nymphs and sylvan gods make their rounds — and occasionally even higher deities!

106.

Music as advocate. — "I thirst for a master of composing," said an innovator to his disciple, "so that he could learn my thoughts[114] from me and henceforth speak them in his own language: thus I will better reach the ears and hearts of people. With tones one can seduce people to every error and every truth: who is capable of *refuting* a tone?" — "So you want to be regarded as irrefutable?" said his disciple. The innovator replied: "I wish[115] for the seed to become a tree. In order for a teaching to become a tree, it has to be believed for a good while: for it to be believed, it has to be regarded as irrefutable. A tree needs storms, doubts, worms, malice, so that it can reveal the nature and the strength of its seed; let it break if it is not strong enough! But a seed is always merely annihilated — not refuted!" — When he had said this, his disciple cried agitatedly: "But I believe in your cause and consider it so strong that I will say everything, absolutely everything that I still have in my heart against it." — The innovator laughed to himself and wagged his finger[116] at the disciple. "This kind of discipleship," he said, "is the best, but it is dangerous and not every kind of teaching can withstand it."

107.[117]

Our ultimate gratitude to art. — If we had not given our blessing to the arts and invented this kind of cult of the untrue: then our insight into the general untruth and mendacity that is now provided to us by science — our insight into delusion and error as a condition of our cognating and sensing existence — would be totally unbearable. *Honesty* would have nausea and suicide in its wake. Now, however, our honesty has a counterforce that helps us to avoid such consequences: art, as the *good* will to appearance. We do not always block our eyes from rounding off, from composing something to the end: and then it is no longer eternal imperfection that we carry across the river of becoming — then we think we are carrying a *goddess* and are proud and childish in performing this service.[118] As an aesthetic phenomenon existence is still *bearable* to us, and through art we are granted the eye and hand and above all the good conscience to *be able* to make such a phenomenon of ourselves. At times we have to take a break from ourselves, by looking out and down upon ourselves and, from an artistic distance, laughing *over* ourselves or weeping *over* ourselves; we have to discover the *hero* and likewise the *fool* who resides in our passion for knowledge, we have to be glad of our folly from time to time, in order to be able to stay glad of our wisdom! And precisely because in the final analysis we are heavy and somber human beings and more weights than humans, nothing does us more good than the *fool's cap*: we need it for our own sake — we need all exuberant, soaring, dancing, mocking, childish and blissful art in order not to lose that *freedom over things* that our ideal demands of us. It would be a *relapse* for us, especially given our irritable honesty, to become completely embroiled in morality, or even turn into virtuous monsters and scarecrows due to the overly stringent demands we place on ourselves in these matters. We should also *be capable* of standing *above* morality: and not only standing with the timid stiffness of someone who is afraid at every moment of slipping and falling, but instead soaring and playing above it! How could we dispense with art for this, or with the fool? — And as long as you are still in any way *ashamed* of yourselves, you do not yet belong among us![119]

Book Three

108.[1]

New struggles. — After Buddha was dead, his shadow was still shown for centuries in a cave — a colossal horrific shadow. God is dead: but given the way of humanity, there will perhaps be caves for thousands of years in which his shadow will be shown. — And we — we still have to conquer his shadow too!

109.[2]

Let us beware! — Let us beware of thinking that the world is a living being. Where is it supposed to expand? What is it supposed to live on? How could it grow and multiply? We know more or less what the organic is: and we're supposed to reinterpret the unspeakably derivative, late, rare, accidental that we perceive only on the crust of the earth into the essential, universal and eternal, as do those who call the universe an organism? This disgusts me. Let us beware of believing that the universe is a machine; it is certainly not constructed for one purpose, we do it much too high an honor with the word "machine." Let us beware of positing generally and everywhere something as perfectly formed as the cyclical movements of our neighboring stars; a mere glance into the Milky Way raises doubts whether much rougher and more contradictory movements do not exist there, likewise stars with eternally linear[3] descent paths and such. The astral order in which we live is an exception; this order and the considerable duration that is conditioned by it has in turn made possible the exception of exceptions: the

formation of the organic. The overall character of the world
on the other hand is chaos in all eternity, not in the sense of a
lack of necessity, but lack of order, structuring, form, beauty,
wisdom and whatever all our aesthetic anthropomorphisms are
called. Judged from the standpoint of our reason, the unsuccessful attempts are by far the rule, the exceptions are not the
secret goal, and the entire music box eternally repeats its tune
that must never be called a melody — and ultimately even
the expression "unsuccessful attempt" is already an anthropomorphism with inherent reproach. But how could we blame
or praise the universe! Let us beware of attributing to it heartlessness and unreason or their opposites: it is neither perfect,
nor beautiful, nor noble, and it doesn't want to become any
of that, it absolutely does not strive to imitate human being!
It is absolutely not affected by any of our aesthetic and moral
judgments![4] Nor does it have any drive for self-preservation or
any drive at all; it also knows no laws. Let us beware of saying
there are laws in nature. There are only necessities: there is no
one who commands, no one who obeys, no one who trespasses.
When you know that there are no purposes, then you also know
there is no accident: for only beside a world of purposes does
the word "accident" have meaning. Let us beware of saying that
death is opposed to life. The living is only a variety of the dead,
and a very rare variety. — Let us beware of thinking the world
eternally creates new things. There are no eternally enduring
substances; matter is just such an error, as is the God of the
Eleatics.[5] But when will we ever be done with our caution and
care! When will all these shadows of God no longer eclipse us?
When will we have totally de-deified nature! When will we be
permitted to begin to *naturalize* us human beings with a pure,
newly discovered, newly redeemed nature!

110.[6]

Origin of knowledge. — The intellect has produced nothing
but errors for tremendous stretches of time; some of them turned
out to be useful and species-preserving: whoever bumped into

them, or acquired them through heredity, fought his struggle for himself and his progeny with greater success. Such erroneous articles of faith, which were repeatedly inherited and finally became almost the basic constitution of the human species, include for example: that there are[7] enduring things; that there are equal things; that there are things, substances, bodies; that a thing is what it appears to be; that our willing is free; that what is good for me is also good in and for itself. Only very late did the deniers and doubters of such propositions appear — only very late did truth appear, as the least strongest form of knowledge. It seemed as though we were unable to live with it, our organism was attuned to its opposite; all of its higher functions, the perceptions of the senses and every kind of sensation generally, worked with those ancient embodied basic errors. Even more: those propositions themselves became norms within knowledge, according to which one measured "true" and "untrue" — right down to the remotest regions of pure logic. Therefore:[8] the *strength* of knowledge does not lie in its degree of truth, but in its age, its incorporation, its character as a condition of life. Where living and knowing appeared to be contradictory, there was never any serious struggle; back then denial and doubt were regarded as madness.[9] Those exceptional thinkers, like the Eleatics, who nevertheless posited and held on to the opposites of natural errors, believed that it was even possible to *live* this opposition: they invented the sage as the human being of immutability, impersonality, universality of intuition, as the one and all simultaneously, with its own faculty for that inverted knowledge; they were of the belief that their knowledge was simultaneously the principle of *life*. But in order to assert all this, they had to *deceive* themselves about their own state: they had to ascribe a fictional impersonality and permanence without change[10] to themselves, to misunderstand the nature of the knower, deny the power of drives in knowledge and generally comprehend reason as totally free activity emanating from itself; they kept their eyes closed to the fact that they, too, had arrived[11] at their propositions by contradicting valid norms, or by craving tranquility or sole possession or dominance. The[12] more refined development of honesty and of skepticism ultimately made these people impossible as well; even their life and judgments proved to be dependent on the ancient drives and basic errors of all sentient existence. — That more refined honesty and skepticism had its origin wherever two opposing propositions seemed *applicable* to life, because both were compatible with the basic errors, hence wherever there could be argument regarding the higher or lesser degree of *utility* for life; likewise wherever new propositions revealed themselves to be not exactly useful, but then at least not harmful to life, as expressions of an intellectual play drive[13] which, like all play, is innocent and happy. Gradually the human brain filled itself with such judgments and convictions, thus a ferment, struggle and lust for power arose in this tangle. Not only utility and pleasure, but every kind of drive took part in the struggle for "truths"; intellectual struggle became an occupation, stimulus, profession, duty, dignity — : knowing and striving for the true, as needs in themselves, finally settled in among the other needs. From then on not only faith and conviction, but also testing, denial, suspicion, contradiction were a *power*, all "evil" instincts were subordinated to knowledge and placed in its service, and they acquired the luster of the permitted, the revered, the useful and ultimately the eye and the innocence of the *good*. Thus knowledge became a part of life itself and as life it grew into an ever-increasing power: until finally knowledge and those ancient basic errors collided; both as life, both as power, both in the same human being. A thinker: this is now a being in whom the drive for truth and those life-preserving errors are fighting their first fight, after the drive for truth also *proved* itself to be a life-preserving power. Compared to the importance of this struggle everything else is a matter of indifference: the ultimate question concerning the condition of life is posed here, and the first attempt is made here to answer this question using experiment. To what extent does truth tolerate incorporation? — that is the question, that is the experiment.[14]

III.

Descent of the logical. — From where did the logic of the human mind originate? Certainly from unlogic, whose sphere must have originally been vast. But countless multitudes of beings who made inferences differently than we do today, have perished: yet theirs could have been more true! For example, whoever was not able to identify the "same" often enough, with respect to nourishment or with respect to hostile animals, hence whoever subsumed too slowly and was too cautious in subsuming, had only a lesser probability of surviving than someone who immediately guessed in favor of the same in all things similar. The preponderant inclination, however, of treating the similar as the same, an illogical inclination — for as such there is nothing identical — first created the entire foundation of logic. Likewise, for the concept of substance to originate, which is indispensable for logic even though in the strictest sense nothing real corresponds to it — the mutability of things must have gone unseen and unperceived for a long time; those beings that did not see with precision had an advantage over those who saw everything "in flux." In and for itself, every high degree of caution in inferring, every skeptical tendency is already a great danger for life. No living beings would have survived unless the countertendency — preferring to affirm rather than suspend judgment, to err and to make things up rather than wait, to agree rather than deny, to judge rather than to be just — had not been cultivated with extraordinary strength. — The course of logical thoughts and inferences in our current brain corresponds to a process and struggle of drives that are inherently and individually all very illogical and unjust; we usually experience only the result of the struggle: so rapidly and so furtively does this ancient mechanism now play itself out in us.[15]

112.[16]

Cause and effect. — "Explanation" we call it: but "description" is what distinguishes us from older stages of knowledge and science. We describe better — we explain just as little as all our predecessors. We have uncovered a multifarious succession where the naïve human being and inquirer of older cultures saw only two things, "cause" and "effect," as the saying went; we have perfected the image of becoming but we have not gotten beyond the image, behind the image. The series of "causes" stands before us in every case much more completely, so we infer: this and that must first precede it, so that that can follow — but we have *understood* nothing with this. For example, the quality of every chemical process appears to be a "miracle" now as before, likewise every locomotion; no one has "explained" thrust. And how could we explain! We operate exclusively with things that do not exist, with lines, planes, bodies, atoms, divisible times, divisible spaces — how should explanation even be possible when we first turn everything into an *image,* into our image! It is sufficient to regard science as the most accurate possible humanization of things; we learn to describe ourselves ever more accurately, insofar as we describe things and their succession. Cause and effect: such a duality probably never exists — in truth a continuum stands before us, from which we isolate a couple of pieces; just as we always perceive a motion only as isolated points, therefore not seeing it but rather inferring it. The suddenness with which many effects stand out leads us astray; but it is a suddenness only for us. There is an infinite multitude of events that eludes us in this second of suddenness. An intellect that could see cause and effect as a continuum, not according to our mode as an arbitrary state of being divided and fragmented, that could see the flux of events — would dismiss the concept of cause and effect and deny all conditionality.

113.

On the doctrine of poisons. — So much has to come together in order for scientific thinking to originate: and all these required forces had to be separately invented, practiced, cultivated! But in their separation they frequently had a quite different effect than now, where in the context of scientific thinking they mutually limit and hold each in check: — they have acted as poisons; for instance the impulse to doubt, to deny, to wait, to collect, to dissolve. Many hecatombs of human beings[17] were sacrificed before these impulses learned to comprehend their coexistence and to feel themselves collectively as the function of a single organizing power in a single human being! And how far are we still from the point where artistic strengths and the practical wisdom of life will also find their way into scientific thinking, where a higher organic system will form, in relation to which the scholar, physician, artist and legislator as we know them today would have to seem like paltry antiquities![18]

114.

The scope of morality. — Once we see a new image[19] we immediately construct it with the help of all the old experiences we have had, *depending on the degree* of our honesty and justice. There simply are no experiences other than moral ones, even in the realm of sense perception.

115.[20]

The four errors. — Human beings have been educated by their errors: first, we always saw ourselves only incompletely; second, we conferred fictional qualities on ourselves; third, we felt ourselves in a false order of rank in relation to animals and nature; fourth, we invented ever-new tablets of goods and took them for a time as eternal and unconditional, so that now this, now that human drive and state took first place and was ennobled as a result of this estimation. If one were to reckon away the effect of these four errors, then humanity, humaneness and "human dignity" have also been reckoned away.

116.

Herd instinct. — Wherever we encounter a morality we find an estimation and order of rank of human drives and actions. These estimations and orders of rank are always the expression of the needs of a community and herd: what is of primary benefit to *it* — and then secondary and tertiary — that is also the uppermost standard for the value of all individuals. Through morality the individual is instructed to be a function of the herd and to assign value to himself only as a function. Since the conditions of the preservation of one community have been very different from those of another, there have been very different moralities; and with respect to the impending essential restructurings of herds and communities, states and societies, one can prophesy that there will be more very divergent moralities. Morality is herd instinct in the individual.

117.

Herd stings of conscience. — In the longest and most distant times of humankind there were quite different stings of conscience than now. Today one feels responsible only for what one wants and does, and takes pride in oneself: all our teachers of law proceed from this feeling of self and pleasure of the individual, as if the source of law had sprung from this well all along. But for the longest period of humankind there was nothing more terrifying than feeling like an individual. Being alone, perceiving things individually, neither obeying nor ruling, signifying an individual — back then it was no pleasure, but a punishment instead; one was sentenced "to individuality." Freedom of thought was regarded as discomfort itself. Whereas we perceive law and conformity as compulsion and forfeit, formerly one perceived egoism as a painful thing, as a genuine distress. To be oneself, to value oneself according to one's own measure and weight — that was offensive to taste at that time. The tendency for this would have been perceived as madness: for being alone was associated with every misery and every fear. Back then "free will" was in the closest proximity to bad conscience: and the more unfreely one acted, the more the herd instinct and not personal meaning spoke through the action, the more one deemed oneself moral. Everything that did damage to the herd, whether the individual wanted it or not, used to cause the individual stings of conscience — and his neighbor too, indeed the whole herd! — In this we have learned most of all to rethink things.[21]

118.

Benevolence. — Is it virtuous when a cell transforms into the function of a stronger cell? It has to. And is it evil when the stronger one assimilates it? It likewise has to; this is a necessity for it, since it strives for superabundant substitutes and wants to regenerate itself. Accordingly, in benevolence a distinction must be made: the impulse to appropriate and the impulse to submit, depending on whether the stronger or the weaker feels benevolence. Joy and desire are together in the stronger one, who wants to reshape something into his function: joy and a wish to be desired are together in the weaker one, who would like to become a function. — Compassion is essentially the former, a pleasant stimulus of the drive to appropriate, at the sight of the weaker: bearing in mind of course that "strong" and "weak" are relative concepts.

119.

No altruism! — In many people I see an excessive force and desire for wanting to be a function; they rush there and have the finest sense for all those spots where precisely *they* can be a function. Here belong those women who transform themselves into that function of a man that happens to be weakly developed in him, thereby becoming his pocketbook or his politics or his conviviality. Such beings preserve themselves best when they attach to a foreign organism; if they don't succeed in this, they become angry, irritable and devour themselves.

120.

Health of the soul. — The beloved medicinal moral formula (whose author is Ariston of Chios): "Virtue is the health of the soul"[22] — would have to be revised, in order to be useful, at least to something like: "your virtue is the health of your soul."

For there is no health in itself, and all attempts to define a thing in this manner are miserable failures. It depends on your goal, your horizon, your strengths, your inspirations, your errors and especially your ideals and the phantasms of your soul, to determine *what* healthy means even for your *body.* Thus there are countless healths of the body; and the more one allows the individual and the incomparable to raise its head again, the more one unlearns the dogma of "equality of human being," the more, too, must the concept of a normal health be abandoned by our medical practitioners, along with normal diet and normal course of an illness. And only then would it be the proper time to reflect on the health and illness of the *soul* and to situate the unique virtue of each person in its health: which, by the way, might look in one person like the opposite of health in another. In the end the great question would remain, whether we could *dispense* with illness, even for the development of our virtue, and especially whether our thirst for knowledge and self-knowledge might need the sick soul just as much as the healthy: in sum, whether the singular will to health is not a prejudice, a cowardice and perhaps a piece of the subtlest barbarism and regression.

121.

Life no argument. — We have contrived for ourselves a world in which we can live — by postulating bodies, lines, planes, causes and effects, motion and rest, form and content: without these articles of faith no one now could bear to live! But for all that they are still unproven. Life is no argument; error could be among the conditions of life.

122.[23]

Moral skepticism in Christianity. — Christianity also made a big contribution to the Enlightenment: it taught moral skepticism in a very obtrusive and effective way: lamentingly, embitteringly, but with inexhaustible patience and subtlety: it annihilated in every single person the belief in their "virtues":

it caused the disappearance forever of those great virtuous figures of whom there was no lack in antiquity, those popular human beings who roamed about in the belief of their own perfection with the dignity of heroic matadors. Today when we read the moral books of the ancients, for instance those of Seneca and Epictetus, educated as we are in this Christian school of skepticism, we feel an amused superiority and are full of mysterious insights and overviews; it makes us feel as though a child were saying before an old man or a girlish beautiful enthusiast before La Rochefoucauld: we know better what virtue is! But ultimately we have applied this same skepticism as well to all *religious* states and events, like sin, repentance, grace, sanctification, and we've allowed the worm to dig so well that now even in reading all Christian books we have the same feeling of subtle superiority and insight: — we also know the religious feelings better! And it is high time to know them well and describe them well, for the pious of the old faith are also dying out: — let us rescue their image and their type at least for knowledge's sake!

123.[24]

Knowledge more than a means. — Even *without* this new passion — I mean the passion for knowledge — science would be promoted: so far science has grown and matured without it. Good faith in science, the prejudice that favors it and now dominates our nation-states (formerly even the Church), at bottom rests on the fact that this unconditional urge and stress has so rarely manifested itself in it, and that science simply is *not* regarded as passion but as a condition and "ethos." Indeed, often enough *amour-plaisir* for knowledge (curiosity) suffices, *amour-vanité*[25] suffices, habituation to it with the ulterior motive of honor and bread, it even suffices for many that they know nothing better to do with an excess of leisure than to read, collect, organize, observe, recount: their "scientific urge" is their boredom. Pope Leo X[26] once (in his brief to Beroaldo) sang the praises of science: he describes it as the most beautiful ornament and the greatest pride of our life, as a noble occupation in times of fortune and misfortune; "without it," he says finally, "all human endeavor would be without a firm foundation — even with it things are still fickle and uncertain enough!" But this tolerably skeptical Pope suppresses his ultimate judgment about it, like all other ecclesiastical eulogists of science. Even if one might choose to hear in these words what is remarkable enough for such a friend of art, namely, that he ranks science above art; in the end, it is still a mere courtesy that he does not speak here of what he too ranks high above all science: of the "revealed truth" and of the "eternal salvation of the soul" — what are ornament, pride, entertainment, security of life compared to this! "Science is something second class, not ultimate, absolute, not an object of passion," — this judgment remained in Leo's soul: the genuinely Christian judgment concerning science! In antiquity, its dignity and recognition were diminished by the fact that even among its most zealous disciples the striving for *virtue* was paramount, and that one believed oneself to have granted science its highest praise when one celebrated it as the best means to virtue. It is something new in history that knowledge wants to be more than a means.

124.[27]

In the horizon of the infinite. — We've left land and gone to sea! The bridge is behind us — what's more, we've broken off the land behind us! Now, little ship, see to it! Beside you lies the ocean, and truth be told, it does not always roar, and sometimes it lies there like silk and gold and dreamy kindness. But hours will come when you will realize that it is infinite and that there is nothing more terrifying than infinity. Oh the poor bird that felt itself free and now slams against the walls of this cage! Woe to you, should homesickness for land befall you, as if more *freedom* existed there — and there is no "land" anymore!

125.[28]

The madman. — Haven't you heard about that madman who lit a lantern in the bright light of morning, ran into the

marketplace and shouted incessantly: "I seek God! I seek God!"
— Since there were many standing around at the time who did
not believe in God, he prompted great laughter. Has he gotten
lost? said one of them. Did he lose his way like a child? said
another. Or is he hiding somewhere? Is he scared of us? Did he
go to sea? Did he emigrate? — thus they shouted and laughed,
everyone talking at once. The madman leaped into their midst
and pierced them with his stare. "Where has God gone?" he
cried, "I'll tell you! *We have killed him* — you and I! All of us
are his murderers! But how did we do this? How did we manage to drink up the sea? Who gave us the sponge to wipe away
the entire horizon? What did we do when we unchained this
earth from its sun? Where is it moving to now? Where are we
moving to? Away from all suns? Are we not constantly plummeting? And backward, sideways, forward, in all directions? Do
up and down still exist? Aren't we just straying as if through
an endless nothing? Don't we feel the breath of empty space?
Hasn't it grown colder? Isn't night and ever more night closing
in on us? Don't we have to light lanterns in the morning? Don't
we hear anything yet of the noise of the gravediggers who are
burying God? Don't we smell anything yet of the divine decay
— even gods decay! God is dead! God stays dead! And we have
killed him! How do we console ourselves, we murderers of all
murderers? The holiest and mightiest that the world possessed
so far, it's bled to death under our knives — who will wipe
this blood off us? What water could help us clean ourselves?
What festivals of atonement, what holy games will we have to
invent? Isn't the magnitude of this deed too big for us? Don't we
have to become gods ourselves just to seem worthy of it? There
has never been a greater deed — and whoever is born after us
will belong to a higher history than all history to this day, on
account of this deed!" — Here the madman fell silent and again
looked at his listeners: they too were silent and gazed at him
in astonishment. Finally he threw his lantern to the ground,
where it broke to pieces and was extinguished. "I've come too
early," he said then, "it's not yet my time. This tremendous event

is still on its way and wandering — it hasn't yet reached the ears of human beings. Lightning and thunder need time, the light of stars needs time, deeds need time, even after they are done, in order to be seen and heard. This deed is still more distant from them than the remotest stars — *and yet they did it themselves!*" — It is also said that on the same day, the madman forced his way into various churches and started singing his *requiem aeternam deo*[29] there. When escorted out and held to account, he always answered only: "What are these churches anymore, if they are not the tombs and sepulchers of God?" —

126.[30]

Mystical explanations. — Mystical explanations are considered profound; the truth is, they are not even superficial.

127.[31]

Aftereffect of the oldest religiosity. — Every thoughtless person thinks the will is the sole effective thing; willing is supposed to be something simple, merely given, underivable, self-evident. He is convinced, whenever he does something, for example striking something, that it is *he* who strikes, and he struck because he *willed* to strike. He notices no problem at all in this, but instead the feeling of *willing* suffices for him not only to assume cause and effect, but also to believe that he *understands* their relationship. He knows nothing of the mechanism of events and the hundredfold subtle work that must be absolved in order for the strike to occur, likewise of the incapacity of willing in itself to perform even the very least part of this work. Will for him is a magically effective force: the belief in the will, as the cause of effects, is the belief in magically effective forces. Now, originally human beings believed that wherever they saw an event, there was a will as cause and personally willing beings were in the background at work — the concept of mechanics was quite remote to them. But because humans for staggering periods of time believed only in persons (and not in matter, forces, objects and so forth), the belief in cause and effect has become their fundamental belief, which they apply wherever anything happens — still to this day, instinctively, and as a piece of atavism of the most ancient lineage. The propositions "no effect without cause," "every effect in turn a cause," appear as generalizations of much narrower propositions: "where effecting is, willing has been," "effects can only happen to willing beings," "there is never a pure, inconsequential suffering of an effect, rather all suffering is an agitation of the will" (to deed, resistance, revenge, retribution) — but in the prehistory of humankind, the latter and the former propositions were identical, and the former were not generalizations of the latter, but the latter were commentaries on the former. — Schopenhauer with his assumption that everything that exists consists only of willing, elevated a primeval mythology to the throne; he seems to have never attempted an analysis of the will, because he *believed* in the simplicity and immediacy of all willing, like everyone: — whereas willing is only a mechanism that is so well rehearsed that it practically escapes the observing eye. I posit these propositions against him: first, in order for will to originate, an idea of pleasure and displeasure is needed. Second: when a vehement stimulus is perceived as pleasure or displeasure, this is the concern of the *interpreting* intellect, which of course mostly works unconsciously for us; and one and the same stimulus *can* be interpreted as pleasure or displeasure. Third: only in intellectual beings is there pleasure, displeasure and will; the tremendous majority of organisms have nothing of this.

128.[32]

The value of prayer. — Prayer has been invented for those human beings who really never have thoughts of their own and for whom an elevation of the soul is unknown or goes unnoticed: what are they supposed to do at sacred sites and in all important situations in life that demand calm and a kind of dignity? So that they at least do not *disturb* others, the wisdom of all religion founders, the small and the great, has prescribed the formula of prayer to them, as a time-consuming mechanical work for the lips, along with exertion of the memory and the same fixed position for the hands and feet and eyes! So they may ruminate their "*om mane padme hum*"[33] countless times like the Tibetans, or, as in Benares, count the name of the God Ram-Ram-Ram (and so forth with or without grace) on their fingers: or honor Vishnu with his thousand invocation names, Allah with his ninety-nine: or they may avail themselves of prayer mills and rosaries — the main thing is that they are preoccupied with this work for a time and make themselves tolerably presentable: their kind of prayer has been invented for the benefit of the pious who indeed have their own thoughts and elevations. And even they have their weary hours, when a series of venerating words and sounds and pious mechanical activity do them good. But supposing these rare human beings — in every religion the religious person is an exception — actually know what they are doing: those poor in spirit[34] do not, and to forbid them the prayer-prattle amounts to taking away their religion: as Protestantism brings to light more and more. From them, religion simply wants no more than that they *stay quiet,* with their eyes, hands, legs and organs of every kind: this way they become more beautiful for a time and — more like human beings!

129.

The conditions of God. — "God himself cannot exist without wise human beings" — said Luther,[35] and he was right to; but "God can exist even less without unwise human beings" — that good Luther failed to mention!

130.

A dangerous decision. — The Christian decision to find the world ugly and bad has made the world ugly and bad.

131.

Christianity and suicide. — Christianity turned the longing for suicide that was prodigious at the time it originated into a lever of its power: it allowed only two forms of suicide to remain, draped them in the highest dignity and the highest hopes, and forbade all others in a terrible way. But martyrdom and the slow self-disembodiment of ascetics were permitted.

132.

Against Christianity. — Now our taste is decisive in rejecting Christianity, no longer our reasons.

133.

Principle. — An unavoidable hypothesis on which humankind must fall back again and again is *more powerful* in the long run than the best-believed faith in something untrue (like the Christian faith). In the long run: here this means for a hundred thousand years.

134.[36]

Pessimists as victims. — Where a deep displeasure in existence gains the upper hand, what comes to light are the aftereffects of a major dietary blunder of which a people has been guilty for a long time. Thus the spread of Buddhism (*not* its origin) is in large part dependent on the excessive and almost exclusive rice diet of the Indians and the general enervation conditioned by it.[37] Perhaps our European dissatisfaction of modern times can be viewed from the standpoint that the world that preceded us, the entire Middle Ages, was addicted to drinking, thanks to the influence of our Germanic inclinations on Europe: the Middle Ages, that is, the alcohol poisoning of Europe. — The German dissatisfaction with living is essentially winter debility, including the effects of cellar air and of the noxious stove fumes in German living rooms.

135.[38]

Origin of sin. — Sin, as it is now perceived wherever Christianity reigns or once reigned: sin is a Jewish feeling and a Jewish invention, and with respect to this background of all Christian morality, Christianity in fact aimed to "Judaize" the entire world. The degree to which it succeeded in doing this in Europe can be detected most precisely by the degree of strangeness that Greek antiquity — a world without feelings of guilt — still has for our sensibility, despite all the good will for approaching and incorporating it, that has been mustered by entire generations and many outstanding individuals. "Only when you *repent* is God merciful to you" — this is laughable and annoying to a Greek: he would say "that is how slaves might feel." Here a powerful, superpowerful and yet vengeful being is assumed: his power is so great that harm cannot even be inflicted on him, except in a point of honor. Every sin is an affront to respect, a *crimen laesae majestatis divinae*[39] — and nothing more! Contrition, degradation, groveling in the dust — this is the first and last condition on which his grace hinges: hence the restoration of his divine honor! Whether sin might otherwise cause damage, whether a deep, growing harm might be planted alongside it, that seizes and chokes one human being after another like an illness — this honor-craving Oriental in heaven does not care: sin is a transgression against him, not against humankind! — those on whom he has conferred grace are also those on whom he has conferred this unconcern for the natural consequences of sin. God and humankind are thought of here so separately, in such an oppositional way, that at bottom there can be no sinning at all against humankind — every deed is supposed to be scrutinized *only according to its supernatural consequences:* not its natural consequences: thus Jewish feeling would have it, for which everything natural is indignity in itself. The *Greeks* on the other hand were closer to thinking that even sacrilege could have dignity — even theft, as in Prometheus, even the slaughtering of cattle as an expression of insane jealousy, as in Ajax: in their need to poeticize and incorporate dignity into sacrilege, they invented *tragedy* — an art and a joy that has remained in its deepest essence foreign to the Jew, despite all his poetic talent and his inclination for the sublime.

136.

The chosen people. — The Jews, who feel themselves to be the chosen people among the peoples, specifically because they are the moral genius among the peoples (owing to their capacity *for having more deeply despised* the human in themselves than any other people) — the Jews have a similar pleasure in their divine monarch and saint to that which the French nobility had in Louis XIV. This nobility had allowed all its power and self-glorification to be taken away, and had become contemptible: in order to not feel this, in order to forget this, it required a royal luster, a royal authority and fullness of power *without peer,* whose portal was open only to the nobility. Inasmuch as they rose to the heights at court in accordance with this prerogative, and from that vantage point looked down upon everything and saw it as contemptible, they got beyond all irritability of the conscience. Thus they deliberately built the tower of royal power ever higher into the clouds and wagered the last building blocks of their own power on it.

137.[40]

Spoken in a parable. — A Jesus Christ was possible only in a Jewish landscape — I mean in one over which the gloomy and sublime thunder cloud of wrathful Jehovah was constantly hanging. Here alone was the rare and sudden penetrating of a single ray of sunshine through this horrific universal and ceaseless day-night greeted like a miracle of "love," as the ray of the most undeserved "grace." Here alone could Christ dream his rainbow and his heavenly ladder, on which God climbed down to human beings; everywhere else the bright weather and the sun were regarded too much as the rule and the commonplace.

138.

Christ's mistake. — The founder of Christianity believed that humans suffered from nothing so much as from their sins: — it was his mistake, the mistake of someone who felt himself without sin, who lacked experience in this matter! And so his soul filled up with that wondrous fantastical mercy, deemed a necessity, that even among his people, the inventors of sin, was rarely a great necessity! — But Christians knew how to retroactively prove their master right and to sanctify his mistake into "truth."

139.[41]

The color of passions. — Natures such as the Apostle Paul have the evil eye for passions; they are familiar with only what is dirty, disfiguring and heartbreaking in them — therefore their ideal craving is for annihilating the passions: in the divine they see the complete cleansing of passions. Quite differently than Paul and the Jews, the Greeks applied their ideal craving precisely to the passions, loving, elevating, gilding and deifying them; apparently they not only felt happier in passion but also purer and more divine than usual. — And now the Christians? Did they want to become Jews in this point? Have they perhaps already done so?

140.[42]

Too Jewish. — If God wanted to become an object of love, then he should first have had to renounce judging and justice: — a judge, and even a merciful judge, is no object of love. In this point the founder of Christianity did not sense things finely enough — as a Jew.

141.[43]

Too Oriental. — What? A God who loves human beings on condition that they believe in him, and who hurls terrifying scowls and threats at anyone who does not believe in this love! What? a legalistically stipulated love as the sensibility of an almighty God! A love that has not even mastered the feeling of honor and inflamed vengefulness! How Oriental is all this! "If I love you, what does it concern you?"[44] is already a sufficient critique of all Christianity.

142.

Incense. — Buddha says: "Do not flatter your benefactor!"[45] Just repeat this proverb in a Christian church: — it instantly cleans the air of all things Christian.

143.[46]

Greatest advantage of polytheism. — That an individual would posit his *own* ideal and derive his law, his joys and his rights from it — that to date surely was regarded as the most monstrous of all human aberrations and as idolatry itself; in fact, the few who dared this always needed to have an apology for themselves, and this usually amounted to: "not I! not I! rather *a god* through me!" The wonderful art and power to create gods — polytheism — was where this drive was permitted to discharge itself, where it purified, perfected and ennobled itself: for originally it was a base and inappropriate drive, related to stubbornness, disobedience and envy. To be *hostile* to this drive to one's own ideal: formerly this was the law of every morality. There[47] was only a single norm: "*the* human being" — and every people believed it *possessed* this singular and ultimate norm. But beyond oneself and outside, in a distant superworld, one was permitted to see a *plurality of norms:* one god was not the denial of or blasphemy against another god! Here for the first time individuals were allowed, here for the first time one respected the rights of individuals. The invention of gods, heroes and superhumans[48] of all kinds, as well as secondary humans and subhumans, of dwarves, fairies, centaurs, satyrs, demons and devils, was invaluable training for justifying the selfishness and self-glorification of the individual: the freedom granted to one god in relation to other gods was in turn granted to oneself in relation to laws and customs and neighbors. Monotheism on the other hand, this rigid consequence of the doctrine of a single normal human being — hence the belief in a normal god beside whom there are only false fairy-tale gods — was perhaps the greatest danger to humankind so far: here it was threatened by that premature stagnation which, as far as we can tell, most other animal species have reached long ago; for they all believe in one normal animal and ideal in their species, and they have translated the morality of customs definitively into their flesh and blood. In polytheism the free-spiritedness and multispiritedness of human beings was modeled: the power to create our own new eyes for ourselves and ever newer and more our own: so that for human beings alone, among all animals, there are no eternal horizons and perspectives.

144.[49]

Religious wars. — The greatest progress of the masses until now has been religious war: for it proves that the masses have begun to treat concepts with respect. Religious wars only arise when reason in general is refined by the subtler quarrels of the sects: so that even the rabble learns to split hairs and takes details seriously, indeed even considers it possible that the "eternal salvation of the soul" depends on the small differences among concepts.

145.

Danger to vegetarians. — The preponderant tremendous consumption of rice drives people to use opium and narcotics in the same way as the preponderant tremendous consumption of potatoes drives people to use distilled liquor — : but it also drives people, in its subtler aftereffect, to modes of thinking and feeling that have narcotic effects. This corresponds with the fact that the promoters of narcotic modes of thinking and feeling, like certain Indian teachers, like to praise precisely a diet that is strictly vegetarian, and they would like to make it a law for the masses: in this manner, they strive to evoke and intensify the need that *they* are in a position to satisfy.[50]

146.[51]

German hopes. — Let's not forget that the names of peoples are usually terms of abuse. The Tartars for instance are "the dogs" according to their name: they were dubbed this by the Chinese. The "Germans": this originally meant "the pagans": so the Goths after their conversion referred to the great mass of their unbaptized tribal relatives, in accordance with their translation of the Septuagint, in which the pagans are described with the word that means "the peoples" in Greek: see Ulfilas.[52] — It would still be possible for the Germans to retroactively turn their name of abuse into a name of honor, if they were to become Europe's first *un-Christian* people: something for which they are highly suited according to the honor ascribed to them by Schopenhauer.[53] Thus *Luther's* work would be completed, who taught them to be un-Roman and to say: "here *I* stand! *I* cannot do otherwise!" —[54]

147.

Question and answer. — What do savage tribes today adopt first from the Europeans? Liquor and Christianity, the European narcotics. — And from what do they perish most quickly? — From the European narcotics.[55]

148.

Where reformations arise. — At the time of the great corruption of the Church, the Church was least corrupt in Germany: this is why the Reformation arose *here,* as a sign that even the beginnings of corruption were felt to be intolerable. For relatively speaking, no people was ever more Christian than the Germans of Luther's time: their Christian culture was simply ready to burst into a hundredfold magnificence of blossoms — only one more night was missing; but this night brought the storm that put an end to everything.

149.

The failure of reformations. — It speaks in favor of the higher culture of the Greeks even in rather early times, that on several occasions their attempts to found new Greek religions failed; this suggests that already early on there must have been a large number of diverse individuals in Greece whose diverse needs could not be dispatched with a single recipe of faith and hope. Pythagoras and Plato, perhaps Empedocles too, and already much earlier the Orphic enthusiasts aimed to found new religions; and the first two had such genuine religion-founder souls and talents that we cannot be amazed enough by their failure: but they succeeded only in founding sects. Every time a reformation of an entire people fails and only sects rear their head, one can conclude that the people is already heterogeneous in itself and is beginning to free itself from the crude herd instincts and the morality of customs: a meaningful state of hovering that is prone to be disparaged as moral decline and corruption: whereas it really proclaims the maturing of the egg and the imminent breaking of the egg shell. That Luther's Reformation succeeded in the North is a sign that the North was backwards in relation to the South of Europe, and it had rather homogeneous and monotone needs; and there would have been no Christianization of Europe at all if the culture of the ancient world of the South had not been barbarized gradually by an excessive admixture of Germanic barbarian blood and lost its cultural superiority. The more general and unconditional an individual or the idea of an individual can be, the more homogeneous and the lower must be the mass that is being affected there; whereas counterstrivings betray inner counterneeds that also want to satisfy and assert themselves. Conversely, one can always infer a genuine peak of culture if powerful and domineering natures manage only to have a meager and sectarian effect: this applies as well to the individual arts and the realms of knowledge. Where there is ruling, there are masses: where there are masses, there is a need for slavery. Where there is slavery, there are only a few individuals, and these have herd instincts and conscience against them.[56]

150.[57]

On the critique of saints. — In order to have a virtue, must one really want it in its most brutal form? — as the Christian saints wanted and needed it, who only endured life by thinking that the sight of their virtue would spawn contempt for themselves in anyone. But a virtue with such an effect I call brutal.

151.

On the origin of religion. — The metaphysical need is not the origin of religions, as Schopenhauer[58] would have it, but instead only a *late offshoot* of them. Under the rule of religious thinking one has grown accustomed to the idea of "another (behind, below, above) world" and with the annihilation of religious delusion[59] one feels an uncomfortable void and deprivation — and now from this feeling in turn grows "another world," but now only a metaphysical one and no longer religious. But what led in the first place to the assumption of "another world" in primeval times was *not* an impulse and need, rather an *error* in the interpretation of certain natural events, a lapse of the intellect.

152.[60]

The greatest change. — The lighting and the colors of all things have changed! We no longer fully understand how ancient human beings perceived the closest and most frequent things — for instance the day and waking: due to the fact that the ancients believed in dreams, waking life had different lights. And likewise the whole of life, in the reflected light of death and its significance: our "death" is an entirely different death. All experiences shone differently because a god shone through them; all decisions and prospects for the distant future likewise: for they had oracles and secret omens and believed in prophecy. "Truth" was perceived differently, since formerly a madman could be regarded as its mouthpiece — which makes *us* shudder or laugh. Every injustice had a different effect on feelings: for one feared a divine retribution and not just a civil punishment and dishonoring. What was joy in that age when people believed in devils and tempters! What was passion when one saw demons lurking close by! What was philosophy when doubting was felt

as the most dangerous kind of sinning, and in fact as a sacrilege against eternal love, as mistrust of everything that was
good, lofty, pure and merciful! — We have repainted things,
we repaint them continually — but in the meantime, what
are we able to do against the *colorful splendor* of that ancient
mistress![61] — I mean ancient humankind.

153.

Homo poeta. — "I myself, who quite singlehandedly created
this tragedy of tragedies, insofar as it is finished; I who first tied
the knot of morality into existence and pulled it so tight that
only a god can untie it — thus[62] Horace demands after all!
— I myself now in the fourth act have killed all gods — out of
morality! What's to become now of the fifth act! From where
will I take the tragic solution! — Must I begin to consider a
comic solution?"

154.[63]

Different dangers in life. — You do not know what you experience, you walk as if drunk through life and fall down the
stairs on occasion. But thanks to your drunkenness you still
don't break your limbs: your muscles are too slack and your
head too foggy for you to find the stones of these stairs as hard
as we others do! For us life is a great danger: we're made of glass
— woe unto us if we *bump* into anything! And all's lost if we
fall!

155.

What we are lacking. — We love *great* nature and have discovered it: this is because in our minds great human beings are
lacking. With the Greeks it was the other way around: their
sense of nature is different than ours.

156.

The most influential one. — That a human being offers
resistance to his entire age, stops it at the gate and holds it to

account, this *has to* exert influence! Whether he wants to is irrelevant: that he *can* is the issue.

157.

Mentiri.[64] — Watch out! — He's thinking now: shortly he will have a lie ready. This is a stage of culture at which entire peoples have stood. Just consider what the Romans expressed with *mentiri*!

158.

Uncomfortable trait. — To find all things deep — this is an uncomfortable trait: it causes one to constantly strain one's eyes and in the end always find more than one had wished.

159.

Every virtue has its time. — Whoever is steadfast today will often have stings of conscience due to his honesty: for steadfastness is the virtue of a different age than honesty.

160.

Interacting with virtues. — One can also be undignified and flattering toward a virtue.

161.

To the lovers of the age. — The runaway priest and the released prisoner are forever making faces: what they want is a face without a past. — But have you ever seen people who know that the future is reflected in their faces, and are so polite to you, you lovers of the "age," that they make a face without a future? —

162.[65]

Egoism. — Egoism is the *perspectival* law of sensation according to which the closest thing appears big and heavy: whereas receding into the distance all things decrease in size and weight.

163.

After a great victory. — What's best about a great victory is that it removes the fear of defeat from the victor. "Why not be defeated for once?" — he says to himself: "I'm rich enough for that now."

164.

The seekers of rest. — I recognize the spirits who seek rest by the many *dark* objects they set up around themselves: whoever wants to sleep darkens his room or crawls into a cave. — A hint for those who do not know what they actually seek most, and would like to know!

165.[66]

On the happiness of renouncers. — Whoever thoroughly denies himself something and does so for a long time, will almost believe he has discovered that thing when he accidentally encounters it — and every discoverer has such happiness! Let's be wiser than the snakes that lie too long in the same sunlight.

166.

Always in our own company. — Everything that is of my kind, in nature and in history, speaks to me, praises me, drives me forward, comforts me — : the rest I do not hear or I forget right away. We are constantly only in our own company.

167.[67]

Misanthropy and love. — One only brings up the fact that one is sick of people when one can no longer digest them and yet has a stomach full of them. Misanthropy is the result of an all too ardent philanthropy and "cannibalism" — but, dear Prince Hamlet, who asked you to swallow people like oysters?

168.

About a sick man. — "Things look bad for him!" — What's wrong? — "He's suffering from a craving to be praised, and he can't find any nourishment for it." — Incomprehensible! The whole world celebrates him, they not only wait on him hand and foot, they keep him on their lips too! — "Yes, but he has bad hearing for praise. If a friend praises him, then to him it sounds as though the friend is praising himself;[68] if an enemy praises him, then to him it sounds as though this enemy wanted to be praised for it; finally, if anyone else praises him — and there aren't that many left, so famous is he! — then he's offended that he's not wanted as a friend or an enemy; he likes to say: What do I care about someone who is capable of playing the just man even toward me!"

169.[69]

Open enemies. — Courage before the enemy is one thing: with it, one can still be a coward and an irresolute muddlehead. Thus Napoleon judged with respect to the "most courageous human being" known to him, Murat: — which means that open enemies are indispensable to some people if they are to rise to *their* virtue, their manliness and cheerfulness.

170.

With the multitude. — So far he has run with the multitude and been its eulogist: but one day he will be its opponent! For he follows it in the belief that his laziness would meet its match in it: he has not yet experienced that the multitude is not lazy enough for him! that it always pushes on! that it allows no one to stand still! — And he likes so much to stand still!

171.

Fame. — When the gratitude of many toward one casts aside all shame, then fame arises.

172.

The spoiler of taste. — A: "You are a spoiler of taste — people everywhere are saying this!"

B: "Certainly! I spoil everyone's taste for their party: — no party forgives me that."

173.

Being deep and appearing deep. — Whoever knows he is deep strives for clarity; whoever wishes to appear deep to the multitude strives for obscurity. For the multitude considers everything to be deep where it can't see to the bottom: it is so timid and so reluctant to go into the water.

174.

Aside. — Parliamentarianism, that is, public permission to choose between five basic political positions, ingratiates itself to the many who like to *appear* independent and individual and to fight for their opinions. Ultimately, though, it is a matter of indifference whether the herd is commanded to have one opinion or allowed five opinions. — Whoever deviates from the five public opinions and steps aside, always has the entire herd against them.

175.

On eloquence. — Who so far has possessed the most convincing eloquence? The drum roll: and as long as kings have control over this, they are still the best orators and rabble rousers.

176.

Compassion. — The poor reigning princes! All their rights are now unexpectedly turning into claims, and all these claims are starting to sound like presumptions! And if they only say "We" or "my people," then old malicious Europe already smiles. Truly, a chief master of ceremonies of the modern world would scarcely stand on ceremony with them; perhaps he would decree: "*les souverains rangent aux parvenus.*"[70,71]

177.

On "the educational system." — In Germany the superior people are lacking a chief means of education: the laughter of superior people; they don't laugh in Germany.

178.

On moral enlightenment. — One has to talk the Germans out of their Mephistopheles: and their Faust as well. These are two moral prejudices against the value of knowledge.

179.

Thoughts. — Thoughts are the shadows of our sensations — always darker, emptier, simpler than these.

180.[72]

The good times of the free spirits. — Free spirits take liberties even with science — and for the time being they will be given them too — as long as the Church remains standing! — To this extent, they are now having their good times.

181.

Following and going first. — A: "Of the two, one will always follow, the other will always go first to wherever destiny will lead them. And *yet* the former is superior to the other in virtue and by intelligence!" B: "And yet? And yet? This is said for the benefit of others; not for me, not for us! — *Fit secundum regulam.*"[73]

182.

In solitude. — When one lives alone, one does not speak too loudly, one also does not write too loudly: for one fears the hollow echo — the criticism of the nymph Echo. — And all voices sound different in solitude!

183.[74]

The music of the best future. — The foremost musician for me would be the one who knew only the sadness of deepest happiness, and no other sadness: there has never been anyone like this.

184.

Justice. — Better to let oneself be robbed than to be surrounded by scarecrows — this is my taste. And in any case it is a matter of taste — and nothing more!

185.

Poor. — Today he is poor: but not because everything was taken away from him, rather because he threw away everything: — what does he care? He's accustomed to finding. — It's the poor who misunderstand his voluntary poverty.

186.[75]

Bad conscience. — Everything he does now is proper and ordinary[76] — and yet he has a bad conscience nonetheless. For his task is the extraordinary.

187.[77]

Offensively presented. — This artist offends me through the manner in which he presents his ideas, his very good ideas: so broadly and emphatically, and with such crude tricks of persuasion, as if he were speaking to the rabble. After a while, whenever we've spent any time with his art, it's as if we're "in bad company."

188.

Work. — How close now are work and the worker to even the most idle among us! The royal courtesy in the words "we are all workers!" would have still been a cynicism and an indecency under Louis XIV.

189.

The thinker. — He is a thinker: that means, he knows how to take things more simply than they are.

190.[78]

Against the praisers. — A: "One is praised only by one's peers!"
B: "Yes! And whoever praises you says to you: you are my peer!"

191.

Against some defenses. — The most perfidious way to damage
a cause is to defend it on purpose on erroneous grounds.

192.

The good-natured. — What distinguishes those good-natured
people whose faces radiate benevolence, from other human
beings? They have a feeling of well-being in the presence of a
new person and are quickly enamored of her; for this reason,
they become well-wishers, and their first judgment is "I like
her." In them occur successively: the wish for appropriation
(they have few scruples about the value of the other), rapid
appropriation, pleasure of possession and actions in behalf of
their new possession.

193.

Kant's joke. — Kant wanted to prove in a manner that dumb-
founded "the whole world" that "the whole world" was right:
— that was the secret joke of this soul. He wrote against the
scholars in favor of popular prejudice, but for scholars and not
for the common people.

194.

The "open-hearted." — That person probably acts always
according to secret reasons: for he always has communicable
reasons on the tip of his tongue and practically in his open hand.

195.

Laughable! — Look! Look! He's running *away* from people
— : but they're following him because he's running *ahead* of
them — so typical of the herds!

196.

Limits of our sense of hearing. — One hears only those questions for which one is able to find an answer.

197.[79]

Therefore caution! — We communicate nothing more gladly to others than the seal of secrecy — along with what lies beneath.

198.[80]

Annoyance of the proud. — The proud are annoyed even by those who bring them forward: they have dirty looks for the horses of their carriage.

199.

Generosity. — Among the rich, generosity is often merely a kind of shyness.

200.

Laughter. — Laughter means: to have schadenfreude, but with a good conscience.

201.

In applause. — There is always a certain noisiness to applause: even in the applause that we accord ourselves.

202.

A squanderer. — He does not yet have that poverty of the rich man who has already counted out his entire fortune — he squanders his spirit with the unreasonableness of the squanderer called nature.

203.

Hic niger est.[81] — Ordinarily he doesn't have a single thought — but in exceptional cases bad thoughts come to him.

204.

Beggars and courtesy. — "One is not being discourteous by using a stone to knock on the door that's missing its doorbell" — this is how beggars and needy people of all kinds think; but nobody says they're right.

205.

Necessity. — Necessity is supposed to be the cause of something coming to be: in truth it is often only an effect of what has come to be.

206.

In the rain. — It's raining, and I am mindful of the poor people who are now huddled together with their many worries and no practice in concealing them; so each one is ready and more than willing to harm the other and create a miserable kind of gratification even in this nasty weather. — This, and only this is the poverty of the poor!

207.[82]

The envious. — This is an envious man — we shouldn't want him to have children; he would be envious of them because he can no longer be a child.

208.

Big man! — Just because someone is "a big man" doesn't mean we have to infer he's a man: perhaps he's only a boy, or a chameleon of all ages of life, or a bewitched little female.

209.

A way of asking for reasons. — There is a way of asking us for our reasons that not only makes us forget our best reasons, but also feel defiance and aversion rising up in us against reasons generally: — a way of asking that renders us quite stupid and is really a trick used by tyrannical people!

210.[83]

Moderation in industriousness. — One must not want to exceed the industriousness of his father — that makes one sick.

211.

Secret enemies. — Being able to afford a secret enemy — this is a luxury for which the morality of even high-minded spirits usually is not rich enough.

212.

Not letting oneself be deceived. — His spirit has bad manners, it's hasty and always stammers with impatience: thus one scarcely has any idea in what a deep-breathed and broad-chested soul this spirit dwells.

213.

The way to happiness. — A wise man asked a fool what was the way to happiness. The latter answered without hesitating, like someone who had been asked for directions to the nearest city: "Admire yourself and live in the street!" "Stop," cried the wise man, "you demand too much, it is already sufficient to admire oneself!" The fool retorted: "But how can one constantly admire without constantly despising?"

214.

Faith makes blessed. — Virtue gives happiness and a kind of blessedness only to those who have good faith in their virtue: — but not to those subtler souls whose virtue consists in deep mistrust of themselves and all virtue. Ultimately here, too, "faith makes blessed!" — and mind you, *not* virtue!

215.

Ideal and material. — You envision a noble ideal: but are *you* that kind of noble stone out of which such a divine image could be formed? And besides — is not your whole work just a barbaric sculpting? A blasphemy against your ideal?

216.

Danger in the voice. — With a very loud voice in one's throat, one is almost incapable of thinking subtle things.

217.

Cause and effect. — Before the effect one believes in different causes than after the effect.

218.

My antipathy. — I don't love people who have to explode before they can even have an effect, like bombs, and in whose proximity one is always in danger of suddenly losing one's hearing — or losing even more.

219.[84]

Purpose of punishment. — Punishment has the purpose of improving the one *who punishes* — this is the last refuge for the defenders of punishment.

220.

Sacrifices. — Sacrificial animals think differently about sacrifice and sacrificing than the spectators: but since time immemorial they haven't been allowed to comment.

221.

Forbearance. — Fathers and sons are much more forbearing toward one another than mothers and daughters.

222.

Poets and liars. — The poet sees in the liar a foster brother whose milk he has drunk up; so the latter has remained miserable and hasn't even gotten as far as a good conscience.

223.

Vicariousness of the senses. — "One also has eyes for hearing" — said an old father confessor who had gone deaf; "and among the blind whoever has the longest ears is king."[85]

224.

Critique by animals. — I fear that animals regard humans as a being of their kind, that has lost its healthy animal common sense in a most dangerous way — as the insane animal, as the laughing animal, as the weeping animal, as the miserable animal.

225.[86]

The natural ones. — "Evil has always had great effects in its favor! And nature is evil! So let's be natural!" — this is how the great effect-mongers of humankind secretly reason, who all too often have been counted among the great human beings.

226.[87]

The mistrustful and style. — We say the strongest things simply, provided we are surrounded by people who believe in our strength: — this kind of environment trains us in "simplicity of style." The mistrustful speak emphatically; the mistrustful make us emphatic.

227.[88]

Bad claim, bad aim.[89] — He can't control himself: and so this woman concludes it will be easy to control him and casts her net to catch him — the poor thing, who very soon will be his slave.

228.

Against the mediators. — One who wishes to mediate between two resolute thinkers is shown to be mediocre: he has no eye for seeing what is unique; always seeing similarities and making things equal is a sign of weak eyes.

229.[90]

Stubbornness and loyalty. — Out of stubbornness he holds on tight to a cause that he already sees through — but he calls it his "loyalty."

230.[91]

Lack of keeping silent. — His entire being does not *persuade* — this is due to the fact that he never kept silent about any of his good deeds.

231.[92]

The "thorough." — Those slow in knowledge believe that slowness is essential to knowledge.

232.

Dreaming. — One dreams interestingly or not at all. — One must learn to be awake in the same way: — not at all, or interestingly.

233.

Most dangerous viewpoint. — What I now do or choose not to do is as important *for everything to come* as the greatest event of the past: in this tremendous perspective of effect, all actions are equally great and small.

234.[93]

Consoling words for a musician. — "Your life makes no sound in people's ears: for them you live a mute life, and all subtlety of melody, all tender resolution in following or leading the way, remain hidden to them. It's true: you do not approach on a broad street to regimental music — but this still does not give these good people the right to say your way of life lacks music. Let those who have ears hear!"[94]

235.[95]

Spirit and character. — Some reach their peak as a character, but their spirit is just not up to this height — and some the other way around.

236.[96]

In order to stir the multitude. — If someone wants to stir the multitude, must he not be the actor of himself? Must he not first translate himself into what is grotesquely obvious and *perform* his entire person and cause in this crudeness and simplification?

237.[97]

The courteous one. — "He is so courteous!" — Yes, he always has a cake ready for Cerberus and is so timid that he considers everyone to be Cerberus, even you and me — that is his "courtesy."

238.[98]

Without envy. — He is entirely without envy, but there is no merit in this: for he wants to conquer a land that no one yet has possessed and scarcely anyone has even seen.

239.

The joyless one. — A single joyless human being already suffices to plunge an entire household into protracted discouragement and gloomy skies; and it takes a miracle for this one person to be missing! — Happiness is not nearly so contagious a disease — why is that?

240.[99]

Seaside. — I wouldn't build myself a house (and I count myself lucky not to be a homeowner!). But if I had to, then like some Romans, I would build it right into the sea — I would indeed like to share a few secrets with this beautiful monster.

241.

Work and artist. — This artist is ambitious and nothing more: ultimately his work is merely a magnifying glass that he offers to anyone who looks his way.

242.

Suum cuique.[100] — However great the greed of my knowledge is: I can extract nothing from things besides what already belongs to me — the possessions of others remain behind in things. How is it possible that a human being could be a thief or a robber!

243.

Origin of "good" and "bad." — Only he invents an improvement who is able to feel: "This is not good."

244.

Thoughts and words. — Even one's thoughts one cannot reproduce entirely in words.

245.

Praise by choice. — The artist chooses his subjects: this is his way of praising.

246.

Mathematics. — We want to instill the subtlety and rigor of mathematics into all sciences as far as humanly possible, not in the belief that we will know things in this manner, rather in order to *determine* our human relation to things. Mathematics is only the means to general and ultimate knowledge of human beings.

247.

Habit. — All habit makes our hand wittier and our wit less handy.

248.

Books. — What does a book matter if it doesn't even carry us beyond all books?

249.[101]

The sigh of the knower. — "Oh my greed! In this soul no self-lessness dwells — instead, an all-craving self that would like to use many individuals to see as if through *his* eyes and to grab as if with *his* hands — a self that also wants to retrieve the whole past, that wants to lose nothing that could ever belong to it! Oh this flame of my greed! Oh that I could be born again into a hundred beings!" — Whoever does not know this sigh from experience, also doesn't know the passion of the knower.

250.[102]

Guilt. — Although the most perspicacious judges of witches and even the witches themselves were convinced of the guilt of witchery, the guilt was nevertheless nonexistent. This is how it is with all guilt.

251.

Unappreciated sufferers. — The magnificent natures suffer differently than their admirers imagine:[103] they suffer most harshly from the ignoble, petty tantrums of some evil moments, in sum, from their doubts about their own magnificence — but not from the sacrifices and martyrdoms that their task demands of them. As long as Prometheus has compassion for humans and sacrifices himself for them, he is happy and great in himself; but when he becomes envious of Zeus and the homage that mortals pay him — then he suffers!

252.

Better in debt. — "Better to stay in debt than to pay with a coin that does not carry our image!" — thus our sovereignty wills it.

253.

Always at home. — One day we reach our *goal* — and now we proudly point out how long were the trips we made to get there. In truth we didn't notice that we were traveling. But we came so far because we fancied ourselves *at home* at every point along the way.

254.[104]

Against embarrassment. — Whoever is always deeply occupied is far beyond all embarrassment.

255.

Imitators. — A: "What? You don't want imitators?" B: "I don't want people to imitate me, I want everyone to show what they can do: the same as *I* do." A: "So — ?"

256.[105]

Skinfulness.[106] — All human beings of depth have their occasional joy in resembling flying fish and playing in the outermost crests of the waves; they treasure as the best of things — that they have a surface: their skinfulness — *sit venia verbo.*[107]

257.[108]

From experience. — Some do not know how rich they are until they discover how many rich people become thieves on their account.

258.[109]

The deniers of chance. — No victor believes in chance.

259.[110]

From paradise. — "Good and evil are the prejudices of God" — said the serpent.

260.

Times table. — One is always wrong: but with two truth begins. — One cannot prove himself: but two are already irrefutable.

261.[III]

Originality. — What is originality? *Seeing* something that does not yet have a name, cannot yet be named, even though it lies in plain view for everyone. As human beings usually are, it takes a name to make a thing visible to them in the first place. — The originals have usually also been the name-givers.

262.

Sub specie aeterni.[112] — A: "You withdraw ever faster from the living: soon they will strike you from their lists!" — B: "It is the only means of participating in the privilege of the dead." — A: "In what privilege?" — B: "No longer to die."

263.

Without vanity. — When we love, we want our flaws to remain hidden — not out of vanity, but instead because our loved one should not suffer. Indeed, the lover would like to resemble a god — and this, too, not out of vanity.

264.

What we do. — What we do is never understood, but always just praised and blamed.

265.[113]

Ultimate skepticism. — What ultimately are the truths of humanity? — They are the *irrefutable* errors of humanity.

266.

Where cruelty is needed. — Whoever has greatness is cruel to his virtues and to second-rate considerations.

267.[114]

With a great goal. — With a great goal one is superior even to justice, not only to one's deeds and one's judges.

268.[115]

What makes one heroic? — To approach one's highest suffering and one's highest hope at the same time.

269.[116]

In what do you believe? — In this: that the weights of all things must be redetermined.

270.

What does your conscience say? — "You shall become who you are."[117]

271.

Where do your greatest dangers lie? — In compassion.

272.

What do you love about others? — My hopes.

273.[118]

Whom do you call bad? — The person who always wants to shame.

274.

What do you regard as most humane? — Sparing someone shame.

275.

What is the seal of freedom achieved? — No longer being ashamed before oneself.

Book Four: Sanctus Januarius

You who with your lances burning
Melt the ice sheets of my soul,
Speed it toward the ocean yearning
For its highest hope and goal:
Ever healthier it rises,
Free in fate most amorous: —
Thus your miracle it prizes
Fairest Januarius![1]
                    Genoa in January 1882

276.[2]

For the new year. — I still live, I still think: I must still live, for I must still think. *Sum, ergo cogito: cogito, ergo sum.*[3] Today everyone permits themselves to express their wish and favorite thought: well, so I too want to say what I wished of myself today and which thought first entered my heart this year — which thought shall be the ground, guarantee and sweetness of my entire future life! I[4] want to learn more and more to see the necessity in all things as the beautiful: — then I will be one of those who make things beautiful. *Amor fati:*[5] let that be my love from now on! I do not want to wage any war against ugliness. I do not want to accuse, I do not even want to accuse the accusers. Let *looking away* be my sole negation! And, all in all and on the whole: I want at some point for once to be only a Yes-sayer!

277.[6]

Personal providence. — There is a certain high point of life: once we've reached it, then for all our freedom, and as much as we have contested all providential reason and goodness in the beautiful chaos of existence, we are once more in greatest danger of spiritual unfreedom and will have to withstand our hardest test. For only now the idea of a personal providence confronts us with the most intrusive force and has the best advocate, appearance, on its side; now when it has become palpable that all, truly all things that happen to us are constantly *for the best.* The life of every day and every hour seems to want nothing more than to prove this proposition again and again; be it whatever, bad or good weather, the loss of a friend, an illness, a slander, the letter that never arrives, the spraining of an ankle, a glance into a shop, a counterargument, opening a book, a dream, a fraud: it immediately or very soon after proves to be a thing that "was indispensable" — it is full of deep meaning and utility precisely *for us*! Is there a more dangerous seduction than renouncing faith in those uncaring, unknown gods of Epicurus and instead believing in some caring petty deity who personally knows every tiny hair on our head and finds no disgust in the most miserable performance of a service? Well — I think, in spite of all this! we should leave the gods in peace, and likewise the service-oriented geniuses, and content ourselves with the assumption that our own practical and theoretical skill in interpreting and arranging events has now reached its high point. Nor do we want to think too highly of this dexterity of our wisdom when occasionally we are all too greatly surprised by the wonderful harmony arising from how we play our instrument: a harmony that sounds too good for us to dare claim it as our own. In fact, here and there someone is playing along *with* us — good old chance: it guides our hand from time to time, and then the wisest providence of all could not conceive a more beautiful music than what our foolish hand is able to produce.

278.[7]

The thought of death. — It gives me a melancholy happiness to live in the midst of this tangle of little streets, of needs, of voices: how much enjoyment, impatience, desire, how much thirsty life and drunkenness of life come to light here at every moment! And yet, soon it will be so quiet for all these loud, living, life-thirsty ones! See how behind everyone stands their shadow, their dark travel companion! It is always like the last moment before the departure of a ship of emigrants: people have more to say to each other than ever, time is pressing, the ocean and its desolate silence waits impatiently behind all the noise — so covetously, so sure of its prey. And all of them, all of them are thinking that the past was nothing or only a little, the imminent future is everything: this explains the haste, the shouting, this drowning-out and overreaching of one another! Each wants to be the first in this future — and yet death and deathly silence are the only certainty and what all will have in common in this future! How odd that this singular certainty and commonality has almost no influence on humanity and that we are *furthest* removed from a feeling of brotherhood with death! It makes me happy to see that people absolutely do not want to think about death! I would gladly do something to make the thought of life even a hundred times *more worthy of thinking* to them.

279.[8]

Astral friendship. — We were friends and have become estranged. But this is alright and we don't want to conceal and obscure it, as if it were something to be ashamed of. We are two ships, each with its own goal and course; our paths could indeed cross and we could celebrate, as we did — that's when the good ships lay so calmly together in one harbor and under one sun, so that it seemed they were already at their goal and both had but one goal. But then the almighty force of our task drove us apart again, into different seas and sunlit zones, and perhaps we will never see each other again — or perhaps we will indeed see but not recognize each other: the different seas and suns will have changed us! That we have to become estranged is the law *above* us: this is precisely why we should also become more venerable to one another! This is precisely why the thought of our former friendship should become more sacred! There is probably a tremendous invisible arc and stellar orbit in which our so different paths and goals might be *encompassed* as small stretches along the way — let us rise to this thought! But our lives are too short and our vision too feeble for us to be anything more than friends in the sense of this sublime possibility. — And so let us *believe* in our astral friendship even if we have to be earthly enemies.

280.[9]

Architecture for knowers. — What is really needed, and probably very soon, is the realization of what above all is lacking in our big cities: quiet and broad, expansive spaces for reflection, spaces with long, high-ceilinged galleries for inclement or all too sunny weather, where no noise from the carriages and hawkers penetrates and where a more refined decorum would prohibit even priests from praying out loud: structures and facilities that, as a whole, would express the sublimity of mindfulness and stepping aside. The times are past in which the Church possessed a monopoly on reflection, in which the *vita contemplativa* always had first to be *vita religiosa:* and everything the Church has built expresses this idea. I do not know how we could content ourselves with its buildings, even if they were stripped of their ecclesiastical mission; these buildings speak a much too emotional and biased language, as houses of God and ostentatious monuments of an other-worldly intercourse, for us godless ones to be able to think *our thoughts* here. We want to have *ourselves* translated into stone and plants, we want to promenade *in ourselves* when we walk these halls and gardens.[10]

281.[11]

Knowing how to end. — Masters of the first rank are distinguished by the fact that in matters great and small, they know perfectly how to find the end, be it the end of a melody or a thought, be it the fifth act of a tragedy or an act of government. The leaders of the second rank always get restless toward the end, and they plunge into the sea without such proud and calm symmetry, for example, as the mountains at Portofino — where the bay of Genoa sings its melody to the end.

282.

The gait. — There are manners of the spirit by which even great spirits betray that they stem from rabble or semi-rabble: — for it is the gait and stride of their thoughts that betray them; they cannot *walk.* Thus, to his deep frustration, Napoleon himself could not walk like a prince and "legitimately," on those occasions when one really must know how, as in great coronation processions and the like: even there he was always merely the lead in a column — proud and hasty at the same time and very self-conscious of it. — It's laughable to see certain writers who love to rustle in the pleated flowing robes of their long sentences: this is how they want to cover their *feet.*

283.[12]

Preparatory human beings. — I welcome all signs that a manlier, more warlike age is beginning, that above all will restore honor to courageousness! For it shall pave the way for an even-higher age and marshal the strength that the new age will require someday — the age that will carry heroism into knowledge and *wage wars* for the sake of ideas and their consequences. For now, this will require many preparatory brave human beings, who cannot just spring up out of nowhere — and likewise not from the sand and mud of contemporary civilization and metropolitan culture: human beings who know how to be silent, solitary, resolute; content and steadfast in invisible activity: human beings with an authentic urge to seek what can be *overcome* in all things: human beings for whom cheerfulness, patience, simplicity and contempt for the great vanities are just as genuine as magnanimity in victory and indulgence toward the small vanities of all the vanquished: human beings with sharp and free judgment about all victors and about the contribution of chance to every victory and fame: human beings with their own festivals, their own workdays, their own periods of mourning, practiced and secure in commanding and equally prepared, when needed, to obey; equally proud of both, equally serving their own cause in both: more endangered human beings, more fruitful human beings, happier human beings! For, believe me! — the secret to harvesting the greatest fruitfulness and the greatest enjoyment from existence is: *live dangerously*! Build your cities on the slopes of Vesuvius! Send your ships into unexplored seas! Live at war with your peers and with yourselves! Be robbers and conquerors as long as you cannot be rulers and possessors, you knowers! The time will soon be past when it could suffice for you to live hidden in the woods like shy deer! In the end, knowledge will reach out for its due — it will want to *rule* and *possess*, and you will too!

284.[13]

Faith in oneself. — Few people at all have faith in themselves: — and of these few, some get it as a useful blindness or partial dimming of their mind — (what would they behold if they could see *to the bottom* of themselves!), others have to acquire it first: everything good, skillful, great that they do is chiefly an argument against the skeptic who dwells within: the goal is to convince or persuade *him*, and for this practically genius is required. They are the great self-insufficient.[14]

285.[15]

Excelsior![16] — "You will never pray again, never worship again, never rest again in endless trust — you forbid yourself to stand still before any ultimate wisdom, ultimate goodness, ultimate power and unharness your thoughts — you have no constant guardian and friend for your seven solitudes — you live without a view of a mountain range with snowy peaks and glowing coals in its heart — for you there is no avenger, no final improver anymore — there is no reason anymore in what happens, no love in what will happen to you — there is no resting place available to your heart anymore, where it only has to find and no longer to seek, you resist any kind of ultimate peace,[17] you want the eternal recurrence[18] of war and peace:[19] — human being of renunciation, all of this you want to renounce? Who will give you the strength for this? No one has ever had this strength!" — There is a lake that one day forbade itself to run off, and built up a dam where it ran off up till now: since then this lake has risen ever higher. Perhaps that very renunciation will also give us the strength with which to bear renunciation itself; perhaps human beings will rise ever higher from the point where they no longer *flow out* into a god.

286.[20]

Interruption. — Here are some hopes; but what will you see and hear of them if in your own souls you have not experienced luster and radiance and dawns? I can only remind — I cannot do more! Moving stones, turning animals into humans — is this what you want of me? Oh, if you are still stones and animals, then go find yourselves your Orpheus!

287.[21]

Pleasure in blindness. — "My thoughts," said the wanderer to his shadow, "should show me where I stand: but they shouldn't reveal to me *where I'm going.* I love my ignorance of the future

and do not want to perish of impatience and tasting in advance
things that are promised."

288.[22]

Elevated moods. — It seems to me, most people do not
believe in elevated moods, except those lasting for moments
or perhaps a quarter of an hour — with the exception of those
few who know the longer duration of an elevated feeling from
experience. But to be someone of a single elevated feeling, the
embodiment of an individual great mood — until now this has
only been a dream and a delightful possibility: history does not
yet provide us with a clear example of this. Nevertheless, one
day it could produce such human beings — once a number
of favorable preconditions have been created and maintained
that are now beyond the capability of even the luckiest dice
throws of chance. Perhaps for these future souls the normal
state would be precisely what entered our souls in the past from
time to time as the exception we perceived with shuddering: an
unrelenting movement between high and low and the feeling
of high and low, a constant sensation of climbing stairs and
resting on clouds at the same time.

289.

To the ships! — If one considers the effect that an overall
philosophical justification has on each individual's manner of
living and thinking — namely that of a warming, blessing,
fructifying sun that shines for him only; how it makes one
independent of praise or blame, self-sufficient, rich, generous
in happiness and benevolence; how it incessantly turns evil into
good, brings all forces to blossom and ripen and prevents the
small and big weeds of grief and frustration from sprouting
at all: — then one finally exclaims with longing: oh if only
many more new suns like this could be created! Even the evil,
even the unhappy, even the exceptional human being should
have his philosophy, his good right, his sunshine! What they
don't need is compassion! — we have to disabuse ourselves of

this arrogant notion, however long humankind has learned and practiced it so far — we shouldn't be providing them with confessors, soul-conjurers and sin-forgivers! Instead, they need a new *justice*! And a new slogan! And new philosophers! The moral earth is round, too! The moral earth has its antipodes, too! The antipodes have their right to existence, too! There is yet another world to be discovered — and more than one! To the ships, you philosophers!

290.[23]

One thing is essential. — "Giving style" to one's character — a great and rare art! It is practiced by the one who surveys everything that his nature offers in strengths and weaknesses, and then subjects it to an artistic plan until each thing appears as art and reason and even weakness delights the eye. Here a large mass of second nature has been added, there a piece of first nature has been deleted: — each time with long practice and after working on it daily. Here the ugly part that could not be deleted is hidden, there it is reinterpreted into the sublime. Much that is vague and resistant to shaping is saved and exploited for distant vistas: — it is meant to beckon into the distance and the infinite. In the end, when the work is complete, it is revealed how the compulsion of the same taste ruled and formed things big and small: whether the taste was a good or bad one means less than one thinks — it's enough that it was a single taste! — The strong, domineering natures are the ones who enjoy their finest delight in such compulsion, in such constraint and perfection under their own law; the passion of their mighty will relaxes at the sight of all stylized nature, all conquered and serving nature; even when they have palaces to build and gardens to design, they resist giving nature a free hand. — Conversely, it is the weak characters who cannot control themselves who *hate* the constraints of style: they feel that if this bitter-evil compulsion were imposed on them, they would have to become *debased* by it: — they become slaves as soon as they serve, they hate serving. Such spirits

— and they can be first-class spirits — are always out to shape
or construe themselves and their environment as *free* nature:
— wild, arbitrary, fantastical, disorderly, surprising — and
they do well to do so, because only in this way do they do
themselves any good! For one thing is essential: that a human
being *attain* satisfaction with themself — be it by this or that
fiction and art: only then is a human being bearable to look
at in the first place! Whoever is dissatisfied with themself is
constantly prepared to avenge themself for it: we others will
be their victims, if only because we will always have to tolerate the ugly sight of them. For the sight of the ugly makes us
bad and gloomy.

291.[24]

Genoa. — For a good while now I've looked at this city, its
villas and pleasure gardens and the broad ambit of its inhabited
heights and slopes, and finally I must say: I see *faces* from past
generations — this region is strewn with the images of bold
and self-glorifying human beings. They *lived* and wanted to go
on living — this is what they tell me with their houses, built
and ornamented for the centuries and not for the fleeting hour:
they were well disposed to life, however evil they often were
toward one another. I always see the builder, how he rests his
gaze on all the buildings lying distant and near around him,
likewise on city, sea and mountain contours, how he exerts a
force and conquest with this gaze: He wants to assimilate all
this into *his* plan and ultimately make it his *property*, insofar
as it will become part of his plan. This whole region is overgrown with this magnificent insatiable selfishness of lust for
property and spoils; and just as these people acknowledged no
boundary in the distance and in their thirst for the new erected
a new world beside the old one, so too in their homeland each
was outraged by the other and invented a way of expressing
his superiority and laying his personal infinity between himself
and his neighbor. Each reconquered his homeland once more
for himself by overwhelming it with his architectural ideas and

more or less re-creating it as his domestic feast for the eyes. In the North one is struck by the law and the general pleasure in lawfulness and obedience when viewing the architectural style of the cities: one divines the internal self-equalizing and self-conforming that must have dominated the souls of all builders. But here as you turn every corner you find a human being on his own, who knows the sea, adventure and the Orient, a human being who is averse to law and neighbors as a kind of boredom and measures everything established and old with envious looks: he wishes, with the wonderful cunning of his imagination, that he could newly establish all this at least in his thoughts, place his hand upon it and his meaning into it — be it only for the moment of a sunny afternoon, when his insatiable and melancholy soul feels sated for once, and only his own and nothing foreign is permitted to show itself to him.[25]

292.

To the preachers of morality. — I don't want to moralize, but to those who do I give this advice: if in the end you want to deprive the best things and states of all honor and value, then just keep talking about them as you have been! Place them at the pinnacle of your morality and talk from morning till night about the happiness of virtue, about the peace of the soul, about righteousness and immanent retribution: the way you're carrying on, all these good things will finally acquire a popularity and a noisy street reputation: but then, too, all that's gold on them will be worn off and even worse: all that's gold *in them* will have turned into lead. Truly, you're good at the reverse art of alchemy, at the devaluation of the most valuable! Reach for once for a different recipe, if you don't want to keep achieving the opposite of what you seek: *deny* those good things, withdraw from them the rabble's acclaim and easy circulation, restore them to being concealed modesties of solitary souls, say that *morality is something forbidden*! Maybe this way you'll win over the kind of human beings who are the only ones that matter for these things, I mean the *heroic*.

But then there has to be an element of fear to it and not, as before, of disgust! Shouldn't we be saying today what Meister Eckhart said in relation to morality: "I ask of God that he rid me of God."[26]

293.

Our air. — We know it alright: whoever glances casually at science, as if while taking a walk, in the manner of women and unfortunately also many artists: for him the rigor of its service, this relentlessness in small as well as big things, this speed in weighing, judging, and passing judgment are something that induces dizziness and fear. What terrifies him in particular is that here the hardest is demanded, and the best is done, in the absence of praise and awards; on the contrary, as if among soldiers, here almost only blame and sharp reproaches *are heard* — for doing well is considered the rule and failure the exception, while the rule here as everywhere keeps its mouth shut. Now with this "rigor of science" matters stand much as they do with the formality and courtesy of the very best society: — they terrify the uninitiated. But those who are accustomed to it would never live anywhere else but in this bright, transparent, robust, and highly electrified air, in this *manly* air. Everywhere else is for him not pure and airy enough: he suspects that *else-where* his best art will not be of real use to anyone nor even a joy to himself, that half of his life will slip through his fingers due to misunderstandings, that much caution, much conceal-ment and restraint will be required at all times — nothing but major and useless forfeitures of energy! But in *this* rigorous and clear element he has his energy intact: here he can fly! Why should he descend again into those murky waters where one has to swim and wallow and get his wings dirty! — No! It's too hard for us to live there: it's not our fault we were born for the air, for the pure air, we rivals of the sunbeam, and that like the sunbeam we would far prefer to ride on specks of ether and not away from the sun, but *toward the sun*! But this we cannot do: — so we want instead to do the only thing we

can do: bring light to the earth, be "the light of the earth"!
And this is why we have our wings and our speed and our
rigor, for this purpose we are manly and even terrible, like
fire. Let those be terrified of us who do not know how to
warm and enlighten themselves by us!

294.[27]

Against the slanderers of nature. — I regard as unpleasant
those people in whom every natural inclination immediately
becomes an illness, or something distorting or even disgraceful
— *they* have seduced us to the opinion that a human being's
inclinations and instincts are evil; *they* are the cause of our
great injustice toward our nature, toward all nature! There are
enough human beings who *could* rely on their instincts with
grace and nonchalance: but they don't do it, out of fear of that
imagined "evil essence" of nature! *This is why* it's gotten to
the point that so little nobility is to be found among human
beings, the mark of which will always be: to have no fear of
oneself, to expect nothing disgraceful of oneself, to fly without hesitation wherever we feel like — we freeborn birds! And
wherever we end up, there will always be freedom and sunlight
around us.

295.[28]

Brief habits. — I love brief habits and consider them an
invaluable means of getting to know *many* things and states,
and right down to the bottom of their sweetness and their
bitterness; my nature is made for brief habits even in the needs
of my bodily health and generally *as far* as I can see at all,
from the lowest to the highest. I always believe *this* will satisfy
me all the time now — even a brief habit has this passionate
faith, this faith in eternity — and I am to be envied for having
found and recognized it: — and now it nourishes me at noon
and in the evening and spreads deep contentment all around and
into me, so that I desire nothing else, without my having to
compare or to despise or to hate. And then one day its time is

up: this good thing takes leave of me, not as something that now makes me nauseous — but peacefully and sated by me, as I am by it, and as if we should be grateful to one another and *so* shake hands in parting. And already the new thing is waiting at the door and likewise my faith — this indestructible fool and sage! — that this new thing will be the right one, the last right thing. This is how I am with food, ideas, people, cities, poems, music, doctrines, daily plans, lifestyles. — On the other hand, I hate *enduring* habits and feel that a tyrant has invaded my space and that my life's air *thickens,* where events structure themselves such that enduring habits seem to spring from them by necessity: for example, through an official duty, through constant intimacy with the same people, through a permanent residence, through a consistent state of health. Indeed, I am gratefully disposed to all my misery and sickness, and to whatever is imperfect in me — from the very bottom of my soul, because all this leaves me a hundred back doors through which I can escape my enduring habits. — However, the most unbearable, the genuinely terrifying thing to me would be a life entirely without habits, a life that constantly demanded improvisation: — this would be my exile and my Siberia.

296.[29]

The solid reputation. — The solid reputation used to be a matter of the utmost utility; and wherever society is still ruled by the herd instinct, today it is still most expedient for every individual *to pretend* his character and his activity are unchangeable — even when at bottom they are not. "One can trust him, he stays the same": — this is in all dangerous social situations the praise that means most. Society feels with gratification that it has a dependable and ever-ready *tool* in the virtue of this one, in the ambition of another, and in the pensiveness and passion of a third — it honors this *tool-nature,* this staying true to oneself, this steadfastness in opinions, ambitions, and even in vices with its highest honors. Such a valuation, that blossoms and has blossomed everywhere at the same time as the morality of customs, breeds "character" and renders *disreputable* all change, relearning, and self-transformation. Now this in any case is the most damaging kind of general judgment for *knowledge,* however big the advantage of this way of thinking may be otherwise: for precisely the good will of the knower undauntedly to declare himself *against* his previous opinion at any time, and generally to be suspicious with respect to everything that wants to become *firm* in us — is condemned here and rendered disreputable. The attitude of the knower, at odds with the "solid reputation," is considered *dishonorable,* while the fossilizing of opinions monopolizes all honor: — even today we must live under the spell of such sentiments! The living is so hard when one has the judgment of many millennia against and around oneself! It is probable that knowledge was burdened for many millennia with a bad conscience, and that there must have been much self-contempt and secret misery in the history of the greatest minds.

297.[30]

Being able to contradict. — These days everyone knows that being able to bear contradiction is a high indicator of culture. A few even know that the superior human being wishes for and provokes contradiction, in order to get a hint of his as yet unrealized injustice. But *being able* to contradict, the *good* conscience achieved with hostility toward the customary, traditional, hallowed — this is more than both of the former and the genuinely great, innovative, amazing thing about our culture, the step of steps of the liberated spirit: who knows this? —

298.

Sigh. — I snatched this insight along the way and quickly took the closest paltry words to secure it, so that it wouldn't fly away from me again. And now it's gone and died on me because of these shriveled words and it hangs and dangles in them — I hardly know anymore, when I look at it, how I could have been so happy when I caught this bird.

299.[31]

What one should learn from artists. — What means do we have to make things beautiful, attractive, desirable to ourselves when they are not? — and in my opinion, in themselves they never are! There is something we can learn from physicians here, when for example they dilute what is bitter or add wine and sugar into the mixing bowl; but even more from the artists who are actually bent on making such inventions and feats all the time. Distancing oneself from things until there is much about them that one no longer sees and much that the eye has to add, *in order still to see them* — or seeing things around the corner and as if in a cutout — or[32] positioning them so that they partially eclipse one another and allow only perspectival vistas — or viewing them through colored glass or in the light of the sunset — or giving them a surface and a skin that lacks full transparency: we should learn all this from the artists[33] and for the rest be wiser than they are. For among them, this subtle power of theirs usually stops where art stops and life begins; *we* however want to be the poets of our life, and first of all in the smallest and most mundane things.

300.

Preludes to science. — Do you really believe the sciences would have originated and matured if they hadn't been preceded by magicians, alchemists, astrologers and witches who had first to create the thirst, hunger and taste for *hidden and forbidden* powers by means of their promises and pretenses? Indeed, that infinitely more had to be *promised* than could ever be fulfilled in order for anything at all to be fulfilled in the realm of knowledge? — Perhaps in the same way that we now see these as preludes and rehearsals for science, though they were absolutely *not* practiced and perceived as such at the time, the whole of *religion* will also appear to some distant age as mere rehearsal and prelude: perhaps it could have been the strange means for individual human beings to enjoy for once the whole self-sufficiency of a god and all his power of self-redemption: Indeed! — one may ask — would humans have ever learned to sense a hunger and thirst for *themselves* and experienced satiety and fullness in *themselves* without such religious schooling and prehistory? Did Prometheus first have to *imagine* that he *stole* light and then pay for it — in order to finally discover that he had created light *by desiring light*, and that not only human beings but even *gods* were the work *of his* hands and were clay in his hands? Everything just images of the sculptor? — just like the delusion, the thievery, the Caucasus, the vulture and the whole tragic *Prometheia*[34] of all knowers?

301.[35]

Delusion of the contemplative. — Superior human beings distinguish themselves from the inferior in that they see and hear unspeakably more and do so thoughtfully — and precisely this distinguishes humans from animals and the higher animals from the lower. The world becomes ever fuller for someone who grows into the heights of humanity; ever more fishhooks of potential interest are cast toward him; the number of stimuli is constantly growing in him and likewise the number of different types of pleasure and displeasure — the superior human being becomes ever happier and unhappier at the same time. But a *delusion* is his constant companion here: he feels as though he has been placed as a *spectator* and *listener* before the great visual and musical spectacle that is life: he refers to his nature as a *contemplative* one and overlooks the fact that he himself is also the actual and the ongoing poet of life — that he indeed differs greatly from the *actor* of this drama, from the so-called man of action, but even more from a mere spectator and festival guest *before* the stage. As a poet, he certainly possesses *vis contemplativa*[36] and retrospective ability for his own work, but at the same time and primarily he has *vis creativa*,[37] which is *lacking* in the man of action regardless of what appearance and all the world may say. We who are simultaneously thinking and feeling are the ones who really and continually *make* something that doesn't already exist: the whole eternally growing world of valuations, colors, weights,[38] perspectives, scales, affirmations and negations. This poem invented by us is constantly being internalized, rehearsed, translated into flesh and reality, indeed into the mundane by the so-called practical people (our actors, as mentioned). Whatever has *value* in the current world does not have it intrinsically, according to its nature — nature is always valueless: — rather, its value has been given by someone at some point, bestowed, and *we* were the givers and bestowers! We first created the world *that concerns human beings*! — But this very knowledge is what we lack, and when we are able to seize it for a moment, then in the next moment we've forgotten it again: we contemplative types fail to recognize our best strength and underestimate ourselves a bit — we are *neither as proud nor as happy* as we could be.

302.[39]

Danger of the happiest. — To have refined senses and refined taste; to be accustomed to the choicest and very best things of the spirit as well as the proper and closest food; to enjoy a strong, bold, daring soul; to go through life with a calm eye and a steady gait, always prepared for extremes, as if for a celebration and full of longing for undiscovered worlds and seas, human beings and gods; to heed every cheerful music, as if perhaps brave men, soldiers, seafarers were taking a brief respite and enjoying themselves there, and in the deepest savoring of the moment becoming overwhelmed by tears and by the whole purple melancholy of the happy one: who would not wish that all this were precisely *his* possession, his state! It was the *happiness of Homer*! The state of the one who invented the gods for the Greeks — nay, who invented *his* own gods for himself! But one should not fool oneself: with this Homeric happiness in one's soul one is also more capable of suffering than any creature under the sun! And it is only at this price that one may purchase the most exquisite shell that the waves of existence have ever washed on shore! As its possessor, one becomes ever more refined in pain and in the end too refined: a petty vexation and disgust sufficed in the end to spoil life for Homer. He wasn't able to solve a foolish little riddle[40] that young fishermen had posed him! Indeed, for the happiest, the little riddles pose the greatest danger! —

303.[41]

Two happy types. — Truly, this person, despite his youth, is adept at the *improvisation of life* and astonishes even the subtlest observer: — for it seems he makes no mistakes even though he is continually playing the riskiest game. One is reminded of those improvising musical masters whose hands the listeners also wish to regard as possessing divine *infallibility,* despite the fact that they err now and again like every mortal. But they are practiced and inventive, and in a moment, they're always prepared to deftly reintegrate into the thematic structure even the most accidental note to which a touch of the finger or a whim has driven them, thus breathing a beautiful meaning and a soul into an accident. — But here is quite a different person: he basically fails at everything that he wants and plans. The things that he occasionally had his heart set on already brought him several times to the abyss and into the closest proximity of ruin; and if he managed to escape it, then certainly not only "with a black eye."[42] Do you think he's unhappy about this? Long ago he made a resolution not to take certain wishes and plans too seriously. "If I don't succeed at this," he says to himself at such times, "then maybe I'll succeed at something else; and on the whole I don't know whether I owe more to my failures than to any success. Am I made to be stubborn and to have the horns of a bull? What counts to *me* as the value and outcome of life lies elsewhere; my pride and likewise my misery lie elsewhere. I know more about life because so often I was at the point of losing it: and this is precisely why I *have* more from life than all of you!"

304.[43]

The don'ts within our do's. — At bottom I'm repulsed by all those moralities that say: "Don't do this! Renounce! Overcome yourself!" — on the other hand, I'm inclined toward those moralities that drive me to do something and do it again from morning till night, and to dream about it at night, and to think of absolutely nothing but: do this *well,* as well as ever *I* alone can do it! For someone who lives like this, one thing after another will continually fall away if it doesn't belong to such a life: without hatred and aversion, he watches today this and tomorrow that depart from him, like yellowed leaves that are stripped from the trees by any stronger puff of air: or he doesn't even see that it departs, so rigidly do his eyes train on his goal and generally forward, not sideward, backward, downward. "Our do's shall determine what we don't: by doing, we don't" — that's how I like it, that's *my placitum.*[44] But I don't want to strive for my impoverishment with open eyes, I dislike all negative virtues — virtues whose very essence is negating and self-denial.

305.[45]

Self-control. — Those moral teachers whose first and chief command is that a human being should gain control of himself, thereby afflict him with a peculiar disease: namely a constant irritability at all natural stirrings and inclinations and a kind of itch, so to speak. Henceforth whatever may push, pull, attract, drive him, from within or from without — always it will seem to this irritable one as if now his self-control were endangered: he may no longer permit himself a single instinct, a single free beat of his wings; instead, he stands there constantly in a defensive stance, armed against himself, with sharp and mistrustful eyes, the eternal guardian of his fortress, which he has turned himself into. Yes, he can be *great* in this way!

But how unbearable he has become to others, how difficult for himself, how impoverished and cut off from the loveliest fortuities of the soul! Indeed, from all further *instruction*. For one must be able to lose oneself from time to time if one wants to learn something from those things that we ourselves are not.

306.[46]

Stoics and Epicureans. — The Epicurean looks for the situation, the persons and even the events that suit his extremely irritable intellectual constitution, he forgoes the rest — that is, most everything else — because it would be too strong and heavy a meal for him. The Stoic, on the other hand, practices swallowing stones and worms, glass splinters and scorpions without becoming nauseous; ultimately his stomach is supposed to become indifferent to everything that the chance of existence dumps into it: — he is reminiscent of that Arabian sect of the Aissawa[47] one encounters in Algiers; and like these insensitive ones, he too likes to have an invited audience when he performs his insensitivity, which is precisely what the Epicurean prefers to dispense with: — he has his "garden" after all! For people with whom fate improvises, for those who live in violent times and are dependent on rash and mercurial human beings, Stoicism may be well advised. But whoever more or less *foresees* that fate will allow him to spin *a long thread* does well to adapt in an Epicurean way; all people engaged in intellectual work have done so thus far! For them, after all, it would be the loss of losses to forfeit their subtle irritability and receive in exchange the gift of a Stoic's hide with porcupine quills.

307.[48]

In favor of criticism. — Now something that you used to love as a truth or probability seems like an error to you: you shed it and suppose that your reason has now gained a victory. But perhaps the error of that time, when you were still another

— you are always another — was just as necessary for you as all your current "truths," as a skin, so to speak, that concealed and covered a lot that you were not yet permitted to see. Your new life killed that opinion for you, not your reason: *you no longer need it,* and now it collapses on its own and unreason crawls out of it like a worm into the light. When we practice criticism, it is not something voluntary and impersonal — it is, quite often at least, proof that living dynamic forces are in us that are shedding their husk. We negate and must negate because something in us lives and *wants* to affirm itself, something that we perhaps do not yet know, do not yet see! — This in favor of criticism.

308.

The history of each day. — What in you constitutes the history of each day? Look at your habits, of which this history consists: are they the result of countless little acts of cowardice and sloth, or of your bravery and inventive reason? As different as the two cases are, it would be possible for people to praise you equally, and for you to actually benefit them equally anyway. However, praise and benefit and respectability may be enough for someone who just wants to have a good conscience — but not for you, diagnostician,[49] for whom *conscience is a matter of science!*[50]

309.[51]

From the seventh solitude. — One day the wanderer slammed the door behind him, stopped and wept. Then he said: "This yearning and urge for what is true, real, nonappearance, certain! How it angers me! Why does this gloomy and zealous taskmaster follow *me* of all people? I would like to rest, but he won't allow it. How many things there are that seduce me to linger! Everywhere there are gardens of Armida[52] for me: and therefore ever-new painful partings and new bitterness of the heart! I must lift my foot once more, this weary and wounded foot: and because I must, I often have a wrathful look back at the most beautiful things that could not hold me — *because* they could not hold me!"

310.[53]

Will and wave. — How greedily this wave approaches, as if it were a matter of reaching something! How it crawls with terrifying haste into the innermost nooks of the rocky cliff! It seems it wants to get there before someone; it seems that something is hidden there, something of value, perhaps high value. — And now it returns, somewhat more slowly, still white all over with excitement — is it disappointed? Did it find what it was looking for? Does it merely pretend to be disappointed? — But already another wave approaches, even greedier and wilder than the first, and its soul also seems to be full of secrets and a yearning to dig for treasure. Thus live the waves — thus we live, we who will! — I'll say no more. — So? You don't trust me? You're angry with me, you beautiful monsters? Are you afraid I'll reveal your whole secret? Well! Go ahead and be angry with me, swell your dangerous emerald bodies as high as you can, build a wall between me and the sun — just like now! Truly, there's nothing left of the world anymore but green twilight and green lightning. Do exactly as you will, you emboldened ones, roar with joy and malice — or dive below again, scatter your emeralds into the deepest depths, toss your infinite white mane of foam and spray over them — everything's fine with me, for everything suits you and I love you so for everything: how could I betray *you*! For — hear me well! — I know you and your secret, I know your kind! You and I, we're of the same kind! — You and I, we've got just one secret!

311.[54]

Refracted light. — One is not always brave, and when one gets tired, then the likes of us will probably also lament someday as follows: "It's so hard to hurt people — oh, what a shame that it's necessary! What use is it to us to live in seclusion if we don't want to keep to ourselves what gives offense? Wouldn't it be smarter to live in the throng and to make good to individuals whatever should and must be sinned against all? To be foolish to the fools, vain to the vain, fanatic to the fanatics? Wouldn't it be fair, given such an overblown degree of deviation on the whole? When I hear about the malicious things others say against me — isn't my first feeling one of satisfaction? You're right! — I seem to be saying to them — I am so ill-suited to you and have so much truth on my side: go ahead and have a good day at my expense, as often as you can! Here are my faults and mistakes, here is my delusion, my bad taste, my confusion, my tears, my vanity, my owlish seclusion, my contradictions! Here's something to laugh at! So just laugh and enjoy yourselves! I'm not angry at the law and nature of things, which prefer that faults and mistakes give pleasure! — To be sure, there were 'nicer' times once,[55] when one could still feel so *indispensable* that he could step into the street with any halfway innovative idea and shout to everyone: 'Look! The kingdom of heaven is nigh!' — I wouldn't miss myself, if I were absent.[56] All of us are dispensable!" — But as I said, we don't think this way when we're brave; we don't think *about it.*

312.[57]

My dog. — I've given my pain a name and I call it "dog" — it is just as loyal, just as obtrusive and shameless, just as entertaining, just as clever as any other dog — and I can scold it and vent my bad moods on it: the way others do with their dogs, servants and wives.

313.

No torture images. — I want to follow Raphael's example and paint no more images of torture. There are sufficient sublime things for us not to have to seek sublimity where it dwells in sisterhood with cruelty; and moreover, my ambition would not find satisfaction if I were to make myself into a sublime torturer.[58]

314.

New house pets. — I want to have my lion and my eagle around me, so that I always have hints and omens to know how great or small my strength is. Must I look down at them today and fear them? And will the hour return when they look up at me and in fear? —

315.[59]

On the last hour. — Storms are my danger: will I have my storm to die of, as Oliver Cromwell died of his storm? Or will I die out like a light not blown out by the wind but that became tired and sated of itself — a burned out light? Or finally: will I blow myself out, in order not to burn out? —

316.[60]

Prophetic human beings. — You have no feeling for the fact that prophetic human beings are very suffering types: you merely suppose they were given a beautiful "gift," and you probably would like to have it yourself — but I wish to express myself in a parable. How greatly may animals suffer from the electricity in the air and the clouds! We see that a few species have a prophetic faculty with respect to weather, for example monkeys (as one can well observe even in Europe, and not only in zoos, but on Gibraltar in particular). But we do not think of their *pains* — as serving as prophets for them! When highly positive electricity suddenly switches into negative electricity under the influence of an approaching but yet not nearly visible cloud, such that a change in the weather is in the offing, then these animals behave as if an enemy were drawing near and they brace themselves for defense or flight; most often they hide away — they don't understand bad weather as weather, but as an enemy whose hand they already *feel*!

317.[61]

Retrospection. — We seldom become aware of the actual pathos of each period of life as such, as long as we are still in it, rather, we always think it is the only possible and reasonable state for us now and regard it as thoroughly *ethos,* not pathos — as the Greeks would say and differentiate. A couple of notes of music today reminded me of a winter and a house and a highly reclusive life and simultaneously of the feeling in which I lived at that time: — I thought I could go on living that way forever. But now I understand that it was pathos and passion through and through, a thing comparable to this painfully courageous and confidently consoling music — it's the sort of thing one should not have for years at a time or worse, for eternities: it would make one too "superterrestrial" for this planet.

318.[62]

Wisdom in pain. — There is as much wisdom in pain as in pleasure: like pleasure, it belongs among the principal species-preserving forces. If it weren't this, it would have perished long ago; that it hurts is no argument against it, it is its essence. In pain I hear the ship's captain command: "Take in the sails!" The bold seafarer "human being" will need to have drilled a thousand ways to set the sails, or else he would be ruined all too quickly, and the ocean would have swallowed him too soon. We must also know how to live with reduced energy: the moment pain issues its safety signal, it's time for a reduction — a great danger of some kind, a storm is brewing, and we do well to "inflate" ourselves as little as possible. — It's true there are human beings who hear the exact opposite command when great pain is approaching, who are never prouder, more warlike and happier than when facing down the storm that blows in; indeed, pain itself gives them their greatest moments! These are the heroic human beings, the great *pain bringers* of humankind: those few or rare types who deserve precisely the same apology as pain in general — and truly, it should not be denied them! They are species-preserving, species-promoting forces of the first order: if only for the fact that they eschew comfort and cannot conceal their disgust for this kind of happiness.

319.

As interpreters of our experiences. — One kind of honesty has remained foreign to all religion founders and their kind: — they've never made their experiences into a matter of conscience for knowledge. "What did I actually experience? What was happening in and around me at the time? Was my reason bright enough? Was my will trained upon all the deceptions of the senses and valiant in opposing the fantastical?" — none of them ever questioned in this manner, and to this day the precious religious ones still don't ask: instead, they have a thirst for things that run *counter to reason* and they don't want to make it too hard for themselves to satisfy it — and so they experience their "miracles" and "rebirths" and hear the voices of little angels! But we, we others, we reason-thirsty ones want to look our experiences as sternly in the face as a scientific experiment, hour by hour, day after day! We want to be our own experiments and guinea pigs!

320.

On meeting again. — A: Do I still understand you correctly? You're searching? Where in the midst of the actual current world is *your* nook and star? Where can *you* lie down in the sun so that an abundance of well-being comes to you, too, and your existence is justified? Let each do that for himself — you seem to be telling me — and let each put out of his mind generalities and worrying about others and society! — B: I want more, I'm no seeker. I want to create my own sun for myself.

321.

New caution. — Let's not think any more so much about punishing, blaming and improving! We will rarely change an individual; and if we should succeed at it, then perhaps something else succeeded inadvertently at the same time: *we* were changed by him! Let's see to it instead that our own influence *on everything to come* balances and outweighs his influence! Let's not struggle in a direct fight! — and that's what all blaming, punishing and wanting to improve people amounts to. Rather, let's raise ourselves that much higher! Let's give our own example ever more vibrant colors! Let's eclipse the other with our light! No! We don't want to become *darker* ourselves on his account, like all who punish and are dissatisfied! Let's turn aside instead! Let's look away!

322.

Parable. — Those thinkers in whom all stars move in cyclical orbits are not the deepest; whoever looks into himself as if into vast space and bears galaxies within himself, also knows how irregular all galaxies are; they lead into chaos and the labyrinth of existence.

323.

Luck in fate. — Fate renders us the greatest distinction when it has allowed us for a time to fight on the side of our opponents. This way we are *predestined* for a great victory.

324.[63]

In media vita.[64] No! Life has not disappointed me! On the contrary, from year to year I find it truer,[65] more desirable and mysterious — from that day on, when the great liberator came over me, that idea that life could be an experiment of the knower — and not a duty, not a disaster, not a deception! — And knowledge itself: whatever it may be for others, for example, a bed to rest on or the way to such a bed, or entertainment, or idleness — for me it is a world of dangers and victories in which even heroic feelings have their dance- and playgrounds.[66] "*Life as a means to knowledge*" — with this principle at heart one can not only live bravely, but even *live cheerfully and laugh cheerfully*! And who after all would know how to laugh well and

live well if they did not first have a good understanding of war
and victory?

325.[67]

What belongs to greatness. — Who will attain something great
if he doesn't feel the strength and the will in himself to *inflict*
great pains! The ability to suffer is the least thing: weak women
and even slaves often accomplish this masterfully. But not to
perish of inner distress and uncertainty when one inflicts great
suffering and hears the cry of this suffering — that is great, that
belongs to greatness.

326.[68]

The physicians of the psyche and pain. — All preachers of
morality, as well as all theologians, have a bad habit in common: all seek to convince people that they are in very poor
health and a harsh, ultimate and radical cure is needed. And
because the whole of humanity has lent its ear too eagerly and for
entire centuries to those teachings, in the end some part of
the superstition about feeling very poorly actually transferred
over to them; so that now they are all too ready to sigh, to
find nothing good in life anymore and to sit around together
making gloomy faces as if life were in fact really hard to *bear.* In
truth, they are uninhibitedly sure of their lives and enamored
of it, and they're full of untold tricks and subtleties for breaking
what is unpleasant and for plucking the thorn out of pain and
misfortune. It seems to me that pain and misfortune are always
talked about in *exaggeration,* as if it were a matter of good manners to exaggerate here: on the other hand, one assiduously fails
to mention that there are innumerable palliatives against pain,
like anesthesia, or the feverish haste of thoughts, or lying in a
comfortable position, or good and bad memories, intentions,
hopes and many kinds of pride and sympathy that have nearly
the same effect as anesthetics, whereas with the highest degrees
of pain, fainting sets in automatically. We are very good at driz-
zling sweetness on our bitterness, particularly on the bitterness

of the psyche; we have remedies in our bravery and sublimity, as well as in the nobler deliria of submission and resignation. A loss is a loss to us for scarcely an hour: somehow even it represents a gift from heaven — new strength, for example, and be it only a new opportunity for strength! What have these moral preachers fantasized about the inner "misery" of evil human beings! What furthermore have they *lied* to us about the unhappiness of passionate human beings! — indeed, lying is the right word here: they knew full well about the super-abundant happiness of this kind of human being, but they hushed it up because it was a refutation of their theory that all happiness first originates with the annihilation of passion and the silencing of the will! And finally, regarding the prescription of all these physicians of the psyche and their praise of a harsh radical cure, it is permitted to ask: is this our life really painful and burdensome enough to exchange it advantageously for a Stoic lifestyle and fossilization? Our health is *not poor enough* for us to have to be in poor health according to Stoic standards!

327.

Taking seriously. — The intellect in most people by far is an unwieldy, gloomy and creaking machine that is hard to get going: they call it "*taking* the matter *seriously*" when they want to work with this machine and to think well — oh how burdensome thinking well must be to them! The lovely beast human being, so it seems, loses its good mood every time it thinks well; it becomes "serious"! And "where laughing and joy are present, thinking is good for nothing": — thus speaks the prejudice of this serious beast against all "joyful science." Well then! Let's demonstrate that it is a prejudice!

328.

Doing damage to stupidity. — Certainly the belief in the rep-rehensibility of egoism, preached so stubbornly and with such conviction, has done damage to egoism on the whole (*to the benefit*, as I will repeat a hundred times, *of the herd instincts!*), in particular by taking away its good conscience and commanding that we seek the genuine source of all misfortune in it. "Your selfishness is the disaster of your life" — this was the sermon for millennia: it did damage to selfishness, as mentioned, and deprived it of much spirit, much cheerfulness, much inventiveness, much beauty; it made selfishness stupid and ugly and it poisoned it! — Philosophical antiquity, on the other hand, taught a different main source of disaster: from Socrates on, thinkers never tired of preaching: "Your thoughtlessness and stupidity, your heedless living by the rules, your subordination to the opinion of neighbors is the reason why you so seldom achieve happiness — we thinkers, as thinkers, are the happiest ones." Let's not decide here whether this sermon against stupidity had better reasons on its side than did that sermon against selfishness; but what is certain is that it deprived stupidity of its good conscience: — these philosophers *did damage* to stupidity.

329.[69]

Leisure and idleness. — There is an Indian-like savageness, peculiar to Indian blood, in the way Americans strive for gold: and their breathless haste for working — the genuine vice of the New World — is already beginning to infect old Europe with savageness and to cover it in a mindlessness that is quite odd. Today one is already ashamed of resting; reflecting for a long time nearly causes stings of conscience. One thinks with watch in hand, as one eats lunch, with an eye on the financial pages — one lives like someone who constantly "could be missing out on something." "Better to do anything at all than nothing" — this principle is likewise just a guideline for putting an end to all culture and superior taste. And so, just as all forms visibly perish from this haste of the workers, so, too, the feeling for form itself perishes, the ear and eye for the melody of movements. The proof of this lies in the *clumsy obviousness* demanded everywhere today in all situations where someone wants to be honest with people for once, in relation to friends,

women, relatives, children, teachers, pupils, leaders and princes
— one no longer has time and energy for ceremonies, for civil-
ity with detours, for all *esprit*[70] of conversation and generally
for all *otium*.[71] For life on the hunt for profit constantly compels one to squander his spirit to the point of exhaustion, in
ceaseless dissembling or outwitting or outdoing; now the real
virtue is doing something in less time than it takes another.
And so only rarely are there hours of *permitted* honesty; in these,
however, one is tired and not only wants to "let oneself go," but
also to *stretch out* long and wide and clumsy. It is in keeping
with this urge that one now writes *letters* whose style and spirit
will always be the genuine "sign of the times." If there is any
pleasure remaining in socializing and in the arts, then it is
a pleasure as contrived by slaves who are worked to exhaustion.
Oh, this frugality of "joy" in our educated and uneducated! Oh,
this increasing suspicion of all joy! More and more it is *work* that
entices the good conscience to its side: the inclination to joy
already refers to itself as a "need for recuperation" and is beginning to be ashamed of itself. "One owes it to one's health" —
this is what they say if they're caught visiting the countryside.
Indeed, it could soon get to the point where we couldn't give in
to our inclination to the *vita contemplativa* (that is, to strolling
with thoughts and friends) without a certain self-loathing and
bad conscience. — Well then! It was the opposite in the past:
work had bad conscience associated with it. A human being
of good lineage *concealed* his work, if need compelled him to
work. The slave worked under the pressure of the feeling that
he did something contemptible: — "doing" itself was something contemptible. "Nobility and honor are found in *otium*
and *bellum*[72] alone": so spoke the voice of antiquity's prejudice!

330.[73]

Applause. — A thinker does not need applause and the clapping of hands, assuming he is assured of his own clapping of
hands: but this he cannot[74] forgo. Are there human beings who
can also dispense with this and with any variety of applause at

all? I doubt it: and Tacitus, who was no slanderer of wise men, says even in reference to the wisest: *quando etiam sapientibus gloriae cupido novissima exuitur*[75] — for him that means: never.

331.[76]

Better deaf than deadened. — It used to be, one wanted a *name* to speak for oneself: that no longer suffices, since the market has become too big — now it has to be a *shout*. The result is that even good voices shout themselves hoarse, and the best wares are offered by raspy voices; without the shouting of vendors and hoarseness there is no genius anymore. — Of course this is an evil time for a thinker: he has to learn how to find his own quiet between two clamors, and pretend to be deaf until he actually is. As long as he has not yet learned this, to be sure, he is in danger of perishing of impatience and headache.

332.[77]

The evil hour. — Probably every philosopher has had an evil hour when he thought: What do I matter if one does not believe my bad arguments too! — And then some gloating little bird flew past him and twittered: "What do you matter? What do you matter?"[78]

333.[79]

What is meant by knowing. — *Non ridere, non lugere, neque detestari, sed intelligere!* says Spinoza,[80] so simply and sublimely in his typical manner. Meanwhile: what else is this *intelligere* at bottom than the form in which precisely all three of these things become sensible to us at once? One result of the different and mutually contradicting drives to laugh, mourn and curse? Before knowing is possible, each of these drives must have manifested its one-sided view of the thing or event; afterwards arose the struggle of these one-sided views and out of it sometimes a middle ground, a calming down, a conceding that all three sides are right, a kind of justice and contract:

after all, by virtue of justice and contract all these drives can assert their existence and maintain their rights in relation to one another. We, who become conscious only of the last reconciliation scenes and final accounts of this lengthy process, later infer that *intelligere* is something conciliatory, just, good, something essentially opposed to the drives, whereas it is only a *certain behavior of the drives toward one another.* For the longest time, conscious thinking was regarded as thinking itself: only now is the truth dawning on us that the biggest part by far of our intellectual activity takes place unconsciously and unfelt by us; but in my opinion, these drives that are fighting each other here will know very well indeed how to make themselves felt by and to hurt *each other* — : that powerful sudden exhaustion that afflicts all thinkers might have its origin in this (it is the exhaustion on the battlefield). Indeed, perhaps there is some kind of hidden *heroism* in our warring depths, but certainly nothing divine, nothing resting eternally in itself, as Spinoza thought. *Conscious* thinking, and in particular that of the philosopher, is the least vigorous and therefore also the relatively mildest and calmest kind of thinking: and so it is precisely the philosopher who can most easily be led astray about the nature of knowing.[81]

334.

One must learn to love. — This is how we are with music: first one must *learn to hear* a figure and a melody at all, to make it out and distinguish it, isolate and delimit it as a life of its own; then effort and good will are required to *tolerate* it despite its strangeness, to practice patience toward its appearance and expression as well as indulgence toward its oddness: — finally a moment arrives when we are *accustomed* to it, when we expect it, when we intuit that we would miss it if it were missing; and now it exerts its pressure and allure on and on and doesn't stop until we have become its humble and enchanted lovers, who want nothing better from the world now than it and it again. — But this is not only how we are with music: this is exactly how we *learned to love* all things that we now love. In the end, we are always rewarded for our good will, our patience, fairness, gentleness toward what is strange, in that the strange gradually removes its veil and manifests itself as new unspeakable beauty: — this is its *gratitude* for our hospitality. Even those who love themselves will have learned it in this manner: there is no other way. Love, too, must be learned.

335.

Long live physics! — How many people really understand how to observe! And of the few who understand how — how many observe themselves? "Everyone is farthest from himself"[82] — this is known by all diagnosticians, to their consternation; and the saying "know thyself!" on the lips of a god and spoken to humans is practically malicious! But *that* the situation of self-observation is so desperate has no better evidence than the way *almost everyone* speaks about the essence of a moral action, this quick, obliging, convinced, loquacious way, with its look, its smile, its obliging zeal! One seems to want to say to you: "But my dear fellow, that's *my* subject exactly! You're addressing your question to someone who's *allowed* to answer: it just so happens that there's nothing I'm so wise about as this. Therefore: when someone judges '*this is right,*' when he then concludes '*therefore it must happen!*' and now *does* what he thus recognizes as right and designates to be necessary — then the essence of his action is *moral!*" But, my friend, you're talking here about three actions instead of one: for example, your judging "this is right" is an action — couldn't there be judging in a moral and in an immoral manner? — *Why* do you consider this and this exclusively to be right? — "Because my conscience tells me this; conscience never speaks immorally, since it alone determines what is supposed to be moral!" — But why do you *listen* to the voice of your conscience? And why do you have the right to regard such a judgment as true and infallible? For this *belief* — isn't there a conscience anymore? Don't you know anything about an intellectual conscience? A conscience behind your "conscience"? Your judgment "this is right" has a prehistory in your drives, likes, dislikes, experiences and non-experiences; "*how* did it originate there?" you must ask, and then later: "*what* is really driving me to listen to it?" You can obey its command like a good soldier who hears the command of his officer. Or like a woman who loves the man who is commanding. Or like a sycophant and coward who is afraid of the commander. Or like a blockhead who obeys because he has nothing to say against it. In sum, there are a hundred ways you can listen to your conscience. But *that* you hear this or that judgment as the voice of conscience, therefore *that* you perceive something to be right could have its cause in the fact that you've never reflected on who you are, you blindly accepted as *right* whatever had been designated as such to you since childhood: or in the fact that until now, your ability to make a living and your honor have been inseparable from what you call your duty — you consider it "right" because it seems to be *your* "condition of existence" (but that you should have a *right* to existence strikes you as irrefutable!). The *firmness* of your moral judgment could still be proof in fact of your personal wretchedness, of impersonality; your "moral strength" could have its source in your stubbornness — or in your inability to behold new ideals! And, to put it briefly: if you had thought more subtly, observed better and learned more, you would not in any case have continued to call this "duty" of yours and this "conscience" of yours duty and conscience: your insight into *how moral judgments ever developed at all* would spoil these lofty words for you — just as other lofty words, for instance "sin," "salvation of the soul," "redemption" have already been spoiled for you. — And now don't talk to me about the categorical imperative, my friend! — this word tickles my ear and I have to laugh, despite your very solemn bearing; it reminds me of old Kant who, as punishment for having *swindled* "the thing in itself" — also a very ridiculous thing! — into existence, was in turn waylaid[83] by the "categorical imperative," and with it in his heart *strayed his way back* to "God," "soul," "freedom"

and "immortality," like a fox that strays its way back to its cage
— and yet it was *his* strength and cleverness that had *broken
open* the cage! — What? You admire the categorical imperative in yourself? This "firmness" of your so-called moral judgment? This "absoluteness" of the feeling "all must judge as I do
in this matter"? Admire your *selfishness* in this instead! And the
blindness, pettiness and unpretentiousness of your selfishness!
For it is selfishness, after all, to perceive *your* judgment as a
universal law; and moreover a blind, petty and unpretentious
selfishness, because it reveals that you have not yet discovered
yourself, not yet created your own, your very own ideal: — for
this could never be anyone's else's, let alone everyone's, everyone's! — — Anyone who still judges "in this case everyone
would have to act like this," has not yet taken five steps in the
direction of self-knowledge: otherwise he would know that
the same actions neither exist nor can exist — that every action
taken was taken in an entirely unique and irretrievable manner,
and that it would be likewise with every future action — that
all prescriptions of action refer only to the crude exterior (and
even the innermost and subtlest prescriptions of all previous
moralities) — that with them perhaps an appearance of same-
ness, *but precisely only an appearance* can ever be reached — that
every action, upon inspection or retrospection, is and remains
an impenetrable issue — that our opinions of "good," "noble,"
"great" can never be *proven* by our actions because every action
is unknowable — that certainly our opinions, valuations and
tablets of goods are among the mightiest levers in the machinery of our actions, but that for each individual case the law of
their mechanism is unprovable. Therefore, let's *limit* ourselves
to the purification of our opinions and valuations and to the
creation of our own new tablets of goods: — but let's not brood
anymore about the "moral value of our actions"! Indeed, my
friends! Regarding the whole moral babbling of someone about
another, it's time to become nauseous! To sit in moral judgment
should offend our taste! We should leave this babbling and this
nasty taste to those who have nothing better to do than drag the

past a bit further through time and who themselves are never
in the present — leave it to the many therefore, to the most by
far! But we *want to become who we are* — the new, the unique,
the incomparable, the ones who give themselves their own laws
and create themselves! And for this we must become the best
learners and discoverers of all that is lawlike and necessary in
the world: we must be *physicists* in order to be able to be *creators*
in this sense — whereas until now all valuations and ideals
were built on *ignorance* of physics or in *contradiction* to it. And
therefore: Long live physics! And longer yet that which *compels* us to it — our honesty![84]

336.[85]

Nature's stinginess. — Why has nature been so parsimonious
toward human beings that it didn't allow them to shine, this
one more, that one less, each according to his inner luminosity?
Why are great human beings not so beautifully spectacular in
their rising and setting as the sun? How much more unambiguous life among humans would be!

337.[86]

Future "humaneness." — When I look at this age with the
eyes of a distant age, then I can find nothing more remarkable
in the human being of the present than the peculiar virtue and
disease known as "the historical sense." It is the start of something entirely new and strange in history: if this seed were given
a few centuries and more, it could finally turn into a wonderful
plant with an equally wonderful fragrance, for whose sake our
old earth would be more pleasant to dwell on than before. We
of the present day are just beginning to fashion the chain of a
future and very mighty feeling, link by link — we scarcely know
what we're doing. It almost seems to us as though it were not
a matter of a new feeling but a decrease of all the old feelings:
— the historical sense is still something so poor and cold, and
many are afflicted by it as by a frost, making them even poorer
and colder. To others it seems like a sign of old age creeping up,

and our planet seems to them a melancholy invalid who writes the story of his youth in order to forget the present. This is in fact one color of this new feeling: whoever has the capacity to feel the history of humanity overall as *their own history* feels in one tremendous generalization all the sorrow of the invalid who thinks of health, of the old man who thinks of his youthful dream, of the lover deprived of his beloved, of the martyr whose ideal perishes, of the hero on the eve of a battle that decided nothing and yet brought him wounds and the loss of his friend — but bearing this tremendous quantum of sorrow of all kinds, being able to bear it and still be the hero who greets the dawn and his fortune at the start of a second day of battle, as the human being with a horizon of millennia before him and after him, as the heir of all nobility of all past spirit and the heir who is liable for it, as the noblest of all old nobles and at the same time the firstborn of a new nobility whose like no age has ever seen or dreamed: to take all this on one's soul, the oldest, the newest, losses, hopes, conquests, triumphs of humankind: finally to have all this in a single soul and to compress it into a single feeling: — this would surely have to yield a happiness never before known to human beings — a god's happiness full of power and love, full of tears and laughter, happiness that, like the sun in the evening, unceasingly lavishes its inexhaustible riches and pours them into the sea and, like the sun, only feels richest when even the poorest fisherman rows with golden oars! This divine feeling would then be called — humaneness!

338.

The will to suffer and the compassionate ones. — Is it beneficial to you personally to be compassionate human beings above all? And is it beneficial to those who suffer if you behave like this? But let's leave the first question unanswered for a moment. — That from which we suffer most deeply and personally is incomprehensible and inaccessible to almost all others: in this we remain a mystery to our neighbor, even if we eat from the same pot. But wherever we get *noticed* as sufferers, our suffering will be superficially interpreted; it belongs to the essence of compassionate emotion that it *strips* another's suffering of its genuine personal component: — our "benefactors" more than our enemies are the belittlers of our value and will. With most good deeds performed for the misfortunate, there is something outrageous in the intellectual nonchalance with which the compassionate play the role of fate: they know nothing of the whole inner sequence and entanglement that constitute misfortune for *me* or for *you*! The overall economy of my psyche and the way it is offset by "misfortune," the breaking open of new sources and needs, the closing of old wounds, the shedding of entire pasts — all these things that can be bound up with misfortune are of no concern to our dear compassionate ones: they want to *help* and don't think about the fact that there is a personal necessity of misfortune, that for me and you terrors, deprivations, impoverishments, midnights, adventures, risks, blunders are as necessary as their opposite, indeed, to put it in mystical terms, that the path to one's own heaven always goes through the voluptuousness of one's own hell. No, they know nothing of that: the "religion of compassion" (or "of the heart") commands them to help, and they believe they've helped most when they've helped fastest! If you adherents of this religion really had the same attitude toward yourselves as you have toward your fellow human beings, if you did not want to endure your own suffering for a single hour, and constantly tried to prevent all possible misfortune way ahead of time, if you feel your suffering and displeasure generally to be evil, despicable, worthy of annihilation, as a stain upon existence: well, now in addition to your religion of compassion you have yet another religion in your heart, and this is perhaps the mother of the former: — the *religion of contentment.* Oh, how little you know of the *happiness* of human beings, you contented and good-natured ones! — for happiness and misfortune are two siblings and twins who grow up together or, as in your case, together — *stay small*! But now back to the first question — How is it even possible to stay on *one's own*

path! Constantly some cry or another calls us aside; seldom
does our eye see anything there that does not necessitate aban-
doning our own cause immediately and coming to someone's
aid. I know: there are a hundred decent and praiseworthy ways
to lose *my own way,* and truly the most highly "moral" ways!
Indeed, the opinion of today's morality preachers of compassion even goes so far as to say that precisely this and this alone
is moral: — to lose *one's own* way like this and come to the aid
of one's neighbor. I likewise know with certainty: I need only
expose myself to the sight of genuine distress and I too *am* lost!
And if a suffering friend were to say to me: "Look, I'm going to
die soon; promise me that you will die with me" — I'd promise
it, just as the sight of some small clan of mountain dwellers
fighting for their freedom would inspire me to offer them my
hand and my life — selecting bad examples here for good reasons. Indeed, there is even a secret seduction in all this arousing
of compassion and crying for help: for our "own way" is a cause
too difficult and demanding and too far from the love and gratitude of others — not at all unwillingly we escape it, along with
our very own conscience, and flee into the conscience of others
and into the lovely temple of "religion of compassion." Now
as soon as any war breaks out, a lust always also breaks out in
precisely the noblest men of a people, secretly harbored to be
sure: they hurl themselves with delight into the new danger
of *death* because they believe that in sacrificing themselves for
the fatherland they finally have that long-sought permission
— permission *to evade their goal*: — war is for them a detour
to suicide, but a detour with a good conscience. And, while I
will remain silent about some things here, I will not remain
silent regarding my morality, which tells me: Live in seclusion,
so that you *can* live yourself! Live *ignorant* of what seems most
important to your age! Lay the skin of at least three centuries
between yourself and today! And the shouting of today, the
clamor of wars and revolutions shall be a mere murmur to you!
You too will want to help: but only those whose distress you
entirely *understand* because you are one with their suffering and

one with their hope — your *friends:* and only in the manner in
which you also help yourself — I want to make them braver,
more persevering, simpler, more joyful! I want to teach them
what so few understand today and least of all those preachers
of compassion: — to share *joy*![87]

339.[88]

Vita femina.[89] — In order to see the ultimate beauties of a work
— for this, all knowledge and all good will do not suffice; the
rarest fortunate accidents are needed so that for once, the veil of
clouds can recede from these peaks and we see the sun glowing
on them. Not only must we be standing in precisely the right
spot to see this; our very soul has to have pulled aside the veil
from its heights, needing an external expression and parable,
as if to have a foothold and maintain control of itself. But all
this so rarely coincides that[90] I'm inclined to believe the highest
heights of all things good, be it a work, deed, human being
or nature, have so far been concealed and veiled from most
people and even from the best: — but what does unveil itself
to us *unveils itself just once*![91] — The Greeks surely prayed:
"Twice and three times everything beautiful!"[92] Oh, they had
a good reason to invoke the gods, for ungodly reality gives us
the beautiful not at all or just once! What I mean is, the world
is overflowing with beautiful things but nevertheless poor, very
poor in beautiful moments and unveilings of these things. But
maybe this is the strongest magic of life: a gold-threaded veil of
beautiful possibilities lies over it, promising, resisting, bashful,
mocking, compassionate, seductive. Yes, life is a woman![93]

340.[94]

The dying Socrates. — I admire the bravery and wisdom of
Socrates in everything he did, said — and did not say. This
mocking and enamored monster and pied piper of Athens,
who made the most impudent youths tremble and sob, was not
only the wisest babbler there ever was: he was just as great in
silence. I wish he had also been taciturn in the last moment of

his life — maybe then he would belong in an even-higher order
of minds. Whether it was death or poison or piety or malice —
something loosened his tongue in that moment[95] and he said:
"Oh Crito, I owe Asclepius a rooster."[96] These ridiculous and
terrible "last words" mean this for those who have ears: "Oh
Crito, *life is a disease!*" Is it possible? A man like him, who lived
his life cheerfully and like a soldier for everyone to see — was
a pessimist! He just put on a good face to life and his whole
life long he concealed his ultimate judgment, his innermost
feeling! Socrates, Socrates *suffered from life!* And he even took
his revenge for this — with those disguised, horrible, pious
and blasphemous words![97] Did a Socrates have to avenge himself too? Was there one ounce too little of magnanimity in his
super-rich virtue? — Oh my friends! We will have to overcome
the Greeks too!

341.[98]

The greatest weight. — What if, one day or night, a demon
sneaked into your loneliest loneliness and said to you: "This
life, as you live it now and have lived it, you will have to live
once more and countless times more; and there will be nothing
new in it, rather every pain and every joy and every thought
and sigh and everything unspeakably small and great in your
life must recur for you, and everything in the same succession
and sequence — and likewise this spider and this moonlight
between the trees, and likewise this moment and I myself. The
eternal hourglass of existence is turned over again and again
— and you along with it, tiniest speak of dust!" — Wouldn't
you throw yourself to the floor and gnash your teeth and curse
the demon that spoke like this? Or have you once experienced
a colossal moment where you would answer him: "you are a
god and I've never heard anything more divine!" If this thought
were to gain power over you, it would transform and perhaps
crush you as you are; the question with each and every thing
"do you want this once more and countless times more?"
would bear upon your actions as the greatest weight! Or how

fond would you have to become[99] of yourself and of life, *to crave* nothing *more* than this ultimate eternal confirmation and seal?[100,101] —

342.[102,103]

Incipit tragoedia.[104] — When Zarathustra was thirty years old, he left his homeland and Lake Urmi and went into the mountains.[105] Here he took delight in his brilliance and his solitude and did not grow weary of this for ten years. But at last he had a change of heart — and one morning he arose with the dawn, approached the sun and spoke to it in this way: "You great star! How could you be happy if you did not have those for whom you shine! For ten years you have been coming up here to my cave: without me, my eagle, and my serpent you would have grown sick and tired of your light and this path; but we waited for you every morning, took your overflow from you and blessed you for it. Behold! I have had my fill of wisdom, like a bee that has gathered too much honey, I need the hands that reach out, I would like to give of what I have and share it, until those human beings who are wise have rejoiced once again in their folly[106] and until those human beings who are poor have rejoiced once again in their riches.[107] For this I must descend into the depths: as you do in the evening, when you go down behind the ocean and still bring light to the underworld, you superabundant star! — like you, I must *descend,* as people say, into the depths where these people live. So bless me, then, you serene eye, that can look without envy even upon all too great a happiness! Bless the goblet that wants to overflow, so that the water flows from it in hues of gold and carries the reflection of your delight everywhere! Behold! This cup wants to become empty again, and Zarathustra wants to become human again." And so began Zarathustra's descent.

Book Five:[1]
We Fearless Ones

Carcasse, tu trembles? Tu tremblerais bien
davantage, si tu savais, où je te mène.[2]
Turenne.

343.[3]

The significance of our cheerfulness. — The greatest recent event — that "God is dead," that belief in the Christian God has become unbelievable — is already beginning to cast its first shadows over Europe. For the few at least, whose eyes, whose *suspicion* in their eyes is strong and subtle enough for this spectacle, a sun appears just to have set, and some old deep trust appears to have turned to doubt: to them our old world must seem daily more evening-like, more mistrustful, stranger, "older." But for the most part one would have to say: the event itself is much too great, too distant, too far afield from the comprehension ability of many, for us to say that even news of it could be said to have *arrived*; let alone that many already would know *what* actually took place here — and what kinds of things have to cave in now that this belief has been undermined, because they were built on it, leaned on it, grew into it: for example, our entire European morality. This long profusion and sequence of demolition, destruction, decline, overthrow that now lies ahead: who could guess enough of it today to have to serve as the teacher and foreteller of this monstrous logic of horrors, the prophet of a dimming and a solar eclipse whose like has probably never existed yet on earth? . . . Even we born guessers of riddles who are waiting atop the mountains, so to speak, poised between today and tomorrow and harnessed to the contradiction between today and tomorrow; we firstborn and premature births of the coming century who really *should* already have caught a glimpse of the shadows that must soon envelop Europe: why is it that even we look forward to the approach of this dimming without real engagement, and above all without worry and fear for *ourselves?* Are we perhaps still influenced too much by the *closest consequences* of this event — and these closest consequences, its consequences for *us*, are the opposite of what one might expect: absolutely not sad and gloomy, on the contrary, like a new and hard to describe kind of light, happiness, relief, amusement, encouragement, dawn . . . Indeed, we philosophers and "free spirits" feel as if we're illuminated by a new dawn at the news that the "old God is dead"; our heart overflows with gratitude, amazement, presentiment, expectation — finally the horizon seems open again to us, even presupposing it is not bright; finally our ships can put to sea again, put to sea against any danger; every risk of the knower is permitted again, the sea, *our* sea lies there open again, perhaps there has never before been such an "open sea." —

344.

How we, too, are still pious. — In science convictions have no rights of citizenship, so people say with good reason: only when they resolve to step down to the modesty of a hypothesis, of a preliminary experimental standpoint, a regulative fiction may they be allowed access to and even a certain value within the realm of knowledge — although with the restriction to remain under police observation, under the police of mistrust. — On closer scrutiny, doesn't this mean: only when conviction *ceases* to be conviction, is it allowed to achieve access to science? Would the rigor of the scientific spirit not begin by no longer allowing itself convictions? . . . This is probably how it is: only the question remains, whether *for this rigor to begin,* a conviction must already exist, and moreover such a commanding and unconditional one that it sacrifices all other convictions to itself. One sees that science, too, is based on a faith, there is no science at all "free of presuppositions." The question of whether *truth* is required must not only be affirmed in advance, but affirmed to the degree that the proposition, the belief, the conviction gets expressed in it that "*nothing* is required *more* than truth, and in relation to it everything else has only a second-class value." — This unconditional will to truth: what is it? Is it the will *not to let oneself be deceived?* Is it the will *not to deceive?* After all, the will to truth could be interpreted in this latter way, too, assuming one includes under the generalization "I do not want to deceive" also the individual case "I do not want to deceive *myself.*" But why not deceive? But why not let oneself be deceived? — Observe that the reasons for the former lie in a completely different sphere than those for the latter: one does not want to let oneself be deceived on the assumption that it is damaging, dangerous, disastrous to be deceived — in this sense science would be a long prudence, a caution, a usefulness against which, however, one could with fairness object: how is that? is wanting not to let oneself be deceived really less damaging, less dangerous, less disastrous: What do you know from the outset about the character of existence to be able to decide whether there is greater advantage on the side of the unconditionally mistrustful or the unconditionally trusting? But in case both should be necessary, much trust *and* much mistrust: where then is science supposed to acquire its unconditional faith, its underlying conviction that truth is more important than any other thing, even than any other conviction? Precisely this conviction could not have arisen if both truth *and* untruth had constantly proven useful: as is indeed the case. Therefore — the faith in science, which after all exists indisputably, cannot have arisen from such a calculus of utility, but on the contrary *in spite of* the uselessness and dangerousness of the "will to truth," of "truth at any price" that is constantly being proved to it. "At any price": oh we understand that well enough, after we've offered and slaughtered one belief after another on this altar! — Consequently, "will to truth" does *not* mean "I do not want to let myself be deceived," but — no other alternative remains — "I do not want to deceive, not even myself": — *and with this we're on the turf of morality.* For one should just ask oneself the fundamental question: "why do you not want to deceive?" especially if it should appear — and it does appear! — as if life were aiming at semblance, I mean at error, deception, dissimulation, blinding, self-blinding, and if on the other hand the great form of life has in fact always shown itself to be on the side of the most unscrupulous πολύτροποι.[4] Such a precept could perhaps be, charitably interpreted, a mere quixotism, a petty fanatic folly; but it could also be something worse, namely a destructive principle hostile to life . . . "Will to truth" — that could be a hidden will to death. — So the question: why science? leads back to the moral problem: *why morality at all* if life, nature, history are "immoral"? There is no doubt, the truthful man, in that daring and ultimate sense in which faith in science presupposes him, *thus affirms a different world* from that of life, nature and history; and insofar as he affirms this "different world," how is that? must he not then — deny its counterpart, this world, *our* world? . . . Surely one will have grasped what I am getting at, namely that it is still a *metaphysical faith* on which our faith in science is based — that even we knowing ones of today, we godless and anti-metaphysical ones also still take *our* fire from the conflagration kindled by an ancient faith that is thousands of years old, that Christian faith that was also the faith of Plato, that God is the truth, that the truth is divine . . .[5] But what if precisely this becomes more and more unbelievable, if nothing proves itself divine anymore, unless it were error, blindness, the lie — if God himself proved to be our longest lie?[6,7] —

345.[8]

Morality as a problem. — The lack of personality is avenging itself everywhere; a weakened, thin, extinguished personality that denies and renounces itself is no longer fit for a single good thing — it is least fit for philosophy. "Selflessness" has no value in heaven and on earth; the great problems all demand *great love,* and only the strong, round, secure spirits are capable of it, those who lean firmly on themselves. It makes the most substantial difference whether a thinker approaches his problems personally,[9] so that he has his destiny, his distress and also his best happiness in them, or "impersonally": that is, he knows how to touch and grasp them only with the feelers of cold curious thought. In the latter case nothing will come of it, this much can be promised: for the great problems, supposing they allowed themselves to be grasped, do not allow themselves to be *held* by frogs and weaklings, this is their taste through the ages — a taste, incidentally, they share with all worthy little females. — So how is it now that I've never met anyone, not even in books, who approached morality personally in this manner, who knew morality as a problem and this problem as *his* personal distress, agony, voluptuousness, passion? Evidently morality so far has not been a problem at all, on the contrary, simply that on which people agreed after all the mistrust, discord and contradiction, the hallowed ground of peace where thinkers rested even from themselves, took deep breaths, revived. I see no one who would have ventured a *critique* of moral valuations; for this I miss even the experiments of scientific curiosity, of the pampered experimental imagination of psychologists and historians that easily anticipates a problem and seizes it on the fly, without quite knowing what it managed to seize. I have scarcely been able to find a few meager preludes to arrive at a *history of the emergence* of these feelings and valuations (which is something different than a critique of them and even more different than the history of ethical systems): in one individual case[10] I did everything to encourage an inclination and talent for this kind of history — in vain, as it seems to me now. These moral historians (in particular the English) are of little significance: they themselves are usually still guilelessly obedient to a particular morality and without knowing it, play the role of its shield-bearer and retinue; for example, with that still so ingenuously parroted folk-superstition of Christian Europe that what is characteristic of moral actions is exemplified by selflessness, self-denial, self-sacrifice or by sympathy and compassion. Their usual erroneous presupposition is that they assert some kind of consensus of peoples, at least the tame peoples regarding certain moral propositions and from them infer they are unconditionally binding for you and me as well; or conversely, when they begin to see the truth that moral valuations are *necessarily* different among different peoples, they infer *all* morality is nonbinding: which are both equally great examples of childishness. The error of the subtler among them is that they discover and criticize the perhaps foolish opinions of a people regarding its morality, or of human beings generally regarding all human morality, such as its descent, religious sanction, the superstition of free will and the like, and therefore imagine that they have criticized this morality itself. But the value of a precept "thou shalt" is still thoroughly different from and independent of such opinions about it and from the weeds of error that have perhaps overgrown it: just as surely as the value of a medication for a sick man is still completely independent of whether the sick man thinks about medicine scientifically or like an old woman. A morality could even have grown *out of* an error: even with this insight the problem of its value would not be touched in the least. — No one therefore has so far examined the *value* of that most famous of all medicines, the one called morality: which requires, first of all and for once — that we *question* it. Well then! Precisely this is our work. —

346.[II]

Our question mark. — But you don't understand this? Indeed, it will take effort to understand us. We're looking for words, perhaps we're looking for ears, too. Who are we after all? If we wanted to refer to ourselves simply with an older expression as godless or unbelievers or even immoralists, we would not believe in the least that we have described ourselves: we are all three in a stage that is too late for anyone, for *you* my curious gentlemen to be able to comprehend what it feels like for us. No! no more of the bitterness and passion of the one who tore himself free, who has to contrive a faith out of his unfaith, a purpose, a martyrdom! We have been steeped in the realization, and have grown cold and hard in it, that what happens in the world is absolutely not divine, indeed not even reasonable, merciful or just according to human standards: we know it; the world in which we live is ungodly, immoral, "inhuman" — all too long we have interpreted it wrongly and mendaciously for ourselves, but in keeping with the wish and will of our veneration, that is, in keeping with our *need.* For the human being is a venerating animal! But he is also a mistrustful one: and that the world is *not* worth what we believed is just about the most certain thing that our mistrust has finally laid hands on. The more mistrust, the more philosophy. We are wary of saying that it is worth *less:* we would even find it laughable today if humans were to lay claim to inventing values that *exceed* the value of the real world — we've returned already from precisely this, as if from having extravagantly lost our way due to human vanity and unreason that long went unrecognized as such. It had its last expression in modern pessimism, an older, stronger one in the teaching of Buddha; but Christianity also contains it, more dubiously and ambiguously to be sure, but no less seductively for that. The whole attitude "human being *against* the world," human being as "world-negating" principle, human being as the value-measure of things, as the world-judge who ultimately places existence itself on his scales and finds it too light — we've become aware of the tremendous absurdity of this attitude as such and it disgusts us — we already laugh when we find "human being *and* world" juxtaposed, separated by the sublime presumptuousness of the little word "and"! But wait? In laughing like this, haven't we just taken another step in the contempt for human beings? And therefore also in pessimism, in contempt for the existence knowable *to us?* Haven't we just exposed ourselves to the suspicion of an opposition, an opposition consisting of the world in which we were previously at home with our venerations — for whose sake we perhaps *endured* living — and another world *which we ourselves are:* a relentless, foundational, deepest suspicion about ourselves that is gaining ever-more, ever-worse control over us Europeans, and could easily confront the coming generations with a terrible either/or: "either abolish your venerations or — *yourselves!*" The latter would be nihilism; but wouldn't the former also be — nihilism? — This is *our* question mark.

347.

Believers and their need for believing. — How much someone needs *faith* in order to thrive, how much "firmness" that he doesn't want shaken because he *clings* to it — is a measure of his strength (or, spoken more clearly, of his weakness). It seems to me that in old Europe even today most people still need Christianity: that's why it still finds believers. For this is how people are: a principle of faith could be refuted to them a thousand times — but supposing they needed it, they would again and again regard it as "true" — in keeping with that famous "demonstration of power" of which the Bible speaks.[12] A few still need metaphysics; but also that impetuous *demand for certainty* that scientifically-positivistically discharges itself today among the broad masses, the demand absolutely to *will* to have something firm (while the establishing of certainty is easier and more lenient given the fervor of this demand): this, too, is still the demand for foothold, support, in sum, that *instinct of weakness* that does not exactly create religions, forms of metaphysics and convictions of all kinds but — conserves them. In fact, all these positivistic systems are enveloped by the vapors of a certain pessimistic dimming, a kind of weariness, fatalism, disappointment, fear of new disappointment — or instead ostentatious rage, bad mood, outrage-anarchism and whatever kinds of symptoms or masquerades exist for the feeling of weakness. Even the vehemence with which our cleverest contemporaries lose themselves in miserable corners and crannies,[13] for instance in fatherlandishness (this is the name I give to what is called *chauvinisme* in France and "German" in Germany) or in obscure aesthetic creeds in the manner of Parisian *naturalisme* (which highlights and reveals only that part of nature that inspires disgust and astonishment simultaneously — today one likes to call this part *la vérité vraie*[14,15] —) or in nihilism according to the St. Petersburg model (that is, in the *belief in unbelief* to the point of martyrdom for it) always demonstrates primarily the *need* for faith, foothold, backbone, backstop . . . Faith is always coveted most and needed most urgently where there is a lack of will: for will, as the affect of commanding, is the decisive sign of self-glorification and strength. This means the less one is able to command, the more urgently he craves for someone who commands, who commands strictly, for a god, prince, class, physician, father confessor, dogma, party conscience. From which it may perhaps be deduced that both world religions, Buddhism and Christianity, may have had their originating motivation, and especially their precipitous spread, in a tremendous *sickening of the will*. And so it was in truth: both religions were faced with an absurdly pent-up demand for a "thou shalt" through sickening of the will, to the point of desperation;[16] both religions were teachers of fanaticism in periods of will-exhaustion and therefore offered countless people a foothold, a new possibility for willing, a pleasure in willing. Fanaticism after all is the only "strength of will" to which even the weak and insecure can be motivated, as a kind of hypnotization of the entire sensual-intellectual system for the sake of superabundantly nourishing (hypertrophy) a single point of view and emotion that henceforth dominates — a Christian calls it his *faith*. When a human being arrives at the basic conviction that he *must* be commanded, he becomes a "believer"; conversely, a delight and strength in self-determination would

be conceivable, a *freedom* of the will in which a spirit bids farewell to every faith, every wish for certainty, practiced as he is in
sustaining himself on light ropes and possibilities and dancing
even beside abysses. Such a spirit would be the *free spirit* par
excellence.

348.

On the descent of scholars. — The scholar in Europe grows
out of every kind of class and social condition, like a plant that
requires no specific soil: this is why he belongs essentially and
involuntarily among the carriers of the democratic idea. But
this descent betrays itself. Once one has trained his eye a bit
to recognize the intellectual *idiosyncrasy* of the scholar — every
scholar has one — and to catch it in the act in a scholarly book
or a scientific treatise, then almost always behind it one will
catch sight of the "prehistory" of the scholar, his family, especially its kinds of occupations and crafts. Wherever the feeling
expresses itself "this is now proven, herewith I am finished,"
there generally speaking it is the ancestor in the scholar's blood
and instinct who is vouching for the "finished job" from his
point of view — the belief in the proof is merely a symptom of
what had for ages been regarded as "good work" in an industrious family. An example: the sons of registrars and office
scribes of all kinds, whose main task had always been to classify
multifarious materials, catalogue it in drawers and generally to
schematize it, demonstrate, in the event they become scholars,
an inclination to consider a problem nearly solved if only they
have schematized it. There are philosophers who at bottom are
merely schematic minds — they have internalized the formal
dimension of their father's craft. The talent for classifications
and for tables of categories betrays something; one pays the
price for being the child of one's parents. The son of an advocate will also have to become an advocate as a scholar: his first
consideration is for his cause to be proven right in court, his
second, perhaps, to be right. The sons of Protestant clerics and
schoolteachers are recognized by the naïve certainty with which

they as scholars regard their cause to be already proven, when in fact it has just been robustly and warmly advanced by them: they are simply and thoroughly accustomed to being *believed* — among their fathers this was part of their "craft"! A Jew, conversely, in keeping with the business circles and the past of his people, is least accustomed precisely to being believed: in this regard consider Jewish scholars — they all think highly of logic, that is, of *compelling* agreement by using reasons; they know that they must triumph using logic, even where racial and class aversion exists against them, and where they are reluctantly believed. Nothing after all is more democratic than logic: it knows no regard for persons and takes even a crooked nose for straight. (Incidentally: precisely with respect to logicization, to *purer* mental habits Europe owes the Jews no small thanks; foremost the Germans, as a lamentably *déraisonnable*[17] race that even today still needs to have "its head examined"[18] first. Wherever Jews have gained influence, they have taught people to make finer distinctions, draw sharper inferences, and write more clearly and cleanly: their task has always been to bring a people "to *raison*."[19])

349.[20]

Once more the descent of scholars. — Wanting to preserve oneself is the expression of a distressed state, of a curtailing of the actual basic instinct of life that is aimed at *expansion of power* and, in willing in this manner, often enough jeopardizes and sacrifices self-preservation. One should consider it symptomatic when some philosophers, like for example the consumptive Spinoza, considered precisely the so-called drive for self-preservation to be decisive, and had to: — after all they were human beings in distressed states. That our modern natural sciences have become so entangled with Spinozistic dogma (most recently and crudely in Darwinism with its incomprehensibly one-sided doctrine of the "struggle for existence" —) probably stems from the descent of most natural scientists: in this respect they belong to the "common people," their ancestors were poor and inconsequential people, who knew all too well and from experience the difficulty of making ends meet. The whole of English Darwinism exudes something like stuffy English overpopulation air, like the petty-people odor of distress and overcrowding. But as a natural scientist one should come out of his human nook: and in nature it is not the state of distress that *rules,* but superabundance, squandering, even to the point of absurdity. The struggle for existence is only an *exception,* a temporary restriction of the life will; the great and small struggle everywhere revolves around superiority, around growth and expansion, around power in accordance with the will to power, which is simply the will of life.

350.

In honor of the homines religiosi.[21] — The struggle against the Church is quite certainly among other things — for it means many things — also the struggle of the baser, more contented, more trusting and superficial natures against the rule of the more somber, deeper, contemplative people, that is the more evil and suspicious ones who brooded with prolonged suspicion over the value of existence and also over their own value: — the base instinct of the common people, its sensual merriness, its "good heart" rebelled against them. The whole Roman Church rests on a southern European suspicion of the nature of human beings, which is always falsely understood on the part of northerners: in this suspicion, the European South has become the heir of the deep Orient, of ancient mysterious Asia and its contemplation. Protestantism is already a popular rebellion for the benefit of the comfortable, the guileless, the superficial (the North was always more good-natured and shallow than the South); but only the French Revolution succeeded in completely and solemnly handing the scepter to the "good person" (the sheep, the ass, the goose and everyone who is incurably shallow and a screamer and ripe for the madhouse of "modern ideas").

351.

In honor of the priestly natures. — I think that what the common people mean by wisdom (and today who is not "common
people"? —), that prudent bovine peace of mind, piety and
country pastor mildness that lies in the meadow and earnestly
and ruminatingly *observes* life — is something precisely the
philosophers have always felt was most distant from themselves, probably because they were not "common people"
enough for it, not country pastor enough. And surely they
again will also be the last to learn to believe that the common
people are *allowed* to understand anything about what is most
remote from them, about the great *passion* of the knower who
lives constantly in the thundercloud of the highest problems
and gravest responsibilities, and must live there (hence not in
the least observing, outside, indifferent, safe, objective . . .). The
common people revere an entirely different kind of human
being when they create an ideal of the "sage" for themselves,
and they have a thousandfold right to pay homage to this particular kind of human being with the best words and honors:
these are the mild, earnestly simple-minded and chaste priest
natures and whatever is related to them[22] — they are the objects
of praise in the revering of wisdom practiced by the common
people. And to whom would the common people have any reason to show more gratitude than to these men, who belong to
them and come from their midst, but as consecrated, as chosen
ones, as *those sacrificed* for their common good — they themselves believe they are sacrificed to God — before whom they
can pour their hearts out with impunity, to whom they can *get
rid of* their secrets, their worries and worse (— for the person
who "communicates"[23] gets rid of himself; and whoever has
"confessed," forgets). Here a great and dire need commands:
after all, even psychic garbage needs drainage ditches filled
with pure and cleansing water, needs rapid streams of love and
strong, humble and pure hearts who make themselves available and sacrifice themselves for such a service of nonpublic

hygiene — for it *is* a sacrifice, a priest is and remains a human sacrifice . . . The common people perceive such sacrificed, subdued, earnest human beings of "faith" as *wise,* that is, as those who have become knowing, as "certain ones" compared to their own uncertainty: who would want to deprive them of this word and this reverence? — But conversely, as is also fair, among philosophers even a priest is still regarded as "common people" and *not* as a knower, above all because philosophers themselves do not believe in "knowers" and in this particular belief and superstition they already smell "common people." It was *modesty* that invented the word "philosopher" in Greece and left the splendid impudence of calling oneself wise to the actors of the spirit — the modesty of such monsters of pride and self-glorification as Pythagoras, as Plato — .

352.

How morality is scarcely dispensable. — A naked human being is generally speaking a scandalous sight — I am speaking of us Europeans (and not even of European women!). Supposing the merriest dinner party saw itself suddenly exposed and undressed through the trickery of a magician, I believe that not only the merriment would be lost and the strongest appetite discouraged — it seems we Europeans absolutely cannot dispense with that masquerade we call clothing. But shouldn't the disguising of "moral human beings," their veiling under moral formulas and concepts of decency, the whole benevolent concealment of our actions beneath the concepts of duty, virtue, common purpose, honorableness, self-denial not have equally valid reasons of its own? Not that I am suggesting that perhaps human malice and baseness, in sum the bad wild animal in us is masked here; my thought is the opposite, that precisely as *tame animals* we are a scandalous sight and need moral disguise — that the "inner human being" in Europe is not bad enough by far to "show itself" as such (to be *beautiful* as such —). The European disguises himself *in morality* because he has become a sick, sickly, crippled animal that has good reasons to be "tame," because he is nearly a monstrosity, something half-done, weak, awkward. It is not the terribleness of the predator that finds moral disguise necessary, but the herd animal with its deep mediocrity, fear and boredom of itself. *Morality dresses up the European* — let's confess it! — into something more noble, more meaningful, more attractive, into something "divine" —

353.

On the origin of religions. — The genuine invention of the founders of religions is first: to posit a specific way of life and daily routine, that acts as a *disciplina voluntatis*[24] and at the same time eliminates boredom; next: to give precisely this life an *interpretation* by virtue of which it appears to be illuminated by supreme value, so that henceforth it becomes a good for which one fights and, under certain circumstances, abandons one's life. In truth, the second of these two inventions is more essential: the first one, the way of life, was ordinarily already there, but alongside other ways of life and without awareness for the kind of value inherent in it. The significance, the originality of the religion founder usually comes to light insofar as he *sees* it, *selects* it and *guesses* for the first time what this way of life can be used for and how it can be interpreted. Jesus (or Paul) for instance, found the life of the small people of the Roman provinces, a modest, virtuous and depressed life: he interpreted it, he infused it with the highest meaning and value — and therewith the courage to despise every other way of life, the quiet Herrnhut[25] fanaticism, the secret subterranean self-confidence that grows and grows and ultimately is prepared "to conquer the world" (that is, Rome and the higher classes throughout the empire). Buddha likewise found this kind of human being, and moreover scattered among all the classes and social strata of his people; they are good and good-natured out of inertia (above all inoffensive), and likewise out of inertia they live abstinently and nearly without needs: he understood how a human being of this kind had to be rolled inevitably with its entire *vis inertiae*[26] into a single faith that promises to *prevent* the return of earthly toil (that is, of work, of action in general) — this "understanding" was his genius. To be a religion founder requires psychological infallibility in knowing about a specific average kind of souls, who have not yet *recognized* that they belong together. He's the one who brings them together; the founding of a religion always becomes to this extent a protracted festival of recognition. —

354.

On the "genius of the species." — The problem of consciousness (more correctly: of becoming conscious of something) only confronts us when we begin to grasp the extent to which we can dispense with it: and now physiology and animal history place us at this starting point of comprehension (both of which have needed two centuries to catch up to the prescient suspicion of *Leibniz*). For we could think, feel, will, remember; we could likewise "act" in every sense of the word, and yet all this would not need to "enter our consciousness" (as we say metaphorically). The whole of life would be possible, without its having to see itself in the mirror, so to speak: just as indeed even now, by far the preponderant portion of our life takes place without this mirroring — and specifically also of our thinking, feeling, willing life, as insulting as this might sound to an older philosopher. *Why* consciousness at all if it is mainly *superfluous?* — Now it seems to me, if one were inclined to listen to my answer to this question and its perhaps extravagant conjecture, the subtlety and strength of consciousness is always related to the *capacity for communication* of a human being (or animal), while the capacity for communication in turn is related to the *need for communication:* the latter not to be understood as if precisely the individual human being itself, who happens to be a master of communicating and making its needs understood, must also be most dependent at the same time on others with its needs. However, it does indeed seem to me to be the case with respect to entire races and series of generations: where need, where urgency has long compelled human beings to communicate, to understand one another quickly and subtly, there, finally, an excess of this strength and art of communication exists, a capacity so to speak that has gradually accumulated and now awaits its heir, who will squander it lavishly (— the so-called artists are these heirs, likewise the orators, preachers, writers, all of them human beings who always come at the end of a long chain, "late born" each one, in the best sense of the word and, as mentioned, *squanderers* by nature). Assuming this observation is correct, I may proceed to the conjecture that *consciousness generally developed only under the pressure of the need for communication* — that from the outset it was only necessary and useful between human and human (between commanders and obeyers in particular) and it also developed only in proportion to the degree of this utility. Consciousness is really only a network of connections between human and human — only as such has it had to develop: the hermit-like and predatory human being would not have needed it. That our actions, thoughts, feelings, movements even enter into consciousness — at least a portion of them — is the result of a terrible "must" that has long ruled over human beings: as the most endangered animal, they *needed* help, protection, they needed their peers, they had to express their distress, had to know how to make themselves understood — and for all these they first needed "consciousness," thus to "know" on their own what was wrong with them, to "know" how they felt, to "know" what they thought. For to repeat myself: the human being like every living creature is constantly thinking but does not know it; the thinking that becomes *conscious* is only the smallest portion thereof, let's say: the most superficial, the worst portion: — for only this conscious thinking *occurs in words, that is in signs of communication,* which betrays the descent of consciousness itself. In sum, the development of language and the development of consciousness (*not* of reason, but solely of the coming to consciousness of reason) go hand in hand. One should add that not only language serves as the bridge between human and human, but also look, touch, gesture; becoming

conscious of our own sense impressions, and being able to fix
them and as it were posit them outside ourselves, increased to
the degree that the necessity increased to communicate them
in signs *to others.* The sign-inventing human being is simultaneously the human being who becomes increasingly conscious
of himself; only as a social animal did the human being learn
to become conscious of himself — he is still doing it, he does it
more and more. — My idea is, as one can see: that consciousness does not actually belong to the individual existence of the
human being, but instead to its communal and herd nature;
that consequently it is also only in relation to communal and
herd utility that it is finely developed, and that consequently
each of us, even with our best effort to *understand* ourselves
as individually as possible, "to know ourselves," will nonetheless succeed only in bringing to consciousness precisely that
which is nonindividual as such, our "average" — that our very
thoughts — through the "genius of the species" that governs
in the character of consciousness — are continuously being
outvoted, as it were, and translated back into the herd perspective. Our actions at bottom are all personal, unique, bound-
lessly individual in an incomparable way, no doubt; but as soon
as we translate them into consciousness, *they no longer appear
to be* . . . This is genuine phenomenalism and perspectivism
as *I* see it: the nature of *animal consciousness* is such that the
world of which we can become conscious is merely a world of
surfaces and signs, a generalized and a debased world[27] — that
whatever we become conscious of for the same reason *becomes*
shallow, thin, relatively stupid, general, sign, herd marker; that
with all coming to consciousness a great thorough corruption,
falsification, superficialization and generalization is involved.
Ultimately, the growing consciousness is a danger: and whoever lives among the most conscious Europeans even knows
that it is a sickness. As one can guess, it is not the opposition
of subject and object that concerns me here: this distinction I
leave to the epistemologists, who have become tangled up in
the snares of grammar (of folk-metaphysics). Even[28] less am I

concerned with the opposition between "thing in itself" and appearance: for we do not "know" enough by far to even try to *distinguish* in this manner. We simply have no organ for *knowing,* for the "truth": we "know" (or believe or imagine) precisely as much as may be *useful* in the interest of the human herd, the species: and even what is called "utility" here is ultimately also a mere belief, something imagined and perhaps precisely that most disastrous stupidity of which we will someday perish.

355.

The origin of our concept of "knowledge." — I take this explanation from the street; I heard someone from the common people say "he recognized[29] me" — : at which I asked myself: what do the common people actually mean by knowledge? What do they want, when they want "knowledge"? Nothing more than this: something strange is supposed to be traced to something *known.*[30] And we philosophers — have we really meant anything *more* by knowledge? The familiar, that is: what we are used to, so that we no longer wonder about it; our daily routine, some rule that we stick to, everything and anything in which we know ourselves to be at home: — what? isn't our need for knowledge simply this need for the familiar, the will to discover something that no longer unsettles us among all that is strange, unusual and questionable? Couldn't it be the *instinct of fear* that commands us to know? Couldn't the rejoicing of the knower simply be a rejoicing at a restored sense of security? . . . This philosopher deemed the world "known" when he had reduced it to the "idea": alas, was it not because the "idea" was so familiar to him, so habituated? because now he feared the "idea" so little anymore? — Oh how easily satisfied these knowers are! as proof, just look at their principles and solutions to the riddle of the world! When they rediscover something in things, among things, behind things that unfortunately is well known to us, for example our multiplication tables or our logic or our willing and desiring, how happy they are all of a sudden! For "what is familiar is known":[31] in this they agree.

Even the most cautious among them believe that at least the familiar is *more easily knowable* than the strange; it would be the dictate of sound method, for example, to proceed from the "inner world," from the "facts of consciousness," because they are the world *more familiar to us*! Error of errors! The familiar is the habitual; and the habitual is hardest to "know," that is, to see as a problem, that is, to see as strange, as distant, as "outside us" . . . The great certainty of the natural sciences in comparison to psychology and the critique of the elements of consciousness — the *unnatural* sciences as one may almost call them — rests precisely on the fact that they take the *strange* as their object: whereas it is something almost contradictory and absurd to even *want* to take the not-strange as one's object . . .

356.

The extent to which things in Europe will become ever more "artistic." — Even today the need to make a living — in our transitional period when so much ceases to be compelling — still compels a certain *role* on almost all male Europeans, their so-called profession;[32] in this a few retain the freedom, an apparent freedom, of choosing this role themselves, but for most it is chosen. The result is odd enough: almost all Europeans of advanced age mistake themselves for their role, they themselves are the victims of their "good performance," they themselves have forgotten how much chance, whim, caprice reigned over them at the time their "profession" was determined — and how many different roles they perhaps *could* have played: for now it is too late! Examined more closely, character has actually *arisen* from the role, and nature from art. There were ages in which one believed with rigid confidence, indeed with piety in one's predestination for precisely this business, this way of earning a living, and simply refused to recognize any chance, role, arbitrariness in it:[33] classes, guilds and hereditary trade privileges managed with the help of this faith to erect those monsters of broad social towers that distinguish the Middle Ages and can be celebrated for at least one thing: durability (— and duration is a value of the highest order on earth!). But there are opposite ages, the actual democratic ones, when this faith is unlearned more and more and a certain impudent faith and opposing viewpoint come to the fore, that Athenian faith first noted in the Periclean age, that American faith of today that wants more and more to become the European faith as well: where the individual is convinced of being able to do just about anything, of being *capable* of just about *any role*; where each person experiments with himself, improvises, experiments anew, experiments joyfully; where all nature ceases and becomes art . . . The Greeks, once they entered into this *faith in roles* — a faith in artists, if you will — underwent step by step, as is well known, an odd transformation that does not merit imitation in every respect: *they actually became actors*; as such they enchanted, they overcame the whole world and ultimately even the "one who overcame the world" (for the *Graeculus histrio*[34] conquered Rome, and *not* Greek culture, as the innocent tend to say . . .) But what I fear, what is already palpable today if one had any desire to grasp it, is that we modern human beings are already wholly on the same path; and every time the human being begins to discover the extent to which he plays a role and the extent to which he *can* be an actor, he *becomes* an actor . . . A new human flora and fauna then emerge, which cannot grow in firmer and more restricted times — or would be left "below," under the ban and suspicion of being dishonorable — and emerging with this each time are the most interesting and craziest historical ages, in which "actors," *all* kinds of actors are the genuine masters. But for this very reason a different species of human being becomes ever more deeply disadvantaged, finally to be rendered impossible, above all the great "master builders"; now the power to build becomes paralyzed; the courage to make plans into the distant future gets discouraged; the organizational geniuses start[35] to go missing: — who would dare anymore to undertake works whose completion would *require* millennia? That fundamental belief is simply dying out, upon which someone could sufficiently calculate, promise, anticipate the future through planning and sacrifice it to one's plan, the belief namely that the human being only has value, has meaning, insofar as he is *a stone in a great edifice:* for which he first of all must be *firm,* must be "stone" . . . And above all not — an actor! In sum — oh, it will yet be suppressed for a long time! — what from now on will no longer be built, no longer *can* be built, is — a society in the ancient sense of the word; everything is lacking for building this edifice, and foremost the material. *All of us are no longer material for a society:* this is a truth whose time has come! I'm indifferent to the fact that currently the most myopic, perhaps most honest, in any case noisiest kind of human being today, our gentlemen socialists, for the time being still believe, hope, dream and above all scream and write more or less the opposite: one already reads their slogan of the future, "free society," on all tables and walls. Free society? Yes! Yes! But surely you gentlemen know what it is built of? Of wooden iron![36] Of the famous wooden iron! And not even wooden . . .

357.

On the old problem: "What is German?" — In doing one's own tally of the genuine achievements of philosophical ideas for which we have German minds to thank: can they in any legitimate sense also be credited to the entire race? Is it permitted to say: they are simultaneously the work of the "German soul," at least its symptoms, in the sense in which we are accustomed to construing perhaps Plato's ideomania, his almost religious mania for forms as an event and testimony of the "Greek soul"? Or would the opposite be true? would they be so strictly individual, so abundantly the *exception* from the spirit of the race, as was for example Goethe's paganism with a good conscience? Or as is Bismarck's Machiavellianism with a good conscience, his so-called *Realpolitik,* among Germans? Do our philosophers perhaps not contradict even the *need* of the "German soul"? In sum, were the German philosophers really — philosophical *Germans?* — I recall three cases. First there is

Leibniz's incomparable insight, in which he was right not only in relation to Descartes, but to everyone who had philosophized before him — that consciousness is merely an accident of representation, *not* its necessary and essential attribute, hence that what we call consciousness constitutes only a state of our intellectual and psychic world (perhaps a pathological state) and *not nearly this world itself:* — in this idea, whose profundity has yet to be exhausted even today, is there anything German? Is there reason to conjecture that a Latin would not have come up with this reversal of appearances? — for it is a reversal. Second, let us recall *Kant's* tremendous question mark, which he inserted after the concept of "causality" — not that he would have doubted its overall legitimacy like Hume: instead, he began cautiously to demarcate the realm within which this concept has meaning at all (to this day we have yet to complete this demarcation).[37] Let us take, third, *Hegel's* astonishing stroke of genius, with which he struck through all logical habits and indulgences by daring to teach that species concepts develop *out of each other*: a proposition that predisposed European minds to the latest great scientific movement, to Darwinism — for without Hegel there is no Darwin. Is there anything German about this Hegelian innovation, which first brought the decisive concept "development" into science? — Indeed, without any doubt: in all three cases we feel something of ourselves has been "revealed" and surmised, and we are simultaneously grateful for it and surprised; each of these three propositions is a thoughtful piece of German self-knowledge, self-experience, self-understanding. "Our inner world is much richer, more comprehensive, more concealed," thus we perceive with Leibniz;[38] as Germans we doubt with Kant the ultimate validity of knowledge gained by the natural sciences and generally of everything that *allows* itself to be explained *causaliter*:[39] what is know*able* as such already seems of *less* value to us. We Germans are Hegelians, even if there had never been a Hegel, insofar as we (in contrast to all Latins) instinctively ascribe a deeper meaning and richer value to becoming, to development, than to what "is" — we scarcely believe in the justification of the concept "being" — ; likewise insofar as we are not inclined to concede that our human logic is logic in itself, the sole kind of logic (on the contrary we would like to convince ourselves that it is merely a special case, and maybe one of the oddest and most stupid —[40]). A fourth question would be whether *Schopenhauer* too, with his pessimism, that is, the problem of the *value of existence,* would have to be specifically a German. I believe not. The event *following* which this problem was to be expected with certainty, such that an astronomer of the psyche would have been able to predict its day and hour, namely the decline of belief in the Christian God, the triumph of scientific atheism, is a pan-European event in which all the races should have their share of credit and honor. Conversely it should be imputed to precisely the Germans — those Germans who were contemporaneous with Schopenhauer — that they *delayed* the triumph of atheism for the longest time and most dangerously; Hegel in particular was its delayer par excellence, in keeping with the grandiose attempt he made to convince us of the divinity of existence, as a last resort even engaging the help of our sixth sense, the "historical sense." Schopenhauer as a philosopher was the *first* admitted and unyielding atheist we Germans have ever had: his[41] enmity toward Hegel had its background in this. The nondivinity of existence was something he regarded as given, palpable, indisputable; he would lose his philosophical presence of mind and become indignant each time he saw anyone hesitate here and beat around the bush. This is the spot where his entire integrity lies: unconditional, honest atheism is simply the *prerequisite* of his approach to problems, as a triumph of the European conscience achieved finally and with difficulty, as the most consequential act of two millennia of cultivating for truth that in the end forbids itself the *lie* of belief in God . . . One sees *what* actually triumphed over the Christian God: Christian morality itself, the concept of truthfulness taken ever more rigorously, the father-confessor's refinement of the Christian conscience translated and sublimated into scientific conscience, into intellectual cleanliness at any price. To regard nature as if it were a proof of the goodness and stewardship of a god; to interpret history in honor of a divine reason, as a constant demonstration of a moral world order and moral ultimate purposes; to interpret one's own experiences as the pious have long enough interpreted them, as if everything were providence, a sign, thought out and ordained for the sake of the soul's salvation: all this is *over* now, this has conscience *against* it, this is regarded by all finer consciences as indecent, dishonest, as mendacity, feminism, weakness, cowardice — with this rigor, if with anything, we are precisely *good* Europeans and heirs of Europe's longest and most courageous self-overcoming. By rejecting Christian interpretation in this way and condemning its "meaning" as counterfeit, the *Schopenhauerian* question immediately befalls us in a terrifying way: *does existence have any meaning at all?* — that question that will require a couple of centuries in order merely to be heard completely and in all its profundity. What[42] Schopenhauer himself answered to this question was — forgive me — something hasty, youthful, merely a compromise, a standing still and remaining stuck in those same Christian-ascetic moral perspectives which, along with belief in God, *had been disavowed* . . . But he *posed* the question — as a good European, as I mentioned already, and *not* as a German. — Or could the Germans, at least given the manner in which they appropriated Schopenhauer's question, perhaps have demonstrated their inner compatibility and affinity, their preparedness, their *need* for his problem? It certainly doesn't suffice to judge in favor of this closer compatibility that after Schopenhauer in Germany, too — late enough, incidentally! — people were thinking and publishing about the problem he posited; one could even adduce the peculiar *ineptitude* of this post-Schopenhauerian pessimism against this notion — obviously the Germans did not behave in this as if they were in their element. Here I am not in the least alluding to Eduard von Hartmann; on the contrary, to this day I maintain my suspicion that he is *too competent* for us, I mean that as an archrogue from the outset, perhaps he did not only make fun of German pessimism — that in the end maybe he could even officially "bequeath" to the Germans in his will how deeply they could be made fools of, even in the age of foundings.[43] But I ask: should the old humming-top Bahnsen perhaps be credited to the Germans, who voluptuously spun for his whole life around his real-dialectical misery and "personal misfortune" — maybe that would be precisely German? (incidentally I recommend his writings for what I myself used them for, as an anti-pessimistic diet, especially on account of their *elegantia psychologicae,*[44] which works, it seems to me, for even the most constipated bodies and minds). Or is one permitted to count among true Germans such dilettantes and old spinsters as that saccharine apostle of virginity Mainländer? In the end he must have been a Jew (— all Jews become saccharine when they moralize). Neither Bahnsen nor Mainländer nor even Eduard von Hartmann give us a firm handle on the question of whether Schopenhauer's pessimism, his horrified look into a world become de-deified, stupid, blind, insane and questionable, his *honest* horror . . . was not merely an exception among Germans but instead a *German* event: whereas everything else that stands in the foreground, our brave politics, our cheerful fatherlandishness, which resolutely enough regard all things in accordance with a scarcely philosophical principle ("Germany, Germany above all"[45]), therefore *sub specie speciei,*[46] namely the German species, testifies with great clarity to the opposite. No! the Germans of today are *no* pessimists![47] And Schopenhauer, I repeat, was a pessimist as a good European and *not* as a German. —

358.

The peasant rebellion of the spirit.[48] — We Europeans find ourselves facing a tremendous world of ruins, where some things are still towering, where many things stand there decaying and uncanny, but most things are already lying on the ground, picturesque enough — where have there ever been lovelier ruins? — and overgrown with weeds large and small. The Church is this city of decline: we see the religious society of Christianity shaken to its lowest foundations — faith in God has collapsed, faith in the Christian-ascetic ideal is just now fighting its last fight. A work like Christianity, built for so long and so methodically — it was the last Roman construction! — naturally could not be destroyed all at once; all kinds of earthquakes had to shake, all kinds of spirits that bore, dig, gnaw and dampen had to pitch in. But the strangest thing is: Those who made the greatest effort to hold on to Christianity, to uphold it, became precisely its best destroyers — the Germans. It seems the Germans do not understand the essence of a church. Are they not spiritual enough for it? Not mistrustful enough? In any case, the edifice of the Church rests on a *southern* freedom and liberality of the spirit and likewise on a southern suspicion of nature, human beings and spirit — it rests on an entirely different knowledge and experience of human beings than the North possessed. The[49] Lutheran Reformation in its entire breadth was the outrage of simplicity against "multiplicity," to choose one's word carefully,[50] a crude, upright misunderstanding in which there is much to forgive — one did not understand the expression of a *triumphant* Church and saw only corruption; one misunderstood the noble skepticism, that *luxury* of skepticism and tolerance which every triumphant and self-confident power permits itself . . . Today[51] one overlooks easily enough how in all cardinal questions of power, Luther was disastrously myopic, superficial and careless by disposition, and above all as a man of the common people, who lacked all inheritance from a ruling caste, all instinct for power:[52] so that his work, his will to restore that work of Rome, became only the beginning of a work of destruction without his wanting or knowing it. In his honest wrath he unraveled, he tore up what the ancient spider had woven so carefully and for so long. He delivered the sacred books to everyone — until ultimately, they got into the hands of the philologists, that is, the annihilators of every faith that is based on books. He destroyed the concept of "Church" by throwing away the faith in the inspiration of the church councils: for only under the assumption that the inspiring spirit that had founded the Church still lives in it, still builds, still continues to build its house, does the concept of "Church" retain its power. He gave back to priests sexual intercourse with woman: but two-thirds of the veneration of which the common people are capable, especially women from the common people, is based on the belief that an exceptional person on this point will also be an exception on other points — here in particular the popular belief in something superhuman in human beings, in miracles, in the redeeming God in human beings has its subtlest and most insidious advocate. Luther had to *take* auricular confession away from priests after he had given them woman, this was psychologically proper: but at bottom this also did away with the Christian priest himself, whose deepest utility has always been to serve as a holy ear, a silent well, a tomb for secrets. "Everyone his own priest" — hiding behind such formulas and their peasant cunning were Luther's abysmal hatred of the "superior human beings" and the rule of "superior human beings," as the Church had conceived of them: — he smashed an ideal that he was unable to attain, while he seemed to struggle against and abhor the degeneration of this very ideal. In fact he, the impossible monk, spurned the *rule* of the *homines religiosi*; he himself personally conducted within the ecclesiastical social order what he so intolerantly fought with respect to the civil order — a "peasant rebellion." — Whatever else grew out of his Reformation, both good and bad, and might be assessed today in some manner — who would be naïve enough to praise or blame Luther on account of these results? He is innocent of everything, he knew not what he did.[53] There's no doubt that the European mind became shallower, especially in the North; it became *more good-natured,* if one prefers to hear it characterized with a moral expression, and this took a major step forward with the Lutheran Reformation; and likewise this shallowing contributed to the nimbleness and restlessness of the mind, its thirst for independence, its faith in a right to freedom, its "naturalness." If one wishes to grant, with regard to the latter point, the value of having prepared and promoted what we venerate today as "modern science," then to be sure one must add that it is also complicit in the degeneration of the modern scholar, in his lack of reverence, shame and profundity,[54] in the whole naïve ingenuousness and bourgeois respectability in matters of knowledge, in sum, in that *plebeianism of the spirit* that is peculiar to the last two centuries and from which even our pessimism to date has in no way redeemed us — "modern ideas" also belong to this peasant rebellion of the North against the colder, more ambiguous, more mistrustful spirit of the South, which has built its greatest monument in the Christian Church. Let's not forget in the end what a church is, and specifically in contrast to every "state": a church is above all a structure for ruling that ensures its *more spiritual* human beings the highest rank and *believes* in the power of spirituality to the extent of forbidding itself all cruder means of force — with this alone the Church is under all circumstances a *nobler* institution than the state. —

359.

The revenge on the intellect and other ulterior motives of morality. — Morality — where do you suppose it has its most dangerous and trickiest advocates? . . . There's a human being who turned out badly, who doesn't possess enough intelligence to be able to enjoy it, but just enough education to know it; bored, tired of everything, a self-despiser; unfortunately cheated out of the last comfort, the "blessing of work," self-forgetfulness in "daily labor" by some inherited wealth; someone who at bottom is ashamed of his existence — perhaps he also harbors a couple of small vices — and on the other hand he can't avoid spoiling himself more and more and irritating his vanity by reading books to which he has no right, or keeping more intelligent company than he is able to digest: such a human being, poisoned through and through — for intelligence becomes poison, education becomes poison, possessions become poison, loneliness becomes poison in those who turn out badly like this — ultimately falls into a habitual state of revenge, of the will to revenge . . . *what* do you suppose he needs, and needs unconditionally, in order to create for himself in his own mind the appearance of superiority over more intelligent human beings, in order to create the joy of *accomplished revenge,* at least in his imagination? Always *morality,* one can bet on this, always the big moral words, always the boom-boom of justice, wisdom, holiness, virtue, always the stoicism of gestures (— how well stoicism conceals what someone does *not* have! . . .), always the cloak of prudent silence, of affability, of mildness and whatever all these idealist-cloaks are called, under which the incurable self-despisers as well as the incurably vain go about. Do not misunderstand me: out of such born *enemies of the intellect* occasionally arises that rare piece of humanity that is revered by the common people under the name of saint, of sage; out of such human beings come those monsters of morality who make noise, make history — St. Augustine belongs among them. The fear of the intellect, revenge on the intellect — oh how often these propulsive vices became the roots of virtues! Indeed *became* virtues! — And, asked in confidence, even that philosopher's claim to *wisdom,* which has been made here and there at times on earth, the craziest and most immodest of all claims — in the past hasn't it always been, in India as in Greece, *above all a hiding place?* Occasionally perhaps motivated by the viewpoint of education, which sanctifies so many lies, as tender consideration for forming, growing minds, for disciples who often need to be protected from themselves by faith in a person (by an error) . . . But in most cases it has been a hiding place of the philosopher, behind which he rescues himself due to exhaustion, old age, growing cold, hardening; as a feeling that the end is near, as the prudence of that instinct displayed by animals before death — they go off to the side, become silent, opt for solitude, crawl into caves, become

wise . . . What? Wisdom a hiding place of the philosopher from
— the intellect? —

360.

Two kinds of causes that are mistaken for each other. — This
seems to me one of my most essential steps and advances: I
learned to distinguish the cause of acting from the cause of
acting in a certain way, in a certain direction, toward a certain
goal. The first kind of cause is a quantum of stored energy that
is waiting to be used in some way, toward some goal; the second kind on the other hand is quite insignificant compared to
this energy, mostly a small accident according to which this
quantum now "discharges" itself in one particular way: a match
in relation to a powder keg. Among these small accidents and
matches I reckon all so-called "purposes," likewise the even
more so-called "vocations": they are relatively random, arbitrary, almost indifferent compared to the tremendous quantum
of energy that strains, as mentioned, to be used up somehow.
One commonly sees it differently: one is accustomed to seeing the *driving* force in precisely the goal (purposes, vocations
etc.), in keeping with an ancient error — but it is only the
directing force; one has mistaken the helmsman for the steam.
And not even always the helmsman, the directing force . . . Isn't
the "goal," the "purpose" not often enough merely a beautify-
ing pretext, a retroactive self-blinding of vanity that does not
wish to grant that the ship *follows* the current into which it has
accidentally gotten itself? That it "wills" to go there *because* it
— *must* go there? That it has a direction, to be sure, but in no
way — a helmsman? A critique of the concept of "purpose" is
still needed.

361.

On the problem of the actor. — The problem of the actor
has disturbed me for the longest time; I was uncertain (and
at times still am) as to whether it is only from this vantage
point that one can get at the dangerous concept of "artist" — a

concept that has so far been treated with unpardonable affability. Falseness with a good conscience; pleasure in dissimulation erupting as a force, sidelining one's so-called "character," flooding it, sometimes extinguishing it; the inner craving for a role and mask, for a *semblance*; an excess of adaptive capacities of all kinds, that can no longer be satisfied in the service of the closest and narrowest utility: all of this is perhaps not *only* the actor himself? . . . This type of instinct will have developed itself most easily among families of the lower classes who had to assert their lives under changing pressure and coercion, in deep dependency; who had to flexibly make ends meet, always readapting to new circumstances, always posing and posturing in different ways until they were eventually able to trim their sails to *every* wind and thereby nearly become sails themselves, as masters of that incorporated and incarnated art of eternal hide-and-seek that among animals we call mimicry:[55] until ultimately this whole capacity, stored up from generation to generation, becomes domineering, irrational, uncontrollable, until it learns as instinct to command other instincts and produces the actor, the "artist," (the joker, the teller of tall tales, the buffoon, the fool, the clown at first, also the classical servant, the Gil Blas: for in such types we have the prehistory of the artist and often enough even of the "genius"). Even in superior social conditions a similar kind of human being arises under similar pressure: only then the actorly instinct is just barely kept in check by another instinct, for example in the "diplomat" — incidentally I believe a good diplomat would be free at any time to also serve as a good stage actor, assuming he were actually "free" to do so. But as concerns the *Jews,* that people of the art of adaptability par excellence, in them one might see from the outset, in keeping with this train of thought, a world-historical event for the cultivation, so to speak, of actors, a genuine breeding ground for actors; and in fact it is high time for the question: what good actor today is *not* — a Jew? Also the Jew as born man of letters, as the true dominator of the European press exercises his power in this respect on the basis of his actorly ability: for the literatus is essentially an actor — namely, he plays the "expert," the "specialist." — Finally *women*: let's reflect on the entire history of women[56] — *must* they not be actresses first and foremost? Just listen to the physicians who have hypnotized females;[57] in the end, love them — let yourself be "hypnotized" by them! What will be the result time after time? That they "give themselves airs," even when they — give themselves.[58] . . . Woman[59] is so artistic . . .[60]

362.

Our faith in a masculinization of Europe. — We have Napoleon to thank (and by no means the French Revolution, which was bent on "fraternity" among the peoples and on the universal flowery exchange of hearts), that now a couple of warlike centuries in a row can unfold, whose like has not existed in history, in brief, that we have entered the *classical age of war,* of academic as well as popular war on the grandest scale (in resources, talents, discipline), on which all future centuries will look back with envy and reverence as on a model of perfection: — for the nationalistic movement out of which this war-glory springs is merely the countershock against Napoleon and would not exist without Napoleon. It will someday be possible to credit him, then, with the fact that the *man* in Europe has again become master over the merchant and philistine; perhaps even over "woman," who has been coddled by Christianity and the fanatic spirit of the eighteenth century, even more by "modern ideas." Napoleon, who in modern ideas and specifically in civilization saw[61] something akin to a personal enemy, has proven himself with this enmity as one of the greatest continuators of the Renaissance: he brought to the fore an entire block of antiquity's essence, maybe even the most decisive piece, the granite part. And who knows whether this piece of antiquity will also eventually become master again over the nationalistic movement, and whether in the *affirming* sense it will have to make itself the heir and continuator of Napoleon: — who wanted one Europe, as is well known, and this as *mistress[62] of the earth.* —

363.

How each sex has its prejudice regarding love. — For all the concessions I am willing to make to the prejudice we call monogamy, still I will never sanction talk of *equal* rights in love for man and woman: these do not exist. This is due to the fact that man and woman each mean something different by love — and it belongs among the conditions of love for both sexes that one sex does *not* presuppose the same feeling, the same concept of "love" in the other sex. What woman means by love is clear enough: complete devotion (not merely surrender) with soul and body, without any consideration, any reserve, rather with shame and horror at the thought of a devotion governed by clauses, by conditions. In this absence of conditions her love is simply a *faith:* woman has no other faith. — Man, when he loves a woman, *wants* precisely this love from her, and so for his part he is furthest removed from the presupposition of feminine love; supposing, however, that there are also men who for their part are no strangers to the craving for complete devotion, well, they simply — aren't men. A man who loves like a woman thereby becomes a slave; but a woman who loves like a woman thereby becomes a *more perfect* woman . . . The passion of woman, in its unconditional renunciation of her own rights, has the exact presupposition that on the other side an equal pathos, an equal will to renounce does *not* exist: for if both were to renounce themselves out of love, then what stems from that would be — well, I don't know what, maybe empty space?[63] — Woman wants to be taken, accepted as a possession, wants to be absorbed in the concept "possession," "possessed"; consequently she wants someone who *takes,* who does not give himself and give himself away, who on the contrary is supposed to be made even richer in "himself" — through the increase in strength, happiness, faith, that woman gives him in giving herself. Woman gives herself away, man takes in more — I don't think social contracts, nor even the very best will to justice could overcome this natural opposition: as desirable as it may be not constantly to face how harsh, horrid, enigmatic and immoral this antagonism is. For love, when it is thought entirely, grandly, fully is nature, and as nature, it is for all eternity something "immoral." — Accordingly *loyalty* is included in woman's love, and it follows from its definition; in man it *can* easily arise in the course of his love, perhaps as gratitude or as idiosyncrasy of taste and so-called elective affinity, but it doesn't belong to the *essence* of his love — in fact it belongs so little that one could almost justifiably speak of a natural counterplay between love and loyalty in man: his love after all is a wanting-to-have and *not* a renunciation and giving away; but wanting-to-have comes to an end each time with *having* . . . In fact it is the subtler and more suspicious thirst for possession on the part of the man, who seldom and only late admits to himself this "having," that makes his love last; it is even possible that it grows after the surrender — he doesn't readily admit that a woman would have nothing more "to give up" for him. —

364.

The hermit speaks. — The art of interacting with people rests essentially on the skill (that requires long practice) of accepting and ingesting a meal whose kitchen one does not trust. Supposing one comes to the table with a ravenous hunger, everything will be fine ("the meanest company lets you[64] *feel* — ," as Mephistopheles says[65]); but one doesn't have it, this ravenous hunger, when it's needed! Oh, how hard it is to digest one's fellow man! First principle: muster your courage as in a mishap, dig in bravely, admire yourself meanwhile, bite down on your revulsion, swallow down your nausea. Second principle: "improve" your fellow man, for example through praise, so that he starts sweating out his happiness with himself; or grab a snippet of his good or "interesting" qualities and pull on it until the whole virtue comes out and you can hide your fellow man in its folds. Third principle: autohypnosis. Focus on your object of association as if on a glass button until you cease to feel pleasure and displeasure, fall asleep unnoticed, grow rigid, gain your composure: a home remedy found in marriages and friendships, richly tested, celebrated as indispensable but not yet scientifically formulated. Its popular name is — patience. —

365.

The hermit speaks again. — We, too, interact with "people," we, too, modestly don the dress in which (*as* which) we are known, respected, sought, and we appear in society with it, in other words among disguised people who do not want to be called that; we, too, do like all clever masks and politely bar the door to every curiosity that does not concern our "dress." But there are also other ways and tricks to "interact" among people, with people: for example as a ghost — which is really advisable if one wants to get rid of them and make them scared. Example: they reach for us and don't get hold of us. That scares them. Or: we walk through a closed door. Or: when all the lights go out. Or: after we've died. The latter is the trick of *posthumous* people par excellence. ("What do you think?" someone like this once said impatiently, "would we have any desire to tolerate this strangeness, coldness, grave-yard stillness around us, this whole subterranean, hidden, mute, undiscovered solitude that among us is called life and could just as well be called death, if we didn't know what would *become* of us — and that we first come to *our* life and become alive after death, oh! very alive! we posthumous people!" —)

366.

Faced with a scholarly book. — We do not belong to those who only get ideas among books, or occasioned by books — it's our habit to think outdoors, walking, leaping, climbing, dancing, preferably on solitary mountains or right by the sea, where even the paths become thoughtful. Our first questions regarding the value of a book, human being and music are: "can they walk? even better, can they dance?" ... We read rarely, yet we do not read worse — oh how quickly we guess how someone has gotten his ideas, whether sitting in front of an inkwell, with stomach clenched, his head bowed over the paper: oh how quickly we too are finished with his book! Cramped bowels betray themselves, one can bet on that, just as stuffy air, low ceiling, and crowded room betray themselves.[66] — Those were my feelings just now as I closed a righteous scholarly book, grateful, very grateful but also relieved . . . In a scholar's book there is almost always something oppressive, oppressed as well: the "specialist" comes to the fore somewhere, his eagerness, his earnestness, his wrath, his overestimation of the nook in which he sits and spins, his hunchback — every specialist has his hunchback. A scholar's book also always reflects a crooked psyche: every craft makes crooked.[67] Just look at your friends again, those you grew up with, after they've taken possession of their academic specialization: oh, how always the opposite too has occurred! Oh, how they themselves are now and forever occupied and possessed by it! Grown into their corner, squashed beyond recognition, unfree, deprived of their equilibrium, emaciated and jagged all over, yet a paragon of roundness in only a single place — one is moved and speechless to see them again this way. Every[68] craft, even supposing it has a golden floor, also has a leaden ceiling over it that presses and presses on the psyche until it is bizarre and bent crooked. There's nothing that can be done about it. Don't believe for a moment that it's possible to circumvent this disfigurement through any kind of educational artifice. Every kind of *mastery* is dearly paid for on this earth, where perhaps everything is too dearly paid for; one is master of his trade at the price of also being victim of his trade. But you would have it differently — "cheaper," above all more comfortable — right, my dear contemporaries? Well then! But then you immediately get something else too, namely instead of a craftsman and master, a man of letters, a dexterous "polydexterous" man of letters, who of course is lacking a hunchback — except for the deep bow[69] he takes before you as the shopkeeper of the spirit and "carrier" of culture — the man of letters, who actually *is* nothing but "represents" most everything, who plays and "portrays" the expert, who even takes it upon himself in all modesty to *make* himself paid, honored and celebrated in place of the expert. — No, my

scholarly friends! I bless you even for the sake of your hunch-
backs! And for the fact that like me, you despise the men of letters and the cultural parasites! And that you do not know how
to make a business of the intellect! And that you have genuine
opinions that can't be expressed in monetary values! And that
you represent nothing that you yourselves *are* not! That your
sole will is to be master of your craft, with reverence for every
kind of mastery and competence, ruthlessly rejecting everything
that is mere semblance, half-genuine, dressed up, virtuoso-like,
demagogic, or actorly *in litteris et artibus*[70] — everything that
cannot prove itself to you in terms of the unconditional *probity* of discipline and prior schooling! (Even genius does not
help to overcome such a deficiency, as much as it knows how to
obscure it: this is understood as soon as one has observed our
most talented painters and composers up close — all of whom,
almost without exception, know how to appropriate artificially
and retroactively the *semblance* of that probity, that solidity of
schooling and culture through a cunning inventiveness of manners, of stopgap measures, even of principles, without of course
deceiving themselves, without constantly muzzling their own
bad conscience. For, surely you know this? all great modern artists suffer from a bad conscience . . .)

367.

The first distinction that should be made among artworks.
— Everything that is thought, written, painted, composed or
even built and sculpted belongs either to monologic art or to
art before witnesses. Among the latter we should also include
that seemingly monologue art that involves faith in God, the
entire lyricism of prayer: after all, for the pious there is still
no solitude — this invention was first made by us, us godless
ones. I know no deeper distinction in the overall optics of an
artist than this: whether he looks at his budding artwork (at
"himself" —) with the eyes of a witness or whether he "has
forgotten the world": which is the essence of every monologic
art — it rests *on forgetting,* it is the music of forgetting.

368.[71]

The cynic speaks. — My objections to Wagner's music are physiological objections: why disguise them first with aesthetic formulas? My "fact of the matter" is that I no longer breathe freely when this music starts to affect me; that suddenly my *foot* becomes angry at it and revolts — it has a need for rhythm, dance, marching, it demands from music above all the delights found in *good* walking, striding, leaping and dancing — But doesn't my stomach also protest? My heart? My blood pressure? My bowels? Doesn't all this unnoticeably make me hoarse? — And so I ask myself: what does my entire body actually *want* from music anyway? I believe, its own *relief:* as if all animal functions could be accelerated by light, bold, unbridled and self-assured rhythms; as if iron and leaden life could be gilded by golden, good and tender harmonies. My melancholy wants to relax in the hiding places and abysses of *perfection:* for this I need music. What do I care about drama! About the cramps of its moral ecstasies, from which the "common people" derive their satisfaction? About the whole gesture-hocus pocus of an actor! . . . One can guess, I am essentially anti-theatrical by disposition — but conversely, Wagner was essentially a man of the theater and an actor, the most enthusiastic mimomaniac that ever existed, even as a musician! . . . And, incidentally speaking: if it has been Wagner's theory that "drama is the end, while music is always merely its means"[72] — his *practice* on the contrary was from start to finish "the pose is the end and drama, even the music is always merely *its* means." Music as a means to clarification, intensification, internalization of the dramatic gesture and the actor's convincingness; and Wagnerian drama merely an opportunity for many dramatic poses! He possessed, along with all other instincts, the commanding instincts of a great actor in all and sundry: and, as mentioned, also as a musician. — I once made this clear to a righteous Wagnerian, with considerable effort; and I had reason to add "just be a bit more honest with yourself: we're not in the theater after all! In the theater, one is only honest as one of the masses; as an individual one lies and lies to oneself. One leaves oneself at home when one goes to the theater, one dispenses with the right to one's own tongue and choice, to one's taste, even to one's courage as one possesses and practices it before God and human within one's own four walls. No one brings into the theater the finest senses of his art, not even the artist who works for the theater: there, one is common people, the public, herd, woman, Pharisee, voting cattle, democrat, neighbor, fellow man; there, even the most personal conscience succumbs to the leveling magic of 'the greatest number'; there, stupidity acts as lechery and contagion; there, the 'neighbor' rules; there, one *becomes* neighbor . . ." (I forgot to tell you what my enlightened Wagnerian replied to my physiological objections: "So you're really not healthy enough for our music?" —)

369.

Our simultaneity. — Don't we have to confess to ourselves, we artists, that there is an uncanny differentness in us, that our taste and on the other hand our creative power in an odd way stand alone for themselves, remain standing alone and have their own growth — I mean entirely different degrees and tempos of old, young, ripe, wilted, rotten? So that for example, a musician could create things his whole life long that *contradict* what his pampered listener-ear, listener-heart esteems, savors and prefers: — he doesn't even need to be aware of this contradiction! In one's taste, as demonstrated by an almost painfully regular experience, one can easily grow beyond the taste of one's power, even without the latter becoming paralyzed or inhibited in its productivity; but something opposite can happen as well — and it is to precisely this that I would like to draw the attention of artists. A constantly creating type, a "mother" of a human being in the grand sense of the word, someone who doesn't know and hear anything anymore besides pregnancies and delivering the babies of his spirit, who has no time at all to reflect on himself and his work, to compare things; who also is no longer willing to exercise his own taste and simply forgets it, just letting it stand, lie or fall — maybe someone like this finally produces works *with which his judgment can no longer keep pace:* so that he says stupid things about them and himself — says and thinks them. To me this seems nearly to be the normal state of affairs with fertile artists — no one knows their child worse than its parents — and this even applies, to cite a tremendous example, in relation to the entire Greek world of poetry and art: it never did "know" what it had done . . .

370.[73]

What is romanticism? — One may perhaps recall, at least among my friends, that in the beginning I went at this modern world with a few hefty errors and overestimations and in any case as someone who was *hopeful.* I understood — who knows based on what personal experience? — the philosophical pessimism of the nineteenth century as if it were the symptom of a superior force of thought, of a more daring courage, of a more triumphant *fullness* of life than had characterized the eighteenth century, the age of Hume, Kant, Condillac and the sensualists: so that tragic knowledge appeared to me as the genuine *luxury* of our culture, as its most precious, noble and dangerous kind of squandering, but nevertheless, based on its superabundance, as its *permitted* luxury. Likewise,[74] I made a point of construing German music as the expression of a Dionysian mightiness of the German soul: in it I believed I heard the earthquake that was finally released by a primal force dammed up since time immemorial — indifferent to whether it made everything else known as culture tremble. One sees that back then, I failed to recognize both in philosophical pessimism and in German music what constitutes their actual character — their *romanticism.* What is romanticism? Every art, every philosophy may be regarded as a remedy and aid in the service of growing, struggling life: they always presuppose suffering and sufferers. But there are two kinds of sufferers; first those who suffer from the *superabundance of life,* who want a Dionysian art and likewise a tragic view and insight into life — and then those who suffer from the *impoverishment of life,* who seek rest, quiet, smooth seas, redemption from themselves through art and knowledge, or intoxication, spasms, numbness, madness. All romanticism in art and knowledge corresponds to the dual needs of the *latter type*; it corresponded (and still does) to Schopenhauer as much as to Richard Wagner, to mention those most famous and explicit romantics who were *misunderstood* by me at the time — incidentally *not* to their disadvantage, as should be conceded to me in all fairness. The one richest in fullness of life, namely the Dionysian god and human being, can allow himself not only the sight of what is terrible and questionable, but the terrible deed itself and that luxury of destruction, disintegration, negation; in him, what is evil, absurd and ugly appears permitted, as it were, as the result of a superabundance of begetting, fertilizing energies that are still capable of turning any desert into a lush farmland. Conversely, the most suffering and poorest in life would mostly need mildness, peacefulness, goodness in thought and in deed, if possible a god who would actually be a god for the sick, a "savior"; logic as well, the conceptual comprehensibility of existence — for logic calms, inspires confidence — in sum, a certain warm, fear-repelling narrowness and enclosure in optimistic horizons. This is how I gradually came to understand Epicurus, the opposite of a Dionysian pessimist, likewise the "Christian," who in fact is merely a kind of Epicurean and like him, essentially a romantic — and my eye grew ever sharper for that most difficult and trickiest form of *backward inference* in which most mistakes are made — the backward inference from the work to the maker, from the deed to the doer, from the ideal to the one who *needs* it, from every manner of thinking and valuing to the commanding *need* behind it. — Regarding all aesthetic values I now avail myself of this major distinction: I ask, in each individual case, "is it hunger or superabundance that has become creative here?" From the outset a different distinction might seem to recommend itself more — it is far more obvious — namely attending to whether the desire for fixing, eternalizing, for *being* is the cause of creativity, or rather the desire for destruction, for change, for the new, for future, for *becoming*. But both kinds of desire, on closer analysis, still prove to be equivocal and are indeed interpretable according to the former scheme which is justifiably preferred, in my view. The desire for *destruction,* change, becoming can be the expression of superabundant energy that is pregnant with the future (my term for this, as is known, is the word "Dionysian"), but it can also be the hatred of the failure, the deprived, underprivileged who destroys, *must* destroy because what exists, indeed all existing, all being itself outrages and provokes him — in order to understand this affect, just look closely at our anarchists. The will to *eternalize* likewise requires[75] a dual interpretation. On the one hand it can stem from gratitude and love: — an art of this origin will always be an apotheosis art, dithyrambic perhaps like Rubens, blissfully mocking like Hafiz, bright and gracious like Goethe and spreading[76] a Homeric radiance and halo over all things. But it can also be that tyrannical will of a deeply suffering, struggling, tortured man who would like to stamp what is most personal, individual, and private, the real idiosyncrasy of his suffering into a binding law and compulsion, and who takes revenge as it were on all things by pressing, squeezing, branding *his* image, the image of *his* torture on them. The latter is *romantic pessimism* in its most expressive form, be it as Schopenhauerian philosophy of will, be it as Wagnerian music: — romantic pessimism, the last *great* event in the fate of our culture. (That there *could* exist an entirely different pessimism, a classical one — this intuition and vision belongs to me, as inseparable from me, as my *proprium* and *ipsissimum:*[77] only my ears are offended by the word "classical," it is far too trite, too rounded and unrecognizable. I call this pessimism of the future — for it is coming! I see it coming! — *Dionysian* pessimism.)

371.

We incomprehensible ones. — Have we ever complained about being misunderstood, misjudged, mistaken for others, maligned, misheard and unheard? Precisely this is our fate

— oh, for a long time yet! let's say, to be modest, until 1901 — it is also our distinction; we wouldn't honor ourselves sufficiently if we wished it otherwise. We are mistaken for others — this is because we ourselves are growing, we're constantly changing, we shed old bark, we still shed our skin each spring, we're becoming ever younger, more futuristic, taller, stronger, we drive our roots ever more powerfully into the depths — into evil — while at the same time we embrace the sky ever more lovingly, ever more broadly and suck its light into ourselves ever more thirstily with all our branches and leaves. We grow as trees do — this is hard to understand, like all life! — not in one spot but everywhere, not in one direction but just as upward and outward as inward and downward — our energy drives simultaneously into the trunk, boughs and roots, we are no longer free to do anything individual, still to *be* anything individual . . . This is our fate, as mentioned: we grow into the *heights*; and supposing it were even our doom — for we're living ever closer to the lightning! — well then, we don't honor it less on that account, it remains that which we do not want to share, to communicate, the doom of the heights, *our* doom . . .

372.

Why we are no idealists. — Formerly philosophers were afraid of the senses: have we perhaps — unlearned this fear all too much? Today we are all sensualists, we who are the present and the future in philosophy, *not* in theory but in praxis, in practice . . . The former, on the other hand, believed themselves to be lured by the senses out of *their* world, the cold realm of "ideas," onto a dangerous southern island: there, they feared, their philosopher-virtues would melt away like snow in the sun. "Wax in one's ears" was practically a condition of philosophizing back then; a genuine philosopher no longer heard life, insofar as life is music; he *denied* the music of life — it is an old philosopher's superstition that all music is sirens' music. — Today, however, we might be inclined to judge totally opposite (which in itself could still be just as wrong): namely, that *ideas* are worse

seductresses than the senses, with all their cold, anemic semblance and not even in spite of this semblance — they always
lived off the "blood" of the philosopher, they always drained his
senses, indeed, if we can be believed, his "heart" too. These old
philosophers were heartless: philosophizing was always a kind
of vampirism. In figures even such as Spinoza, don't you feel
something profoundly enigmatic and uncanny? Don't you see
the drama that is playing out here, this steady *turning paler*
— this desensualization that is interpreted ever more ideally?
Don't you suspect some long-concealed bloodsucker in the
background, who begins with the senses and ultimately is left
with, and leaves behind, only bones and rattling? — I mean
categories, formulas, *words* (after all, forgive me, what was *left
of* Spinoza, *amor intellectualis dei,*[78] is rattling, nothing more!
what is *amor,* what is *deus* if they lack any drop of blood? . . .)
In sum: all philosophical idealism to date was something like
sickness, when it was not, as in Plato's case, the caution of a
superabundant and dangerous health, the fear of *superpowerful* senses, the cleverness of a clever Socratic. — Perhaps we
moderns are just not healthy enough *to have need* of Plato's
idealism? And we don't fear the senses, because — —

373.[79]

"Science" as prejudice. — It follows from the laws of the order
of rank that scholars, insofar as they belong to the intellectual
middle class, are not allowed even to glimpse the genuine *great*
problems and question marks: furthermore their courage and
likewise their vision don't reach that far — above all, the need
that makes them scholars, their inner anticipation and desire for
things to be *thus and such,* their fears and hopes are too quickly
laid to rest and satisfied. What makes the pedantic Englishman
Herbert Spencer rave in his way, for example, and draw a line
of hope, a horizon-line of desirability, namely that ultimate
reconciliation of "egoism and altruism" that he fibs about; this
makes the likes of us almost nauseated: — a humankind with
such Spencerian perspectives as its ultimate perspectives would

seem to us worthy of contempt, of annihilation! But even *that* something has to be perceived by him as the highest hope, when it is regarded and should be regarded by others merely as an odious possibility, is a question mark that Spencer would not have been able to foresee . . . Matters are the same for that faith with which so many materialistic natural scientists are content now, that faith in a world that is supposed to have its equivalent and measure in human thinking, in human value concepts, in a "world of truth" that one is ultimately capable of figuring out with our little four-square human reason — what? do we really want to allow existence to be degraded like this to an exercise for a calculating machine and parlor game for mathematicians? Above all one should not want to strip it of its *ambiguous* character: that is what *good* taste requires, gentlemen, the taste of reverence for everything that goes beyond your horizon! That the only justified world interpretation would be one in which *you* are justified, in which research is conducted and maintained scientifically in *your* sense (— you really mean *mechanistically?*), one that allows counting, calculating, weighing, seeing and touching and nothing else; this is clumsiness and naïveté, assuming it is not mental illness or idiocy. Would it not conversely be quite probable that precisely the most superficial and external aspects of existence — its most apparent qualities, its skin and sensualization — would be grasped first? would perhaps even be the only thing grasped? A "scientific" world interpretation as you understand it could then still be one of the *most stupid,* that is, most lacking in meaning of all possible interpretations: this I whisper into the ear and conscience of our dear mechanics, who like to consort with philosophers these days and brazenly suppose that mechanics is the doctrine of first and last laws, upon which all existence must be constructed as if upon a ground floor. But an essentially mechanistic world would be an essentially *meaningless* world! Supposing one appraised the *value* of a music according to how much of it could be counted, calculated, put into formulas — how absurd would such a "scientific" appraisal of music be! What would anyone have comprehended, understood, known about it? Nothing, virtually nothing of what is really "music" in it! . . .

374.

Our new "infinite." — How far the perspectival character of existence reaches or even whether it has some other character; whether an existence without interpretation, without "sense" does not simply become "nonsense"; whether, conversely, all existence is not essentially an *interpreting* existence — this, as is only fair, cannot be ascertained even by the most industrious and scrupulously conscientious analysis and self-examination of the intellect: since human intellect in this analysis cannot help seeing itself under its perspectival forms and *only* in them. We cannot see around our corner: it is a hopeless curiosity to want to know what other kinds of intellect and perspective *could* exist: for instance, whether some kinds of beings could perceive time backward or alternatingly forward and backward (which would give a different direction for life and a different concept of cause and effect). But I think that today we are at least far removed from the ridiculous immodesty of decreeing from our corner that one is *permitted* to have perspectives only from this corner. On the contrary, the world for us has become "infinite" again: insofar as we cannot reject the possibility that it *includes infinite interpretations.* Once more, we are seized by the great shudder — but who would desire immediately to re-deify in the old manner *this* monster of an unknown world? And perhaps worship *what* is unknown from now on as the "unknown *one*"? Oh, there are just too many *ungodly* possibilities of interpretation included in this unknown, too much devilry, stupidity, foolishness of interpretation — even our own human, all too human variety, which we know . . .

375.

Why we seem like Epicureans. — We are cautious, we modern human beings, about ultimate convictions; our mistrust lies in wait for enchantments and deceptions of the conscience that lie in every strong faith, every unconditional Yes and No: how can this be explained? Perhaps, one could see here to a large extent the caution of the "burned child," the disappointed idealist; but to a different and better extent also the jubilating curiosity of someone who formerly stood in his corner, who was driven to despair by his corner and now revels and raves in the opposite of his corner, in the infinite, in the "open as such." With this, a nearly Epicurean penchant for knowledge develops, which does not want cheaply to let go of the question-mark character of things; likewise an aversion for big moral words and gestures, a taste that rejects all clumsy foursquare oppositions and is consciously proud of its practice in being reserved. For *this* is what constitutes our pride, this gentle tugging on the reins of our forward-charging urge for certainty, this self-mastery of the rider on his wildest rides: for we still have the same crazy and fiery steeds beneath us, and if we hesitate, then surely danger is least of all what makes us hesitate . . .[80]

376.

Our slow times. — This is how all artists and people of "works" feel, the motherly kind of person: they always believe, at every segment of their lives — which is segmented each time by a work — they are already at their goal, they would always patiently accept death with the feeling: "we are ripe for it." This is not the expression of exhaustion — rather that of a certain autumnal sunniness and mildness that is left behind every time by the work itself for its author, by the work's having ripened. Then the tempo of life slows down and becomes thick and flows like honey — to the point of long *fermatas,*[81] to the point of faith in *the* long *fermata* . . .

377.

We homeless ones. — There is no lack among the Europeans of today of those who have a right to call themselves homeless in a distinguishing and honorable sense, and it is on them precisely that I cordially and expressly enjoin my secret wisdom and *gaya scienza*! For their lot is hard, their hope uncertain, it is a feat to invent any solace for them — but what good does it do![82] We children of the future, how *could* we be at home in this today? We disfavor all ideals according to which anyone could still feel at home even in this brittle and broken time of transition; but as concerns its "realities," we do not believe they are *durable*. The ice that still holds today has already become very thin: the thaw wind is blowing, we ourselves, we home-less ones, are something that breaks up ice and other all too thin "realities" . . . We "conserve" nothing, nor do we want to go back to any past; we[83] are absolutely not "liberal," we do not work for "progress," we don't need to first plug our ears to the marketplace's sirens of the future — what they sing: "equal rights," "free society," "no more masters and no servants," this doesn't lure us! — we regard it as totally undesirable that the realm of justice and concord be established on earth (because in any case it would be the realm of deepest mediocritizing and Chinesery[84]), we delight in all who, like us, love danger, war, adventure, who do not permit themselves to be compromised, captured, reconciled and castrated; we count ourselves among the conquerors, we contemplate the necessity of new orders, even a new slavery — for every strengthening and enhancement of the type "human being" entails adding a new kind of slavery — right? With all this, must it not be difficult for us to feel at home in an age that loves to lay claim to the honor of being the most humane, mildest, most righteous age ever to have existed under the sun? It's bad enough that precisely these beautiful words bring to mind ulterior motives that are all the more ugly! That in them we see only the expression — and also the mas-querade — of deep weakening, of exhaustion, of old age, of waning strength! Of what concern can it be to us what kind of tinsel the sick use to adorn their weakness! Let them sport it as their *virtue* — indeed, there is no doubt that weakness makes us mild, oh so mild, so righteous, so inoffensive, so "humane"! — The "religion of compassion" to which one would like to persuade us — oh, we know well enough the hysterical little

men and little women who today need precisely this religion
as a veil and adornment! We are no humanitarians; we would
never permit ourselves to dare to speak about our "love for
humankind" — the likes of us is not sufficiently actor for that!
Or not sufficiently Saint-Simonist,[85] not French enough. One
must indeed be burdened by a *Gallic* superabundance of erotic
irritability and amorous impatience even to approach humankind in such an honest way with one's ardor . . . Humankind!
Was there ever a more hideous old hag among all old hags?
(— unless it were perhaps "truth": a question for philosophers).
No, we do not love humankind; but on the other hand, we
are by far not "German" enough in the sense that the word
"German" is commonplace today for endorsing nationalism
and racial hatred, for being capable of deriving pleasure from
the nationalistic scabies of the heart and blood poisoning on
whose account today the peoples of Europe distance and bar-
ricade themselves from each other as if by quarantine. For this
we are too uninhibited, too malicious, too pampered, also too
well informed, too "well traveled": we prefer by far to live on
mountains, isolated, "untimely," in past or future centuries,
just to spare ourselves the silent rage to which we know we'd
be condemned as eyewitnesses of a politics that desolates the
German spirit by making it vain, and moreover is *petty* politics:
— so that its own creation doesn't immediately fall apart again,
doesn't it need to plant it between two deadly hatreds? *must* it
not desire the perpetuation of Europe's system of petty states?
. . . We homeless ones, in keeping with our race and descent,
are too multifarious and mixed, as "modern human beings,"
and consequently scarcely tempted to participate in that mendacious racial self-admiration and obscenity that parades today
in Germany as a sign of German mentality, making the people
of the "historical sense" look doubly false and indecent. We
are, in a word — and it shall be our word of honor! — *good
Europeans,* the heirs of Europe, the rich, overprovisioned but
also overly obligated heirs of millennia of the European spirit:
as such, we also outgrew Christianity and are averse to it, and

precisely because we grew *out* of it, because our ancestors were Christians whose Christianity was ruthlessly righteous, who willingly sacrificed blood and treasure, status and fatherland for their faith. We — do the same. And for what? For our unbelief? For every kind of unbelief? No, you know better, my friends! The hidden *Yes* in you is stronger than all the Nos and Maybes that sicken you and your times; and if you have to put to sea, you emigrants, then you too are compelled by — a *faith*![86] . . .

378.

"And become clear again." — We generous and wealthy of spirit, who stand by the road like open wells, wishing to stop no one drawing from us: unfortunately we don't know how to defend ourselves when we would like to, we have nothing to prevent people from *clouding* and darkening us — prevent the times in which we live from throwing their "timeliest" into us, their dirty birds throwing their filth, the little boys their rubbish, and exhausted wanderers who rest by us their misery small and great. But we will do as we have always done: whatever gets thrown into us, we take it down into our depths — for we are deep, we do not forget — *and become clear again* . . .

379.

The fool's interruption.[87] — That's no misanthrope, the one who wrote this book: hatred of humanity is paid for too dearly these days. In order to hate in the manner one used to hate *the* human being, Timonically,[88] on the whole, without exception, wholeheartedly, with the full *love* of hatred — for that, one would have to renounce contempt: — and how much fine joy, how much patience, how much graciousness even do we owe precisely to our contempt! Moreover, because of it we are "God's chosen": subtle contempt is our taste and privilege, our art, our virtue perhaps, we most modern among moderns! . . . Hatred on the other hand puts us on a par and face to face, there is honor in hatred, finally: in hatred there is *fear*, a large and good measure of fear. We fearless ones, however, we more spiritual human beings of this age, we know our advantage sufficiently well, as precisely the more spiritual ones, to live without fear of this age. We will hardly be decapitated, imprisoned, or exiled; not even our books will be banned and burned. The age loves the spirit, it loves us and needs us, even if we had to let it know that we are artists of contempt; that every interaction with human beings makes us shudder a bit; that for all our mildness, patience, congeniality, courtesy, we cannot persuade our noses to desist from their prejudice against the proximity of a human being; that we love nature the less humanly things occur in it, and art, *when* it is the artist's escape from human being or the artist's mockery of the human being or the artist's mockery of himself . . .

380.

"The wanderer" speaks.[89] — In order to view our European morality for once from a distance, in order to measure it against other, earlier or future moralities, one must do as a wanderer does when he wants to know how tall are the towers of a city: for this he *leaves* the city. "Thoughts about moral prejudices," if they are not to be prejudices about prejudices, presuppose a position *outside* morality, some beyond good and evil to which one must ascend, climb, fly — and, in the present case, at least a beyond *our* good and evil, a freedom from all "Europe," the latter understood as a sum of commanding value judgments that have entered into our flesh and blood. That anyone *wants* precisely to go out there, up there, is perhaps a bit crazy, a peculiar and unreasonable "you must," — for we knowers, too, have our idiosyncrasies of "unfree will" — : the question is whether one *can* actually get up there. This might depend on numerous conditions, but mainly it is a question of how light or heavy we are, the problem of our "specific gravity." One has to be *very light* to drive one's will to knowledge into such a distance and, as it were, beyond one's times; to create eyes for oneself for surveying millennia, and moreover clear skies[90] in these eyes! One will have to have untethered oneself from much that pressures,

inhibits, holds down and makes heavy precisely us Europeans
of today. The human being of such a beyond, who wants to
catch sight of the supreme value measures of his time itself,
first needs to "overcome" this time in himself — it is the test
of his strength[91] — and consequently not only his time, but also
his previous aversion and contradiction *against* this time, his
suffering from this time, his un-timeliness, his *romanticism* . . .

381.[92]

On the question of comprehensibility. — One does not merely
want to be understood when one writes, but likewise certainly
also *not* understood. It is by no means an objection to a book if
just anyone finds it incomprehensible: perhaps this was exactly
part of the writer's intention — he did not *want* to be understood by "just anyone." Each nobler spirit and taste also selects his
listeners when he wants to communicate; by selecting them, he
simultaneously establishes boundaries against "the others." All the
subtler laws of style have their origins in this: they simultaneously
keep away, they create distance, they prohibit "entry," comprehension, as mentioned — while they open the ears of those who
are related to us by ear. And to say it just between you and me
and in my case — I don't want to prevent myself either through
my ignorance or through the vivaciousness of my temperament
from being comprehensible to *you*, my friends: not through vivaciousness, no matter how much it compels me to get at a matter
swiftly in order to get at it at all. For I approach deep problems
as I do a cold bath — get in fast, get out fast. That one doesn't
get deep enough, doesn't get deep *down* enough in this manner
is the superstition of those who fear water, of the enemies of cold
water; they speak without experience. Oh, great cold makes us
swift! — And I ask, incidentally: does a matter really remain
uncomprehended and unknown merely because it is brushed
on the fly, glanced at, flashed at? Must one absolutely sit firmly on
top of it first? as if having hatched an egg? *Diu noctuque incu-
bando*[93] as Newton said of himself? At least there are truths of
a particular shyness and ticklishness that we cannot get hold

of except suddenly — that we must either *surprise* or let go . . .
Finally, my brevity has yet another value: given such questions as
occupy me, I must say much briefly, so that it is heard even more
briefly. For as an immoralist one must guard against corrupt-
ing innocence, I mean the asses and the old maids of both sexes,
who have nothing from life besides their innocence; even more,
my writings should inspire, elevate and encourage them to virtue.
What on earth could be funnier than seeing inspired old asses and
old maids who are aroused by the sweet emotions of virtue:
and "this I have seen" — thus spoke Zarathustra. So much by way
of brevity; things are worse with my ignorance, which I do not
conceal from myself. There are hours when I am ashamed of it;
of course, likewise hours when I am ashamed of this shame. Perhaps all of us philosophers today are in a difficult position regarding knowledge: science is growing, the most scholarly among us
are close to discovering that they know too little. But it would be
even worse if matters were different — if we knew *too much*; our
task is and remains first of all not to mistake ourselves for others.
We *are* something different from scholars: although it cannot be
avoided that we are also, among other things, scholarly. We have
different needs, a different growth pattern, a different digestion:
we need more, we also need less. There is no formula for how
much a spirit needs for his nourishment; but if his taste aims for
independence, for coming and going swiftly, for wandering, perhaps for adventures to which only the swiftest are equal, then he
would rather live free with meagre fare than unfree and stuffed.
It's not fat, but the greatest suppleness and strength that a good
dancer wants from his nourishment — and I would not know
what the spirit of a philosopher would prefer more to be than a
good dancer. For dance is his ideal, also his art, and ultimately
also his single piety, his "divine worship" . . .

382.

The great health. — We new, nameless, hard-to-understand
ones, we premature births of a still-unproven future — for
a new end we also need a new means, namely a new health,

a stronger, savvier, tougher, more daring, merrier one than all
healths of the past. Someone whose soul thirsts to have experienced the entire scope of previous values and desiderata, to have
circumnavigated all coasts of this ideal "Mediterranean sea";
who wants to know from the adventures of his most authentic
experiences how a conqueror and discoverer of the ideal feels,
likewise an artist, a saint, a legislator, a sage, a scholar, a pious
man, a soothsayer, an old-fashioned divine loner: for this he
needs one thing above all, *the great health* — of the kind that
one does not merely have, but also continuously acquires and
must acquire, because one gives it up again and again, must give
it up! . . . And now, after we've been underway for a long time
in this manner, we argonauts of the ideal, more courageously
perhaps than is prudent, and often enough shipwrecked and
damaged but, as mentioned, healthier than one would like to
give us credit for, dangerously healthy, healthy again and again
— now it seems to us as though, as a reward for this, we have
a yet undiscovered land before us, whose boundaries no one
has yet surveyed, something beyond all previous lands and corners of the ideal, a world so superabundant in what is beautiful,
strange, questionable, terrible and divine, that our curiosity as
well as our craving to possess are beside themselves — oh, that
nothing is capable of sating us anymore! How could we, after
such vistas and with such ravenousness in our conscience and
science,[94] still be satisfied with the *current human being?* Bad
enough: but it is inevitable that we look upon his worthiest
goals and hopes with merely a poorly maintained seriousness
and perhaps don't look upon it at all anymore. A different
ideal runs ahead of us, a marvelous, seductive, dangerous ideal
to which we want to persuade no one because we do not so
easily concede anyone the *right to it:* the ideal of a spirit who
plays naïvely, that is, involuntarily and from overflowing fullness and power, with everything that has so far passed for holy,
good, untouchable, divine; for whom the supreme, which is
justifiably the measure of value of the common people, would
instead equate with danger, decline, debasement or at least to

recuperation, blindness, temporary self-oblivion; the ideal of a human-superhuman well-being and benevolence, that will often enough appear *inhuman,* for instance, when it shows up next to all previous earthly seriousness, next to every kind of solemnity of gesture, word, tone, look, morality and task looking like their incarnate and involuntary parody — and perhaps only with it, in spite of everything, *the great seriousness* begins, the real question mark is posed for the first time, the destiny of the soul turns, the clock hand advances, the tragedy *begins* . . .

383.

Epilogue. — But as I, in conclusion, ever so slowly finish painting this gloomy question mark, still willing to remind my readers of the virtues of proper reading[95] — oh what forgotten and unknown virtues! — I notice that all around me the most malicious, lively, hobgoblin laughter rings out: the very spirits of my book fall upon me, tug on my ears and call me to order. "We can't stand it anymore" — they shout to me — : "away, away with this raven-black music. Is it not bright morning all around us? And green soft ground and grass, the kingdom of dance? Was there ever a better hour to be cheerful? Who'll sing us a song, a morning song, so sunny, so light, so fully fledged that it does *not* chase away the bad mood[96] — that instead it invites the crickets to sing along, to dance along? And better a simple, rustic bagpipe than these mysterious tones, these toad calls, tomb voices and marmot whistles with which you have regaled us so far in your wilderness, Mr. Hermit and Musician of the Future! No! No more of these sounds! Rather, let's strike up more pleasant and joyful ones!"[97] — Do you like it like *this,* my impatient friends? Well then! Who wouldn't comply with your wishes? My bagpipe is already waiting, my throat too — it may sound a bit raspy, but put up with it! we're in the mountains after all. But at least what you get to hear is new; and if you don't understand it, if you misunderstand the *singer,* so what! That just happens to be the "the singer's curse."[98] All the more clearly you can hear his music and melody, and dance all the better — to his pipe. Do you *want* that? . . .

An Goethe.

Das Unvergängliche
Ist nur dein Gleichniss!
Gott der Verfängliche
Ist Dichter-Erschleichniss . . .

Welt-Rad, das rollende,
Streift Ziel auf Ziel:
Noth — nennt's der Grollende,
Der Narr nennt's — Spiel . . .

Welt-Spiel, das herrische,
Mischt Sein und Schein: —
Das Ewig-Närrische
Mischt *uns* — hinein! . . .

Dichters Berufung.

Als ich jüngst, mich zu erquicken,
Unter dunklen Bäumen sass,
Hört' ich ticken, leise ticken,
Zierlich, wie nach Takt und Maass.
Böse wurd' ich, zog Gesichter, —
Endlich aber gab ich nach,
Bis ich gar, gleich einem Dichter,
Selber mit im Tiktak sprach.

To Goethe[2]

The ever-enduring
Is merely your parable!
God the all-blurring
Your fiction unbearable . . .

World-wheel, the turning one
Spawns goals each day:
Fate — sighs the yearning one,
The fool calls it — play . . .

World-play, the ruling one,
Blends truth and tricks: —
The eternally fooling one
Blends *us* — in the mix! . . .

Poet's Calling[3]

Stopped to rest one day, while walking,
Seated under shady trees,
When I heard a ticking tocking,
Dainty rhythm on the breeze.
I grew angry — made some faces —
But I lost my anger quick,
And, as if in poet's paces,
Started speaking tick tock tick.

Wie mir so im Verse-Machen
Silb' um Silb' ihr Hopsa sprang,
Musst' ich plötzlich lachen, lachen
Eine Viertelstunde lang.
Du ein Dichter? Du ein Dichter?
Steht's mit deinem Kopf so schlecht?
— „Ja, mein Herr, Sie sind ein Dichter"
Achselzuckt der Vogel Specht.

Wessen harr' ich hier im Busche?
Wem doch laur' ich Räuber auf?
Ist's ein Spruch? Ein Bild? Im Husche
Sitzt mein Reim ihm hintendrauf.
Was nur schlüpft und hüpft, gleich sticht der
Dichter sich's zum Vers zurecht.
— „Ja, mein Herr, Sie sind ein Dichter"
Achselzuckt der Vogel Specht.

Reime, mein' ich, sind wie Pfeile?
Wie das zappelt, zittert, springt,
Wenn der Pfeil in edle Theile
Des Lacerten-Leibchens dringt!
Ach, ihr sterbt dran, arme Wichter,
Oder taumelt wie bezecht!
— „Ja, mein Herr, Sie sind ein Dichter"
Achselzuckt der Vogel Specht.

Schiefe Sprüchlein voller Eile,
Trunkne Wörtlein, wie sich's drängt!
Bis ihr Alle, Zeil' an Zeile,
An der Tiktak-Kette hängt.
Und es giebt grausam Gelichter,
Das dies — freut? Sind Dichter — schlecht?
— „Ja, mein Herr, Sie sind ein Dichter"
Achselzuckt der Vogel Specht.

As I sat, my verses making
Syllables and sounds did pour,
Till I burst out laughing, shaking
For a quarter hour or more.
You a poet? You a poet?
Is your mind no longer good?
— "Yes, my man, you are a poet"
Shrugs the pecker in the wood.

Whom do I await[4] in bushes?
Whom do I, a robber, stalk?
Proverb? Image? My rhyme rushes
After it and makes it talk.
Anything that moves,[5] you know it
Serves to fuel my poet's mood.
— "Yes, my man, you are a poet"
Shrugs the pecker in the wood.

Rhymes, I think, must be like arrows:
When they pierce the lizard's heart,[6]
How he twitches, how it harrows,
How he leaps in fits and starts!
Wretched creatures, full of woe, it
Kills you or it boils your blood!
— "Yes, my man, you are a poet"
Shrugs the pecker in the wood.

Crooked proverbs full of hurry,
Drunken wordlets how you throng!
See each word and sentence scurry,
To the tick tock chain so long.
Worthless souls who can't forgo it,
Find it — fun? Are poets — crude?
— "Yes, my man, you are a poet"
Shrugs the pecker in the wood.

Höhnst du, Vogel? Willst du scherzen?
Steht's mit meinem Kopf schon schlimm,
Schlimmer stünd's mit meinem Herzen?
Fürchte, fürchte meinen Grimm! —
Doch der Dichter — Reime flicht er
Selbst im Grimm noch schlecht und recht.
— „Ja, mein Herr, Sie sind ein Dichter"
Achselzuckt der Vogel Specht.

Im Süden.

So häng' ich denn auf krummem Aste
Und schaukle meine Müdigkeit.
Ein Vogel lud mich her zu Gaste,
Ein Vogelnest ist's, drin ich raste.
Wo bin ich doch? Ach, weit! Ach, weit!

Das weisse Meer liegt eingeschlafen,
Und purpurn steht ein Segel drauf.
Fels, Feigenbäume, Thurm und Hafen,
Idylle rings, Geblök von Schafen, —
Unschuld des Südens, nimm mich auf!

Nur Schritt für Schritt — das ist kein Leben,
Stets Bein vor Bein macht deutsch und schwer.
Ich hiess den Wind mich aufwärts heben,
Ich lernte mit den Vögeln schweben, —
Nach Süden flog ich über's Meer.

Vernunft! Verdriessliches Geschäfte!
Das bringt uns allzubald an's Ziel!
Im Fliegen lernt' ich, was mich äffte, —
Schon fühl' ich Muth und Blut und Säfte
Zu neuem Leben, neuem Spiel . . .

Einsam zu denken nenn' ich weise,
Doch einsam singen — wäre dumm!
So hört ein Lied zu eurem Preise

Do you mock me feathered joker?
Mentally I'm in rough shape,
Might my feelings too be broken?
Fear my rage you jackanapes! —
Still, the poet rhymes — and though it
Spoiled his mood 'twas all he could.
— "Yes, my man, you are a poet"
Shrugs the pecker in the wood.

In the South[7]

I perch now midst the crooked arbor
And leave my weariness to sway.
A bird enticed me to this harbor,
Within this nest I cool my ardor.
Yet where am I? Away! Away!

The sleeping sea, its color fleeting,
A purple sail, pure indolence.
Rocks, fig trees, spires and harbor meeting,
Around me idylls, sheep are bleating —
Absorb me, southern innocence!

Just step by step — that is not living,
The German stride's too dull for me.
I asked the wind to lift me heaving,
With[8] birds I soared without misgiving —
And south I flew across the sea.

Reason! A grim preoccupation!
Too soon it brings us all the way!
In flight I saw my limitation —
Now juices flow for new creation
For life renewed and dawn of play . . .

It's wise to think in solitary,
But sing alone? — There wisdom ends!
I've come to sing your praises merry

Und setzt euch still um mich im Kreise,
Ihr schlimmen Vögelchen, herum!

So jung, so falsch, so umgetrieben
Scheint ganz ihr mir gemacht zum Lieben
Und jedem schönen Zeitvertreib?
Im Norden — ich gesteh's mit Zaudern —
Liebt' ich ein Weibchen, alt zum Schaudern:
„Die Wahrheit" hiess dies alte Weib . . .

Die fromme Beppa.

So lang noch hübsch mein Leibchen,
Lohnt's sich schon, fromm zu sein.
Man weiss, Gott liebt die Weibchen,
Die hübschen obendrein.
Er wird's dem armen Mönchlein
Gewisslich gern verzeih'n,
Dass er, gleich manchem Mönchlein,
So gern will bei mir sein.

Kein grauer Kirchenvater!
Nein, jung noch und oft roth,
Oft trotz dem grausten Kater
Voll Eifersucht und Noth.
Ich liebe nicht die Greise,
Er liebt die Alten nicht:
Wie wunderlich und weise
Hat Gott dies eingericht!

Die Kirche weiss zu leben,
Sie prüft Herz und Gesicht.
Stets will sie mir vergeben, —
Ja, wer vergiebt mir nicht!
Man lispelt mit dem Mündchen,
Man knixt und geht hinaus,
Und mit dem neuen Sündchen
Löscht man das alte aus.

Be still, sit down, and with me tarry,
My little birds, my naughty friends!

So young, so false, and so beguiling
It seems love looks upon me smiling
And offers ev'ry charm of youth?
Up north — I say it though I waver —
I loved a crone so old I quaver:
This woman bore the name of "truth" . . .

Pious Beppa[9]

As long as I'm curvaceous,
Being pious is no test.
To young girls God is gracious,
He loves the cute ones best.
He will forgive the friar
Forgive him certainly,
That he, like other friars,
So wants to be with me.

He is no gray Church Father!
No, young and full of sap,
Hung over he'll still bother
To play the jealous chap.
I do not love the ageing,
He does not love the old:
How wondrous and engaging
When God's designs unfold!

The Church, it knows of living,
It checks us thoroughly.
And always it's forgiving —
Who would not pardon me!
One whispers low and steady,
One kneels and wipes at tears,
And when the new sin's ready
The old one disappears.

Gelobt sei Gott auf Erden,
Der hübsche Mädchen liebt
Und derlei Herzbeschwerden
Sich selber gern vergiebt.
So lang noch hübsch mein Leibchen,
Lohnt sich's schon, fromm zu sein:
Als altes Wackelweibchen
Mag mich der Teufel frein!

Der geheimnissvolle Nachen.

Gestern Nachts, als Alles schlief,
Kaum der Wind mit ungewissen
Seufzern durch die Gassen lief,
Gab mir Ruhe nicht das Kissen,
Noch der Mohn, noch, was sonst tief
Schlafen macht, — ein gut Gewissen.

Endlich schlug ich mir den Schlaf
Aus dem Sinn und lief zum Strande.
Mondhell war's und mild, — ich traf
Mann und Kahn auf warmem Sande,
Schläfrig beide, Hirt und Schaf: —
Schläfrig stiess der Kahn vom Lande.

Eine Stunde, leicht auch zwei,
Oder war's ein Jahr? — da sanken
Plötzlich mir Sinn und Gedanken
In ein ew'ges Einerlei,
Und ein Abgrund ohne Schranken
That sich auf: — da war's vorbei! —

— Morgen kam: auf schwarzen Tiefen
Steht ein Kahn und ruht und ruht . . .
Was geschah? so rief's, so riefen
Hundert bald: was gab es? Blut? — —
Nichts geschah! Wir schliefen, schliefen
Alle — ach, so gut! so gut!

Praise God who loves a maiden,
As pretty as she lives,
His heart by sin is laden,
Which he himself forgives.
As long as I'm curvaceous,
Being pious is no test:
When old and unsalacious,
The devil take the rest!

The Mysterious Bark[10]

Yesternight, all were asleep,
How the wind with steps uncertain
Sighing through the streets did creep,
Rest was not in pillow, curtain,
Poppy, slumber potion deep
Nor good conscience — which unburdens.

Finally I left my bed
Dressed and ran down to the shoreline.
Tender mild the night — I met
Man and bark on sand in moonshine,
Sleepy both, the man and pet: —
Sleepily the bark took to the brine.

Just one hour, more than one,
Or was it a year? — my thinking
And feeling left me, sinking
Down to timeless tedium,
Chasms opened, I stood shrinking
Bounds dissolved: — then it was done!

— Morning came: On blackness seeping
Rests a bark, it rides the swell . . .
What took place? Thus crying, weeping
Hundreds ask: what was this? Hell? — —
Nothing happened! We were sleeping
Sleeping *all* — so well! so well!

Liebeserklärung.
(bei der aber der Dichter in eine Grube fiel —).

Oh Wunder! Fliegt er noch?
Er steigt empor, und seine Flügel ruhn?
    Was hebt und trägt ihn doch?
Was ist ihm Ziel und Zug und Zügel nun?

    Gleich Stern und Ewigkeit
Lebt er in Höhn jetzt, die das Leben flieht,
    Mitleidig selbst dem Neid — :
Und hoch flog, wer ihn auch nur schweben sieht!

    Oh Vogel Albatross!
Zur Höhe treibt's mit ew'gem Triebe mich.
    Ich dachte dein: da floss
Mir Thrän' um Thräne, — ja, ich liebe dich!

Lied eines theokritischen Ziegenhirten.
Da lieg' ich, krank im Gedärm, —
Mich fressen die Wanzen.
Und drüben noch Licht und Lärm!
Ich hör's, sie tanzen . . .

Sie wollte um diese Stund'
Zu mir sich schleichen.
Ich warte wie ein Hund, —
Es kommt kein Zeichen.

Das Kreuz, als sie's versprach?
Wie konnte sie lügen?
— Oder läuft sie Jedem nach,
Wie meine Ziegen?

Woher ihr seid'ner Rock? —
Ah, meine Stolze?

Declaration of Love[11]
(whereby however the poet fell into a ditch —)

Oh wonder! Does he fly?
He climbs aloft, and yet his pinions rest?
    What lifts and bears him high?
What are his goal and course and limit's test?

    Star and eternity
He lives now in the heights that living shuns,
    Forgives all jealousy — :
Who sees him fly, they too are soaring ones!

    Oh albatross! I know
That to the heights I am forever lured.
    I thought of you: tears flow
And do not cease — I love you noble bird!

Song of a Theocritical Goatherd[12,13]

I lie here, stomach aching —
With bedbugs in my pants.
Close by, the noise they're making!
I hear it, how they dance . . .

She was supposed to slip away
And join me as my lover.
I wait here like a stray —
There's no sign of her.

The cross, on which she swore to come?
How could she be untrue?
— Does she chase everyone,
Like my old goats do?

That silken dress, pray tell?
Proud girl, have you been good?

Es wohnt noch mancher Bock
An diesem Holze?

— Wie kraus und giftig macht
Verliebtes Warten!
So wächst bei schwüler Nacht
Giftpilz im Garten.

Die Liebe zehrt an mir
Gleich sieben Uebeln, —
Nichts mag ich essen schier.
Lebt wohl, ihr Zwiebeln!

Der Mond gieng schon in's Meer,
Müd sind alle Sterne,
Grau kommt der Tag daher, —
Ich stürbe gerne.

„Diesen ungewissen Seelen".
Diesen ungewissen Seelen
Bin ich grimmig gram.
All ihr Ehren ist ein Quälen,
All ihr Lob ist Selbstverdruss und Scham.

Dass ich nicht an *ihrem* Stricke
Ziehe durch die Zeit,
Dafür grüsst mich ihrer Blicke
Giftig-süsser hoffnungsloser Neid.

Möchten sie mir herzhaft fluchen
Und die Nase drehn!
Dieser Augen hülflos Suchen
Soll bei mir auf ewig irre gehn.

Narr in Verzweiflung.
Ach! Was ich schrieb auf Tisch und Wand
Mit Narrenherz und Narrenhand,

Does more than one buck dwell
In this little wood?

— Lethally love makes us wait,
It burns, it hardens!
As hot nights germinate
Toadstools in gardens.

Love eats away at me
Like seven deadly sins —
I can barely eat or see.
Farewell dear onions!

The moon sets in the sea,
And stars fade from the sky,
Gray dawn comes 'round for me —
I just want to die.

"People Who Are Vacillating"[14]

People who are vacillating
Make my anger flame.
When they honor they are hating,[15]
All their praise is self-contempt and shame.

I'm not bound by *their* convention
As I wander free,
In their gaze is apprehension,
Poison-laced their hopeless jealousy.

May they curse me all to blazes,
Spit for all to see!
Though they seek with helpless gazes,
None will ever find their mark in me.

Fool in Despair

Oh! What I wrote on board and wall
With foolish heart and foolish scrawl,[16]

Das sollte Tisch und Wand mir zieren? . . .

Doch *ihr* sagt: „Narrenhände schmieren, —
Und Tisch und Wand soll man purgieren,
Bis auch die letzte Spur verschwand!"

Erlaubt! Ich lege Hand mit an —,
Ich lernte Schwamm und Besen führen,
Als Kritiker, als Wassermann.

Doch, wenn die Arbeit abgethan,
Säh' gern ich euch, ihr Ueberweisen,
Mit Weisheit Tisch und Wand besch . . . . . .

Rimus remedium.
Oder: Wie kranke Dichter sich trösten.

Aus deinem Munde,
Du speichelflüssige Hexe Zeit,
Tropft langsam Stund' auf Stunde.
Umsonst, dass all mein Ekel schreit:
„Fluch, Fluch dem Schlunde
    Der Ewigkeit!"

Welt — ist von Erz:
Ein glühender Stier, — der hört kein Schrein.
Mit fliegenden Dolchen schreibt der Schmerz
Mir in's Gebein:
    „Welt hat kein Herz,
Und Dummheit wär's, ihr gram drum sein!"

Giess alle Mohne,
Giess, Fieber! Gift mir in's Gehirn!
Zu lang schon prüfst du mir Hand und Stirn.
Was frägst du? Was? „Zu welchem — Lohne?"
    — — Ha! Fluch der Dirn'
Und ihrem Hohne!

Was meant to help me decorate? . . .

But *you* say: "Foolish hands desecrate —
And we the walls must expurgate,
Remove all traces big and small!"

Allow me! This I can enjoy —
I've wielded sponge and broom for all,
As critic and as water boy.

But, when I've finished your employ,
I ask you, you of super wit,
Your wisdom on the walls to sh . . . . . .

Rimus remedium[17]
Or: How Sick Poets Console Themselves

Time is dour,
A witch who drools incessantly,
Drips hour upon hour.
In vain, disgust cries out of me:
    "Curse, curse the power
    Of eternity!"

World — brazen hard:
A glowing bull[18] — it hears no moan.
Pain shoots through me and bores like a dart
Into my bone:
    "World has no heart,
And stupid he, who'd therefore groan!"

Your poppies pour,
Pour, fever! poison in my brain!
Too long already you bring me pain.
What would you ask? What? "For what *reward*?"
    — — Ha! Curse the whore
And her disdain!

Nein! Komm zurück!
Draussen ist's kalt, ich höre regnen —
Ich sollte dir zärtlicher begegnen?
— Nimm! Hier ist Gold: wie glänzt das Stück! —
    Dich heissen „Glück"?
Dich, Fieber, segnen? —

    Die Thür springt auf!
Der Regen sprüht nach meinem Bette!
Wind löscht das Licht, — Unheil in Hauf'!
— Wer jetzt nicht hundert *Reime* hätte,
    Ich wette, wette,
Der gienge drauf!

                    „*Mein Glück*!"
Die Tauben von San Marco seh ich wieder:
Still ist der Platz, Vormittag ruht darauf.
In sanfter Kühle schick' ich müssig Lieder
Gleich Taubenschwärmen in das Blau hinauf —
    Und locke sie zurück,
Noch einen Reim zu hängen in's Gefieder
— mein Glück! Mein Glück!

Du stilles Himmels-Dach, blau-licht, von Seide,
Wie schwebst du schirmend ob des bunten Bau's,
Den ich — was sag ich? — liebe, fürchte, *neide* . . .
Die Seele wahrlich tränk' ich gern ihm aus!
    Gäb' ich sie je zurück? —
Nein, still davon, du Augen-Wunderweide!
— mein Glück! Mein Glück!

Du strenger Thurm, mit welchem Löwendrange
Stiegst du empor hier, siegreich, sonder Müh!
Du überklingst den Platz mit tiefem Klange — :
Französisch, wärst du sein accent aigu?
Blieb ich gleich dir zurück,

No! Please don't go!
Outside it's cold, I hear it raining —
I'll cherish you without complaining?
— Here! Take my gold: it glitters so! —
     "Happiness" — No?
Fever is sustaining? —

     The door panes fly!
Rain lashes in, to my bed it climbs!
The lamp blows out — havoc is nigh!
— Who did not own a hundred *rhymes,*
     Betimes, betimes,
Would surely die!

                    "*My Happiness!*"[19]
I see again the pigeons of San Marco:
The square is still, all bathed in sunny leisure.
In gentle morn I idly let my songs flow
Like swarms of pigeons high into the azure —
     And still caress,
Them, tucking one more rhyme into their feathers
— my happiness!

You silent, blue-lit, silky heaven's awning,
Protectively above the colored stone,
I love, and fear, and *envy* — you are yawning . . .
Indeed I'd drink its soul into my own!
     Would I let it egress? —
No, silence, feast for eyes, in splendor dawning!
— my happiness!

You tower stern, with lion force ascending
Triumphantly, no effort, in full view!
Across the square your throaty peal suspending — :
In French you'd be its own *accent aigu?*
     To stay would be duress,

Ich wüsste, aus welch seidenweichem Zwange . . .
— mein Glück! Mein Glück!

Fort, fort, Musik! Lass erst die Schatten dunkeln
Und wachsen bis zur braunen lauen Nacht!
Zum Tone ist's zu früh am Tag, noch funkeln
Die Gold-Zieraten nicht in Rosen-Pracht,
Noch blieb viel Tag zurück,
Viel Tag für Dichten, Schleichen, Einsam-Munkeln
— mein Glück! Mein Glück!

Nach neuen Meeren.

Dorthin — *will* ich; und ich traue
Mir fortan und meinem Griff.
Offen liegt das Meer, in's Blaue
Treibt mein Genueser Schiff.

Alles glänzt mir neu und neuer,
Mittag schläft auf Raum und Zeit — :
Nur *dein* Auge — ungeheuer
Blickt mich's an, Unendlichkeit!

Sils-Maria.

Hier sass ich, wartend, wartend, — doch auf Nichts,
Jenseits von Gut und Böse, bald des Lichts
Geniessend, bald des Schattens, ganz nur Spiel,
Ganz See, ganz Mittag, ganz Zeit ohne Ziel.

Da, plötzlich, Freundin! wurde Eins zu Zwei —
— Und Zarathustra gieng an mir vorbei . . .

An den Mistral.
Ein Tanzlied.

Mistral-Wind, du Wolken-Jäger,
Trübsal-Mörder, Himmels-Feger,
Brausender, wie lieb' ich dich!

Like yours, a bond of silken strands unending . . .
— my happiness!

Go, music, go! Let shadows start preparing
To grow into the brown and balmy night!
Too early in the day for chimes, the flaring
Of gilded trim awaits a rosy light,
 Much does the day compress,
Much time for verses, prowling, secret sharing
— my happiness!

On to New Seas[20]

Out there — thus I *will*; so doing
Trust myself now and my grip.
Open lies the sea, its blueing
Swallows my Genoese ship.

All things now are new and beaming,
Space and time their noon decree — :,
Only *your* eye — monstrous, gleaming
Stares at me, infinity![21]

Sils-Maria[22]

There I sat, waiting, waiting — yet for naught,
Transcending good and evil, sometimes caught
In light, sometimes caught in shadow, all game,
All sea, all midday, all time without aim.

At once then, my friend! One turned into Two —
— And Zarathustra strode into my view . . .

To the Mistral
A Dance Song

Mistral wind, you rain-cloud reaper,
Sadness slayer, heaven sweeper,
Blustering, how I love you!

Sind wir Zwei nicht Eines Schoosses
Erstlingsgabe, Eines Looses
Vorbestimmte ewiglich?

Hier auf glatten Felsenwegen
Lauf' ich tanzend dir entgegen,
Tanzend, wie du pfeifst und singst:
Der du ohne Schiff und Ruder
Als der Freiheit freister Bruder
Ueber wilde Meere springst.

Kaum erwacht, hört' ich dein Rufen,
Stürmte zu den Felsenstufen,
Hin zur gelben Wand am Meer.
Heil! da kamst du schon gleich hellen
Diamantnen Stromesschnellen
Sieghaft von den Bergen her.

Auf den ebnen Himmels-Tennen
Sah ich deine Rosse rennen,
Sah den Wagen, der dich trägt,
Sah die Hand dir selber zücken,
Wenn sie auf der Rosse Rücken
Blitzesgleich die Geissel schlägt, —

Sah dich aus dem Wagen springen,
Schneller dich hinabzuschwingen,
Sah dich wie zum Pfeil verkürzt
Senkrecht in die Tiefe stossen, —
Wie ein Goldstrahl durch die Rosen
Erster Morgenröthen stürzt.

Tanze nun auf tausend Rücken,
Wellen-Rücken, Wellen-Tücken —
Heil, wer *neue* Tänze schafft!
Tanzen wir in tausend Weisen,

Are we not of one womb's making,
First born of one fate unbreaking,
Predetermined just we two?

Here on stony pathways sliding
I run to you dancing, gliding,
Dancing as you pipe and sing:
You without a ship and rudder
You as freedom's freest brother
Over raging seas do spring.

Scarce awake, I heard you calling,
Rushed to where the cliffs are falling
Golden walled into the sea.
Hail! You came like rapids teeming,
Glitter bright and diamond gleaming
From the peaks triumphantly.

'Cross the plains of heaven dashing
I saw horses, hooves a-flashing,
Saw the carriage where you stand,
Saw your hand and how it quivered,
When it to the steeds delivered
Lightning-like the whip's command —

Saw you toss the reins and plummet,
Faster from your airy summit,[23]
Diving like an arrow bright
Glowing as the distances closes —
Like a ray of gold on roses[24]
Struck by daybreak's early light.

On a thousand backs we're dancing,
Billow-backs and backs of chancing —
Hail to dances *new,* say we!
Let us dance in every manner,

Frei — sei *unsre* Kunst geheissen,
Fröhlich — *unsre* Wissenschaft!

Raffen wir von jeder Blume
Eine Blüthe uns zum Ruhme
Und zwei Blätter noch zum Kranz!
Tanzen wir gleich Troubadouren
Zwischen Heiligen und Huren,
Zwischen Gott und Welt den Tanz!

Wer nicht tanzen kann mit Winden,
Wer sich wickeln muss mit Binden,
Angebunden, Krüppel-Greis,
Wer da gleicht den Heuchel-Hänsen,
Ehren-Tölpeln, Tugend-Gänsen,
Fort aus unsrem Paradeis!

Wirbeln wir den Staub der Strassen
Allen Kranken in die Nasen,
Scheuchen wir die Kranken-Brut!
Lösen wir die ganze Küste
Von dem Odem dürrer Brüste,
Von den Augen ohne Muth!

Jagen wir die Himmels-Trüber,
Welten-Schwärzer, Wolken-Schieber,
Hellen wir das Himmelreich!
Brausen wir . . . oh aller freien
Geister Geist, mit dir zu Zweien
Braust mein Glück dem Sturme gleich. —

— Und dass ewig das Gedächtniss
Solchen Glücks, nimm sein Vermächtniss,
Nimm den *Kranz* hier mit hinauf!
Wirf ihn höher, ferner, weiter,
Stürm' empor die Himmelsleiter,
Häng ihn — an den Sternen auf!

Free — so shall be *our* art's banner,
Joyful — shall *our* science be!

From each flower let us garner
Just one blossom for our honor,
For our wreath just two leaves worth!
Then like troubadours in riches
We shall dance 'tween saints and bitches,
Dance our dance 'tween God and Earth!

He who cannot dance with twisters,
Bandages his wounds and blisters,
Bound and old and paralyzed;
He who reeks of sanctimony,
Honor-fools and virtues phony,
Out of our paradise!

Let us whirl the dust in doses
Into sickly people's noses,
Let us shoo these sickly flies!
This whole coast we must unshackle
From their shrivel-breasted cackle,
From these courage-vacant eyes!

Let us chase the overcasters,
World maligners, rain-cloud pastors,
Let us tear the dark sky's veil!
Let us roar . . . free spirit's spirit
Joy uplifts me when you're near it
Makes me *bluster* like a gale! —

— And to mark this joy forever,
Leave a will that time can't sever,
Take this *wreath* up where you are!
Hurl it higher, further, madder,
Storm the sky on heaven's ladder,
Hang it there — upon a star!

Idylls from Messina.[1]

Prinz Vogelfrei.

So hang ich denn auf krummem Aste
Hoch über Meer und Hügelchen:
Ein Vogel lud mich her zu Gaste —
Ich flog ihm nach und rast' und raste
Und schlage mit den Flügelchen.

Das weisse Meer ist eingeschlafen,
Es schläft mir jedes Weh und Ach.
Vergessen hab' ich Ziel und Hafen,
Vergessen Furcht und Lob und Strafen:
Jetzt flieg ich jedem Vogel nach.

Nur Schritt für Schritt — das ist kein Leben!
Stäts Bein vor Bein macht müd und schwer!
Ich lass mich von den Winden heben,
Ich liebe es, mit Flügeln schweben
Und hinter jedem Vogel her.

Vernunft? — das ist ein bös Geschäfte:
Vernunft und Zunge stolpern viel!
Das Fliegen gab mir neue Kräfte
Und lehrt' mich schönere Geschäfte,
Gesang und Scherz und Liederspiel.

Einsam zu denken — das ist weise.
Einsam zu singen — das ist dumm!
So horcht mir denn auf meine Weise
Und setzt euch still um mich im Kreise,
Ihr schönen Vögelchen, herum!

Die kleine Brigg, genannt „das Engelchen".

Engelchen: so nennt man mich —
Jetzt ein Schiff, dereinst ein Mädchen,
Ach, noch immer sehr ein Mädchen!

Prince Vogelfrei [2]

I perched then midst the crooked arbor
High above sea and[3] little hill.
A bird enticed me to this harbor,
I flew after and cooled[4] my ardor
Until my beating wings lay still.

The[5] sea's asleep, its color fleeting,
Within me sleep all woes and sighs.
Forgotten goal[6] and port, retreating,
Fear, praise,[7] punishment are receding:
I'll follow any bird that flies!

Just[8] step by step — that life is boring!
Dull plodding makes[9] one heavy, spent!
I let the wind embrace me, roaring,
I love to stretch my wings for soaring,
For chasing birds in steep ascent.

Reason?[10] — that's[11] a thing that glowers:
The tongue and reason stumble along!
But flying gave me novel[12] powers,
Taught me how to spend the hours
Singing, joking,[13] and playing songs.

Thinking alone — that's wise as can be.
But sing alone? — There wisdom ends!
So listen to my melody
Be still, and form a circle 'round me,
You lovely little feathered friends!

The Small[14] *Brig Called "The Little Angel"*[15]

Little Angel: so I'm called —
Now a ship, but once a maiden
Oh, still very much a maiden!

Denn es dreht um Liebe sich
Stäts mein feines Steuerrädchen.

Engelchen: so nennt man mich —
Bin geschmückt mit hundert Fähnchen,
Und das schönste Kapitänchen
Bläht an meinem Steuer sich,
Als das hundert erste Fähnchen.

Engelchen: so nennt man mich —
Ueberall hin, wo ein Flämmchen
Für mich glüht, lauf ich ein Lämmchen
Meinen Weg sehnsüchtiglich:
Immer war ich solch ein Lämmchen.

Engelchen: so nennt man mich —
Glaubt ihr wohl, dass wie ein Hündchen
Bell'n ich kann und dass mein Mündchen
Dampf und Feuer wirft um sich?
Ach, des Teufels ist mein Mündchen!

Engelchen: so nennt man mich —
Sprach ein bitterböses Wörtchen
Einst, dass schnell zum letzten Oertchen
Mein Geliebtester entwich:
Ja, er starb an diesem Wörtchen!

Engelchen: so nennt man mich —
Kaum gehört, sprang ich vom Klippchen
In den Grund und brach ein Rippchen,
Dass die liebe Seele wich:
Ja, sie wich durch dieses Rippchen!

Engelchen: so nennt man mich —
Meine Seele, wie ein Kätzchen,
That eins, zwei, drei, vier, fünf Sätzchen,

For my little helm's enthralled
By love, and constant waiting.

Little Angel: so they say —
Decked with little banners streaming,
At my helm puffed up and beaming
Handsome little captain sways,
Hundred-first of banners streaming.

Little Angel: they call me —
Wherever a little flicker
Glows, I little lamb, am quicker,
Run toward it longingly:
Ever little lamb, and quicker.

Little Angel: as I'm known —
My little mouth can bark as well
As a little dog, can you tell
It spews smoke and is fire-prone?
Oh, my little mouth is hell!

Little Angel: that's my name —
Once spoke a wicked little word
To my most beloved, which he heard,
Then to that last little place he came:
Yes, he died of this little word!

Little Angel: yes that's me —
Then I sprang from a little height
And broke a little rib that night,
Out of which my soul broke free:
Yes, it issued from my rib that night.

Little Angel: one may quip —
My soul, with little kitty's feet,
Made one to three four little leaps,

Schwang dann in dies Schiffchen sich —
Ja, sie hat geschwinde Tätzchen.

Engelchen: so nennt man mich —
Jetzt ein Schiff, dereinst ein Mädchen,
Ach, noch immer sehr ein Mädchen!
Denn es dreht um Liebe sich
Stäts mein feines Steuerrädchen.

Lied des Ziegenhirten.
(An meinen Nachbar Theokrit von Syrakusa.)

Da lieg ich, krank im Gedärm —
Mich fressen die Wanzen.
Und drüben noch Licht und Lärm:
Ich hör's, sie tanzen.

Sie wollte um diese Stund'
Zu mir sich schleichen:
Ich warte wie ein Hund —
Es kommt kein Zeichen!

Das Kreuz, als sie's versprach!
Wie konnte sie lügen?
Oder läuft sie Jedem nach,
Wie meine Ziegen?

Woher ihr seidner Rock? —
Ah, meine Stolze?
Es wohnt noch mancher Bock
An diesem Holze?

Wie kraus und giftig macht
Verliebtes Warten!
So wächst bei schwüler Nacht
Giftpilz im Garten.

And landed in this little ship —
Yes, its little paws are fleet.

Little Angel: so I'm called —
Now a ship, but once a maiden
Oh, still very much a maiden!
For my little helm's enthralled
By love, and constant waiting.

Song of the Goatherd[16]
(To my neighbor Theocritus of Syracuse)

I lie here, stomach aching —
With bed bugs in my pants.
Close by, the noise they're making:
I hear it, how they dance.

She[17] was supposed to slip away
And join me as my lover:
I wait here like a stray —
There's no sign of her!

The cross, on which she swore to come!
How could she be untrue?
Does she chase everyone,
Like my old goats do?

That silken dress, pray tell? —
Proud girl, have you been good?
Does more than one buck dwell
In this little wood?

Lethally love makes us wait,
It burns, it hardens!
As hot nights germinate
Toadstools in gardens.

Die Liebe zehrt an mir
Gleich sieben Uebeln —
Nichts mag ich essen schier,
Lebt wohl, ihr Zwiebeln!

Der Mond ging schon in's Meer,
Müd sind alle Sterne,
Grau kommt der Tag daher —
Ich stürbe gerne.

Die kleine Hexe.

So lang noch hübsch mein Leibchen,
Lohnt sichs schon, fromm zu sein.
Man weiss, Gott liebt die Weibchen,
Die hübschen obendrein.
Er wird's dem art'gen Mönchlein
Gewisslich gern verzeihn,
Dass er, gleich manchem Mönchlein,
So gern will bei mir sein.

Kein grauer Kirchenvater!
Nein, jung noch und oft roth,
Oft gleich dem grausten Kater
Voll Eifersucht und Noth!
Ich liebe nicht die Greise,
Er liebt die Alten nicht:
Wie wunderlich und weise
Hat Gott dies eingericht!

Die Kirche zu leben,
Sie prüft Herz und Gesicht.
Stäts will sie mir vergeben: —
Ja wer vergiebt mir nicht!
Man lispelt mit dem Mündchen,
Man knixt und geht hinaus

Love eats away at me
Like seven deadly sins —
I can barely eat or see,
Farewell, dear onions!

The moon sets in the sea,
Spent stars fade from the sky,
Grey dawn comes 'round for me —
I just want to die.

The Little Witch[18],[19]

As long as I'm curvaceous,
Being pious is no test.
To young girls God is gracious,
He loves the cute ones best.
He will forgive the friar,
Forgive him certainly
That he, like other friars,
So wants to be with me.

He is no gray Church Father!
No, young and full of sap,
As tomcat he'll still bother
To play the jealous chap.[20]
I do not love the ageing,
He does not love the old:[21]
How wondrous and engaging
When God's designs unfold!

The Church, it knows of living,
It checks us thoroughly.
And always it's forgiving: —
Who would not pardon me!
One whispers low and steady,
One kneels and wipes at tears,

Und mit dem neuen Sündchen
Löscht man das alte aus.

Gelobt sei Gott auf Erden,
Der hübsche Mädchen liebt
Und derlei Herzbeschwerden
Sich selber gern vergiebt!
So lang noch hübsch mein Leibchen,
Lohnt sich's schon, fromm zu sein:
Als altes Wackelweibchen
Mag mich der Teufel frein!

Das nächtliche Geheimniss.

Gestern Nachts, als Alles schlief,
Kaum der Wind mit ungewissen
Seufzern durch die Gassen lief,
Gab mir Ruhe nicht das Kissen,
Noch der Mohn, noch, was sonst tief
Schlafen macht — ein gut Gewissen.

Endlich schlug ich mir den Schlaf
Aus dem Sinn und lief zum Strande.
Mondhell war's und mild — ich traf
Mann und Kahn auf warmem Sande,
Schläfrig beide, Hirt und Schaf: —
Schläfrig stiess der Kahn vom Lande.

Eine Stunde, leicht auch zwei,
Oder war's ein Jahr? — da sanken
Plötzlich mir Sinn und Gedanken
In ein ew'ges Einerlei,
Und ein Abgrund ohne Schranken
That sich auf: — da war's vorbei! —

Morgen kam: auf schwarzen Tiefen
Steht ein Kahn und ruht und ruht — —

And when the new sin's ready
The old one disappears.

Praise God who loves a maiden,
As pretty as she lives,
His heart by sin is laden,
Which he himself forgives.
As long as I'm curvaceous,
Being pious is no test:
When old and unsalacious,
The devil take[22] the rest!

The Nocturnal Mystery[23]

Yesternight, all were asleep,
How the wind with steps uncertain
Sighing through the streets did creep.
Rest was not in pillow, curtain,
Poppy, slumber potion deep,
Nor good conscience — which unburdens.

Finally I left my bed,
Dressed and ran down to the shoreline.
Tender mild the night — I met
Man and bark on sand in moonshine,
Sleepy both, the man and pet: —
Sleepily the bark took to the brine.

Just one hour, more than one,
Or was it a year? — my thinking
And feeling left me, sinking
Down to timeless tedium.
Chasms opened, I stood shrinking,
Bounds dissolved: — then it was done!

— Morning came: On blackness seeping
Rests a bark, it rides the swell . . .

Was geschah? so riefs, so riefen
Hundert bald — was gab es? Blut? —
Nichts geschah! Wir schliefen, schliefen
Alle — ach, so gut! so gut!

„Pia, caritatevole, amorosissima".
(Auf dem campo santo.)

O Mädchen, das dem Lamme
Das zarte Fellchen kraut,
Dem Beides, Licht und Flamme,
Aus beiden Augen schaut,
Du lieblich Ding zum Scherzen,
Du Liebling weit und nah,
So fromm, so mild von Herzen,
Amorosissima!

Was riss so früh die Kette?
Wer hat dein Herz betrübt?
Und liebtest du, wer hätte
Dich nicht genug geliebt? —
Du schweigst — doch sind die Thränen
Den milden Augen nah:
Du schwiegst — und starbst vor Sehnen,
Amorosissima?

Vogel Albatross.

O Wunder! Fliegt er noch?
Er steigt empor und seine Flügel ruhn!
Was hebt und trägt ihn doch?
Was ist ihm Ziel und Zug und Zügel nun?

Er flog zu höchst — nun hebt
Der Himmel selbst den siegreich Fliegenden:
Nun ruht er still und schwebt,
Den Sieg vergessend und den Siegenden.

What took place? Thus crying, weeping
Hundreds ask: what was this? Hell?[24] — —
Nothing happened! We were sleeping,
Sleeping all — so well, so well.

"Pia, caritatevole, amorosissima"[25]
(On Campo Santo)

Oh maiden sweetly petting
A curly lamb that plays,
With flashing eyes begetting
A bright and fiery gaze;
You lovely friend of jesting,
You favorite wide and far,
So pious, so arresting
Amorosissima!

What broke the chain so early?
Who caused your heart to yearn?
And if you loved, then surely
One loved you in return? —
You're still — yet tears are thronging,
How moist your mild eyes are:
Were still — you died of longing,
Amorosissima?

Bird Albatross[26,27]

Oh wonder! Does he fly?
He climbs aloft, and yet his pinions rest?
What lifts and bears him high?
What are his goal and course and limit's test?

He flew highest — the sky
Itself lifts him where the air is thinner:
Now motionless on high
He soars, heedless both of win and winner.[28]

Gleich Stern und Ewigkeit
Lebt er in Höhn jetzt, die das Leben flieht,
Mitleidig selbst dem Neid — :
Und hoch flog, wer ihn auch nur schweben sieht!

O Vogel Albatross!
Zur Höhe treibt's mit ew'gem Triebe mich!
Ich dachte dein: da floss
Mir Thrän' um Thräne — ja, ich liebe dich!

Vogel-Urtheil.

Als ich jüngst, mich zu erquicken,
Unter dunklen Bäumen sass,
Hört' ich ticken, leise ticken,
Zierlich, wie nach Takt und Maass.
Böse wurd' ich, zog Gesichter,
Endlich aber gab ich nach,
Bis ich gar, gleich einem Dichter,
Selber mit im Tiktak sprach.

Wie mir so im Versemachen
Silb' um Silb' ihr Hopsa sprang,
Musst ich plötzlich lachen, lachen
Eine Viertelstunde lang,
Du ein Dichter? Du ein Dichter?
Stehts mit deinem Kopf so schlecht? —
„Ja, mein Herr! Sie sind ein Dichter!"
— Also sprach der Vogel Specht.

Star and eternity,
He lives now in the heights[29] that living shuns,
Forgives all jealousy — :
Who sees him fly, they too are soaring ones!

Oh albatross! I know
That to the heights I am forever lured.
I thought of you: tears flow
And do not cease — I love you noble bird!

Bird-Judgment[30]

Stopped to rest one day, while walking,
Seated under shady trees,
When I heard a ticking tocking
Dainty rhythm on the breeze.
I grew angry, made some faces —
But I lost my anger quick
And, as if in poet's paces
Started speaking tick tock tick.

As I sat, my verses making,
Syllables and sounds did pour,
Till I burst out laughing, shaking
For a quarter hour or more.
You a poet? You a poet?
Is your mind no longer good?
"Yes, my man! You are a poet!"
— Spoke the pecker in the wood.

Unpublished Fragments
(Spring 1881–Summer 1882)

11[1]

Make oneself indifferent to praise and blame; recipes for this. Establish a circle against it, that knows about our goals and standards and signifies praise and blame *for us*.

11[2]

Expand the concept of nutrition; do not design one's life incorrectly, as do those who have an eye merely for their preservation.

We must not let our life slip through our hands, through a "goal" — rather harvest the fruits of *all* our seasons.

We want to strive for the other, for everything that is external to us, as for our nourishment. Often they are the fruits that have grown ripe precisely for our year. — Must one always have the egoism of a robber or thief? Why not that of a gardener? Pleasure in caring for others, like caring for a garden!

11[3]

Formerly, in alchemy, it was believed that everything could be explained with *moral* concepts (affinity friendship drive etc.). The realm of morals grows ever smaller.

Use a single medication (e.g., quinine) and its "*moral*" effects for example!

11[4]

La Rochef⟨oucauld⟩ errs only in the fact that he estimates the motives he considers true to be lower than the other alleged motives: i.e., *at bottom he still believes* in the others and takes his *standard* from them: he disparages the human being in that he considers him *incapable* of certain motives.

11[5]

Our instinct of drives reaches in every case for the closest agreeable thing: but *not* for what is useful. Of course, in countless cases (especially due to selective breeding) what is agreeable to the drives is likewise simply what is useful! — The human being, arrogant even where he senses reasons and purposes, shuts his eyes in matters of morality when faced by the agreeable: *he* in particular wants his actions to appear as the consequence of a reasonable intent for lasting utility: he despises what is *momentarily agreeable* — : even though *precisely this* is the lever of all his powers.

The trick to a happy life is *to find the place* where the momentarily agreeable is also the enduringly most useful thing, where the senses and one's taste pronounce the same thing to be good as do reason and caution.

11[6]

The manner of living of women, who are essentially nurtured and do not work, could *immediately* be transformed into a philosophical existence! But just look at them in front of a display window full of finery and lingerie!

11[7]

Main thought! It is *not* nature that deceives us individuals and promotes its goals through our deception: rather, individuals explain the whole of existence to themselves according to individual i.e., false measures; we want to be right about this and consequently "nature" must appear as the deceiver. In truth there are no *individual truths,* rather nothing but individual

errors — the *individual* itself is an *error.* Everything that tran-
spires in us is in itself *something different* that we do not know:
it is we who insert intent and deception and morality into
nature. — But I differentiate between: the imagined individuals and the true "life-systems" of which each of us is an example — we throw them both together, whereas "the individual"
is merely a sum of conscious perceptions and judgments and
errors, a *belief,* a little piece of true life-system or many little pieces thought together and fabled together, a "unity" that
does not stand up. We are buds on a single tree — what do we
know of what can become of us in the interest of the tree! But
we have a consciousness as if we wanted to be and should be
everything, a fantasy of "ego" and *everything* "non-ego." *Cease
feeling ourselves to be such fantastical ego*! Learn step by step to
throw off the reputed individual! Discover the errors of the ego!
Realize *egoism as error*! Certainly do not construe altruism as
the opposite! That would be the love of the *other reputed* individuals! No! Get **beyond** "*me*" and "*you*"! **Perceive cosmically!**

11[8][1]

Egoism as the universal "megalomania" — to be inferred
likewise — physiologically.

11[9]

To cultivate the evil but indispensable drives just as that of
dissimulation (in art) hence harmlessly. Seek the *parallels* to
"art"!

11[10]

Wanting to know things as they are — that alone is the *good*
inclination: not looking over at others and seeing with other
eyes — that would merely be a *change of place* of egoistic seeing!
We want to heal ourselves of the great fundamental madness
of measuring everything according to ourselves: self-love is a false
and too-narrow expression; self-hatred and all affects are constantly active with this short leap; as if everything were *striving*

over to us. One walks through the lanes and thinks every eye is on us: and what would it amount to, if one eye and one word actually was on us! — no more than concerns *us* when someone's gaze and word are on someone else — we should personally be able to be just as indifferent! An increase in indifference! And *for this, practice* at seeing with *other* eyes: practice at seeing without human relationships, hence *objectively*! Cure the human-megalomania! Where does it come from? From *fear*: all intellectual power always had to snap back to personal-seeing. It's already a form of animal suffering. The highest selfishness does *not* have its opposite in the love for others!! Rather in neutral objective seeing! The *passion for this* despite all personal considerations, despite all "agreeable" and disagreeable "*truth*" is supreme — therefore the rarest to date!

11[11]

One must give human beings the courage for a new great **contempt,** e.g., for the rich, bureaucrats etc. Every *impersonal* form of life must be regarded as base and contemptible.

A. How much do I need in order to live in good health and pleasantly for myself?

B. How do I acquire this, in such a way that the acquisition is healthy and pleasant and useful to my mind, especially as recuperation?

c. How should I be thinking about others, in order to think as highly as possible of myself and to grow in my feeling of power?

d. How do I bring others to acknowledge my power?

e. How will the new nobility organize itself as the power-holding class? How will it distance others from itself, without making them into enemies and rivals?

11[12]

What precedes a purposeful action, in consciousness e.g., the image of chewing prior to chewing, is completely indefinite: and if I make it more scientifically exact, then this itself is without influence on the action. Innumerable individual movements are executed, of which we know nothing at all beforehand, and the *cleverness* of the tongue e.g., is much greater than the *cleverness of our consciousness* generally. I deny that these movements are produced by our will; they play out, and *remain unknown to us* — even their process we are only able to grasp in symbols (of touch hearing seeing of colors) and in individual pieces and moments — its essence, just like its continuing *course* remain foreign to us. **Perhaps imagination opposes** the real course and essence with something, a **fiction** that we are *accustomed* to taking as the essence.

11[13][2]

We hear only a little and uncertainly when we do not understand a language that is spoken around us. Likewise in the case of music that is foreign to *us,* like Chinese. Hearing *well* is therefore probably a continuous *guessing* and *filling in* of the few actually perceived sensations. *Understanding* is an amazingly fast considerate fantasizing and inferring: from two words we guess the sentence (when reading): from one vowel and 2 consonants we guess a word when listening, indeed many words we do *not* hear, yet *think* them heard. — What really *occurred* is hard to say after our *semblance* — since we were constantly making things up and judging throughout. Often when speaking with people I have their facial expression more clearly before me than my eyes are capable of perceiving: there is a fiction to their words, an interpreting of the facial gestures.

I suspect that we only see what we *know*; our eyes are constantly in practice in the manipulation of countless forms: — the biggest part of the picture is not sense impressions, but *products of the imagination.* Only small occasions and motives are taken from the senses and then this is used to make up things. *Imagination* should replace the "*unconscious*": imagination does not provide unconscious inferences so much as it *throws out possibilities* (when e.g., *sousreliefs*[3] turn into *reliefs* for the beholder).

Our "external world" is a *product of the imagination,* whereby earlier imaginings are reused for construction as habituated practiced activities. Colors, sounds are imaginings, they do not in the least correspond exactly to mechanical real events, but to our individual state. — —

11[14]

The ego[4] — not to be confused with the organic feeling of unity. —

11[15]

Obscure sneaky violent and pampered early on, by a petty and servile environment. — he upholds *obscurity above all principles,* in order to position himself this way and that in keeping with his own advantage.

11[16]

Purported expediency of nature, in selfishness, in the sex drive, where it is said that it uses the individual, in the sun's outpouring of light etc. — all fabrications! It is perhaps the last form of a *God*-representation — but this God is not very smart and is very unmerciful. Leopardi has the evil stepmother nature, Schopenhauer the "will." — Maybe with such apparent purposivenesses the purposiveness of humans can be illuminated. Something is achieved, and what gets achieved and everything that occurs in addition is *totally different* from the image that exists beforehand in the mind of the willing person — no bridge leads to the other side. "I eat in order to sate myself" — but what do I *know* about what satiety is! — In truth, satiety is achieved, but not *willed* — the momentary pleasure sensation with each bite, as long as hunger remains, is the motive: not the intention "in order," but as experiment with each bite to see *whether* it still tastes good. Our actions are, to the most convoluted degree, *experiments* as to *whether* this or that drive takes its pleasure in something; playful expressions of the urge for activity, which we misinterpret through the theory of purposes and incorrectly understand. We move our tentacles — and some drive or another finds its prey in what we catch, and makes us believe we *intended* to satisfy that drive.

11[17]

His bad character follows him to the highest peaks of his genius. —

11[18]

Scope of *fictionalizing* power: we can't do anything without previously drafting a *free image* of it — (though of course we don't know *how* this image relates to the action; the action is something essentially different and takes place in regions that are *inaccessible* to us). This image is very general, a schema — we think it is not only the guiding principle, but the kinetic force itself. Countless images are not followed by an activity, we close our eyes to this: the cases where something later occurs that "we willed" stay in our memory. — An *ideal image* precedes all of our development, the product of imagination: the real development is unknown to us. We *must* produce this image. The history of the human being and humankind runs its course unknown to us, but the ideal images and their history appears to us as development itself. Science cannot create it, but science is a main *nourishment* for this drive: in the long term we shy away from everything uncertain and mendacious, this fear and this disgust promote science. That fictionalizing drive should *guess,* not fantasize; guess something unknown from actual elements: it needs science i.e., the sum of what is certain and probable, in order to make up things with this material. This process exists already in *seeing*. It is a free production in all the senses, the biggest share of sense perception is *guessing*. All scientific books bore us if they do not feed this drive that wants to guess: the *certain does not do us good* if it doesn't want to be nourishment for this drive!

11[19]

Maybe all moral impulses can be traced to wanting-to-*have* and wanting-to-*hold.* The concept of having is constantly refining itself, we comprehend ever more how hard it is to have and how apparent possession still knows how to *withdraw* from us — so we practice having more subtly: until ultimately the complete *knowing* of a thing is the prerequisite for striving for it: often complete knowing already suffices us as possession, it has no more hiding place from us and can no longer run away from us. In this sense, knowledge would be the last stage of morality. Earlier examples are: to fantasize something for oneself and to now believe that one possesses it entirely, like the lover with his beloved, the father with his child: what pleasure there is now in possessing! — but appearance suffices here for us. We think of the things *that we can attain* in such a way that their possession seems highly valuable to us: we fabricate the enemy over whom we *hope* to triumph for the sake of our pride: and likewise the beloved woman and child. We first have an approximate calculation of the kinds of things we generally *can abscond with* — and now our imagination is busy making these future possessions extremely *valuable* to us (also offices honors interactions etc.). *We seek the philosophy that suits our possession* i.e., gilds it. The great reformers, like Mohammed, understand how to give the habits and ⟨the⟩⁵ possessions of human beings a new luster — not command them to strive for "something else," rather to see what they *want to and can have* as something higher (to "discover" more reason and wisdom and happiness in these things than they previously found in them). — Wanting to *have* oneself: self-mastery etc.

11[20]

Main question: according to what has the *table of values of goods* been made and changed? So that one property seemed more desirable than another?

What was easy to have (like e.g., nourishment) was relatively *underestimated.* The table of values does **not** *at all* correspond with the *degree of utility* (against Spencer).

11[21]

To describe the history of the *ego-feeling:* and to show how even in altruism this wanting-to-possess is the essential thing. To show that the main progress of morality does not lie in the concept "non-ego and ego," but in a sharper comprehension of what is true in others and in me and in nature, hence increasingly to liberate wanting-to-possess from the appearance of possession, from made-up possessions; hence to cleanse the ego-feeling of self-deception. Perhaps it ends with the fact that instead of the ego, we recognize the affinities and enmities of things, *multiplicities* therefore and their laws: that we *try to free* ourselves from the *error* of the ego (altruism has also so far been an error). Not "for the sake of others," but "live for the sake of the true"! Not "I and you!" How could we be permitted to promote "the other" (who himself is a *sum of delusion*!)! Re-create the ego-feeling! Weaken the personal inclination! Accustom the eye to the reality of things. Look away *temporarily as much as possible from persons*! What effects must this have! Seek to become master over *things* and thus satisfy one's wanting-to-possess! Do not want to possess human beings! — But doesn't this also mean that individuals are weakened? Something new has to be created: not *ego* and not *tu* and not *omnes*! [6]

NB. Not to *have to* and *want to* strive for *possessions* in youth!: likewise no *prestige,* in order to command others — these two impulses we should *not develop at all*! **Let** ourselves be **possessed** by things (not by persons) and by the greatest possible scope *of true things*! What *grows* from this remains to be seen: we are *arable land* for things. *Images of existence* should sprout from us: and we should be as this fertility requires us to be: our inclinations disinclinations are those of the arable land that is supposed to yield such fruits. The images of existence are the *most important thing* so far — they rule over humankind.

11[22]

The education of the genius.

11[23]

NB! Love science without thinking about its utility! But maybe it is a means of turning the human being into an artist in an unheard-of sense! Up till now it was supposed to *serve*. — A series of beautiful experiments is one of the highest pleasures of the theater.

11[24]

NB. "The chemical process is always greater than the net efficiency" Mayer.[7] "In good steam engines approximately 1/20, in guns 1/10, in mammals 1/5 of the combustion heat is converted to mechanical effect." On the squandering in nature! Then solar heat in Proctor![8] The state in relation to its utility! The great mind! Our intellectual work in relation to the utility that the drives derive from it! Therefore no false "utility as norm"! Squandering is simply not a fault: perhaps it is *necessary*. Also *the vehemence of the drives belongs here*.

11[25][9]

Innervation "exerts its control over muscle activity, probably without a noticeable expenditure of physical force, without an electric current and without a chemical process generally" according to Mayer — "as the energy expenditure of a *machinist* is something *infinitely small*." (Contact — influence of the motor nerves.)

11[26]

In the progress of civilization, the senses of human beings have become weaker, eyes and ears: because *fear* became smaller and the understanding more refined. Perhaps with the *increase of security* the *refinement of understanding* will no longer be necessary: and will *decrease*: as in China! In Europe the *struggle* against Christianity, the *anarchy* of opinions and the *competition* among *princes peoples and merchants* has so far *refined the understanding.*

11[27]

We are entering the age of *anarchy:* — but this is simultaneously the age of the smartest and freest individuals. Tremendously much intellectual energy is in reversal. Age of the genius: hitherto prevented by customs morality[10] etc.

11[28]

Depression as *thwarted* discharge. Principle: it was not the discharges, as powerful as they may have been, that caused humankind the greatest damage, but the thwarting of them. Depression, pathologically unpleasant sensations need to be eliminated — but this requires the *courage* to judge the terribleness of discharges differently and more favorably. Assassination attempts are better than creeping annoyances. Murders wars etc. open violence the evil of power should be given approval: if the evil of weakness from now on should be called *evil.*

11[29]

To demonstrate the error of positive philosophy: it wants to annihilate the anarchy of minds, and it will bring about the dull pressure of unsatisfied discharge (like China)!

11[30]

There is no beautiful and healthy custom governing our occupation with science. One thoughtlessly transfers the habits of other occupations e.g., of bureaucrats, clerks, gardeners, laborers. The aristocracy is so fruitful on the whole because it added on noble customs: the noblest is being able to tolerate boredom. Indeed, the scientific human being must limit himself daily for several hours to himself, and since often the ideas do not come right away, he must endure much boredom without impatience. The Indians understood this!

11[31]

Many of our drives find their discharge in a mechanically robust activity that *can be* expediently selected: without this there are corruptive and harmful discharges. Hatred rage sex drive etc. could be *put* to the *machine* and learn to work usefully, e.g., chopping wood or carrying letters or guiding a plow. One must work out one's drives. The life of a scholar in particular demands something of the sort. A few hours of the day absolutely must be withheld from meditation. All *sour mood* should be discharged: keep manual labor close by! Or running jumping riding. As a thinker one could do quite well at breaking in horses. Or commanding.

11[32]

The general history of science ultimately provides a concept for how the most ordinary intellectual arrangements come about.

11[33]

NB! In the molecule the history of the solar system could still play ⟨itself⟩ out and heat be produced from fall and thrust.

11[34]

The Chinese: without shame, without prejudices, loquacious, moderate: their passions opium gambling women. They love cleanliness.

11[35]

To acquire the advantages of a dead person for ourselves — no one cares about us, neither pro nor contra. To think oneself out of humankind, to unlearn desires of all kind: and apply the whole superabundance of strength to *looking* **on**. Be the *invisible onlooker*!!

11[36]

We are somehow in the *middle* — in respect of the magnitude of the world and the smallness of the infinite world. Or is an atom closer to us than the outermost end of the world? — *Is* the world for us not merely a summarizing of relations under one standard? As soon as this arbitrary standard is gone, our world *melts away*!

11[37]

We do not know a) the motives of an action; b) we do not know the action we perform; c) we do not know what becomes of it. But we believe the *opposite* about all three: the alleged motive, the alleged action and the alleged consequences belong to our known history of humanity, but they also affect its unknown history, as the sum each time of three errors.

In *any* case there is no *single* action to be done, but as many as there are *ideals* of the perfect human being. Useful, corruptive — are no "in-itself"; ideals are fictions atop more or less meager knowledge of mankind. — I deny absolute morality because I do not know an absolute goal of mankind. One has to know a healthy state in order to recognize an unhealthy one — but health itself is a representation that produces itself in us in keeping with *what already exists.* Spencer p. 302.[11] "Transitional states permeated by misery that rests on nonadaptability": says Spencer — and yet precisely this misery could be the most useful thing!

11[38]

I *seek* for myself and my peers the sunny nook in the midst of the actual current world, those sunny representations with which an abundance of well-being comes to us. Let each do this for himself and put aside generalities and concerns about "society"!

11[39]

Afflicted with oneself as if with a sickness — thus talents seemed to me.

11[40]

The *presupposition* of Spencer's ideal of the future, however, is what he **does not see,** the *greatest possible similarity* of all human beings, so that one really sees oneself in the *alter*.[12] Only thus is altruism possible! But I think of the ever-enduring *dissimilarity* and greatest possible *sovereignty* of the individual: therefore altruistic pleasures must become rare, or must *acquire the form* of *pleasure in others,* like our *current pleasure in nature.*

11[41]

The emergence of the thinker and the dangers by which such an emergence usually comes to an end. 1) parents want to make him into their likeness 2) one accustoms him to activities that deprive him of the energy and time for thinking; professions etc. 3) he is raised to adopt an expensive lifestyle, on which he must now expend much energy in creating the means to sustain it 4) one accustoms him to joys that make those of thinking seem drab, and to a mood of discomfort in the presence of thinkers and their works 5) his sex drive wants to induce him to a union with a woman and henceforth to live *for* children — no longer for himself 6) his talent is accompanied by honors: and these lead him to influential persons who have an interest in making an instrument of him 7) his delight in scientific success makes him an apostate of further goals: he remains stuck on the means and forgets the end. — From these the maxims for educating an independent thinker can be deduced. And precepts, for imprinting these precepts *most*[13] *effectively* (namely *distance* from danger, *compulsion* to think through *other* kinds of inactivity etc.) I am concerned with the *preservation of my kind*!! —

11[42]

To expose for once the whole tyranny of the *expediency of the species*! What! We're even supposed to promote it? Not supposed to instead *reconquer as much as possible* for the individual? All morality is supposed to be absorbed in it: what is inheritable by the entire species is supposed to constitute value? — Let's look instead at the *random throws* that must occur here — to see whether some things don't happen here, assuming they're ever achieved, that contradict the species-ideal!

11[43]

These glorifiers of selection-expediency[14] (like Spencer) believe they know what *favorable circumstances* of a development are! and fail to reckon *evil* among them! And what would have become of human beings without fear envy greed! They wouldn't exist anymore: and if one thinks of the richest noblest and most fruitful human being, *without* evil — then one is thinking a contradiction. Treated benevolently on all sides and being benevolent oneself — here a genius would have to suffer *terribly,* for all of his fruitfulness wants to nourish itself egoistically from others, wants to dominate, suck them dry etc. In sum, if today a virtuous person suffers from the strength of his egoism, then *subsequently* from the strength of his altruism: all activity galls him because it *contradicts* his primary inclination and seems evil to him. To do something for himself, put something aside, to create — it would all be with an evil conscience: *pleasure* would set in if one repressed his creative urges and perceived things *generally.* In this manner, too, a beautiful resting humanity would be possible, nourished and blossoming on all sides, but a quite different humanity than *our best one* — for which some things also have to be asserted.

Incidentally, as an individual one could *anticipate* the tremendously slow process of selection,[15] in many respects and temporarily reveal the human being in their goal — my ideal! *Set aside* the unfavorable circumstances by setting *oneself* aside (solitude) *selection*[16] of influences (nature books elevated events) with which to reflect on this! Maintain only benevolent rivals in one's memory! Independent friends! Banish all lower stages of humankind from one's sight! Or refuse to see and hear them! Blindness deafness of the sage!

11[44]

The *anticipators.* — I doubt whether that *enduring human being* whom the expediency of species-selection ultimately produces will stand much higher than the *Chinese.* Among the throws there are many *useless* ones and with respect to that species goal transitory and *ineffective* ones — but *higher*: let's focus on those! Let's emancipate ourselves from the *morality* of species-expediency! — Obviously the goal is to make human beings just as steady and firm as has already happened in connection with *most animal species:* they have *adapted* to the conditions of the earth etc. and do not change essentially. The human being is still changeable — is still becoming.

11[45]

We have no overview over the biggest effects: we could still destroy the race, for we measure effects by individuals, at best by centuries. Whether e.g., coffee or alcohol are not poisons which, consumed *regularly* as they now are, will have annihilated humankind in 2000 years?

11[46]

"Rudimentary human beings," those who now no longer serve the expediency of the type: but have not become self-sufficient beings.

Inexpedient with respect to the species, not yet with respect to small complexes and *not* with respect to the individual! Are the goals of the individual *necessarily* the goals of the species? No. Individual morality: as the result of a random throw in a game of dice, a being exists who seeks *its* conditions of existence — let's take *this* seriously and not be fools to *sacrifice for the unknown*!

11[47]

The drive for possessions — continuation of the *drive* for *nourishment* and hunting. Even the drive for knowledge is a higher drive for possessions.

11[48]

People remain stuck on the *means* if they derive pleasure in achieving them. Rohde.[17]

11[49][18]

Whoever does not achieve the beautiful seeks the wildly sublime, because there even the ugly can show its "beauty." Likewise he seeks the wildly sublime morality.

11[50]

In heroism *disgust* is very strong (likewise in non-self-interest — one despises the limitation of the "ego" — the intellect has its expansion). The *weakness* of disgust characterizes industrial and utilitarian culture.

11[51]

Two origins of art 1) to be deceived in a harmless manner (conjuror actor storyteller etc.) also architecture *as if* the stone could speak (of the house or temple dweller) 2) to be *overwhelmed* in a harmless manner: intoxication, music, lyric poetry etc. At first worry and amazement that nothing evil results, no danger is there — with both. Thus the states that are *most* **feared** and exert the highest charm become *worthy of pursuing:* deception and being overwhelmed. Thus when viewed from the side of *those who enjoy.*

11[52]

Interest ("usury") and the evil conscience.
Theater and the evil conscience.

11[53][19]

Purification of the soul. — **First** origin of *higher and lower.*[20]
What is *aesthetically* repulsive about the inner human being without skin — bloody masses, colon, bowels, all those sucking and pumping monsters — formless or ugly or grotesque, also painful to the sense of smell. Hence *think it away*! But what emerges from this arouses shame (feces urine saliva sperm) Women can't stand to hear about digestion. Byron not watch a woman eating[21] (Thus do ulterior motives make their rounds) This body *covered* by skin, which seems to be *ashamed* of itself!

Clothing on those parts where its essence sticks out: or holding one's hand to one's mouth when salivating. Therefore: there are things that arouse disgust; the more ignorant a human being is about the organism, the more raw meat decay stench maggots coincide for him. The human being, to the extent that he is not shape, is disgusting to himself — he does everything so as *not to think about it.* — *Lust,* which is obviously related to this inner human being, is considered as *lower* — aftereffect of aesthetic judgment. The idealists of love are fanatics of beautiful *forms,* they want to deceive themselves and are often indignant at the representation of coitus and sperm. — Everything that is painful torturous overly ardent has been relegated by humans to this inner body: all the higher did he elevate seeing hearing shape and thinking. The *disgusting* is supposed to be the source of *unhappiness*! — *We are rethinking disgust*!

Second origin the distinction between *higher* and *lower.* Everything that is *fear*-inspiring as the more powerful is regarded as *higher*; everything else as lower or even as contemptible. As **the highest** — inspire fear and *yet* do good and mean well!

11[54]

What are the *profound transformations* that must emanate from the *teachings* that no *God* cares for us and that there is no eternal moral law (atheistically immoral humankind)? that we are *animals?* That our life passes? That we are not responsible? *The sage and the animal* will *converge* and produce a new *type*!

11[55]

Those who have *benefited* from a helpful benevolent disposition have glorified it so! *Praise* as a function of *utility*! And the benefactor would put up with being *compensated* with praise?

11[56]

How do drive, taste, *passion* arise? The latter *sacrifices to itself other drives* that are weaker (different craving for pleasure) — : this is not unegoistic! *One* drive rules the others, also the so-called drive of self-preservation! "Heroism" etc. have **not** been **understood** as passions, but *because* they were very *useful* to other people, as something *superior* nobler different! — since most of the other passions were dangerous to other people. This was very myopic! *Also* the *heroism* of love of the fatherland of loyalty of "truth," of research etc. are highly *dangerous* to *other people* — only they are too stupid to see it! otherwise they would put the unegoistic virtues under the same ban in which belong *greed* sexuality, cruelty lust to conquer etc. But the former were called *good* and perceived as good, and eventually *permeated* entirely by the nobler and purer feelings — and **idealized**! made ideal! Thus *work,* poverty, *interest, pederasty* were degraded at various times, yet made ideal at other times.

11[57]

People admire and praise the actions of another which appear *inexpedient* for him personally insofar as they are useful to *them.* (Inexpediency with respect to pleasure or utility.) Earlier one understood enjoyment or utility very crudely and narrowly: and whoever e.g., did something for *gloria*[22] was already *inexpedient* in the opinion of *crude* people, of the masses. Because one did not see **subtler** *kinds* of enjoyment, one assumed the realm of the selfless to be *so large.* The lack of psychological refinement is a reason for **much** *praising* and admiring! Because the masses have *no* passion, they *admired* passion because it is associated with sacrifice and is imprudent — they could not imagine the **enjoyment** of passion, they *denied it.* The multitude **despises** everything *ordinary, easy, petty.*

11[58]

Before all doing good and doing harm looms the question: *who* is the other factor, *who* is the other person? in sum, knowledge of the world! The *what for* of doing good and doing harm — must first be decided! Up till now all beneficence and doing harm happened in **error,** as if one knew *what?* and *what for?* Our esteem for doing good has yet to be *proven,* namely its *degree*!

11[59]

Not happiness, but the longest possible *preservation* is the content of all morality hitherto in community and society (indeed at the expense of the happiness of all individuals). Therefore not utility either. Who has an interest in *preservation?* The *chieftains* at the head of families, classes etc. who want to live on in the continuation of their institutions, which drive their *feeling of power* into the *distance.* All *old people:* whoever strongly senses his personally *too short* or *still-short* life, seeks to *impress* himself upon the psyche and customs of the new generation and to thus *live on, continue to rule.* It is vanity. — The individual *against* the society-morality and *aloof* of it — when the greatest danger for *everyone* is past, *individual* trees can grow tall with *their* existential conditions.

11[60]

New look at the world with respect to intelligence and kindness. Is humankind an exception? Is its degree of intelligence and kindness on the *whole on a par* with that in nature? Yes. — But now we have to understand the "expediency" and "intelligence" of nature — they *do not exist at all*! Just as little as the unegoistic! From here infer back to humankind: perhaps our *expediency*, too, is only a sum of favorable accidents, and our "kindness" likewise an error. From the great flourishes of nature try to understand our tiny script! — We can propose a series of sequences that lead to an end — but 1) it is not the *complete* series, just a miserable selection 2) we cannot *make* a link in the series of our own free will, we only know more or less that *it will make itself.* Wherever we are expedient, we act nevertheless in ignorance of means and end, seen on the *whole.* We cannot get beyond this fatalism.

11[61][23]

Human beings have observed with astonishment that some people *neglect their own advantage* (in passion, or as a matter of taste): they were blind to the inner advantages of pride,

of mood etc. and regarded these people either as 1) *crazy* or
2) as *good,* particularly in case an advantage arose for *them:*
they now expand on the belief that actions are done solely
to benefit *them.* The glorification of such actions and human
beings had the value of *encouraging* similar personally inexpedient actions. The *egoism* of those who *need* help and beneficence
has elevated the unegoistic so highly!

11[62]

The Jesuits contrary to Pascal represented the Enlightenment
and humaneness.

11[63]

new practice.

To see the other human being chiefly as a *thing,* an *object of
knowledge* that must be permitted to enjoy its *justice: honesty*
forbids that we *mistake* him, indeed that we treat him according to any kind of presuppositions that are made up and superficial. *Beneficence* is the same thing as moving a plant into the
light in order to see it better — *doing harm* can also be a necessary means for nature to reveal itself. Not treat everyone as
a human being, but as a human being who is constituted *thus*
and *such:* first viewpoint! As something that must be *known*
before it can be treated thus and such. Morality with *general*
precepts does *each* individual injustice. Or are there *means* for
the *preparation of knowledge* that are *first* applicable to every
being, as a preliminary stage of the experiment? — The way
we interact with things, in order to know them, so also with
living beings, so also with ourselves. — But before we have
knowledge or after we admit that we *cannot* acquire it, how to
act then? And how, *when* we have known them? — *Use* them
as forces for our goals — how else? Just as humans have always
done (even when they *subjugated* themselves: they promoted
their advantage through the power of those to whom they subjugated themselves) — Our interaction with human beings
must have the aim of *discovering* the existing *forces,* those of

peoples classes etc. — then positioning these forces for the benefit of our goals (possibly allowing them to mutually annihilate themselves, should need arise).

New: **honesty** denies *the* human being, it wants no moral *general* practice, it denies *common* goals. *Humankind* is the **quantum of power** for whose *utilization* and *direction* individuals **compete**. It is a *part of ruling over nature:* above all, nature must be known, then *guided* and *used.* — My *goal* again would be *knowledge?* To place a quantum of power in the service of know⟨ledge⟩?

11[64]

To evaluate *higher* and *lower* properties according to my *goal* — to treat all judgments as prejudices in this realm. What people think about chastity should be indifferent to me — so long as it is better *for knowledge,* it will be recommended. To test *all* things with regard to their value for knowing, e.g., art political conditions etc. commerce.

11[65]

Task: to *see things as they are*! *Means:* to be able to look at them from a hundred eyes, from *many* persons! It was a wrong approach to stress the impersonal and to characterize seeing through the eyes of one's neighbor as moral. *Many* neighbors and to see from *many* eyes and from purely personal eyes — is the right thing. The "impersonal" is merely the *weakened-* personal, the feeble — can be useful, too, here and there, namely where it is a matter of removing from sight the obscurity caused by passion. *The* branches of knowledge where **weak** personalities[24] are useful, are cultivated *best* (mathematics etc.). The best *soil* for knowledge, the strong powerful natures, are conquered only late for knowing (made arable etc.) — Here the driving forces are greatest: but completely getting lost and going wild and sprouting weeds (religion and mysticism) is still the *most probable* outcome (the "*philosophers*" are such *powerful* natures, who are not yet arable for knowledge; they cultivate, tyrannize reality, insert themselves *into* it. Wherever love hate etc. are **possible**, science was still entirely **wrong**: here the "impersonal" ones are *without* eyes for the real phenomena, and the strong natures see only *themselves* and measure everything according to *themselves*. — *New* beings will have to form.

11[66]

To seek "truth for the sake of truth" — superficial! We do not want to be cheated, it offends our pride.

11[67]

The harmfulness of "virtues," the usefulness of "nonvirtues" has never been seen in its full breadth. Without fear and craving — what would a human being be! Or even without errors!

11[68]

The extent to which the *sense of honesty* is capable of *stimulating* the fantastic *counter*force of nature! Whether humans are really becoming *more sober?* — Indeed, we **comprehend** only through a fantastic *anticipation* and experimenting, whether reality has *accidentally* been attained in the fantasy image; namely in *history* etc. Thucydides and Tacitus *must* be *poets*. Even in the science of the simplest events imagination is necessary (e.g., Mayer[25]) — but *here* **deception** can still arise, as if sobriety were productive!

11[69]

The passion of knowledge sees *itself* as the *purpose* of existence — if it denies purposes, then it sees itself as the *most valu*able *result* of all accidents. Will it *deny* values? it cannot claim to **be** the supreme *pleasure?* But to search for **it**? *to construct the most pleasure-worthy being,* as the means and task of this passion? To intensify the senses and pride and thirst etc.

To climb down a mountain, to embrace the landscape with one's eyes, amidst an unsatisfied craving. The passionately loving ones who do not know how to reach *union* (— in

Lucretius[26]) The knower *longs* for union with things and sees himself as *secluded* — this is his passion. Either everything is supposed to dissolve into knowledge or he dissolves himself into things — this is his tragedy (the latter his death and its *pathos.* The former his striving to *make* everything into spirit — : *pleasure* of mastering, of evaporating, of raping etc. *matter.* Pleasure in the atomistics of mathematical points. *Greed*!

11[70]

Fundamentally false *valu*ation of the *sensate* world toward the *dead one.* Because *we* are it! We *belong* to it! And yet, with sensation *superficiality* breaks out, and deception: what do pain and pleasure have to do with *real* events! — they are secondary things that do not penetrate to the depths! But *we* call it the *interior* and we see the dead world as *exterior* — fundamentally false! The "dead" world! eternally animated and without error, force against force! And in the sensate world everything false, conceited! It is a *festival* to cross over from this world into the "dead world" — and the greatest desire of knowledge aims to counter this false conceited world with the eternal laws, where there is no pleasure and no pain and no deception. Is this the *self-denial* of sensation, in the intellect? The meaning of truth is: to understand sensation as the exterior side of existence, as a mistake of being, an adventure. Its duration is short enough after all! Let's see through this comedy and thus *enjoy* it! Let's *not* think of our return to the insensate as a regression! We become entirely *true,* we perfect ourselves. *Death* must be *reinterpreted*! We *reconcile* ⟨ourselves⟩ thus with what is real i.e., with the dead world.

11[71]

Insofar as the world reveals itself to be *countable* and *measurable,* therefore *reliable* — it receives *dignity* from us. Formerly the *unpredictable* world (of spirits — of the spirit) had dignity, it inspired more fear. *We* however see the eternal **power** somewhere else entirely. Our perception of the world **is turning around: pessimism** of the *intellect.*

11[72]²⁷

Magnificent discovery: everything is not unpredictable, indefinite! There are laws that remain *true beyond* the measure of the **individual**! A *different* result **could** have been yielded after all!

The individual no longer as the *eternal oddity* and venerable! Instead, as the *most complicated* fact in the world, the *supreme* **accident**. We believe also in *his* conformity to law, even if we don't see it. — **Or**? As removed from knowability, but a means of knowledge, also a hindrance to knowledge — *not* venerable, something dubious!

11[73]

We can dispense with neither evil nor the passions — the complete *adaptation* of everyone to everything and each thing in itself (as in Spencer) is an error, it would be the deepest atrophy. — The most beautiful and physically powerful predator has the strongest affects: its hatred and its greed in this strength will be necessary for its health, and if satisfied, will develop its health magnificently. Even for cognition I need all my drives, the good as well as the evil, and I would soon be done for if I failed to approach things hostilely suspiciously cruelly cunningly vengefully and by dissembling etc. All great human beings were great through the strength of their affects. Even health is worthless if it is not the equal of great affects, indeed if it doesn't need them. Great affects concentrate and hold power in a state of tension. Of course they are often the reason one perishes — but this is no argument against their *useful* effect on the whole. Our morality, however, wants the opposite, amiable and credit-worthy payers and borrowers.

11[74]

The damage of virtues has not yet been proven!

11[75]

We can comprehend only intellectual events: hence whatever in matter becomes *visible audible tangible* — whatever *can*! i.e., we comprehend *our* changes in the seeing, hearing, feeling that arise from this. Anything for which we have no *senses,* ⟨that⟩[28] does *not* exist for us — but the world does not have to end because of it. Electricity — e.g., our sense very poorly developed. — Even in the case of a passion, a drive, we comprehend it only as an *intellectual* event — not the physiological, essential, but the bit of sensation that accompanies it. Reduce *everything* to willing — very naïve distortion! — then to be sure everything would be more comprehensible! But that was always the tendency, to **reduce** everything to an intellectual or sensory event — e.g., to[29] purposes etc.

11[76]
   Transformation of valuation — is my task.

    The body and the mind
    passion
    evil
    the community — morality
    life and death
    conscience punishment sin
    praise and blame
    purposes volition
    indifference
    life as aberration.[30]

11[77][31]
   The human being as the animal gone mad: lives in pure delusion, up till now, more than anyone has dreamed. This is how I came across it.

11[78]
   The *aesthetic* judgments (taste, displeasure, disgust etc.) are what constitute the basis of the *tablets of good.* These in turn are the basis of *moral* judgments.

11[79]

The beautiful, the disgusting etc. is the older judgment. As soon as it lays claim to *absolute truth,* aesthetic judgment changes over to moral *demand.*

As soon as we *deny* absolute truth, we must give up all *absolute demands* and retreat into *aesthetic judgments. This is the task* — to create an abundance *of aesthetic valu*ations *with equal rights:* each one for an individual the ultimate fact and the measure of things.

Reduction of morality to aesthetics ! ! !

11[80]

Knowledge has the value 1) of refuting "absolute knowledge" 2) of discovering the objective computable world of necessary succession.

11[81]

For us there is not cause and effect, but only consequences ("discharges") NB.

11[82]

I.

The wise must acquire a monopoly of the *financial market:* soaring above it through their lifestyle and goals and providing direction for wealth — it is absolutely necessary that the highest intelligence provide direction to wealth.

2.

Marriage. Most of our married women are treasured too highly. — Sexual gratification should *never* be the goal of marriage. — A population of laborers needs good whorehouses. — Temporary marriages.

3.

Suicide as an ordinary kind of death: new pride of the human being who puts an end to himself and invents a new *celebration* — dying.

11[83]

The science of 1650–1800 wanted to *demonstrate* the wisdom and kindness of God: the opposite was the result. Now one is tempted to concede deceptive and evil detours to good etc. *to a remnant of God,* to a faulty intellect. But 1) *entirely different* degrees of unreason are being displayed 2) and likewise of kindness: it would be a being *without* character. Why *accept* such a *being?* — The world is neither good nor evil! And the human being as well! —

11[84]

Our entire world is the *ashes* of countless *living* beings: and even if there is still so little of the living in comparison to the whole: thus *everything* has already been transposed once into life, and it continues so. Let us assume an eternal duration, and consequently an eternal change of substances —

11[85]

Researchers like Lecky[32] can never explain the *decline* of an opinion after its great dominance. *Opinions* (on the basis of taste) are great *diseases* across many generations, physiologically *healing themselves* in the end and dying out — and opinions themselves are only the expression that is known to us of a physiological event. There are individual and superindividual diseases. One must study the human beings in whom *counteropinions* or skepticism surfaces: there is a new physiological marker in them, probably the germ of a *different* disease. — Human beings as the *insane* animals.[33]

11[86]

The fact about *witchcraft* is that at the time, tremendous multitudes of human beings felt pleasure in harming others and in thinking of themselves as harmful, likewise in dissipating themselves sensuously in their thoughts and feeling themselves to be *powerful* in evil and in the meanest things. Where did *that* come from? — is the question.

11[87]

Those human beings with the *virtue* of steadfastness self-overcoming heroism demonstrate in their callous harsh and cruelly excessive thinking and treatment of others *where* this virtue has its foundation. They behave *toward others* as they *behave toward themselves* — but because the latter seems useful and rare to people, and is therefore honorable, while the former is very painful, one divides them into good and evil halves! Ultimately this callous harshness has probably been quite useful to humankind on the whole, it kept opinions and strivings intact and gave entire peoples and ages precisely *those* virtues of steadfastness self-overcoming heroism, made them great and strong and dominant.

11[88]

I must give up not only the doctrine of *sin,* but also that of *merit* (virtue). As in nature — the *aesthetic* judgments remain! "disgusting, ordinary, rare, attractive, harmonious, abrupt, garish, contradictory, torturous, enchanting" etc. But these judgments have to be placed on a *scientific* basis! "rare" what is *actually* rare. Much that is "ordinary" as *exceedingly* valuable, more than the rare etc.

11[89]

Wanting to *harm,* the *pleasure in cruelty* — have a major history. Christians in their behavior toward pagans; peoples toward their neighbors and opponents; philosophers toward people of a different opinion; all freethinkers; journalists; all who live anomalously, like saints. Almost all writers. Even in artworks there are those features that suggest designs upon rivals. Or like with Heinrich von Kleist, who wants to do violence to the reader with his imagination; Shakespeare too. — Likewise all laughter, and comedy.

Likewise the pleasure in *dissembling*: major history. —

Is the human being therefore *evil*?

11[90]

The people of the Middle Ages, the steadfast ones, would *despise* us, we are beneath their taste.

11[91]

A great stride in cruelty, to make do with mental instead of physical tortures and even in imagining these tortures and no longer wanting to see.

11[92]

Witches wanted to *see* harm, Christian persecutors and inquisitors too, even God before hell. This the influence of barbarians (Germans) on Europe — a regression. Slaves brought humility and barbarians brought cruelty into Christianity.

11[93]

We are constantly *perceiving* very much and *thinking* very much (remembering, imagining) that doesn't become conscious. It is of a lesser and weaker quality, and it suffices.

11[94]

To the believers in morality.

Deus nudus est,[34]
Seneca.[35]

11[95]

Deus nudus est says Seneca. I fear he's completely clothed. And even more: clothes not only make the man, but make gods too.

11[96]

Do you think a Greek, to whom one described *our* culture, would admire it or find it worthy of emulating? Or even a savage? Every condition has its ideal from itself: one that is entirely different is always a kind of contradiction to this ideal and therefore *painful* and *contemptible*. According to what should we measure the concept "progress of culture"! Everyone believes he is at the top and *his* ideal is the ideal of humanity. The history of these tastes in ideals! — Also missing in every ideal is that which provides another ideal its value, its *tastefulness* for its admirers. Now, is there progress in *cooking,* then? Yes, within a few circles, peoples cities families, the ideal develops. — A free *individual* has his private taste, he has to be very *strong,* otherwise he will be merely a *tiny craving* and nothing more, in comparison to the taste of families and peoples.

11[97]

The emergence **of many** *free* individuals among the Greeks: marriage *not* on account of lust. Exercise and development of the art of coi⟨tus⟩. Pederasty as a derivation of the worship and coddling of women — and hence prevention of hypernervousness and weakness in women. The agon and the sanction of envy. The simple lifestyle. Slaves and the taxation of labor. Religion no preacher of morality, hence letting go the mores, on the whole. The killing of the embryo; elimination of the fruits of infelicitous coitus etc.

11[98]

From each moment in the state of a being, countless ways are available for its *development:* the dominant drive, however, pronounces only a single one of them *good,* that which accords with its ideal. Thus Spencer's image of the future of humankind is not a *natural-scientific necessity,* rather a *wish* projected from contemporary ideals.

11[99]

What is tolerance! And recognition of foreign ideals! Whoever promotes his own ideal quite deeply and strongly *can* not believe in others at all, without judging them disparagingly — ideals of *lesser* beings than he is. The absolute peak of *our* standard is simply the belief in the ideal. — Thus tolerance historical sense so-called justice are proof of the mistrust of one's own ideal, or the absence of an ideal. What therefore is the *scientific sense? Perhaps* the demand for an ideal and the belief that here one has a path to the absolute, to an *irrefutable* ideal: hence under the assumption that one *has* no ideal and suffers *from this*! — In many it may be *revenge* for not having an ideal, when they *destroy* the others. There is a kind of playacting (as in Bacon) as if one had an ideal. "Truth for its own sake" is a cliché, something *completely impossible,* like love of one's neighbor for its own sake.

11[100]

History of cruelty; of dissimulation; of *lust to kill* (the latter in the killing of opinions, passing sentence on works, persons, peoples, the past — a judge is a sublimated executioner).

11[101]

In what an age perceives as evil I see what contradicts its ideal, therefore an *atavism of the former good:* e.g., a cruder kind of cruelty lust to kill than is tolerated today. At some time or other the deed of every criminal was a *virtue.* But now he himself perceives it with the conscience of the *age* — he interprets it as evil. *Interpreting* as *evil* everything or most things that human beings do and think, occurs when the ideal does not correspond at all with human nature (Christianity): then everything becomes original sin, whereas actually it is *original virtue.*

11[102]

Wretch! Now you've also seen through the life of the solitary, free individual: and again, as before, you have *barred* the way to him for yourself precisely through your knowledge.

I want to arrange everything that I deny, and sing the whole song: there is no retribution no wisdom no kindness no purposes no will: in order to act, you must believe in errors; and you will still act according to these errors even after you have seen through them as errors.

11[103]

What is morality! A human being, a people has suffered a physiological change, senses this in *communal feeling* and interprets it in the language of its affects and *according to the degree* of its knowledge, without noticing that the seat of the change is in its *physis*.[36] As if someone were hungry and believed they could satisfy their hunger with concepts and customs, with praise and blame!

11[104]

Courtesy a *refined* benevolence, because it acknowledges distance and lets us feel it as pleasant, while the crude intellect becomes angry at it or does not see it.

11[105]

In the most highly praised actions and characters murder theft cruelty dissimulation are as necessary elements of strength. In the most reprehensible actions and characters there is *love* (esteeming and overesteeming of something whose possession one covets) and *benevolence* (esteeming of something whose possession one has, that one wants to keep)

Love and cruelty not opposites: they are always found together in the best and sturdiest natures. (The Christian God — a person imagined to be very wise and without moral prejudices!)

People do not see the small sublimated doses and they deny them: they deny e.g., the cruelty in the thinker, the love in the robber. Or they have good names for *everything* that stands out in a being, as long as it satisfies their *taste.* A "child" displays all qualities shamelessly, as a plant displays its sexual organs — both know nothing of praise and blame. Education is learning to rename or to feel differently.

11[106]

"Useful-harmful"! "Utilitarian"! Such talk is based on the prejudice that it is already *established* which *direction* the development of human nature (or also animal plant) *should* take. As if countless thousands of developments were not possible from every point! As if the decision about what would be *best highest* were not purely a matter of *taste*! (A measuring according to an ideal that must *not* be that of a different time, a different human being!)

11[107]

How valuable it is that human beings have learned so much *joy* at the sight or sensation of *pain*! Human beings have also elevated themselves mightily through the scope of their schadenfreude! (Joy also in one's own pain — motif in many moralities and religions.)

11[108][37]

There is no self-preservation drive!

11[109]

These preachers of tolerance! They always exempt a couple of dogmas ("fundamental truths") after all! They distinguish themselves from their persecutors only in their opinion of what is necessary for salvation.

To stick to reason would be nice, if there were only *one* reason! But the tolerant one must make himself dependent on *his* reason, on its weakness! In addition: in the end it *is* not even the latter that lends its ear to the proofs and refutations and decides. It is inclinations and disinclinations of *taste*. The persecutors have certainly not been less *logical* than the freethinkers.

11[110]

Indifference! A thing does not concern us, we can think about it as we like, there is no use or disadvantage for us — *this* is a foundation of the scientific mind. The number of these things has always grown; the world has become ever more indifferent — thus impartial knowledge increased, which eventually became a *taste* and finally will *become* a passion.

11[111]

Paracelsi mirabilia.[38] Adapted by F. N. — Of all the wondrous things — so Paracelsus told me — that I ever saw and heard, one is the most amazing, and in order to report it exactly as it took place, I must have not only a courageous heart like a lion, but also the innocent patience of a lamb. For supposing it had been the chimera of a spirit that wished evil upon me, then I never had a more vexing temptation: and if what appeared to me spoke the truth —

11[112]

The essence of every action is as distasteful to a human being as the essence of every food: he would rather starve than eat it, so strong is his *disgust* for the most part. It needs *spices,* we have to be seduced to all meals: and so too to all actions. *Taste* and its relation to hunger, and its relation to the needs of the organism! Moral judgments are the spices. But taste will be seen in both cases as what *decides* the *value of the food, value of the action:* the biggest error!

How does taste change? When does it become sluggish and unfree? When is it tyrannical? — And likewise with judgments concerning good and evil; a physiological fact is the reason for every change in moral taste; but this physiological change is not something that necessarily promoted what was *advantageous* to the organism each time. Rather, the *history of taste* is a history for itself, and likewise degenerations of the whole as progress are equally the consequences of this taste. Healthy taste, sick taste — these are false distinctions — there are countless possibilities of development: whatever leads each time to one development, is healthy: but it can be contradictory to another development. Only in the context of an *ideal* that is supposed to be reached is there a meaning to "healthy" and "sick." But the ideal is always extremely changeable, even in the individual (that of the child and of the man!) — and the *knowledge* of what is necessary to reach it is almost entirely lacking.

We follow our *taste* and refer to it with the most sublime words, as duty and virtue and sacrifice. We do not acknowledge the *useful,* indeed we despise it, just as we despise the inside of our bodies; everything is bearable to us only when it is concealed in a smooth skin.

11[113]

From its taste, it was established incidentally whether a remedy killed, whether it satisfied etc. — not how it functioned when taken for any *length of time* (across generations). Also, one did not know how *unevenly* the body was maintained and how these strong vacillations functioned. Depression as a result of insufficient nourishment or digestion determines the *ideal.*

11[114]

Consecration has been given to lust for spoils, gluttony, lasciviousness, cruelty, dissimulation, lying, weakness, insanity, St. Vitus' dance, drunkenness, sensibility, sloth, ignorance, having no possessions, feeble-mindedness, schadenfreude, fear — all opposing properties that were produced somewhere by taste and invincible proclivity (each time people slandered the opposite and were disgusted by it and called it bad or base)

11[115]

In *benevolence* are refined avarice, refined lasciviousness, refined dissipation of the one who is safe etc.

As soon as refinement is *there,* the *earlier* stage is no longer felt as a stage, but as the opposite. It is *easier* to think opposites than degrees.

Even a very complicated drive, if it has a *name,* is regarded as a *unity* and tyrannizes all thinkers who look for its definition.

11[116]

Let us not be slaves of pleasure and pain, not in science either! Painlessness, indeed pleasure do *not* prove health — and *pain is no proof* against health (rather only a strong stimulus).

11[117]

Moral judgments are epidemics that have *their time.*

11[118]

A slave class is being formed — let's make sure that an aristocracy also gets formed.

11[119]

"Science" allegedly on the basis of the love for truth for its own sake! Allegedly on the basis of the pure silence of the "will"! In truth *all our drives* are active, but in a special, so to speak, political order and adaptation to one another, so that their result is no phantasm: one drive stimulates the other, each one fantasizes and wants to assert *its* kind of error: but each of these errors immediately becomes the handle for another drive (e.g., contradiction analysis etc.). With all these many phantasms one finally almost necessarily guesses the reality and the truth, one posits so many images that finally one of them *hits,* like shooting from many many rifles at a single deer; a great game of dice, often not playing out in a single person, but in several, in generations: then, where a single scholar asserts even only a single phantasm, and when it in turn is dispelled by another, the *number of possibilities* (in which the truth *must* be contained) has **diminished** — a success! It is a hunt. The more individuals someone has inside himself, the more he alone will have the prospect of finding a truth — then the struggle is *in* him: and he must put *all* his powers at the disposal of the individual phantasm and later once more oppose another: great buoyancy, great revulsion for what is immaterial, copious and sudden disgust are a must for him. — Those natures who merely compare what other individuals have already fantasized, need *coldness* above all: they speak of the "coldness of science," they are the unproductive, an important class of human beings, since they bring about an *exchange* between the producers, a kind of merchant type, they estimate the value of products. *This capacity* can ultimately still be found also in a single human being who is otherwise productive. But also one more *important capacity:* the **enjoyment** of all the rejected phantasms, having the spectacle of their struggle etc. — *seeing nature in them.*

11[120]

I need *all* my gall for science. —

11[121]

Chaos is constantly still at work in our mind: concepts images sensations are **randomly** brought alongside each other, thrown about like dice. This process spawns proximities that force the mind to *stop short:* it remembers *similarities,* it senses a *taste* for them, it holds on to and works on them both, according to its art and its way of knowing. — Here is the last tiny particle of world, where something new is combined, at least as far as the human eye can reach. And ultimately it will be at bottom simply another new superlatively subtle chemical combination, that really does not yet have its equal in the becoming of the world.

11[122][39]

All the animal-human drives have preserved themselves, since time immemorial, they would have *perished* if they were harmful to the *preservation of the species:* this is why they can still be harmful and painful to the individual — but species-expediency is the principle of the preserving force. First of all, *exterminating* those drives and passions in the individual is *impossible* — he *consists* of them, just as probably in the structure and ⟨in⟩ the movement of an organism the same drives are at work; and secondly it would mean: the suicide of the species. The bifurcation of these drives is just as necessary as all struggle: for suffering has as little to do with the preservation of the species as the perishing of countless individuals. These are indeed not the most reasonable and direct means of preservation thinkable, but the *only real ones.* — In the *individual* the drives are quite often thrown together inexpediently, then the individual perishes of

this; *on the whole* the result is the preservation of the species. —
The praising and blaming of drives, the temporary *taste* for these
or those is a rather **superficial** phenomenon, dependent on the
consciousness of "useful" "harmful" — which is very *unscientific*!
— This is why the detested drives were active anyway, under
other names or unnoticed. Not so much depends on the ethical
systems that have dominated!

11[123]

Whence the changes in *taste* in matters of morality? Does
this go deep down? Like the lack of appetite during eating,
like the feeling of disgust and of unpleasantness around putre-
faction smoke etc.? Is it that for a state (of a people of a person) its taste is in proportion to *expediency?* Or at least to what
is thought to be expedient? — Does its taste say "this I *need
now,* that I do not need"? — Or is it changing habits, like a
taste for foods, brought about by the present easier gratification through this or that, so that habit stimulus and craving
arise and the opposite is *perceived* in the face *of the opposite* and
unknown? Or both?

11[124]

When a drive becomes *more intellectual,* then it gets a new
name, a new charm and a new estimation. It is often *juxtaposed*
with the drive of the older phase, as if it were its opposite (cruelty e.g.) — Some drives, e.g., the sex drive are capable of major
refinements by the intellect (philanthropy, worship of Mary and
saints, artistic enthusiasm; Plato[40] believes love of knowledge
and philosophy is a sublimated sex drive) meanwhile *alongside,*
its old direct effect remains intact.

11[125]

To be redeemed from life and to become dead nature again
can be perceived as a *celebration* — by those who want to die.
To love nature! To again venerate what is dead! It is not the
opposite, but instead the maternal womb, the rule, which

makes more sense than its exception: for unreason and pain are merely in the so-called "expedient" world, in the living.

11[126]

The strongest individuals[41] will be those who oppose the species laws and yet do not perish from it, the singular ones. From them the *new nobility* is formed: but countless singular ones *must* perish when it emerges! Because they *alone* lose the preserving lawfulness and the accustomed air.

11[127]

Remarkable activity of the intellect! With the sex drive one person desires another as the means to release their seed or to fertilize their egg. Precisely this the intellect does not know: it asks: *why* this desiring? It weighs *what* kinds of things make a person desirable and now says: that person *must* have all these properties that make someone desirable! — thus it *concludes* and from now on *believes* as firmly in it, as in dreaming we believe in the dream image. Believing in its conclusions is characteristic. With all affects the intellect is animalistically primitive to this extent, as in dreams. — To prove these animalistic conclusions for all affects. — What then is skepticism? *When* and in which state then does the intellect become so refined, so suspicious of its conclusions? so minimally dreamlike?

11[128][42]

Now one has rediscovered *struggle* everywhere and speaks of struggle of cells, tissues, organs, organisms. But one *can* find in them all the affects of which we are aware — ultimately, once this has happened, *we reverse the issue* and say: What is really taking place during the activity of our human affects are those physiological movements, and the affects (struggles etc.) are merely intellectual interpretations where the intellect knows absolutely nothing yet *thinks* it knows everything. With the words "anger"[43] "love" "hate" it thinks it has explained the Why?, the *reason* for the movement; likewise with the word "will" etc. — Our natural science is now undertaking to clarify the tiniest events through our acquired affect-feelings, in sum to create a *discourse* for those events: very good! But it remains metaphorical speech.

11[129]

Capacity *to hear intelligently*!

11[130][44]

Our drives and passions have been cultivated over tremendous stretches of time in *social* and *tribal communities* (previously perhaps in ape-*herds*): thus as social drives and passions they are stronger than individual ones, even today. One *hates* more, more precipitously, *more innocently* (innocence belongs among the oldest inherited feelings) as a patriot than as an individual; one sacrifices oneself faster for one's family than for oneself: or for a church, party. Honor is the strongest emotion for many i.e., their estimation of themselves is subordinate to the estimation of others and craves its sanction there. — This nonindividual egoism is the more ancient, more original; hence so much subordination, piety (as with the Chinese) thoughtlessness about one's own character and well-being, the well-being of the group means more to us. Hence the easiness of wars: here a human being falls back into his more ancient character. — The *cell* is foremost more member than individual; the individual *becomes* ever more complicated in the course of development, ever more a group of members, society. The free human being is a state and a society of individuals. — The development of herd animals and social plants is an entirely different one than that of individually living things. — Individually living humans, if they do not perish, develop into societies, a multitude of work zones is developed, and likewise much struggle among the drives for nourishment space time. Self-regulation isn't just there all at once. Indeed, on the whole a human is a being that necessarily perishes because it has not yet achieved self-regulation. We all die too young from a thousand errors and unknowns of practice. — The freest human being has the greatest *feeling of power* over himself, the greatest *knowledge* of himself, the greatest *order* in the necessary *struggle* of his forces, the relatively greatest *independence* of his individual forces, the relatively greatest *struggle* within himself: he is the most *discordant* being and the *most fickle* and the *most long-lived* and the superabundantly craving, and self-nourishing one, the one who *excretes* and *renews* himself the most.

11[131][45]

A movement occurs 1) through a direct *stimulus* e.g., in a frog whose cerebral hemisphere has been excised and is lacking automatic response 2) through *representation* of the movement, through the image of the event in us. This is an extremely *superficial* image — what do humans *know* about chewing when they imagine chewing! — but countless times the event produced by a stimulus has followed the image of the event in our eye and brain and *finally* a bond is there, so firmly that the *reverse* process sets in: as soon as that image arises, the corresponding movement arises, *the image serves as the triggering stimulus.*

In order for a stimulus really to have a triggering effect, it must be stronger than the counterstimulus that is also always present e.g., the pleasure of calm of indolence must be suspended. Thus the *image* of an event does *not always* act as a triggering stimulus, because an actual counterstimulus is present, which is stronger. Here we speak of "being-willing-and-not-able" — the counterstimulus is frequently not in our consciousness, but we notice an opposing force that deprives the image's stimulus of its force *however distinct it may be.* A struggle is present, even though we do not know *who* is struggling. Will that leads to action occurs when the opposing stimulus is weaker — we *always* notice something like resistance, and this provides, **falsely interpreted**, *that secondary feeling of* **triumph** when something willed succeeds. In this false interpretation we have the origin of the belief in free will. "*We*" are not the ones who cause its representation to triumph — rather, it triumphs because the counterstimulus is weaker. But the very fact that the mechanism advances has absolutely nothing to do with our willfulness — we do not even know the mechanism! How could we even "will" it! What e.g., does extending our arm mean for our consciousness!!

11[132][46]

Reason! *Without knowledge* it is something quite foolish, even in the greatest philosophers. How Spinoza fantasizes about *reason*! A *fundamental error* is the belief in harmony and the absence of struggle — this would simply be death! Where there is life, there is a cooperative formation, where the comrades struggle for nourishment for space, where the weaker adapt, have shorter lives, fewer progeny: diversity rules in the smallest things, spermatozoa, eggs — equality is a grand delusion. Countless beings perish from struggle — a few rare cases preserve themselves. — Whether reason to date on the whole has maintained more than it destroyed, with its conceit of knowing everything, of knowing the body, of "willing" — ? Centralization is by no means so perfect — and the *conceit that reason* **is** this center is certainly the greatest deficiency of this perfection.

11[133]

We can only "will" what we have *seen* — therefore it is only since the development of the eye that there are *representations* in our memory, and if these stimulate strongly enough, they are followed by actions. Before this, afferent stimuli are needed in order to produce actions.

1[134][47]

When we translate the properties of the lowest animate beings into our "reason," then *moral* drives result. Such a being assimilates its neighbor, transforms it into its property (property is chiefly nourishment and storing of nourishment), it seeks to incorporate as much as possible, not only to *compensate* for loss — it is **greedy**. Thus it *grows* on its own and thus finally it becomes *reproductive* — it splits into 2 beings. Growth and generation follow the unbounded *drive of appropriation.* — This drive leads it to the exploitation of the weaker, and to competition with beings of similar strength, it struggles i.e., it **hates**, *fears, disguises itself.* Assimilation after all is: *making* something foreign the same as oneself, *tyrannizing* — **cruelty**.

It subordinates itself, it transforms itself into *function* and dispenses with many more original strengths and freedoms almost entirely, and lives on in this manner — *slavery* is essential for the development of a higher organism, like *castes.* Craving "*honor*" is — wanting to have one's function acknowledged. Obedience is compulsion condition of life, ultimately stimulus to life. — Whoever has the most power to reduce others to functions, ends up ruling — but the subordinated have their own subordinates in turn — their ongoing struggles: whose maintenance to a certain degree is the condition of life for the whole. The whole in turn seeks its advantage and finds opponents. — If everyone had wanted to stand their posts with "reason" and not constantly expend as much energy and hostility as they needed to *live* — then this driving force would be *lacking* on the whole: the functions of similar degree struggle, *caution* has to be exercised continuously, every sluggishness is exploited, the opponent is *on guard.* An association must strive to become superabundant (overpopulation) in order to produce a new one (colonies), in order to split into 2 independent beings. Measures to provide the organism with duration *without* giving it the goal of reproduction drive it to ruin, are unnatural — like now the clever "nations" of Europe. — Every body is constantly *excreting,* it separates what is *not* useful to it in the assimilated being: what the human being despises, what causes him disgust, what he calls evil are the *excrements.* But his ignorant "reason" often characterizes as evil the things that cause him trouble, are uncomfortable, the others, the enemy, he **mistakes** as *useless* that which is hard to gain, hard to conquer hard to incorporate. When he "*shares*" with others, is "*unselfish*" — then maybe this is merely the excretion of his *useless* **feces**, which he *must* pass, in order not to suffer from them. He knows that this dung is *useful* to the foreign field and makes himself a *virtue* of his "generosity." — "Love" is a sensation for property or that which we desire as property.

11[135]

"Effect." The stimulus that someone exerts, the impulse he provides, on which others discharge their energies (e.g., the religion founder) has ordinarily been mistaken for the *effect:* one infers great "causes" from great discharges of force. False! These could be insignificant stimuli and human beings: but the force had accumulated and was primed to explode! — A glance at world history!

11[136]

When a researcher arrives at uncommon results (like Mayer), this in itself is *no* proof of uncommon power: his talent *accidentally* became active at the point where discovery was already prepared. If chance had made Mayer a philologist, he would have done something notable with the same acumen, but nothing for which he would be trumpeted as a "genius." — It is not the results that prove the great knower: nor even the method, since at any given time different doctrines and demands exist in regard to it. Rather, it is the multitude, particularly of the heterogeneous, the mastering of great masses and unifying, looking at things with new eyes — the old etc. —

11[137]

Moses Mendelsohn[48] this archangel of precociousness believed with regard to purposes that Spinoza would surely not be so foolish as to deny them! —

11[138]

Our *memory* is based on seeing *the same* and taking things to be the same: therefore on seeing *inaccurately*; it is originally of the greatest *crudeness* and sees almost everything as *the same.* — That our representations act as discharging stimuli comes from the fact that we always imagine and perceive many representations as *the same,* hence due to our crude memory that *sees* the same, and imagination, that out of laziness *creates* **the same** from what in reality is different. — The movement of the foot as representation is extremely different from the ensuing movement!

11[139]

In the smallest organism there is an incessant developing of force that must then discharge itself: either on its own, when *fullness* is reached, or when an external stimulus arrives. *Where* does the force turn? certainly to what is *habitual:* hence *wherever the stimuli lead,* the *spontaneous* discharge will also go there. The more frequent stimuli **also** *train the direction of the spontaneous* discharge.

11[140]

Oh the false opposites! War *and* "**peace**"! Reason and passion! Subject object! Such things do not *exist*!

11[141]⁴⁹

The Recurrence of the Same.
Draft.

1. The incorporation of basic errors.
2. The incorporation of passions.
3. The incorporation of knowing and of the knowing that renounces. (Passion of knowledge)
4. The innocent one. The individual as experiment. The alleviation of life, debasement, weakening — transition.
5. The new *weight: the eternal recurrence of the same.* Infinite importance of our knowing, erring, our habits, lifestyles for everything coming. What do we do with the *rest* of our life — we who have spent the greatest portion of it in the vastest ignorance? We *teach the teaching* — it is the strongest means of *incorporating*

it into ourselves. Our kind of bliss, as teachers of the greatest teaching.

> Beginning of August 1881 in Sils-Maria,
> 6000 feet above sea level and much higher above all
> human affairs! —

Re 4) Philosophy of indifference. What earlier stimulated most powerfully now has an entirely different effect, it is looked upon and allowed to pass as mere *play* (passions and works) on principle rejected as a life in untruth, but as form and charm aesthetically savored and cultivated, we position ourselves like children vis-à-vis what earlier constituted the *seriousness of existence.* But all our striving for seriousness has to be understood as becoming, denying oneself as an individual, looking into the world with as *many* eyes as possible, *living* in our drives and activities, **in order** to create eyes for oneself, *temporarily* entrusting oneself to life, in order then temporarily to let our eyes rest on it: to *maintain* the drives as the foundation of all knowing, but know where they become opponents of knowing: in sum **wait to see** how extensively *knowing* and *truth* can be **incorporated** — and to what extent a transformation of the human being ensues, once he finally lives only *for the sake of knowing.* — This is the consequence of the passion of knowledge: there *are no other means for its existence* than also to preserve the sources and powers of knowledge, errors and pas⟨sions⟩, from their *struggle* it derives its sustaining force. — How will this life look with respect to its sum of well-being? *The playing of children,* gazed upon by the eye of the sage, having control over *this* **and** *that* state — and over death, if something like this is not possible. — Now, however, comes the hardest knowledge and makes all kinds of life terribly full of misgiving: an absolute excess of joy **must** be demonstrated, otherwise the choice is the annihilation of our self with respect to humankind as a means of annihilating humankind. Even this: we have to place the past, ours and that of all humankind, on the scale and *also* outweigh it — no! this piece of humankind's history *will* and must eternally repeat, *this* we may exclude from the bottom line, on this we have no influence: though it immediately burdens our empathy and prejudices us against life generally. In order not to be toppled by this, our compassion must not be great. Indifference has to have affected us deeply and also the pleasure of looking on. Even the misery of future humankind should *not* be of concern to us. But whether *we* still *want to live* is the question: and how!

To consider: the various *sublime states* that I had, as foundations of the various *chapters* and their material — as the regulator of the expression, presentation, pathos reigning in each chapter — thus gaining an illustration of my ideal, as it were through *addition*. And then upward!

11[142]

Do I speak like someone who has had a revelation? Then despise me and do not listen to me. — Are you the kind who need gods? Does your reason not yet become nauseous from letting itself be fed so cheaply and poorly?

11[143]

"But if everything is necessary, what control do I have over my actions?" This thought and belief is a weight that presses on you along with all other weights, and more than them. You say nourishment location air society transform and condition you? Well, your opinions do it even more, for they condition you to this nourishment location air society. — If you incorporate the thought of thoughts, then it will transform you. The question with everything that you want to do: "is it such that I want to do it countless times?" is the *greatest* weight.[50]

11[144]

It would be appalling if we still believed in *sin:* instead, whatever we will do, in countless repetition, it is *innocent.* If the thought of the eternal recurrence of all things does not over-whelm you, then it is not a fault: and it is no merit if it does. — We think more charitably of all our ancestors than they themselves thought, we mourn for their incorporated errors, not for their evil.

1. *The most powerful knowledge.*
2. Opinions and errors transform human beings and pro-vide them their drives — or: *their incorporated errors.*
3. *Necessity and innocence.*
4. *The play of life.*

11[145]

The *new education* will have to *prevent* humans from suc-cumbing to a single exclusive impulse and becoming an organ, counter to the natural tendency toward division of labor. Rul-ing and surveying beings must be created, who view the play of life and *play along,* now here, now there, *without all too impet-uously* being drawn in. *Power* must ultimately devolve to them, it will be entrusted to them because they will not make intense use of it exclusively for *one* goal. At first they will have control of the finances, for the purpose of education (the first educators must educate themselves!), then because the finances are most secure in their control (otherwise it will be used everywhere for *overly intense one-sided tendencies*). Thus a new governing caste is formed.

11[146]

Aversion to life is rare. We sustain ourselves in it and even at the end and in difficult circumstances we are on good terms with it, *not* out of fear of something worse, *not* out of hope for something better, *not* out of habit (which would be boredom) *not* on account of occasional pleasure — rather on account of *variety* and because at bottom nothing is a *repetition,* yet it reminds us of something experienced. The allure of what is new and yet echoes our old taste — like a piece of music with much ugly content.

11[147]

A new teaching reaches its best representatives last of all, those long-established and establishing natures, because in them, earlier thoughts have become intertwined, with the fertility of a primeval forest, and are *impenetrable.* The weaker emptier sicklier needier are the ones who take on the new infection — the early adherents prove nothing *against* a teaching. I believe the first Christians were the most insufferable people with their "virtues."

11[148]⁵¹

The world of forces sustains no decrease: for otherwise it would have become weak and perished over infinite time. The world of forces sustains no standstill: for otherwise it would have been reached, and the clock of existence would stand still. Therefore the world of forces never arrives at an equilibrium, it never has a moment of rest, its force and its motion are equally great at any time. Whatever state this world *can* ever reach, it must have reached and not once, but countless times. Likewise this moment: it was already here once and many times and it will likewise recur, all forces apportioned precisely as now: and likewise for the moment that bore this one and with the one that is the child of the current moment. Human being! Your entire life is turned over again and again like an hourglass and will run out again and again — with one prodigious minute of time in between, until all the conditions from which you have sprung, in the circuit of the world, come together again. And then you rediscover every pain and every pleasure and every friend and enemy and every hope and every error and every blade of grass and every ray of sunshine, the entire coherence of all things. This ring, in which you are a kernel, sparkles again and again. And in every ring of human existence generally there ⟨is⟩⁵² always one hour when the most powerful thought surfaces first to one, then to many, then to all, the thought of the eternal recurrence of all things — each time for humankind it is the hour of *noon.*

11[149]

Even chemical qualities flow and change: even if the time span is tremendous before the current formula of a compound is *refuted* by its successor. For the time being the formulas are true: for they are crude; what after all is 9 parts oxygen to 11 parts hydrogen! This 9:11 is thoroughly impossible to make precise, there is always an error in its realization, consequently a certain range within which the experiment succeeds. But likewise within the same range there is eternal change, the eternal flux of all things, in no moment is oxygen precisely the same as in the previous, but something new instead: even if this novelty is too fine for all measurements, indeed if the whole development of all the innovations during the duration of the human race is perhaps not yet great enough to refute the formula. — *Forms* exist no more than *qualities*.

11[150]

We cannot conceive of *becoming* as anything other than the transition from an enduring "dead" state into a different enduring "dead" state. Oh, we call what is "dead" motionless! As if something motionless existed! The living is no opposite of the dead, but a special case.

11[151]

Our assumption that bodies planes lines forms exist is only the result of our assumption that substances and things, enduring things exist. As certain as our concepts are fictions, so too are the formations of mathematics. Such things do not exist — we can no more *realize* a plane, a circle, a line than a concept. The whole infinity always lies as reality and obstacle between 2 points.

11[152]

If *all* possibilities in the order and relation of forces were not already exhausted, then no infinity could have yet gone by. But because this *must* be, there is no new possibility anymore and everything must have already existed, countless times.

11[153]

Our intellect is not equipped to comprehend becoming, it strives to prove universal rigidity, thanks to its lineage from *images*. All philosophers have had the goal of proving eternal duration, because in this the intellect feels its own form and effect.

11[154]

Nothing is *congruent* in reality, for no planes exist there.

11[155]

Our senses never show us simultaneity but always succession. Space and the human laws of space *presuppose* the reality of images forms substances and their longevity, i.e., our space amounts to an imaginary world. We know nothing of the space that belongs to the eternal flux of things.

11[156]

At bottom the aim of science is to determine how *the human being* — **not** the individual — perceives in relation to all things and to himself, therefore to *weed out* the idiosyncrasy of individuals and groups and determine the *enduring* relationship. Not truth, but *the human being* becomes known and moreover within all ages in which it exists. I.e., a phantom is *constructed,* everyone works constantly on finding that on which one *must agree,* because it belongs to the nature of human being. One learned in the process that countless things were not essential, as one had long believed, and that with the determination of the essential nothing was proved for reality except *that the existence of human beings has so far* depended *on faith* in this "reality" (like bodies duration substance etc.) Science therefore merely *continues* the process that has *constituted* the essence of the species, making the faith in certain things endemic and weeding out the nonbelievers and letting them die out. The achieved *similarity* of perception (about space, or the temporal feeling or the feeling of big and small) has become an existential condition of the species, but it has nothing to do with truth. The "crazy person," the idiosyncrasy prove not the untruth of a representation, but its abnormality; it is impossible for a mass of people to *live* with it. It is the *mass* instinct that also reigns in knowledge: it wants to know *its* existential conditions better and better, in order to live longer. *Uniformity of perception,* formerly striven for by society religion, is now striven for by science: the *normal taste* in all things determined; knowledge, based on the faith in permanence, stands in the service of *cruder* forms of permanence (masses, common people humankind) and wants to weed out and kill the finer forms, idiosyncratic *taste* — it works against *individualization,* the *taste* that is a condition of life for only *one* person. — The species is the cruder error, the individual the finer error, it comes *later.* It *struggles* for its existence, for its new taste, for its relatively *singular* position to all things — it considers this better than the general taste and despises it. It wants *to rule.* But then it discovers that it itself is something changeable and has a variable taste, with its subtlety it gets behind the secret that there is no individual, that in the briefest moment it is something different than in the next and that its existential conditions are those of countless individuals: the *infinitely tiny moment* is the higher reality and truth, a lightning image out of the eternal flux. This is what it learns: how all *enjoying* knowledge rests on the cruder error of the species, the finer errors of the individual, and the finest error of the creative moment.

11[157][53]

Let us beware of attributing any kind of *striving* to this circuit, a goal: or assessing it in keeping with our needs as *boring,* stupid etc. Certainly the highest degree of unreason occurs in it just as well as the opposite: but it should not be measured according to this, rationality or irrationality are *not* predicates for the universe. — Let us beware of thinking of the *law of this circle* as *having become,* in keeping with the false analogy of the circular motion *within* the ring: there was *not* first a chaos and afterward gradually a more harmonious and finally a steadily circular motion of all forces: rather everything is eternal, not developed:[54] if a chaos of forces existed, then the chaos too was eternal and returned in each ring. The *circuit* is not *something that has become,* it is the primal law, just as *quantum of force* is primal law, without exception and infringement. All becoming is within the circuit and the quantum of force; therefore, not to use, through false analogy, the becoming and passing circuits e.g., of the stars or ebb and flood day and night the seasons for characterizing the eternal circuit.

11[158]

Let us beware of teaching such a teaching like a sudden religion! It must seep in slowly, entire generations have to build on it and become fertile — so that they become a great tree that provides shade for all of future humankind. What are the couple of millennia in which Christianity has sustained itself! For the mightiest thought many millennia are needed — for a *long long* time it must be small and impotent!

11[159]

Let us press the image of eternity on *our* life! This thought contains more than all religions that despise this life as fleeting and taught us to look toward an unspecified *different* life.

11[160]

This teaching is mild toward those who do not believe in it, it has no hells or threats. Whoever does not believe has a *fleeting* life in his consciousness.

11[161][55]

Not to gaze out on distant unknown blisses and *blessings* and *pardons,* but to live in such a way that we want to live again and live *this way* in eternity! — Our task approaches us in every moment.

11[162]

So that some degree of consciousness could exist in the world, an unreal world of error had to — emerge: beings with a belief in permanence in individuals etc. Only after an imaginary counterworld had arisen in contradiction to absolute flux, could something *be known on this foundation* — indeed, ultimately the basic error on which everything rests can be appreciated (because opposites can be *conceived of*) — yet there is no other way to annihilate this error than with life: the ultimate truth of the flux of things does not tolerate *incorporation,* our **organs** (for *living*) are equipped for error. Thus in the sage *contradiction to life* arises and to its final decisions; his *drive* for knowledge presupposes faith in error and the life it contains.

Life is the condition of knowing. Erring the condition of life and in particular erring in the deepest sense. Knowing about erring does not suspend it! This is not something bitter!

We must love and nourish erring, it is the womb of knowledge. Art as the nourishing of delusion — our cult.

Love and promote life for the sake of knowledge, love and promote erring imagining for the sake of life. Giving existence an aesthetic significance, *increasing our taste for it,* is the basic condition of all passion for knowledge.

Thus we discover here, too, a night and a day as a condition of life for *us:* wanting to know and wanting to err are ebb and flood. If *one* rules absolutely, then the human being perishes; and *capacity at the same time.*

11[163]

The political delusion that just now makes me smile, as my contemporaries smile about the religious delusion of earlier ages, is above all *secularization,* belief in the *world* and ridding one's mind of "beyond" and "hinterworld." Its goal is the well-being of the **fleeting** individual: which is why socialism is its fruit, i.e., *fleeting* **individuals** want to capture their happiness through socialization, they have no reason to *wait* like human beings with eternal souls and eternal becoming and future improvement. My teaching says: live *in such a way* that you must *wish* to live again is the task — you will do so *anyway*! Whoever feels best from striving, let him strive: whoever feels best from resting, let him rest;[56] whoever feels best from arrangement conformity obedience, let him obey. Only **may** *he be aware of* **what** makes him feel best and spare *no means*! At stake is *eternity*!

11[164]

I speak of *instinct* when some *judgment* (*taste* in its lowest stage) is incorporated, so that it now moves spontaneously and no longer needs to wait for stimuli. It has its growth for itself and consequently also its externally directed sense of activity. Intermediate stage: the semi-instinct that only reacts to stimuli and is otherwise dead.

11[165]

We want to experience an artwork again and again! Thus one should shape one's life so that one has the same wish with respect to its individual parts! This the main idea! Only at the end is the *teaching* then presented of the repetition of all that has been, after the tendency has been implanted to *create* something that can *flourish* a hundred times more strongly under the sunshine of this teaching!

11[166]

The similar is not a degree of the same: rather, something completely different from the same.

11[167]

How can one give significance to the closest the small the fleeting? A) By comprehending it as the root of habits B) as eternal and likewise conditioning eternal things.

11[168]

Whoever sows on the spirit plants trees that grow tall very late. What the son inherits from the father are the *most practiced* habits (*not* the most esteemed!) The son *betrays* the father. The industriousness of a scholar corresponds to the activity of his father: e.g., when the latter is always at the office or "works" only like a country preacher. The Greeks of the higher classes became so individually productive because they did not inherit any thoughtless *industriousness*.

11[169]

We *resist* all wild energies as long as we do not know how to use them (as force) and this is also how long we call them *evil*. But no longer afterward! Question: how does one make crime useful? How does one make one's own wildness useful?

11[170]⁵⁷

Against the art of artworks I want to teach a higher art: that of the invention of *festivals*.

11[171]

I perceive something true only in opposition to a real live untruth: hence the true comes into the world quite feeble, as a concept, and must first acquire *powers* by *merging with live errors*! And this is why we need to let errors live and concede a large realm to them. — Likewise: in order to be able to live individually, society must first be highly promoted and continue to be promoted on and on — the opposite: only in association with it, does what is individual acquire some strength. — In the end a point appears where we want to get beyond what is individual and idiosyncratic: but only in association with the individual, the opposite, can we energize this striving.

11[172]

How do we give weight to the inner life without making it evil and fanatic toward those who think differently? Religious faith diminishes and human beings learn to comprehend themselves as fleeting and as unessential, until this finally weakens them; they do not exert themselves so much in striving, bearing, they want the momentary pleasure, they make things easy for themselves — and perhaps they expend much spirit in doing so.

11[173]
How feeble has all physiological *knowledge* been so far! whereas the old physiological *errors* have acquired spontaneous force! For a long long time we can only use new knowledge as stimuli — in order to discharge the spontaneous forces.

11[174]
How evil has *diminished*! Formerly one presupposed harmful intention in every natural event!

11[175]
How churlishly Christianity has behaved toward antiquity, insofar as it completely *demonized*[58] it! Pinnacle of all slanderous malice!

11[176][59]
Slave labor! Free man's labor! The former labor is all labor that is not done for our own sake and has no satisfaction to it. Much intelligence will yet have to be found, before everyone is able *satisfactorily* to organize his labors.

11[177]
The age of experiments! Darwin's claims have to be proven — through experiments! Likewise the origin of higher organisms from lower ones. Experiments lasting 1000s of years have to be conducted! Educate apes into humans!

11[178]
This is an incorrect viewpoint: *in order* to preserve the species, countless[60] exemplars are sacrificed. Such an "in order" does not exist! Likewise no species exists, but instead nothing but different individual beings! Hence there is no sacrifice

either, no waste! Hence *no unreason* to it either! — Nature does not want to "preserve the species"! The fact of the matter is that numerous similar beings with similar existential conditions preserve themselves more easily than abnormal beings.

11[179]

Whereas in very many cases the first child of a marriage provides sufficient reason to bring no further children into the world: the marriage is not dissolved on this account, but instead *maintained* despite the anticipated disadvantage of new children (to the harm of all later generations!)! How myopic! But the state does not and did not want better quality, but *masses*! This is why it cares nothing about the *cultivation of human beings*! — A few outstanding men should have the opportunity to reproduce with several women; and a few women with especially favorable conditions should not be bound to the accident of one man. Marriage should be taken more seriously! Because the state is not necessary anymore.

11[180]

Today we speak of *luxury* as the strongest stimulus on poor people, overburdened workers and married people: ⟨on⟩[61] account of it they strive for *wealth:* we shun satisfaction and idyllic philosophy as ravagers of the *national wealth* and *work*-force. As much wealth as possible, as much envy and displeasure as possible, as much competition as possible! In *rich* states the arts are supposed to have been promoted best, by the luxury class, art as a means to arouse the envy of the lower classes, as a piece of luxury. — On the other hand their *ascent in luxury* is supposed to be an **apology** for luxury and for designs upon dissatisfaction: arts temporarily allaying and anaesthetizing the displeasure of such conditions, glorifying them in any case.

11[181]

A h⟨uman being⟩ sinks in my estimation 1) if he has 200–300 thalers a year and yet still *becomes* a merchant official or soldier

in choosing a profession 2) if he earns this much and nevertheless seeks an even more time-consuming office (including as
scholar). What! Are these intellectual human beings! Wanting
to marry and losing the *meaning* of life in doing so!

11[182]⁶²

A strong free h⟨uman being⟩ senses vis-à-vis everything else
the *properties of the* **organism**

1) self-regulation: in the form of *fear* of all foreign intrusions,
   in *hatred* of the enemy, in maintaining moderation etc.
2) superabundant compensation: in the form of *greed* craving of appropriation craving of power
3) assimilation in itself: in the form of praising blaming
   making others dependent on oneself, in tandem with
   dissembling cunning, learning, habituation commanding incorporating of judgments and experiences
4) secretion and excretion: in the form of nausea contempt
   for properties per se that are *no longer* useful to him;
   communicating the excrescent, benevolence
5) metabolic force: temporarily venerating admiring making oneself dependent conforming, almost dispensing
   with the practice of other organic properties, transforming oneself into an "organ," being able to serve
6) Regeneration: in the form of sexual drive, didactic drive
   etc.

Now one would err in presupposing these organic properties
occur in a human being *first:* on the contrary, he receives all
these *last,* as an emancipated human being. He instead began
as a part of a *whole,* which had *its own* organic properties and
made the individual into one of its organs — so that over
unspeakably long habituation human beings **primarily** sense
the *affects of society* against other societies and individuals and
everything that is living and dead, and *not* as individuals! E.g.,
he *fears* and *hates* more strongly and most strongly as a member
of a tribe or state, *not* his personal enemy, but the public one;
indeed, he perceives his personal enemy essentially as a public

one (blood vengeance) He goes to war in order to enrich his state and his chief and to aid in their overcompensation, with every personal danger of atrophy sacrifice maiming. He assimilates the unknown into himself as a member of his society, learns for their benefit; he despises whatever properties no longer promote the maintenance of society, he spurns the highest individuals if they contradict *this* advantage. He thoroughly transforms into an organ in the service of his society and makes only accordingly *limited* use of all properties: **more accurately**: he does not yet *have* those other qualities and *first acquires them as an organ of the community: as an organ he receives the first stirrings of the overall properties of the organic.* Society first raises the individual being, forms it into a semi- or whole individual, it does **not** form itself *from* individual beings, not from contracts of these! Rather, an individual is necessary at best as a central point (a chief) and even the latter is only "free" in relation to the lower or higher stage of others. Therefore: the state does *not* originally oppress individuals: they do not even exist yet! It makes the human being's existence possible in the first place, as herd animals. Our *drives affects* are only then *taught* to us: *they are nothing original*! There is no "natural state" for them! As parts of a whole we participate in its existential conditions and functions and *incorporate into ourselves the experiences and judgments made in the process.* These later end up in struggle and relation with one another, when the bonds of society disintegrate: in himself he has to *suffer to the end* the aftereffects of the social organism, he has to do penance for the inexpediency of existential conditions judgments and experiences that were suitable *for a whole,* and finally he gets to the point where he creates in himself *his own existential possibility as an individual* through *re*arrangement and assimilation excretion of drives. Usually these *experimental individuals* perish. The ages in which they arise are those of demoralization, of so-called corruption i.e., all the drives now want to test themselves personally and up to this time not having *adapted* to that personal utility they destroy the individual through excess. Or they tear it to pieces, in their struggle with one another. Then the ethicists come around and try to demonstrate to human beings how they can still live without suffering so from themselves — usually by recommending the *old conditioned lifestyle* beneath the yoke of society, only such that in place of society a concept appears — they are *reactionaries.* But they *preserve* many, if only by leading them back to constraints. Their claim is that an *eternal moral law* exists; they do not want to acknowledge the individual law and they call striving for it unethical and destructive. — In someone who wants to become free, the functions that inevitably predominate in force are those with which he (or his ancestors) served society: these outstanding functions steer and promote or limit the rest — but he needs them *all* in order to *live* as an organism himself, they are *conditions of life*!

But for a long time we are *deformities,* and this corresponds with the much *greater discontent* of individuals who are becoming free — compared to the older dependent stage and perishing in mass numbers.

11[183]

Major tendencies: 1) to plant the love for life, for *one's own* life using *all* means! *Whatever* each individual devises *for this,* others will let it stand, and will have to acquire a new great tolerance for it: as often as it runs counter to his taste when the individual really increases his joy in his own life!

2) To be of one mind in *enmity* toward everything and everyone that tries to impugn the value of life: against the gloomy and dissatisfied and the grumblers. Prohibit their reproduction! But our very enmity must also become a means to our friends! Therefore laugh, mock, annihilate without bitterness! This is our *struggle to the death.*

This life—your eternal life!

11[184]

The real course of things must also have a corresponding *real* time, to say nothing of the *feeling* of long or brief time spans, as knowing beings have them. Real time is probably unspeakably far *slower* than we humans sense time: we perceive *so little,* even though for us, too, a day seems very long, compared to that same day in the feeling of an insect. But our blood circulation could in truth have the duration of an earth- and solar-orbit. — Thus we probably perceive ourselves as *much too big* and overestimate ourselves because we are sensing too big a measure into space. It's possible that everything is much smaller. Hence the real world *smaller,* but *moving much more slowly,* but infinitely *richer in movements* than we *suspect.*

11[185][63]

Egoism is something late and still rare: herd-feelings are more powerful and older! E.g., a human being still *esteems* himself as highly as others esteem him (vanity) He still wants *equal* rights with the others and has a feeling of well-being when thinking about it, even when he treats people equally (which strongly contradicts the justice of *suum cuique!*[64]) He doesn't in the least focus on himself as something new, but strives to adapt himself to the opinions of the rulers, likewise he raises his children in this way. It is the *pre-stage* of egoism, not its opposite: the human being *is* really not yet individual and ego; as a function of the whole he still feels *its* existence as supreme and most justified. This is why he lets himself be commanded, by parents teachers castes princes in order to achieve a kind of **self-respect** — even in matters of love he is much more the conditioned than the conditioner. Obedience duty seem like "morality" to him i.e., he *glorifies* his herd drives by setting them up as *weighty virtues.* — Even in the *awakened* individual the primal stock of herd feelings is still overly powerful and associated with *good* conscience. The Christian with his *extra ecclesiam nulla salus*[65] is *cruel* toward the opponents of the Christian herd; the citizen imposes *horrific* punishments on the criminal, not as ego, but out of ancient instinct — the *deed* of the cruelty of murder of slavery (prison) doesn't offend him once he sees it from the perspective of herd instinct. — All more liberated h⟨uman beings⟩ of the Middle Ages believed that the herd feeling was to be preserved above all, that the rare individual must practice dissimulation in *this* respect, that without shepherds and faith in universal laws everything would become topsy-turvy. We no longer believe this — because we've seen that the *tendency toward the herd* is so great that it breaks through again and again, counter to all freedom of thought! Even now, quite simply, *there is very rarely* an ego! The demand for state, social foundations, churches etc. has not weakened. *v⟨ide⟩*[66] wars! And "nations"!

11[186]

The Greek lawgivers promoted the agon in such a way as to distract the idea of competition from the *state* and to gain political tranquility. (Today the competition of commerce comes to mind) Ruminating about the state was supposed to be distracted by agonistic fervor — indeed people were supposed to engage in gymnastics and poetry — this had the ancillary success of making citizens strong beautiful and refined. — Likewise they promoted pederasty, first in order to prevent overpopulation (which produces restless impoverished circles, even within the aristocracy), then as an educational means for the agon: the young and the elders were supposed to stay together, not separate from each other and uphold the interests of the young — otherwise the ambition of the disengaged elders would have thrown itself upon the state, but with boys one couldn't speak of the state. Thus perhaps Richelieu used the gallantry of men to distract the ambitious drives and to initiate different *conversations* than those about the state.

11[187]

Of what did Alexandrian culture perish? For all its useful discoveries and the pleasure in knowledge of *this* world it was still **not** able *to give this world,* **this life** *the ultimate importance, the beyond remained more important*! Even now the main thing is to *teach* differently in this matter — perhaps *when* metaphysics

hits precisely *this* life with the *heaviest* accent — in accordance
with my teaching!

11[188]

In general the direction of socialism like that of nationalism
is a reaction, against becoming individual. One has *difficulties*
with the ego, the *semi-mature crazy* ego: one wants to put a lid
on it again.

11[189]

The amoeba-*unity*[67] of the individual arrives last! And philosophers proceeded from it as if it existed in everyone! — Morality is
the main counterevidence: everywhere the individual appears *moral
degradation* appears i.e., the individual standard of pleasure and displeasure is manipulated for the first time, and there it is revealed
how the drives within an individual have not yet learned to adapt
in the least, unity is not yet there, or in the form of the crudest tyranny of a single drive over the others — so that the whole usually
perishes! — Therewith begins the period of the *free* human being
— countless perish. — At the sight of this the "sages" invoke the
old morality and seek to prove that it is pleasant and useful *for
the individual.*

11[190]

An unstable equilibrium occurs in nature as rarely as two
congruent triangles. Consequently no standstill at all of force
either. If standstill were *possible,* it would have occurred!

11[191]

The *herd human beings* and the *self-reliant* human beings: the
latter first as shepherds. —

11[192]

Wanting to harm as a tendency is now stripped of its reproach
in the struggle of *parties* (political and also scientific ones), likewise in the competition among merchants, states: one forgoes

certain means, but *not* the tendency! Criticism practiced against everything is a final expression of power of those without influence — a continuation of witchcraft

Wanting to be useful through *prayers* and elevation of the imagination was formerly regarded as a major activity of human beings, violating a god and conditioning him to good — it is the counterpart to magic: violating a devil and compelling him to evil: which was surely also a major activity. *Reveling* in desire and in the image of the achieved purpose and the belief that *this* was the *means* to *achieving* the purpose: in this everyone was in agreement. One believed in a secret *way* in addition to that of action and mechanics, in order to arrive at the same goal.

11[193][68]

Spinoza: we are conditioned only by desires and affects in our actions. Knowledge must be affect, in order to be motive.[69] — I say: it must be *passion,* in order to be motive.

ex virtute absolute agere = ex ductu rationis agere, vivere, suum Esse conservare.[70] "fundamentally seek nothing but one's *own advantage*" "no one strives for the sake of another being to preserve one's own existence."[71] "Striving for self-preservation is the prerequisite of all virtue."[72]

"Human beings are mutually most useful when they seek their own advantage." "No single being in the world is as useful to the human being as the one who lives by the guiding principle of his reason *ex ductu rationis.*"[73]

"*Good* is everything that truly serves knowledge; *bad* by contrast is everything that hinders it."[74]

Our reason is our greatest power. Among all goods it is the only one that pleases everyone equally, that no one envies anyone else, that everyone wishes the other and wishes all the more when he himself has some. — People are united only in reason. They cannot be more unified than when they live according to reason. — They cannot be more powerful than when they agree completely. — In any case, we live more powerfully in a state of agreement with others and with ourselves than in a state of division. The passions divide us; they bring us into conflict with other human beings and with ourselves, they make us hostile externally and unstable internally.[75] — **ego**: all this is **prejudice**. *There is* no reason at all of this kind, and *without* struggle and passion everything becomes *weak,* humans and society.

("*Desire* is the essence of the human being himself, namely the striving on the strength of which a human being wants permanence of being."[76]

"Everyone is impotent to the degree that he neglects his advantage i.e., his self-preservation."

"Striving for self-preservation is the first and sole foundation of virtue."[77]

There is no free will in the spirit, instead the spirit is conditioned to will this or that, by a cause, which likewise is conditioned by another, and this in turn by another, and so on to infinity.[78]

The will is the capacity to affirm and to deny: nothing else.[79]

I say on the other hand: *pre*-egoism, herd drives are older than "wanting-to-preserve-oneself." The human being is first *developed* as a *function:* from this, the individual later detached itself again once it *as function* **got to know** countless conditions of the *whole,* of the organism, and eventually *incorporated* them.

11[194]

The *Jesuits* sided with empiricism, adherents of Gassendi, opponents of Descartes (whom they attack on the grounds of sensualism): like Father Bourdin. Therefore they are for Thomas Aristotle Gassendi — *against* Augustine Plato Descartes idealism. (Congregation of the Fathers of the Oratory of Jesus[80] and likewise Port-Royal[81,82]) Pascal

Arnold *Geulin{c}x* (born in the Netherlands 1625): *impossibile est ut is faciat, qui nescit quomodo fiat. Quod nescio, quomodo fiat, id non facio. — Qua fronte dicam, id me facere quod quomodo fiat nescio?*[83] — My will should extend no further than my capacity. *Ubi nihil vales, ibi nihil velis.*[84,85]

Virtus est amor rationis.[86] — *Amor rationis hoc agit in amante, ut se ipse deserat, a se penitus recedat. Humilitas est incuria sui. Partes humilitatis sunt duae: inspectio sui et despectio sui.*[87]

Malebranche: "The senses may be regarded as false witnesses with respect to truth, but as loyal counselors in consideration of the preservation and utility of life!" We err as soon as our thinking starts to become dependent on the senses, if the intellect makes itself dependent on the body. It is *sin* that lays the blame on this dependency. Wanting to know through the senses, the source of error — is sin. *Error* caused by *sin*! Error becomes possible through *spurning* God, through subjugation beneath the yoke of the body.[88]

Spinoza or teleology as *Asylum ignorantiae.*[89,90]

11[195][91]

Noon and Eternity.
Hints toward a new life.

Zarathustra, born at Lake Urmi, left his homeland in his thirtieth year, went to the province of Aria and wrote the Zend-Avesta[92] in the ten years of his solitude in the mountains.

11[196]

The sun of knowledge stands once more at noon: and the snake of eternity lies curled in its light — — it is *your* time, you brothers of noon!

11[197]

For "Draft of a new kind of living."

First Book in the style of the first movement of the ninth symphony. *Chaos sive natura:*[93] "*on the dehumanization of nature.*" Prometheus is chained to the Caucasus. Written with the cruelty of Κράτος,[94] "of power."

Second Book. Fleeting-skeptical-Mephistophelian. "*On the incorporation of experiences.*" Knowledge = error that becomes organic and organized.[95]

Third Book. The most sincere and soaring-over-the-heavens writing that will ever be: "on the *ultimate happiness of the solitary one*" — he's the one who has developed from "belonging" into "self-reliant" to the highest degree: the perfect *ego:* only *this* ego has *love*; in the earlier stages where supreme solitude and self-glorification are not yet achieved, there is something different than love.

Fourth Book. Dithyrambically comprehensive. "*Annulus aeternitatis.*"[96] Craving to experience everything once more and endless times.

Incessant *metamorphosis* — in a short time frame you must go through many individuals. The means is *incessant struggle*.

Sils-Maria   26 August 1881

("avoid everything pretty and pleasing, as a world-despising brute" says J. Burckhardt at Palazzo Pitti)[97]

11[198]

The great form of an artwork will come to light if the artist has the great form in *his essence*! In itself the great form is silly and it ruins art, it means seducing the artist to hypocrisy or wanting to restamp the great and rare into conventional coin. An honest artist who does not have this shaping force in his *character* is *honest* for not wanting to have it in his works either: — if he generally denies and maligns it, then this is understandable and at least it can be excused: he *can't* go beyond himself. Thus Wagner. But the "infinite melody" is wooden iron[98] — "the shape that did not take shape, become complete" — this is an expression for the incapacity of form and a kind of principle made out of incapacity. Dramatic music and in general poser-music of course is most compatible with formless, flowing music — but it is therefore of a *baser* species.

11[199]

Obedience feeling of function feeling of weakness have raised the value "of the **unegoistical**": especially when one believed the complete dependency on *one god.* Contempt toward oneself, but seeking a purpose for the fact that one is *active* anyway, namely **must** *be:* therefore for *God's* sake, and ultimately, when one no longer believed in the god, for the sake of the *other*: a conceit, a powerful thought that made the existence of human beings easier. Our conditions also want slavery, and the individual is supposed to be impeded — hence culture of altruism. In truth one behaves "unegoistically" because it is the *sole* condition under which one *continues to exist i.e.,* one thinks habitually of the existence of the other before thinking of one's own (e.g., the prince thinks of the people, the mother of the child) because otherwise the prince could not exist as prince, the mother not as mother: they want the preservation of *their* feeling of power, even if it demands constant attention and countless self-sacrifices for the sake of the dependents: or, in other cases, for the *sake* of the *powerful,* if our existence (sense of well-being, e.g., in the service of a genius etc.) is only asserted in this manner.

11[200]

Rights: the more powerful one establishes the functionaries *against one another*: and *duties:* the more powerful one establishes the functionaries *against himself:* each has something to accomplish, and in order to achieve this **regularly**, the more powerful one *dispenses* with further intrusions and *submits himself* to an *order*: this belongs to self-regulation. With respect to the *duties of the functions* the powerful one and the function correspond. There is nothing "unegoistical" about it.

11[201][99]

The modern-scientific counterpart to faith in God is faith in the *universe as organism:* this disgusts me. So, what is quite rare, unspeakably derivative, the organic that we perceive only atop the crust of the earth is made into the essential universal eternal! This is still anthropomorphizing of nature! And a veiled polytheism in the monads, which collectively form the universal-organism! With foresight! Monads that know how to prevent certain possible mechanical events such as the equilibrium of forces! Fantasizing! — If the universe could become an organism, it would have become one. We must think of it as a whole precisely as far removed as possible from the organic! I believe even our chemical affinity and coherence are perhaps late-developed appearances belonging to specific epochs *in* individual systems. Let's believe in absolute necessity in the universe, but let's beware of claiming of any law, be it even a primitive mechanical one of our experience, that necessity governs in it and is an eternal property. — All chemical qualities can have developed and pass away and come again. Countless "properties" may have developed, for which we, from the vantage point of our nook in space and time, have no possible basis of observation. The *change* of a chemical quality is perhaps taking place even now, only to such a subtle degree that it escapes our finest monitoring.

11[202]

The measure of universal force is *determined,* nothing "infinite": let's beware of such conceptual extravagances! Consequently the number of states changes combinations and developments of this force is indeed tremendously large and practically *"immeasurable,"* but in any case also determined and not infinite. To be sure, however, the time in which the universe exerts its force is infinite, i.e., force is eternally the same and eternally active: — up to this moment an infinity has already run its course, i.e., all possible developments must already *have been. Consequently* the momentary development must be a repetition and likewise the one[100] that bore it and the one[101] that arises from it and thus on and on forward and backward! Everything has been here countless times, insofar as the overall state of all forces always returns. Whether *apart from this* anything identical has ever existed, is entirely indemonstrable. It appears that the overall state forms new *properties* in the smallest detail, so that two different overall states can have nothing identical. Whether something identical can exist in a single overall state, e.g., *two leaves?* I doubt it: it would presuppose they had an absolutely identical origin, and then we would have to *assume* that something identical has existed *back to all eternity,* despite all changes in overall states and the creation of new properties — an impossible assumption!

11[203]

Let's test how the *thought* that *something repeats* has affected things so far (the year e.g., or periodic illnesses, waking and sleeping etc.) If circular repetition is even a mere probability or possibility, even the *thought of a possibility* can shatter and reshape us, not only perceptions or specific expectations! See how the *possibility* of eternal damnation has affected us!

11[204]

The **situation** in which human beings find themselves, in relation to nature and to human beings, *constitutes their properties* — it's like atoms.

11[205]

Let's beware of believing that the universe has a tendency to achieve certain *forms,* that it is supposed to become more beautiful, more perfect, more complicated! All this is anthropomorphizing! Anarchy, ugly, form — are inappropriate concepts. In mechanics there is nothing imperfect.

11[206][102]

Everything has recurred: Sirius and the spider and your thought in this hour and this your thought that everything recurs.

11[207]

How strange and superior we act with respect to the dead, to the inorganic, and in the meantime we are three-fourths a water column, and have inorganic salts in us that probably do more to determine our well-being and woe than all of living society!

11[208]

The philosophers have done the same as the peoples: inserted their narrow *morality* into the essence of things. The ideal of every philosopher should also reside in the in-itself of things.

11[209]

Herd human beings and *special human beings*!

11[210]

The inorganic *conditions* us part and parcel: water air soil topography electricity etc. Under such conditions we are plants.

11[211]

My task: the dehumanizing of nature and then the naturalizing of humans, once they have gained the pure concept of "nature."

11[212]

All habituations (e.g., to a certain food, like coffee, or a certain timing) in the long run have the result of *cultivating a certain kind of* human being. Therefore look around you! Test the smallest thing! Where does it want to go? Does it belong to *your* kind, to *your* goal?

11[213][103]

Infinitely new becoming is a contradiction, it would presuppose an infinitely *growing* force. But *from what* is it supposed to grow! From what nourish itself, nourish itself to *excess*! The assumption that the universe is an organism contradicts the *essence of the organic.*

11[214]

Friends of salt are *no* "meat eaters." There are always those pretenders to nobility and wealth who would like to conceal that *little* meat gets eaten: one should watch out for whether persons use much or little salt!

11[215]

Tea a dull or sharp or insignificant aroma and taste: consequently one should add blossoms!

11[216]

Foods (e.g., onions and stimulant narcotics like tobacco) prove that what is most important to human beings is not pleasure and the avoidance of displeasure, but being *stimulated*. *Stimulation* is in itself something different than pleasure or displeasure (or the latter two[104] are its extremes)

11[217]

We occasionally need blindness and must leave certain articles of faith and errors untouched in ourselves — as long as they *preserve* us in life.

We must be *without conscience* with respect to truth and error, as long as *life* is at stake — precisely **so that** we then consume life once more in the service of truth and of the intellectual conscience. This is our ebb and flow, the energy of our contraction and expansion.

11[218]

Reproduction often *without* any individual inclination.

11[219]

These slaves are often *weary* and regularly weary — this is why they are so content with their *pleasures* (which is the most curious sign of our times) Their beer- and wine-houses, their quantum of pleasant entertainment, their festivals, their churches — everything is so mediocre, for not much intellect and strength is supposed to be used on this, nor should they be demanded — one wants to rest. — Indeed! Otium! This is the idleness of those who still have all their strength about them.

11[220]

The most powerful thought consumes much energy that formerly was available to other goals, so its effect is *reshaping,* it creates new laws of motion for energy, but no new energy. But therein lies the possibility to determine and organize individual human beings in their affects anew.

11[221]

Slavery is universally visible, although it does not admit this to itself; — we must strive to be everywhere, to know all of its circumstances, to best represent all its opinions, only thus can we master and use it. Our nature must remain concealed: like that of the Jesuits, who practiced a dictatorship amidst general anarchy, but introduced themselves as *instrument* and *function.* What is our function, our cloak of slavery? Teacherhood? — Slavery should not be abolished, it is necessary. Only we want to see to it that again and again those arise *for whom* others work, so that this tremendous mass of political-commercial forces does not consume itself in vain. At the very least, that there are *spectators* and *those who no longer play along*!

11[222]

Using the spirit of function as a vantage point, philosophers are now reflecting on transforming humankind into a single organism — it is the opposite of *my* tendency. Instead, *the greatest possible number of variable differing* organisms, which drop their fruit when they reach their *ripeness and rottenness*; the individuals, of whom to be sure the majority perish, but what matters is the few. — Socialism is a ferment that proclaims countless experiments of state, hence also of declines of states and new eggs. The ripening of contemporary states happens more rapidly; military violence is becoming greater and greater.

11[223]

I sense exertion ponderousness and the desire to possess intelligence in every turn!

11[224][105]

We have rendered lightning harmless: we must be inventive in making it *useful,* in letting it work.

11[225]

The "chaos of the universe" as the exclusion of every purposive activity does *not* contradict the thought of the circuit: the latter is simply an *irrational necessity,* without any formal ethical aesthetic consideration. Caprice is lacking, in the smallest and on the whole.

11[226][106]

Egoism is *still* infinitely weak! This is what one calls the effects of *herd-forming affects,* quite inaccurately: one is greedy and hoards wealth (drive of the family the tribe), another is extravagant *in Venere,*[107] another vain (taxation of himself in keeping with the standard of the herd), one speaks of the egoism of the conqueror, of the statesman etc. — they think only of themselves, but of "themselves" insofar as the ego is developed by the herd-forming affect. Egoism of mothers, of teachers. For once we must ask how few thoroughly examine: *why* do you live here? *why* do you go around with him? How did you arrive at this religion? What influence does this or that diet have on you? Has this house been built for *you?* etc. Nothing is rarer than the *establishment of the ego* to our ourselves. The *prejudice* prevails that one *knows the ego,* it *does not fail* to assert itself constantly: but almost no work and intelligence at all are spent *on this* — as if we were exempted from self-knowledge by an intuition of research!

11[227]

Here the mountains show their 3 hummocks: with a sharper telescope I see a number of new hummocks, the line renews itself with each sharper telescope, the old one becomes an arbitrary phantasm. Finally I get to the point where the line can no longer be observed, because the *motion* of the *weathering* escapes our eye. But the motion *suspends* the *line*!

11[228]

On a large scale we can protect ourselves only little: at any moment a comet could smash the sun, or an electrical force could appear in which the solar system is vaporized all at once. What are "statistics" in these matters! We have maybe a couple of million years for the earth and sun in which something like this has *not* occurred: it proves nothing at all. — The naturalizing of the human being requires readiness for the absolutely sudden and annihilating.

Sudden things have accustomed human beings to a false contrast, they call it enduring regular etc. — but suddenness is constantly there in the smallest thing, in every nerve; and it is precisely regular, although in time it seems unpredictable *to us*. *Enduring* is that whose changes we don't see, because they are too gradual and too subtle for us.

11[229]

When we gradually formulate the *opposites* to all our fundamental opinions, we begin to approach the *truth*. At first there is a cold dead world of concepts; we animate it with our other errors and drives and thus move *into life* one piece at a time. *Only in adapting to living errors can the truth that is at first always* **dead** *be brought to life.*

11[230]

People speak of those with stomach illness and mean those who suffer from digestion problems — as if the stomach alone were what digests! And the educated speak of "gastric juice." — It's a very good thing that such errors have no effect on the organic structure, or we would have perished long ago. — And through their healing method and dietary nonsense they *have* had a sufficiently lethal effect! —

11[231]

The coexistence of 2 complete equals is impossible: it would presuppose an *absolutely equal existential history* back to all eternity. *This* however would presuppose a *generally* absolutely equal history of emergence i.e., everything else would also have to be absolutely equal in all times i.e., the entire *remainder* would have to repeat itself continually, in itself and *detached* from the 2 equals. — But likewise one can already prove absolute difference and inequality in coexistence using a single difference: a *detachment* is inconceivable; if one thing changes, then the aftereffect penetrates into everything.

11[232]

There have been infinitely *many* states of force, but not infinitely *different* ones: the latter would presuppose an *indefinite* force. It has only a "number" of possible properties.

11[233]

Mechanics takes force as something absolutely *divisible:* but it must first check each of its possibilities against reality. In that force, there is simply nothing divisible into equal parts; in each state it is a property, and properties cannot be *halved:* which is why there has never been an equilibrium of force

11[234]

It is wonderful that for *our* needs (machines bridges etc.) the assumptions of mechanics suffice, for they are very big needs and the "small errors" are not a factor.

11[235]

We cannot conceive of motion without lines: its essence is concealed from us. "Force" in mathematical points and mathematical lines — is the final consequence and demonstrates the whole nonsense. — They are ultimately *practical* sciences, emanating from the fundamental errors of human beings that things and the like exist.

11[236]

f{rom} Analysis o⟨f⟩ R⟨eality⟩[108]

We can *perceive* the same motion as sound color heat electricity. *Perception* makes the properties of things so colorful and manifold for us. In truth everything could be much simpler and different! How do we distinguish between red and blue, how does it differently affect the mind, nam⟨ely⟩ of the insane! — and yet! Perception make the chasms, the differences much *greater* than they are in nature.

11[237]

"*Archetype*" is a fiction like purpose, line etc. The *similar* in shape is never striven for in nature, rather it arises where *negligibly different* degrees in the quantity of forces prevail. "Negligibly" different *for us*! and "similar" *for us*!

Similar qualities we should say, instead of "identical" — even in chemistry. And "similar" for us. Nothing occurs twice, the oxygen atom is without its likeness, in truth, for *us* it **suffices** to assume that countless[109] equals exist.

11[238]

H⟨uman beings⟩ and philosophers earlier fictionalized humans *into nature* — let's de-anthropomorphize nature! Later they will *fictionalize* more *into* themselves, in the place of philosophies and artworks there will be ideal human beings, who every 5 years form a new ideal from themselves.

11[239]

49 centals less — atmosph⟨eric⟩ pressure here at an altitude of 6000 feet: if I let my sensations put it into words, they tell me on the contrary: "two pounds less to carry than down at sea level — and maybe not even that much less!"

11[240]

First human beings must learn the new *desire* — and for this someone has to be there who arouses it in them, a teacher: I trust that they will then indeed be subtle and inventive enough to find the paths to satisfaction of this desire on their own — in steps, experimentally, as they're accustomed to. — It doesn't matter if my suggestions are "impracticable" — they're only supposed to provide stimulus to the appetite (e.g., the treatment of criminals).

11[241][110]

If our affects are the means to sustain the movements and formations of a *social* organism, then surely nothing would be more erroneous than now to infer back that in the lowest organism it is also precisely the affects that here self-regulate, assimilate, excrete transform, regenerate — hence to presuppose affects even here, pleasure displeasure will inclination disinclination. It would be as crazy a mistake as if one were to infer a similar blood circulation for the lowest organisms based on the fact of blood circulation in the human body. — Our affects presuppose thoughts and tastes, these in turn a nervous system etc.

11[242]

We see as far as we sense — but sensation is idiosyncrasy, therefore seeing too (periphery and degree of clarity) is idiosyncrasy.

11[243][111]

Odd: what human beings are most proud of, their self-regulation through reason, is likewise achieved by the lowest organism, and better, more reliably! But acting according to goals is in fact only the smallest possible part of our self-regulation: if humankind really acted according to its reason i.e., according to the foundation of its *opining* and *knowing*, then it would have long since perished. Reason is a slowly developing ancillary organ that fortunately had *little* strength for conditioning human beings throughout tremendous stretches of time, it works in the *service* of the organic drives and emancipates itself slowly *to equal rights* with them — so that reason (opinion and knowing) struggles with the drives, as its own new drive — and late, really late *gains the upper hand.*

11[244]

Temperamental differences are perhaps conditioned more by the different distribution and amount of inorganic salts than by anything else. Bilious people have too little sulfuric natrium, the melancholic lacks sulfuric and phosphoric potassium; too little phosphoric calcium among phlegmatics. The most courageous natures have an excess of phosphoric iron.[112]

11[245]

If an equilibrium of force had ever been achieved, then it would still exist: therefore it has never occurred. The current state *contradicts* the assumption. If one assumes that there was once a state absolutely identical to the current one, then this assumption is *not* contradicted by the current state. Among the infinite possibilities, however, this case *must* have existed, for up till now an infinity has already passed. If equilibrium were possible, then it must have occurred. — And if this current state existed, then also the one that bore it and its pre-state backward — from which it emerges that it already *existed* a second third etc. time — likewise that it will exist a second third time — countless times, forward — and backward. I.e., all becoming moves in the repetition of a specific number of perfectly identical states. — Of course it cannot be left to the human mind to think out whatever is *possible:* but under any circumstances the present state is a possible one, quite apart from our capacity or incapacity for judgment with respect to the possible — for it is a real one. Thus it would have to be said: all *real states* must have already had *their equal,* assuming that the number of cases is not infinite, and in the process of infinite time only a finite number had to occur? because from every moment counting backward always an infinity has already passed? The standstill of forces, their equilibrium is a conceivable case: but it has not occurred, consequently the number of possibilities is greater than that of the realities. — That nothing identical recurs could be explained not by chance, but only by an intentionality inserted into the nature of force: for, presupposing a tremendous quantity of cases, the random achievement *of the same throw* is more probable than absolute never-identity.

11[246]

Basic idea of the merchant culture: the lower multitude with its modest possessions is made dissatisfied by the sight of the rich, it believes the *rich man is the happy one.* — The laboring overworked rarely resting slave multitude believes, the human being *without physical labor* is the happy one (e.g., even the monk — which is why slaves so gladly became monks). — The one who is plagued by and rarely free from cravings believes the *scholar and steadfast one* and also clerics are the happy ones. — The nervous one who is torn back and forth believes that the human being possessed by a *great single passion* is the happy one. — The person who has experienced minor distinctions thinks that the most honored one is the happy one. That which is *rare and possessed to a small degree* is what prods the human imagination to images of the *happy one — not* that which he is lacking — *what is lacking produces indifference toward the opposite of what is lacking.*

11[247]

In the molecule there are explosions and changes of the orbit of all atoms, and sudden discharges of force. Our entire solar system could also experience in a single moment the same kind of stimulus that a nerve exerts on a muscle. That this *never* happened or will happen cannot be proved.

11[248]

Hypothesis in the long run more powerful than any belief — presupposing that it *remains in place much longer* than a rel⟨igious⟩ dogma.

11[249]

Boldness toward the inside and *modesty* toward the outside, toward *all* "outside" — a German union of virtues, as one formerly believed — I have so far found most beautifully among Swiss artists and scholars: in Switzerland, where to me it seems all German properties generally grow up more abundantly by far because more protected by far than in today's Germany. And which writer would Germany have to compare to the Swiss Gottfried *Keller*? Does it have a similarly *pioneering* painter like *Böcklin*? A similarly *wise* knower like J. *Burckhardt*? Does the great fame of the natural scientist Haeckel do anything to diminish the greater fame-worthiness of *Rütimeyer*? — by way of merely beginning a series of good names. There alpine and alpine valley plants of the mind are still growing, and just as in the time of young Goethe one fetched even one's lofty German motivations from Switzerland, just as Voltaire Gibbon and Byron learned there to surrender to their own supernational perceptions, so too, in our day, a temporary *Helvetiation* is an advisable means of gazing out for a bit beyond the German economy of the moment.[113]

11[250]

Not regret! rather compensate for evil by a good deed!

11[251]

In *Lohengrin*[114] there is much *blue* music. Wagner knows the opiatic and narcotic effects and uses them against the nervous flightiness of his musical inventiveness, of which he was very much aware.

11[252]

I am always amazed, when stepping outdoors, to think of how magnificently distinct everything appears to us, the woods just so and mountain just so and that there is no confusion and mistake and hesitation in us in the least with respect to all perceptions. And yet there must have been the greatest possible uncertainty and something chaotic, all this is only *firmly* inherited over vast stretches of time; humans who perceived essentially differently, about distance in space, light and color etc. were pushed aside and were poorly capable of reproducing. This manner of perceiving *differently* must have been perceived and avoided over long millennia as "*the craziness.*" People no longer understood each other, one let the "exception" perish off to the side. There existed from the beginning of everything organic a tremendous cruelty, weeding out everything that "*perceived differently.*" *Science* is perhaps merely a continuation of this weeding-out process, it is completely impossible if it does not recognize the "normal human being" as uppermost, as the "standard" to be preserved by all means! — We live in the remains of the perceptions of our ancient ancestors: in fossils of emotion so to speak. They fictionalized and fantasized — but the decision as to whether such a fiction and phantasm was allowed to live was provided by the experience of whether one could *live* with it or whether one perished with it. Errors or truths — *if* only **life** were possible with them! Gradually here an impenetrable *net* arose! *Entangled* in it we come into this life, and even science does not extricate us.

11[253]

If moral *sufferings* have made life difficult — it comes from the fact that it is absolutely impossible to take a moral perception relatively; it is essentially *absolute,* as bodies seem absolute to us, likewise the state, the soul, the community. However much we remind ourselves that we *developed* from all that: it *works* on us as the undeveloped, the eternal and it imposes *absolute* duties. Likewise "our neighbor," however wise we might be about him. *The drive to take things absolutely* is very powerfully *bred into us.*

11[254]

There would be no suffering if there were nothing organic i.e., without the belief in **equality** i.e., without *this error there would be no suffering* in the world!

11[255]

Science increasingly has the task of determining the *succession* of things in their course, so that events become *practicable* for us (e.g., as they are practicable in machines) This does not create *insight* into cause and effect, but a *power over nature* can be acquired in this manner. The demonstration soon comes to an end and a further refinement has no utility for human beings. — So far this has been the great feat of human beings, achieving the *best possible* accuracy in their observation of succession in many things and *thus* imitating this for their purposes

11[256]¹¹⁵

Our parents still grow in us after the fact, their later acquired properties that are also present in the embryo need time. The properties of the father back when he was a man we only get to know as a man.

11[257]

I saw tragedy with music high above Wagner — and high above Schopenhauer I heard the music in the tragedy of existence.

11[258]¹¹⁶

On the "Cure of the Individual"

1) he should proceed from the closest and smallest things and determine the entire dependency into which he was born and raised

2) he should likewise comprehend the accustomed rhythm of his thinking and feeling, his intellectual needs of nourishment

3) Then he should attempt *change* of all kind, chiefly in order to break his habits (much dietary change, with sharpest observation

4) he should lean intellectually on his opponents for once, he should try to sample their food. He should *travel* in every sense of the word. In this period he will be

"unstable and fleeting." From time to time he should
rest from his experiences — and digest.

5) Then comes the higher part: the attempt to *create* an
ideal. This anticipates what is even higher — living
precisely this ideal.

6) He must pass through a series of ideals.

11[259]

Principle: that which is to be *revered* must not be *pleasant*.
Consequently — — —

11[260][117]

There is a part of the night of which I say "here *time* is stopping!" After all night watches, especially after nocturnal travels
and wanderings one has with respect to this period of time an
odd feeling: it was always much too short or much too long, our
perception of time feels an anomaly. It may be that we also have
to do penance in waking because we ordinarily spend that time
in the time-chaos of dream! enough, at night from 1–3 o'clock
we no longer have a clock in our heads. To me it seems that this
is precisely what the ancients also expressed with *intempestiva
nocte* and ἐν ἀωρονυκτί[118] (Aeschylus) "there in the night where
time does not exist"; and I also use this thought to explain to
myself etymologically an obscure phrase of Homer for describing the deepest stillest part of the night: even if the translators
have reproduced it with "time of the night milking"[119] — where
in the whole wide world did people ever milk the cows at one
o'clock at night! Where was anybody that stupid!

11[261]

It is our task to maintain the *purity* of music and to prevent
it from being abused now for mystical semireligious purposes,
after it has been made capable of *tremendously sudden* effects
in the form of the baroque style and after prolonged incorporation: — every future sorcerer and Cagliostro will try to
achieve effect with music and spiritism, and reawakenings of

religious and moral instincts are possible on this path — perhaps one will attempt to restore an inner glow to the Christian Last Supper through music. — That it doesn't need words is its greatest advantage over poetry, which appeals to concepts and consequently *pushes* against philosophy and science — : but one doesn't notice when music leads us *away,* misleads[120] us from philosophy and science!

11[262]

The history of philosophy so far is only *brief:* it is a beginning, it hasn't waged any wars yet and brought the peoples together; the high point of its pre-stage has been the *religious* wars, the age of religion is by far not over yet. Later one will regard *philosophical* opinions for once as questions of life and existence, as formerly on occasion religious and political ones were — taste and disgust in opinions will become so great that one *will no longer want to live* as long as a different opinion persists. The whole of philosophy will be lived through in this forum of mass-taste and mass-disgust — prior to the age of religions there were probably already preliminary but completely indifferent religious individuals, corresponding to the preliminary and indifferent individual philosophers. — "Truth" will always be asserted as that which corresponds to necessary vital conditions of the age, the group: in the long term humankind's *sum of opinions* will be *incorporated,* with which it has its greatest advantage i.e., the possibility of the longest duration. The most essential of these opinions, on which the duration of humankind rests, are those longest incorporated, e.g., the belief in identity number space etc. *Around these* the struggle will *not* revolve — it can only be an *extension* of these erroneous *foundations* of our animal existence. — Important as the most significant monument of the *spirit of duration* is the *Chinese* way of thinking. — Hence it will scarcely become the history of "truth," but that of an organic structure of errors that transitions into body and soul and ultimately dominates *sensations* and *instincts.* There will be a practicing of a continuous selection of what belongs to life. The demand for *preservation of life* will appear ever more tyrannically in place of the "sense of truth" i.e., it will *take* its *name* from this sense and keep it. — Let us individuals live our preliminary existence, let us leave it to the coming generations to wage wars for our opinions — we live in the *middle* of human time: **greatest fortune**!

11[263]

Deepest error in the *judgment of human beings:* we evaluate them according to their *effects,* using the standard *effectus aequat causam.*[121] But human beings only exert stimuli on other human beings, it depends ⟨on⟩[122] *what* is *present* in other human beings whether the powder explodes or whether the stimulus amounts to almost nothing. Who would evaluate a match by the fact that in its aftereffect it destroyed a city! But this is what we do! Effects prove *which elements* were present in the other human beings of the time: that he exerted a stimulus: and by what means and with what kind of *actual* intentions one must still ask! — It is teleology to believe that the great man *must* come at the time when precisely those elements are present and ready to explode. What's important, in any case, is that the *stimulating* force of a human being can survive his death, through his works or through the myth that forms around his life: this is what *those* should think about who themselves exert *no* "*stimulus*" *on the times.*

Ultimately: we err likewise *about things,* because we judge them according to the *effects in us:* how different blue and red seem to us, and what's at stake are nerves whose length is a little more or less! Or the same chemical components yield different results when arranged so and so, and *how* we perceive this difference! We measure *everything in keeping with the explosion* that a *stimulus* produces in us, as big small etc.

11[264]

Impact is not the first mechanical fact, but that something is there that can impact, that aggregate herd state of atoms that is not like dust but instead holds together: here precisely is *non-impact* and yet force, not only of counterstriving, resistance, but above all of arrangement, classification, attachment, of *conducting* and *attaching force*. Such a particle can then "*impact*" as a whole!

11[265]

Complete equilibrium must either be an impossibility in itself, *or* the changes of force enter the circuit before that intrinsically possible equilibrium has set in. — To attribute "feeling for self-preservation" to being! Insanity! To atoms "striving for pleasure and displeasure"!

11[266]

One refrained from eating meat, because one did not want to dine on the souls of human beings, thus it was just an aversion to cannibalism, in Pythagoras as well as the Indians. *Not* sympathy with animals! Inflicting pain through killing is not necessary at all: and with respect to the probable *natural* death, the human being who kills animals generally **alleviated** the *lot of the animal world,* especially since they have no anticipation of death. — Whoever does not want to live "off living things" should also refrain from plants! — The sympathy of Christian saints was sympathy with beings in whom the devil dwells — not with "*living things.*"

11[267][123]

"The immorality" of Boc⟨c⟩accio is of Indian origin.

11[268]

In order for a *subject* to exist in the first place there must be something enduring and likewise much identity and similarity. What is *unconditionally different* in continuous change would not be maintainable, there would be nothing to maintain, it would run off like rain on stone. And without something enduring there would be no mirror at all in which simultaneity and succession could show themselves: the mirror already pre-supposes something that endures. — Now, however, I believe: the subject could arise while the error of identity arises e.g., if a protoplasm of different forces (light electricity pressure) always receives only one stimulus and after the one stimulus infers the identity of causes: or *is only capable of one stimulus* in the first place and *perceives everything else as identical* — and this is how it must be in organisms of the lowest stage. The belief in enduring and identity *outside ourselves* arises first — and only later do we comprehend *ourselves* after tremendous training in what is outside ourselves as *something enduring and like itself,* as something unconditional. The *belief* (the judgment) therefore must have arisen **before** self-consciousness: in the process of *assimilation* of the organic this belief is already there — i.e., this *error*! — This is the secret: how did the organic arrive at the judgment of identity and similarity and enduring? Pleasure and displeasure are only *consequences* of this judgment and its incorporation, they already presuppose the accustomed stimuli of nourishment from identity and similarity!

11[269]

Formerly one thought that infinite activity in time required an *infinite* force that no consumption could exhaust. Now one thinks of force as constantly equal, and it no longer needs to become *infinitely great.* It is eternally active, but it can no longer create infinite cases, it must repeat itself: this is *my* conclusion.

11[270]

Stimulus and *inducing* thing mistaken for each other from the beginning! The identity of stimuli gave rise to the belief in "*identical* things": the *enduringly identical* stimuli created the belief in "things," "substances."

In the manner in which the firstborn of organic formations perceived stimuli and evaluated what was outside themselves, we must seek the *life-preserving principle:* the belief *that enabled life to continue* triumphed, maintained itself; *not* the one that was most true, but the belief that was most useful. "Subject" is the life condition of organic existence, therefore not "true," rather, subject-feeling *can* be essentially false, but as the sole means of preservation. *Error the father of the living*!

This *primal error* is to be understood as an *accident*! To be guessed!

In the most developed states we still commit the oldest error: e.g., we posit the state as something whole enduring real as thing and *accordingly* we adapt ourselves to it, as function. Without the protoplasm's representation of an "enduring thing" outside itself there would be no adaptation, no assimilation.

There are very few stimuli vis-à-vis the true *multiple* stimulating occasions — on this the oldest error was based.

11[271]

In the forest the tree grows quickly, in its craving for air and light, but "it drives few roots and is therefore scarcely enduring: whereas the trees to which light and air have open access stand for centuries: the *depth and spread of the roots* are proportionate to duration. But consequently *slow* growing!"[124]

11[272]

My opposition to the spirit of *commerce,* as to the spirit of the epoch.

11[273]

I wish Germany would conquer *Mexico,* in order to set the tone on earth through an exemplary *forest culture* in the conservationist interest of *future* humankind. — The time is coming when the struggle for ruling the earth will be waged — it will be waged in the name of *philosophical principles.* Already now the first power-groupings are forming, people are acquiring training in the great principle of blood- and race-affinity. "*Nations*" are much finer concepts than races, at bottom a discovery of science, which one now *incorporates into feeling: wars* are the great teachers of such concepts and will be so. — Then come *social wars* — and again concepts will be incorporated! Until finally *concepts* no longer yield mere pretexts, names etc. for popular movements, but instead the *most powerful concept* must prevail.

The *social wars* are namely wars against the spirit of commerce and limitations of the national spirit. *Climatic* decisions about populations and races in America. — *Slavic-Germanic-Nordic* culture! — the *smaller,* but more energetic and industrious one!

11[274]¹²⁵

A constant progress in *climatic adaptation* is taking place, and now it is tremendously accelerated because the *weeding out* of unsuitable persons is so easy: and likewise because now adaptation is supported by science (e.g., heat, groundwater etc.).

The animal species, like the plants, have for the most part *reached* an adaptation to a specific continent, and in this they now have something firm and confirming for their character, they are essentially *no longer changing.* Unlike human beings, who are always unstable and do not want to adapt ultimately to a single climate, humankind is pushing toward the production of a being that *can cope* with *all* climates (even through such phantasms as "equality of human beings"): a universal earth human being is meant to arise, *this is why* humans are still *changing* (wherever they have adapted e.g., in China they have remained almost unchanged throughout millennia). The superclimatic artificial human being, who knows how to compensate for the disadvantages of every climate and hauls into every climate the substitutions for what it is lacking (e.g., stoves) — a demanding being, difficult to maintain! "Workers' plight" prevails where the climate *contradicts* human beings! and only a few are able to acquire the substitutions (through struggle naturally, and tyrannically).

In the educated circles of the North *winter*-atrophy prevails. — Maybe the stoves are causing prolonged poisoning! Compared to the French, a German looks like a stunted stove hugger.

11[275]

Be no despiser of lasciviousness!

11[276]

The transformation of the human being first requires millennia for the formation of the type, then generations: finally a *single* human being goes through *several* individuals during his life.

Why should we not succeed in doing for human beings what the Chinese are able to do with a tree — making it bear roses on one side and pears on the other?

Those natural processes of *cultivation of human beings* e.g., which up till now have been practiced with infinite slowness and awkwardly, could be taken in hand by human beings: and the old clumsiness of races, race struggles nationalist fevers and personal jealousies could be compressed into small periods, at least experimentally. — *Entire sections* of the earth could *dedicate themselves to conscious experimentation*!

11[277]

It would be possible to conceive of noses whose olfactory nerves would only be tickled by the eruptions of a volcano. In fact the surfaces of all things that smell appear to be in a constant state of explosion; the force with which small quantities are expelled must be tremendous — I'm thinking e.g., about the effect of camphor[126] on water. — Thus the whole earth is always veiled in thick clouds of the finest materials: without these, *water vapor* would never be able to form into clouds.

11[278]

In order to deduce from large to small: we see everywhere the effect of *currents,* but these are not lines! It is probably like this in the realm of atoms too, the *forces flow* and in doing so exert just as much pressure horizontally as they do with respect to the things they impact. A line is an abstraction compared to the probable facts: a moved force cannot be painted by any symbol, instead we *conceptually isolate* 1) the direction 2) what is moved 3) the pressure etc. In reality these isolated things do *not* exist!

11[279]

The principle of "doing something for the sake of one's neighbor" is either an *atavism* of feeling at the time when the bond with the community has become weak or an *obscure* feeling of the herd sense, which does not at all think of people outside the community because they are so distant, and with respect to the neighbor focuses only on the member of the community (e.g., with "freedom" and "equality" where one certainly is not thinking of the Hottentots) Or it is a mask for that feeling: a community *shall* be formed, e.g., the Christian one. Where that principle appears, one usually *wants* to form communities e.g., the followers of Comte.

11[280][127]

Laws are *not* the expression of the character of a people: I mean, the *flaws of character,* as they appear to the *most powerful* (as obstacles to their power and intentions) are emphasized. In addition, they stand *firm* and the people develops: so that very soon a disproportion arises.

11[281]

Only succession produces *temporal* representation. Supposing we did not perceive causes and effects, but a continuum, then we would not believe in time. For the motion of becoming does *not* consist of *resting* points, of equal periods of rest. ◎ The outer periphery of a wheel is always moving just as much as the inner periphery, and though slower, still compared to the faster-moving inner wheel *it does not rest.* With "time" there can be no deciding between slower and faster motion. In absolute becoming, force can never rest, *never* be nonforce: "slow and fast motion of the same" is *not* measured by a unit that is lacking there. A continuum of force is *without succession* and *without simultaneity* (the latter too would again presuppose human intellect and gaps between things). Without succession and without simultaneity there is *for us* no becoming, no multiplicity — we *could* only claim that such a continuum was unified, calm, immutable, no becoming, without time and space. But precisely this is merely the human *opposite*.

11[282]

Which articles of faith are *indispensable* for the **ennoblement** of the human being? — First of all so as *not* to regress to savagery and nonsociety. Here, too, there could be indispensable errors.

11[283][128]

Jesus was a big egoist.

11[284][129]

The feeling of power first conquering, then dominating (organizing) — it regulates the vanquished for *its own* preservation and *for this it preserves the vanquished itself.* — Even function has arisen from the feeling of power, in the struggle with still-weaker forces. Function preserves itself in overwhelming and ruling over still-lower functions — *in this it*[130] *is supported by a higher power*!

11[285][131]

I used to think our existence was the artistic dream of a god, all our thoughts and perceptions at bottom *his* inventions in writing out his drama — even that we believed "*I* thought" "*I* acted" was *his* thought. Nature's conformity to law would be comprehensible as the conformity to law of his representations — or also that it *would suffice* that he thought of *us* as beings who perceive nature the way we perceive it. — Not a happy god, but simply an artist-god!

11[286]

Without the tremendous certainty of *faith* and the readiness of *faith* humans and animals would not be *capable of life.* To generalize on the basis of the *smallest* induction, to make a rule for one's behavior, to believe that a one-time event that proved itself was the *sole* means to a goal — *this,* at bottom *crude* intellectuality, has preserved humans and animals. To err countless times in this way and suffer from wrong conclusions is not so damaging by far, on the whole, as skepticism and indecision and caution. It is a *basic feature* of humans to regard *success* and *failure* as proofs and counterproofs against faith: "whatever *succeeds,*" its idea is *true.* — How certainly the world stands before us as a result of this raging greedy faith! How certainly we execute all movements! "*I* strike" — how certainly one perceives this! — Thus *base* intellectuality, the *un*scientific nature is a *condition* of existence, of action, we would starve without this, skepticism and caution are only permitted late and always only rarely. *Habit* and *unconditional faith* that it must be the way it is are the foundation of all growth and becoming strong. — Our entire worldview has arisen in such a way that it was proven by the *success* of our being able to *live* with it (faith in external things, freedom of will). Likewise every morality is only proven *in this manner.* — Here now the great counterquestion arises: there can probably be countless ways of life and consequently also of imagining and believing. If we establish everything *necessary* in our current way of thinking, then we haven't proven anything for the "true in itself," but only "the true for us" i.e., that which enables our existence on the basis of experience — and the process is so ancient that rethinking is impossible. Everything a priori belongs here.

11[287]

The dissolution of custom, of society is a state in which the new *egg* (or multiple *eggs*) emerge — eggs (individuals) as seeds of new societies and unities. The appearance of individuals is the sign of an achieved *reproductive capacity of society:* as soon as it shows up, *the old society dies off.* This is not a metaphor. — Our eternal "states" are something unnatural. — As many new formations as possible! — Or conversely: if the tendency toward *eternalization* of the state shows itself, then also decrease in individuals and infertility of the whole: this is why the Chinese regard great men as a national calamity; they keep eternal duration in focus. Individuals are signs of decline.

11[288]

There is something intoxicating in *lasciviousness,* ancient religions used this. And even now poets and musicians seek to make use of this portion of intoxicating energy through stimulation of erotic sympathies. — Artists act with all *possible effective means,* very uninhibitedly.

11[289]

First *compulsion* compels us to do something often, and later the *need* arises, once the compulsion has been incorporated (e.g., to walk, when an animal no longer can swim, is first compulsion, and the opposite of craving: later it becomes need)

11[290]

The last benefit of knowledge and science is to enable the detachment of new eggs from the ovary and to allow ever-new species to emerge: for science brings knowledge of the means of preservation for new individuals. — Without progress of knowledge new individuals would always quickly perish, the existential conditions would be too difficult and random. Just the torment of internal contradiction!

11[291]

There are probably many kinds of intelligence, but each has *its conformity to law,* which makes the *idea* of a **different** conformity to law *impossible.* Therefore because we *can* have nothing *empirical* about the different kinds of intelligence, any path to insight into the *origin* of intelligence is also blocked. The *general* phenomenon of intelligence is unknown to us, we have only the *special case,* and *are not able to generalize.* Here alone we are entirely slaves, even if we wanted to be visionaries! On the other hand from the standpoint of *every* kind of intelligence there must be an *understanding of the world* — but I believe it is merely the ultimate adaptation of conformity to law within the individual kind of intelligence — it asserts itself everywhere. Every intelligence believes in itself

11[292]

Let's go backward for once. If the world had a *goal* then it must have been reached: if an (unintended) *final state* existed for it, then it likewise must have been reached. If it were generally capable of stopping and becoming fixed, if in its course it had only a single moment of "being" in the strictest sense, then there could be no more becoming, also no more thinking, no observation of a becoming. If it were *eternally becoming new,* then through this it would be posited ⟨as⟩ something *wondrous* in itself and something freely and *self-creatively divine.* Eternally becoming *new* presupposes: that force would arbitrarily increase itself, that it would have not only the intention but also the means to *guard* itself against repetition, against ending up back in an old form, hence ⟨to⟩[132] control any movement toward this avoidance at any moment — or the *inability* to end up in the same situation: this would mean that the quantum of force was not *fixed* and likewise the properties of force. An *un*fixed kind of energy, something undulating is entirely *inconceivable to us.* If we don't want to fantasize into the inconceivable and regress to the old creator concept (increase out of nothing, decrease out of nothing, absolute whimsy and freedom in growth and in properties) —

11[293]

With respect to all *our* experience we must always remain *skeptical* and e.g., say: we can claim an eternal validity for no "law of nature," we can claim eternal permanence for no chemical quality, we are not *refined* enough to see the alleged *absolute flux of events:* the *enduring* exists only by virtue of our crude organs, which summarize and lay out as planes what does not in the least exist *like this*. A tree is in every moment something *new:* we assert the *form* because we cannot perceive the subtlest absolute motion: we insert a *mathematical average line* into absolute motion, *we add* lines and planes in general, on the foundation of the intellect, which is *error*: the assumption of identity and permanence because we can *see* only permanence and we *remember* only through similarity (identity). But things are different in themselves: we should not transfer our skepticism into the essence.

11[294]

Prosperity, comfort that brings sensual gratification are now coveted, the whole world wants them above all. Consequently it will approach a *spiritual slavery* that has never before existed. For this goal *can* be reached, the biggest disturbances of the day should not deceive us. The Chinese are proof that it can also endure. *Spiritual Caesarism* hovers over all the striving of merchants and philosophers.

11[295]

Our current education has the value of a kind of *compulsion to wander* in the period of the Middle Ages and the guilds. The counterweight of setting oneself up comfortably at home according to local standards used to be effective. Now what is effective is having designs upon sensual prosperity *alongside* the image of all other cultures that wanted something *over* or *against* sensual prosperity.

Compulsory guild membership taught people *to learn:* in the end an individual drive to learn arose, through heredity. *Learning* is originally *more sour* than all work, hence hated. This is why scholars have the upper hand in the Middle Ages.

11[296]

Whoever hates or despises foreign blood is not yet an individual, but a kind of human protoplasm.

11[297]

Just go on becoming the one that you are — the teacher and sculptor of yourself! You're no writer, you write only for yourself! Thus you will keep the memory of your good moments and find their coherence, the golden chain of your self! Thus you will prepare yourself for the time when you must speak! Maybe then you will be ashamed of your speaking, as you have occasionally been ashamed of your writing, that it is still necessary to interpret yourself, that actions and nonactions do not suffice to *communicate* yourself. Yes, you want to communicate yourself! One day the etiquette will arrive by which reading widely is considered bad form: then you won't have to be ashamed anymore of being read; whereas now anyone who addresses you as a writer offends you; and whoever *praises* you on account of your writings signals to you that his tact is not subtle, he creates a gap between himself and you — he hasn't the slightest inkling of how he debases himself in believing he elevates you *thus.* I know the state of current human beings when they *read:* Phooey! Who wants to care and create for this state!

11[298][133]

When people are at odds over opinions and blood is shed and sacrificed, then the culture is high: then opinions have become goods.

11[299]

Hellwald, Haeckel and consorts — they have the disposition of specialists, and a frog-nosed wisdom. The tiny particle of brain that is open to knowledge of their world has nothing to do with its totality, it is a little nook of a talent, as when someone draws, or another plays piano; they remind me of old honest David Strauß,[134] who recounts quite innocuously how he first had to pinch and pull at himself in order to determine *whether* he even had a sensation for existence in general. These specialists do not have one and this is why they're so "cold"; cultural camels upon whose humps many good insights and much good knowledge sits, without changing the fact that the whole is still simply a camel.

11[300]

Vegetarian diet and wine — that would be the craziest of all possible lifestyles!

11[301]

Without imagination and memory there would be no pleasure and no pain. The affects stimulated by them instantly have available to them past similar cases and bad possibilities, they interpret, they insert. This is why a *pain* generally is quite disproportionate to its significance for life — it is inexpedient. But wherever an injury is not perceived by the eye or by touch, it is much less painful, in that case imagination is untrained. Pain is greatest on fingers, on teeth, on the head etc.

11[302]

The magnificence of nature, all sensations of the lofty noble gracious beautiful kindly austere violent thrilling that we have in nature and with human beings and history, are not *direct feelings* but aftereffects of countless *errors* incorporated by us — everything would be cold and dead for us without this long schooling. Even the definite lines of the mountains, the definite gradations of color, the different pleasure in each color are heirlooms: at some remote time this color was less connected with dangerously threatening appearances than another and gradually it acquired a *calming* effect (like blue)

11[303]

Egoism has been rendered heretical by those who *practiced* it (communities princes party leaders religion founders philosophers like Plato); they needed the opposite sentiment among those human beings who were supposed to perform a *function* for them. — Where a period a people a city stands out, it is always because its *egoism* becomes aware of itself and no

longer spares any means (*no longer* is *ashamed* of itself). Rich
in individuals means rich in those who are no longer ashamed
of their authenticity and deviation. When a people becomes
proud and seeks foes, it grows in strength and goodness. — By
contrast glorify selflessness! and admit, like Kant, that probably
never a deed was done by it! Therefore to diminish the opposite
principle, to suppress its value, only prejudice human beings
coldly and contemptuously, ergo *unimaginatively* against egoism! — For up till now it has been the *lack* of refined planned
resourceful egoism that has kept human beings as a whole on
such a low level! *Equality* is regarded as unifying and desirable!
We are haunted by a false concept of harmony and peace, as the
most useful condition. In truth a strong *antagonism* needs to be
added everywhere, to marriage friendship state league of states
corporation scholarly societies religion, so that something
proper can grow. Resistance is the form of *force* — in peace as
in war, consequently diverse forces and not equal ones should
exist, for the latter would hold on to the equilibrium!

11[304]¹³⁵

   Drain your life situations and accidents — and then transition to others! It does not suffice to be *one person,* even though
it happens to be the necessary beginning! Ultimately this
would mean challenging yourselves to become limited! But to
transition from one into another and to live through *a series
of beings*!

11[305]

   Infinitely new changes and states of a *specific* force is a contradiction, however big a force and however frugal a change
one were to imagine, presupposing that it is eternal. Thus we
would have to conclude 1) either it has only become active at a
specific point in time and will likewise cease at some time —
but it is *absurd* to think of a beginning of activity; if it were in
equilibrium, then it would be so eternally! 2) or infinitely new
changes do *not* exist, but instead a circuit of a specific number

of changes plays itself out again and again: activity is eternal, the number of products and states of force finite.

11[306][136]

Nature does not build for the eye, *form* is a random outcome. Think of how in one egg cell *all* atoms execute their motions, how *forms exist only for eyes* and how atoms without eyes could not *want* them either.

11[307]

Schopenhauer surely set his heart on one idea of Spinoza's: that the essence of each thing is *appetitus*[137] and that this *appetitus* consists of persisting to exist. This dawned on him once and dawned on him in such a way that he never again carefully reflected on the event "will" (no more so than all his basic concepts — with respect to which he was without doubt, because he arrived at them without proper reason and empiricism).

11[308]

How irregular is the *Milky Way*! (Vogt.[138] p 110)

11[309]

To observe how a pleasure *arises,* how *many* representations must come together! and in the end it is a unity and a whole, and no longer wants to be recognized as a multiplicity. This is how it could be with *every* pleasure and every pain! They are *brain* phenomena! But multiplicities long since incorporated into us and now only presenting themselves as a whole! *Why* does a *cut* finger hurt? *In itself* it does not hurt (even if it experiences "stimuli"), someone whose brain is chloroformed has no "pain" in the finger. Should a *judgment* first have been necessary about the injury of a functioning organ on the part of the representing *unity?* Is it the unity alone that imagines the damage and — now gives it to us to perceive as pain, by sending the *strongest* **stimuli** to the place where the harm was done? Could therefore the intent to flight defense caution rescue also reside in pain? Means of preventing further damage? Simultaneously rage about the injury, feeling of revenge in one? *Everything* **together** — pain? Thus rising to consciousness in **us**, as a jumble and unity of feeling?

11[310]

He was ashamed of his holiness and disguised it.

11[311]

Is not the existence of *any kind of* difference and the not complete circularity of the world around us already a *sufficient* **counter***proof* against a symmetrical circularity of everything that exists? Whence the difference within the circle? Whence the duration in time of this lapsing difference? Isn't everything *much too manifold* to have arisen from *one thing?* And are not the many *chemical* laws and again *organic* species and forms inexplicable from one thing? Or from two things? — Supposing there were a symmetrical "contraction energy"[139] in all the force centers of the universe, then the question arises, whence could even the slightest difference arise? Then the universe would have to dissolve into countless *completely identical* rings and existential globes, and we would have countless *completely identical worlds* **simultaneously**. Is it necessary for me to assume this? For the eternal succession of identical worlds an eternal simultaneity? But the *multiplicity and disorder* in the *world known to us so far* contradicts, there *can* not have been *such* a universal homogeneousness of development, it would have to have yielded a symmetrical globe-being for our part as well! Should in fact the emergence of qualities *not have been in conformity to law* in itself? Should different things be able to emerge from "force"? Arbitrary things? Should *conformity to law,* which *we* see, deceive us? Not be a primal law? Should the multiplicity of qualities in our world also be a result of the absolute emergence of arbitrary properties? Only it no longer occurs in our corner of the world? Or has it assumed a *rule* that we call *cause and effect,* without it being this (**a caprice turned into a rule,** e.g., oxygen and hydrogen chemically)??? Should this "rule" be simply a longer **whim**? — — —

11[312]

Whoever does not believe in a *circular process of the universe, must* believe in an *arbitrary* God — this is how my observation is conditioned in opposition to all previous theistic ones! (see Vogt p. 90.)[140]

11[313]

My **objections** *as a* **counter***hypothesis against the circular process:*

Should it be possible to deduce the laws of the *mechanical* world likewise as exceptions and to some extent *accidents* of existence *generally,* as *one* possibility among *many* countless possibilities? That we have been accidentally thrown into this mechanistic corner of the world order? That in turn all *chemism* in the mechanistic world order is the exception and the accident and ultimately the *organism* within the *chemical world* is the exception and accident? — Wouldn't we have to assume as *the most general* form of existence actually a *not yet mechanistic* world, one removed from mechanical laws (even though not inaccessible to them)? Which would in fact be the most general even now and forever? So that the emergence of the mechanistic world would be a lawless game, which in the end would gain precisely the same consistency as organic laws have now for our observation? So that *all* our *mechanistic* laws would *not be eternal,* but would have developed, among countless *diverse* mechanistic laws, as their remainder, or would have achieved mastery in individual parts of the world, not in others? — It appears that we need a *caprice,* a real nonconformity to law, only a capacity to become law-conforming, a primal-stupidity that is not suited even for mechanics? The *emergence of qualities* presupposes the emerging of quantities, and these again could emerge in keeping with thousands of kinds of mechanics.

11[314]

Our *higher* pains, the so-called pains of the soul whose dialectic we often still see with the appearance of some event, are *slow* and *protracted* compared to more base pain (e.g., from a wound), whose character is suddenness. But at bottom the latter is just as complicated and dialectical, and intellectual — the essential thing is that many affects fly off suddenly and fly *into one another* — this sudden confusion and chaos is *physical pain* for consciousness. — Pleasure and pain are not "direct facts," as representations are. A multitude of *representations, incorporated* in *drives,* show up with lightning speed and against one another. The opposite happens with pleasure, representations show up just as quickly, are in harmony and equilibrium and — *this* is perceived by the intellect as pleasure.

11[315]

There have been countless *modi cogitandi*[141] but only those that advanced organic life have been preserved — will these have been the subtlest? — *Simplification* is the main need of the organic; seeing[142] relations as much more compressed, comprehending cause and effect without the numerous intermediary members, finding much that is dissimilar to be similar — this was necessary — thus an incomparably *greater search* for nourishment and assimilation took place, because the *belief* that something nourishing could be found was much more frequently aroused — a great advantage in the growth of the organic! *Desire* multiplied a thousandfold by the thousandfold probability of gratification, the organs of *search strengthened* — : erring and making mistakes may mount innumerably, but the *favorable* moves grow **more frequent**! "*Error*" is the means to *lucky accident*!

11[316]

The **final** *organisms* whose formation we see (peoples states societies) must be used for instruction about the first organisms. Self-consciousness is the last thing to be added when an organism functions perfectly, *almost* something superfluous: the consciousness of *unity*, in any case something extremely imperfect and mistake-prone compared to the actually innate incorporated working unity of all functions. The great majority of activity is unconscious. Consciousness usually *appears* first when the whole wants to subordinate itself again to a higher whole — chiefly as the consciousness of this *higher whole*, of the outside-itself. Consciousness arises in relation to the being *for whom we could be a function* — it is the means of incorporating ourselves. As long as self-preservation is at stake, consciousness of the self is unnecessary. — Thus surely already in the lowest organism. The foreign greater stronger is first *imagined* as such. — Our judgments about our "self" limp behind, and are enacted after the introduction of the outside-of-us, of the power that rules over us. We *signify to ourselves that for which we are regarded in the* **higher** *organism* — universal law.

The sensations and the affects of the organic are all long since fully developed before the feeling of unity of consciousness arises.

Oldest organisms: chemically slow processes, sealed within even much slower processes as if in husks, exploding from time to time and then grasping about and pulling in new nourishment.

11[317][143]

You say: "those errors were necessary for that stage, as remedy — the *cure* of the human race has a necessarily rational course!" In this sense I deny rationality. It is *random* that this and any article of faith triumphed, *not* necessary — the same healing effect would perhaps have emanated as well from a different one. But above all! The *consequence* of the healing effects has been very capricious, very irrational! In addition, almost all of them brought along a deep *different* malady! But this whole *cure* of humankind has *been tolerated* by it — this is what is most remarkable! It was certainly not the most rational one, nor the *only* possible! But it was *possible*!

11[318]

You think you would have a long rest until your rebirth
— but don't deceive yourselves! Between the final moment of
consciousness and the first glow of the new life there is "no
time" — it's gone as fast as a lightning strike, even if living
creatures measure it according to billions of years and couldn't
even measure it in the first place. Timelessness and succession
are compatible once the intellect is gone.

11[319]

Measured intellectually, how *error-prone* are pleasure and
pain! How incorrectly would judgments be made if one wanted
to draw conclusions about the value for life in keeping with the
degree of pleasure or pain! In *pain* there is as much stupidity as
in blind affects, indeed it *is* wrath revenge flight disgust hatred
overfilling of imagination (exaggeration) itself, pain is a mass
of affects, undifferentiated and flowing together, *without intellect* there is no pain, but the basest form of intellect manifests
there; the intellect of "matter," of "atoms." — There is a way of
being *surprised* by an injury (like the man who was sitting on
the cherry tree and took a bullet through his cheek), such that
one does not even *feel the pain*. Pain is a *product of the brain*.

11[320]

If it's understood how even now *life* on a grand scale (in the
course of states moralities etc.) is generated by *errors:* but how
the errors must become ever higher and subtler: then it becomes
probable that what *originally* generated life was precisely the
crudest conceivable *error* — that this error first developed itself
and that generally the oldest, best-incorporated errors were
those on which the continuation of society rests. Not truth,
but the utility and longevity of opinions have to prove themselves in the course of the empirical world; it is a delusion contradicted by even our current experience that the most vitally
favorable condition is the greatest possible adaptation to the
real facts. — There could have been very many *approaches*

to representations about things, which were truer (and these still exist) but they perish, they no longer want to incorporate themselves — the foundation of errors upon which everything now rests has a selecting effect, regulating, it demands from all that is "known" an adaptation as function — otherwise[144] it will weed it out. — Within every small circle the process repeats itself: numerous approaches to new opinions will be made, but a selection takes place, the decision is made by that which lives and wants to continue living. Opinions have never caused anything to perish — *but in all perishing* those opinions shoot up freely that were previously suppressed. Every new knowledge is damaging, until it has transformed itself into an organ of the old and it acknowledges the hierarchy of old and young within it — for a long time it must remain embryonically weak; ideas often appear only late in its nature, they needed time to incorporate themselves and grow up.

11[321][145]

Untruth must be derivable from the "authentic true essence" of things: the collapsing into subject and object must correspond to actual facts. *Not* knowledge, but error belongs to the essence of things. The belief in the absolute must be derivable from the essence of *esse*,[146] from the general state of being conditioned! Evil[147] and pain belong to what is real: but not as enduring properties of *esse*. For evil and pain are only *consequences* of representing, and that representing is an eternal and universal property of all being, whether there can even be enduring properties, whether becoming does not exclude everything identical and enduring, except in the form of error and illusion, whereas representation itself is an event *without* identity and duration? — Has error *emerged* as a property of being? Erring is then a continuous becoming and changing?

11[322]

The higher the intellect, the more the scope of pain and pleasure increases, in realm and degree.

11[323]

How entirely *erroneous* is *sensation*! All our movements on the basis of sensations are underlain by judgments — incorporated opinions about specific causes and effects, about a mechanism, about our "ego" etc. But everything is false! Still: we may *know* better, but as soon as we act practically, we must act *against* our better knowing and place ourselves in the service of sensation-judgments! This is the *stage of knowledge* that is even much older than the stage of language invention — mostly animal!

11[324]

Representation itself is *no* opposite of the properties of *esse:* but only its content and the laws thereof. — Feeling and will are known to us only as representations, with this their existence is *not* proven. If they are known to us only as the content of representation and in keeping with the law of representation, then they must appear to us as equally similar enduring etc. In fact, *every* feeling is comprehended by us as something somehow enduring (a sudden blow?) and not as something new and authentic in itself, but similar and identical to what is known.

11[325]

Without the assumption of a kind of being that is opposed to true reality, we would have nothing by which it could measure and compare and copy itself: error is the prerequisite of knowing. Partial permanence, relative bodies, identical events, similar events — with these we *falsify* the true facts, but it would be impossible to know anything about them without first having falsified them. Thus to be sure every knowledge is still false, but *thus* too a *representing exists,* and among the representations in turn a *multitude of degrees* **of falseness**. To determine the degree of falseness and the necessity of basic error as the **life** *condition of being that represents* — task of science. Not how is error possible is the question, but instead: *how is a kind of truth possible* at all *despite* the fundamental untruth in knowing? — The being that represents is **certain**, indeed our only certainty: *what* it represents and *how* it must represent is the problem. That being represents is not a problem, it is simply *the fact:* **whether** a different being than the one that represents exists at all, whether representation does not belong to the *property* of being, is a problem.

11[326][148]

I am learning more and more: what *distinguishes* between human beings is *how long* they can maintain an *elevated mood.* Some for scarcely an hour, and with a few one might even doubt whether they are capable of elevated moods. There is something physiological about it.

11[327]

Women who are all too lively and would like to temper that impression choose *blue* colors: and likewise there are blue color shades in books, with which their author tries to balance his bouncy irritability.

11[328]

A human being who has to choke down so many poisonous broths each day is always to be admired when he experiences periods of great sensations and does not simply display a principled disgust of "greatness."

11[329][149]

The *antinomy:* "the elements in given reality that are *foreign* to the true essence of things can *not* stem from it, therefore *must* have been added — but from where? since nothing exists besides the true essence — consequently an explanation of the world is just as necessary as impossible." This I solve as follows: the true essence of things is a *fiction* of representing being, without which being is unable to represent. Those elements in given reality that are foreign to this fictionalized "true essence" are the properties of being, have *not* been added. But representing being, too, whose existence is bound to *erroneous* belief, *must have emerged,* provided that those properties (those of change, of relativity) are properties of *esse:* representation *and* faith in the self-identical and permanence must have emerged *simultaneously:* — I believe that already *everything organic* presupposes representation.

11[330]

Basic Certainty.

"I represent, therefore there is a being" *cogito, ergo est.*[150] — That I am this representing being, that representing is an *activity of the ego,* is no longer certain: no more so than *what* I represent. — The only being that we know is *representing being.* If we *describe* it *correctly,* then the predicates of being generally must be in it. (But insofar as we take representation itself as the object of representing, doesn't it become soaked, falsified, uncertain there by the *laws of representation?*—) *Change* belongs to representation, *not motion:* surely passing and emerging, and in representation itself all permanence is lacking; on the other hand it posits two kinds of permanence, it *believes* in permanence 1) of an ego 2) of a content: this faith in the permanence of substance i.e., in its staying *the same* with itself is a contrast to the event of representation itself. (Even when I speak quite generally about representation, as here, still I'm making a permanent thing of it) What is *in itself clear,* however, is that representation is *not something at rest,* not something immutable and identical to itself: thus the only *kind* of *being* that is granted to us, is *changing, not identical to itself,* has *relations* (conditioned, thinking *must* have a content in order to be thinking). — This is the *basic certainty of being.* Now representation *claims* the very opposite about being! But it does not therefore have to be *true!* Rather, perhaps this claiming of the opposite is simply an *existential condition* of this *kind* of being, of the *representing* kind! That is: thinking would be impossible if it did not thoroughly *misjudge* the essence of *esse:* it must *assert* substance and identity because a knowing of complete flux is impossible, it must *add fictional* properties to being in order to exist itself. *No subject or object needs to exist* for representation to be possible, but surely representation *must* believe in them both. — In sum: what thinking comprehends as reality, *must comprehend,* can be the opposite of what exists!

11[331]

We *are milder* and more humane! All mildness and humaneness, however, consists in the fact that we attribute much to *circumstances* and no longer everything to the person! and that in numerous ways we grant egoism its validity and no longer regard it as the incarnation of evil and reprehensibility (as it was regarded in the *community*). Therefore: *relenting* in our belief in the absolute responsibility of the person and our belief in the reprehensibility of the individual constitutes our *progress away from barbarism*!

11[332]

You say: "certain articles of faith are *salutary* for humankind, consequently they must be believed" (thus every community has judged[151]). But it has been **my** achievement to have promoted the *counterclaim* for the first time! — thus to have asked: what unspeakable misery, what worsening of the human being has arisen from the fact that one posited the ideal of selflessness, *therefore* proclaiming egoism evil and letting it *be perceived as evil*!! — from the fact that one proclaimed human will to be free and saddled humans with complete responsibility hence *responsibility* for everything egoistic — everything "called evil" — i.e., the natural necessities of human nature: this is how he got a bad name and a bad conscience: — from the fact that one thought of a sacred God above human beings and therewith imposed an evil essence on *all* deeds, and especially for those human beings who perceived more subtly and nobly? — *Relenting* in these terrible articles of faith and relenting generally in the forcing and enforcing of faith banished barbarism! — To be sure: an *even earlier* barbarism, a cruder one could only be banished by those "salutary" articles of delusion.

11[333]

All *representing* comes into being with the help of memory, and is the product of countless experiences judgments errors pleasures displeasures of past moments in a human being: however suddenly it appears. When I imagine a mountain lake, then an entirely different past in me works on this representation than if someone from Berlin imagines it. Or: "church" "philosopher" "nobleman" "loafer" etc.

11[334]

Every *pleasure* and *displeasure* in us is now an extremely complicated event, no matter how suddenly it appears; they are accompanied by the whole of experience and an immense sum of valuations and errors. The measure of pain is not proportionate to danger; our insight contradicts. Likewise the measure of pleasure is not proportionate to our current knowledge — but surely to the "knowledge" of the most primitive and longest pre-period of humankind and animality. We are subject to the law of the past i.e., *its assumptions and valuations.*

11[335][152]

Only those kinds of assumptions have been preserved with which a continuation of life was *possible* — this is the most ancient *critique* and for a long time the only one! Through this the crudest errors have been incorporated by us, ineradicably — for often they did not hinder the continuation of life. Whether an assumption brought damage *in the long run* (e.g., the assumption that a drink was healthy, yet in the long run it shortened one's life), this was not considered. The short life span of human beings may be the *consequence* of erroneous incorporated assumptions.

At the beginning of all mental activity stand the *crudest assumptions* and fictions, e.g., identity thing permanence. They are of the same age as the intellect and it modeled its nature after them. — Only those assumptions remained with which organic life was compatible.

11[336]¹⁵³

To E. R.¹⁵⁴

If I read me, then I read into me
A friend construes me more objectively.
And should he on his own true path ascend,
He bears on high the image of his friend.

February 1882.

11[337]¹⁵⁵

Gaya Scienza.

Albas	Morning songs
Serenas	Evening songs
Tenzoni	Battle songs
Sirventes	Songs of praise and censure
Sontas	Songs of joy
Laïs	Songs of sorrow

11[338]

Future history: *this* thought will triumph more and more —
and those who do not believe in it will have to *die out* finally in
keeping with their nature!

Only those who consider their existence capable of eternal
repetition will *survive:* among *these,* however, a state¹⁵⁶ is *possible* for which no utopian has ever reached!

11[339]

Are you now *prepared?* You must have lived through every
degree of skepticism and have bathed lasciviously in ice-cold
streams — otherwise you have no right to this thought; I want
to defend myself well against the gullible and the fanatics! I
want to *defend* my thought in advance! It should be the religion
of the freest most cheerful and most sublime souls — a lovely
stretch of meadow between gilded ice and pure blue sky!

11[340]
1) Tremendous fact: all our moral judgments have arisen from their *opposites: how* did this happen?
2) how did the *older* moral judgment *emerge?*

11[341]
Punishment is not *dishonoring* as long as it also applies to the *unintentional* harm-doer.

11[342]
Sting of conscience also following *unintentional* sacrilege. E.g., Oedipus.
essential: *disgust* at oneself!
aesthetic basic nature of judgment.

11[343][157]
Against Spencer: "it is not expedient this way" — this is *no moral* judgment
"It is not right, *even though* it is expedient"
"it debases me" "it makes me appalled and disgusted."
Consideration for one's own advantage **or** *that of society still does not* make the matter "moral"! "It is harmful to others, advantageous for me" — *what has to happen* so that this is perceived as "demeaning," as disgusting? — In and of itself it is the *just* deed that is natural, with which everything blossoms and flourishes.
Free will, knowledge of the **purposes** *of actions* were perceived as *immoral:* this is herd instinct. *Science*[158] has had bad conscience in its favor.

11[344]
In the herd *no* love of thy neighbor: but a sense for the whole and *indifference* toward the neighbor. This indifference is something very *elevated*!

11[345]

Which proposition and belief best expresses the decisive turn that manifested through the preponderance of scientific spirit over religious divinely fictionalized spirit? We insist on the fact that the world, as a force, cannot be thought of as unlimited — we forbid ourselves the concept of an infinite force as incompatible with the concept of "force."

11[346]

human beings taking *nature* into service and overwhelming it

the scientific human being works under the instinct of this *will to power* and feels himself justified

progress in knowledge as progress in power (but *not* as an individual). On the contrary, this slave-like use of the scholar makes the individual *baser.*

11[347]

Antagonism:

| Enhancement and strengthening of the type!
| Enhancement and strengthening of its individual organs and functions.

11[348]

In and of myself — what for? —

12[1][1]

>   At night, before the starry sky:
>   — Oh this deathly silent din! —

12[2]
Wordplays:
>   *Ridiculture* of a person
>   the *intellectual dessert* now for many: Gorgon-Zola
>   — in *the Grotto of his Nymph Angeria*.[2]

12[3]
>   Genoa, *this bleached South.*

12[4][3]
Artists who with their urging and their longing know how to make an effect, whereas they are incapable of reaching *their* own goals. But they communicate the impulse — and occasionally the other has the mightier energy for reaching or at least *anticipating* the goal.

12[5]
sci⟨ence⟩ displays *where humans have become rigid* (not *where* things have — even though it expresses itself like this today!) Polyps become *aware* of the tremendous mountain that they have built and that consists of them, that they are a *living* mountain of terrible rigidity.

12[6]⁴

This terrible *reality*, this *terribleness* of reality is just as visible in moral phenomena as in physical, indeed more distinctly: how here [+++] at bottom everything **fiction! This is what I must prove!** — It is as if in a dream, it exerts an entirely real power, the belief that here is *something real* (e.g., in a murder, an execution, a funeral procession)

12[7]⁵

Without the imagining of other beings besides humans everything is and remains small-town, small-humanity. The invention of gods and heroes was inestimable. We *need* beings for comparison, even the falsely interpreted human beings, the saints and heroes have been a powerful means. Of course: this drive *consumed* a portion of the energy that could have been expended on finding our *own* ideal. — But seeking one's own ideals was not for earlier times, the most important thing was no longer to allow humans *to sink below* an average and this was helped by the fact that they were virtually chained to a universal image of humans, that selflessness was preached to them.

12[8]⁶

How I have sought the human being who is higher than I and who really surveys me! I didn't find him. I'm not permitted to compare myself to W⟨agner⟩ — but I belong to a higher rank, apart from "energy."

12[9]

If we do not make a magnificent *renunciation* and an ongoing *triumph over ourselves* out of the *death of God,* then we have the *loss to bear.*

12[10]

The new problem: whether *part of humanity* should not be cultivated at the expense of another to a higher race. Cultivation — — — —

12[11]

Ultimately: our idealistic fantasizing *also* belongs to *existence* and must appear in the *latter's character.* It is not the *source,* but that is why it is present at all. Our highest and most daring thoughts are character pieces of "reality." Our thought is of the same stuff as all things.

12[12]

We despise someone who is without property — *therefore* also someone who cannot control himself, who is not in possession of himself. In our perception he is not despicable as an egoist, but as a weathervane of impulses and lack of self.

12[13]

In a clever ruthless rogue and criminal it is not his *egoism* as such that we censure, which expresses itself in the finest manner, but that it aims for such *base goals* and *limits* itself to them. If the goals are great, then humankind has a different standard and does *not* estimate "crime" as such, even the most terrible means. — What is disgusting is a good intellect in the service of a miserable insipidity of taste — we are *disgusted* by the **kind** of ego not by ego in itself.

12[14]⁷

Music now *represents* feelings — it *does not arouse them*!

12[15]

inorganic matter, even if it was mostly organic, *did not learn anything,* is always without a past! *If it were otherwise,* then there could never be a repetition — for something would always emerge from stuff with *new* qualities, with *new* pasts.

12[16]

To experience different things with the same *music*!

12[17]⁸

A thing, all alone, would not exist at all — it would have no relations at all. E.g., my book.

12[18]⁹

I pretend to myself to be irate about the coldness and neglect I experience from friends — but at the deepest bottom this leaves me unperturbed, and I almost *wish* to make it a motive that might agitate me somewhat. I seek reasons against boredom and don't find much.

12[19]

That someone does not desire certain things, does not love them, this we begrudge him as a sign of his *lowness* and baseness. "Selflessness" as *counterpart* — he loves certain things and makes a sacrifice of other drives that are *not comprehensible* to most people as the object of such love — this is why they assume the *miracle* of "selflessness"!

12[20]¹⁰

Human beings have always misunderstood love — they believe themselves to be selfless here, because they desire the advantage of another being, often against their own. Do they want to **possess** that other being *for this reason?* Often not even that!

12[21]

The first book as the *eulogy* for the death of *God.* —

12[22]

A hundred Tannhäusers.¹¹ — To not believe in Wotan! Interpretation of the past.

12[23]¹²

This loneliest of the lonely, the human being, no longer seeks a God, but a *companion.* This will be the *myth-building* drive of the future. He seeks the *friend of human beings.*

12[24]¹³

This world we created, oh how we have *loved* it!

How profoundly *foreign* to us is the world discovered through science!

12[25]

We are constantly making sacrifices. Now this inclination triumphs over the others and their demands, now that one. You would be amazed if I calculated in advance how much sacrifice each day costs me.

12[26]¹⁴

Everything that human beings posited out of themselves, *into* the outside world, they have thereby made *foreign* to themselves and ever more so: so that it now functions like a non-ego and bears and endures all the moral predicates that humans no longer dare to ascribe to themselves. "Nature." Thus they have *debased* and *impoverished* themselves: the richer their outside-themselves became (color movement likewise beauty lines sublimity).

12[27]¹⁵

Whereas the melancholic is all too deficient in phosphoric calcium in his blood and brain, he sees the reason for his feeling of insufficiency and his depression in the *moral* conditions of human beings, of things, or himself!!!

12[28]

Children who have recall of punishments become sneaky and secretive. But usually they forget them — and so they remain in innocence.

12[29]¹⁶

We cannot get beyond aesthetics — I used to believe that a god takes pleasure in beholding the world: but we have the essence of a world that *humans* have gradually *created: their* aesthetics.

12[30]¹⁷

Music — a disguised gratification of the *religiosi*.¹⁸ *Look away* from words! This is their advantage! Indeed even from images! So that the intellect is not *ashamed* of itself! Thus it is *healthy* and an alleviation for those drives that *really do want to be gratified*!

12[31]

to hunt for truth — it is also merely a form of the *hunt for happiness*

12[32]

Alas, *now* we must embrace untruth and only now error becomes *lie* and the lie in front of us becomes a *necessity of life*!

12[33]

Alas, I have seen through the masquerade of great men, of great successes, of great losses. Everything has to be observed perspectivally — if one does not classify oneself among the petty, then all one gets in return is noise and grounds for laughter and heartbreak.

12[34]¹⁹

My task: to reclaim all the beauty and sublimity that we have conferred on things real and imagined as the *property and productivity of human beings* and as their most beautiful ornamentation, most beautiful apology. The human being as poet, as thinker, as god, as power, as compassion. Oh to think of the royal generosity with which he bestowed things, *in order to impoverish himself* and feel miserable! This is his greatest "selflessness," as he admires and worships and neither knows nor wants to know that he *created* what he admires. — These are the *poems* and *paintings* of *primitive* humankind, these "real" nature scenes — back when one did not yet know how else to write and to paint except by *projecting* something into things. And we have received *this inheritance*. — This sublime line, this feeling of mournful grandeur, this feeling of the restless sea have all been *created* by our ancestors. This *viewing* of things as fixed and definite in general!

12[35]
How is it that we satisfy our stronger inclinations at the expense of our weaker inclinations? — In itself, if we were a unity, this split could not exist. In fact we are a multiplicity *that has imagined a unity for itself.* The intellect as the means of deception with its obligatory forms "substance" "identity" "duration" — *it* was the first to get multiplicity out of its head.

12[36]
Music is my and our *predecessor* — to speak so personally and so well and nobly! Unspeakably ⟨much⟩[20] has found no words and no thoughts — this is what our music *proves* — *not* that no thought and no word were to be found.

12[37][21]
nox intemp⟨esta⟩[22] where cause and effect seem to have become unhinged and at any moment something can emerge from nothing. (Richard Wagner set it to music in "Hagen's Vigil"[23])

12[38][24]
This beauty and sublimity of *nature,* before which every human being seems small, was first *imposed* on nature by us — consequently humankind has been *deprived* of this portion. It will have to atone for it.

12[39]
Wherever we believe we recognize something quite estimable and want to acquire and keep it, hence in the craving for *possessions,* our noblest drives are awakened. The lover is a *superior* human being: even though he is more egoist than ever. But 1. his egoism is concentrated, 2. a single drive has decisively *triumphed* over the others and produces the *extraordinary.*

12[40]

The bulwark of science and its rational universality must first be erected, then the unchaining *of indi⟨viduals⟩* can proceed: this must be brought about without error, because the *borders* of rationality were established in advance and incorporated into the conscience and body. *First* incorporation of science — then:

12[41]²⁵

My feeling distinguishes between superior and lower human beings: what and how it distinguishes here is something I want someday to articulate as harshly and definitely as possible.

12[42]²⁶

One thing is always more necessary than the other.

12[43]

Actions through which we *satisfy* an affect (whether that of love inclination disinclination toward someone) are not called "selfless," unless in an imprecise manner of speaking. The lover obviously affirms himself more than ever — and if he has to dispense with the actions of love and sacrifice, then he suffers greatly — The problem is not here — we also carry out seemingly selfless actions toward indifferent or even unpleasant persons and things. On this my [—]. — But the problem remains: how can one love someone? Even a brother? Such a brother.

12[44]²⁷

The thinker who usually has to find his quiet between two clamors, if he knows how to find it all!   26 Oct. 1881.

12[45]

How many different *ages of life* our moral qualities have!

12[46]

What becomes of the excess of divine feelings? Or does *this* not exist?

12[47]

Conversations in solitude.

12[48]

12 summers.

12[49]

Mockery in someone who *calmly* enjoys, as a sign that the intellect is not falling asleep! But hatred — — —

12[50]

But the world that science discovers — where does *it* come from? If everything came from *us,* then *something* like this should not even exist! Or is it only our *forgotten* world? Was everything at some time surface and skin and *object* of consciousness, until there was a new surface and skin and the old one was forgotten?

12[51]

aesthetic judgments are *remnants* of our judgments about happy-unhappy e.g., in a landscape the *abundance* of colors, of things to savor, of peace, of definite lines — they are all the signs and symbols of someone once considered by us to be the happy one. Thus at other times the *passionate* zone — we also considered passion to be the state of happiness. The pious zone, the sacred zone, the venerated zone, the ancient, the childish, the feminine, the proud, the sleeping

12[52]

When I speak of Plato Pascal[28] Spinoza and Goethe, then I know that their blood flows in mine — I am *proud* when I speak the truth about them — the family is good enough that it doesn't need to invent or to conceal; and thus I stand in relation to everything that has been, *I am proud of humaneness,* and proud precisely in unconditional truthfulness

12[53]

For the thoughtless an abbreviated philosophy and morality is needed: God. Especially when the evil hours come!

12[54]

High chambers!

Many stupid women do not consider milk to be food, and yet beets indeed.[29]

12[55][30]

A woman is the creature that *should love* — and loves — its enemy and robber.

12[56]

To perish of a bad tendency — not so terrible! To *expose* the fantasies about evil as well as about *pain*!!

12[57]

To what extent any brighter horizon appears as nihilism

12[58]

We aestheticians of the highest order also do not want to *miss* crimes and vices and agonies of the soul and errors — and a society of *sages* would probably *create an additional* evil world for itself. I mean, it is no proof against the artistry of God that evil and pain exist — but surely against his "*goodness*"? — But then what is goodness! Wanting to help and wanting to do good deeds, which likewise presupposes those for whom things are *worse*! and who are *worse*!

12[59]

Extraordinarily *small* changes of valuation suffice to obtain quite tremendously *different images of value* (arrangement of goods)

12[60]

We are *not* the remains and remnants of humankind (as we are this certainly of the organic world of *becoming*) Much that is new can still emanate from us, that *will change* the character of humankind.

12[61]

Who will invent for us the tragic ballet with music? Especially necessary among peoples who cannot sing and who have broken their throats through dramatic music!

12[62]

"I have forgotten my umbrella"[31]

12[63][32]

Cause and effect. At bottom what we mean by this is simply that which we think, when we think *ourselves* as the cause of a blow etc. "I want" is the prerequisite, actually it is the belief in a magically acting force, this belief in cause and effect — the belief that *all* causes are as *personally willing* as a human being. In sum, this proposition a priori is a piece of primal mythology — nothing more!

12[64]

We should not develop the reason of humankind *against the grain,* but it is already ensured that we are unable to.

12[65]

the *reconciling* human beings are fatal to me

12[66][33]

the *ash-gray light* that the moon obtains from the illuminated earth

12[67][34]

Pain is so well developed on account of its great utility — it is just as useful as pleasure

12[68]

Emerson

I have never felt myself so at home and in my home in a book as — I must not praise it, it's too close to me.

12[69]³⁵

Masks occur to us in the case of Ital⟨ian⟩ music.

12[70]³⁶

I want to write the whole thing quite personally and as a kind of *Manfred.*³⁷ From human beings I seek *neither "praise nor compassion nor help"* — on the contrary I want them *"overwhelmed* by me."

12[71]³⁸

through alcohol one regresses to stages of culture that one has overcome. All foods have some kind of revelation about the past from which we *became.*

12[72]

No! I do not want to be older than I am. Perhaps the time will one day come when even the eagles must look up timidly to me (as to S⟨aint⟩ John³⁹)

12[73]

Textual scholars⁴⁰ — natural scholars

12[74]⁴¹

That each and every event is the result of acts of will and *thereby* explained or not further explicable — this belief the savages have in common with Schopenhauer: it used to dominate all human beings and it was a mere *atavism* still to have and to preach it in the 19th century in the middle of Europe. The opposite — that with all events the will is not involved, however much it seems to be — has *practically* been proven! (And this for the unspeakably tiny piece of event where a will could be involved at all!)

12[75]

I *guard against* separating reason *and love,* justice and love from each other, or even juxtaposing them and assigning a higher rank to love! Love is *comes,*[42] in reason and justice, it is the joy of something, pleasure in owning it, desire to own it entirely and in its complete beauty — the *aesthetic side* of justice and reason, a secondary drive.

After we *have reason* and *justice,* we must *smash* the ladders that led us there; it is our sad duty that these highest achievements force us to summon our parents and grandparents to court, so to speak. *To be just toward the past, to want to know it, in all love!* Here our nobility is put to the hardest test! I notice when someone speaks of Christianity with a vengeful heart — this is base!

12[76][43]

Science gives us our *noble* family tree, our heraldry: it gives us ancestors. Compared to us all previous human beings were "ephemera"[44] and rabble, who had only a *short* memory.

The *historic feeling* is the new, here something *quite great* is growing! At first harmful, like everything new! It will have to accustom itself for a long time before it becomes *healthy* and produces rich blossoms! We hear how much our ancestors — heroes *possessed* — we have to let go of much, but counter all losses with *higher gains.*

Reason and *justice* are the hardest to dignify, because *young* and *weak* and often harmful!

12[77][45]

God is dead[46] — then who *killed* him? Even this feeling *of having killed the most sacred and most powerful* must still come over *individual* human beings — now it is still too early! too weak! Murder of murders! We awaken as murderers! How does someone like this console himself? How does he cleanse himself? *Must he not himself become the most omnipotent and sacred poet?*

12[78]

Our laws are attempts to create out of paper the wise man who is equal to all circumstances and whose justice is just as great as his intrepidity — oh, where has the awe-inspiring face of the lawgiver gone, who must signify more than the law, namely the desire *to keep it holy out of love and reverence?*

12[79][47]

I have a *descent* — this is pride, contrasted with *cupido gloriae.*[48] It is not unknown to me that Zarathustra — — —

12[80][49]

What is original in the human being is that he *sees* a thing that all do not *see.*

12[81][50]

The dissatisfied must have something to which they can attach their affections: e.g., God. Now that the latter is *lacking, socialism* gets many of those who would have formerly clung to God — or *patria*[51] (like Mazzini). An occasion for magnificent self-sacrifice, and a *public one* (because it disciplines and holds together, also provides courage!) should always be there! Here are opportunities for *invention*!

12[82]

We ourselves, like God, must be just merciful sunny toward all things and always re-create them, just as we created them.

12[83]

One incorrectly transposes perceptions (that are explicable according to contemporary circumstances e.g., *marriage*) into ancient times, when marriage was different and could not in the least produce *love* between the spouses!

12[84]

R⟨ichard⟩ W⟨agner⟩ wanted a grand culture in order to have a place for his art — but he lacked the new idea. So he went borrowing everywhere: ultimately Christian sentiments, even if not Christian ideas etc.

12[85]⁵²

Give up the lower degrees of power in order to arrive at higher ones

12[86]⁵³

To me as a *man* the dreamy constitution of the world is *repulsive* — but as a *man* I tell the truth, even the repulsive one.

12[87]

That kind of egoism that compels us *to do or not do something for the neighbor's sake.*

12[88]

To collect situations

12[89]

First principle of *my* morality: one shall not strive for *states,* neither for one's happiness, nor one's calm, nor one's mastery of himself. One's *state* should always be *only comes,* never *dux virtutis!*⁵⁴ Why? — Also not "the ideal" — rather, execute *every small and big action* as sublimely and beautifully as possible and also visibly! *The way and manner shall distinguish us!*

12[90]⁵⁵

Sci⟨ence⟩ suddenly is soaring upward so rapidly that its disciples can scarcely catch their breath — and precisely in this all too thin air it *pains* them as far and as clearly as their eye can see. Humankind will have to catch it up — it will have to do as it has done *so far!* All the prudence and reason on which our life now rests has been the invention of individuals and quite gradually has become forced upon, imposed upon, drilled into and incorporated by humankind — so that now it appears to belong to the unshakeable essence of human beings!

12[91]

Someone who studies nutrition e.g., or heating learns a multitude of rules of conduct. Formerly all these rules were subsumed by "morality" — now their instruction is no longer so solemn and is not associated with the salvation of the soul. Just as magic has been infinitely overtaken by science in force and feats — so too:

12[92]

We old inveterate Wagnerians are indeed the most grateful listeners of Bellini and Rossini.

12[93]

I see the disproportion between science and human beings all the time — it never disappears from my sight: was there ever anything similar? Priest and human being, prophet and human being, prince and human being, judge and human being. Each time the challenge seemed to *raise* the individual

12[94]

The *fioriture* and cadenzas of music are like sweet ice cream in summer.

12[95]⁵⁶

All who do not want to show themselves naked reach for the periodic style, as if for a costume — whether because they are formless, whether because they have all too shamefully gotten used to things. Their thoughts are timid and awkward without a veil — the bit of *grace* of which they are capable only shows when the pleats of the period inspire them with courage and faith in their own dignity. We want to tolerate this in them and even commend it: only we request that these cloak-wearing, pleat-replete ones not make a law of morality and beauty of themselves: the periodic style is and remains a stopgap and — — —

12[96][57]

M⟨y⟩ brothers! Let us not hide it from ourselves! The sci⟨ence⟩ or, more honestly, the *passion of knowledge* is here; a tremendous new growing power, whose like has never been seen before, with the eagle's sweep, owl's eyes and the feet of a dragon — indeed already it is so strong that it sees itself as a problem and asks: "how am *I* even possible among *human beings*! How are human beings henceforth possible *with me*!"

12[97][58]

This passion of kno⟨wledge⟩ attacks itself, it enquires into its Why? Into its "Where from?" — and — — —

12[98][59]

humankind has become worse

12[99]

The feeling of moral disdain is now common!

12[100]

a monster of time spans, for which we speech-starved again are not prepared with any word — we would have to say: a small eternity of time —

12[101]

Here I am this living shellfish, beneath all the cliffs on the shore

12[102]

Whoever enjoys tragedy *morally* still has a few levels to *climb*

12[103]

The best music isn't much if a male or female singer cannot transport us through voice and artistry into gentle drunkenness — and in *this* case *inferior* music is elevated unspeakably!

12[104]

Are these things *important* after all? I walk through great cities and find no one who would consider them to be such — or those who fake it — for the sake of their profession. *But what is important is that they no longer take it to be important*! Savonarola in Florence is over! entirely!

12[105]

The builder asks: who is *regarded as* having the best taste as an architect? His taste I *want* to have — and he accustoms himself to this, it becomes his *need*. Thus do cities finally acquire a taste

12[106]⁶⁰

Happiness, broad and slow stairs

12[107]⁶¹

The thoughts of the ancients have tremendous effect, because faith in the ancients has accumulated for centuries. My thoughts concern things that are too lofty and difficult to be capable of effect without the greatest *personal pressure* —

12[108]⁶²

If this h⟨uman being⟩ does not become great in virtue, then he will become terrible, to himself and others. With others it is of no use if they strive so urgently for virtue — through their mediocrity they will deprive even virtue of its prestige.

12[109]

Is not simply everything ready for this revolution? The situation has to be described.

12[110][63]

Paradox in woman and her education — very secretive and interesting. — *This* meaning all morality has

12[111]

There is no partiality for the living or against the dead in nature. When something living does not survive, *then no purpose has failed*!

the character "useful" "expedient" is accessorial, human

12[112][64]

"If Z⟨arathustra⟩ wants to move the multitude, then he must be the actor of himself"

"Zarathustra's idleness is the root of all evil"[65]

12[113][66]

Is there then in the whole world now a human being who is sitting like me on the seashore and —

12[114][67]

Genoese idleness.

If I've observed properly, then I'm the only idler here.

12[115]

The middle classes strive with every enthusiasm to bring the workers into *their* circumstances: are they perhaps *happier?*

12[116][68]

What I have noticed in the real Jew-haters[69] (like W⟨agner⟩) is more their affinity with Judaism than their dissimilarity — it is a tremendous jealousy. The Germans would divide now into Jews and Jew-haters, i.e., — — —

12[117][70]

A new kind of *stultification* — through pleasure in activity and enterprise.

12[118]⁷¹

S⟨omeone⟩ with a pale face, bent deeply over my table. This image lasted a moment: in the next I perceived a cat, a *couple of steps further*

12[119]⁷²

Music as the *art* of the *dawn*!

12[120]

What R⟨ichard⟩ W⟨agner⟩ is worth, that will only be told us by the one who makes the best use of him. For the time being we have believed about W⟨agner⟩ what he would like to have believed

12[121]

Chamfort and his way of making us laugh in one moment and reflect in many moments.

12[122]⁷³

Ennoblement of prostitution

12[123]⁷⁴

In honor of old women

12[124]

in Germany, where the best voices are ruined by the ugly language so that ultimately beautiful brass instruments remain and nothing more —

12[125]⁷⁵

Marriage has had a bad conscience — can you believe it? Yes one should believe it

12[126]

My art of alleviating and breaking what is pathetic.

12[127]

I take the liberty of *forgetting* myself. Why not contradicting!

12[128]

You contradict today what you taught yesterday — But that is why yesterday is not today, said Zarathustra.

12[129]⁷⁶

Ready for the utmost

All kinds of brave h⟨uman beings⟩ in order — — —

an unspeakable feeling of grief that life just flows away.

One day I said to myself: everything comes back, and this wonderful drop of melancholy in the happiness of the conqueror is perhaps the most beautiful thing.

To his disciple he said: "that is the purple melancholy, the loveliest mussel that you can collect at the sea of existence

the feeling of impending *farewell,* the evening lighting of things

for **kings**

12[130]⁷⁷

You are harsh against your earlier ideal and the people with whom it bound you. — In fact, I have climbed over and beyond them, in order to look around for a higher ideal. It was a stair for me — and those others thought that was where I wanted to retire.

12[131]⁷⁸

2 youths were brought to Z⟨arathustra⟩. "this one will do everything in a mediocre way — this one will not want to harm anyone, he is not heroically cruel enough."

12[132]⁷⁹

Not species- but herd-egoism

12[133]

barbaric, to take precisely the weakness of a thing, the opposite, to take a thing in such a way that one knows how to posit one's own strength in place of its weakness and thus *bestow* on it

12[134][80]

the terrible screams signs riddles everything that the digestion of humankind cannot finish — the "*feces of existence*" have been the most fertile dung

12[135]

Whoever triumphs much must have had many opponents. All our strengths constantly want to fight. Morality wants: *first and foremost opponents! and war!*

12[136]

How *many* noble and fine goats[81] I have met on my travels! said Z⟨arathustra⟩.

12[137]

Verdi is poor in inventions of beautiful sensuality and even lets it show that he has to deal with them extremely sparsely. But he manages to keep his audience together with his few ideas — they have all grown poorer, like him, and yet they want nothing else, just like him — so he is their man and master. W⟨agner⟩ too has a poor sensuality and with respect to melody an obstinacy of poverty that borders on the crazy — but how successfully he knew how to use this to build a bridge to the ideal!

12[138]

W⟨agner's⟩ music is like a cloud — and one would have to be like Rosencrantz and Guildenstern,[82] and some aestheticians, to see a *camel* in this cloud and nothing more

12[139]

Of the German poets Clemens Brentano has the most *music* in his body

12[140][83]

Heroism is the power to suffer pain and *to inflict it.*

12[141]

Stoicism in composed suffering is a sign of paralyzed strength, one places his laziness in countering pain on the scale — lack of heroism, which always fights (not suffers) which "voluntarily seeks" pain.

12[142][84]

"How did I even bear living until now!" on Posillipo[85] as the carriage rolled — evening light

12[143]

Those people do not matter who would sooner return a greeting on the street than recognize the person

12[144][86]

To "*Mediterraneanize*" one's tea or water (using orange-water)

12[145][87]

That emperor constantly reminds himself of the transitoriness of all things, in order not to take them too seriously and to stay *calm.* Transitoriness has an entirely different effect on me — to me everything seems to be far more valuable than to be permitted to be so fleeting — to me it's as if the precious wines and ointments were being poured into the sea.

12[146]

Lest our happiness malign us, we must wear visible defects.

12[147]

Noble: to what extent a different standard of morality than that of compassion? the superior one — the *degree of capacity for contempt.*

One can *ask:* has morality been a means of *ennoblement* of human beings? What does "ennoblement" mean here? A finer kind of morality itself? — "To think *more highly* of oneself"? —
prophetic crimes

12[148]

Without the feeling "I am responsible" — what will become of human beings? Without *faith in conscience* — what will become of them? For they can have stings of conscience, but be *skeptical* of them, as they are of other drives that stir

12[149]

Pilgrimages as the spa journeys of the poor — and the churches their palace and their nobility

12[150]

Inscription of the poet-room

12[151]

the author richest in ideas so far this cen⟨tury⟩ is an American[88] (unfortunately obscured by German philosophy — frosted glass)
Three[89] errors 1) compensation[90] — — —

12[152]

Goethe who keeps accounts even regarding his passions.

12[153][91]

I still follow everything that illuminates — and you shield your eyes with your hand when you look out.

12[154][92]

I swim on the uppermost wave.

12[155]

Foul smell a prejudice. All excretions disgusting — why? As foul-smelling? Why foul? they are not harmful. Saliva mucus sweat sperm urine feces skin residue, nasal discharges etc. It is inexpedient! — Disgust increasing with refinement. The functions associated with them, also disgusting. — Disgust to be understood as nausea: excretions arouse the impulse to evacuate nourishment undigested (*like a poison*) Judgment from the standpoint of *edibility:* this cannot be eaten! Basic judgment of morality.

12[156][93]

Those who are made ever more spiritual and sweeter by age, like a good wine — human beings like Goethe and Epicurus — think back also on their erotic experiences.

12[157][94]

Here Z⟨arathustra⟩ fell silent again and sank into deep reflection. Finally he said as if dreaming: "Or did he kill himself? Were we merely his hands?"

12[158]

In order to see the beauty of this woman entirely, one must see her with weak eyes: but in order to see her mind entirely, one will have to use the sharpest magnifying glass — for she hides it in her[95] face out of vanity, to the fullest extent it can be hidden: for intelligence makes women old.

12[159]

   Oh happiness, you fairest prey,
   ever near, never near enough,
   ever morrow, just not today —
   is your hunter's youth too rough?
   Are you really the path to sin,

of every sin
the sinful loveliest stuff

12[160]

Each thing measurable against each thing: but outside of things there is no standard: which is why in itself each magnitude is infinitely big and infinitely small.

By contrast there is perhaps a unit of *time* that is fixed. Forces need definite times in order to become definite qualities.

12[161][96]

I wouldn't miss me!

12[162]

The dawn has glowed — but where is the sun? This day will bring storm — storm clouds drift along the horizon.

12[163]

the simplest organism is the perfect one — all more complicated ones are more defective and countless of the superior kind perish. Herds and states are the highest known to us — very imperfect organisms. Finally there emerges, *behind* the state, the human individual — the highest and *most imperfect* being, which perishes *as a rule* and annihilates the creations from which he emerges. The entire *pensum*[97] of herd- and state-instincts is concentrated within him. He can live alone, according to his own laws — he is *not* a lawgiver and does *not* **want** to rule. His *feeling of power* strikes *inward*. The Socratic *virtues*!

12[164]

Comfort for those who *perish*! regard their passions as an unfortunate lottery outcome. Observe *that* most throws must fail, that perishing is as *useful* as becoming. *No* regret. Abbreviating suicide.

12[165]

A word to those who believe in God — they might wish to consider whether a God can will the annihilation of something or is even *able* to annihilate anything — whether precisely this is not the divine incapacity

12[166]

The brain-unease that wine—and be it only a tablespoon, produces in me is insufferable.

12[167][98]

*Youth has no virtue[99]

12[168][100]

A music could still come along, compared to which Wagner's entire art would fall under the category and the justification of *recitativo secco:*[101] and whoever surrenders himself to the sublime question of morality in music will also have to take that possibility into consideration.

12[169]

Hostility greed for power cruelty envy revenge lust for mocking and blaming lying penchant for lasciviousness and possessions

12[170][102]

Voltaire's noble decency and gracefulness

12[171][103]

Malherbe says to his father confessor, who spoke to him of bliss in clumsy and crude terms: "Enough! leave it alone! Your bad style is making me nauseous."

12[172][104]

That Indian who got it into his head that if he voided his urine he would flood the whole of Disnajan.[105]

12[173]
"this very bridge was built here"[106] provincial simplicity

12[174][107]
Friendship — different than love

12[175][108]
Cardinal Richelieu wanted to be proclaimed holy

12[176]
From whom have you learned all that, asked Saadi[109] of a wise man. "From the blind man who does not lift his foot until he has first tested with his cane the ground on which he is to step"[110]

12[177][111]
Posillipo and all the blind people whose eyes are opened.[112]

12[178][113]
My thoughts are supposed to show me *where I stand,* but they should not betray where I am going — I love the uncertainty of the future and do not want to perish of impatience and anticipation of *promised* things.

I will fall until I hit the ground — and no longer want to say: "I am investigating the grounds!"

My invisible nature is perhaps at bottom far-sighted and long-winded:[114] but perhaps my spirit is too short for it, with a quick glance it snatches up a few of my nature's last fringes and never tires of being amazed by its colorfulness and apparent irrationality.

12[179][115]
"from this chalice *foams* infinity."

12[180]
Sophocles concedes that each person is right or makes them so.

12[181][116]

I don't have enough energy for the North: there rule the
ponderous and artificial souls who work as incessantly and
urgently on rules of caution as beavers on their lodge.[117]
Among them I misspent my entire youth! this took hold of
me, when I saw evening descend over Naples for the 1st time,
with its velvet gray and red ⟨of the⟩ sky[118] — like a shudder of
compassion for myself, for having begun my life with being
old, and tears and the feeling of still being rescued, at the last
minute.

I have enough spirit for the South

12[182]

A h⟨uman being⟩ who is without all love and sympathy
for others is in my eyes someone who does not want to gain,
forbids himself enjoyment or has a dearth of smartness, he
lacks variety, a poor h⟨uman being⟩

12[183]

Cultivation of the Greeks.

The men more beautiful than the women.

12[184][119]

Grillparzer:[120] "Schiller rises to the heights, Goethe comes
from on high"

Distinguishing between higher natures

12[185]

Spencer[121] believes that what is essentially moral is to take
into consideration the real natural consequences of an action
— not praise blame punishment. But *this "taking into consideration" was immoral*! The deed is done, *whatever may result from
it*! — Consideration for the *overall consequences* of an action
has never before been demanded — and whoever demanded
it would bring humans to a standstill. The consequences are

unspeakable and inscrutable: the closest consequences would be outweighed by the further: every crime could be justified in this way.

12[186]

The individual for a long time was *"immoral"* — consequently he concealed himself, e.g., the genius (like Homer) beneath the name of a hero. Or one made a god responsible.

12[187]

"The superior human being worth more than the knowing one, who can be base and stupid. The achievements are of no importance. The human being is most valuable as an instrument and function — the geniuses are rare."

12[188]

One practices to oneself, long before one knows what one will later need to say, the gestures, the stance, the tone of voice, the style that is best suited for it: the aesthetic drives and inclinations of youth are the adumbrations of something that is more than aesthetic. Odd!

12[189][122]

We do not want to do as Wagner's Wotan, who with tremendous urgency awakens ancient Erda from her sleep in order to tell her that she can just go on sleeping.[123] Nor as Wagner's Parsifal — a physician who heals his patient, to be sure, yet so that she dies immediately after the healing[124] — and of course with retroactive force; for some old grandfather also has to die because of it. Indeed, we want to be awakeners and physicians, yet in such a way that the awakened don't have to fall asleep again and the healed don't have to perish from the healing.

12[190]

Praise of Voltaire

12[191]

How amazed I am by M⟨arcus⟩ Aurelius and by Gracián!

12[192]

An entirely different eternalization — fame moves forward in a false dimension. We must add eternal depth, eternal repeatability.

12[193][125]

* Are we not wandering lost around the desolate universe?

12[194]

A long love is possible because — even if it is happy — it is not easy to finish possessing a human being, or finish conquering — ever-new and undiscovered floors and back rooms of the soul are opened up, and the endless greed of love reaches out for these too. — But love ends as soon as we perceive its essence to be *limited*.

The conflict of long and short passion arises when one believes they have finished possessing the other and the other does not yet — then the former turns away, withdraws and by this *distance* spurs the other even more to seek new values — ultimately often with the resolve to kill him rather than to let him become the possession of another. — Fortunately objects have no soul; otherwise we would see this conflict continuously: and nature, if it had really loved the infinite h⟨uman being⟩, would long ago have devoured him out of love — if only so as not to allow him to fall prey e.g., to a god.

12[195]

To every morality belongs a certain kind of *analysis* of *actions:* each is *wrong.* But every morality has its perspectives and illuminations — its *doctrine* of "motives."

12[196]

"Let each do whatever he considers to be his duty" — with this we would have regression and standstill.

12[197]

One calls it knowing: in truth the lov⟨ing⟩ human being goes — — —

12[198]¹²⁶

Nothing is wiser than a proverb — said the sea urchin, as the sun stabbed him: then he promptly created twenty-five of them.

12[199]

The Good Human Being

	but also	
1. who does his (legal) duty		1. who follows his heart
2. the brave one		2. the kindly conciliatory one
3. the one who masters himself		3. the one of good nature, without compulsion
4. the reverential one		4. the friend of truth
5. the pious one		5. the one who obeys himself
6. the aristocratic, noble		6. the one who does not despise
7. the good-natured one		7. the one who is avid for battles and victories.

the opposite of this has also always been called *good*

12[200]¹²⁷

Contempt for the actor (its effect rebounds on him, even on Shakespeare, Voltaire liberators.

12[201]¹²⁸

as long as we are young and not yet sure of ourselves, there is no little danger that science will be spoiled for us by scientific types — or art by the artists — or even life by ourselves.

12[202]¹²⁹

God

We loved him more than ourselves and sacrificed to him not only our "only begotten son."¹³⁰

You make it too easy on yourselves, you godless ones! Good, it may be as you say: humans created God — is this any reason not to care about him anymore? Up till now we have reasoned conversely, God, *because* he the — — —

Oh friend, what have human beings done then for thousands of years besides caring for their God etc. If now despite all this he can no longer live, and no food can keep up his strength anymore — : then — — —

12[203]

That was a proud human being! "I'd rather die than have a benefactor" — he said and leaped into the water. A half hour later he had a benefactor and was alive: a poor laborer had jumped in after him and prevented him from dying.

12[204]¹³¹

Logic in thievery. Being able to be a thief. — Everyone buys as cheaply as he can: i.e., everyone steals from his neighbor as long as the latter *must* put up with it.

12[205]¹³²

I stand still, suddenly I am tired. Up ahead, it seems, it's downhill, lightning fast, into an abyss — I don't want to look. Behind me looms the mountain. I reach trembling for a hold. What! has everything around me suddenly turned to stone and precipice? Here this shrub — it crumbles in my hand and wilted leaves and pitiful little roots rain down. I shudder and ⟨I⟩ close my eyes. — Where am I? I look into a purple night, it pulls me to itself and summons me — what's happening to me?¹³³ what happened to make your voice suddenly fail and you feel as if buried under a burden of drunken and opaque emotions?

What are you suffering from now? — yes I'm *suffering* — that's the right word! — What worm bit into my heart?[134]

12[206]

I thought of the age today when I saw someone perform an entrechat to avoid[135] a suddenly approaching carriage.

12[207][136]

The anxieties of a cowardly fearful and suspicious soul, the inability to restrain any kind of malicious idea if it was witty, constitute the comedy in R⟨ousseau⟩'s life.

12[208]

I am most obliging toward people who know me very well (including myself): toward a stranger I am cautious until he has made note of my foothills and cliffs: I don't want him to bump into me and become annoyed with himself because of it.

12[209]

Stings of conscience with the invocation of state justice (instead of revenge)
    when getting married
    when working
    when visiting a teacher
    the merchant
    the actor

12[210][137]

Well, I know a cure for a palate that has become so tasty! — And it would be? — He should go ahead and swallow a toad. After that, good things such as praise would taste good to him again!

12[211]

The defenders of prejudices must have a lot of intelligence if they don't believe in these prejudices — and if someone has a lot of it, then he's usually fighting the prejudices.

12[212]

Ultimate prudence. He fears the envy of the gods and the good: he knows how to render his merit questionable through foolishness and thereby atone for it once more.

12[213][138]

Ego as the felt opposite of the herd (self — herd) and the *herd member feeling,* which is unable to distinguish itself from the interest of the herd — not to be mistaken for each other!

12[214]

People become so rich because the things they *like* are not worth so much — they are not inventive in their joy.

12[215]

Whoever you may be, beloved stranger, whom I meet here for the first time: make note of this cheerful hour and the stillness around us and above us and let me tell you about a thought that rose before me, like a star, that would like to shine down on you and everyone as is the nature of light.

12[216]

For this thought we do not want 30 years of glory with drums and fifes and 30 years of gravedigger labor and then an eternity of deathly silence, as with so many famous thoughts.

Simple and almost dry, the thought should not need eloquence.

Don't you notice — suddenly it grows quiet quiet, quiet around you —

12[217][139]

Cruelty is the remedy of injured pride.

12[218]

The error in being praised consists in the fact that the one who is being praised reads *his* own understanding into the praiser's words and not that of the praiser — which for the most part he cannot even know at all. Usually, however, the understanding in the mind of the praiser is something much smaller duller poorer than in the mind of the praised: such that the latter would often enough be quite annoyed to know *what* actually has been praised about him and his work.

12[219]

The stomach, morally described

Recommend *themata*.

12[220]

⁂ These are temporary settlements with what obstructed and promoted me most in life, attempts to put some things behind me by disparaging or glorifying it (— oh, gratitude in good and evil has always been so challenging for me!

As far as I know from my contemporaries, I made the best use of Schopenhauer and Wagner: perhaps not to their advantage, for I got to know them too deeply by an inch.

I could name them *Juvenilia et Juvenalia*,[140] clearly enough I would think, but in a Latinity that makes me blush. Much youthful love and youthful hate is in them, of every kind.

Birth of Tragedy
  1) against Wagner's proposition "music is the means to an end" and simultaneously an apology for my taste in Wagner
  2) against Schopenhauer and the moral interpretation of existence — I posited **the aesthetic interpretation above it,** *without denying the moral one* or changing it.

12[221]

Köselitz: Eckermann on Voltaire "too noble was he — — —"[141]

12[222]

   It is the same old story here
   "Much ado but nothing to see,"[142]
   this is what the people say, it will appear —
   As happens, two times or three.

12[223][143]

Incipit tragoedia.[144]

12[224]

     "Music Poet Thinker et hoc genus omne."[145]
   Occasions Observations and Questions by F. N.

12[225][146]

Zarathustra's Idleness.
By F. N.
fluid fiery glowing — but bright:
the last book —
it should roll in majestically and blissfully. — So spoke
Z⟨arathustra⟩ *"I do not accuse, I do not even want to accuse the accusers"*

12[226]

   From the moment when this thought is present, all color is
transformed, and there is a different *history.*

12[227]

   To collect passages of happiness e.g., Em⟨erson⟩

12[228][147]

   Philosophy of the *superfluous.* Against sacrifice as harmful in
the long run.

12[229][148]

   Colony — corruption.

12[230]¹⁴⁹

> *Form* only for the eye.

12[231]

> Friedrich Nietzsche
> at the end of his second
> sojourn in Genoa.¹⁵⁰
> [*lux mea crux*]
> [*crux mea lux*]¹⁵¹

[13 = Copy of Emerson.[1] Autumn 1881]

13[1][2]

Those errors were necessary for that stage, as remedy — the education of the human race[3] as a *cure* has a necessarily rational course. — So you say.

In this sense I deny necessity. It is random that this and that article of faith triumphed — the same healing effect would have emanated as well from a *different* one. And above all! the *consequence* of the healing effects is very capricious, very *irrational*! Almost always a profound malady was the result of the new faith and not a *cure*!

13[2][4]

You live through life like drunks, unconsciously — and occasionally you fall down the stairs and do *not* break your limbs, *on account* of your drunkenness and unconsciousness. — Here lies **our** danger! Our muscles are not limp and suffer terribly much *more* than yours!

13[3][5]

Drain *out* your life situations and accidents — and then transition to others! It does not suffice to be *one* person! This would mean challenging yourselves to become limited! But from one into another!

13[4][6]

The capacity for pain is an excellent preserver, a kind of insurance for life: *this is what pain has preserved:* it is as useful as pleasure — not to say too much. I laugh about the enumerations of pain and misery with which pessimism attempts to prove itself — Hamlet and Schopenhauer and Voltaire and Leopardi and Byron.

"Life is something that should not be, if it can only preserve itself in this manner!" — you say. I laugh about this "should" and position myself on life in order to help life to grow as abundantly as possible from pain — security, caution, patience, wisdom, variety, all the subtle colors of bright and dark, bitter and sweet — in all of this we are indebted to pain, and an entire canon of beauty exaltation divinity is only properly possible in a world of deep and changing and manifold pain. That which commands you to pronounce judgment on life cannot be justice — for justice would know that pain and evil — — — friends! We must increase the pain in the world if we want to increase pleasure and wisdom.

13[5][7]

Do you want to become a universal just eye? Then you must do so as someone who has gone through *many* individuals and whose final individual *uses* all previous ones as functions.

13[6][8]

Be a plate of gold — then things will inscribe themselves on you in golden script.

13[7][9]

Oh our greed! I feel nothing of selflessness, on the contrary a self that craves everything, which sees through many individuals — as if through its own eyes and grasps as if with its own hands, a self that also retrieves the entire past, which does not want to lose anything that even *could* belong to it.

13[8][10]

We honor and protect all *accumulations of power* because we hope to *inherit* them — the *sages*. We likewise want to be the heirs of morality once we h⟨ave⟩ destroyed morals

13[9][11]

There is a lot to answer when a riddle is posed and to *believe* that one has solved it — sometimes the sphinx has already plunged into the depths due to the *courage* of the *answer* to the riddle of life.

13[10][12]

My way of being sick *and* healthy is a good portion of my character — it justifies itself and me.

13[11][13]

Supposing my book existed only in the minds of human beings, then in a certain sense everything would consist of **their** thoughts and essence — it would be a *"sum of relations."* Is it nothing more on that account? Metaphor for all things. Likewise our "neighbor."

That something dissolves into a sum of relations proves nothing *against* its reality.

13[12][14]

My philosophy — to extricate human beings from *appearance* at *any* risk! Also no fear of the perishing of life!

13[13][15]

Why do the opposite natures attract me most vehemently? They allow me the feeling of *needing* to become *full,* they belong in me.

13[14][16]

The real human being is far behind the embryonic one, who only emerges from it after 3 generations.

13[15][17]

All forms are *our* work — *we* express *ourselves* in the manner in which we *must* know things now.

13[16][18]

What have I learned, up to today (15 October 1881[19])? To *benefit* myself from all circumstances and *not need* others.

13[17][20]

What do I care about the errors of philosophers!

13[18][21]

Character = organism.

13[19][22]

To see the new greatness not above oneself, not outside oneself, but to make a new function of our self from it.

We are the ocean into which all rivers of greatness must flow.

How dangerous it is if faith in the universality of our self is *lacking*! Many kinds of faith are *necessary.*

13[20][23]

To proceed from the smallest closest things:
1) to determine the entire dependency into which one was born and raised
2) the accustomed rhythm of our thinking, feeling, our intellectual needs and modes of nourishment
3) *Attempts*[24] at change, chiefly in order to break habits (e.g., diet
   Lean intellectually on one's opponents for once, try to live in their air
   travel in every sense of the word
   "Unstable and fleeting"[25] — for a time.
   From time to time *rest* on one's experiences, *digest* them.
4) *Attempts* at an ideal *creation* and later at an ideal *life.*

13[21][26]

beyond love and hate, also good and evil, a deceiver with a good conscience, cruel to the point of self-mutilation, undiscovered and for all to see, a tempter, who lives off the blood of other souls, who loves virtue as an experiment, like vice.

13[22][27]

Here you sit, as ruthless as my curiosity that compelled me to you: well then, sphinx, I am a questioner like you: we have this abyss in common — would it be possible that we are speaking with one voice?

14[1]¹

This is something *new* in today's music, as I just heard it! It *represents* feelings, it *no longer arouses them* — one is satisfied to *understand* with its help! How modest!

14[2]²

How cold and foreign to us so far are the worlds that science discovered! How different e.g., is the body as we perceive, see, feel, fear, admire it and the "body" as the anatomist teaches it! Plants, food, mountains and whatever science shows us — everything is a *totally unknown* freshly discovered *new* world, the greatest contradiction with our perception! And yet supposedly "the truth" will gradually link up with our dreams and — we shall one day *dream more truthfully*! — — — —

14[3]³

It is an *entirely new situation* — it too has its sublimity, it too can be conceived of as heroic: even though no one has done so yet. Certainly not scientific people: they are common souls, with a sphere of intellectual activity closed off to their perception: for them science is primarily something rigorous, cold, sober — no shattering moment, no daring, no standing alone against all demons and gods. Science does not concern them — this gives them the *capacity for it*! If they had fear or a hint of the colossal — then they wouldn't touch it. It is this kind of science alone that the state has promoted *so far*! — the striving

for knowledge *without heroism,* as business, useful application
of the powers of understanding etc.

14[4][4]

At night, with a starry sky surely a feeling stirs, how miserable is our capacity for hearing. Oh this deathly silent din! —

14[5][5]

Now I seem to myself to be someone who has learned to
travel with all winds — and *his* road! Today I am entirely in
my Genoese boldness and scarcely know where in the world I
should travel — : it's as if existence were too narrow for me and
as if I had to invent or create a new one. *I need space,* a very big
broad unknown undiscovered world, otherwise I'm disgusted.[6]

14[6][7]

Why do I not find human beings among the living who
gaze out higher than I, and have to look down on me? Have
I merely *searched* poorly? — And I crave precisely *such types*!!

14[7]

With my half-blind and work-shy eyes I now prefer most to
walk on those paths where my feet no longer need to *think* —
I can and want no longer to live in mountains and in poorly
maintained small towns, where living *and stumbling* go together.

14[8][8]

This entire world that really concerns us somewhat, in which
our needs desires joys hopes colors lines fantasies prayers and
curses are rooted — this entire world we *humans created* —
and we've *forgotten* it, so that we retroactively thought up our
own creator for all this, or tortured ourselves with the problem
of Whence? Just as language is the primal poem of a people, so
the whole vivid perceived world is the primal poem of humankind, and even the animals have begun to create here. **This** we
inherit all at once, as if it were reality itself.

14[9]⁹

This entire world we created, oh how we *loved* it! Everything poets feel toward their work is nothing compared to the countless outpourings of happiness that human beings in prehistoric times felt as they *invented nature.*

14[10]¹⁰

Where will we find, we loneliest of the lonely, we human beings — for this is certainly what we will one day *become,* through the aftereffects of science — where will we find a *companion for the human being!* Formerly we sought a king, a father, a judge for everything, because there was a shortage of proper kings, proper fathers, proper judges. Later we will *seek* the *friend* — human beings will have become self-sufficient majesties and solar orbits — but *lonely.* The myth-building drive will then turn outward toward the friend.

14[11]¹¹

I would wish that I had just once encountered a human being who asked himself, regarding everything that he touched: "couldn't this be improved?" Meals and diet and the disposition of the day etc.

14[12]¹²

The way our big and small cities are now, a thinker today has to understand how to find his place between two clamors — or he will not find it and he'll cease to be a thinker. Ancient Rome had more humanity for thinkers than our world! —

14[13]¹³

This is how we all live! — we greedily seize things, with insatiable lust in our eyes, then we just as greedily plunder them for what tastes good and is serviceable — and finally we leave the rest — everything that our appetite and our teeth could not finish — to other human beings and to nature, especially everything that we swallowed without being able to incorporate — :

our excrements. In this we are inexhaustibly benevolent and not in the least stingy: we *dung* humankind with these undigested components of our intellect and our experiences.

14[14]¹⁴

Wherever there is venerating, admiring, blessing, fearing, hoping, anticipating, the God still remains whom we have pronounced dead — he sneaks about on all paths and simply does not want to be known and named. For then he would *vanish* like Buddha's shadow in the cave — he *continues* to live under the odd and new condition that one *no longer believes in him.* But he has become a ghost! Indeed!

14[15]¹⁵

At bottom all civilizations have a profound fear of the "great human being," which only the Chinese have admitted to themselves, with their proverb "the great human being is a public calamity." Basically all institutions are arranged in such a way that he emerges as seldom as possible and grows under the least favorable conditions possible: no wonder! The little people have cared for themselves, for the little people!

14[16]

Permission to procreate should be granted as a distinction, and the potential for reproduction should be removed in every way from all too common sexual intercourse: otherwise more and more the *base-minded* human beings will gain the upper hand — for the superior minds are not too eager in erotic matters. Indeed these are the brave and warlike — and on the whole they are to be thanked for the better kind of human being that still exists. But if the commercial spirit becomes preponderant over the warlike, then — Criminals should be treated like the sick: even in the sense that one *abhors* allowing them to reproduce. This is the first general improvement of customs that I wish for: the sick and the criminal should not be deemed reproductive.

14[17][16]

So I just want to admit — I pretend *to myself* to be irate about the occasional coldness and neglect I experience from friends and former confidants — at the deepest bottom all this leaves me *unperturbed,* and it is the feeling of this ordinary imperturbability that sometimes makes me wish that something really powerful would shake me and turn me around. I seek a remedy against *boredom* when I pretend to be irate about such things, and this doesn't work for me — I mean **you** well and remain someone of the most conciliatory heart! —

14[18][17]

It is a major finding that in the valuation of all things, human beings gave everything *ordinary* and what's more everything simply *indispensable* a lower value. The ordinary was juxtaposed with the uncommon, as the "common" — : the indispensable as a compulsion was juxtaposed with what the free human being can or cannot arbitrarily acquire on his own, the excess and the luxurious in life. Thus everything that is *necessary* and everything *ordinary* became humble: everything fated became baseness. Mood caprice free will the aristocratic penchant of the ruler and capricious commander, the passion for all things rare hard to get — this was the sign of *superior* humanity: here humans first believed they were no longer animals. Prudence and experience of course prescribed their laws to the *active* human being and pointed unrelentingly to the *necessary* and the *ordinary* — but *superior* perception departed often enough from prudence and gave *priority* to the unnecessary and the extraordinary and therefore also mostly imprudent. Thus in the long run the soil of our life and of our entire *style of living* — which is and still remains of course the necessary and the habituated — has been stripped of the higher perceptions! Eating and dwelling and reproducing, commerce, making a living, business indeed even social life have *dis*engaged from the ideal — and caring for oneself, even in its finest form, has been burdened with a stigma that intimates blame for egoism and praise for selflessness.

14[19][18]

To *ally* oneself with someone in order then to oppress him or push him into obscurity — a trick of politicians of all times, which is subtler than reshaping someone else into a rival, so that one can achieve fame for oneself using the rival's already established notoriety.

14[20][19]

The *proud* man hates to tremble and takes revenge on whoever made him tremble: this is the reason for his cruelty. He has the greatest joy in seeing before him the one who no longer causes him to tremble, even if he inflicts the most degrading and painful things on him. — The proud one does not admit to himself what oppresses him, as long as he does not see the possibility of taking revenge for this oppression. His *hatred* erupts in the moment he catches sight of this possibility. All *strong ones,* who break themselves and subject themselves to a law, are cruel: earlier it gave them similar pleasure to break the will of others and to knead the clay in keeping with their will. All who are misjudged, neglected, bored are cruel, for their pride is always irritated. Also all who are *weak* are cruel, and especially insofar as they *want* compassion from others. That is: they *demand* that others also suffer when *they* suffer and are weak. This is why it is only a half misfortune that *socios habuisse malorum.*[20] Finally: how cruel are all *artists,* for they want by all means that their experiences exert force and acquire it, that their sufferings become ours! And even the *preachers of repentance,* who intuit their demonic goad and spur in the fact that they publicly despise great power, that they want to compel the very mightiest as well as the lowest to the same contrition and abstinence — this is a cruelty of pride without equal! In sum, human beings take much pleasure in cruelty, it is the most common of all enjoyments, regardless of how the "cruel" are maligned!

14[21]

Oh this new ambition of the current generation! Among its artists it is the age of imitated originality and in particular imitated passions: for they have the old fear of foreign lands, one doesn't believe them capable of sufficient passion and of passions generally, so they immediately make grimaces and become excessive in tone and gesture, not from the strength of their emotion, but in order to convince themselves of ⟨the⟩ strength of their emotion. Their dramatic characters as well as the figures in their paintings chase the passions in such a way that anyone who acted like this in real life would be considered crazy. It is to be feared that this public schooling will also compel G⟨ermans⟩ to crazy behavior in life e.g., in politics. Their former predilection for the comfortable and the cozy now makes them ashamed; they suspect that with such inclinations they have sentenced themselves to mediocrity of the spirit and are incapable of contributing to the discussion about great things e.g., about the question of happiness. One does not now want happiness itself, but in any case, one wants the pride of belonging to the ultimate judges and measuring artists of happiness — one has simultaneously the ambition of the intellect and of passion. So for example with respect to *the happiness of love:* German artists are now making a vampiric creature of this: their "love" in happiness wants to gouge out, drain and as it were leave behind the whole dried-up world: and if it doesn't succeed at this, then at least it wants to take revenge on everything that otherwise remains of happiness. But this is love in the insane asylum — or it belongs in the insane asylum: or it *creates* an insane asylum. —

14[22]

With piano music the main thing is that one lets the song *sing* and the accompaniment *accompany.* Now I can only tolerate as a brief interlude a piece of music in which there is no separation between music and accompaniment in this manner, as an ideal noise that makes us yearn for the song to begin again.

14[23]

The human voice is the apology of music.

14[24][21]

With what gratitude *Goethe* in his old age looked upon the erotic sensations of all kinds as life had offered them to him! It was a bad hour when Sophocles spoke of Eros as if of a raging demon[22] — either this most lovable of all Athenians was too loving toward himself and as a result became temporarily malicious and devious and weary of himself — or, more probably, he was reviling the god and making him pay for having *abandoned* him.[23]

14[25][24]

Where has God gone? What have we done? have we drunk up the sea? What kind of sponge was that, with which we wiped away the entire horizon around us? How did we manage to wipe away this eternal fixed line, on which heretofore all lines and standards were based, according to which all architects of life have built, without which there seemed to exist no perspectives, no order, no architecture at all? Do we even stand on our own feet anymore? Are we not constantly *plummeting?* And as it were downward, backward, sideways, in all directions? Have we not donned infinite space like a cloak of icy air? And lost all gravity, because for us there is no up, no down anymore? And if we still live and drink light, seemingly as we have always lived, is it not so to speak through the glowing and sparkling of stars that have extinguished? We do not yet see our death, our ashes, and this deceives us and makes us believe that we ourselves are the light and the life — but it is only the old previous life in the light, the humankind of the past and the God of the past, whose rays and glowing still reach us — light also needs time, death and ashes also need time! And finally, we living and luminous ones: what is the status of our luminosity? compared with that of past generations? Is it more than that ash-gray light that the moon obtains from the illuminated earth?

14[26]²⁵

It is still too early, this tremendous event has still not reached the ears and hearts of human beings — great news requires a long time to be understood, whereas the small tidings of the day have a loud voice and the universal understanding of the moment. God is dead! *And we have killed him*! This feeling, to have killed the most powerful and most holy that the world ever possessed, will yet come over human beings, it is a colossal *new* feeling! How does the murderer of all murderers ever console himself! How will he cleanse himself!

15[1][1]

This I have become aware of: in what an odd *simplification of things and human beings* we live! how we have made it *easy* and *comfortable* for ourselves, and given our senses a free pass for *superficial* observations, and our thinking for the *craziest* boldest leaps and *false* conclusions! The picture that science gradually details is *not* drawn from different sources of knowledge: the same senses, the same judging and reasoning, but as it were *turned moral,* stoically patient, brave, just, tireless, not to be offended, not to be delighted. These are good senses, this is good thinking at work in science. And this science now is finally exposing the superficiality and false conclusions of *the good human being,* the foundations of his valuations, even his *superstition* that *the moral* human being has developed humankind to this point: the immoral human being has no less participation — and even in science, hostility mistrust revenge sense of contradiction cunning suspicion are active and needed in fine doses: this evil element exists in all of science's bravery, justice and ἀταραξία.[2] If individual researchers were not one-sidedly prejudiced in favor of their idea, if they did not want to have *their* entertainment, did not fear being disrespected — if they did not mutually keep each other within bounds through envy and suspicion, then *science would lack its just and brave character.* But as a whole it trains us to certain *valuations* — the *res publica*[3] of scholars compels a certain moral way of doing things, at least the expression thereof: *it sublimates evil into virtues*!

15[2][4]

I confess that the world as it presents itself to me upon most mature reflection, this continuously growing phantom of the human mind, on which all of us work, invent, love, create in complete blindness — this is an outcome that frankly is repulsive to my manly instinct: let women and artists amuse themselves with it, in keeping with their instincts and their affinity for everything phantom-like. The sight of it makes me fear for manly virtues, and I don't rightly know where bravery and justice and hard patient rationality can still prevail, if everything is so transitional, so fantastic, so uncertain, so groundless. Well, at least this should remain to us: as men we do indeed want to speak precisely this truth, if it now is the truth, and not conceal it from ourselves! Even the anatomist is often repulsed by the cadaver — but his manliness reveals itself in steadfastness. *I want to know.*

15[3][5]

This drives me to despair: from history we are taught that all great human beings were extremely unjust, and that without the brazen overestimation of their thought and plan, without a deep internal unbroken unquestionable injustice they would not have risen to their greatness — not even Jesus, who truly did not judge human beings justly. What? And now this training in justice that we have promoted, as it is held up to us, is supposed to *prevent* people from becoming great? Deprive them of magnificent traits and verve and practically all instinct? And instead, we're supposed to close the eyes of those who are destined for greatness, and throw the noose of *delusion* around their necks and be grateful when their fate strikes them completely blind? — Be that as it may: we want to become just in this matter and take it as far as we possibly can.[6] Perhaps, too, we were deceived, and many of those great h⟨uman beings⟩ were not great, but simply unjust, and others among them simply through the fact that they practiced their justice as far as their insight, their times, their education, their opponents enabled them to do. *They believed in their justice* perhaps more surely than we in their injustice!

15[4][7]

Human beings created God, there is no doubt: should we therefore not believe in him? He so needs faith in order to live: let's be merciful!

15[5][8]

The sun set behind the sea, and the cliffs on which it had rested[9] during the day exhale a warm breath.

15[6][10]

There is much that has to be enjoyed like the South Americans their tea — they drink it without looking at it: for it is constantly becoming *blacker*. We also taste the *colors* of all foods — a metaphor.

15[7]

Is it then "truth" that eventually gets established by science? Is it not instead the human being who establishes himself — who gives birth to an abundance of optical errors and limitations or derives them from one another, until the whole tablet is inscribed and the human being *stands firm* in his relations to all remaining forces — science only carries on this tremendous process, which began with the first organic being, it is a creating shaping constitutive force and not the opposite of a creating shaping constitutive force, as the poorly educated believe. We promote science — my friends! in the long run this means absolutely nothing more than: *we promote human beings* and make them firmer and less changeable, as much as appearance may occasionally be against us, and just as surely as we pull the rug out from under many things in which more limited ages saw all human firmness and longevity justified, e.g., the usual morality.

15[8][11]

Humankind would have perished from each and every moral system if on the whole it had lived in accordance with it — this is easy to agree with: humankind still exists by means of its unconquerable "immorality." However, what perhaps dawns on us less and yet is no less certain is: even the individual who believed himself perfect as the executor of *his* moral will, a Jesus, an Epictetus, a Zarathustra, a Buddha, even such a type had likewise only lived and continued to live by virtue of the deepest and most thorough "immorality," as little as they may have been aware of it.

15[9]

Ultimately we do no more with knowledge than the spider with its web-spinning and hunting and blood-sucking: it wants to live by virtue of these talents and activities and have its satisfaction — and we also want precisely this, when we knowers seize and hold on to and as it were establish suns and atoms — in this we are on a detour *to ourselves,* to our needs, which in the long run remain dissatisfied with each erroneous inhuman and purely arbitrary perspective, and which *cause* us *trouble.* Science has a fine ear for the cry for help of needs, and often a prophetic ear. In order to see things in such a way that we can satisfy our needs with them, we must drive our human optics into its ultimate consequences. You human being yourself, with your five or six feet of height — you yourself belong to this optics, you are constructed by yourself in keeping with the weakness of your sensory organs — and woe if it were otherwise, if our organs were even weaker and our eye did not even reach our hand or only saw it hovering in some indefinite distance, so that an overall construction of the human being for the human being himself were impossible — Our knowledge is not knowledge in itself and generally not so much a knowing as a continuing to infer and spinning things out: it is the magnificent outcome, growing for thousands of years, consisting of purely necessary optical errors — necessary, in case we even want to live — errors, in case all laws of perspective must be errors in themselves. It is *our* laws and conformity to laws that we insert into the world — as much as appearance dictates the contrary and seems to reveal us as the consequence of that world, and those laws as its laws in their effect on us. Our eye is growing — and we believe the world is growing. Our eye, which is simultaneously an unconscious poet and a logician! Which now represents a mirror in which things do not show up as surfaces, but as bodies — and existing and enduring, as foreign and not belonging to us, as power next to our power! *This* mirror *image* of the eye paints science to its conclusion! — and therewith it *describes* the power that human beings have exerted up till now while continuing to exert it — our poetic-logical power of determining the perspectives to all things, by virtue of which we *stay alive.*

15[10]

The ordinary thoughts (and everything we mean by healthy human understanding) enjoy such high respect and are at bottom made obligatory for everyone because this kind of thinking has its own great validation: *with it humankind has not perished:* this suffices to bring humankind to the conclusion — we conclude so gladly and so quickly!! — that healthy human understanding has *the truth* on its side. "True" — generally speaking this merely amounts to: expedient for the preservation of humankind. If it's something I would perish of if I were to believe it — thus people conclude — then that's *not true* for me — it's an arbitrary inappropriate relation of my being to other things.

15[11]

There is also a kind of optics for morality. How weakly human beings feel responsible for their indirect and distant effects! And how cruelly and exaggeratedly the closest effect that we exert pounces on us — the effect we see, for which our myopic vision is still just sharp enough! How heavy is the guilt we bear, simply because it stands so close before our eyes! How we measure *weight* differently *according to its distance* from us!

15[12]

Formerly the doctrine of the *unfree will* was proven by readily pointing to the prophets, who enjoyed serious credibility even among skeptical philosophers: but the art of prophecy presupposes a world that is nothing but fate, and consequently this world likewise enjoyed serious credibility. But when prophets became discredited, along with them the doctrine of the unfree will also became discredited: in keeping with a wrong way of reasoning, which is more common than the right way.

15[13]

We moderns, however religious or moral we may be, are deeply unreligious compared to religious people of the Middle Ages, and deeply immoral compared to the moralists of antiquity. Ancient philosophers one and all had a moral fanaticism and a triumphant lack of scruples in the belief in *their* "salvation of the soul," such that they finally contributed to antiquity's bad reputation and its doubt in itself: that excessive value they laid on the "salvation of the soul" was the most useful preparation for Christianity, which became its heir, without showing any gratitude for it. (Religious human beings have never been distinguished by their gratitude.)

15[14]

The way I think of life and the world: it is as if I were sitting in the midst of *tragic household goods,* and wherever I look there are inspirations to write tragedies — indeed I can scarcely prevent these solemn and passionate masks from playing a tragedy themselves, and luring me into their play: this kind of urge surrounds me now.

15[15]

"And what will be after the end of morality?" Oh you curious ones! Why pose the question *already now*! But let's run through it quickly — quickly — otherwise we'll fall — for here everything is ice and slipperiness.

Each and every way of acting that morality *demands* was demanded by it on the basis of inadequate knowledge about human beings and many deep and difficult prejudices: once one has proven this inadequacy and this fiction, then one has *annihilated* the *moral* obligation for these actions — there is no doubt! — and specifically for the simple reason that morality itself demands truth and honesty above all and thus placed around its own neck the noose with which it can be strangled — *must* be strangled: the *suicide of morality* is its own ultimate moral demand! — Even so, the demand for doing this and not doing that might not yet be annihilated, only henceforth the moral impulse would be lacking — and only in the event that no further impulse for an action existed other than this would the demand itself be strangled along with morality. Now, however, the utilitarians speak up and point to utility as the occasion for the same demand — to utility as the necessary detour to happiness; then the aestheticians, who repeat the demand in the name of the beautiful and the exalted or of good taste (which is the same thing); the friends of knowledge come along to demonstrate that living this or that way is the best preparation for knowing and that it would not only be a sign of bad taste, but of obstinacy toward wisdom if one even *wanted* to live differently, at odds with the former demands of morality. — And finally, idealists of all degrees stream forth and gesture toward that edifice that hovers before them: "oh, to reach this edifice, to embrace it, to press it upon ourselves like a seal and henceforth *to be* this image — what we wouldn't do and not do *for its sake*! What do we care about utility and taste and wisdom, what to us are grounds and groundlessness compared to this *craving* for our ideal, for this my ideal!" — and so they reestablish that demand, each for *himself* — as a remedy for their craving, as a tonic for their thirst.

15[16][12]

To have more refined senses and more refined taste, to be accustomed to the choicest and very best as well as proper and natural food, to enjoy a strong and bold body that is deployed as a guard and protector and even more as an instrument of an even stronger, bolder, more daring, more danger-seeking spirit: who would not wish that all this were precisely his possession, his state! But he should not fool himself: with this possession and this state one is the creature *most capable of suffering* under the sun, and it is only at *this* price that one may purchase the distinction of also being the *creature most capable of happiness* under the sun! The abundance of *varieties* of suffering falls on such a man like a never-ending snow flurry, just as the most powerful strokes of lightning discharge themselves on him. Only under the condition of always remaining open to pain on all sides and down to his innermost soul, can he remain open to the finest and supreme varieties of happiness: as the most sensitive most delicate healthiest most changeable and longest-lasting organ of joy and all cruder and finer delights of the mind and the senses: if in fact the gods take him only partially under their protection and do not make of him (as usual, unfortunately!) a lightning rod of their envy and mockery of humankind. For a couple of centuries Athens was very rich in such human beings, in other ages Florence had its turn, and more recently Paris. And, in the face of such ultimate and supreme products of culture to date, the good belief of Enlightenment thinkers still prevails that happiness, more happiness will be the fruit of growing enlightenment and culture, and no one adds: also unhappiness, more unhappiness, more capacity for suffering, more diversified and greater suffering than ever! — Why then did the philosophical schools of Athens in the 4th century burst forth so mightily precisely in the midst of the highest enlightenment and culture ever attained, and why did they, each in their own manner, try to sell the Athenians of that time on the notion of a harsh and partially horrific or at least completely arduous and wretched lifestyle whose goals were painlessness and a kind of paralysis? They were surrounded by human beings who were capable of the highest suffering and they belonged to them — they all dispensed with happiness in the lap of this supreme culture, because this "happiness" was not to be had without the brake of pain and its eternal goading! That, *properly calculated,* a life dedicated to knowledge and to *nil admirari*[13] even under the harshest renunciations and discomforts was *more bearable* than the life of the happy wealthy healthy educated enjoying admiring admirers of such a "supreme culture" — philosophy in Athens introduced itself with this paradox and on the whole indeed it found many believers and emulators! and certainly not merely among the friends of paradox! — One never tires of staring at the oddness of this fact. — — — —

15[17][14]

In antiquity every superior human being had a craving for fame — it stemmed from the fact that each believed humankind began with him, and he could only infuse himself with sufficient breadth and duration by thinking himself into the whole of posterity, as a tragedian acting along on the eternal stage. My pride on the contrary is "I have an *ancestry*" — which is why I don't need fame. In whatever moved Zarathustra, Moses, Mohammed Jesus Plato Brutus Spinoza Mirabeau, I, too, am already living, and what embryonically took a couple of millennia first saw the light of day by ripening in me. We are the first aristocrats in the history of the spirit — the historical sense begins only now.

15[18][15]

Let's not forget: the new instinct is simply new — still weak vulnerable, often childish, often harmful, without finer selection, so that occasionally it attacks lesser natures and is fearful of the great natures: it often acts like an illness, is sour, bitter — no wonder that it gets incorrectly described, because one is unable to guess the tree from its fruits and compares the new growth in its earliest form with known growths and their effects: one probably says, it's a poisonous shrub.

15[19]

Is it not a degree of desecration when the lover thinks "I do not actually long for this beloved, but for love" — is not every generalization of the goal a desecration? Indeed even this is crude and offensive "I long for this beloved" — rather, the language of passion wants only a little, only something singular, only a sign and symbol. Even to name anything whole as a goal is desecrating. The ideal must be too big as a whole — you're supposed to be able to pluck out only individual rays.

15[20]

First what is necessary — and this as beautifully and completely as you can! "Love that which is necessary" — *amor fati*[16] this would be my morality, do all good things to it and lift it up to you beyond its horrifying descent.[17]

15[21][18]

The two greatest opponents of appearance are Copernicus and Boscovich, both Poles[19] and both clerics — the latter was the first to annihilate the superstition of materiality, with the doctrine of the mathematical character of the atom

15[22][20]

Chamfort — a human being of *great* character and *profound* intellect — but neither for his character nor for his intellect has the hour of recognition arrived. The virtues must always first make *a pair* — otherwise people won't believe them. Mirabeau called him his *best* friend: "Chamfort is of my kind in mind and heart."[21]

15[23]

The gestures of sudden fright are by no means a language of fright, as if it wanted to *communicate* — but the most immediate precautionary measures and therefore very different: I learned this when a carriage suddenly threatened to fall on me.

15[24]

How differently one perceives the business[22] and the work of one's life, if one is the first in the family to do it or his father and grandfather had already practiced the same! There is much more inner turmoil, a much more sudden pride in it, but the good conscience for it has not yet been created, and we perceive something as "capricious" in it.

15[25]

Nettle rash: now a sickness, appears to me to have originally been a defensive reaction of the skin against insects and the like, from the time when humans still had longer and bristlier hair:[23] perhaps humans were able voluntarily to produce this condition of hardened patches of skin: now an atavism. In some people it emerges when they eat certain fruits e.g., strawberries: perhaps because the insects against which we used to protect ourselves this way swarmed around these very fruits and we used the protective remedy *in order* to be able to enjoy these fruits?

15[26][24]

All passion obscures vision 1) for the object 2) for the one who is afflicted by it. And now! *Paradox!* Passion of knowledge, that wants to know precisely this knowledge and likewise the one who is afflicted by the passion! *Impossible*!!! Is beautiful impossibility perhaps its ultimate magic?

15[27][25]

Must not precisely the *best* human beings be the *most evil?* Those in whom science and conscience are most finely and robustly developed, so that everything they do they perceive as unjust, and themselves as the *ever-evil, ever-unjust,* as the necessarily evil? But whoever perceives himself to be like this *is like this*!

15[28]²⁶

Whoever has made a *climbing mistake* in the mountains must beware above all not to regard the danger of his situation as *greater* than it is!

15[29]

In the North people shy away from *warm colors* — there they are considered base, rabble-like. In this therefore *I* belong to the rabble — but no longer *in the South*!

15[30]

The first thing one has to learn in a foreign language are the courtesies of the foreign country — the *second thing* is the names of needs. But focusing first on the second — in the worst case one could make do just with courtesies: who would let a courteous person (who is not lacking in decency and money) *starve?*

15[31]

When people curse the lotteries, they usually forget *how much happiness* and cheerful horizons constitute the pleasant hopes *of everyone* collectively! And how much poorer a people is without lotteries — namely in pleasant sensations! The disappointment is only one-time and is shaken off seemingly quickly — but how often does one dream of winnings and make plans! How it enhances the *taste for venturing*!

15[32]

No, I'm not made for burdening even further the conscience of human beings! I want them to be more mindful of their happiness, "all the hundred wells"²⁷ even in the desert! as a German poet says — and that they themselves think better of their unhappiness and inability and nonvirtues than before — that way they too are useful, and it's even probable that *there* is where their own conditions of pleasure and happiness and strength and virtue lie.

15[33]²⁸

What we love shall not find blemishes in itself — : thus wills the egoism of this most refined *lust to possess,* which is called love.

Supposing one were the lover of a female singer, with what fearful ears does one hear her singing there in front of various listeners! One judges subtly and supersubtly, not in the least biasedly, enamored, sealed: rather, none of her tiniest errors elude us, not even the most fleeting slip or omission; we know, even if the listeners are jubilating and clapping, that for the singer herself everything did not sound and go quite like her subtlest conscience had demanded of her — and because we feel that all her failures small and big are known to her, *we suffer indescribably at this* and are grateful and touched for everything in which she succeeded. This is also how it is with masters of an art who are our friends; for their sake we are invigorated by their success, indeed we give up our own taste entirely as soon as we become aware of *their* way of tasting themselves.

15[34]²⁹

At bottom morality is inimically disposed to science: already Socrates was, and specifically because it holds things to be important that have nothing to do with good and evil, and therefore *withhold importance* from "good and evil" — morality wants all the powers of human beings to be at its disposal; it regards it as a waste for someone *who is not sufficiently rich for it,* that one concerns himself with stars and plants.

15[35]

Those Greek philosophers of rigorous observation had the choice of becoming evil animals or austere and joyless animal tamers: so even Socrates. They were smart enough to comprehend that when someone becomes a human predator, he will always *tear to pieces* himself first. But now they believed that *everyone* was in danger like they themselves of becoming *this predator* — this is *the great faith of all* great moralists, their power and their error! — Faith in the proximity of terrible animality in everyone. — These were scarcely beautiful human beings.

15[36]

Our eyes and our aesthetics are also seated at the table, and many delicate morsels are withheld from us because our eyes say "this looks abhorrent," "these lines are unfamiliar to my taste." With oysters — and even these are something impossible for many people — it is the noble work of the shell that intercedes for the disgusting slimy mass and as it were pleads with the eyes not to look when it's about to be swallowed. — Perhaps for the same reason, the best women are withheld from us, the true morsels of goodness and strength of the soul. A couple of different lines (or, as the physiologists say, some fat more or less — that

15[37]³⁰

The rationality in the French Revolution — this is the rationality of Chamfort and Mirabeau — the irrationality of it: this is the irrationality of Rousseau.

15[38]³¹

Is this my task: *déniaiser les savants?*³² They knew not what they did³³ and they did not think about it much, but there was a silly arrogance to everything they did, as if virtue itself had come into the world through them.

15[39]³⁴

Taste is stronger than any morality; I cannot stand to live next to someone who is constantly spitting, or who is eating soup — I'd rather live with a thief or a perjurer. Formerly the innovators of ideas were perceived to be as embarrassing as a violation of decency.

15[40]³⁵

My thoughts concern things that are too lofty and difficult, they can only have effect if the strongest personal pressure were

added. Perhaps it will take centuries for faith in my authority to grow strong enough to enable human beings to interpret the book of this authority, without modesty, as rigorously and seriously as an ancient classic (e.g., Aristotle). — *Faith in humanity must grow,* so that its work just finds the necessary degree of accommodating intelligence: faith therefore and prejudice. This is why one formerly insisted so on "inspiration": now
— — — —

15[41]

The sea is shrinking, the human being *the solid ground* is always increasing — but because he only sees that everything is changing, he believes and feels the opposite, and thinks that his instability is growing and ultimately he won't be able to resist the sea. — The *slowness* of events in the history of human beings is not suited to the human sense of time — and the subtlety and smallness of all growth defies human vision. This is why it will always be just an article of faith: this *real* human history! and this is why it has such a hard struggle against all other articles of faith, it cannot likewise demonstrate itself *ad oculos.*[36] — Indeed, appearance testifies against all our "truths" and thereby easily becomes the advocate of all semblance and even of lies.

15[42][37]

I imagined the most horrifying life for *me:* that of a courtier attorney toll collector registrar bank clerk king grocer domestic servant and all those others whose surplus of performance consists of *waiting* — waiting, until someone comes and speaks — while it is not possible in the meantime to occupy oneself better ("it conflicts with duty") Now I notice that most people by far who have any kind of job in the big cities are employed in precisely this manner and undergo training toward this goal — hence this mandatory waiting must seem quite bearable to them.

15[43]³⁸

From a distance and abroad one does not see things in the homeland as simply black or white, but certainly not as colorfully as they really are: one simplifies the colors. As an example of a major simplification of colors I offer this judgment: "the Germans are now divided into Jews and Jew-haters: the latter would like all too much to be real Germans."

15[44]³⁹

Is it not laughable that one still believes in a sacred inviolable law "thou shalt not lie" "thou shalt not kill"⁴⁰ — given an existence whose character is constant lying, constant killing! What *blindness* to the real essence of this existence must have been produced by the fact that one believed one could *live* with those laws alone! How much blindness about ourselves! What misinterpretation of all our intentions and explanations! How much pathetic lying, how much murder of *honest people* — i.e., annihilation of those who dared to be evil and to appear to be themselves — has once more entered the world because of it! The credit of morality itself has only lasted this long through immorality.

15[45]

Luxury is the form of a continuous *triumph* — over all the poor disadvantaged impotent sickly covetous. Not that one enjoys much of the luxury items themselves — what does the triumphant one care about golden wheels and the slaves chained to his carriage! — but one does enjoy how the carriage *rolls over* countless people and *presses* or *crushes* them.

15[46]

Humankind would have died out if the sex drive did not have such a blind careless hasty thoughtless character. In itself, its gratification is absolutely not associated with the reproduction of the species. How unspeakably seldom is coitus the intent of reproduction! — And so, too, with pugnacity and rivalry: only a couple more degrees of *cooling of the drives* — and life would stand still! It is dependent on a high temperature and a boiling heat of unreason.

15[47][41]

We may well talk of all kinds of immorality! But being able to endure it! E.g., I would not *endure* a broken promise or far worse a murder: long or brief invalidism and destruction would be my lot! quite apart from publicity of the misdeed and its punishment.

15[48]

If you could see more sharply, then you would see everything *in motion:* just as burning paper curls up, so too everything is constantly passing and curling up in the process.

15[49][42]

Up till now God was responsible for every living thing that emerged — one could not guess what his intentions were for it; and precisely when the stamp of suffering and infirmity was imprinted on life, one presumed that it was to be healed more quickly than other beings of the pleasure of "living" and of the "world," and thus marked by a sign of mercy and hope. But as soon as one no longer believes in God and the destiny of human beings in a hereafter, *humans become responsible for all living things* that arise through suffering and are predestined for displeasure in life. "Thou shalt not kill" — belongs to an order of things where a God disposes over life and death.

15[50][43]

Friends, said Z⟨arathustra⟩ this is a new teaching and bitter medicine, you will not like its taste. Therefore do as clever sick people — drink it down in one long swallow and quickly chase it with something sweet and spicy that rinses your palate clean again and tricks your memory. The effect will not be lost in any case: for henceforth you have "the devil in your flesh" — as the priests will tell you, who I am not fond of.

15[51][44]

Have you no compassion for the past? Do you not see how it is abandoned and depends like a poor old woman on the mercy the spirit of fairness of every generation? Couldn't some great monster come at any moment, who would force us to misjudge her entirely, who would render our ears deaf to her or even place into our hands the whip for abusing her? Does she not suffer the same lot as music, the best music we have? A new evil Orpheus, who could be spawned at any hour, would likely be capable of persuading us through his sounds that we did not yet have any music, and it would be best to run away from everything called music to this day.

15[52][45]

"You come too early!" — "you come too late" — these are the cries surrounding all those who come *forever*, said Z⟨arathustra⟩.

15[53]

"To think well of human beings — this is understandable in you! they dissemble in your presence and probably become even better — enough that you become acquainted with them as if they were mirrors in which you yourself are reflected." Traveling! ego.

15[54][46]

You feel that you will take your *leave*, perhaps soon — and the sunset of this feeling shines into your happiness. Pay heed to this testimony: it means that you love life and yourself, and especially life as it has affected you and shaped you so far — and *that you are longing for its eternalization. non alia sed haec vita sempiterna!* [47]

But know also! — that the past sings its brief song again and again and that when listening to the first strophe, one almost dies of longing at the thought that it might be gone forever.

15[55]

I believe that Stoicism has been misjudged. What is essential in this mental state — that is what it was even before philosophy appropriated it — is one's comportment toward pain and representations of displeasure: a certain *heaviness pressure* and *indolence* is intensified to the extreme, in order to sense pain only slightly: *rigidity* and *coldness* are the trick, in other words anesthetics. The main purpose of Stoic training, to annihilate *easy irritability,* increasingly to limit the number of objects that may even *move,* faith in the despicability and the scant worth of most things that excite, hatred and hostility toward excitement, passion themselves as if they were a disease *or* something unworthy: attention to all the ugly and painful manifestations of passion — in sum: *petrification* as an antidote to suffering, and henceforth relegating all exalted names of the divinity of virtue to the statue. What harm to embrace a statue in winter if one has become dulled to the cold? — what harm for a statue to embrace a statue? If the Stoic achieves the condition that he wants to have — *usually he brings this with him* and this is why he chooses *this* philosophy! — then he has the *pressure of a bond* that produces insensitivity. — This way of thinking is quite repugnant to me: it underestimates the value of *pain* (it is as useful and conducive as pleasure), the value of *excitement* and *passion,* he is ultimately compelled to say: everything is fine with me as it comes, I want nothing else — he no longer *eliminates any emergencies* because he has killed the sensitivity for emergencies. This he expresses religiously, as complete agreement with all actions of the deity (e.g., in Epictetus).

15[56][48]

I scarcely brush the outermost crests of the waves — the existence in which I am supposed to swim is as if *outside of me* and I feel with a shudder of ecstasy its undulating skin: have I turned into a flying fish? —

15[57][49]

When I looked up just now, I thought I saw, quick as a flash of lightning, a pale person next to my table, deeply bent over: in the next moment, as my eyes tried to focus more sharply on this object, I see a *cat* a couple of steps away from the table: my imagination used its color and likewise presupposed a different perspective. In an animated conversation I often see the face of the person with extreme clarity and full of the subtlest muscle movement and expression of the eyes, adapting to the thoughts they express or which I believe I have produced in them: my actual capacity to see *cannot see* these subtleties and therefore they *must* be made up. The person is probably making quite a different face or none at all. —

15[58]

The thought never occurred to me for a moment that something I have written would simply be dead after a few years and so would have to have success in the near term, if it wanted to be successful at all. Without ever having had the thought of glory, the doubt never crept into me that these writings would not outlive me. If I ever thought of readers, then always only of scattered individuals sown across the centuries: and my situation is different from that of the singer who requires a full house to make his voice supple, his eyes expressive and his hands communicative.

15[59][50]

As concerns practice: I regard the individual moral schools as sites of experimentation where a number of techniques for prudent living were thoroughly drilled and thought to their conclusion: the results of all these schools and all their experiences belong *to us,* therefore we accept a Stoic technique no less gladly just because we have already adopted Epicurean ones. That *one-sidedness* of the schools was very useful, indeed it was indispensable for the determination of these experiments. Stoicism e.g., demonstrated that human beings were voluntarily capable of giving themselves a harder skin and as it were a kind of nettle rash: from it I learned to say in the midst of distress and storms: "what does *that* matter?" "what do I matter?" From Epicureanism I took the readiness to enjoy and the eye for all those places where nature set its table for us.

15[60][51]

Moreover my eyesight is poor and my imagination (in dreams and in waking) is accustomed to certain things and considers some things possible that others would not be prepared for. — I fly in dreams, I know that it is my prerogative, I do not recall a state in which I was not capable of flying. Executing every kind of curve and angle with a light impulse, a flying mathematics — this is such a singular happiness that in the long run it certainly permeated my basic perception of happiness. When I start to feel really good, I am always in such a free soaring state, upward and downward arbitrarily, the one without *tension* and the other without condescension and *debasement.* "Upswing" — as many describe *this* is too muscular and violent for me. — My best understanding of the Corybants[52] and even the Dionysian essence sees them as attempts by nonwinged animals to imagine themselves with wings and lift themselves above the earth. The noise of extremely powerful motion like a monstrous beating of wings — its effect is almost *as if* they were suspended on high.

15[61]

Wherever *court* is being held, I cannot abide it: why stand like a colorful flamingo for hours in shallow water! All courtiers regard *sitting* as one of the joys of "life after death."

15[62][53]

Being compassionate sarcastic seductive with a single sound — only women know how to do this.

15[63]⁵⁴

In the petty and miserable life the chords of the *great life of past* human beings nevertheless ring through: every *valuation* has its origin in great movements of individual souls.

15[64]

And as a lover speaks: her coldness makes my memories numb: have I ever felt this heart glowing and beating next to me? — so — — —

15[65]⁵⁵

Perhaps one must now seek among *merchants* for the properties that formerly made human beings great — impetuous sense of honor entrepreneurial spirit etc. also the corporate spirit.

15[66]⁵⁶

On the whole the morality of Europe is *Jewish* — a profound alienation still separates us from the Greeks. But the Jews, just as much as they despised human beings and perceived them to be *evil and despicable simultaneously,* formed their God to be purer and more distant than any people: they *nurtured him* with all the goodness and loftiness that grows in the breast of human beings — and this rarest of all sacrifices eventually allowed a breach to emerge between God and human beings, that was perceived as *terrible.* Only among Jews was it possible, indeed necessary, that ultimately a being hurled himself *into* this breach — and again "the God" who did this had to be the only one deemed capable of something exalted: those human beings themselves, who felt like *mediators, first had to feel like God* in order to assign themselves this mediator task. Where the breach was not so great, there probably a human being could step in *without* having to be completely superhuman, but as a *hero,* and spread that feeling of well-being that was perhaps the *pinnacle of more ancient humankind: to witness harmony and transition from God to human being.*

15[67]⁵⁷

Why am I overcome at almost regular intervals by such a longing for *Gil Blas*⁵⁸ and again for the novellas of Mérimée? Hasn't *Carmen*⁵⁹ enchanted me more than any opera, in which this beloved world (that I basically leave for only a half year at a time) echoes?

15[68]⁶⁰

Behind every tragedy there is something *witty and absurd,* a joy in paradox, e.g., the concluding words of the most recent tragic opera: "yes *I* have killed her, my Carmen, my adored Carmen!" This kind of pepper is completely lacking in the epic — it is more innocent and appeals to more childish and clumsier spirits, who are still repulsed by everything sour bitter and sharp. Tragedy is an omen that a people wants to become witty — that *esprit* wants to make its appearance.

15[69]⁶¹

"Use, useful": for this now everyone thinks of prudence caution coldness moderation etc., in sum of psychic states that are contrasted with affect. Nevertheless there must have been tremendous stretches of time when humans did *what was useful to them* only under the prompting of affects and when prudence and cold reasoning were still lacking in them generally. Back then the highest *utile*⁶² still spoke the language of passion, of madness, of horror: without such a powerful eloquence it wasn't possible to condition humans to something "useful" — i.e., to a *detour* from "pleasure" i.e., to a *temporary preference for the unpleasant.* Back then morality was not yet the intuition of prudence — one had to *unlearn* reason as it were and the usual kind of willing, for a time, in order to do something moral in this sense.

15[70]⁶³

I want to have my heraldry and knowledge about the entire noble family tree of my spirit — only *history* provides it.

Without it we are all merely ephemeral flies and rabble: our remembrance goes back to our grandfather — time comes to an end with him.

15[71][64]

"Whoever is not a misanthrope by age 40, never loved human beings," Chamfort was fond of saying.

15[72]

Balzac: *pour moraliser en littérature, le procédé a toujours été de* montrer la plaie.[65] —

[16 = M III 6a. December 1881–January 1882]

16[1][1]

Continuation of "*Dawn*."[2]

Genoa, January 1882.

16[2][3]

One has convalesced only when one has forgotten physicians and illnesses.

16[3][4]

I want only a single equality: the one that is produced by the gravest danger and gun smoke around us. Then all of us have but one rank! Then all of us can have fun together!

16[4]

You complain that I make use of screaming colors? Well, I take the colors from nature — what can I do about nature! — But you say, this is only my nature and not yours and that of everyone else! And maybe you're right: maybe I have a nature that *screams* — "as the hart pants after the water brooks."[5] If you yourselves were these water brooks, how pleasing would my voice sound to you! But you are annoyed at not being able to help me slake my thirst — and maybe you would so like to help me? — —

16[5][6]

Am I really a researcher? I am merely *heavy:* I fall, fall, constantly — until I get *to the bottom*.

16[6][7]

Our virtues must come *and go* like the verses of Homer.

16[7]

Those types have a need to make night in order to let their light shine — what would I have to do with them, I who am no good for the light of night? Indeed, more often than is helpful I deny the night, if it doesn't first have to be made.

16[8]

The Epicureans had the most dignified conception of the gods. How could the unconditional have anything to do with the conditional? How could it be the conditional's cause or law or justice or love and providence! "If there are gods, then they are not concerned about us"[8] — this is the sole true proposition of all philosophy of religion.

16[9][9]

"But where then do all the rivers of what is great and greatest in humans ultimately flow? Are they alone in having no ocean?" — Be this ocean: then one exists.

16[10][10]

If one climbs over and beyond someone, it is hard to do so without seeming harsh. No one is going to grant you the right to see nothing in him but a *step*. — But you *must* climb the entire stairway!

16[11][11]

Prescription against medicine. — "Those are entirely new teachings and entirely new medicines" — you say to me; "we don't like the taste of it!" Well, just do as all clever sick people do — drink it down in one long swallow and quickly chase it with something sweet and spicy that rinses your palate clean again and tricks your memory! The "effect" will not be lost in any case — rest assured! For henceforth you have "the devil in your flesh," as all the old medicine men will tell you.

16[12][12]

Egoism! If we did not revolve around ourselves first and foremost and continuously, we could not bear to chase any sun!

16[13][13]

One has a keen ear for the clinking of chains if one was ever bound in chains.

16[14][14]

Whoever desires fame must occasionally practice being able to live without honor.

16[15][15]

Forward! As soon as I decide to stop here, I would think I had lost my way — there's no gain for me in standing still, but the terrible possibility that I'll become dizzy. Hence forward!

16[16][16]

Aftereffect of the oldest religiosity. — We all believe rigidly and firmly in cause and effect; and some philosophers call this faith "knowledge a priori" on account of its rigidity and firmness — doubting and weighing whether perhaps here a type of knowledge and wisdom of superhuman origin could not to be assumed: in any case they regard humans on this issue to be incomprehensibly wise. Now to me, however, the origin of this invincible faith seems fairly transparent and more an object of ridicule than of pride. Human beings think, whenever they do something, for example executing a stroke, it is *they* who then strike, and they struck because they *willed* to strike, in sum, their will was the cause. They notice no problem at all in this, but instead the feeling of *willing* suffices for them to make the connection between cause and effect understandable for themselves. They know nothing of the mechanism of events and the hundredfold subtle work that must be done in order for the stroke to occur, likewise of the incapacity of willing in itself to perform even the very least part of this work. Will for them is a magically effective force: the belief in the will, as in the cause of effects, is the belief in magically effective forces, in the direct influence of thoughts on unmoved or moved substances. Now originally human beings believed that wherever they saw an event, there was a will as cause, in sum: personally willing beings in the background were thought to be at work — the concept of mechanics was quite remote to them. But because humans for staggering periods of time believed *only in persons* (and not in matter, forces, objects etc.), the belief in cause and effect became their fundamental belief, which they apply wherever anything happens — still to this day, instinctively, and as a piece of atavism of the most ancient lineage. The propositions "no effect without cause," "every effect in turn a cause," appear as generalizations of much narrower propositions: "where effecting is, willing has been," "effects can only happen to willing beings," "there is never a pure, inconsequential suffering of an effect, rather all suffering is an agitation of the will" (to deed, resistance, revenge, retribution) — but in the prehistory of humankind, the latter and the former propositions were identical, and the former were not generalizations of the latter, but the latter were commentaries on the former: all on the foundation of the idea "nature is a sum of persons." If on the other hand nature had appeared to humankind from the beginning as something impersonal, consequently as something nonwilling, then the opposite belief — of *fieri e nihilo*,[17] of effect without cause — would have developed: and perhaps *it* would then have the reputation of superhuman wisdom. — This "knowledge a priori" is therefore no knowledge, but an incarnate *primal mythology* from the time of deepest ignorance!

16[17][18]

A: "The way he publicly misunderstands me proves to me that he has understood me only far too well." — B: "Look on the bright side! You have risen mightily in his esteem; he already considers it necessary to slander you."

16[18][19]

Someone who wants to surpass considerably the industriousness of his father will become ill; and it is the same way with all virtues — our task is always to preserve a virtue at the level on which it was *handed down* to us, for *at this level* it is part of our health: to augment it — — —

16[19]

To have descendants — this alone makes humans steady, coherent and capable of doing without: it is the best upbringing. It is always the parents who are raised by the children, and indeed by the children in every sense, also intellectually. Only our works and pupils give the ship of our life its compass and its great direction.

16[20][20]

"The best things have become distasteful to him!" — Well, there's a remedy for that: he should go ahead and swallow a toad!

16[21][21]

What happened to me yesterday at this place? I was never before so happy, and the tide of existence threw to me on the highest waves of happiness its most precious mussel, purple melancholy. What was I not ready for! Which danger would I not have defied! Did space not seem too narrow for me — — —

16[22]

"Yes! From now on I want to love only that which is necessary! Yes! *Amor fati* shall be my ultimate love!" — Perhaps you will get to this point: but first you will have to be the lover of the Furies: I confess, the snakes would drive me insane.

— "What do you know of the Furies! Furies — that is merely a bad word for the Graces." — He is insane! —

16[23]²²

You self-reliant ones! You self-glorifying ones! All those whose *essence* is *belonging,* those uncounted countless work only for you, even if it seems otherwise to the superficial! Those princes merchants officials farmers soldiers who perhaps believe themselves to be above you — they are all *slaves* and work with an eternal necessity not for themselves: never have slaves existed without masters — and *you* will always be these masters, for whom the work gets done: a later century will surely have eyes for this spectacle! Let them have their views and their conceits, with which they justify and hide from themselves their slave labor — do not fight against opinions that are a charity for slaves! But always bear in mind that this massive exertion, this sweat dust and working noise of civilization exists for those who know how to use all this, without having to work themselves: that there must be *surplus people* who are sustained by the general overwork, and that the surplus people are the meaning and the apology of the whole enterprise! So be millers then and let your wheel be turned by these streams! And do not be worried about their struggles and the wild roaring of these waterfalls! Whatever forms of state and society may result, *all will eternally be mere forms of slavery* — and among all the forms you will be the rulers, because you alone belong to yourselves, and they must always be *belongings*!²³

[17 = M III 7. Excerpts from Emerson's *Essays*.[1] Beginning of 1882]

17[1][2]

In every action is the abbreviated history of all becoming. ego.

17[2][3]

I hear the commendations of the world, but they are not for me: I hear in them only the praise of the character for which I strive, much lovelier to my ears, and which I hear in every word, in every fact — in the running river and in the rustling corn.

17[3][4]

That which I do today has as deep a significance as anything from the past.

17[4][5]

I want to live all history in my own person and appropriate all power and force, and bow neither before kings nor any kind of greatness.

17[5][6]

The creative instinct of the mind[7] reveals itself in the use we are able to extract from history: there is *only* biography. Each human being must know *his* entire lesson. — This wild savage preposterous There and Then must be done away with and be replaced by the Now and the Here.

17[6][8]
To make one's most precious ornament from the remains of our animality: just as in Isis nothing is left of her metamorphosis except the lunar horns.

17[7][9]
Who can draw a tree without becoming a tree!

17[8][10]
The artist has the power of awakening the *energy* slumbering in other souls.

17[9][11]
The true poem is the poet's mind: there lies the sufficient reason for the last flourish itself. St. Peter's is a lame copy.

17[10][12]
The genii in the woods wait until the wayfarer has passed onward.

17[11][13]
When nature has accustomed the eye to huge dimensions, art cannot move on a smaller scale without degrading itself. (*Caverns —*)[14]

17[12][15]
To be reminded of cathedrals on a road cut through spruce woods: the forest exerted an *overpowering* influence on the builder.

17[13][16]
Intellectual nomadism is the talent of objectivity or the talent of finding feasts for the eyes everywhere. Every human being,

every thing is my discovery, my property: the love that animates him for everything *smooths* his brow.

17[14][17]

It must be impossible for my eye to squint here and there when looking: rather, I must always turn my whole head — so is it noble.

17[15][18]

Neither the poet nor the hero can look with condescension on the words or gestures of a *child.* A childlike nature next to inborn energy. A nature who pays so little attention to his hardship, sunk in contemplation, a haughty beneficiary of alms, begging in the name of God.

17[16][19]

The obligation of reverence is onerous to him, he would steal the fire of the Creator and live apart from him.

17[17][20]

When a god comes among men, then they do not know him.

17[18][21]

There is *a lot* to answer when such a riddle is posed: and it is much to *believe* that one has solved such a riddle. The sphinx already plunges into the depths due to the *courage* of the answer to the riddle of life (ego).

17[19][22]

He shall be a Temple of Fame, he shall walk about in a robe painted all over with wonderful events and experiences.

17[20][23]

To believe your own thought — to believe that what is true for you in your private heart is also true for all men: that is genius.

17[21]²⁴

In every work of genius we recognize our own rejected thoughts: they come back to us with a certain alienating majesty.

17[22]²⁵

There is a time in every man's education when he arrives at the conviction that envy is only ignorance, imitation is assassination: that though the wide universe is full of good, not even a kernel of corn can come to him but through his toil, that he bestows on that plot of land.

17[23]²⁶

We usually but half express ourselves and are ashamed of the divine idea that is represented by us. — One must have put his whole heart into his work: in the mere attempt our genius deserts us; no muse, no hope stands by us.

17[24]²⁷

That divided, rebel mind, the lofty skill of computing what could oppose the strength and means of our purpose: these the children do not have; when we look into the face of a child, we are disconcerted. They bend to nothing, everything conforms to them; they never worry themselves with the consequences or the interests of others: they give an independent genuine verdict. They do not seek your favor: *you* must court them.

17[25]²⁸

To make one's observations anew, again and again from the same unbribable, intrepid standpoint of innocence — that is formidable: the power of such immortal youth is felt.

17[26]²⁹

No law can be sacred to me but that of my nature. The only right is what is according to my nature, the only wrong what is against my nature.

17[27][30]

That I think only of that which seems right to me, but not about what the people think about it — serves as the distinction between sublimity and meanness. This is the harder, because you will everywhere find those who think they know your duty better than you do.

Great is he who can maintain with perfect clarity in the midst of the crowd the independence that solitude grants us.

17[28][31]

When the poor and the ignorant are also aroused, when the unintelligent brute mass growls and grimaces — there great souls are needed, to shove this aside in a godlike manner and as a trifle. NB.

17[29][32]

Human beings cannot violate their nature: character, read forward, backward, or across, tells me the same. What are the tallest mountains measured against the entire globe!

17[30][33]

The strength of character appears on its own: the foregone days full of virtue work their spiritual health on you. Through consciousness of a great series of victories comes the majestic nature of the hero.

17[31][34]

Honor is so venerable to us because it is not of today: it is always an ancient virtue.

17[32][35]

The true man is the center of things: he takes possession of the whole of creation, he reminds you of no other, all circumstances are overshadowed by him, he requires infinite space, numbers and time to fully accomplish his design: — posterity follows his steps like a procession.

17[33]³⁶

The actions of kings have instructed the world: they act from a broad point of view: they teach through a colossal symbolism the reverence that is due from man to man. There has always been joyful loyalty to the one who moved among them by laws of his own, made his own value scale of humans and things and overturned the existing one, and *represented* the *law in his person.*

17[34]³⁷

History is an impertinence and injury, if it wants to be anything more than a cheerful story and parable of my being and becoming. — With reverted eye he laments the past or stands on tiptoe to foresee something of the future. But he should live in the present with nature, *sublimely above time.*

17[35]³⁸

Virtue is inner strength: a human being who penetrates to *creative* primal force overpowers by the law of nature all cities nations kings, the rich and the poets.

17[36]³⁹

What we love, that is ours: but by desire for it we bereave ourselves of it.

17[37]⁴⁰

The power men possess to annoy me, I give them myself. Do not stoop so low, assert your dignity; do not let yourself be taken in for a moment by their circumstances, by their shouting: let the light of your inner law penetrate the confusion.

17[38]⁴¹

It demands something godlike in him who has cast off the common motives of humanity. High-heartedness loyalty and a clear understanding: these must be his properties, if he wants to be doctrine society and law to himself: so that a *simple purpose may be to him as strong as iron necessity is to others.* p. 57.

17[39]⁴²

Our housekeeping is mendicant; our arts, our occupations, our marriages — we have not chosen them, but society has chosen for us. The *rugged battle with fate,* where our inner strength is born, we shun.

[18 = Mp XVIII 3. February–March 1882]

500 *Inscriptions*
On Table and Wall
For Fools
by
Fool's Scrawl.[1]

18[1][2]
The proud one even hates the mare,
That pulls his carriage anywhere.[3]

18[2]
The writing ball's[4] like me: it's iron-fisted
And yet on trips it easily gets twisted.
While tact and patience one must never shirk
It's help from subtle fingers makes us work.[5]

18[3][6]
Here gold rolled here I played with gold —
In truth gold played with me — I rolled![7]

18[4]
The poets formerly had a different concept of property:
memory was the mother of all muses. Novelty passed for inspiration. One felt oneself only a little responsible.

18[5][8]

Emerson says, after my heart: To the poet to the philosopher just as to the saint all things are friendly and sacred, all events useful, all days holy, all human beings divine.

18[6][9]
From Paradise.

"Good and evil show the biased taste
of God" — spoke the snake and fled in haste.[10]

18[7][11]

Just as all the victors say,
You say: "Chance is not in play."
You said nothing yesterday,
No one knows what happen may.[12]

[19 = M III 6b. Spring 1882]

19[1]

Two categorical imperatives. — Certainly! One must have a skeleton — otherwise the dear flesh has no support! But you gentlemen without flesh, you skeletons of the Stoa, your sermon should be: "one should also have flesh on one's bones!"

19[2]

"I treasured this too highly and paid too dearly for it — as with so many things! I fancied I was paying and I was bestowing. I have become poor because I believed in some things as if they were exceedingly estimable — oh, and the way I am, I will become poorer still!"

19[3]

Omnia naturalia affirmanti sunt indifferentia, neganti vero vel abstinenti aut mala aut bona.[1]

19[4]

> *Knowing how to find one's company.*
> It's good to crack wise with wise crackers:
> Of tickling the ticklish are backers.[2]

19[5]

> *From the Barrel of Diogenes.*[3]
> "Pissing is cheap, happiness has no price:
> I can't sit on gold, my rump must suffice."[4]

19[6]

Timon⁵ speaks:

"Not so lavish: only dogs shit
All the time as they see fit!"⁶

19[7]

Concluding Rhyme.

Laughing is a serious art
If I'm to have a better start,
Tell me: how'd it go today?
Was heart-felt joy the guiding light?
A joking mind is not so bright
Unless the heart-light shines the way.

Dare to taste my fare, dear diner!
Come tomorrow it tastes finer
And day after — even good!
If you still want more, I'll make it
From past inspiration take it,
Turning food for thought to food.⁷

19[8]⁸

Rules for Life.

To live life with elation
You must stand at its crown!
Improve your elevation!
Work hard on — looking down!

The noblest of your urges
Ennoble and maintain:
For ev'ry pound love surges
Take one grain of self-disdain!

Stay not where the lowlands are,
Climb not into the sky!
The world looks best by far
When viewed from halfway high.⁹

19[9][10]

Desperate.

Terrible for me to bear
Are those spitting knaves!
I can run, of course, but where?
Leap into the waves?

Mouths forever pursed and splayed,
Their throats a-gurgling phlegm,
Walls and floors forever sprayed —
Spittle souls, a curse on them!

Rather live just poor and plain
Free as birds on wires,
Rather join a thieving strain,
Adulterers and liars!

Curse on culture, when it spits!
And curse the churchly fold!
Even holiness admits
Its mouth does not wear gold.[11,12]

19[10]

Nausicaa Songs.[13]

Yesterday, girl, I turned sage,
Seventeen since yesterday: —
And now like those advanced in age
I'm graying — but my hair's not gray!

Yesterday a thought came to me —
A thought? Oh, laughter pealing!
Since when did one thought come to you?
Maybe a tiny feeling!

Seldom would a woman need
To think, for wise old proverbs say:
The woman should obey, not lead;

If she thinks, she can't obey.

What else they say I won't believe,
The proverbs hop like fleas and sting!
"If some rare thought she should achieve,
It can't amount to anything!"

Wisdom of the ages binding,
I bow to you in reverence!
Hear now my new wisdom's finding,
Its most recent quintessence!

Yesterday a voice inside me
Spoke as never — hear who can:
"Woman's beauty can't denied be,
More interesting is — the man!"[14]

19[11][15]
Sanctus Januarius
Woman God and Sin
Art and Writing
Maxims

19[12][16]

The Joyful Science.
1. Sanctus Januarius.
2. On Artists and Women.
3. Thoughts of a Godless One.
4. From the "Moral Diary."
5. "Jokes Cunning and Revenge." Maxims.

19[13]

Songs and Maxims.
Beat to open, rhyme to shut,
And as soul ever music:
Godlike squeaking, when we use it,

Is called song. More briefly put,
Song means: "Words as music."

A maxim's message isn't long:
It can mock, rave, teach,
A maxim is beyond song's reach:
Maxim means: "Pith without song." —

May I bring you some of each?[17]

19[14][18]

Sanctus Januarius.
By
Friedrich Nietzsche

To my Friends
as
Gift and Greeting.

[20 = M III 3a. Spring–Summer 1882]

20[1][1]

BOOK OF FOOLS
Songs and Maxims
by
Friedrich Nietzsche

20[2]
One always has only a single virtue — or none.

20[3]
The moral words are the same in different periods of a people:
on the other hand, the feeling that accompanies them when
they are spoken is always changing. Each period colors anew
the same old words: each period places some of these in the
foreground and others in the background — well, these things
are known! Allow me to make a few observations about the
mor⟨al⟩ linguistic usage of today. — In the circles in which I
have lived, people distinguish between good, noble, and great
human beings. The word good is used in keeping with the
most varying viewpoints: indeed even opposing ones: as I will
soon demonstrate in detail. Whoever is called noble is distinguished thereby as a character who is more than good — not
as especially good but as different from good human beings
specifically insofar as this word allocates him to a superior classification of rank. A great human being in keeping with today's
linguistic usage needs to be neither a good nor a noble human

being — I can recall only one example of a human being of this century who received all three predicates, and even from his enemies — Mazzini.[2]

Studies of all Kinds
for
"The Joyful Science."
(*la gaya scienza*)

21[1]

The introduction from the point of the view of the troubadour.

21[2]¹

I've been taught to trace the ancestry of my blood and name to Polish nobility whose name was Niëtzky, who roughly a hundred years ago gave up their homeland and their nobility, finally succumbing to intolerable religious oppression: for they were Protestants. I will not deny that as a boy I took no small pride in this my Polish ancestry: what is of German blood in me stems solely from my mother, from the Oehler family, and the mother of my father, from the Krause family, and to me it always seemed as though I nevertheless remained a Pole in all essential aspects. It has often been confirmed to me that to this day my outer appearance bears the Polish stamp; abroad, as in Switzerland and in Italy, I have often been addressed as a Pole; in Sorrento, where I spent a winter, the locals referred to me as *il Polacco*; and especially during a summer sojourn in Marienbad, I was reminded of my Polish nature numerous times in a notable way: Poles approached me, greeting me in Polish and mistaking me for one of their acquaintances, and one of them, to whom I denied any Polishness and to whom I introduced myself as a Swiss, looked at me sadly for a long time and finally said "it *is* still the ancient race, but God knows where its heart has turned in the meantime."[2] A small booklet of mazurkas that I composed as a boy bore the title "In Remembrance of Our Forebears!" — and I *did* remember them, in various judgments and prejudices. I regarded the Poles as the most talented and courtliest among the Slavic peoples; and the talent of the Slavs seemed to me superior to that of Germans, indeed, I thought the Germans only managed to join the ranks of talented nations through a strong mixture of Slavic blood. It felt good to me to think about the right of a Polish nobleman to overturn the edict of an assembly with his simple veto;[3] and the Pole Copernicus[4] only seemed to have made precisely the greatest and most dignified use of this veto by opposing the edict and appearance of all other people. The political unruliness and weakness of Poles, likewise their extravagance, were for me sooner evidence in favor of than against their talent. In Chopin I admired in particular how he liberated music from German influences, from the tendency to the ugly, dull, petit bourgeois, awkward, boastful: beauty and nobility of spirit and especially noble cheerfulness, casualness and magnificence of the soul, likewise the southerly glow and melancholy of sensibility were still without expression in music prior to him. Compared to him, even Beethoven seemed to me a semi-barbarian nature, whose great soul was poorly educated, so that it never had learned properly to distinguish the sublime from the adventurous, the simple from the paltry and tasteless. (Unfortunately, as I must also add now, Chopin dwelled too close to a dangerous current of the French spirit, and there is not a little music by him that is pale, sunless, subdued and yet richly costumed and elegant in its entrance — the more robust Slav was unable to ward off the narcotics of an overrefined culture.)

21[3]⁵

1. Abandon what is superfluous. Sacrificing in the long run is harmful to wholeness.

2. Stings of conscience when invoking
     the state (instead of revenge)
     work
     marriage
     teacher   modesty
     merchant craftsman interest
     actor
     great men

3. Cultivation of the race among the Greeks. Ennoblement of prostitution. 34. 38b. 39b. 72⁶

4. Voluntary death as festival 27. 73b⁷

5. Drive humans to ultimate consequences and compel those with the denial of value to dispense with reproduction, p. 70⁸ (cf. no. 11 note)⁹

6. Homer: the hidden individual

7. The wars of the future. 45.¹⁰

8. New order of rank of spirits: no longer the tragic natures in front.

9. No drive for knowledge, intell⟨igence⟩ in the service of different instincts 41. 45.¹¹

10. Preparation of the thought p. 79.¹²

11. Ways of propagating it, 79. 57. 58b 62, 67, 72¹³

The "knowledge of the future has always worked *selectively* — so that those who are permitted to hope survive.

12. As judgment sword of religions. Antichrist.

13. Value tablets of good whence? 11b.¹⁴

14. The ultimate value of existence is not the consequence of insight, but state,¹⁵ prerequisite of knowledge.

15. New valuations — my task
     body and mind
     passion   marriage 66¹⁶

      evil
      community — morality.
      life and death
      conscience punishment sin
      praise and blame
      purposes wills
      indifference 53[17]

16. Rehabilitate injustice — be positive
17. On the damage of virtues.
18. Prerequisite of absolute morality: *my* valuation the ultimate! Feeling of power! 52b.[18]
19. The sage and the gold market. 56.[19]
20. Witchcraft — use of every *power*. Conversion. 74.[20]
21. Feeling of power and function. 33b, 66,[21]
22. Power, function — and *conscience.*
23. Cause and effect. Description. 34b.[22]
24. Lasciviousness in the service of religion. Likewise enjoyment of meals. Consecration p. 40[23]
25. Scientific sense — demand for an absolute morality. Tolerance? p. 35. 38.[24]
26. Evil — atavism of the former good. 36. 37b.[25]
27. Elements of force p. 32.[26]
28. Taste, not utility imparts value p. 39. 40.[27]
29. The human among animals p. 43b[28]
30. All drives exist for the preservation of the species 57. 43. 44.[29]
31. We assess humans in keeping with their effects p. 44. 50. Results no proof of strength 50.[30]
32. Protoplasm and morality. 45. 48. 58.[31]
    Struggle as the *essence of peace.*
32. Our instincts herd instincts 46.[32]
33. Freedom of the will p. 47.[33]
34. the individual powers of knowledge as poisons p. 48.[34]
35. Cure of the individual p. 49b[35]
36. What lower culture takes from the higher (Schopenhauer's use)

37. The lesser degrees and dissatisfaction, p. 55b[36]
38. Beware! p. 55. 61. 71b[37]
39. Now time to believe in innocence! 56.[38]
40. History of aversion to life p. 56.[39]
41. Elevate *ourselves* — instead of punishing!
42. Incorporation of error. 64. 62.[40]
43. how meagre is egoism! p. 63b, 71,[41]
44. An antidote to the striving for happiness of the *fleeting* individual is needed p. 63. 65. 72.[42]
45. Against the apologists of luxury 66.[43]
46. Wagner's art through Schopenhauer false. 66.[44]
    Only my philosophy is right for it. Siegfried.
47. The free human being as perfection of the organic p. 67. 73.[45]
48. the universe no organism p. 73.[46]
49. Unegoistic 74b[47]
50. the great form in a being as condition of the great form in an artwork. 76.[48]
51. The idealizing power of stings of conscience. What matter are the believed motives, not the actual ones, for ennoblement.
52. To portray my kind of "idealism" — and for this the absolute necessity of even the crudest error. All sensation contains valuation; all valuation fantasizes and invents. We live as heirs of these phantasms: we can*not* shed them. Their "reality" is entirely *different* than the reality of the law of falling bodies.
53. The contradiction must be in "force," to speak *logically.* Struggle etc. As unity and as existence there would be no change.
54. There is no substance, no space (no *actio in distans*[49]), no form, no body and no soul. No "creation," no "omniscience" — no God: indeed no human.
55. *Chaos sive Natura.*[50] 71b 73b 70b 63b 55 43b 23a.[51]

21[4]

Responsibility long since separate from "conscience."

21[5]⁵²

various instincts are satisfied in such a way that we feel *inferior*. Our entire pride and courage turns limp in the awareness of the *smallest* defeats of each day

21[6]⁵³

Once I learn on one leg to stand
Soon both will be at my command⁵⁴

21[7]

If you wa⟨nt⟩ to stay young, grow old soon

21[8]

Experience dangerous⁵⁵
Sudden⟨ly⟩ time passes

21[9]

hearing is surely a delicate thing

21[10]

toss a wax candle down here, so that it is extinguished
[—] to ring a little bell

21[11]

In the state of pregnancy we hide and are fearful: for we feel that it is hard for us to defend ourselves now, even more, that it would be harmful to what we love more than ourselves if we had to defend ourselves.

21[12]

The odd fate of a human! He lives 70 years and thinks during this time that he is something new and never seen before — and yet he is merely a wave in which the past of humans continues to move, and he is always laboring on a work of tremendous duration, no matter how much he may feel himself to be an ephemeral fly. For: he considers himself free, and yet he is only a wound-up clockwork, without the power even to see this mechanism clearly, let alone to change it however he might wish.

21[13]

When modesty is the cause of love: wherever the gratification of an instinct is blocked, a new state arises, and a certain more modest agony and gratification, in this manner an ideal begins to germinate — something sensually supersensual.

Reference Matter

Notes

The following symbols are used throughout the text and notes:

[ ]	Deletion by Nietzsche
| |	Addition by Nietzsche
{ }	Addition by the translator or editors
⟨ ⟩	Addition by the editors (Colli and Montinari)
[?]	Unsure reading
[+++]	Gap in the manuscript
— — —	Unfinished or incomplete sentence or thought
Italics	Underlined once by Nietzsche
Bold	Underlined twice or more by Nietzsche
NL	Books in Nietzsche's personal library

Variants and editions of Nietzsche's works are referred to by the following abbreviations:

CW	*The Complete Works of Friedrich Nietzsche*
KGB	*Briefwechsel: Kritische Gesamtausgabe*
KGW	*Kritische Gesamtausgabe*
KSA	*Kritische Studienausgabe*
Cp	Correction in the proofs
Fe	First edition
Fe²	First printing of the 1887 second edition of *JS*

Le	Twenty-volume 1894 Leipzig edition of Nietzsche's works (*Großoktav-Ausgabe*)
Le²	*Großoktav-Ausgabe*, second edition (1897, edited by Fritz Koegel)
Ms	Manuscript
Pd	Preliminary draft
Pm	Printer's manuscript (clean final copy of handwritten MS)
PmG	Change made by Gast in the printer's manuscript
PmN	Change made by Nietzsche in the printer's manuscript
Pp	Page proofs
Sd	Second draft
Se	Subsequent emendation
Up	Uncorrected proofs

Titles of Nietzsche's works are referred to by the following abbreviations:

AC	*The Antichrist*
BGE	*Beyond Good and Evil*
BT	*The Birth of Tragedy*
D	*Dawn*
DD	*Dionysus Dithyrambs*
DS	*David Strauss the Confessor and the Writer*
EH	*Ecce Homo*
GM	*On the Genealogy of Morality*
HAH	*Human, All Too Human*
HL	*On the Utility and Liability of History for Life*
IM	*Idylls from Messina*
JS	*The Joyful Science*
JSA	*The Joyful Science, Appendix: Songs of Prince Vogelfrei*
JSP	*The Joyful Science, Prelude in German Rhymes*
MM	*Mixed Opinions and Maxims*
NCW	*Nietzsche Contra Wagner*
SE	*Schopenhauer as Educator*

TI	*Twilight of the Idols*
UO	*Unfashionable Observations*
WA	*The Case of Wagner*
WB	*Richard Wagner in Bayreuth*
WP	*The Will to Power*
WS	*The Wanderer and His Shadow*
Z	*Thus Spoke Zarathustra*

The editorial apparatus has been supplemented with information drawn from Sebastian Kaufmann's commentary to *The Joyful Science:*

> *Kommentar zu Nietzsches* Die fröhliche Wissenschaft. In: *Historischer und kritischer Kommentar zu Friedrich Nietzsches Werken.* Herausgegeben von der Heidelberger Akademie der Wissenschaften: Bd. 3.2. Berlin: Walter de Gruyter, 2022.
> References to Kaufmann's commentary are cited as "Kaufmann," followed by page numbers.

Citations from Emerson's works will provide volume number, volume title, essay title, and page number from the *The Collected Works of Ralph Waldo Emerson:*

> Volume II: *Essays: First Series.* Cambridge, MA: Belknap Press of Harvard University Press, 1979.
> Volume III: *Essays: Second Series.* Cambridge, MA: Belknap Press of Harvard University Press, 1983.

Citations from Schopenhauer's works will provide the page number from the German edition in Nietzsche's possession: the Julius Frauenstädt editions of the *Sämtliche Werke* (Leipzig: F. A. Brockhaus, 1873–74) and *Arthur Schopenhauer's handschriftlichem Nachlaß* (Leipzig: F. A. Brockhaus, 1864), followed by the page number from the following English translations and using these abbreviated titles:

Ethics	*The Two Fundamental Problems of Ethics.* Translated by Christopher Janaway. Cambridge: Cambridge University Press, 2009.
Manuscript	*Manuscript Remains in Four Volumes.* Edited by Arthur Hübscher. Translated by E. F. J. Payne. Oxford: Berg, 1988–90.
Parerga 1	*Parerga and Paralipomena.* Vol. 1. Translated and edited by Sabine Roehr and Christopher Janaway. Cambridge: Cambridge University Press, 2014.
Parerga 2	*Parerga and Paralipomena.* Vol. 2. Translated and edited by Adrian Del Caro and Christopher Janaway. Cambridge: Cambridge University Press, 2015.
World 1	*The World as Will and Representation.* Vol. 1. Translated by Judith Norman, Alistair Welchman, and Christopher Janaway. Cambridge: Cambridge University Press, 2010.
World 2	*The World as Will and Representation.* Vol. 2. Translated and edited by Judith Norman, Alistair Welchman, and Christopher Janaway. Cambridge: Cambridge University Press, 2017.

Note to Volume 6

In order to distinguish the Colli-Montinari editorial apparatus in *KSA 14* from Nietzsche's variants and letters and from the translator's and editors' notes, this volume follows the *KSA* convention of italicizing Colli's and Montinari's editors' notes.

The Joyful Science

The Joyful Science was at first conceived by N as a continuation of *Dawn.* On {25} January 1882 he communicated to Peter Gast {*KGB* III:1, 159}: "A few days ago I finished books VI, VII and VIII of 'Dawn,' and my work on it is done for the time being. For I want to reserve books 9 and 10 for next winter — I am not yet ripe enough for the elemental thoughts I want to present in these concluding books. Among them is one thought that in fact will require 'millennia' to *become* something. Where will I find the courage to utter it!" For his work on the new book, N had until now reached back into writings that stemmed both from *Dawn* material that remained unused as well as later material originating between spring and autumn of 1881, the latter, however, with the exception of those writings contained in a notebook (M III 1) from spring–autumn 1881. {Montinari could be more clear here: what he means is that for his work thus far on *JS* (Books 1–3 = "Dawn" VI, VII, VII), N had drawn upon material not yet used in *D* and *Nachlass* material from spring–autumn 1881, but he had not yet drawn from writings in M III 1 (305–421), which he used for *JS* Book 4.} In this notebook we find the thought that required "millennia" in order "to *become* something," the thought of the eternal recurrence of the same. N still referred to this note dated "beginning of August 1881 in Sils-Maria" (cf. 11[141]) in *Ecce Homo* ("Books" *Z*1, *CW* 9, 278). Shortly after his acquaintance with Lou von Salomé and during his sojourn in Switzerland with Lou and Rée, N changed his plans, and on 8 May he wrote to his publisher {*KGB* III:1, 191}: "By autumn you will have a manuscript by me: title 'The Joyful Science' (with many epigrams in *verses*!!!)." The printer's manuscript was produced by N in Naumburg, with the help of his sister and a "bankrupt merchant." Some of its parts N wrote himself, for example, "Jokes, Cunning and Revenge." The printer's manuscript was sent to Schmeitzner bit by bit between 19 June and 3 July; with the exception of "Jokes, Cunning and Revenge" and a few other pages handwritten by N, it has not been preserved. The surviving proofs were read by N and Gast together between 29 June and 3 August. *The Joyful Science* (= *JS*) appeared shortly before 20 August 1882 in Chemnitz from the Ernst Schmeitzner Verlag. N had reserved "approximately a fourth of the original material for a scholarly treatise" (to Gast, 14 August 1882 {*KGB* III:1, 237}). At stake were the unpublished fragments from M III 1 (cf. pp. 305–421).

The "thought" surfaced only as a suggestive question in aphorism 341.

In 1887 N undertook a "new edition" of his book, by adding to the first edition a preface, a fifth book and the "Songs of Prince Vogelfrei." This time, too, the book was not newly printed, but the unsold copies were given these supplements. Now it was called *The Joyful Science* ("*la gaya scienza*"): *New Edition with an Appendix, Songs of Prince Vogelfrei* (Leipzig: E. W. Fritzsch Verlag). The subtitle clarified the origin of the title itself as stemming from Provençal poetry (cf. 11[337] and the corresponding note). An author's copy of the second edition with N's notations has been preserved.

{The title page now appeared as:

Die
fröhliche Wissenschaft.
("la gaya scienza")

Von
FRIEDRICH NIETZSCHE.

Ich wohne in meinem eignen Haus,
Hab Niemandem nie nichts nachgemacht
Und — lachte noch jeden Meister aus,
Der nicht sich selber ausgelacht.

Ueber meiner Hausthür.

Neue Ausgabe
mit einem Anhange:
Lieder des Prinzen Vogelfrei.

✸

Leipzig.
Verlag von E. W. Fritzsch.
1887.

The following advertisement, written by N, appeared on the back cover of the first edition:

> With this book we arrive at the conclusion of a series of writings by FRIEDRICH NIETZSCHE, whose common goal is to erect a new image and ideal of the free spirit. In this series belongs:
>
> *Human, All Too Human.* With Appendix: Mixed Opinions and Maxims.
>
> *The Wander and His Shadow.*
>
> *Dawn.* Thoughts on the Presumptions of Morality.
>
> *The Joyful Science.*

——————

> Earlier writings by the same author:
>
> *The Birth of Tragedy Out of the Spirit of Music.*
>
> *Unfashionable Observations.* 1. *David Strauss the Confessor and the Writer.* 2. *On the Utility and Liability of History for Life.* 3. *Schopenhauer as Educator.* 4. *Richard Wagner in Bayreuth.*

——————}

Notes

The Joyful Science

1. *Emerson]* Cf. 18[5] and note. {Cf. vol. 2: *Essays: First Series,* "History," 8: "To the poet, to the philosopher, to the saint, all things are friendly and sacred, all events profitable, all days holy, all men divine." Although in 18[5], N accurately transcribes the Emerson quotation from the German translation that he was reading (*Versuche,* trans. G. Fabricius [pseudonym] [Hanover: Carl Meyer, 1858], 9, *NL*), here he is not quoting but slightly paraphrasing. Hence the substitution of *Erlebnisse* ("experiences") for *Ereignisse* ("events") — which links directly to the first sentence of the preface to the 2nd edition.}

Preface to the Second Edition

1. *Preface to the Second Edition.] Sd*: 2 — But the goal of this preface should be different than reminding my readers of the virtues of a reader — good will, indulgence, caution, insight, subtlety; it would be a deception if I left it at that. I know too well why this book [has to be] will be misunderstood: or [rather] more clearly, why its cheerfulness, its almost capricious pleasure in what is bright, close, light, flippant does not communicate, rather acts as a problem, disconcerts like a problem . . . This cheerfulness conceals something, this will to the surface betrays a *knowing* about the depths, these depths exhale their breath, a cold breath that makes one shiver; and supposing that one learned to dance to the music of such "cheerfulness," then maybe not for the purpose of dancing but instead to keep warm? — I may as well confess: we humans of the depths *need* our cheerfulness too much not to make it suspicious, and if we "could only believe in a God who knew how to dance," {cf. *CW* 14, 3[1] 137 (p. 57); *Z* I "On Reading and Writing"} then it might be because we believe too much in the devil, namely in the *spirit of gravity*, by whom we are too often, too hard, too thoroughly burdened. No, there is something pessimistic about us, that *reveals* itself even in our cheerfulness, we know about this appearance, about every appearance — for we love appearance, we even worship it — but only because we have our suspicions about "being" itself . . . Oh if only you could grasp completely why we need precisely *art*, a mocking, divinely undisturbed art, that blazes up like a bright flame into a cloudless sky! And why we [now no longer] surely least resemble those tragic [buffoons] fanatics, who make temples unsafe at night, embrace statues and unveil and uncover absolutely everything that is kept covered with good reason, want to [must] expose it to bright light [those [friends] wooers of truth at any cost, the romantics of knowledge! Oh! This craving has left us, this youth's insanity in love, this Egyptian earnestness, this grisly "will to truth" terrifies us even as a remembrance]. No, this bad taste and youth's insanity is spoiled for us, we are too experienced for it, too burned, too profound . . . [*What follows is almost verbatim Preface §4, pp. 8–9*: "In retrospect we have . . . 1886." *Hence the preface was here planned as two sections. For this also the following partially preserved preliminary draft*:] NB!

Conclusion of the *last* section! — . . . Oh if only you could completely understand why [we love and require precisely such an art! Were we not previously all too long the same] precisely we require art — and especially a mocking and divinely undisturbed art! [and why we are not in the least romantics anymore!] that blazes up like a bright flame into a cloudless sky. — In our youth we may have all too long resembled those fanatics who make temples unsafe at night, who secretly embrace statues and [want to] unveil and uncover absolutely everything that is kept covered, must expose it to bright light — those friends of truth at any cost, the romantics of knowledge! Oh! This craving has left us, this youth's insanity [in love], this Egyptian earnestness, this grisly "will to truth" terrifies us even as a remembrance! *We no longer believe* that truth remains truth when one removes its veil, we have reason to believe this . . . Today we regard it as a matter of decency that one not [want to] see everything naked [; also that one] not [want to] be present for everything [; also that one] not want to "know" everything . . . [What? *Tout comprendre c'est tout pardonner?* {To know everything is to pardon everything} On the contrary!] [What follows here almost verbatim Preface §4, p. 9]: "Is it true . . . artists?"

2. *willful tenderness . . . lured.]* Pm: willfulness even at the cost of serious things and things held sacred, much play and playing around with problems that otherwise arouse fear and are not made for laughing

3. *romanticism]* Pm: idealism

4. *"Incipit tragoedia"]* "The tragedy begins" {N underlines *tragoedia*.}

5. *incipit parodia]* "the parody begins" {N underlines *parodia*.}

6. {In German, *Pferd* (horse) and *Erd*[e] (earth) do rhyme.}

7. *led and misled]* geführt und verführt

8. {Sections 3 and 4 of this preface were revised and used as §§1 and 2 of the "Epilogue" to *Nietzsche Contra Wagner* (cf. *CW* 9, 405–7).}

9. *from our pain . . . of]* Pm: and live, achieve, act nothing but our thoughts, that they {are}

10. *We are no . . . doom.]* Pd:— — — [through that] with that we distinguish ourselves from frogs, [the so-called thinkers] that which the common people call a thinker — that one [knows] feels

precisely his thoughts and nothing but his thoughts as [his] blood, heart, fire, joy [sorrow] pain, reality destiny, doom — that one lives them, achieves them, *acts* them.

11. *an X out of every U]* {To try to convince someone that a U is an X is an idiom for hoodwinking or duping someone.}

12. *Now whether . . . tortured;]* {Cf. Stendhal, *De l'amour* ("On love") (Paris: Michel Lévy Frères, 1868), 110–11.}

13. *And as concerns illness: . . . unsaid:]* In Mp XV 2, 23 *first written down as an aphorism*: 372. *In favor of illness.* — Between you and me: pain is the great schoolmaster of suspicion, that long slow pain in which so to speak we are burned as if on green wood. It compels us to descend into our ultimate depth and rid ourselves of all trust, all that is good-natured, cloaking, mild, mediating in which perhaps we had formerly placed our humanity. I doubt whether pain "improves" humans — ; but I know that it *deepens* them. Now whether it is because we learn to counter it with our pride, our scorn, our will power, as does the American Indian who repays his torturer with the malice of his tongue, no matter how badly he is tortured; whether we withdraw from pain into that oriental nothing, into that mute, rigid, deaf self-surrender, self-forgetting, self-extinguishing: one emerges from such long dangerous exercises as a different human being, with a few more question marks, above all with the *will* henceforth to question more, more deeply, more rigorously, more harshly, more evilly than one had questioned before. The trust in life is gone: life itself became a problem . . . But we should not believe that this necessarily turns one into a gloom monger. The joy in everything problematic in more spiritual human beings is too great for this joy not to smolder again and again like a bright ember over all the *adversity* of the problematic, over all danger of uncertainty. Finally, to ensure that the most essential point does not go unsaid: if life is a riddle, why should it be forbidden from the outset to reflect upon a *comical* solution to it? [+++] [here the page was cut off]

14. *elevated, deviated]* Gehobenen, Verschrobenen {"elevated," "perverse"; "deviated" to preserve the rhyme}

15. *remain concealed]* {Cf. Friedrich Schiller's poem "Das verschleierte Bild zu Sais" ("The veiled image at Sais") and Novalis's

fragmentary novel "Die Lehrlinge zu Sais" ("The apprentices at Sais"); both romantic texts allude to the goddess Isis and the Egyptian myths as handed down to Plutarch.}

16. *grounds for . . . seen] das Gründe hat, ihre Gründe nicht sehn zu lassen*

17. *Baubo]* {Also known as Iambe, daughter of Echo and Pan, servant in Demeter's house who cured Demeter's depression by exposing her genitalia to her.}

18. *worshipping appearance . . . appearance!] Pd*: to worship appearance, to deify forms, sounds, words, the moment

19. *autumn] Pm*; *Le*: autumn of the year

"Jokes, Cunning, and Revenge"

1. *Jokes . . . Revenge]* On the title: cf. Goethe, *Scherz, List und Rache: Ein Singspiel* {"Jokes, cunning and revenge: A musical comedy"} (1790): Peter Gast set it to music in 1880.

2. *Invitation] Sd*: *Concluding Rhyme*

3. *Undaunted] Sd*: *The Depths*

4. *obscurantists] Sd*: grave diggers; *Pd*: gloomy birds

5. Cf. 16[2].

6. *Pd*: 16[6]; *Pm*: *To our Virtues*

7. Originally the third strophe of 19[8], p. 514.

8. *Worldly Wisdom] Up*: Rules of life

9. *Vademecum — Vadetecum]* {*Vademecum* "go with me" refers to a book one carries always. *Vadetecum* is N's playful revision: "go with yourself."}

10. *Pd*: *The Wanderer's Encouragement.* – Vademecum. Vadetecum. That means, in German style and language — : / follow only *yourself* — / thus you follow me without trouble, / and break the spell as I broke it! *Peter Gast's handwriting*

11. *Pd*: Already my skin cracks and breaks / Already the old snake dies / And a new snake gazes / forth with a new urge

12. *Among . . . what's] Pd*: I crave the old food / With each [new] die and become! / I still eat

13. *In Pd crossed-out version*: Wise and foolish, crude and fine, / sharp and mild, water and wine: / All this shall be my proverb!

14. *Friend of Light] Sd*: *Brother of the Sun*; cf. N to Peter Gast, 17 February 1882 {*KGB* III:1, 171}.

15. *Pd*: Light and warmth soon make weary / And push one finally to any shadow.

16. *For Dancers] Sd*: *Slippery Ice [Dancer-Wisdom]*; cf. N to Peter Gast, 17 February 1882 {*KGB* III:1, 171}.

17. *The Good Man] Sd*: *The Resolute One [At the Crossroads]*; cf. N to Peter Gast, 17 February 1882 {*KGB* III:1, 171}.

18. *Pd*: Better a [fresh] whole enmity than a glued friendship!

19. Cf. N to Peter Gast, 17 February 1882 {*KGB* III:1, 171}.

20. *Upward] Sd*: *The Wanderer*; cf. N to Peter Gast, 17 February 1882 {*KGB* III:1, 171}.

21. *Motto of a Brute] Sd*: *The Brute Speaks*

22. *Pd*: *Mp XVIII 3, 25*: Only ask for what one owes you. For all else, don't ask, just take! *N V 7*: Better to steal something than to ask for it.

23. *Pd*: *N V 7, 51*: The evil are only a small burden: / Yet narrow souls I despise. *N V 7, 100*: *narrow* souls

24. *Consider This] Sd*: *Let's Consider It!*

25. *Pd*: One bears 2 pains more easily than a single pain.

26. *Pd*: One calls it conquering — in truth the loving man goes out to rob, but the loving woman wants to steal — unnoticed she sometimes steals the robber.

27. Cf. 11[336].

28. *Medication for Pessimists] Sd*: *Radical Cure [Medication of Pessimists]*

29. Cf. 15[50]; 16[11, 20]; 12[210]; note to *CW* 12, 21[21]; cf. also Chamfort, maxim 863: "*M. de Lassay, homme très doux, mais qui avait une grande connaissance de la société, disait qu'il faudrait avaler un crapaud tous les matins, pour ne trouver plus rien de dégoûtant le reste de la journée, quand on devait la passer dans le monde.*" ("M. de Lassay, a very indulgent man, but with a great knowledge of society, said that we should swallow a toad every morning, in order to fortify ourselves against the disgust of the rest of the day, when we have to spend it in society.") {*Chamfort: Pensées — maximes — anecdotes — dialogues. Précédé de l'histoire de Chamfort* by P.-J. Stahl (Paris: Michel Lévy Frères, 1860), 187–88.} *NL*.

30. *too. / Come]* too. / [The Greeks call it dyspepsia —] / Come; *Sd crossed out at the end*: A toad is the main medication / For all pessimist-gnats!

31. *Pd*: 16[10]; cf. 12[130].

32. Cf. 16[15]; 15[28].

33. Cf. 21[6]; *Sd crossed out*: Yes! I still resemble early wine, / Yes! You should see me foam! / Insolently, I should think, / I will yet go my way! / Once I stand on both feet, / Soon I'll stand on one. / *Next to it also the following crossed-out variant*: Laborious my appearance seems to you / Wait! Soon it will be better! / Once I stand on both feet, / Soon I'll stand on one. / If I still resemble sour wine today, / Soon you shall see me foam; / Insolently, I should think / I will yet go my way!

34. *Pd*: 16[12]; *crossed out in M III 3, Pd*: If I did not, year in year out, / Want to roll around myself, / How would I, star, bear so long, / To chase the sun? / If I wanted — — —

35. *Joy . . . concealing,] Pd*: As if out of shame for your happiness

36. *Joy . . . dress.] Pd*: With the devil's wit and trickery / Now you wear the devil's dress —

37. Cf. 16[13].

38. *N V 8, first version*: If I don't want to follow, I must hide, / I cannot rule, nor can I seduce. / Whoever is not frightening, frightens no one, / Whoever fears himself — always will he rule. *N V 8, second version*: Obey? No! And no again! Rule! / Whoever is not frightening to himself, frightens no one. / And only he who frightens can rule / [Thus I love *solitude*] Thus I live in my own hiding place / Ready to seduce myself to me / To *discover* alone my happiness in my own caves; *M III 3, 26 first version*: Obey? No! And no again! Rule! / Whoever is not frightening to himself, frightens no one, / And only he who frightens, can lead others / Thus I live in caves and hiding places, / Ready to uncover the treasures of the depths, / [And to speak scorn to everyone] And to mock all who rule. / If I want to follow myself, I must seduce myself!; *M III 3, 27, second version*: [If I want to follow myself, I must seduce myself.] I hate following and leading. / Obey? No! And no again — to rule! / Whoever is not frightening to himself, frightens no one / And only he who frightens, can lead others. /

Thus I live in caves and hiding places, / Ready to uncover [the deep] solitary treasures, / Ready to mock all who rule — / Ready to seduce myself to me.

39. *myself a while]* Pm: myself for a little hour

40. *and brood in]* Pm: and despair

41. *But just . . . features.]* M III 3, 27, Pd: I do hate to seduce myself, / Thus I live in caves and hiding places, / To uncover the lonely one's [treasures] works, / Ready to mock all who rule, / Ready to seduce you to yourselves. / I love to misjudge myself. / I hate to know myself / To call myself both master and servant. / I love to lose myself, / To seduce myself to me, / To separate myself from me for a good hour or two, / To crouch in lovely confusion and despair / To lose myself for an hour or two, / To lure myself back home from afar / And to finally seduce myself.

42. *Seneca . . . omne.]* "Seneca and his lot."

43. *In Pd crossed out:* Don't want to read anymore these gentlemen's / philosophical la-di-da-di: / They think: *primum scribere / deinde philosophari.* {"first write, then philosophize"}

44. *primum . . . philosophari]* "first write, then philosophize"

45. *Juvenilia]* Pd: *To My First Five Little Books;* cf. N to Rée, September 1879 {*KGB* II:5, 440}: *To My First Five Little Books.* / Formerly I thought, A and O / My wisdom was in them; / Now I no longer think so: / Only the eternal Ah! and Oh! / Of my *youth* I find inside.

46. *A and O]* {Alpha and omega are the first and last letters of the Greek alphabet, hence proverbially "the alpha and omega" are said to comprise or to be everything. Cf. also Revelation 1:8.}

47. *Pd:* I love God because [he] I created [me] him / And you — you want to deny him for that?? / The conclusion doesn't stand up well / It limps: because of its cloven hoof

48. *In Summer]* Sd: *Solar-Morality*

49. *Beneath . . . bread]* Pd: Beneath the sweat of your brow you have to drink your wine {Cf. Genesis 3:19: "In the sweat of thy face shalt thou eat bread."}

50. Cf. 16[35]; *Pd at the end:* Swarmed by all flies

51. *Principle of the All Too Refined]* Sd: *The All Too-Refined;* Pd: *Motto of the Refined Spirits*

52. Cf. 16[14].

53. *The Well-Grounded One] Der Gründliche* {"the thorough one," based on *Grund* ("ground," "reason")}

54. Cf. 16[5]; 12[178].

55. *Pd*: "You come too early! you come too late!" — that gets shouted about all who come forever. Cf. 15[52].

56. *Pd*: When it's hot, we judge the value of trees by their shade. —

57. *Going Down] Niedergang* {"decline," or literally "going down"}

58. *Going Down] Sd*: The Divine One

59. *"He sinks . . . walking!] Pd*: From his superhappiness's hardship / He, like the sun, follows you cold ones

60. *His superjoy . . . air.] Pd*: It was the highest flight he ever flew! / And if he hadn't flown up to the sky, / What would have ever pulled him down to you?

61. *Pd*: Since yesterday you have a clock — / And only from now on do you have a need / To check the time

62. *The Wise Man Speaks] Sd*: The Wise Man; *Pd*: *N V 7, 55*: How pleasant the common people! A foreign tongue speaks to me; *N V 7, 56*: With foreign tongue among foreign people / To live: so lives the sun despite the cloud. / I am like the sun: below me the cloud!

63. *Pd*: *Mp XVIII 3, 25*: In love the man loses his understanding, / But woman first gets hers entirely. — *N V 7, 55*: In love the man loses his understanding, but woman gets hers, she alone also has puberty first entirely in her head.

64. *Pious Wishes] Sd*: Pious Wish

65. *Skeletons] Dietrich* {German for skeleton key, or a combination key capable of opening any lock. It is also a common given name for males.}

66. *Writing . . . foot.] Sd*: The Wanderer [*The Author Speaks*]

67. *"Human . . . Book] Sd*: To the Book Called "Human All Too Human"; cf. N to Rée, September 1879 {*KGB* II:5, 441}: To My **Last** Book. / Melancholy proud, when you look back, / Carelessly bold, when you trust the future: / O bird, I count you among the eagles? / Are you Athena's owl hoot-hoot?

68. *Minerva's]* {Minerva, Roman goddess of wisdom, arts and crafts, and medicine, was identified with the Greek goddess Athena, whose symbol was the sacred and wise owl.}

69. *hoot hoot]* *Uhu* {German for eagle-owl, as well as the sound (hooting) made by owls.}

70. *To My]* Pd: *To my*

71. *To My Reader]* Sd: *To the Reader* [dedicated to "Dawn."]

72. *The . . . Painter]* Sd: *The Realist*; Sd: *Impossibility of Realism*

73. *two!]* In Sd crossed out after two! / Know then: this maxim's glue / Were — "rhyme" "glue" "wood" and "pride"!; *in Sd crossed out:* Did you know how proud of rhymes / Every poet glues his wood! {In the original German, N rhymes *Leime/Reime* (glue/rhymes) and *Holz/Stolz* (wood, pride)}.

74. Pd: The best place in paradise is outside its door.

75. Pd: Notwithstanding this and that / Surely you will fall on your nose. —

76. *rhino]* *Nashorn* {From *Nase* ("nose") and *Horn* ("horn"), a loan translation from the Greek.}

77. *The . . . Scribbles]* Sd: *What I write no one reads* [*To My Readers*]

78. Cf. 12[184].

79. *The . . . Speaks]* Sd: *In media vita* [*Last Ground for Existence*]

80. *The . . . Speaks]* Pd: *In media vita* {at midlife} / My life is halfway over, / The clock hand falls, my soul shudders — / Long already does it roam / And [wants out — and yet! it] sought and found nothing — and it wavers here! / My life is halfway over: / [Pain it was to live here] groundless pain to live here hour upon hour! / Shall I run around the track? / And in the end yet find — ground upon ground for it?

81. Pd: I am like a flame / I wish to seize everything / All I hold glows / All I leave turns to coal.

82. *Beyond . . . deserves]* Pd: stellar distant / You shall be light for those to come / The furthest distance is your

Book One
1. Cf. *CW* 13, 6[438].
2. *species]* *Gattung*

3. *species*] Art

4. *I no longer . . . words*] Sd: With such a look at the tremendous whole and its advantages you must agree, my dear fellow human being and closest neighbor, that you not at all

5. *and*] Sd: the real "egoist"

6. *"waves . . . laughter"*] Incorrect translation of Aeschylus, *Prometheus Bound*, 89–90 {ποντίων τε κυμάτων ἀνήριθμον γέλασμα, "countless laughing waves of the sea"}.

7. *exists, its*] Sd: exists, [he must have an interest of knowledge in this, to prefer to be than not to be] its

8. *this new . . . flow?*] Sd: that now there are *two opposing conditions* in human nature, *that want to form a rhythm in their sequence?* Do you understand *why* we all have to have our ebb and flow? *Which* we cannot have simultaneously? *Which* we must not *be* simultaneously? — Well then! Let us be the inventors of this new rhythm! Each for himself and his music!

9. *We too . . . time!*] Missing in Up.

10. *women . . . genius*] Pd: women seemed to me, once I saw the light about them one day, as base and — degraded: what was genius to me

11. *rerum . . . discors*] "discordant concord of things" {Horace, *Epistles* I, 12, 19.}

12. Cf. *CW* 13, 6[175]; Pd: To common natures all noble feelings seem to be inexpedient and therefore improbable, implausible: if they believe in them, they regard anyone who does something that is inexpedient as a fool. A goal is an advantage for him: he [*sic*] probably comprehends the *pleasure* in noble actions, but he [*sic*] does not honor *these* as goals. "How can someone be glad to be or to put themselves at a disadvantage, as the sacrificing one does?" asks the common one. A sickness of reason must be connected with the noble affection, that is why he thinks dismissively of this pleasure, just as we do with the joy that the madman derives from his fixed idea. — Ordinarily however he thinks: "this sacrifice will surely be the means to a richly compensating *advantage*" — this is why he is suspicious of the magnanimous. — In fact the noble can be determined by a pleasure- and displeasure-feeling *without thought,* just as we chew

our food now on this, now on that side of our mouths, without thinking about it but according to whether it is more pleasant one way or the other. A certain lack of bright intellect is peculiar to the magnanimous: Napoleon does not comprehend the *pausing of thinking*. The animals that risk their lives to protect their young do not think about *their danger*, because the pleasure in their brood and the fear of being robbed of this controls them entirely, it renders them stupid. In itself this is *no more ethical* than when a man exposes himself to the most abhorrent diseases by following his sex drive. — The common nature is therefore distinguished by the fact that it never forgets its advantage and that this *thinking is stronger* than his drives: his wisdom consists of not being led astray to inexpedient actions for the sake of his drives. Therefore: *the superior nature is the more unreasonable.*

Cf. also in J. J. Baumann, *Handbuch der Moral nebst Abriß der Rechtsphilosophie* {"Manual of morality along with a philosophy of law"} (Leipzig{: Hirzel,} 1879), 13. *NL.* This passage underlined by N: "Conversely the person of common or egoistical disposition interprets everything in keeping with himself, because a disinterested and noble way of thinking is entirely incomprehensible to him . . ."

13. *those] Sd, Le*: his

14. *more unreasonable] unvernünftigere*

15. *unreason or antireason] Unvernunft oder Quervernunft*

16. *values and unvalues] Werthe und Unwerthe*

17. *Pd*: The strongest individuals have so far carried humankind forward the most, again and again they ignited the sleeping passions and awakened the spirit by setting models against each other and forcing humans to form opinions about new things — whereas without this, humans just lie down to sleep on their opinions. Mostly with weapons, by toppling the boundary markers, and through violating pieties: but also through new contrasting teachings! A conqueror possesses the same malice as a philosopher: only in the latter it is more sublimated, it does not at first set his muscles in motion so much. The so-called good human beings of every epoch are those who dig the old thoughts deep into the ground and bear fruit with them — they are the

plowmen. But all land becomes exhausted, the great plowshare must come, otherwise the good make humankind into a stale barren region. The marriages of the good gradually produce imbecile progeny.

18. Cf. *CW* 13, 6[116].

19. *Pd*: What is needed is the working-through of all *passions*, according to people period basic value judgments, and the whole rationality of it must come to light.

20. *cyclopic buildings]* {Cf. *WS* 275, *CW* 4, 265.}

21. *Pd*: What humankind embryonically acquired thousands of years earlier, perhaps first makes its appearance in *us*, though very feebly. — So e.g., the influence of the café on Europe can only become evident in perhaps thousands of years. Cf. 11[212].

22. *Pd*: The *rare* humans: my conception of them as atavism, very *instructive* for the past! There was a time when their properties were *ordinary* and *base*. Ordinarily products of the reserved conservative families.

23. *Consciousness. — Consciousness]* Bewußtsein. — Bewußtheit {N uses *Bewußtsein* for the title, but *Bewußtheit* (roughly: the state of being conscious) for most of this aphorism.}

24. *"beyond . . . says.]* Cf. the Homeric expressions ὑπὲρ μόρον, *hyper moron* (*Odyssey,* bk. 1, line 34; *Iliad,* bk. 20, line 30, etc.), ὑπὲρ μοῖραν, *hyper moiran* (*Iliad,* bk. 20, line 336, etc.), ὑπὲρ μορα, *hyper mora* (*Iliad,* bk. 2, line 155, etc.).

25. Cf. 13[14]; *Pd*: I assume that *pain* has *grown* tremendously in civilization, and that its degree and its diversity are becoming ever greater as culture becomes greater. — At the zenith is always the *most suffering* human being — because he is simultaneously the one *richest in joys.* — Well, what do the Stoics and the Christians think about it? *The former* wanted as little pleasure and displeasure as possible — they strove for the *stone* as the Epicureans did for the *plant.* All socialists and philanthropists who want to create a lasting happiness, i.e., *painlessness* for humanity, have to **suppress** the *joys* of humans just as much as their pains — humans can no longer be jubilating to high heaven according to this morality, if they want to escape being "depressed to death!" But perhaps science will help *here.*

26. *ultimate . . . if]* Pd: happiness, the greatest possible pleasure and least possible displeasure is the goal of morality? If

27. *were . . . that]* Pd: were, as Socrates once said, that

28. *"jubilate . . . to death"]* Goethe, *Egmont* III:2. {The phrase *"himmelhoch jauchzend, zum Tode betrübt"* has become a proverb in German, encapsulating the Storm and Stress and romantic emotionalism that characterized Goethe's early work.}

29. *Stoics . . . this]* Sd: Stoics [and the Christians] (and at bottom [even the Epicureans] all ancients) knew it

30. *An easy prey is something . . . delightful.]* Pd: Compassion as a feeling of well-being arises at the sight of someone who is inferior, whom we perhaps can win over to us, he seems an easy prey. Indeed: an *easy* prey is something contemptuous to very proud natures, they perceive a feeling of *well-being* at the sight of unbroken new *enemies*. The *suffering* are not worthy of their striving for possessions — they are harsh toward them. But they are refined and obliging to their enemy, who is worthy of them

31. *Compassion . . . prostitutes.]* Sd: Hence it is an emotion of women and of the subjugated

32. Cf. 12[174, 20], 14[24]; *CW* 13, 4[72]; 6[54, 164, 446, 454]; 10[A 3].

33. *"raging . . . Sophocles]* Quote not verbatim from Sophocles, but cf. Sophocles, *Antigone* 790, *Women of Trachis* 441–46; also Plato on Sophocles in *Republic* 329b–d; Schopenhauer also refers to this passage in Plato, in "On the Different Stages of Life," *Parerga 1*, 524/431.

34. *time . . . favorites]* Pd: at his gray-haired blasphemer and favorite

35. *probably here . . . friendship.]* Sd: a very rare idealization of love: it is called friendship. [But whoever knows or intuits it,]

— — —

36. Pd: This mountain makes the entire region that it dominates unspeakably *charming*. This ceases when you climb it. — Distance for some kinds of magnitude, not letting oneself be lured into wanting to see them without distance.

37. Pd: "Come Cross the Footbridge!"

38. *Pd adds*: This is perhaps how Bossuet felt at times.

39. *more disgusted] Sd, Fe; in Le and all subsequent editions*: nobler

40. *Pd*: Only with respect to the community are actions *good* or *bad*: how the neighbor feels about it is indifferent.

41. *stimuli. (The) Sd*: stimuli. (Even the personal reward and advantage of industriousness is ultimately only ever — industriousness itself. Education is a deceiver insofar as it lures the individual forward with bait that ultimately proves to be unenjoyable. Only through such frequent failures and semi-failures of education does the meaning and taste in personal advantage more or less get preserved, for instance the real enjoyment of wealth and honor: hence through the fact that in a given case, the individual ultimately did not allow the incorporation of that blind raging industriousness to which he was supposed to be condemned: that he reserved time and energy to find the spirit of enjoyment and to become an inventor in enjoyment.) The

42. *it] Sd, Le; Fe*: {refutes} itself

43. *individuals.] In Sd later added, then crossed out*: i.e., by a being who would see [seek] the purpose of [this] existence in both renunciation and perishing! The doctrine of selflessness is consistent only in the mouth [of pessimistic nihilism (hence for example in the mouth of Buddha)] of a teacher of the absolute depravity of existence.

44. *criterion of what is moral! . . . preached!] Sd*: criterion of what is moral — if it measures its value according to its own principle. — But you will say (with Comte): "it is so pleasant to deny oneself, it is lascivious to renounce! it is the supreme voluptuousness!" — Well then, for the sake of this pleasure and lasciviousness your society would have to *dispense with* precisely its advantage, its promotion and preservation! And in case precisely the renunciation [of individuals] and sacrifice of [indiv] individuals should be the means to this promotion and preservation, well! then it would have to teach the opposite of altruism, the most unbounded individualism! [in sum] i.e., it would have to demand for the sake of its advantage that individuals *refrained* from the pleasure of self-denial — in sum it would need, as mentioned, to preach both "thou shalt" and "thou shalt not!" simultaneously

and contradict itself to its face — in consideration of the fact that society itself is merely a multiplicity of individuals and does not have its own sensorium for pleasantries and voluptuousness standing above individuals. — Or how would you like the formula "you must comprehend yourself as an individual so that as a society you can have the pleasure of renunciation and self-denial"? — — —

45. *L'ordre . . . roi]* "The order of the day for the king"

46. *L'ordre . . . roi]* Pd: *Travailler pour le roi Moi* {"Work for King I"}

47. *"whoever . . . favor."]* Cf. *CW* 13, 6[72].

48. Cf. 12[229].

49. *superstition]* Aberglaube

50. *faith]* Glaube

51. *One should pay . . . enlightenment]* Pd: When *corruption* sets in, then superstition increases, for the latter in its manifoldness is already closer to individual impulses, here the individual can choose: and he detaches himself from the traditional faith; it is the *plebeian* kind of *freethinking*

52. *Just . . . fruits]* Sd:— for the first time this fruit hangs

53. *but the tyrant . . . morality]* Pd: the power holder has the understanding of a common heritage

54. *"I have the right . . . diversion."]* Cf. *CW* 13, 8[116], quote from Madame de Rémusat, *Mémoires 1802–1808*, 3 vols. (Paris{: Calmann Lévy,} 1880), 1:114–15. *NL.*

55. *but on the . . . therefore]* Sd: they love and promote all who know how to provide "consolation" through beautiful speeches and sounds and are

56. *and, when . . . knowledge.]* Pd: that for a disciple of wisdom is just as dangerous as any great vice

57. Cf. 15[44]; *CW* 13, 6[154].

58. {Cf. Exodus 20:13; Deuteronomy 5:17.}

59. Cf. 12[85].

60. *all]* Sd: we

61. *Yes! . . . renounces.]* Pd: thus he reconciles us, and he even harvests our admiration: indeed, many poor people snatch up what he throws away and even become rich in doing so

62. *Pd*: Occasionally our strength drives us forward so far that our weak components (e.g., health self-mastery) become *lethal* to us in the process.

63. Cf. *CW* 13, 7[230].

64. *unities]* {In the *Poetics,* Aristotle spelled out the required features of tragedy, namely, tight controls over time, place, and plot, which later European writers tried to reflect in their own works.}

65. Cf. 14[19]; *CW* 13, 10[A 14].

66. Cf. 15[65].

67. Cf. 12[131, 108].

68. Cf. 12[98]; *Pd*: In order to prove to you that the human being is indeed a good-natured animal, I would remind you of how *gullible* he has been. So science is supposed to be a sign that humankind has become more evil? — One cannot doubt the fact that humankind is more evil than ever: everyone today carries around with him the vinegar of moral dissatisfaction — this wasn't the case in older times and not even among the most savage and unruly humans.

69. *Pd*: A great h⟨uman⟩ has a *retroactive* force, all of history is placed on a scale and a thousand secrets crawl out of their holes, each time it is as if until then one had not known what is essential about the past.

70. *Historia abscondita]* "hidden or concealed history"

71. *Pd*: Thinking differently than is customary — is not the effect of intellect, but of *inclinations,* the kind that detach, isolate, defy or are cowardly or gloating and spiteful: heresy is the counterpart of witchcraft and certainly neither harmless nor worthy of veneration. — As long as the whole world *believes* in the evil in human beings, they will become increasingly evil. Thus the great *doubled* Middle Ages, the Reformation, produced both species of *evil* humans on the grandest scale, witches and heretics, i.e., those who have a desire *to harm* whatever (kind of people or opinions) *dominates*

72. *Plaudite . . . est!]* "Applaud, friends, the comedy is over!" Suetonius, *Augustus,* chap. 90, 1.

73. *qualis . . . pereo!]* "what an artist perishes with me!" Suetonius, *Nero,* chap. 49, 1.

74. *qualis . . . pereo!]* "what a spectator perishes with me!"

75. *knowledge]* Erkenntnis

76. *knowledge]* Wissen

77. *believed]* Pd: believed (something indifferent for the masses of human beings) something

78. Pd: not take the enthusiasm for a thing as the thing itself!

79. *to present them with . . . reasons!]* Sd: not to win them over with reasons. Reasons sooner prompt them to counter-reasons and to opposition. —

80. *more important]* Sd, Le; Fe: more powerful

81. *hoc . . . absurdum]* "this is ridiculous, this is absurd"

82. *physis]* "nature" {in the sense of their physiology}

83. Pd: Soldiers and leaders have a *much higher relationship* with one another than workers and employers. For the time being, all military culture stands above all industrial culture: the latter is the *basest* form of existence to date (not even defeat and enslavement through conquest produces such a base sensation: the respect for the powerful is there). But here quite simply the need of wanting to live is in effect — and *contempt* for the one who *exploits* this need of the worker. The fear-inducing powerful *person* is lacking, it is odd that the debasement and subjugation to a person is perceived as far less painful than this debasement to a state of distress — one sees in the employer a cunning, voraciously sucking dog, *like the usurer of former times.* If the manufacturers had the nobility of the aristocracy, there wouldn't be any socialism: but the absence of higher form gives the impression that only accident and luck elevated one over the other here: on the other hand, the basest man feels that the noble *cannot be improvised* and that he is a creature of long ages. — Since the French Revolution one has believed in the *improvisation of state circumstances*: one proceeds.

84. *form]* Form {The nuances of Nietzsche's usage in this aphorism tend toward "bearing," "composure," "dignity," "formality," but also suggest observance of decorum and distance.}

85. Cf. 11[176].

86. Cf. 11[281].

87. *morality of customs]* Sittlichkeit der Sitte {Nietzsche explains in *GM* Preface 4 that the morality of customs and practices is

the older, original morality, and it needs to be distinguished from abstract morality that arises later.}

88. *Wahhabis]* {Wahhabism is a conservative sect of Islam founded by Muhammad ibn Abd al-Wahhab (1703–92).}

89. *Englishman]* Pd: the Englishman Palgrave [William Gifford Palgrave, author of *A Narrative of a Year's Journey Through Central and Eastern Arabia* {(London: Macmillan and Co., 1865)}.]

90. {N most likely came across this story about Palgrave's conversation with the Wahhabi chieftain in Herbert Spencer, *Einleitung in das Studium der Sociologie*, pt. 2 (Leipzig: Brockhaus, 1875), 118. *NL. The Study of Sociology* (New York: Appleton and Co., 1874), 295.}

91. *Cato . . . wine?]* Cf. Plutarch, *Roman Questions* 6, who, however, ascribes this opinion to "most people" (ὡς οἱ πλεῖστοι νομίζουσιν) and not specifically to Cato.

92. *Pd*: According to what kind of motives they — — —

93. *Such happiness . . . existed.]* Pd: Only a constant sufferer can enjoy in this spectacle the happiness of happiness: and his eye knows something about the voluptuousness of gliding across the surface of existence while merely brushing its skin — this white tender trembling skin of the sea! Cf. also 12[154], 15[56], *JS* 256.

94. *invented by . . . existed.]* Pd: found. — What do I make of it, that during meals he forbade himself aesthetic conversation — he thought too well of eating and of poets to make the one into a side dish of the other!

95. Cf. 11[72]; *CW* 13, 7[78]; *Pd*: What voluptuousness that science discovers things that *withstand*! Historical periods with *firm faith* probably felt similarly when listening to fairy tales and sagas; uncertainty and fluctuation was so charming to them! because so unaccustomed! But we are the *soaring ones*! We planets and comets!

96. *joined . . . necessity]* Up: letters carved into the book of existence

97. *everywhere, . . . written,]* Pd: with astonishment the same sign of the times in German and Italian theater:

98. Cf. 12[140]; *Pd*: I look at human beings with an eye toward whether they know the distress of the soul only from description

— whether they consider it cultured and distinguishing to fake knowledge of it — — even major physical pain is unknown to most of them, they equate it with their tooth- and headaches. This ignorance and this *unfamiliarity with pain* makes them seem much less tolerable than earlier humans — thus the philosophies of pessimism are the sign of great refinement that endeavors to allow even *tormenting ideas* to be perceived as suffering of the highest order. Humans with bodily and psychic distress and good familiarity with them were not pessimists.

99. *order.* — *There] Pd*: order: [somewhat Faustian or Hamletian i⟨deas⟩] but especially with the socialistic portrayal of current "distress," I wouldn't know whether the bungling or the fantasizing or the hypocrisy of the portrayers predominates— but some of all these three I always find there. It

100. *Those paradoxical . . . envy] Pd*: Paradoxical drives like magnanimity (dispensing with revenge and gratification of envy, Talleyrand and Napoleon)

101. *Pd*: one fears more the cold gaze of the small circle of society to which we belong than any reproach of conscience: to inflict something unpleasant on one of *these* circles! And the fear of *their* scorn acts as a restraint on the strongest natures.

102. *Pd*: The closest impulse will be under all circumstances: "Let's try it!"

103. *Pd*: Where our dull eyesight is no longer capable of *recognizing* the evil drive on account of its sublimation, there it posits the *realm of goodness*: and the sensation of having crossed over now into the realm of goodness excites all those opposing drives in concert: no fear, no cunning etc. — but security, comfort, benevolence, letting oneself go etc. The duller the eyesight, the farther the good extends: hence the eternal cheerfulness of common people. The subtlest minds have therefore suffered most from this and were gloomy — "the bad conscience." Up till now the general pardon for so-called evil and the *denial* of *good has been lacking.* — Conversely: all evil is merely a coarsened good — denial of evil. Cf. 11[101].

104. Cf. 17[1]; *Pd*: New relationship to existence! I discovered that ancient humankind continues to dream, suffer, act in me — I awaken in dream from a dream!

105. *perfect comprehension] Allverständlichkeit* {i.e., omni-comprehension}

106. Cf. *CW* 13, 6[175, 178].

107. *without selfishness . . . individual] Sd*: not for oneself; the noblest lover is perhaps the most consistent Christian

108. *Pd*: There are always forces there that *want* to do — that's why above all *work* and need! Neediness is needed!

109. *"states of emergency"] "Nothstände"* {playing off *Noth* ("distress," "neediness," "plight") and *nöthig* ("needed," "necessary")}

Book Two

1. *Pd*: "Reality!" What is "real" for someone in love? And even in a sober state, are we not all still extremely passionate animals compared to fish! And then: in our coldest states we still esteem things in keeping with the habits of millennia — and these estimations have their origin in the passions! Where does the *real* world begin here! Is not each sense impression *certainly* also a phantasm, on which the judgment and passion of the entire human past has worked! Mountain! Cloud! What then is "real" about them! — This against realism, which makes things too easy for itself: it appeals to the cruder prejudices of the sober, who believe themselves to be armed against passion and fantasy.

2. *Sais]* {See Preface §4.}

3. *You sober people . . . you sober ones! . . . you sober ones —]* Cf. Goethe, *The Sorrows of Young Werther,* "On 12 August," Werther's conversation with Albert: "Oh you rational people! . . . Shame on you, you sober ones! Shame on you, you wise ones!"

4. *you sober ones — . . . drunkenness.] Pd*: only this question arises, whether someone must or wants to *continue writing* this *poem* "World" or whether he *can*not and consequently also *must not* — like you! You sober ones! You ruminators!

5. *Pd*: Vastly more depends on *what things are called* — than anyone believes.

6. Cf. 11[53]; *Pd*: The human being beneath the skin is an object of disgust to humans; they don't want to think about it. To hear of "digestion" is unpleasant to some women. This feeling resists the

incorporation of knowledge. *Acknowledging* the surface, shape and skin — is human.

7. *moon- and God-addicts]* Mond- und Gottsüchtigen {N is punning with *Mondsüchtiger,* "sleepwalker": *süchtig* added to a noun indicates an addiction to it.}

8. *Pd: M III 5:* You stand pensively beneath cliffs and all around you breaking is the iron rhythm of the surf. Then, suddenly, as if born out of nothing, not far from you there appears around a bend a great sailing ship, [in ghostly beauty and silence] and its deathly silent beauty seemed truly ghostly to me. We measure the quiet of things in keeping with the noise in which we find ourselves at the time: and so women are regarded as quiet places, whose seclusion is longed for by a man amidst his surf of projectiles and projects: but this is only an *actio in distans* {"action at a distance"}. — *N V 7, 189:* You stand thinking beneath cliffs, and the surf breaks around you — then not far from you the ghostly beauty of a great sailing ship glides past, soundlessly — Cf. Charles Baudelaire, *Fusées VIII:* "*Ces beaux et grands navires, imperceptiblement balancés (dandinés) sur les eaux tranquilles, ces robustes navires, à l'air désœuvré et nostalgique, ne nous disent-ils pas dans une langue muette: Quand partons-nous pour le bonheur?*" {"These beautiful and large ships, imperceptibly swayed (bobbing) on the still waters, these robust ships, with their idle and nostalgic air, do not they say to us in a mute language: When do we leave for happiness?"}, in *Œuvres complètes* (Paris{: Éditions Gallimard,} 1968), 1253.

9. *blaze of the surf]* des Brandes der Brandung

10. *projectiles and projects]* Würfen und Entwürfen {literally, "throws" (as in dice or darts) and "projects," "drafts," "plans," or "sketches"}

11. *talent]* {ancient unit of measure of gold and silver}

12. *give . . . thoughts?]* Pd: bring? — while our thoughts seem to ride on the tramontana {tramontana: cold north wind of western Europe}

13. *Pd:* I fear that women in the last recesses of their heart are greater skeptics than any man

14. {Cf. Matthew 5:3.}

15. *Vivat comoedia]* "Long live comedy"

16. *took . . . man] Pd*: showed Z⟨arathustra⟩ a youth: look! someone said, here is someone who is being ruined by women! . Z⟨arathustra⟩

17. {Cf. Genesis 1:27.}

18. *The wise man] Pd*: Z⟨arathustra⟩

19. *existence] Pd*: being

20. *the wise man] Pd*: Z⟨arathustra⟩

21. *But . . . him.] Missing in Pd*; cf. Matthew 19:22.

22. *Pd*: Up till now my only notion of majestic powerful women has derived from the contralto voices of the theater (e.g., from Biancholini {Marietta Biancolini-Rodriguez (1846–1905), Italian mezzo-soprano opera singer}). — To be sure, according to the intention of theater such voices are not supposed to arouse this notion, but that of male lovers, for instance a Romeo — but this effect they never had on me: I always heard the maternal and the housewifely come through: but the entire *lofty* soul of woman, her capacity for *grandiose* resolutions sacrifices responses suddenness did emerge for me from these voices — an ideal to which certainly even here and there in the real world more corresponds than the sound of a voice.

23. *mistresses of masters] Herrinnen der Herren {Herrinnen*, i.e., "lady masters," as used by N in *Z* "The Stillest Hour" to indicate the "terrible mistress." *Herrin* is on a par with *Herr* in German, and to use circumlocutions to avoid the negative, subservient connotations of "mistress" as it is used today to refer to a female lover is to obscure the symmetry.}

24. Cf. 12[110]; *CW* 13, 8[69].

25. *noble] Missing in Sd.*

26. *in eroticis]* "in matters of erotic love"

27. *shame in contradiction] Up*: to find shamelessness in league

28. *or a penance] Missing in Sd.*

29. *Here, in fact, . . . women!] Pd*: in fact, there one has created a gruesome mystery of the psyche, and the curiosity of even the wisest connoisseur of human nature cannot guess how thousandfold differently each woman comes to terms with the solution of this riddle — especially since afterward the same deep silence as before is

observed — if this charm were missing, how boring women would be to us

30. *In brief, . . . women!]* Missing in Sd.

31. *Pd:* The difference between small women and tall women seems so significant to me that I would not be surprised if people were to speak of 3 sexes instead of 2.

32. *Aristotle]* N is thinking of passages like: *Nicomachean Ethics* 1123b5–6: ὥσπερ καὶ τὸ κάλλος ἐν μεγάλῳ σώματι, οἱ μικροὶ δ'ἀστεῖοι καὶ σύμμετροι, καλοὶ δ'οὔ {"since to be great-souled involves greatness just as handsomeness involves size: small people may be neat and well-made, but not handsome"}; *Rhetoric* 1361a6: . . . θηλειῶν δὲ ἀρετὴ σώματος μὲν κάλλος καὶ μέγεθος . . . {". . . Female bodily excellences are beauty and stature . . ."}

33. *And the greatest . . . rule.]* *Pd:* But now this faith grows and lives, and puts itself in danger — continuously the image of things pushes and displaces itself just as does that which makes the things see, hear and feel — continuously there is [the striving of this faith] a powerful urge in this faith to grow rapidly and suddenly and impatiently i.e., to become insanity! Do not precisely the most gifted suffer most from this impatience and writhe under the boredom of the tempo required by that faith? Are not poets and artists signs of the general joy at the eruption of that insanity and the ones leading the dance, as it were? What's needed therefore is the scientific spirit and the virtuous intellect, what's needed is the unflappable beat-keepers for the tremendous dance of the faithful of that faith: it is a necessity of the first degree that commands and demands here. Without it the earth would have been the insane asylum of humans and this only for a brief span, only one night — for the life and duration of humankind depends on the universality and all-connectedness of that faith, on that which it calls its "reason." — My friends, it is a matter full of wonder and majesty to have and to propagate one's *reason* and to finally give it the force of law: they are fools or humans of base ancestry who mock this wondrousness and majesty, because it, among many other things, also demands a certain slowness of movement — all noble things are slow

34. Cf. 12[69]; *Pd:* The vulgarity occasionally in Gil Blas and in Italian opera does not debase me — but it also does not offend

me because it knows no shame, but is so certain and confident of itself, as "the good."

35. *Gil Blas]* Cf. *CW* 13, 7[81]; {Alain-René Lesage (1668–1747), French writer, published his picaresque novel *Histoire de Gil Blas de Santillane* in four volumes between 1715 and 1735.}

36. *popular] volksthümlich*

37. *On the other . . . sake.] Pd*: The vulgarity in German works (e.g., some expressions in Wagner's *Tannhäuser* and *Flying Dutchman*) offend me *unspeakably* — but there is also shame present, and a degrading condescension in the soul of the artist himself, which I become aware of — I am ashamed along with him

38. Cf. 12[4].

39. *Pd*: Humans who find themselves in a difficult situation and know how to speak well about it. — No illusion! Bright intelligence, the fewest possible depths and backgrounds of passion! Everything has to be able to turn into reason and word! — The manner of the [antique] tragic stage illustrates that it works against illusion: the same thing is taught by the kind of language that all characters of tragedy use. — Conversely: all masters of opera make a point of preventing their characters from being understood. With the exception of an occasional word as the catchword of a situation, they rely on the situation to explain itself — none of them had the courage to simply allow la la la to be sung, and to provide the whole thing as musical mime: which is what opera ultimately *is*. Even Wagner's writings, of which no one in the theater community has yet heard anything, were written for readers, not for listeners, and they, too, reveal the resistance of all opera composers to wanting to be understood — they are not supposed *to be taken* at their word, rather by *sound*! — Wagner's writings like his music presuppose that one has learned verses and music by heart before the performance (otherwise one hears neither the words *nor the music*).

40. *remnant of silence] Rest Schweigen* {An allusion to the dying words of Shakespeare's Hamlet ("The rest is silence") in A. W. von Schlegel's renowned German translation ("*Der Rest ist Schweigen*").}

41. {Cf. Aristotle, *Poetics* 1449b. Although *Mitleid* is usually translated as "compassion" in *CW*, here N is referring to Aristotle's ἐλέου, which is typically rendered in English as "pity."}

42. *recitativo secco]* "dry recitative" {A style between speaking and singing; *secco* ("dry") refers to notes played and released abruptly.}

43. *Wagner?]* Sd, Le: Wagner? Perhaps likewise? *Sd crossed out at the end*: — A music could always come along (from France or Russia?), compared to which the whole of Wagnerian art would have to fall into the category and under the justification of *recitativo* (of course as *recitativo umido* {wet} and only rarely *secco*! {dry}) — a possibility that one also has to envisage when one reflects on the delicate relationship between music and morality. — *Cf. as Pd to this*: 12[168].

44. *Even the recitativo . . . itself.]* From: (With Wagner's art things are perhaps just the same, maybe different — meanwhile it seems to me as if one had to have learned [text] word and music *by heart* before the performance: for without this one *hears* neither the words *nor the music*. Often it also seemed otherwise to me.)

45. *Iphigenia]* by Racine

46. *"nothing . . . in it!"]* {Nietzsche is incorrectly recalling Schopenhauer, *The World as Will and Representation*, vol. I, bk. 3, §36 (*World 1*, 213), where Schopenhauer claims that superior mathematicians have "little sensitivity to beautiful works of art," based on an anecdote about a French mathematician who read Racine's *Iphigenia* and asked "What does that prove?"}

47. *Pd*: The builders of antiquity had a mild aversion to strict mathematical proportions; the Middle Ages were indifferent on this point: this is how it is with *logic*. The Greeks are very accurate: the French too, yet they want a little leap into the opposite, apparently (*esprit*). So also in the *beat* of music, and in the sense for what is *emotionally full*.

48. *Est . . . tacere]* "It is a great thing to be silent." Cf. Martial, *Epigrams* IV, 80, 6.

49. Cf. *CW* 13, 10[B 23]; *Pd*: I wish we had the courage to *translate* as the ancients did: namely into the *present*, quite *apart* from when the creator lived and what he was and what he experienced: make it to suit ourselves and make ourselves comfortable in him, raise

ourselves to him, grow into him! (e.g., Horace with Alcaeus — one not only omitted things, but one added allusions to the present — *one even omitted the author's name!*)

50. *imperium Romanum]* "Roman Empire"

51. *after it . . . memory]* Cf. Stendhal, *De l'amour,* 233: "*Les vers furent inventés pour aider la mémoire.*" {"Verse was invented as an aid to memory."}

52. *ferocia animi]* "ferocity of the mind"

53. *poet]* {N uses the archaic *Sänger* here for "poet" as well as in the concluding Homer quote of this section; otherwise, he uses the modern *Dichter.*}

54. *melos]* "melody"

55. *Homer . . . lie!]* According to Aristotle, *Metaphysics* 983a, more likely a proverb: ἀλλὰ κατὰ τὴν παροιμίαν πολλὰ ψεύδονται ἀοιδοί {"But it is impossible for the Deity to be jealous (indeed, as the proverb says, 'poets tell many a lie')"; cf. also Solon, fr. 21 (Diehl) {quoted by Aristotle}.

56. *Pd:* If the day brought you strong and good feelings, then you don't need art — or stand differently before it, with different needs and different taste. You do not crave to be artificially prodded and elevated — it is not the weary who must be given wings —

57. *but of intoxication! . . . culture!] Pd:* but only of intoxication! And the former as a means to the latter? Theater art as a narcotic! And the poets concocters of artificial wines! Narcotics!

58. *"culture" . . . culture!]* "*Bildung*" . . . *Bildung! Sd: Cultur!* — {"culture!"}

59. *musician]* {Cf. *NCW,* "Where I Admire," in *CW* 9, 388–89, which represents a slightly revised version of this aphorism.}

60. *Pd:* 12[37].

61. {N is referring here to Wagner, as is confirmed by his using a revised version of this aphorism in *NCW.*}

62. *mysterious-uncanny] heimlich-unheimlichen*

63. *that we . . . weighty] was wir wichtig nehmen* {"that we consider important [*wichtig*]," from *Gewicht* ("weight"); in the concluding sentence N uses *Gewichte* ("weights").}

64. Cf. 11[170].

65. *Pd*: Some writings are *lights*, from the midst of rays of a knowledge that virtually shines out of us, others are *shadows*, copies in gray and black of whatever my soul used for fortification days ago. Both are material, but of the most differing kind.

66. {Rousseau's autobiographical *Confessions* were published posthumously in 1782; Dante's *Vita Nuova* ("The New Life"), written not in Latin but in Tuscan vernacular, was published in 1294.}

67. *Pd*: The 4 great prose masters

68. *abstractum]* "abstraction"

69. *War . . . things]* Cf. Heraclitus, fr. 53 (Diels-Kranz).

70. *Pd*: What good is a thinker who thinks with a wet pen in his hand! [Or] And those poets who surrender to their passions before an open inkwell, sitting on their chair and staring at their paper! Writing should be a dire need, about which one cannot think without shame — even the metaphor of this subject is disgusting. —

71. {Fontenelle's *Dialogues des morts* ("Dialogues of the Dead") was first published in 1683.}

72. Cf. 12[121]; 15[22, 37, 71]; N's source for Chamfort: P.-J. Stahl, *Histoire de Chamfort* ("History of Chamfort") in Sébastien-Roch-Nicolas Chamfort, *Chamfort: Pensées — maximes — anecdotes — dialogues.* (Paris{: Michel Lévy Frères, 1860)}; (the *Histoire de Chamfort* is dated "Brussels, 4 October 1856). *NL.* {Cf. *JSP* poem 24 and note}. *Pd*: *N V 7, 13*: Ch⟨amfort⟩ whose collection of proverbs and jokes per⟨haps⟩ of all books in the world has the closest power to that of an electric ray {fish}: to make someone convulse; *N V 7, 36*: How does it happen that despite such an advocate as Mirabeau, Ch⟨amfort⟩ is still foreign and uncomfortable to the French to this day, so that even the impartial spirit of S⟨ainte-⟩B⟨euve⟩ {reacted?} to Ch⟨amfort⟩ as if irritated — — — Cf. Stahl, 25: "*La susceptibilité de M. Sainte-Beuve . . .*" {"The susceptibility of M. Sainte-Beuve . . ."}; Stahl polemicized against Sainte-Beuve's essay on Chamfort (*Causeries du lundi,* IV, 414–34, Paris{: Garnier Frères,} 1852); *N V 7, 144*: Chamfort sacrificed to his old people, the people of the ancien régime, and did penance by not standing on the sidelines, but instead coming to the aid of the common people.

73. *perhaps the old . . . mother]* Chamfort was an illegitimate child; cf. Stahl, *Histoire de Chamfort*, 12–13.

74. *Mirabeau . . . Chamfort]* Cf. 15[22]; N had read the letters of Mirabeau to Chamfort as an appendix to the edition by Stahl cited above.

75. *a thinker . . . laughed]* Cf. Chamfort, {*Pensées — maximes — anecdotes — dialogues*}, 66: "*La plus perdue de toutes les journées est celle où l'on n'a pas ri.*" {"The most wasted of all days is the one on which one did not laugh."}

76. *"Ah! Mon ami . . . bronze — ."]* "Ah, my friend, I am finally about to leave this world, where one's heart must either break or become bronzed — ." Georg Brandes wrote about this to N (3 April 1888 {*KGB* III:6, 135}): "The quoted words are not the last by Chamfort, they are found in his writings: *Caractères et anecdotes*: Conversation between M. D. and M. L. as an explanation of the sentence: *Peu de personnes et peu de choses m'intéressent, mais rien ne m'intéresse moins que moi. The end is: en vivant et en voyant les hommes, il faut que le cœur se brise ou se bronze."* {"Few persons and few things have interested me, but nothing interests me less than myself." The end is: "by living and seeing men, one's heart must either break or become bronzed.} Charles Andler (*Nietzsche, sa vie et sa pensée* ["Nietzsche, his life and his thought"], 2nd ed., Paris{: Librairie Gallimard,} 1958, 1:146n4), assumes that N took this anecdote from the introduction by Arsène Houssaye to his edition of the works of Chamfort (Paris{: Delahays,} 1857); in this edition one indeed also finds the conversation to which Brandes alludes (61), however not in the edition by Stahl known to N; Stahl quotes the "last words" of Chamfort from a different work by A. Houssaye (*Portraits du XVIIIe siècle*), in his *Histoire de Chamfort* (50), but he did not know the "conversation" as a fragment of Chamfort. On the issue itself, Andler comments: "*Cependant Chamfort a pu mourir en prononçant un aphorisme cité par lui bien avant.*" {"However, Chamfort may have died pronouncing an aphorism he had quoted long before."}

77. Cf. *CW* 13, 8[91].

78. *two writers.]* *Pd*: the writings of E. Dühring and R. Wagner

79. *inner]* *Sd, Le*: pure

80. *Pd*: *N V 7, 141*: How highly Shakespeare thought of Brutus is revealed by how he characterizes Caesar as "the best friend of Brutus" — such a man, and moreover a magnificent genius, the salt of the earth must be murdered if he is detrimental to freedom — thus thinks Shakespeare: the tragedy should be called *Brutus*: it is Shakesp⟨eare's⟩ belief in great human beings. Cf. also Zelter to Goethe: "Voß claims straightforwardly: the play should not be called *Julius Caesar* but *Brutus*; Brutus this last of the Romans and favorite of the poet is the main character" (30 March 1830); *N V 7, 66*: *I'll know his humor,* when he knows his time — says Brutus of the poet — Brutus was a philosopher. — Brutus, even Brutus loses his patience when the poet approaches with his wisdom and obtrusiveness.

81. *knows] Sd, Le*: knew

82. *perhaps Shakespeare . . . Brutus!] Pd*: perhaps it was Shakespeare's! Perhaps there was also an "evil spirit" for him! And greatness of virtue perhaps sounded like the music of the most nocturnal melancholy and isolation to his ears too!

83. *sounds like . . . self-contempt.] Pd*: sounds and acts — as if he were saying to us: What am I, just throw the poet out! I, a mere worm with all my wisdom and presumption! Why don't they step on me? I should be stepped on — here in the presence of Brutus!

84. *I'll . . . humor]* {N's emphasis.}

85. *I'll . . . fool."]* Cf. Shakespeare, *Julius Caesar,* Act IV, Scene 3. {Shakespeare's actual words are: "I'll know his humour, when he knows his time: What should the wars do with these jigging fools?"}

86. *Pd crossed out at the end*: Even this joy-bringer of humankind suffered from self-contempt! From the contempt of the joy he brought!

87. Cf. *CW* 13, 4[307]; *Pd*: Many an artist makes mistakes his whole life long in *interpreting* the characters he creates, because as a thinker he is too weak and has no great overview of all that's been thought. E.g., Richard Wagner let himself be led astray by Hegel until the middle of his life, and again once more and more crudely, when later he read Schopenhauer's doctrine into *his* characters; it definitely seems to me that the *innocence* of willing, the inner [?] justification of all great passions, the Siegfried-interpretation of *egoism*

(that has the right to kill a being out of disgust and despite piety and gratitude) is profoundly counter to the spirit of Schopenhauer.

88. {Arthur Schopenhauer, *Die Welt als Wille und Vorstellung I* (Leipzig: F. A. Brockhaus, 1873), §60, 387. *NL.* / *World 1,* 354.}

89. {Arthur Schopenhauer, *Parerga und Paralipomena II* (Leipzig: F. A. Brockhaus, 1874), §115, 236. *NL.* / *Parerga 2,* 201.}

90. {Cf. Arthur Schopenhauer, *Die Welt als Wille und Vorstellung II* (Leipzig: F. A. Brockhaus, 1873), bk. 4, §41, 552. *NL.* / *World 2,* 499, where Schopenhauer compares actual lions to Plato's Idea of a lion. Most likely, the source of this remark is Philipp Mainländer, *Die Philosophie der Erlösung* ("The philosophy of redemption") (Berlin: Grieben, 1876), 480, *NL,* where Mainländer, in discussing Schopenhauer's metaphysics, writes: "Alle lebenden Löwen seien im Grunde nur Ein Löwe" ("All living lions are at bottom only a single lion").}

91. {Cf. Mainländer, *Die Philosophie der Erlösung,* 476: "Nicht nur ist, nach Schopenhauer, die Vielheit der Individuen ein Schein, sondern auch die Gattung" ("According to Schopenhauer, not only is the multiplicity of individuals an illusion, but also the species").}

92. {This is not a direct quote from Schopenhauer; N might have in mind the following remark from Schopenhauer's *Ueber den Willen in der Natur* ("On the will in nature") (Leipzig: F. A. Brockhaus, 1867), 44: "ein genialer Irrthum, der ihm, trotz aller darin liegenden Absurdität, noch Ehre macht" ("a brilliant error that, despite all the absurdity contained therein, still honors it"); N might also have in mind *Welt I,* §27, 169 / *World 1,* 166, where Schopenhauer refers to the "absurdity of [Lamarck's] opinion" in his *Zoological Philosophy,* where he "describes life as the simple effect of heat and electricity."}

93. {N alters slightly this quote from *Welt I,* §34, 210–11; cf. also §38, 230 / *World 1,* 201; cf. also 219. Cf. *GM* III 12, *CW* 8, 308, where N also cites the "pure, will-less, painless, timeless subject of knowledge" without referring to Schopenhauer.}

94. {Schopenhauer, *Welt I,* §34, 212 / *World 1,* 202.}

95. {N alters slightly this quote from Schopenhauer, *Welt II,* §49, 732 / *World 2,* 653.}

96. {N alters slightly this quote from Arthur Schopenhauer, *Parerga und Paralipomena I* (Leipzig: F. A. Brockhaus, 1874), 325 / *Parerga 1,* 268.}

97. *of becoming]* Up: of being

98. *And what attracts . . . seducer!]* Up: Indeed, Wagner follows his teacher even along the side paths, indeed down to the individual idiosyncrasies of his taste.

99. *"Be a man . . . instead!"]* Cf. Goethe's motto to the second edition (1775) of *Werther.* {Goethe added this exhortation to later editions of his novel *The Sorrows of Young Werther* (1774) when it became clear that his proto-romantic, epistolary novel about unrequited love had inspired young men to commit suicide.}

100. *that passion . . . Bayreuth p. 94)]* Cf. *WB* 11 {*CW* 2, 327, line 34–328, line 8}.

101. *It is of no . . . Bayreuth p. 94]* Sd: But art — his art as well as all art — should certainly not "want to be the teacher and educator for immediate action; the artist is only an educator and advisor in this sense." Cf. *WB* 4 {*CW* 2, 279, lines 1–3}.

102. *Pd*: Human beings must also learn to pay homage: all who walk on new paths discover with astonishment how clumsy and thoughtless humans are in expressing their gratitude, indeed how seldom they even express gratitude for the highest advancements. The manner in which a reforming and devastating author grows aware of this effect in his readers is often ridiculous — often offensive. It is as if the reader somehow had to unleash his revenge or his resistance on him, as if he had to demonstrate his threatened self-reliance in an especially *rude* manner — the best friends often become insufferable as a result. — After a few generations one learns to be inventive in gratitude — and then usually there is someone on hand who is the *great recipient of thanks,* not only for the good that he himself did. Thus Liszt harvested, after one had practiced for a century to honor virtuosos; thus Wagner harvests, after German music learned to bring joy to the whole earth, one pays homage to this music by paying a toll to its most famous representative. This is how it was with Bernini.

103. Cf. 12[170].

104. *in usum Delphinorum]* "for the use of the Dauphin" {i.e., a special edition of the classics prepared for the education of the French heir apparent. Here, for the royalty of future humanity.}

105. *Pd: N V 1*: If one imagines Beethoven next to Goethe, then he immediately looks like the "untamed human being" (as Goethe himself described him after their encounter in Karlsbad) as the semi-barbarian, the moody one, the self-tormentor, the foolishly ecstatic, the foolishly unhappy, the guilelessly boundless next to the confident one, the visionary next to the artist. Beethoven was roughly what Rousseau would have so gladly been and what he lived in the eyes of his idealistic readers — back then it was called "nature." Today one finds, surely, that this does not mean anything and that Goethe was more natural [*for this cf. the variant from M II 1, 70*: that Goethe too was natural]. In those times one longed for the good-natured semi-barbarian.

106. *"people"] Added in N V 7*: an Italian told me the Germans know more about beautiful noise he ⟨therefore⟩ preferred German music.

107. *gate]* {Allusion to Goethe's ballad "Der Sänger," in which the singer eschews the king's reward of a golden chain in favor of a drink of wine: "I sing as does the bird up there, / That in the branches lives. / The song it puts into the air / Is pay that richly gives." This ballad also quoted by Schopenhauer, *Parerga 2,* §221, 461/386.}

108. *"the knights . . . laps"]* Cf. Goethe's poem "Der Sänger" ("The Singer").

109. *"untamed human being"]* Cf. Goethe's letter to Karl Friedrich Zelter, Karlsbad, 2 September 1812.

110. *In addition . . . spreading] Sd*: in addition, that all German music sounds like a contradiction and mockery of noble knightly courtly elegance and discipline of form and at bottom forbids itself grace, since grace is suspected a little of trying to pass for "elegance": which is why German musicians permit themselves only a certain rural unschooled gruff grace that also appears among the "common people" — a Beethovenesque grace. It appears now from this point of view that

111. *Pd*: The Germans with their respect for everything that comes from the *court,* have {adopted} for their written language (hence in particular for their correspondence, records, wills and so on) the

112. *foreigner] Pd*: Englishman

113. *Germans] Pd*: Prussians

114. *an innovator . . . thoughts] Pd*: Z⟨arathustra⟩, that he could {learn} my thoughts

115. *his disciple . . . wish] Pd*: one of his disciples. I wish, responded Z⟨arathustra⟩

116. *not refuted!" . . . disciple.] Pd*: not refuted. [I thirst for a music that speaks the language of the dawn." Here one of his disciples embraced him and cried] When he said this [someone cried with e⟨nthusiasm⟩ from the crowd: O my], cried the disciple who had asked him, with fervor: "Oh you my true [master] teacher! I consider your cause to be so [good] strong, that I will say everything, absolutely everything that I have against it in my heart." Z⟨arathustra⟩ [smiled] laughed to himself at these words and pointed [to him] his finger at him: Cf. 12[119].

117. Cf. 11[285]; 12 [29]; *Pd*: If we had not given our blessing to the arts and invented this kind of cult of the *untrue*: then our insight into the general untruth and mendacity that is provided to us by science would be unbearable. *Honesty* would have nausea and suicide in its wake. Now, however, our honesty has a counter-force that helps us to avoid such consequences: we remember that we *like* lying and being lied to and *elevate them,* if they are artful. *Ecce homo.*

118. *art, as the good . . . service] Up*: we remember that we like the liar and being lied to, and elevate them, so long as they are artful

119. *bearable to us, and . . . us!] Up*: *bearable* to us. Thus we want to belong among those who make it into that! who make it beautiful!

Book Three

1. Cf. 14[14]; *Pd*: *N V 7, 16*: In sum, beware of the shadow of God. — One also calls it metaphysics. *N V 7, 104*: We must also fight God's shadow — and if it lasted for centuries — still there will be caves for a long long time in which — — —

2. Cf. 11[108, 157, 201, 213]; *Pd*: *M III 1, 49*: Beware of saying that the world is a living being. Where is it supposed to expand? What is it supposed to live on? How could it grow and multiply?

— Beware of saying that death is counter to life. The living is only a variety of the dead: and a rare variety. — Beware of saying the world eternally creates new things. — Beware of saying there are laws in nature. There are only necessities: there is no one who commands, no one who obeys, no one who trespasses. — When you know that there are no purposes, then you also know there is no accident. For only *beside* a world of purposes does the word accident have meaning. — Beware of thinking that there are eternally enduring substances, however tiny: the atom is as much an error as the God of the Eleatics. There are clusters like lines of force, whose ends are mathematical points, but not material ones. Matter exists no more than God does. *M III 1, 34*: The universe is far from a "machine" — that would be to tax its essence too highly. What! constructed in keeping with one goal! *M III 1, 74*: The *deepest* error is to think of *the universe itself* as something *organic* — we can indeed attempt to calculate approximately the emergence of the organic and show the steps that are necessary. What! The inorganic would ultimately be the development and decline of the organic! Asinine!! *M III 1, 18*: Let us beware of positing generally and everywhere something as perfectly formed as the cyclical movements of our stars; a mere glance into the Milky Way already raises doubts whether much rougher and more contradictory movements do not exist there, stars with eternally vertical descent paths etc. We live in an exceptional *order,* and this order and the seeming duration it creates has in turn made possible the exception of exceptions, the formation of the organic. The overall character on the other hand is *chaos* in all eternity, not in the sense of a lack of necessity, but lack of order beauty structuring and whatever all our aesthetic anthropomorphisms are called. Judged from the standpoint of our reason, the *unsuccessful attempts* are by far the rule, the entire game eternally repeats itself, but the exceptions are not the secret goal, even "unsuccessful attempt" is already an anthropomorphism. [*Pp crossed out at the end*:] Prometheus has still not gotten rid of his vulture!

3. *linear] Corrected in Fe², Se, Le; Fe*: vertical; cf. Gast to N, 22 August 1882 {*KGB* III:2, 278}: "The 'eternally vertical descent paths' are impossible . . ."

4. *attributing to it . . . judgments!]* M III *1, 74: slandering* the *value of existence* by inserting into the nature of being "heartlessness mercilessness irrationality lack of noble feeling etc." — like the pessimists, but at bottom also the monadists etc. We must imagine it as entirely irrationally mechanical, that *it cannot be captured in any predicate of aesthetic and moral value* — it wants nothing, it becomes *neither* perfect, nor beautiful, nor noble etc. — Casp⟨ari⟩ p. 288 appeals in a disgraceful way to the "dissuading feeling"! N quotes here from Otto Caspari, *Der Zusammenhang der Dinge: Gesammelte philosophische Aufsätze* {"The Coherence of things. Complete philosophical essays"} (Breslau{: Trewendt,} 1881). *NL.*

5. *Eleatics]* {A school of philosophy founded by Parmenides in the sixth century BCE, in which Being was equated with God. See N's fragment 38[12] in *CW* 16, 168–69, and the Translator's Afterword, 524–25.}

6. Cf. 11[335].

7. *are]* Pd: are (on which language is based)

8. *logic. Therefore:]* Pd: logic (e.g., each thing identical to itself, A = A: such things do not *exist* in truth). Therefore:

9. *and knowing . . . madness.]* Pd: comes into question, is no longer seriously opposed, here a denial is considered madness, and even the opponent must live in keeping with what he calls "error"

10. *permanence without change]* Dauer ohne Wechsel {*Dauer ohne Wechsel* is a playful allusion to Goethe's poem "Dauer im Wechsel" ("Permanence in change"); the poetic allusion is enhanced by the verb *andichten* ("to ascribe fictionally").}

11. *had arrived]* arrived

12. *dominance. The]* Pd: dominance. The ideally reasonable being and life without passion, *virtue* constructed on the judgments opposed to those according to which the *world* lives. The

13. *play drive]* Spieltrieb {*Spieltrieb* is taken from Schiller's *Aesthetic Letters* (1794).}

14. *That more refined honesty . . . experiment.]* Pd: Yet where could the *more refined* sense of truth emerge? Where the propositions for life were *indifferent* or seemed so *or* where the opposing propositions were applicable to life, but there could be argument regarding their utility — *higher utility as an argument for truth*: this is a

long stage of knowledge. Otherwise, the seeking of truth as *play*, on which nothing depends (first of all probably arithmetic). After countless numbers of propositions were once more regarded as fixed, they were gathered together and began to battle one another: the researchers took sides, the curious and the idle likewise, a new occupation arose, a stimulus etc. — knowing and striving for the true classified themselves as a *need*: now conviction was no longer a *power*, but also testing, denial suspicion contradiction, all "*evil*" instincts were ascribed to knowledge. It became a part of *life* itself, and therewith part of *power*: And the latter is *growing*! It is finally bringing forth a struggle in the living, the instinct of truth and the ancient life-conditioning errors are colliding!

15. *In and for . . . us.]* Pd: Even the degree of skepticism and disbelief was and is highly dangerous — for the *continuation* of life — *the* **inclination** *must emerge for preferring* to affirm rather than suspend judgment, *to err* and *to make things up* rather than wait, to judge and to condemn. This illogical inclination for preferring to judge, preferring to affirm and to deny is likewise a foundation of logic. The course of logical thoughts and inferences must correspond to a process in our brain — naturally not a logical one — (what do phosphorus and potassium have to do with "thoughts"!) but a process of *drives* (these must all have been carefully and individually *cultivated*)

16. Cf. 16[16].

17. *Many . . . human beings.]* Pd: Countless generations of scholars

18. *And how far . . . antiquities!]* Pd: And we are still far from the point where artistic strengths and the practical wisdom of life will also have found their way into the system of scientific forces — it is still a *pre-stage*. Goethe intuited what must converge — and how *then* the artist and legislator and *physician* will become paltry antiquities — — —

19. *image]* Pd: thing

20. Pd: The human being educated by his *errors* 1) he saw himself only *incompletely* 2) with made-up properties 3) in a false order of rank 4) with varying tablets of goods, so that *gradually* different drives were *ennobled.*

21. *Freedom of thought . . . things.] Pd*: The feeling of power always summons up a new competition and change of ruler and possession. "Freedom of thought" was regarded as discomfort itself. We perceive law and conformity as compulsion and forfeit: but *the former* perceived the *egoism* of the individual as a painful thing, as an occasional distress. Better *just to follow*! Even the ruler tried to *make* himself dependent through the interpretation of chance and through spirit promptings. *Blasphemy* was *counter* to *taste*. Everything individual is evil, is madness! — Christian morality triumphed as atavism!

22. *"Virtue . . . soul"]* Cf. Hans von Arnim, *Stoicorum Veterum Fragmenta* {(Stuttgart: B. G. Teubner, 1903; 1964), vol. 1,} fr. 359.

23. *Pd*: The great feat of Christianity is *moral skepticism.* Now one must also extend skepticism to one's religious circumstances. And lose the tone of lament and bitterness. Compared to Epictetus we are full of secret subtleties and insights: antiquity is morally naïve. La Rochefoucauld continues the process. (Vauvenargues muddies the tendency)

24. *Pd*: Even without passion of knowledge the sciences would be *promoted* — out of *amour-plaisir* {"love based on pleasure"} and *amour-vanité* {"love based on vanity"}, then out of habit, for the sake of their utility, indeed out of boredom with the one and the other. There the terrible and heroic perspectives are lacking.

25. *amour-plaisir . . . amour-vanité]* "love based on pleasure" . . . "love based on vanity"; based on Stendhal's *De l'amour,* which N knew.

26. *Leo X]* {Giovanni di Lorenzo de' Medici (1475–1521).}

27. *Pd*: We've left land and even more, we've *broken off* not only the bridges but the land and thrown it into the sea. Now, little ship! See to it! Beside you lies the *ocean*! Right beside you and around you infinity!

28. Cf. 14[25, 26] and *Pd* to these; 12[77, 157]. Cf. Eugen Biser, "Die Proklamation von Gottes Tod" {"The proclamation of God's death"}, in *Hochland* 56 (1963): 137–52. *Pd*: Once Z⟨arathustra⟩ lit a lantern in the bright light of morning, ran into the marketplace and shouted: "I seek God! I seek God!" — Since there were many standing around at the time who did not believe in God, he

prompted great laughter. Has he gotten lost? said some of them.
Did he lose his way like a child? said the others. Or is he hiding
somewhere? Is he scared of us? Did he go to sea? Did he emigrate? — thus they shouted and laughed, everyone talking at once.
Zarath⟨ustra⟩ leaped into their midst and pierced them with his
stare. "Where has God gone?" he cried, "I will tell you! *We have*
killed him — you and I! all of us are his murderers. But how did
we do this? How did we manage to drink up the sea? Who gave
us the sponge to wipe away the entire horizon? Without this line
— what will our architecture be from now on! Will our houses
stand firmly anymore? Do we ourselves stand firmly? Are we not
constantly plummeting? And backward, sideways, forward, in all
directions? — Do up and down still exist? Hasn't it grown colder?
Isn't night and ever more night closing in on us? Don't we have to
light lanterns in the morning? Don't we hear anything yet of the
noise of the gravediggers who are burying God? Don't we smell
anything yet [of the fire and the ashes in the air] of the divine
decay? — even gods decay! God is dead! |God stays dead!| And we
have killed him! How do we console ourselves, we murderers of
all murderers? The holiest and mightiest that the world possessed
so far — it's bled to death under our knives — who will wipe this
blood off us? What [|holy|] water could help us clean ourselves?
|What festivals of atonement, what holy games will we have to
[celebrate] invent? Isn't the magnitude of [the] this deed too great
for us? Don't we have to [grow and almost] become gods ourselves
just to seem worthy of it? There has never been a greater deed! —
and whoever is born after us will belong to a higher history than
all history to this day [was], on account of this deed!"| — Here
Z⟨arathustra⟩ fell silent and again looked at his listeners: they
too were silent and [were] gazed at him in astonishment. Finally
Z⟨arathustra⟩ threw his lantern to the ground, where it broke to
pieces and was extinguished. "I've come too early," he said, "it's not
yet [time] my time. [The] This tremendous event |is still on its way
and| wandering [and is still wandering and] — it hasn't yet reached
the ears of human beings. |*Lightning* and thunder need time, the
light of stars needs time, [events] deeds need time, even after they
are done.| [There are [events] deeds, that to you are] This deed is

still more distant from them than the remotest [stars] constellations — *and* [even if you yourselves did] *yet they did it themselves!*"

29. *requiem . . . deo]* "(grant) God eternal rest"

30. *Pd*: the mystical explanations are the most superficial

31. Cf. 12[63, 74, 226].

32. *Pd*: *M III 5*: Human beings who really never think, to whom an elevation of the soul is unknown or goes unnoticed, but who must also fill their time — what are they supposed to do at sacred sites? How in general are they supposed to behave in important situations, in order to behave with relative *dignity?* This is why all religions invented *prayer,* as a *time-consuming mechanical work* with exertion of the memory and the same fixed position for the body, for hands and feet. If the intention was to facilitate the suppression of instincts in these people, then *the whole day* would need to be filled with such work — and this is what the orders of old convents were about. And now our dear Protestants are protesting and they want *uplifting*! As if one could even *order it* up! N V 7: *Prayer* as a venerable pastime — the main thing is that it is mechanical.

33. *"om mane padme hum"]* "*om mani padme hum*" {Sanskrit Buddhist mantra: "The jewel is in the lotus."}

34. *poor in spirit]* {Cf. Matthew 5:3.}

35. {Cf. Ralph Waldo Emerson, "Natur," in *Versuche,* trans. G. Fabricius (Hanover: Carl Meyer, 1858), 405, *NL*: "Für den Dichter, für den Propheten hat das, was er ausspricht, einen viel größeren Werth, wie für irgend einen der Hörer, und darum wird es gesprochen. Der kräftige, selbstgefällige Luther behauptet ausdrücklich, was aber nicht falsch verstanden werden darf, daß 'Gott selbst nicht ohne weise Menschen bestehen kann.'" Vol. 3, *Essays: Second Series,* "Nature," 109: "The poet, the prophet, has a higher value for what he utters than any hearer, and therefore it gets spoken. The strong, self-complacent Luther declares with an emphasis, not to be mistaken, that 'God himself cannot do without wise men.'"}

36. Cf. 11[274]; *JS* 145.

37. *excessive . . . it.] Up*: foolish rejection by the Indians of a meat diet and the overuse and [degeneration] affliction of the stomach caused by it

38. Cf. 15[66].

39. *crimen . . . divinae]* "affront to the divine majesty"

40. Cf. *D* 38; *CW* 13, 8[97].

41. *Pd*: Natures such as Paul only learned what is dirty about all the passions: the Jews did *not* apply their idealism to the passions as the Greeks did, but to the divine cleansing *of them*: which is why *in the state* of the passionate they always perceived the ugliest in them and felt *distant* from their ideality — completely opposite to us! Christians have made an effort to become Jews in this point — and to make the whole world into Jews.

42. Cf. *CW* 13, 8[27].

43. *Pd*: How *good* it feels for someone to believe in us can be recognized from this: no one has found it objectionable that God made his love for human beings dependent on their faith in him. How petty! "If I love you, what does it matter to you?" is *superior.*

44. *"If . . . you?"]* Cf. Goethe, *Wilhelm Meisters Lehrjahre* IV, 9{, in *Sämtliche Werke* ("Complete works") (Stuttgart: Cotta, 1855), 16:281. *NL.*}; *Dichtung und Wahrheit,* III, 14{, in *Sämtliche Werke,* 22:219. *NL.*}.

45. *Buddha . . . benefactor!"]* {Cf. Emerson, *Versuche,* 389; vol. 3, *Essays: Second Series,* "Gifts," 95: "A golden text for these gentlemen is that which I so admire in the Buddhist, who never thanks, and who says, 'Do not flatter your benefactors.'" N underlines "Do not flatter your benefactors." in his personal copy.}

46. Cf. 12[7]; *Pd*: Without the imagining of other beings besides humans everything is and remains small-town, small-humanity: the invention of gods heroes and superhumans of all kinds, as well as of secondary- and subhumans, of dwarves, fairies, centaurs was invaluable. We need beings for comparison, indeed we can scarcely dispense with the *falsely interpreted* human beings, the heroic epics and legends of the saints. Of course: this drive consumed the greatest portion of the energy that could have been expended on inventing and composing our own new ideal. But seeking one's own ideals was scarcely the task of earlier humans, their task rather was no longer to allow humans *to sink below* an average that had been reached. The gods and saints were the cork, as it were, that kept humankind afloat on the sea. "Selflessness"

was a good sermon — back then: which also includes dispensing with a personal ideal. "Uphold with me the *universal image of humanity*, resist anyone who wants something else, expend all your energy *on this*" — thus good humans perceived

47. *disobedience . . . There] Sd:* jealousy and lying. One had *to be* as the law and the omnipotent omnipresent custom decreed: there

48. *superhumans]* {This is the first published use of the word *Übermenschen* to connote a higher human being; the word appears with greater frequency beginning in the unpublished notes of November 1882–February 1883, where it is linked to Zarathustra for the first time.}

49. Cf. 11[298].

50. *This corresponds . . . satisfy.] Pd:* Conversely: the promoters of narcotic ways of thinking prefer the consumption of rice and potatoes (allegedly as nonanimal) and are opponents of alcoholic spirits, *only* to satisfy the emerging need: Praising of asceticism!

51. Cf. N to Gast, 30 July 1882 {*KGB* III:1, 233}.

52. *Ulfilas]* {Gothic Wulfila (ca. 311–383), missionary and bishop of the Visigoths.}

53. {Cf. Schopenhauer, *Parerga 2,* "On Religion," 352–53.}

54. *"here . . . otherwise!"]* {Luther's famous reply at the Diet of Worms in 1521 when he was told to recant.}

55. *And from . . . narcotics.] Pd:* It was always this way. The religions should be examined in this regard

56. *The more general . . . them.] Pd:—* the culture had finally come to a standstill internally, in a few places (university{,} Athens) or in philosophical schools (Epic⟨ureans⟩ Stoics). — The more general and unconditional an individual can be, the more homogeneous must be the mass that is being affected there; the relatively *small* influence of such a domineering nature as Richard Wagner proves the *stature* of musical culture. — *Counterefforts* are simply the *counterneeds* of other beings who also want *to live.*

57. *Pd:* I confess: the sight of most Christian saints is unbearable to me: if they have virtues, then they always have the most brutal kind.

58. {Cf. *World 2,* "On Humanity's Metaphysical Need," 170–71.}

59. *of religious delusion] Pp, Le; Fe:* of religious ideas

60. Cf. *CW* 13, 6[112]; *Pd at the end*: Thus our sensitivity for moral actions and judgments could someday become incomprehensible, through progress in psychology statistics and the doctrine of health. In a given body a given psyche and its movements are necessary to the smallest detail — like the movements of a solar system.

61. *mistress] Meisterin* {i.e., "lady master"; cf. *Z* II "The Stillest Hour."}

62. *can untie it — thus] Sd*: can untie it — *nec deus intersit, nisi dignus vindice nodus inciderit* ("neither let a god interfere, unless a knot worthy of a god's unraveling should happen") {cf. Horace, *Ars poetica*, lines 191–92} — thus

63. Cf. 13[2].

64. *Mentiri]* "To lie" {the root of which is *mens*, "mind"}

65. Cf. 11[8].

66. *Pd*: I have denied myself many things so thoroughly and for such a long time that when I accidentally stumbled upon them again, I almost believed I had discovered them (e.g., friendship, music, drinking wine, conversation).

67. Cf. 15[71].

68. *If a friend . . . himself;] Pd*: "When my enemy praises me, then it sounds to me like he wants to be praised for his praise; when a friend praises me, then it sounds to me only as if he is praising himself" said Timon of Athens.

69. *Pd*: For all one's bravery in facing the enemy, one can be a coward and fool without resolution in all other things: Napoleon about Murat (whom along with Ney he calls "the bravest men" he has known). Cf. {Paul de Rémusat, ed.,} *Mémoires de Madame de Rémusat 1802–1808*{, 3 vols. (Paris: Calmann Levy, 1880); English translation: *Memoirs of Madame de Rémusat 1802–1808*, trans. Mrs. Cashel Hoey and John Lillie (New York: Appleton and Co., 1880).}

70. *"les souverains . . . parvenus."]* "sovereigns rank with parvenus."

71. *Truly, . . . parvenus."] Pd*: I believe Talleyrand would express himself on this as follows if he were to return: *les souverains rangent aux parvenus; il y a partout trop d'arrivés en tout genre* {"sovereigns

rank with parvenus; there are too many arrivals of every kind everywhere"}

72. Cf. *CW* 13, 8[79].

73. *Fit . . . regulam]* "Done according to the rule"

74. *Pd*: The completely cheerful human beings who are saddened by a deeper feeling of happiness — the true musicians

75. Cf. *CW* 13, 6[202].

76. *ordinary] ordentlich* {"orderly," here juxtaposed with *das Ausserordentliche,* "the extraordinary"}

77. *Pd*: The way some artists tell their cause offends me, they consider us too stupid and themselves too sublime, they are broad and emphatic, as if they were speaking to a public meeting, and their tricks for arousing amazement and stirring emotions are lacking good conscience.

78. *Pd*: When we are praised, we have always done something that places us on the same level as the praiser: one is praised only by one's peers: i.e., whoever praises is saying to you: you are my peer. [Cf. Goethe, "When someone praises, he is equating himself with the praised one." *Sämtliche Werke,* 40 Bände {"Complete works," 40 vols.} (Stuttgart: Cotta, 1855/58), 3, 220. *NL*.]

79. *Pd*: What we learn under the seal of confidentiality we share more eagerly than anything else with others, and moreover including the seal.

80. Cf. 18[2].

81. *Hic . . . est]* "This one is black" {i.e., dangerous, treacherous; cf. Horace, *Satires,* I, 4, 85.}

82. *Pd*: On this kind of man you would not wish a son, or maybe an untalented one — he is so envious that he tolerates no talent around him and indeed does not tolerate the child as a child

83. Cf. 16[18].

84. *Pd*: *Vivisectio voluntaria* {"Voluntary vivisection"}. — But you want there to be punishments in the world? Well, let this be your motto: Punishment should improve the one who punishes!

85. *king."] Sd*: king — he added [ironically] good-naturedly.

86. Cf. *CW* 13, 6[414].

87. *Pd*: The superlative is the [invention] fondness of the not quite honest. When others believe in our strength, we say the

strongest things plainly, and when we ourselves believe in them, likewise. One lets himself go when he judges, the other reins himself in when he judges and gives himself a mask through the form of his judgment.

88. *Pd*: He clearly can't *control* himself — and from this the superficial conclude it is possible and even easy to control him and they throw their lasso and reins around his neck — he the proudest one, who gnashes his teeth and feels loathing for his own overwhelming of himself! Just let the wild one run —

89. *Bad claim, bad aim] Fehlschluss, Fehlschuss* {literally, "wrong conclusion, missed shot"}

90. *Pd*: Out of spite we hold tightly to a cause that we have already begun to see through. We must afford ourselves this spite, this deliberate not-wanting-to-see!

91. *Pd*: The good deed of which you remain silent makes you more persuasive and convincing on the whole.

92. *Pd*: Those who are slow to know believe slowness is essential to science.

93. *Pd*: How little human beings see of subtlety! How concealed or misunderstood is all sense of delicacy! If someone [?] does not come marching along as if to regimental music, people believe he is lacking in music.

94. *Let . . . hear!]* {Cf. Matthew 11:15.}

95. Cf. *CW* 13, 6[322].

96. Cf. 12[112].

97. *Pd*: Carrying cake for Cerberus —

98. *Pd*: I want to conquer the land *that no one yet possesses.*

99. *Pd*: I would indeed like to share a few secrets with this beautiful monster.

100. *Suum cuique]* "To each his own"

101. Cf. 13[7].

102. *Pd at the end*: The devil as *means to power* could not remain *unused*! —

103. *Unappreciated . . . imagine:] Pd*: I want to show you the *pudendum* {"object of shame"} of *magnificent* natures: they suffer *differently* than one thinks and they themselves say in their works

104. *Pd*: "I am always deeply preoccupied, why should I be embarrassed?"

105. Cf. 15[56]; 12[154].

106. *Skinfulness] Hautlichkeit* {a Nietzschean coinage, literally "having the quality of skin"}

107. *sit venia verbo]* "pardon the expression"

108. *Pd*: I did not know how rich I was until I invented *such* men as thieves stealing from me.

109. Cf. 18[7].

110. Cf. 18[6]; *Pd at the end*: and fled in haste.

111. Cf. 12[80].

112. *Sub specie aeterni]* "From the point of view of eternity"

113. *Pd*: As far as humans may go: their ultimate truths are always merely — irrefutable errors.

114. Cf. *CW* 13, 9[6]; 8[48].

115. *Pd at the beginning*: *Heroism*: the just human being knows that he

116. *Pd*: *What do you want?* — To recalibrate the weight of things.

117. *"You . . . are."]* This proverb frequently quoted by N stems from Pindar, *Pythian Odes* II, 72: γένοι' οἷος ἐσσὶ μαθών.

118. *Pd at the beginning*: Shame is the *uniquely* human form of suffering; animals do not know shame.

Book Four

1. Der du mit dem Flammenspeere
Meiner Seele Eis zertheilt,
Dass sie brausend nun zum Meere
Ihrer höchsten Hoffnung eilt:
Heller stets und stets gesunder,
Frei im liebevollsten Muss: —
Also preist sie deine Wunder,
Schönster Januarius!

{Januarius is the first month of the Roman civil calendar. The name might (or might not) be connected with that of the deity Janus, the god of doors and entrances. St. Januarius (in Italian San Gennaro) was an early Christian martyr, a vial of whose dried blood is kept in a church in Naples. On certain feast days the blood is said miraculously to become fluid again.}

2. *Pd*: *M III 5*: This I wish myself from myself: may I weigh things more and more with aesthetic scales and less and less with moral! may the surfacing of moral judgments serve as [appear] a hint that in this moment my nature is without its entire strength and stature and, as it were, wanders on the paths of the past and around the graves of its pre-world! May I learn more and more to see things as beautiful and to feel good in doing so! — thus I will be one of those who *make* things *beautiful*! But no war against the ugly! Let *looking away* be my sole negation! And, all in all and on the whole: I want at some point to be only a Yes-sayer! *N V 7*: My wish is that things will be weighed less and less with moral scales and more and more with aesthetic ones and that ultimately morality will be perceived as the sign of retarded ages and of aesthetic incapacity! If we learn to *see* things as *beautiful* and always feel good in doing so: then we will make things beautiful — but let's not wage war against the ugly! *Looking away* is our denial and all in all and on the whole: we want someday to be only Yes-sayers! *N V 8*: I still live, I still think. I must still live for I must still think *sum ergo cogito, cogito ergo sum*! [I must, I will, I can still think — I would no longer live without this Must and Will and Can! Indeed! Certainly! but even more this too!] And so greetings to you, first thought of this year! Ground guarantee and sweetness of my life! My wish, my gift — before myself — for myself! — Nonetheless: *crux mea lux*! *Lux mea crux*! {"cross my light! Light my cross!"} Cf. 12[231]; *M III 1*: I still live, I still think — *sum ergo cogito*.

3. *Sum . . . sum]* "I am, therefore I think: I think, therefore I am."

4. *life! I] Sd*: life! I want to unlearn more from day to day how to weigh with moral scales; I want to take the surfacing of a moral judgment as a hint that in this moment my nature is without its full strength and stature and wanders on the paths of its past and as it were around the graves of its pre-world. I

5. *Amor fati]* "Love of fate"

6. *Pd*: At a high point in life we are most in danger of becoming fools and believers in personal providence: when we notice that

really all things work out best for us. For our practical and theoretical wisdom is then at its peak in interpreting and shifting things to suit.

7. Cf. 12[114]; *Pd*: This tumult of the city, these voices desires impatiences — it brings me a melancholy *happiness*: it is always "*the hour before departure*" of a ⟨great⟩ ship of emigrants — for all, absolutely all it will soon be so quiet.

8. *Pd*: We have become strangers to one another — no harm done. We each have our course. But more strange and more honorable to us!

9. *Pd*: To build quiet places for reflection in the midst of our cities — reconstruct the churches in addition. The sublimity of thinking and coming to one's senses should lie in the structure. The Church should no longer have this monopoly — humanity has had to pay a high price for the fact that the *vita contemplativa* {"contemplative life"} was always supposed to be *religiosa*! {"*religiosa*" underlined by N}

10. *and everything . . . gardens.] Pd*:— but perhaps we could reconstruct, redecorate many of its buildings beside us in our sense, to our purpose. For the time being the feeling of thinking is *captive* in a rich Catholic church — I at least am not *crude* enough to be able to think *my* thoughts in such places. — —

11. *Pd*: The masters of the first order betray themselves in the fact that they come to the end in a perfect way, in *melody* and in life.

12. Cf. *CW* 13, 8[34]; *Pd*: *N V 5, 5*: I welcome a warlike and anarchical age, because it will honor bravery: *and this will carry heroism into knowledge*!! There is nothing important at all except the great questions of morality. *N V 5, 6*: To develop *bravery* as an instinct: it will always seek a substance in which something needs to be overcome. This includes: cheerfulness of the hero, patience and contempt of luxury and of bourgeois ways, lack of vanity on the whole, while indulging petty v⟨anity⟩, magnanimity of the victor (to be victorious over oneself), free discussion among those accustomed to and excited by victory (about the favor of *chance*): the pleasures and recuperations of the brave. No god of revenge, nor of compassion. — Silently solitary resolute, in invisible constant activity: from time to time our *festivals* and

our great *days of mourning* come, in keeping with their own law, without calendar.

13. *Pd in the beginning*: Whoever does not have faith in himself, does not bear it with him, must acquire it on the road to knowledge about himself

14. *dwells within . . . insufficient.*] *Pd*: dwells. They are the superior and finer natures who must first create themselves

15. *Pd*: *N V 7, 80*: Insofar as I deny myself all praying etc., it raises the entire level of my lake, as if there were no flowing off. *N V 7, 187–88*: What! *Never again* pray — worship — devote oneself absolutely and rest in confidence — stand before the ultimate truth, before the ultimate goodness and power, alone — without the constant guard, friend — without avenger — without improver — without the belief that the mountains tower *above us* — without secret aid — without gratitude — without a view to laws that are rooted in an intellect and should *therefore* be admired? What *impoverishment*! And *on what* will all these drives *unleash* themselves? And what quantity of bad *intellectual conscience* will arise, because they have to unleash themselves and are *ashamed* of it! Nothing fixed! Nothing in common with *everyone*! With past and future beings! The rounding-off and fictionalizing force that we continuously use for nature, we *may* no longer use for the *inner* world! On account of *God's death countless others must die*! It is still too early!

16. *Excelsior!*] {Possible reference to Longfellow's poem by the same name; cf. N's letter to Erwin Rohde, 14 April 1876, *KGB* II:5, 150.}

17. *there is no resting place . . . peace,*] *Up*: — henceforth you will forbid your eye to round off things, to finish composing, you will take everything on your back as the eternally imperfect and without the delusion that you are carrying a goddess across the river

18. *recurrence*] *Fe*; *Cp, Le*: return

19. *the eternal recurrence . . . peace:*] *Up*: the eternal war. Your only joy is that of the warrior

20. *Pd*: All this is said for those who have some brilliance and glow and dawn in their own soul.

21. *Pd*: 12[178].

22. Cf. 12[106]; *Pd*: *M III 5*: It seems to me, the better human beings believe in *elevated moods* only as a matter of moments, at best of a quarter of an hour: to believe in the temporal duration of an elevated feeling is already nearly proof that one knows this from his own experience. But to be *someone of such a feeling,* the embodiment of an elevated soul — this is still a dream, yet as I hope, an anticipatory dream that reveals what is possible for humans. A very great deal has to come together, a very great deal of spirit is necessary even to ceaselessly have new objects around one or in one's thoughts, on which one can release the feeling of his stature, be it in making it sense their baseness, be it in lifting them up to one's own level. A continuous sensation of climbing stairs or resting on a cloud is the usual state for such a soul, the movement between high and low and the feeling of high and deep. *N V 7{, 183}*: The better human beings believe in *elevated mood* only as a matter of brief moments and quarter-hours. To believe in the **duration** of an *elevated* feeling is already nearly proof that one *knows this.* But to actually be a *human of such a feeling* — that is still a dream, yet something *possible.* Among other things it takes a very great deal of spirit *ceaselessly* to have new objects, which can be made to feel one's elevation, hence to perceive something base as base and constantly *climb* as if *on stairs.*

23. *Pd*: *N V 4, 71*: The inability to control oneself may disguise itself as free nature. Likewise also the satiety with all too much artificiality and obligedness of characters, as in Pope. Strong natures seek to *stylize* themselves and take pleasure in analogues (in the arts, in their gardens) The deep passion of desiring alleviates itself at the sight of stylized nature: beautiful bonds and perfection in compulsion is its ideal. Even the bad styles exert this force. The weak n⟨atures⟩ who are impotent over themselves find a bitterly evil compulsion in the bonds of style, they feel that if they were to impose it on themselves, they would become *base*: they become slavish when they serve. *N V 4, 72*: The *layout of character*: oversee precisely what nature offers and then *newly motivate* it, in the sense of the overall layout (illusory motives, like the scarcity of water can be explained by gods of the well etc.) Know one's

weaknesses and strengths, but then put them into an artistic plan, where even the weaknesses *delight.* It is not a matter of forming individuals in general: although to be sure this is the fundamental thing! But — Even an evil urge can be used, there are idealizations. Mind you: it is not a matter of interpreting the facts, but of developing, subtracting and adding: a great mass of second nature is to be added, and another m⟨ass⟩ of first nature to be deleted. To sideline the ugly or if needed reform it into the sublime: what is vague, resistant to shaping should be saved for distant vistas to beckon far into the distance, so to speak. Bad taste in these things is better than none at all: for all who think of themselves with revulsion are to be greatly pitied, and they let others pay for it. I do not doubt that all people *in whom there is no inner wellness* are in a permanent *mood of revenge.* NB

24. *Pd*: 6. After Z⟨arathustra⟩ had seen the city its villas and pleasure gardens and the heights and [the] shrub-covered slopes all around he said: this region has been strewn with the images of many bold humans, their houses look at us like faces — [they understood *how to go on living* — and they *lived*! That's what these faces say] they *lived*! — we wanted to go on living! They were well disposed to life, although they were often *evil* to one another.

25. *But here . . . him.] Pd.* Everything here is overgrown with this immeasurable magnificent egoism, leaning around every corner you find the exploitative *appropriator.*

26. *"I . . . God!"*] Cf. Meister Eckhart, *Predigten und Schriften* {"Sermons and writings"} (Frankfurt {: Fischer Bücherei,} 1956), 195.

27. *Pd.* Unpleasant people in whom every urge immediately becomes an illness and as it were causes the scabies to erupt.

28. *Pd*: *N V 7, 177*: My nature: it wants to enjoy the same things (foods, too) — quite regularly for a good long time, without craving any variety — "brief habits." But then, without sensing any disgust, it wants to leave for something new after all. Continuing variety like lasting habit are equally hated by me — also with respect to humans. With my brief habits I penetrate to all the depths of a matter; my love, indeed my faith is great that I would have enough here for the long run. *N V 7, 179*: I love brief habits

and consider them invaluable for getting acquainted with something — but I hate the *lasting ones* that subjugate us.

29. *Pd*: *N V 7*: *Formerly* one had to *have* a *solid reputation,* and at least appear as full of character as one was — it bred characters. Now this is becoming dispensable. — *M III 4*: In dangerous social situations it was expedient to create a *solid reputation* for oneself and to let one's character appear at least as certain and steadfast as it was: this need bred character and the estimation of solidity of opinions gave change, relearning, the transformation of the human a bad reputation. The precondition of the knower: to declare oneself undaunted by one's former opinion and to be suspicious of everything that wants to become fixed in us — was lacking: such a state was regarded as *dishonorable.* That one can *rely* on a human being has its supreme value in times of *war*: even now we are far from also granting the soldier the right to free decisions concerning war. *Fossilization* has had a monopoly on *honor* for a long time. *Sd at the end crossed out*: Perhaps no change of customs will be more useful to the free human being and to knowledge than the spread of the "immoral" way of thinking of Americans: in the United States everyone allows himself to change his lifestyle and way of making a living ten times, never running a risk to his reputation — there one will finally also allow oneself to change one's opinions ten times and to be a different human being ten times.

30. *Pd*: Being able to contradict and being able to bear contradiction are the most important steps in the culture of reason.

31. *Pd*: to distance oneself from things until there is much one no longer sees, or to see them as if around a corner as in a cutout — or to dilute them — or to see them through glass, or give them a surface and skin without full transparency — this way one *makes* things *alluring, desirable, beautiful*! To extend the *feat of art* more and more and make it into an entire art of life!

32. *cutout — or] Pd*: cutout — or diluting them and adding water and wine to their mixing bowl (this last) — or

33. *we should . . . artists] Pd*: these are my means of making things *beautiful, attractive, desirable — which in themselves they never are*! From artists we must learn these feats

34. *Prometheia]* {The trilogy by Aeschylus featuring Prometheus, of which only the first tragedy, *Prometheus Bound,* has survived.}

35. Cf. 14[8]; *Pd:* The superior human being distinguishes himself from the inferior in that he sees and hears unspeakably more and does so thoughtfully — and precisely this distinguishes humans from animals and the higher animals from the lower. The world becomes ever fuller, and the fishhook [*sic*] that are cast at our interest are ever-increasing: the number of stimuli is growing and likewise the number of types of pleasure and displeasure. The visual and musical play that is performed there before us also continues to be written, continues to be composed, in its depth and length — we who take ourselves to be auditors and spectators, we thinking and feeling ones are the ones who also continue to write and to compose here: *our* colors remain clinging to things and will ultimately be visible even to posterity. — And so it has always been, ever since humans and animals existed: the most intellectual and most sensitive of them *fancied* themselves as contemplative and *were* the actual practical ones — they who *did* something that was not yet there: — they misjudged themselves just as we also still misjudge ourselves. What one normally calls "practical people" are those who gradually learn for themselves *our* new valuations, colors, accents, perspectives — our *inventions,* and then pass them on to their children, breed and incorporate them into them. Whatever has *value* in the current world does *not* have it according to its nature — its in-itself — rather, its value has been *given* by someone at some point, *bestowed* — *we created* the world that concerns human beings in the first place!

36. *vis contemplativa]* "power of contemplation"

37. *vis creativa]* "power of creation"

38. *colors, weights]* *Cp, Le; Sd, Fe:* colors, accents

39. *Pd:* 12[129]; cf. 15[16]; 16[21].

40. *riddle]* {Homer was stumped by a young fisherman who posed the riddle: "What we caught, we left behind; what we did not catch, we carry with us." The answer is: lice. Homer supposedly died of vexation days later. Cf. *Vita Homeri Herodotea* ("Herodotus's life of Homer"), ed. and trans. Maria Vasiloudi (Berlin: de Gruyter, 2013).}

41. *Pd*: My life would no longer reveal a mistake to the observer — I understand like the masters of composing how to reinterpret the actual mistake and accident and to reintegrate it *instantly* into the thematic structure. So I even get to the point of recognizing a providential *coincidence* for myself "that all is for the best" — and *deceiving* myself. Cf. *JS* 277.

42. *with a black eye]* mit einem blauen Auge davon kommen {German idiom: "to get off cheaply/lightly"}

43. *Pd*: I am repulsed by all negative paths of virtue! *Do* something — and much has to fall away, and we're not even supposed to look at it!

44. *placitum]* "principle"

45. *Pd*: To gain control of oneself, that is the first thing — say all teachers of morals. Fine! Then the second thing is *to know* precisely where one should exert one's power. We've become *poorer,* there is nothing new and strange anymore, and what has been added is the eternal irritability of the one who fears for his power, the suffering of the Stoic. A few things could be said in favor of the opposite: to live in one's affects and — — —

46. Cf. 15[59]; *Pd*: Epicurean: *to seek* one's situation person and events in keeping with our constitution and then *resign oneself* and not leap beyond one's designated chalk line. — For those people with whom destiny *improvises* Stoicism is advisable, for those to whom destiny spins a long thread and sings a melody, Epicureanism — but for the unspeakably irritable and refined — — —

47. *Aissawa]* {While the source of N's knowledge concerning the Aissawa is uncertain, Kaufmann, 1153, suggests it might have come from Bernhard Schwartz, *Algerien* (Leipzig: Frohberg, 1881), 184.}

48. *Pd*: When we shed an *error* like a dead skin, we think ourselves *arbitrary,* but perhaps it was *time.* Our errors seem like *such* after new principles of life — it is a *sign of life.* This in favor of criticism.

49. *diagnostician]* Nierenprüfer {N's coinage, from the idiom *jemanden auf Herz und Nieren prüfen,* "to subject someone to extreme scrutiny"; literally, "to examine someone's heart and kidney."}

50. *conscience . . . science] der du ein Wissen um das Gewissen hast* {Play on words using *Wissen* ("knowledge") and *Gewissen* ("conscience").}

51. *Pd*: In my soul there is a dark and passionate urge for the true. Oh, I often have such a need for recuperation! Who is seduced as I am to linger! There are too many gardens of Armida for me! And therefore so many partings and bitternesses of the heart! But an indomitable trait drives me, and I follow often as if beaten. I often see what is most beautiful with a grim look back, and I am angry, as if it were seducer: and my honesty tortures me on account of this kind of revenge. "Destiny, I follow you" and if I did not wish to, I would have to beneath your blows and sighing. This moves me to tears. Cf. *D* 195.

52. *Armida]* {Enchantress of crusaders who creates a magical garden in Torquato Tasso's epic poem *Gerusalemme Liberata* (*Jerusalem Delivered*) (1575); also the title character in many operas.}

53. *Pd*: These waves approach so greedily, as if it were a matter of reaching something and they crawl into the innermost nooks of the rocky cliff — is something hidden there, then? Then they return somewhat more slowly — but already another wave approaches, greedier and wilder than the former ones, and it seems again to be full of secrets and a yearning to dig for treasure. Oh you greedy ones, you knowledge-craving ones —

54. Cf. 12[161].

55. *Here are my faults . . . once] Sd*: The way I happen to be, I will probably never lack for actions and thoughts that give you the impression of your own superiority and a good right to this impression. I am not angry with the law and nature of things that bring it about that even someone with his failings and mistakes can cause joy." — Those were of course

56. *I wouldn't . . . absent.]* Cf. Cosima Wagner to N, 22 August 1872, *KGB* II:4, 69.

57. *Pd*: I call my pain "dog" —

58. *paint . . . torturer.] Pd*: paint: there is too much *of the sublime,* for us to need to have associated it with cruelty!

59. *Pd*: Like Oliver Cromwell I will die in a storm.

60. *Pd*: How greatly animals may suffer from the electricity in the clouds! Their pains are prophecies of the weather for them.

61. *Pd*: I have never been aware of the actual *pathos* of any period of life as such, but always believed it was the only possible and reasonable state at the time and absolutely ethos, not pathos — to speak and distinguish like the Greeks. — I erred e.g., when in winter 1880–81 I was working on "Dawn," in Genoa (via Palestro 18 No. 13 *interno*) — this extremely hermit-like frugal life was pathos through and through and now, in feeling a completely different state, it echoes to me from a couple of notes of music that were played in that house: as something so good, painfully courageous and confidently consoling, that such consoling things should not be possessed for years at a time. One would be too rich, too super-proud — indeed it was the soul of Columbus in me.

62. Cf. 13[4]; *Pd*: Our vital energy must occasionally also be able to be *decreased* (this is why pain exists: it is a taking in of the sails).

63. *Pd*: No, life didn't disappoint me — I always found it to be fuller.

64. *In media vita.]* "At midlife."

65. *truer] Sd, Le*: richer

66. *dance- and playgrounds] Tanz- und Tummelplätze* {A *Tanz-platz* is a dancing ground for cultic dancing.}

67. Cf. 12[140].

68. *Pd*: M III 4: All preachers of morality (as well as all theologians) have an error in common: all seek to convince people that they are in poorer health than they are: and a harsh, ultimate and radical cure is needed. To me it seems, conversely, that people are in reality in even better health than they think: overall they have allowed themselves to be persuaded somewhat by those teachings and are too ready to sigh, to find nothing good in life and its "sweet habit" anymore, even to make gloomy faces together as if life were in fact really hard *to bear*. In truth, they are uninhibitedly sure of their lives and enamored of them, and they always [have] practiced many tricks and subtleties for breaking what is unpleasant and for reinterpreting pain as a blessing. One should consider how pain is always spoken of in exaggeration — with a certain ultimate degree

of pain unconsciousness ensues, with lesser degrees there is fever semi-numbness hasty thinking, lying in a comfortable position, good and bad memories and intentions, hopes, pride, sympathy [etc.] Narcotics. Humans drizzle very much sweetness on their bitterness, particularly on bitterness of the psyche, where sublimity and bravery or the delirium of submission and resignation set in. A loss — I will quickly reformulate the matter into a gain! The moral preachers have also fantasized about the unhappiness of *evil* human beings, but certainly about the unhappiness of passionate human beings — here they often lied and tried to lie away their *happiness,* because it was a refutation of their theory that all happiness first originates with the annihilation of passion. Why live so harshly as the Stoics? *Ordinary* life is *not painful* and burdensome *enough* to exchange it advantageously for Stoic harshness. Indeed, if it involved an **eternal danger**, as Christianity would have it! — and precisely insofar as life is "not painful and burdensome enough!" — — *N V 7*: Common error of the preachers of morals and theol⟨ogians⟩, to convince people that they are in worse health than they are, that a radical harsh cure is needed. I am inclined to judge: people are in even better health than they think.

69. Cf. 12[117].

70. *esprit]* "spirit"

71. *otium]* "leisure" {Underlined by N.}

72. *bellum]* "war"

73. *Pd*: to clap hands for oneself

74. *A thinker . . . cannot]* *Sd*: I do not need applause and the clapping of hands [unless] supposing I am assured of my own clapping of hands: but I can

75. *quando . . . exuitur]* "the desire of glory is the last infirmity cast off even by the wise"; Tacitus, *Histories* IV, 6.

76. Cf. 12[44]; 14[12].

77. *Pd*: What do I matter, said Z⟨arathustra⟩ if one does not also believe my bad arguments!

78. *"What do . . . matter?"]* Cf. D 488, 494, 539; cf. *CW* 13, 7[45, 102, 126, 158, 151]; 15[59].

79. *Pd*: *Non ridere, non lugere, neque detestari, sed intelligere!* — Ultimately however *intelligere* is nothing but the last refinement

of those three — a result of the adaptation of different opposing instincts — they must all be made into organs of knowledge, each one must produce its one-sided view of things. *Everyone must have enjoyed the entire availability of intellect at least once*! *Ego contra Spinozam.* {I versus Spinoza.}

80. *Non . . . intelligere!]* "Not to laugh, mourn, or curse, but to understand." Spinoza, *Tractatus Politicus* I, 4. {This line is misidentified in *KSA* 14 as coming from *Ethics* III Preface.}

81. *kind of justice . . . knowing.]* Sd: justice: in sum precisely that *intelligere*! Why did he leave out the opposite of *detestari?* Namely *amare?* {to love}

82. *"Everyone . . . himself"*] {This reverses the German saying "Everyone is closest to himself."}

83. *swindled . . . waylaid]* erschleichen . . . beschleichen {*erschleichen* ("to obtain by stealth") is paired with *beschleichen* ("to stalk," "waylay").}

84. *that which compels . . . honesty!]* Cp: "Well, what then? So speak already, old friend and immoralist! Which word there are you having trouble saying? Oh, you are silent?"

85. *Pd*: I bemoan the fact that great humans are not so beautifully spectacular in their rising and going down as the sun. Why do we not glow! more or less? each in keeping with his fullness of light?

86. Cf. 12[76]; 14[2]; *M III 6, 165*: Hurrah! I too want to write a long period for once! A whole printed page long! But of course for that one needs a bellows for lungs! *Pd*: *M III 5*: Our historical studies on the whole are now still poor and cold in feeling, as far as they concern the history of humanity overall — but here we are just beginning to fashion the *chain* of a *future very mighty feeling,* link by link. Someday, in looking back on the course of humanity, one should be able to feel everything that is felt by the lover and the one deprived of his beloved, the martyr whose ideal perishes, the old man whose dream of youth rekindles, the hero on the eve of a battle — and the hero on the morning of the *second* day of battle. Up till now historical souls have felt this way with small pieces of the past (be it the history of their family their city their country) and *aristocracy* is to be found on the whole wherever

one bears the chain of a long feeling for the past. But the *supreme aristocracy,* the supreme *species* of the historical soul has yet to be created, because that *feeling has yet to be created*: each the heir of all *nobility* of all *past spirit and the* heir *who is liable for it*! — [*This is where the text is immediately joined by fragment 14[2].*] M III 4: In that hour when even the poorest fisherman rows with golden oars; *N V 7*: how the sun pours its treasure into the sea

87. *joy]* Mitfreude {Literally, "shared joy"; plays off *Mitleid,* literally "shared suffering" or "compassion."}

88. Cf. 15[62].

89. *Vita femina]* "Life is a woman"

90. *coincides that]* Pd: coincides and does not let itself be tossed easily, like a throw of dice, that

91. *veiled from most . . . once!]* Pd: always veiled — and *what unveils itself* to them, *does it once,* [it is deception to wait for a return]

92. *The Greeks . . . beautiful!]* Cf. the Greek proverb: δὶς καὶ τρὶς τὸ καλόν, in Plato *Gorgias* 498e and Schol.; *Philebus* 59e–60a; in Empedocles, fr. 25 (Diels-Kranz).

93. *resisting . . . woman!]* Pd: veiling, alluring, and here and there, rarely, *revealing itself* only for the rarest. *Vita femina.*

94. *Sd at the end*: Continuation on p. 91 [= *M III 6, 94*], where *Sd of JS 36 is found; N originally wanted to make a single aphorism from the two notes about "last words"; Pd*: Socrates betrayed himself

95. *something . . . moment]* Pd: but the hemlock loosened his {tongue} again

96. *"Oh . . . rooster."]* Cf. Plato, *Phaedo* 118a.

97. *ridiculous and terrible . . . words!]* Pd: terrible words means to someone who has ears with which to hear: this most autocratic of all Greeks was a pessimist: with his last words he took revenge on *life.*

98. {Cf. 11[141, 143].}

99. *become]* Cp: have become

100. *how fond . . . seal?]* Up: would you become that athlete and hero, who could bear this weight and even climb higher with it? Picture this powerful thought—and you will immediately behold

the ideal that guides the most powerful human beings of the future!

101. *would you . . . seal?] Cp*: would you have to become [be] of your life and yourself in order [to be able to] perceive this weight not as the highest burden, but as the highest joy?

102. Cf. 11[195]; *Z* I "Zarathustra's Preface" 1.

103. *Pd*: and wants to make the wise rejoice again in their wisdom and the poor rejoice again in their poverty

104. *Incipit tragoedia.]* "The tragedy begins."

105. {Kaufmann, 1270, notes that Paolo D'Iorio, in "Beiträge zur Quellenforschung," *Nietzsche-Studien* 22 (1993): 395, discovers the source for this passage in Friedrich von Hellwald, *Culturgeschichte in ihrer natürlichen Entwicklung bis zur Gegenwart* ("Cultural history in its natural development up to the present"), 2nd ed., vol. 1 (Augsburg: Lampart, 1876), 169. There, in the chapter "Zarathustra's Teaching," Hellwald writes: "*Zarathustra,* the great prophet of the Iranians commonly known as Zoroaster (Ζωροάστηρ) in the Greek tradition, whose name in the Zend incidentally holds no special significance, was born in the city of Urmia on the lake by the same name. He moved eastward to the province of Aria and spent ten years there in the isolation of the mountains, working on writing the *Avesta.* After this period had passed, he relocated to Balkh, proclaimed his new teaching and claimed a divine mission." N wrote to Franz Overbeck on 8 July 1881 (*KGB* III:1, 100–101) requesting that he send Hellwald's book to him in Sils-Maria. Cf. 11[195], where N mentions more explicitly some of the details provided by Hellwald.}

106. *folly] Up*: wisdom

107. *their riches] Up*: their poverty

Book Five

1. {The first edition of *JS* was published in 1882 and included only the Prelude "Jokes, Cunning and Revenge" and bks. 1–4. Book 5 was added to the second edition, published in 1887, along with a new preface and the Appendix "Songs of Prince Vogelfrei."}

2. *Carcasse . . . mène.]* "You tremble, carcass? You would tremble even more if you knew where I am taking you."

3. *Pd*: The greatest recent event — that belief in God has become unbelievable, that "God is dead" — is already beginning to cast its dim shadows over Europe. [But what has actually happened, whatever has been abandoned by this abandonment of belief and must yet be abandoned, surely no one today can guess in its entire fullness and consequence;] But who could know entirely what actually took place here? Once this belief has been abandoned, there is *so* much that was built atop it, built on it, grew into it, that must still be abandoned: surely no one today can guess this long profusion and sequence of abandonment and destruction that still lies ahead: — as is only fair: for the greatest events are comprehended last and latest. Conversely, even today there is in the foreground enough gratitude, amazement, cheerfulness in the face of the most immediate consequences of that event, because — — — about that which is achieved through this, namely among us philosophers: for the horizon is open again, even presupposing it is not bright, and the sea has never lain as open as it now lies. — Let us admit it like philosophers: this old God, of whom it is said that he is dead — was he not like our greatest enemy? . . .

4. πολύτροποι] *polytropoi*; "tricksters" {N uses the plural form of this word as a nominalized adjective, while the singular form, meaning "wily" or "crafty," is used in the first line of the *Odyssey* to describe Odysseus.}

5. *that Christian . . . divine . . .] Pd*: the Christian faith [in the value of truth] in God as the truth, because God "is the truth," as a "beyond" and "In Itself" of truth

6. *But what . . . lie? —] Pd*: In other words, there is and was, looking deeply into the matter, until now in Europe only "Christian science" . . . Every anti-Christian science has over its entrance the terrible question mark: "why — precisely — truth?"

7. *blindness . . . lie? —] Pm*: appearance, the lie, folly, the delusion of folly? —

8. *Beginning of an earlier version in Sd: Morality as a Problem.* — It makes a considerable difference in a thinker (— and belongs among the strongest signs [of his innate order of rank in the realm of intellects] of his rank), whether he has, lives, suffers, loves a given problem as *his* problem and destiny, out of necessity, out of

renunciation and passion, or whether he merely reaches it with the tip of a cold curious thought and feels for it so to speak as something strange, new, wondrous.

9. *personally]* *Pd*: with body and soul *personally*

10. *case]* {N is here referring to Paul Rée; cf. *GM* Preface 4 in *CW* 8, 210–11.}

11. *Pd*: [+++] we are unbelievers and godless ones, but both in a late stage, no longer with the bitterness and passion of the one who tore himself free, who must ⟨contrive⟩ a faith out of his unfaith, a purpose, often a martyrdom. We have [grown cold and] been steeped in the realization, and have grown cold and old in it, that ⟨what happens⟩ in the world is absolutely not divine, indeed not even reasonable, merciful or just according to human standards: we know, the world in which we live is ungodly, immoral, "inhuman" — we have [inter⟨preted⟩ it all too long in keeping with our veneration, our lying and self-blinding be it fear be it love] ⟨interpreted⟩ it for ourselves all too long falsely and mendaciously, but in keeping with our veneration, that is, with our need. ⟨For the human being is⟩ a venerating animal — but also a mistrustful one! [+++] ⟨t⟩he world is *not* worth what we believed: [and the last thread of consolation that Schopenhauer spun ⟨in order to⟩ reconnect ⟨with the fa⟩ith of old ⟨has been⟩ torn by us: precisely this, he told us, was the meaning of all history, that finally it would discover its [+++]t and grow sick of it. This becoming weary of existence, this will to no longer willing, the [+++] of willfulness, of personal well-being, in sum "selflessness" as the expression of this inverted willing: this and ⟨only this⟩ Schopenhauer wanted to see honored with the highest honors — in this he saw morality per se, he believed he was securing a value ⟨for⟩ art only insofar as it creates states that could serve as preparations and ⟨bait for⟩ that complete reversal of the gaze, for that final turning away, separation.] this is the most certain thing [we today] our mistrust can lay its hands on. ⟨We⟩ do not ⟨d⟩are say that it is worth less; it seems to us almost laughable if humans were to lay claim to ⟨inventing⟩ values ⟨tha⟩t *exceed* the value of what exists — we've returned from precisely this already, as if from the most extravagant immodesty of humanity [+++]: the world is more valuable than all concepts

we are capable of thinking — but this "*more*" is itself something so incomprehensible, so negative, that it [easily] also becomes something completely indifferent.

12. *Bible speaks]* {Cf. 1 Corinthians 2:4; cf. *AC* 50.}

13. *miserable . . . crannies]* *Pm*: entirely myopic follies

14. *la vérité vraie]* "the real truth" or "the true truth"

15. *of Parisian . . . vraie]* *Pm*: of the Parisian Parnassians (this daintiest and thinnest aftergrowth of the romanticism of 1830) {Parnassianism was a French literary style influenced by Théophile Gautier (1811–72) and his doctrine of "art for art's sake."}

16. *And so . . . desperation]* *Pd*: the demand for a "thou shalt" in both cases ultimately became creative, it laid out, contrived, unified and wrote on the walls of heaven a person, a series of facts according to its needs, e.g., that fact J⟨esus⟩ of N⟨azareth⟩ or, in another case, the f⟨act⟩ that is called B⟨uddha⟩

17. *déraisonnable]* "unreasonable"

18. *"its head examined"]* *"den Kopf zu waschen"* {literally, "its head washed"}

19. *raison]* "reason"

20. {Cf. *BGE* 13; *TI* "Forays" 14; *CW* 15, 26[369]; William H. Rolph, *Biologische Probleme: Zugleich als Versuch zur Entwicklung einer rationellen Ethik* ("Biological problems: At the same time an attempt at developing a rational ethics"), 2nd ed. (Leipzig: Engelmann, 1884), 72–97. *NL.*}

21. *homines religiosi]* "religious people"

22. *them]* *Pd*: them [and truly they also have something to honor and emulate; their favorite saints are the Francis of Assisi types, human beings of the overflowing heart and the forgetful mild hand, who eternally give, give away, must give away, those who are constantly roasted in a fire of compassionate love]

23. *"communicates"]* *"sich mittheilt"* {literally, "shares [knowledge/information] of himself" as in "unburdens himself"}

24. *disciplina voluntatis]* "discipline of the will"

25. *Herrnhut]* {Town in Germany founded in 1722 by the Moravian Brethren sect of Christianity. The Moravians were founded by Nikolaus Ludwig von Zinzendorf as a Protestant movement to return to early Christian practices.}

26. *vis inertiae]* "force of inertia"

27. *generalized and debased world]* eine verallgemeinerte, eine
vergemeinerte Welt

28. *folk-metaphysics.) Even] Pm*: folk-metaphysics[, likewise in
the laughable philosophical arrogance of the past: as if humans
with their concepts could get beyond the perspective given to us,
beyond *our* perspectival nature]. Even

29. *recognized] erkannt* {The verb *erkennen* (to know) is used
also for recognition (cf. English "cognize, cognition").}

30. *known] Bekanntes* {Literally, "something known" or "familiar." In the remainder of §355 N uses *bekannt* ("known" as familiar)
juxtaposed with *erkannt* ("known" as cognized).}

31. *"what is familiar is known"] "was bekannt ist, ist erkannt"*

32. *profession] Beruf* {Whose stem verb is *rufen,* to call, hence
Beruf as "calling" or "that to which one is called."}

33. *There were . . . it:] Pd*: There are ages in which one believes
with rigid confidence in one's chance business and way of making
a living as if in divine providence:

34. *Graeculus historio]* "little Greek actor" {"Little Greek" being
a Roman term of contempt.}

35. *geniuses start] Pd*: geniuses of the stature of a Caesar and a
Napoleon start

36. *wooden iron] hölzernes Eisen* {A common German oxymo-
ron; here, wood that merely gives the appearance of iron.}

37. *instead, . . . demarcation)]* {*Pd*:} rather, insofar as its limits and realm [were questioned, and natural science generally was
admonished to modesty as a science of appearance were rewritten,
as valid for the world of appearance.

38. {Cf. *JS* 354; cf. Otto Liebmann, *Zur Analysis der Wirklichkeit:
Eine Erörterung der Grundprobleme der Philosophie* ("On the analysis of reality: A discussion of the basic problems of philosophy"),
2nd ed. (Straßburg: Trübner, 1880), 212–13. *NL.* These pages show
pencil marks by N.}

39. *causaliter]* "causally"

40. *Indeed, without . . . stupid —] Pd*: I for my part would say
Yes in all three cases: to me Leibniz's discovery of a much greater
scope to our inner world, as well as Kant's doubts about the

ultimate validity of our natural scientific knowledge, but above all Hegel's emphasis on "becoming" vis-à-vis "being" all seem to be a thought-provoking symptom of German self-awareness.

41. *had: his] Pm*: had: [— perhaps this is why today we are the most thorough atheists, because we resisted being so for the longest time.] his

42. *profundity. What] Pm*: profundity. [I am least inclined to admit that one hears it in today's Germany better than elsewhere.] What

43. *age of foundings] Zeitalter der Gründungen* {The Second Reich was founded in 1871, and its earliest years witnessed the founding of many enterprises in an economic boom.}

44. *elegantia psychologicae]* "psychological elegance" {N uses the Latin genitive *elegantiae* because the German *um . . . willen* construction requires a genitive. In English, we have restored the nominative case.}

45. *"Germany, Germany above all"] "Deutschland, Deutschland über Alles"* {Opening words of "Das Lied der Deutschen" ("The song of the Germans") by August Heinrich Hoffmann von Fallersleben, which subsequently became the German national anthem.}

46. *sub specie speciei]* "from the point of view of the species"

47. *pessimists!] Pd*: pessimists! [No more than they are romantics. That R. Wagner's Schopenhauerism was merely a misunderstanding, a romantic embarrassment, I indicated on a different occasion.]

48. *The . . . spirit.] Pd*: *The Germans and the Reformation.*

49. *possessed. The] Pd*: possessed. [But in the North one thinks along with Rousseau "the human being is good."] The

50. *in its entire . . . carefully,] Pd*: from the beginning a northern flat-headedness

51. *itself . . . Today] Pd*: itself (and was it not the luxury of the Renaissance, in which the Church indulged at that time?) Today

52. *Today one overlooks . . . power:] Pd*: In all cardinal questions of power — how is power gained? how is power maintained? — Luther revealed himself, first as a German, then as a man of the common people bereft of all heritage from a ruling caste, to be disastrously brief, trusting, superficial:

53. *he knew not . . . did]* {Cf. Luke 23:34.}

54. *is also complicit in the degeneration . . . profundity,]* *Pm*: is also complicit in its consequences, I mean in the trusting bliss of so-called "modern ideas"

55. *mimicry]* {N's English.}

56. *women]* *Frauen* {preferred, regular usage here}

57. *females]* *Frauenzimmer* {a pejorative term}

58. *That they . . . give themselves.]* Dass sie *"sich geben"*, selbst noch, wenn sie — sich geben. {N's wordplay, whereby *sich geben* means "to pretend, to put on airs" and literally to "give oneself."}

59. *Woman]* *Das Weib* {an archaic, pejorative term}

60. *Just listen . . . artistic . . .]* *Pm*: And at bottom, what do we love in them if not precisely *this*: that when they "give themselves," they are always giving a spectacle? . . .

61. *Napoleon, who . . . saw]* Cf. Madame de Rémusat, *Mémoires 1802–1808*, 1:122; cf. *CW* 13, 8[116].

62. *mistress]* *Herrin* {grammatically feminine form of *Herr*}

63. *empty space]* N in *Se*: *Horror vacui* {"Horror of the void"}

64. *you]* *dich* in *Pm, Le*; cf. Goethe, *Faust* I:1637; in *Fe*, N uses the wrong reflexive pronoun *sich* {"one"}.

65. *says]* {Cf. Goethe's *Faust* I:1637; Mephistopheles is recruiting Faust, persuading him that he is superior: "The meanest company lets you feel, / That you are one human among humans."}

66. *Cramped . . . themselves.]* *Pd*: Let there be no doubt: cramped bowels contribute to the work, the writing, and betray themselves in the form of the sentence: just like a cramped vain hopelessly mediocre [literati] scribe-psyche, above which the sky never can become bright

67. *We do not . . . crooked.]* *Pd*: Scholars would need above all to be artists; just as the stay-at-homes would need to dance and exercise: but they do *not* find it necessary

68. *way. Every]* *Pd*: way [gone blind in columns of books due to transcription errors or got lost in the "inner world" of a bowel worm, never to be seen again: a spectacle that arouses compassion, when one thinks of what they were, what they "promised," at that age when one signs oneself over to the devil in a good-natured and godly mood, and they devoted themselves "to science" because it

struts so devilishly today! They sacrificed themselves, these scholars: there is no doubt: and we shouldn't believe in the least that they could have avoided it, that perhaps they only became victims of some awkward method and art of education, as the superficial world improvers and writer-devils want to convince them. Every decent scholar knows from the bottom of their heart that it's different, that namely without such a sacrifice no decent scholar could even exist.] Every

69. *bow] Buckel* {Here translated as "bow" (the act of bowing); earlier in this section *Buckel* is translated as "hunchback."}

70. *in litteris et artibus]* "in letters and arts"

71. {Cf. *NCW* "Where I Object," in *CW* 9, 389–91, for a slightly more radical version of this aphorism.}

72. *"that drama . . . means"]* {Cf. Richard Wagner, the introduction to *Oper und Drama* ("Opera and drama"), in *Gesammelte Schriften und Dichtungen,* vol. 3 (Leipzig: Fritzsch, 1872), 282. *NL.* Cf. also *CW* 11, 32[52], 328; *WA* 10 (*CW* 9, 24–26); *NCW* "Where I Object" (*CW* 9, 389–91).}

73. {Cf. *NCW* "We Antipodes," in *CW* 9, 395–96, for N's rewrite of this aphorism.}

74. *Likewise]* In *Pm, Se, Le*; in *Fe*: Similarly

75. *eternalize likewise requires] Se: eternalize* [— the Apollonian, in keeping with my old formula —] requires

76. *spreading] Se, Le*: spreading (in this case I am speaking of *Apollonian* art.)

77. *proprium and ipsissimum]* "my own and my own(inner) most"

78. *amor intellectualis dei]* "intellectual love of God"

79. *In Pm crossed out at the end*: The naturalists of the mechanistic persuasion *deny* at bottom, like all deaf people, that music exists, that existence is music, even that ears should be allowed to exist . . . In doing so they *devalue* existence.

80. *rejects all clumsy . . . hesitate . . .] Pd*: rejects foursquare oppositions [of "good and evil"], [and knows how to enjoy precisely in what is immoral and forbidden the charms of its intermediate colors and shades, the lights of its afternoon, the shimmering mirrors of its sea.] a practice, a reserve, a light tugging on the reins in

every forward-charging demand for certainty, [for a Yes or a No without] a pleasure in the self-mastery of steed and rider . . . for beneath us we have, now as before, a fiery animal, we are still now proudly sitting on our impetuous steed.

81. *fermatas]* {In music, a hold or pause on a note for a longer period than indicated by the note.}

82. *There is no . . . do!] Pm*: However few or many they may be, among the Europeans of today there is no lack of those who have a right to call themselves homeless in a distinguishing and honorable sense — and it is primarily to these few or many that this book is addressed, as if to its predestined auditors.

83. *past; we] Pm*: past, we flatter neither the masses nor the dynasts, we

84. *Chinesery] Chineserei* {N means by this term something more critical than the French *chinoiserie,* as is clear from his derogatory portrait of the Chinese at §24.}

85. *Saint-Simonist]* {Follower of Henri de Saint-Simon (1760–1825), French socialist and utopian.}

86. *No, you know . . . faith!] Pm*: We homeless ones, we have no choice at all: we *must* henceforth be conquerors and explorers! Perhaps we who renounce ourselves, we who robbed ourselves, will someday bequeath to our children — new ideals, new realities, a new homeland! — —

87. *The fool's interruption.] Pm*: We artists of contempt. *Pm*: We fearless ones.

88. *Timonically]* {Timon (5th c. BCE), Athenian misanthrope featured in Attic comedy, by Shakespeare in *Timon of Athens.*}

89. *"The wanderer" speaks.] Pm*: On the goal and the way.

90. *clear skies] Pm*: a conscience

91. *it is . . . strength] Pm*: to fly over, when one wants; *Pm crossed out at the end*: But do you know then what romanticism is? — *Earlier*: Yet you do not understand what romanticism means to me?

92. *Pd*: There is a strict optics to which a writer as well as a painter keeps: "stand *there* – or leave my painting in peace!" Every good thing is good only from a certain distance.

93. *Diu noctuque incubando]* "by incubating it night and day" {Kaufmann, 1579–80, suggests that these words might not be from

Newton but that N probably knew them from French writer and painter Eugène Fromentin's *Les maîtres d'autrefois: Belgique – Hollande* ("The old masters: Belgium – Holland") (Paris: E. Plon et Cie, 1882), 135, *NL*, where Fromentin refers to these words as Rubens's "Latin motto." Kaufmann notes that Nietzsche underlined these words in his copy of the book. N also mentions these words in a letter to Overbeck of 14 July 1886 (*KGB* III:3, 208).}

94. *conscience and science]* Gewissen und Wissen {literally, "conscience and knowing"}

95. *reading]* In Pm, Le; in Fe: reader.

96. *bad mood]* Grillen {Literally, "crickets"; used idiomatically here, and literally in the following clause.}

97. *No . . . joyful ones!]* Cf. Schiller, "Ode to Joy"

98. *"the singer's curse"]* Cf. {Ludwig} Uhland, "Des Sängers Fluch" ("The Singer's Curse").

Appendix: Songs of Prince Vogelfrei

1. *Vogelfrei]* {*Vogelfrei* is an archaic expression used to declare someone an outlaw, literally "free as a bird," and therefore not to be sheltered but to be shot on sight. In German the *v* and *f* are both pronounced as *f*, adding alliteration to this name and the title N makes of it. "Prince Vogelfrei" here functions as N's *nom de guerre* or pseudonym.}

2. *To Goethe]* {N is here parodying the "Chorus Mysticus" that concludes Goethe's *Faust*. At issue are the poet's need to fictionalize and Goethe's elevation of womanhood to a metaphysical "eternal feminine." In *Faust*, the "eternal feminine" (*das Ewig-Weibliche*) represented by the blessed Gretchen succeeds in helping to redeem Faust and to pull him up into heaven: "Woman Eternal / Draws us on high" ("Das Ewig-Weibliche / Zieht uns hinan") (lines 12110–11 of *Faust*.}

3. *Poet's Calling]* Cf. *IM* "Bird Judgment."

4. *await]* Pm: wait

5. *Anything . . . moves]* Pm: Anything that slips

6. *When . . . heart]* Pm: When they {pierce} the words' *meaning*

7. Cf. *IM* "Prince Vogelfrei."

8. *With]* Pm: From

9. *Pious Beppa*] Cf. *IM* "The Little Witch."

10. *The Mysterious Bark*] Cf. *IM* "The Nocturnal Secret."

11. *Declaration of Love*] Cf. *IM* "Bird Albatross."

12. *Goatherd*] {The Greek poet Theocritus (3rd c. BCE) is considered the father of pastoral poetry. A "theocritical" [*theokritischen*] goatherd, using wordplay, is thus both pastoral and critical of God (*theo*).}

13. *Song of a Theocritical Goatherd*] Cf. *IM* "Song of the Goatherd"

14. *"People Who Are Vacillating"*] Pm: "*To Certain Eulogists*"; Pd: "*Against Certain Eulogists*"

15. *honor . . . hating*] Pd: take they are stealing

16. *What I wrote . . . scrawl*] {The proverb "*Narrenhände beschmieren Tisch und Wände*," literally, "Fools' hands smear table and walls," is used to suggest that clumsy, incompetent people make a mess.}

17. *Rimus remedium*] "Rhyme as remedy"

18. *bull*] {Phalaris, the tyrant of Akragas (now Agrigento, in Sicily) from approximately 570 to 554 BCE, tortured his enemies by roasting them alive in a brazen bull.}

19. *"My Happiness!"*] Pm: And Once More!

20. *On to New Seas*] Cf. *CW* 14, 1[15, 101]; 3[1, 4]; Pm: "*Toward New Seas*" / or / *Columbus*

21. *infinity*] Pd: immortality

22. *Sils-Maria*] Cf. *CW* 14, 3[3].

23. *Faster . . . summit*] Pm: Whipping waves, taming seas

24. *Glowing . . . roses*] Pm: Striking backward with your heels, / So that your wagon in

Idylls from Messina

1. The *Idylls from Messina* (*IM*) were published in the *Internationale Monatsschrift* 1, no. 5 (May 1882): 269–75, in the Ernst Schmeitzner publishing house in Chemnitz. Our printing is based on this copy. They stem from the same extensive mass of poetic experiments of February–April 1882, from which N later constructed his "Prelude in German Rhymes" for *JS* ("Jokes, Cunning and Revenge"). In mid-May 1882, N sent the printer's

manuscript (still preserved) of *IM* to Schmeitzner. The proofs undertaken by N were concluded on 26 May. Of these eight poems N adopted six (in revised form) for the "Songs of Prince Vogelfrei," the appendix to the second edition of *JS* (1887). This is why the *IM* are missing in all previous editions of N's works. Erich F. Podach published them in his *Ein Blick in Nietzsches Notizbücher* ("A glance into Nietzsche's notebooks") (Heidelberg: Rothe, 1963), 176–82.

2. Cf. *JSA* "In the South"

3. *High . . . and] Pd*: On this Genoese

4. *I . . . cooled] Pd*: So I follow and dream

5. *still. / The] Pd*: still. / [A bird myself certainly! / And sing and gaze far around me / And sing song after song for me? / A bird myself — certainly!] The

6. *goal] Pd*: trip

7. *Fear, praise] Pd*: And goal and path and [reward] fear

8. *flies! / Just] Pd*: flies! / [And sing song after song for me, / A bird myself — certainly!] This

9. *Just . . . makes] Pd*: This "Step by step" — that's no life! / This "dull plodding" makes

10. *ascent. / Reason?] Pd*: ascent. / So I sing song after song for myself, / A bird myself — certainly/ Reason?

11. *Reason? — that's] Pd*: Talking

12. *But . . . novel] Pd*: There are more physical

13. *joking] Pd*: dance

14. *The Small] Sd*: *Song of the Small*; *Sd at the end*: Little angel: so I'm called! {Also in the letter to Gast; cf. note 15 below.}

15. Cf. N to Peter Gast, 15 March 1882 {*KGB* III:1, 178–79}.

16. Cf. *JSA* "Song of a Theocritical Goatherd"

17. *dance. / She] Pd*: dance! / [Where for your curly [hair] head / The silk ribbon! / Is it a new year's gift for] / her

18. Cf. *JSA* "Pious Beppa"

19. *The Little Witch] Pm*: Juanita

20. *To . . . chap.] Pd*: In love, yes, unto death

21. *I . . . old] Pd*: He's truly amazed / He loves my young face!

22. *The devil . . . rest!] Pd*: Let the devil woo me!

23. Cf. *JSA* "The Mysterious Bark"

24. *Hundreds . . . Hell?] Pm*: Skiffs rush through the waters

25. *"Pia, caritatevole, amorosissima."]* "Pious one, charitable, most filled with love." {N found this inscription on a girl's tombstone near Genoa; the stress should be on the fourth syllable: a-mo-ro-*sis*-si-ma.}

26. Cf. *JSA* "Declaration of Love"

27. *Bird Albatross] Pd*: The Triumphant One; *Pd at the beginning*: The heavens will surely bear me / My wings may yet rest! / What happened! I was just flying? / And here I forget how / I rest and yet soar / How can my wings rest?

28. *He flew . . . winner.] Pd*: Who without beating his wings / Flies higher than all flyers / Oh riddle comfort and image! / Oh comfort and [happiness]!! Here lies the triumphing one / the jewel of all victors

29. *Star . . . heights] Pm*: Happiness of deepest solitude! / Living in the heights

30. Cf. *JSA* "Poet's Calling"

[II = M III 1.]

1. Cf. *JS* 162.

2. Cf. *BGE* 192.

3. *sousreliefs]* "sunken reliefs" versus reliefs [in the plastic arts]

4. *ego —] Le*: ego feeling

5. *the] Added in Le and Le²*.

6. *not ego . . . omnes!]* "not I and not you (thou) and not everyone!"

7. *Mayer]* Julius Robert Mayer, *Mechanik der Wärme* ("Mechanics of heat") (Stuttgart{: Cotta}, 1874). Cf. N to Peter Gast, 10 April 1881 {*KGB* III:1, 82}; 16 April 1881 {*KGB* III:1, 84}; 20 March 1882 {*KGB* III:1, 183–84}.

8. *Proctor]* Richard A. Proctor, *Unser Standpunkt im Weltall* ("Our standpoint in the universe") (Heilbronn{: Henninger}, 1877). *NL.*

9. Cf. 11[24].

10. *customs morality] Sitten* ("customs") *Sittlichkeit* ("morality") {versus "morality" as *Moral* (cf. *GM*).}

11. *Spencer p. 302]* {Herbert Spencer,} *Die Thatsachen der Ethik*{: *Autor. dt. Ausgabe nach der zweiten engl. Auflage übersetzt von Benjamin Vetter* ("The data of ethics: Authorized German edition

according to the 2nd English ed., trans. Benjamin Vetter") (Stuttgart: Schweizerbart, 1879), 302. *The Data of Ethics* (London: Williams and Norgate, 1879), 277: "transitional states, full of miseries due to non-adaptation . . .".}

12. *alter]* "other person"

13. *most]* Le, Le²: most = *auf's* {correcting a small slip}; *Ms*: most = *auf*

14. *selection-expediency]* Selektions-Zweckmäßigkeit

15. *selection]* Selection

16. *selection]* Auswahl

17. *Rohde]* [?]

18. Cf. *Z* I "On War and Warrior-Peoples"; *Z* IV "The Festival of the Ass."

19. Cf. *JS* 59.

20. *Purification . . . lower]* Added later.

21. {In a letter to Lady Melbourne on 25 September 1812, Lord Byron writes: "a woman should never be seen eating or drinking, unless it be lobster sallad [*sic*] & Champaigne [*sic*] the only truly feminine & becoming viands." Cf. *Lord Byron: Selected Letters and Journals,* ed. Leslie A. Marchand (Cambridge, MA: Belknap Press of Harvard University Press, 1973), 358–59.}

22. *gloria]* "glory"

23. Cf. *JS* 21.

24. *personalities]* [?]

25. *Mayer]* {Cf. note 7 above.}

26. *Lucretius]* De rerum natura IV, lines 1058–1120.

27. Cf. *JS* 46; *CW* 13, 7[78].

28. ⟨*that*⟩] Added according to Le and Le².

29. *to]* In Le, Le²; *Ms*: in

30. *aberration.]* [?]

31. Cf. 11[85].

32. *Lecky]* N is referring to William Edward Hartpole Lecky, *Geschichte des Ursprungs und Einflusses der Aufklärung in Europa,* trans. from English by H. Jolowicz (Leipzig{: C. F. Winter,} 1873. NL. {*History of the Rise and Influence of the Spirit of Rationalism in Europe,* 2 vols. (London: Longmans, Green, 1865).}

33. *Human . . . animals.]* Cf. 11[77].

34. *Deus nudus est]* "God is naked"

35. *Seneca] Epistulae morales ad Lucilium* ("Moral letters to Lucilius"), letter 7; cf. 11[95]. N is citing Lecky, *Geschichte*, 178n3.

36. *physis]* "nature"

37. Cf. *JS* 109, 349.

38. *Paracelsi mirabilia]* "wonders of Paracelsus"

39. Cf. *JS* 1.

40. *Plato] Symposium* 207c–212a.

41. *individuals] Individuen* {N uses the Latinate noun here, but uses the Germanic noun *Einzelne* ("singular ones") twice in the remainder of this note.}

42. This fragment and fragments 11[130, 131, 132, 134, 182, 241, 243, 256, 284] originated in connection with N's reading of Wilhelm Roux, *Der Kampf der Theile im Organismus: Ein Beitrag zur Vervollständigung der mechanischen Zweckmäßigkeitslehre* {"Struggle of the parts within the organism: A contribution to the completion of the doctrine of mechanical expediency"} (Leipzig{: Engelmann,} 1881). *NL.* We thank Wolfgang Müller-Lauter for this important reference: "Der Organismus als innerer Kampf: Der Einfluß von Wilhelm Roux auf Friedrich Nietzsche" {"The organism as inner struggle: The influence of Wilhelm Roux on Friedrich Nietzsche"}, *Nietzsche-Studien* 7 (1978): 189–223. Müller-Lauter also made available to us the results of his research; cf. also notes 44, 75, 77–95, 145, 159–66 to the fragments of Notebook 7 in *CW* 14.

43. *"anger"]* Müller-Lauter, "Der Organismus als innerer Kampf," 196n30: "When *KGW* writes 'anger,' 'love,' 'hate' in the Nietzsche fragment, I suspect an erroneous reading; the word 'anger' yields no meaning in this context. Harking back to the Roux text the reading of *'Kräfte'* {"forces"} is likely." However, in N's manuscript (M III 1, 69) the word *anger* is incontestably legible.

44. Cf. note to 11[128].

45. Cf. note to 11[128]; Müller-Lauter, "Der Organismus als innerer Kampf," proves that the beginning of this fragment was taken from Michael Foster, *Lehrbuch der Physiologie* {*A Textbook of Physiology* (London: Macmillan, 1876)} (Heidelberg{: C. Winter,} 1881), 524. *NL.*

46. Cf. note to 11[128]; Roux, *Der Kampf der Theile im Organismus,* 65, 71.

47. Cf. note to 11[128].

48. *Mendelsohn]* N misspells "Mendelssohn"

49. Cf. *EH* "Books" *Z* 1. {Cf. *JS* 341.}

50. {Cf. *JS* 341.}

51. {Cf. *Z* III "The Vision and the Riddle."}

52. *is] Added according to Le and Le².*

53. Cf. *JS* 109.

54. *developed] ungeworden* {not become or un-become}

55. Cf. *Z* I "On the Hinterworldly."

56. *rest] Ms*: Rest {i.e., correcting the verb for the noun}

57. Cf. *JS* 89; *crossed out by N.*

58. *demonized] durchteufelte* {literally, "devilized it through and through"}

59. Cf *JS* 42.

60. *countless] Ms*: Countless {i.e., correcting the adjective for the noun}

61. *on] Added according to Le.*

62. Cf. note to 11[128].

63. Cf. 12[213].

64. *suum cuique]* "to each his own"

65. *extra ecclesiam nulla salus]* "outside the Church there is no salvation"

66. *v⟨ide⟩]* "see"

67. *amoeba-unity] Amöben-*Einheit; *Ms: Amöeben* Einheit {"amöeba *unity*"}

68. The source of the Spinoza quotes is Kuno Fischer, *Geschichte der neueren Philosophie I, 2: Descartes' Schule. Geulinx, Malebranche, Baruch Spinoza* ("History of modern philosophy I, 2: Descartes's school; Geulincx, Malebranche, Baruch Spinoza") (Heidelberg{: Bassermann}, 1865. In July 1881 {Cf. N's letter to Overbeck, 8 July 1881 (*KGB* III:1, 101)}, N had Overbeck send this book to him in Sils-Maria (cited as "Fischer," followed by the page number).

69. *we are . . . motive.]* Fischer, 489

70. *ex . . . conservare]* "To act absolutely according to virtue = to act under the guidance of reason, to live so, and to preserve one's being." {Spinoza, *Ethics* IV, Prop. XXIV.} Fischer, 488n.

71. *"fundamentally . . . existence."]* Fischer, 488.

72. *"Striving . . . virtue."]* Fischer, 489.

73. *"Human . . . rationis."]* Fischer, 486.

74. *"Good . . . it."]* Fischer, 487.

75. *Our . . . internally.]* Fischer, 486.

76. *("Craving . . . being."]* Fischer, 483.

77. *"Everyone . . . virtue."]* Fischer, 484.

78. *There . . . eternity.]* Fischer, 480.

79. *The . . . else.]* Fischer, 479.

80. *Congregation . . . Jesus]* {The Congregation of the Oratory of Jesus and Mary Immaculate, also known as the French Oratory, founded in Paris in 1611 by Pierre de Bérulle.}

81. *Port-Royal]* {Originally referred to the Abbey at Port-Royal-des-Champs, then became synonymous with the new abbey relocated to Paris in the 17th century. Port-Royal referred collectively to a style of logic taught in the Catholic schools, then became associated with the Jansenist movement.}

82. *The Jesuits . . . Port-Royal]* Fischer, 32–33.

83. *impossibile . . . nescio?]* "it is impossible for someone who does not know how to do something to do it, when I do not know how it is done, I do not do it. — On which front shall I say that I do and I do not know how it is done?" Fischer, 15n.

84. *My . . . velis.]* Fischer, 18.

85. *Ubi nihil . . . velis.]* "Where you are worth nothing, there you will want nothing."

86. *Virtus . . . rationis.]* "Virtue is the love of reason." Fischer, 24n.

87. *Amor . . . sui.]* "Love of reason has this effect on the lover that he forsakes himself, and thoroughly withdraws from himself. Humility is disregard of oneself. Humility has two parts: inspection of oneself and disregard of oneself." Fischer, 26–27n. {N underlines *incuria sui*.}

88. *"The senses . . . body.]* Fischer, 56–57.

89. *Asylum ignorantiae]* "Asylum of ignorance" {In philosophy dodging the question.}

90. *Spinoza . . . ignorantiae.]* Fischer, 235ff.

91. Cf. *JS* 342 and note 101; *Z* I Preface 1.

92. *Zend-Avesta]* {The scriptures (Avesta) and commentary (Zend) of Zoroastrianism.}

93. *Chaos sive natura]* "Chaos or nature"

94. *Κράτος] Kratos* {In Greek mythology, the divine personification of strength.}

95. *organisirt]* {Unclear whether *organisirt* is used as past participle ("organized") or third person ("organizes").}

96. *Annulus aeternitatis]* "Ring of eternity" {Underlined by N.}

97. *Burckhardt . . . Pitti)]* Cf. *Der Cicerone,* 2nd ed. (Leipzig{: Seemann,} 1869), 175: "One asks oneself, who then is the world-despising brute who, endowed with such means, was able to avoid everything that is merely pretty and pleasing? — The single major variation, namely the limitation of the top story to the middle, by itself already has a colossal effect and gives one the feeling that superhuman beings accounted for the distribution of these masses." {The Palazzo Pitti, or Pitti Palace, is currently a large art museum in Florence, named after Florentine banker Luca Pitti, who built the original structure as his home in 1458; later, during the Renaissance expansion, it became the home of grand dukes and the king of Italy.} *NL.*

98. *wooden iron]* {Cf. *JS* 356 and note 36.}

99. Cf. *JS* 109.

100. *one] Le, Le²*: one = *sie*; *Ms*: one = *ihn* {correcting a small slip}.

101. *one] Le, Le²*: one = *ihr*; *Ms*: one = *ihm* {correcting a small slip}.}

102. Cf. *JS* 341.

103. Cf. *JS* 109.

104. *latter two] Le*: *letztere*; *Ms*: *letzteres* {correcting a small slip}

105. Cf. *Z* IV "On Superior Humans" 8.

106. Cf. 11[185].

107. *in Venere]* "in matters of erotic love," "venereally"

108. *Analysis o⟨f⟩ R⟨eality⟩]* Otto Liebmann, *Zur Analysis der Wirklichkeit* {"On the analysis of reality"} (Straßburg {: Trübner,} 1880). *NL.*

109. *countless] unzählige*; *Ms*: *unzähliche* {correcting a small slip}

110. Cf. note to 11[128].

111. Cf. note to 11[128].

112. {The modern chemical names for these compounds: sodium sulfate, potassium sulfate and phosphate, calcium phosphate, iron phosphate.}

113. *of . . . moment]* Crossed out by N.

114. *Lohengrin]* Wagner's romantic opera of 1850.

115. Cf. 13[14]; cf. note to 11[128].

116. Cf. 13[20].

117. Cf. *CW* 16, 4[5].

118. *intempestiva . . . ἀωρονυκτί]* "untimely night" in Latin and Greek

119. *"time of the night milking"]* {This is "νυκτὸς ἀμολγῷ" (*nuktos amolgoi*), used several times in the *Iliad*.}

120. *leads us away, misleads]* weg *führt* ("leads *away*"), *verführt* (literally, "seduces")

121. *effectus aequat causam]* "the effect is equal to the cause"

122. *on]* Added in Le.

123. {Cf. Friedrich Anton Heller von Hellwald, *Culturgeschichte in ihrer natürlichen Entwicklung von der ältesten Zeiten bis zur Gegenwart* ("Cultural history in its natural development from the earliest times to the present") (Augsburg: Lampart, 1875), 629).}

124. {Cf. Henry Charles Carey, *Lehrbuch der Volkswirthschaft und Socialwissenschaft,* German trans. by Carl Adler, 2nd ed. (Vienna: W. Braumüller, 1870), 121. *NL.* English original: *Principles of Social Science,* 3 vols. (Philadelphia: Lippincott and Co., 1858–59).}

125. Cf. *JS* 134.

126. *camphor]* Ms: canphor

127. Cf. *JS* 43.

128. Cf. *CW* 13, 6[237].

129. Cf. note to 11[128].

130. *it]* Le², Le: it = *sie* {in reference to the grammatical subject "function" (gendered feminine in German)}; *Ms*: it = *es* {in reference to the grammatical subject "feeling" (gendered neuter).}

131. Cf. 12[29].

132. ⟨*as*⟩ ⟨*something . . .* ⟨*to*⟩⟩ Added in Le² and Le.

133. Cf. *JS* 144.

134. *David Strauß]* Cf. *David Strauss, the Confessor and Writer* (1873), in *CW* 2, *UO*.

135. Cf. 13[3].

136. Cf. 12[230].

137. *appetitus]* "appetite"

138. *Vogt]* Johann Gustav Vogt, *Die Kraft: Eine real-monistische Weltanschauung*, Bd. 1: *Die Contraktionsenergie, die letztursächliche einheitliche mechanische Wirkungsform des Weltsubstrates* {"Force: A real-monistic worldview, vol. 1: Contraction energy, the ultimate unified mechanical form of activity of the world's substratum"} (Leipzig{: Haupt & Tischler}, 1878). *NL.* {See Martin Bauer, "Zur Genealogie von Nietzsches Kraftbegriff: Nietzsches Auseinandersetzung mit J. G. Vogt," *Nietzsche-Studien* 13 (1984): 211–27.}

139. *contraction energy]* {The first volume of Vogt's *Die Kraft* is titled *Die Contraktionsenergie* ("Contraction energy").}

140. *Vogt]* Cf. Vogt, *Die Kraft*.

141. *modi cogitandi]* "modes of thinking"

142. *seeing]* In Le, Ms: being

143. Cf. 13[1].

144. *otherwise]* In Le², Le; Ms: rather

145. {Cf. Afrikan Spir, *Denken und Wirklichkeit: Versuch einer Erneuerung der kritischen Philosophie*, Bd. 1: *Das Unbedingte* ("Thought and reality: Attempt at a renewal of critical philosophy, vol. 1: The absolute") (Leipzig: Findel, 1877), 382. *NL.*}

146. *esse]* "to be"

147. *evil]* das Übel

148. Cf. *JS* 80.

149. {Cf. Afrikan Spir, *Denken und Wirklichkeit*, 379–80.}

150. *cogito, ergo est]* "I think, therefore **it (something) is**"

151. *(thus . . . judged)]* Later written above it in pencil.

152. Cf. *JS* 110.

153. Cf. *JSP* 23.

154. *To E. R.]* {To Erwin Rohde?}

155. Forms of Provençal poetry of the troubadours; {Cf. Theodor Gsell-Fels, *Süd-Frankreich, nebst den Kurorten der Riviera di Ponente, Corsica und Algier* ("Southern France including the spas of Riviera di Ponente, Corsica and Algiers") (Leipzig:

Bibliographisches Institut, 1878), 312–13, 316}; on the "joyful science" (*gaya ciencia, gay sabèr*), cf. J. G. Herder, *Briefe zur Beförderung der Humanität: Siebente Sammlung* {"Letters for the advancement of humanity: Seventh collection"} {(Riga: Johann Friedrich Hartknoch, 1796)}, letters 81–90.

156. *state]* Zustand

157. *Crossed out by N.*

158. *Science]* Das Wissen

[12 = N V 7.]

1. Cf. 14[4].

2. *Grotto . . . Angeria]* Grotte seiner Nymphe Ärgeria {Alludes to "Grotto of the Nymph Egeria" by Giovanni Battista Piranesi (*Ärger* = "anger"; "vexation").}

3. Cf. *JS* 79.

4. *Page torn on right margin.*

5. Cf. *JS* 143.

6. Cf. 14[6].

7. Cf. 14[1].

8. Cf. 13[11].

9. Cf. 14[1{7}].

10. Cf. *JS* 14; *CW* 18, 11[89].

11. *Tannhäusers]* {Title figure in Wagner's 1845 opera about the medieval poet (*Minnesänger*).}

12. Cf. 14[10].

13. Cf. 14 [2, 9].

14. Cf. 12[34, 38]; 14[8].

15. Cf. 11[244].

16. Cf. 11[285].

17. Cf. *CW* 18, 11[88].

18. *religiosi]* "religious {people}"

19. Cf. 12[26, 38]; 14[8]; *CW* 18, 11[87].

20. ⟨*much*⟩] *Le*: filled in

21. Cf. *JS* 87; 11[260]; *CW* 17, 4[5].

22. *nox intemp⟨esta⟩]* "dead of night"

23. *"Hagen's vigil"]* {From Wagner's *Götterdämmerung*, Act 2, where Hagen is in a trance-like state.}

24. Cf. 12[26, 34]; 14[8].

25. Cf. *JS* 2, 301; *CW* 18, 11[112].

26. Cf. *Z* IV "At Noon" and "The Last Supper."

27. Cf. *JS* 331; 14[12].

28. *Pascal] Ms*: Paskal

29. Cf. *CW* 18, 11[86]; possible source (according to a suggestion by Jörg Salaquarda): Carl von Linné {Charles Linnaeus}, *Lappländische Reise von 1732* ("Lappland journey of 1732") (Leipzig: {Reclam,} 1980), 57–58: Entry of 6 to 8 June: "The inhabitants of the Lapp March plant many beets, which often grow quite well, and the Lapplanders who truly like beets will often exchange a cheese for a beet, *quae stultitia!* {"what stupidity!"} . . . The women here have their children drink from a sucking-bottle, and I was surprised by the peasant women who did not bother to suckle their children. No one boiled milk, it would have been too burdensome for them, which is why it is also not surprising that the children get worms."

30. Cf. *CW* 18, 20[145].

31. *"I . . . umbrella"]* {This curious remark has become famous as a result of Jacques Derrida's treatment of it in *Éperons: Les styles de Nietzsche* (Paris: Flammarion, 1978); *Spurs: Nietzsche's Styles,* trans. Barbara Harlow (Chicago: University of Chicago Press, 1979).}

32. Cf. *JS* 127.

33. Cf. 14[125]; *JS* 125.

34. Cf. *JS* 12; 13[4].

35. Cf. *JS* 77.

36. Cf. Byron, *Manfred* II, 1.

37. *Manfred]* {Byron's dramatic poem (1817), featuring the eponymous superhuman Manfred.}

38. Cf. *CW* 18, 11[85]

39. *S⟨aint⟩ John]* {The eagle is a symbol of St. John as depicted in Christian heraldry.}

40. *Textual scholars]* *Schriftgelehrte* {The standard term for "scribes" in Luther's German Bible translation.}

41. Cf. *JS* 127.

42. *comes]* "friend"; "companion"

43. Cf. *JS* 337; 15[18, 70].

44. *"ephemera"] "Eintagsfliegen"* {literally, blowflies, dayflies, mayflies}

45. Cf. *JS* 125; 14[26].

46. *God is dead]* {This is the first appearance of the phrase "God is dead" — *Gott ist todt* — in any of N's texts, notebooks, or letters.}

47. Cf. 15[17].

48. *cupido gloriae]* "desire for glory"

49. Cf. *JS* 261.

50. Cf. *JS* 5.

51. *patria]* "homeland"

52. Cf. *JS* 27.

53. Cf. 15[2].

54. *comes . . . virtutis]* "companion . . . guide of virtue" {Reworking of the motto *fortuna comes virtutis,* "fortune is the companion of virtue."}

55. Cf. *JS* 293.

56. Cf. *CW* 14, 1[45, 109].

57. Cf. 12[97]; 15[26].

58. Cf. 12[96]; 15[26].

59. Cf. *JS* 33.

60. Cf. *JS* 288.

61. Cf. 15[40].

62. Cf. *JS* 32; *variant in M III 4:* This person is too mediocre for me to wish he could grasp the subject of virtue. His mediocrity will compromise the prestige of every subject he touches.

63. Cf. *JS* 71; *CW* 13, 8[69].

64. Cf. *JS* 236; *TI* "Sayings and Arrows" 1; *CW* 18, 11[107].

65. *"Zarathustra's . . . evil"]* {Reworking of the proverb *Müssiggang ist aller Laster Anfang,* "Idleness is the root of all evil."}

66. Cf. 12[101].

67. Cf. *JS* 278.

68. Cf. 15[43].

69. *Jew-haters] Misojuden* {*Miso* is a Greek prefix for "hater" or "hatred."}

70. Cf. *JS* 278.

71. Cf. 15[55].

72. Cf. *JS* 106 (variant).

73. Cf. 21[3] no. 3; *CW* 18, 11[91].

74. Cf. *CW* 18, 11[91].

75. Cf. *CW* 14, 1[79]; *CW* 18, 11[91].

76. Cf. *JS* 302; 15[54]; 16[21].

77. Cf. *JSP* 26 {cf. *TI* "Sayings and Arrows" 42}.

78. Cf. *JS* 32.

79. Cf. *JS* 1.

80. Cf. 14[13]; *CW* 18, 11[93].

81. *goats]* [?]

82. *Rosencrantz and Guildenstern]* {False friends of the hero in Shakespeare's tragedy *Hamlet*. In Act III, Scene 2, Hamlet points out to Polonius "yonder cloud that's almost in shape of a camel."}

83. Cf. *JS* 325, 48.

84. Cf. 12[177, 181].

85. *Posillipo]* {A famed and ancient panoramic residential quarter of Naples.}

86. Cf. 11[215].

87. Cf. *CW* 18, 11[94].

88. *an American]* Ralph Waldo Emerson

89. *Three]* Uncertain reading.

90. *compensation]* N is probably referring to the chapter by the same name in Emerson's *Essays*, 70–96 {cf. vol. 2, *Essays: First Series*, "Compensation," 53–73} in the translation used by him (cf. the fragments of Group 13 in this volume).

91. Perhaps in connection with *JS* 16.

92. Cf. *JS* 256; 15[56].

93. Cf. 14[24].

94. Cf. *JS* 125.

95. *in her]* Le, Ms: from her

96. Cf. *JS* 311; Cosima Wagner to N, 22 August 1872 {*KGB* II:4, 69}.

97. *pensum]* "lessons"

98. {In notebook N V 7, N often places a cross before a line. In the three-asterisk mark below (see 12[220], N V 7, 3), one can clearly see that N has placed three crosses at the start. There is no obvious reason why the German editors chose to acknowledge

some of these crosses with asterisks and ignored all of the others, but we follow their decision here and below.}

99. *Youth . . . virtue]* Jugend hat keine Tugend {Proverbially, "Boys will be boys," with the nouns rhyming in German.}

100. Cf. *JS* 80; *variant of the conclusion in N V 7:* a possibility that everyone has to face up to, who reflects on the sublime relationship between music and morality.

101. *recitativo secco]* "dry recitative" {A style between speaking and singing; *secco* ("dry") refers to notes played and released abruptly.}

102. Cf. *JS* 101. {Cf. Claude Adrien Helvétius, *Discurs über den Geist des Menschen* ("Discourse on the mind of human beings"}, trans. from the French by J. G. Forkert (Leipzig: Siegerts, 1760), 532. *NL.*}

103. {Cf. Helvétius, *Discurs,* 534–35.}

104. {Cf. Helvétius, *Discurs,* 552–53.}

105. *Disnajan]* {N's misciting of Helvétius's reference to Bisnagar; cf. *Discurs,* 552.}

106. *"this . . . here"]* {Cf. Helvétius, *Discurs,* 554; an example of provincial simplicity.}

107. Cf. *JS* 14.

108. {Cf. Helvétius, *Discurs,* 614.}

109. *Saadi]* Cf. Saadi, *Gulistan* {("The rose garden"), trans. Edward B. Eastwick (London: Trübner, 1880),} preface, {19}. {Saadi or Sa'dī (formal name: Shaykh Muṣliḥ ud-Dīn Sa'dī Shīrāzī) (1213–91), Persian poet and mystic.}

110. *"From . . . step"]* {Cf. Helvétius, *Discurs,* 624.}

111. Cf. 12[81, 142].

112. *Posillipo . . . opened]* {Cf. Goethe, *Italienische Reise* ("Italian journey"), 2 March 1787: "Von der Lage der Stadt und ihren Herrlichkeiten, die so oft beschrieben und belobt sind, kein Wort. 'Vedi Napoli e poi muori!' sagen sie hier. 'Siehe Neapel und stirb!' ("I will not say a word about the layout of the city and its magnificent views, which have been frequently described and praised. 'See Napoli and then you can die!' they say here. 'See Naples and die!'") N may be referring to his near-ecstatic discovery of the beauty of Naples on his trip with Rée, Brenner, and Meysenbug in October 1876; cf. Paolo D'Iorio, *Nietzsche's Journey to Sorrento:*

Genesis of the Philosophy of the Free Spirit (Chicago: University of Chicago Press, 2016), 22–23; and the Chronicle of N's Life in *CW* 19.}

113. Cf. *JS* 287; *JSP* 44; 16[5].

114. *long-winded]* Crossed out after this: this nature lurks behind my spirit, which pulls only at the last fringes of this nature and is never amazed enough by its fantasizing and apparent patchwork

115. Cf. Schiller, *Die Freundschaft* (*Anthologie auf das Jahr 1782*) {"Friendship (Anthology from the year 1782)"}, 59–60 {cf. Friedrich Schiller, *Sämmtliche Werke* ("Collected works"), vol. 1 (Stuttgart: J. G. Cotta, 1822), 102}: "From the chalice of the whole kingdom of the soul / Foams up for him — infinity."

116. Cf. 12[142, 177].

117. *lodge.]* Crossed out after this: the North of Europe is strewn with them

118. *sky]* Crossed out after this: you could have died without seeing this

119. Cf. *JSP* 60.

120. *Grillparzer] Sämtliche Werke* {"Collected works"}, ed. H. Laube and J. Weilen, vol. 9 (Stuttgart: {Cotta,} 1872), 229. Concerning Grillparzer, whom N expressly quotes in *DS* and *HL,* cf. also N to Erwin Rohde, 7 December 1872 {*KGB* II:3, 98}.

121. *Spencer] The Data of Ethics*; cf. *CW* 13, 1[11].

122. Cf. *WA* 9.

123. *We . . . sleeping]* {In Act 3 of Wagner's opera *Siegfried* (1876).}

124. *healing]* {From Wagner's last opera, *Parsifal* (1882).}

125. Cf. *JS* 125: "Aren't we just groping as if through an endless nothing?"

126. *Perhaps reminiscent of Friedrich Schlegel*: "A fragment must be entirely isolated from the surrounding world like a small artwork, and perfect in itself like a porcupine." Cf. Friedrich Schlegel, *Athenäums-Fragmente* {"Fragments published in the journal *Athenaeum*"}, in *Kritische Schriften* {"Critical writings"}, ed. Wolfdietrich Rasch (Munich{: Hanser,} 1970), 47.

127. Perhaps in connection with Lecky's writings on theater {cf. William Edward Hartpole Lecky, *Geschichte des Ursprungs und Einflusses der Aufklärung in Europa,* trans. from English by

H. Jolowicz (Leipzig: C. F. Winter, 1873), 2:252–58. *NL. History of the Rise and Influence of the Spirit of Rationalism in Europe,* 2 vols. (London: Longmans, Green, 1865), 2:347–53.}.

128. *Pd: N V 7, 26*: Not let science be spoiled b⟨y⟩ the scientific types any more than art by the artists — my danger

129. Cf. *JSP* 38; *JS* 25; 15[4].

130. {Cf. John 3:16.}

131. *The following version crossed out by N in N V 7, 35*: Everyone buys as cheaply as he can i.e., everyone steals from his neighbor, as long as the latter cannot forbid him doing so

132. Cf. the poem "In the Mountains," *CW* 14, 1[105].

133. *into a purple . . . me?] Pm*: a purple night around me, I sank into it, I'm drowning — everything is a roaring plunging ⟨sea⟩ around me, through me, in me — yes even the sea is in me, yes I myself have turned into this purple night

134. *heart?] Crossed out after this*: What shudder and dizziness darken the radiant eye?

135. *perform . . . avoid] Pm*: avoid, yet not without transforming his leap into an entrechat

136. *Fragmentary version N V 7, 83*: cowardly and yet not capable of suppressing a malicious act if it was witty — — — Rousseau said in such a case, who was not the man to suppress a joke, not even *si fractus illabatur orbis* {if the world should break to pieces around him} — — — compliment — — —

137. Cf. *JSP* 24; 16[20].

138. Cf. 11[185].

139. Cf. 14[20].

140. *Juvenilia et Juvenalia]* {"Juvenilia" are the childhood writings of an author; "Juvenalia" are satires written in the style of the Roman writer Juvenal (Decimus Junius Juvenalis, 60?–127? CE.)}

141. *"too noble was he — — —]* {N is misquoting Eckermann's *Conversations with Goethe,* 16 December 1828: "'Ja,' sagte Goethe, 'vornehm war er. Und bei all seiner Freiheit und Verwegenheit hat er sich immer in den Grenzen des Schicklichen zu halten gewußt, welches fast noch mehr sagen will.'" ("'Yes,' said Goethe, 'noble he was. And despite all his freedom and daring, he always knew how to stay within the borders of decency, which is nearly more telling.'")}

142. *"Much . . . see,"*] {Part of a line from August von Platen's poem "Die neuen Propheten" ("The new prophets"); cf. *Gesammelte Werke des Grafen August von Platen* ("Collected works of Count August von Platen"), vol. 3 (Stuttgart: Cotta, 1847), 14. The line also appears in Theodor Fontane's 1866 poem "Die Gardemusik bei Chlum" ("The guard music at Chlum").}

143. Cf. *JS* 342.

144. *Incipit tragoedia*] "The tragedy begins" {Cf. *JS* 342, the final section of the first edition of *JS*.}

145. *et hoc genus omne*] "and everything of this sort"

146. Cf. *JS* 276.

147. Cf. 21[3] no. 1.

148. Cf. *JS* 23; 11[134].

149. Cf. 11[306].

150. *at . . . Genoa.*] End of March 1882.

151. *lux mea crux / crux mea lux*] "the light is my cross / the cross is my light"

[13 = Copy of Emerson.]

1. *Copy of Emerson*] N possessed a copy of Ralph Waldo Emerson, *Versuche (Essays), aus dem Englischen von G. Fabricius* (Hanover: Carl Meyer, 1858) {Essays, translated from the English by G. Fabricius}, in which he wrote all the fragments of this group, though not all are glosses on Emerson. {Quotations from Emerson's *Essays* below are taken from Emerson's English text and not translated from the German translation by Fabricius that appears in *KSA* 14.}

2. On the reverse side of the cover; cf. 11[317].

3. *the education . . . race*] {Allusion to the late work with this title (*Die Erziehung des Menschengeschlechts*, 1780) by Gotthold Ephraim Lessing.}

4. On the reverse side of the cover; cf. *JS* 154.

5. On the reverse side of the cover; cf. 11[304].

6. On the title page; cf. *JS* 12, 318; 12[67].

7. On the reverse side of the title page; cf. 11[65].

8. On the reverse side of the title page.

9. In the margin of p. 1; cf. *JS* 249.

10. At the bottom of p. 3.

11. In the margin of p. 25; cf. 17[18]; 13[22]; refers to the following passage {in "History," vol. 2, *Essays: First Series,* 18}: "As near and proper to us is also that old fable of the Sphinx, who was said to sit in the roadside and put riddles to every passenger. *If the man could not answer,* she swallowed him alive. If he could solve the riddle, the Sphinx was slain"; italics = underlined by N.

12. At the bottom of p. 105.

13. At the bottom of p. 108; cf. 12[17].

14. At the bottom of p. 119.

15. At the bottom of p. 203; probably refers to the following passage {in "The Over-Soul," vol. 2, *Essays: First Series,* 164}: "One mode of the divine teaching is the incarnation of the spirit in a form, — in forms, like my own. I live in society; with persons who answer to thoughts in my own mind, or express a certain obedience to the great instincts to which I live. I see its presence to them. I am certified of a common nature; and these other souls, these separated selves, draw me as nothing else can."

16. At the top of p. 205.

17. In the margin of p. 281; refers to the following passage {in "The Poet," vol. 3, *Essays: Second Series,* 8}: "Things admit of being used as symbols, because nature is a symbol, in the whole and in every part. Every line we can draw in the sand, has expression; and there is no body without its spirit or genius. *All form is an effect of character . . .*"; italics = underlined by N.

18. At the bottom of p. 344.

19. *15 October 1881]* {N's 37th birthday.}

20. At the bottom of p. 346.

21. At the bottom of p. 348.

22. On the {penultimate} blank page {mislocated in *KSA* 14}; cf. 16[9].

23. On the {penultimate} blank page {mislocated in *KSA* 14}; cf. 11[258].

24. *Attempts] Versuche* {I.e., "assays" or "essays" — N is taking his inspiration from the German title of Emerson's book.}

25. *"Unstable and fleeting"] "Unstet und flüchtig"* {Luther's German translation of Cain's self-description as "a fugitive and a vagabond" at Genesis 4:14.}

26. On the last blank page.

27. On the last blank page.; cf. 13[9]; 17[8].

[14 = M III 5.]

1. Cf. 12[14].

2. Originally a continuation of *Pd* for *JS* 337; cf. 12[24].

3. *Pd*: It is an entirely *new* situation — and it has its *sublimity*, for heroic humans! But no one has yet perceived it as such!

4. Cf. 12[1].

5. Cf. 16[21].

6. *it's as if . . . disgusted] Pd*: otherwise sailing and sea travel disgust me

7. Cf. 12[8].

8. Cf. *JS* 301; 12[26]; *Pd*: *This world* that concerns us, we have created! — Let us resign ourselves here!

9. Cf. 12[24].

10. Cf. 12[23].

11. Cf. *JS* 7.

12. Cf. *JS* 331; 12[44].

13. Cf. 12[34]; *Pd*: We seize things and plunder them for what is useful to us and leave the rest to others and to nature — hence our *excrements*. Our constant benevolence!

14. Cf. *JS* 108; *Pd*: In all things of nature and in our veneration, the God still lingers whom we have pronounced dead.

15. *Pd*: Any moment now the magnificent image of the human can awaken — the time is here. But we prevent it artificially — we *fear* the great and beautiful human like the Chinese.

16. Cf. 12[18].

17. *Pd*: Main principle: we have *degraded* the ordinary *indispensable*: even eating is base to us, because it is *necessary*. — Thus the "animalistic" is regarded as base by us, we want to be *more*. — Freedom of the will, indeed *arbitrariness* constitutes our feeling of the noble, which is why we hate all *fate* and believe we become *base* there.

18. Cf. *CW* 13, 10[A14]; *JS* 30.

19. Cf. *D* 362; *CW* 13, 8[52, 57]; *Pd*: the proud man *hates* to tremble: and takes revenge on whoever makes him tremble. Therefore cruel: he has the greatest joy in seeing the one who no longer

causes him to tremble, even if he inflicts the most degrading and painful things on him. — The proud man, as soon as he sees the possibility of taking revenge, *hates* what oppresses him. — There is an extraordinary quantity of pleasure in the world through cruelty: all who are misjudged, neglected, bored, who are proud, are cruel. All who are weak *want* compassion. This will is a sublimation of cruelty: our perception shared by others: hence a half misfortune, *socios habuisse malorum.* Idealized and **consequently** called good and beautiful: the cruelty of the poets, who compel us to suffer along with their experiences.

20. *socios habuisse malorum]* "misery loves company"; cf. Spinoza, *Ethics* IV, Prop. LVII, scholium: "*unde illud proverbium natum: solamen miseris socios habuisse malorum.*" {"whence comes the proverb: misery is easier when one is not alone."}

21. Cf. *JS* 14; 12[156].

22. *Sophocles . . . demon]* {Cf. *Antigone,* lines 781–800.}

23. *made . . . him] Pm*: in doing so was afraid of himself

24. Cf. *JS* 125; 12[66]; *Pd*: Where has God gone? Have we drunk up the sea

25. Cf. *JS* 125; 12[77].

[15 = M III 4a.]

1. Cf. *BGE* 24.

2. *ἀταραξία] ataraxia*; "emotional tranquility"

3. *res publica]* "republic"

4. Cf. 12[86].

5. *Pd*: It drives me to despair! Therefore *injustice* is needed by great humans! Otherwise they will not execute their plan if they do not take it more seriously.

6. *can.] Crossed out after this*: And if we should become "small men on this account: my friends, I wish |it is much| that we would become *men.*

7. Cf. *JSP* 38.

8. Cf. *DD* "The Sun Is Sinking"; *Pd*: The warm breath of the cliffs, on which the sun rested during the day.

9. *had rested] Le, Ms*: rested

10. *Pd*: just as it improves the taste of *maté* {"maté," a traditional South American tea-like beverage} if one drinks it *without looking at it.*

11. Cf. *JS* 1.

12. Cf. *JS* 302; *the addition crossed out by N in M III 4, 193*: Highest culture achieved heretofore ultimately admitted to itself, it seems, that the passion of knowledge — — —

13. *nil admirari]* "to admire nothing"; "to be surprised by nothing"

14. Cf. 12[79].

15. Cf. 12[76]; *JS* 337; *Pd*: Important! *The new drive is beginning*! Expresses itself unclearly, weakly, harmfully, afflicts the bad natures, acts like illness etc. — so that it is misjudged and *incorrectly* described, as if the tree had already grown out and bore blossoms and fruit! We can only *guess*, not *describe*!

16. *amor fati]* "love of fate" {Underlined by N. This is the first appearance of *amor fati* in N's writings.}

17. *beautifully . . . descent.] Pd*: well and beautifully as you can! Love it — then you will rise above the fate in it. Otherwise you are the slave!

18. *Pd*: Only the Pole Boscovich annihilated the prejudice of materiality — the two great opponents of *appearance*!

19. *both Poles]* Boscovich was not a Pole but a Dalmatian. {Cf. Roger Joseph Boscovich, *Philosophiæ Naturalis Theoria Redacta ad Unicam Legem Virium in Natura Existentium* ("Theory of natural philosophy reduced to the single law of forces that exist in nature") (Vienna: Bernard, 1759). *A Theory of Natural Philosophy*, trans. J. M. Child (Chicago: Open Court, 1922).}

20. *Pd*: Chamfort, before whose character and intellect a Mirabeau bowed in homage, and without whose closeness life meant little to him: "he is of my kind in mind and heart," said Mirabeau.

21. {For these references to Mirabeau, cf. his letters to Chamfort of 20 August and 10 November 1784, in *Œuvres complètes de Chamfort*, ed. P. R. Auguis (Paris: Chaumerot Jeune, 1825), 5:388, 418. N would have read these in Sébastien-Roch-Nicolas Chamfort, *Pensées — maximes — anecdotes — dialogues: Précédés de l'histoire de Chamfort par P.-J. Stahl* ("Thoughts — maxims — anecdotes

— dialogues : Preceded by a history of Chamfort by P.-J. Stahl") (Paris: Michel Lévy Frères, n.d.), 327, 350. *NL.*}

22. *business]* *Pd*: business (e.g., science)

23. *hair:]* *Pd*: to protect against insects

24. Cf. 12[96, 97].

25. *Pd*: The best human is simultaneously the most evil.

26. Cf. *JSP* 27; 16[15]

27. *"all . . . wells"]* Cf. Goethe's "Harzreise im Winter." {Goethe's poem "Winter Journey in the Harz" (1777) contains the lines: "Open the clouded gaze / To the thousand wells / Next to the thirsting one / In the desert." Cf. Johann Wolfgang von Goethe, "Harzreise im Winter," in *Goethe's sämmtliche Werke in vierzig Bänden* ("Goethe's collected works in forty volumes") (Stuttgart: J. G. Cotta, 1853), 2:51. *NL.*}

28. *Pd*: We hear its subtlest errors

29. *Pd*: Morality is the opponent of science — "these things do not concern us": Socrates already judged in this manner.

30. Cf. *JS* 95.

31. *Pd*: My task is perhaps: *deniaiser les savants* — they know not what they do and would not forgive themselves if they knew. *Quote from Stendhal?* {N underlines "*deniaiser les savants*"; no link to Stendhal has been located.}

32. *déniaiser les savants]* "disabuse the scholars"

33. *They . . . did]* {Cf. Luke 23:24.}

34. Cf. the poem "Desperate" 19[9]; *CW* 13, 10[B40]; *Pd*: I cannot stand to live next to someone who is always and repeatedly spitting — yet I could live next to a criminal. *Taste* is that much stronger. Formerly a thinking human being was just as disgusting.

35. Cf. 12[107].

36. *ad oculos]* "to the eyes"

37. *Pd*: The life of a toll collector, a cashier and all those who have to wait a long time without being able to occupy themselves better in the meantime (courtiers too) seems terrible to me.

38. Cf. 12[116].

39. Cf. *JS* 26; *Pd*: That there is an eternal sacred law "thou shalt not lie, thou shalt not kill" — in a world whose goodness consists precisely of lying and killing — is ridiculous.

40. {Cf. Exodus 20:13; Deuteronomy 5:17.}

41. *Pd*: I would not endure murder.

42. Cf. *JS* 26.

43. Cf. *JSP* 24; 16[11].

44. Cf. *Z* III "On Old and New Tablets" 11.

45. Cf. *JS* 45.

46. Cf. 12[129].

47. *non . . . sempiterna]* "no other life than this eternal one"

48. Cf. *JS* 45, 256; 12[154].

49. Cf. 12[118]; *BGE* 192.

50. Cf. *JS* 306; *Pd*: to give oneself a harder skin and nettle rash, as it were — Stoicism. Among women. — In the midst of a storm "it does not matter" "I do not matter" — we must have the tricks of the *different* schools of morality at hand.

51. Cf. *CW* 13, 7[37]; *Pd*: On dreams and flying — since I see poorly and my imagination considers much to be possible and is *accustomed to much*

52. *Corybants]* {priests or votaries of Cybele}

53. Cf. *JS* 339.

54. *Pd*: This small life has been (inherited) as the echo of a *great one* — — —

55. Cf. *JS* 31; *Pd*: merchants, what else —

56. Cf. *JS* 135; *Pd*: Jewish — gulf God human — moral

57. Cf. N to Peter Gast, 28 November 1881 {*KGB* III:1,144}.

58. *Gil Blas]* {Picaresque novel (1715–35) by Alain-René Lesage.}

59. *Carmen]* {Bizet's opera (1875), based on a novella by Mérimée.}

60. *Pd*: tragic joke and nonsense

61. *Pd*: Against the English: before *utile* spoke the language of prudence and reason, it had the language of affect, of madness, of horror.

62. *utile]* "useful"; "utility"

63. Cf. 12[76]; *Z* III "On Old and New Tablets" 11.

64. Cf. *JS* 167; Chamfort, *Pensées — maximes — anecdotes — dialogues* (Stahl), 32. "*Le secret du caractère de Chamfort est tout entier dans ces mots qu'il répétait souvent, dit Roederer: 'Tout homme qui, à quarante ans, n'est pas misanthrope, n'a jamais aimé les hommes.'*" {"The secret of Chamfort's character is contained entirely in the words that he would often repeat, said Roederer: 'All people

who are not misanthropes at age forty never loved human beings.'"
Cf. note 21 above.}

65. *pour . . . plaie.]* "to moralize in literature, the procedure
is always *to show the wound.*" {*montrer la plaie* is underlined by
N. Cf. *BGE* 204. The quote from Balzac also appears on p. 32 in
Stahl's introductory history of Chamfort, cited above. Stahl may
be paraphrasing remarks from Balzac's letter to Hippolyte Castille,
11 October 1846; cf. Honoré de Balzac, *Œuvres complètes,* vol. 22
(Paris: Calmann Lévy, 1886), 367.}

[16 = M III 6a.]

1. Cf. Chronicle of N's life in *CW* 19 and preface to the commentary to *JS* above, pp. 532–35.

2. *Continuation of "Dawn"]* {See the Translator's Afterword in
CW 8, 432–33; *JS* was originally conceived as a continuation of *D*;
cf. 532–33 above.}

3. Cf. *JSP* 4.

4. Cf. *JSP* 41.

5. *water.*"] {Cf. Psalms 42: "As the hart panteth after the water
brooks, so panteth my soul after thee, O God". Luther: "Wie der
Hirsch schreiet nach frischem Wasser / So schreiet meine Seele
Gott zu dir."}

6. Cf. *JSP* 44; 12[178].

7. Cf. *JSP* 5.

8. *If . . . us."]* Cf. Diogenes Laertius{, *De vitis philosophorum
libri X cum indice rerum* ("On the lives of the philosophers: Ten
books with an index of subjects"), vol. II, bks. VII–X (Lipsiæ:
C. Tauchnitz, 1833), vol. X, §§}123–24, pp. 234–35. *NL.* (Montinari's reference points to Diogenes Laertius's *Lives of Eminent
Philosophers,* trans. Pamela Mensch [New York: Oxford University
Press, 2018], bk. X: "Epicurus," p. 533: the gods "always favor their
own good qualities and embrace men who are like themselves, but
regard everything that is unlike them as alien.")}

9. Cf. 13[19].

10. Cf. *JSP* 26.

11. In *Pp* to *JS* as no. 268; then replaced. {Cf. *JSP* 24; 15[50].}

12. Cf. *JSP* 29.

13. Cf. *JSP* 32.

14. Cf. *JSP* 43.

15. Cf. *JSP* 27.

16. Original version of *JS* 127.

17. *fieri e nihilo]* "made out of nothing"

18. *Pd*: This man has a high regard for me: he considers it necessary to slander me. — The way he publicly misunderstands me proves to me that he has understood me only all too well.

19. Cf. *JS* 210; *Pd*: Ever [?] the father. Whoever exaggerates the industriousness of his father becomes ill.

20. Cf. *JSP* 24; 12[210]; 15[50].

21. Cf. *JS* 302; 12[129]; 14[5].

22. In *Pp* to *JS* as no. 335; later replaced

23. *belongings] Zubehöre* {Literally, "accessories" or "equipment," used in tandem with *belong*.}

[17 = M III 7.]

1. Excerpts from Emerson's *Essays*: cf. Group 13 {esp. note 1 above, p. 621}. These excerpts were first published by Eduard Baumgarten, *Das Vorbild Emersons in Werk und Leben Nietzsches* {"Emerson as a model in the work and life of Nietzsche"} (Heidelberg{: C. Winter,} 1957). The page references in the notes refer to N's copy of Emerson's *Essays*. {These are excerpts of a sort, but not verbatim, from Emerson's essays "History" and "Self-Reliance." They might more accurately be called paraphrases.}

2. Cf. *JS* 54.

3. P. 5. {Cf. vol. 2, *Essays: First Series,* "History," 5: "He hears the commendation, not of himself, but more sweet, of that character he seeks, in every word that is said concerning character, yea, further, in every fact and circumstance, — in the running river, and the rustling corn."}

4. P. 5. {Cf. vol. 2, *Essays: First Series,* "History," 5: "I have no expectation that any man will read history aright, who thinks that what was done in a remote age, by men whose names have resounded far, has any deeper sense than what he is doing to-day."

5. P. 5. {Cf. vol. 2, *Essays: First Series,* "History," 6: "He should see that he can live all history in his own person. He must sit

solidly at home, and not suffer himself to be bullied by kings or empires, . . ."

6. Pp. 6–7. {Cf. vol. 2, *Essays: First Series,* "History," 6–7: "We are always coming up with the emphatic facts of history in our private experience, and verifying them here. All history becomes subjective; in other words, there is properly no History; only Biography. Every mind must know the whole lesson for itself — [All inquiry into antiquity . . .] is the desire to do away this wild, savage and preposterous There and Then, and introduce in its place the Here and the Now."}

7. *mind]* {It is worth noting that Fabricius translates Emerson's "mind" with *Seele* ("soul").}

8. P. 10. {Cf. vol. 2, *Essays: First Series,* "History," 9: "how changed when as Isis in Egypt she meets Osiris-Jove, a beautiful woman with nothing of the metamorphosis left but the lunar horns as the splendid ornament of her brows."}

9. P. 12. {Cf. vol. 2, *Essays: First Series,* "History," 10: "A painter told me that nobody could draw a tree without in some sort becoming a tree;"}

10. P. 12. {Cf. vol. 2, *Essays: First Series,* "History," 10: "the artist attains the power of awakening other souls to a given activity."}

11. P. 13. {Cf. vol. 2, *Essays: First Series,* "History," 10–11: "Santa Croce and the Dome of St. Peter's are lame copies after a divine model. [. . .] The true poem is the poet's mind; the true ship is the ship-builder. In the man, could we lay him open, we should see the reason for the last flourish and tendril of his work;"}

12. P. 14. {Cf. vol. 2, *Essays: First Series,* "History," 11: "A lady with whom I was riding in the forest said to me that the woods always seemed to her to *wait,* as if the genii who inhabit them suspended their deeds until the wayfarer had passed onward;"}

13. P. 15. {Cf. vol. 2, *Essays: First Series,* "History," 12: "In these caverns, already prepared by nature, the eye was accustomed to dwell on huge shapes and masses, so that when art came to the assistance of nature it could not move on a small scale without degrading itself."}

14. *Caverns]* {This paraphrase is from Emerson's quote of A. H. L. Heeren, *Historical Researches into the Politics, Intercourse, and Trade of the Carthaginians, Ethiopians, and Egyptians* (trans. from the German), vol. 1 (London: D. A. Talboys, 1838).}

15. P. 15. {Cf. vol. 2, *Essays: First Series*, "History," 12: "No one can walk in a road cut through pine woods, without being struck with the architectural appearance of the grove, especially in winter, when the barrenness of all other trees shows the low arch of the Saxons. In the woods in a winter afternoon one will see as readily the origin of the stained glass window, with which the Gothic cathedrals are adorned, in the colors of the western sky seen through the bare and crossing branches of the forest. Nor can any lover of nature enter the old piles of Oxford and the English cathedrals, without feeling that the forest overpowered the mind of the builder [. . .]"}

16. P. 13. {Cf. vol. 2, *Essays: First Series*, "History," 13: "Or perhaps his facility is deeper seated, in the increased range of his faculties of observation, which yield him points of interest wherever fresh objects meet his eyes. [. . .] this intellectual nomadism, in its excess, bankrupts the mind through the dissipation of power on a miscellany of objects. The home-keeping wit, on the other hand, is that continence or content which finds all the elements of life in its own soil; and which has its own perils of monotony and deterioration, if not stimulated by foreign infusions."}

17. P. 18. {Cf. vol. 2, *Essays: First Series*, "History," 14: "it would be impossible for such eyes to squint and take furtive glances on this side and on that, but they must turn the whole head."}

18. P. 20. {Cf. vol. 2, *Essays: First Series*, "History," 16: More than once some individual has appeared to me with such negligence of labor and such commanding contemplation, a haughty beneficiary begging in the name of God . . ."}

19. P. 23. {Cf. vol. 2, *Essays: First Series*, "History," 17: "a discontent with the believed fact that a God exists, and a feeling that the obligation of reverence is onerous. It would steal if it could the fire of the Creator, and live apart from him and independent of him."}

20. P. 24. {Cf. vol. 2, *Essays: First Series*, "History," 18: "When the gods come among men, they are not known."}

21. P. 25 {see the note to 13[9]}; cf. 13[9, 22].

22. P. 29. {Cf. vol. 2, *Essays: First Series*, "History," 22: "A man shall be the Temple of Fame. He shall walk, as the poets have described that goddess, in a robe painted all over with wonderful events and experiences;"}

23. P. 32. {Cf. vol. 2, *Essays: First Series,* "Self-Reliance," 27.}

24. P. 33. {Cf. vol. 2, *Essays: First Series,* "Self-Reliance," 27.}

25. P. 33. {Cf. vol. 2, *Essays: First Series,* "Self-Reliance," 27–28: "There is a time in every man's education when he arrives at the conviction that envy is ignorance; that imitation is suicide; that he must take himself for better for worse as his portion; that though the wide universe is full of good, no kernel of nourishing corn can come to him but through his toil bestowed on that plot of ground which is given to him to till."}

26. P. 34. {Cf. vol. 2, *Essays: First Series,* "Self-Reliance," 28: "We but half express ourselves, and are ashamed of that divine idea which each of us represents. It may be safely trusted as proportionate and of good issues, so it be faithfully imparted, but God will not have his work made manifest by cowards. A man is relieved and gay when he has put his heart into his work and done his best; but what he has said or done otherwise shall give him no peace. It is a deliverance which does not deliver. In the attempt his genius deserts him; no muse befriends; no invention, no hope."}

27. P. 35. {Cf. vol. 2, *Essays: First Series,* "Self-Reliance," 28–29: "That divided and rebel mind, that distrust of a sentiment because our arithmetic has computed the strength and means opposed to our purpose, these have not. Their mind being whole, their eye is as yet unconquered, and when we look in their faces we are disconcerted. Infancy conforms to nobody; all conform to it; [. . .] He cumbers himself never about consequences, about interests; he gives an independent, genuine verdict. You must court him; he does not court you."}

28. P. 36. {Cf. vol. 2, *Essays: First Series,* "Self-Reliance," 29: "Who can thus avoid all pledges and, having observed, observe again from the same unaffected, unbiased, unbribable, unaffrighted innocence, must always be formidable."}

29. P. 37. {Cf. vol. 2, *Essays: First Series,* "Self-Reliance," 30: "No law can be sacred to me but that of my nature. Good and bad are but names very readily transferable to that or this; the only right is what is after my constitution; the only wrong what is against it."}

30. P. 39. {Cf. vol. 2, *Essays: First Series,* "Self-Reliance," 31: "What I must do is all that concerns me, not what the people think. This rule, equally arduous in actual and in intellectual life,

may serve for the whole distinction between greatness and meanness. It is the harder because you will always find those who think
they know what is your duty better than you know it. [. . .] the
great man is he who in the midst of the crowd keeps with perfect
sweetness the independence of solitude."}

31. P. 41. {Cf. vol. 2, *Essays: First Series,* "Self-Reliance," 33:
"when the ignorant and the poor are aroused, when the unintelligent brute force that lies at the bottom of society is made to growl
and mow, it needs the habit of magnanimity and religion to treat
it godlike as a trifle of no concernment."}

32. P. 43. {Cf. vol. 2, *Essays: First Series,* "Self-Reliance," 34: "I
suppose no man can violate his nature. All the sallies of his will
are rounded in by the law of his being, as the inequalities of Andes
and Himmaleh are insignificant in the curve of the sphere. Nor
does it matter how you gauge and try him. A character is like an
acrostic or Alexandrian stanza; — read it forward, backward, or
across, it still spells the same thing."}

33. P. 44. {Cf. vol. 2, *Essays: First Series,* "Self-Reliance," 34–35:
"The force of character is cumulative. All the foregone days of
virtue work their health into this. What makes the majesty of the
heroes of the senate and the field, which so fills the imagination? The consciousness of a train of great days and victories
behind."}

34. P. 44. {Cf. vol. 2, *Essays: First Series,* "Self-Reliance," 35:
"Honor is venerable to us because it is no ephemera. It is always
ancient virtue. We worship it to-day because it is not of to-day."}

35. P. 45. {Cf. vol. 2, *Essays: First Series,* "Self-Reliance," 35: "a true
man belongs to no other time or place, but is the centre of things.
[. . .] Character, reality, reminds you of nothing else; it takes place
of the whole creation. The man must be so much that he must
make all circumstances indifferent. Every true man is a cause, a
country, and an age; requires infinite spaces and numbers and
time fully to accomplish his design; — and posterity seem to follow his steps as a train of clients."}

36. P. 47. {Cf. vol. 2, *Essays: First Series,* "Self-Reliance," 36–37: "The
world has been instructed by its kings, who have so magnetized the
eyes of nations. It has been taught by this colossal symbol the mutual

reverence that is due from man to man. The joyful loyalty with which men have everywhere suffered the king, the noble, or the great proprietor to walk among them by a law of his own, make his own scale of men and things and reverse theirs, pay for benefits not with money but with honor, and represent the law in his person, [. . .]"}

37. P. 50. {Cf. vol. 2, *Essays: First Series,* "Self-Reliance," 38–39: "history is an impertinence and an injury if it be any thing more than a cheerful apologue or parable of my being and becoming. [. . .] with reverted eye laments the past, or, heedless of the riches that surround him, stands on tiptoe to foresee the future. He cannot be happy and strong until he too lives with nature in the present, above time."}

38. P. 53. {Cf. vol. 2, *Essays: First Series,* "Self-Reliance," 40: "We do not yet see that virtue is Height, and that a man or a company of men, plastic and permeable to principles, by the law of nature must overpower and ride all cities, nations, kings, rich men, poets, who are not."}

39. P. 55. {Cf. vol. 2, *Essays: First Series,* "Self-Reliance," 41: "'What we love that we have, but by desire we bereave ourselves of the love.'"}

40. P. 54. {Cf. vol. 2, *Essays: First Series,* "Self-Reliance," 41: "But your isolation must not be mechanical, but spiritual, that is, must be elevation. At times the whole world seems to be in conspiracy to importune you with emphatic trifles. Friend, client, child, sickness, fear, want, charity, all knock at once at thy closet door and say, — 'Come out unto us.' But keep thy state; come not into their confusion. The power men possess to annoy me I give them by a weak curiosity. No man can come near me but through my act.'"}

41. P. 57. {Cf. vol. 2, *Essays: First Series,* "Self-Reliance," 43: "And truly it demands something godlike in him who has cast off the common motives of humanity and has ventured to trust himself for a taskmaster. High be his heart, faithful his will, clear his sight, that he may in good earnest be doctrine, society, law, to himself, that a simple purpose may be to him as strong as iron necessity is to others!"}

42. P. 57. {Cf. vol. 2, *Essays: First Series,* "Self-Reliance," 43: "Our housekeeping is mendicant, our arts, our occupations, our marriages, our religion, we have not chosen, but society has chosen for us. We are parlor soldiers. We shun the rugged battle of fate, where strength is born."}

[18 = Mp XVIII 3.]

   1. For this title, cf. 20[1].

   2. Cf. *JS* 198.

   3. Wer stolz ist, haßt sogar das Pferd,

Das seinen Wagen vorwärts fährt.

   4. *writing ball]* {N was an early adopter of this precursor to the typewriter, the Malling-Hansen Writing Ball (*Schreibkugel*), so named because of the way the keys were arranged. This poem was in fact typed with it.}

   5 Schreibkugel ist ein Ding gleich mir: von Eisen

Und doch leicht zu verdrehn zumal auf Reisen.

Geduld und Takt muss reichlich man besitzen

Und feine Fingerchen, uns zu benuetzen.

   6. Cf. N to Peter Gast, 4 March 1882 {*KGB* III:1, 174}.

   7. Hier rollte Gold hier spielte ich mit Golde —

In Wahrheit spielte Gold mit mir — ich rollte!

   8. Cf. the motto to the first edition of *JS* {which, although the wording is slightly altered, is this same quote from Emerson's essay "History" in vol. 2, *Essays: First Series,* 8: "To the poet, to the philosopher, to the saint, all things are friendly and sacred, all events profitable, all days holy, all men divine."}

   9. Cf. *JS* 259.

   10. „Gut und Böse sind die Vorurtheile

Gottes" — sprach die Schlange und floh in Eile.

   11. Cf. *JS* 258.

   12 So wie jeder Sieger spricht,

Sprichst du: „Zufall giebt es nicht."

Gestern sprachst du also nicht,

Niemand weiß was ihm geschicht.

[19 = M III 6b.]

   1. *Omnia . . . bona]* "All natural things are indifferent to someone who affirms them, for someone who denies or abstains from them, either bad or good."

   2. Mit Witzbolden ist gut zu witzeln:

Wer kitzeln will ist leicht zu kitzeln.

3. *Diogenes]* {Founder of Cynic philosophy, Diogenes was said to have lived for a time in a wine barrel.}

4 „Nothdurft ist wohlfeil, Glück ist ohne Preis:
Drum sitz' ich statt auf Gold auf meinem Steiß."

5. *Timon]* {Cf. *JS* 379; 5th c. BCE Athenian misanthrope featured in Attic comedies and Shakespeare's *Timon of Athens*.}

6. „Nicht zu freigebig: nur Hunde
scheißen zu jeder Stunde!"

7. Eine ernste Kunst ist Lachen
Soll ich's morgen besser machen,
Sagt mir: macht' ich's heute gut?
Kam der Funke stets vom Herzen?
Wenig taugt der Kopf zum Scherzen,
Glüht im Herzen nicht die Gluth.

Wagt's mit meiner Kost, ihr Esser!
Morgen schmeckt sie euch schon besser,
Und schon übermorgen — gut!
Wollt ihr dann noch mehr, so machen
Meine alten sieben Sachen
Mir zu sieben neuen Muth.

8. The third strophe is the *Sd* for *JSP* 6.

9. Das Leben gern zu leben
Mußt du darüber stehn!
Drum lerne dich erheben!
Drum lerne — abwärts sehn!

Den edelsten der Triebe
Veredle mit Bedachtung:
Zu jedem Kilo Liebe
Nimm Ein Gran Selbstverachtung!

Bleib nicht auf ebnem Feld,
Steig nicht zu hoch hinaus!
Am schönsten sieht die Welt
Von halber Höhe aus.

10. Cf. 15[39]; *CW* 13, 10[B40].

11. *Its mouth . . . gold.] Trägt nicht Gold im Munde.* {The German proverb *Morgenstund trägt Gold im Mund* (literally, "The morning hour bears gold in its mouth"; figuratively, "the early bird catches the worm") is based on the Latin "*aurora habet aurem in ore.*"}

12 Fürchterlich sind meinem Sinn
Spuckende Gesellen!
Lauf' ich schon, wo lauf' ich hin?
Spring' ich in die Wellen?

Alle Münder stets gespitzt,
Gurgelnd alle Kehlen,
Wand und Boden stets bespritzt —
Fluch auf Speichelseelen!

Lieber lebt' ich schlecht und schlicht
Vogelfrei auf Dächern,
Lieber unter Diebsgezücht,
Eid- und Ehebrechern!

Fluch der Bildung, wenn sie speit!
Fluch dem Tugendbunde!
Auch die reinste Heiligkeit
Trägt nicht Gold im Munde.

13. *Nausicaa Songs] Pm*: Maiden Song

14. Gestern, Mädchen, ward ich weise,
Gestern ward ich siebzehn Jahr: —
Und dem gräulichsten der Greise
Gleich' ich nun — doch nicht auf's Haar!

Gestern kam mir ein Gedanke —
Ein Gedanke? Spott und Hohn!
Kam euch jemals ein Gedanke?
Ein Gefühlchen eher schon!

Selten, daß ein Weib zu denken
Wagt, denn alte Weisheit spricht:

Folgen soll das Weib, nicht lenken;
Denkt sie, nun, dann folgt sie nicht

Was sie noch sagt, glaubt' ich nimmer;
Wie ein Floh, so springt's, so sticht's!
„Selten denkt das Frauenzimmer,
Denkt es aber, taugt es nichts!"

Alter hergebrachter Weisheit
Meine schönste Reverenz!
Hört jetzt meiner neuen Weisheit
Allerneuste Quintessenz!

Gestern sprach's in mir, wie's nimmer
In mir sprach — nun hört mich an:
„Schöner ist das Frauenzimmer,
Interessanter ist — der Mann!"
15. Arrangement for *JS*.
16. Arrangement for *JS*.
17. Takt als Anfang, Reim als Endung,
Und als Seele stets Musik:
Solch ein göttliches Gequiek
Nennt man Lied. Mit kürzrer Wendung,
Lied heißt: „Worte als Musik".

Sinnspruch hat ein neu Gebiet:
Er kann spotten, schwärmen, springen,
Niemals kann der Sinnspruch singen;
Sinnspruch heißt: „Sinn ohne Lied". —
Darf ich euch von Beidem bringen?
18. Cf. *JS* bk. 4.

[20 = M III 3a.]
   1. Cf. title of Notebook 18.
   2. *Mazzini*] {Giuseppe Mazzini; cf. 12[81].}

[21 = M III 2a.]

1. {On N's Polish origins, cf. *EH* "Why I Am So Wise" 3; N to Heinrich von Stein, beginning of December 1882 (*KGB* III:1, 287); N to Georg Brandes, 10 April 1888 (*KGB* III:5, 288); N to Jean Bourdeau (draft), ca. 17 December 1888 (*KGB* III:5, 533).}

2. *and . . . meantime.]* Cf. N to Peter Gast, Marienbad, 20 August 1880 {*KGB* III:1, 37: "Es *ist* die polnische Rasse, aber das Herz ist Gott weiß wohin gewandert." ("It *is* the Polish race, but God knows where its heart has wandered off to.")}

3. *simple veto]* {N refers here to the *liberum veto,* a parliamentary device in the Polish-Lithuanian Commonwealth (1648–1764) that gave any member of the legislature the right to call an end to the session and nullify any legislation that had been passed during the session.}

4. *the Pole Copernicus]* Cf. 15[21].

5. Classification of the notes in M III 1; N paginated this notebook, and the page numbers he entered into the classification refer to that pagination; in the following, N's data are deciphered{, with page numbers replaced by fragment numbers in Notebook 11}.

6. *Breeding . . . 72]* 11[96, 97, 276, 274, 186].

7. *Voluntary . . . 73b]* 11[70]; *JS* 131; cf. 11[125].

8. *Drive . . . 70]* 11[183].

9. *no. 11 note]* Refers to the two lines that appear below no. 11 below.

10. *The . . . 45.]* 11[262].

11. *No . . . 45.]* 11[119, 127].

12. *Preparation . . . p. 79.]* 11[338].

13. *Ways . . . 72]* 11[338, 147, 240, 158, 159, 160, 161, 187].

14. *Value . . . 11b.]* 11[20].

15. *state]* Zustand

16. *marriage 66]* 11[179].

17. *indifference 53]* 11[141].

18. *Prerequisite . . . 52b.]* 11[253].

19. *The . . . 56.]* 11[145].

20. *Witchcraft . . . 74.]* *JS* 250.

21. *Feeling . . . 66,]* 11[284]; *JS* 119.

22. *Cause . . . 34b.]* *JS* 112.

23. *Lasciviousness . . . 40]* 11[114].

24. *Scientific . . . 38.]* 11[99, 109].

25. *Evil . . . 37b.]* 11[101, 279].

26. *Elements . . . 32.]* 11[87].

27. *Taste . . . 40.]* 11[112, 113].

28. *The . . . 43b]* 11[266].

29. *All . . . 44.]* 11[243, 122, 124].

30. *We . . . 50.]* 11[263, 135, 136].

31. *Protoplasm . . . 58.]* 11[128, 134, 241].

32. *Our . . . 46.]* 11[130].

33. *Freedom . . . 47.]* 11[131].

34. *the . . . 48.] JS* 113.

35. *Cure . . . 49b]* 11[258].

36. *The . . . 59b]* 11[246].

37. *Beware . . . 71b] JS* 109; 11[157, 205].

38. *Now . . . 56.]* 11[144].

39. *History . . . 56.]* 11[146].

40. *Incorporation . . . 62.]* 11[171, 162].

41. *How . . . 71,]* 11[226, 185].

42. *An . . . 72.]* 11[163, 172, 187].

43. *Against . . . 66.]* 11[180].

44. *Wagner's . . . 66.] JS* 99.

45. *The . . . 73.]* 11[182, 189].

46. *the . . . 73.]* 11[201].

47. *Unegoistic 74b]* 11[199].

48. *the . . . 76.]* 11[198].

49. *actio in distans]* "action at a distance"

50. *Chaos sive Natura]* {Cf. 11[197] and note.}

51. *Chaos . . . 23a.]* 11[204, 199, 211, 225]; *JS* 109; 11[60].

52. Cf. *JS* 308.

53. Cf. *JSP* 28.

54. Steh ich erst auf Einem Beine
Steh ich balde auch auf zweien

55. *Experience dangerous] Erfahrung fährlich* {*Erfahrung,* stem *fahr* from *fahren,* to move, travel, drive, vs. *fährlich,* archaic for *gefährlich,* dangerous; N may be suggesting a shared etymology, but erroneously: the verbs stemming from Old High German are not related in meaning.}

Afterword to *The Joyful Science*
Giorgio Colli

Each time one reads *The Joyful Science* it seems different, new, even though the thematics appear to be easily accessible and the language is clear and balanced, without distorted argumentation, without ambiguity. Perhaps it is the distance of a convalescent, the absence of invectives — anyone who inveighs is not joyful, he is sick — that confuses the reader. A hard, polemic stress immediately clarifies the author's purpose and nails down the interpretation firmly and unequivocally.

In *Joyful Science* all of Nietzsche's contradictions can be detected, yet here their effect is neither conspicuous nor offensive, indeed, they scarcely seem to be contradictions. One example among many: in a different text Nietzsche thunders with great persistence against the concept of "appearance" among metaphysicians and simultaneously develops his own conception of the world as a lie, hence as something very similar to "appearance." If one reads aphorism 54 of *Joyful Science*, one finds this crass antinomy softened in a higher, contemplative, clearer view, absent any animosity.

In fact, this book is "central" in Nietzsche's life, not merely in the external sense of occupying a midpoint within his literary production, but also more subtly, insofar as it takes its place among his writings as a magical moment of balance, as the sole experience of complete "health"; all the extremes are present, to be sure, but they are bound together without tension, kept under control and free of any fanaticism. And Nietzsche knew very well that for him fanaticism — or more precisely, the irresistible urge to infinitely intensify personal viewpoints, to deploy thoughts from the blue as murderous weapons — was a sign of illness.

The Joyful Science is "central" also with respect to the juxtaposition of art and science. Nietzsche's uninterrupted passion for this theme reflects the inner struggle between his antithetical callings — and each work to date betrayed the respective outcome of this struggle. Now, on the other hand, even the title suggests a new solution: The inner struggle — an alternative expression for "illness" — does not lead to shutting down either of the two opponents (to suppress or to smother a vitally important part of himself would really not be any kind of convalescence); instead, it leads to a transfigured sphere of coexistence. This is genuine "health": to be poet and scientist in one and to practice a science that is not merely sullen and stiff, but even not always in the least serious. Already in *Human, All Too Human* Nietzsche had suggested an intuitive science, yet at the expense of deeper inner damage to and damnation of art, which nonetheless corresponded more than anything else with his nature. That was not convalescence, and it is no accident that now the new — "joyful" — science is announced, proven or even equated with verses.

For these reasons *The Joyful Science* possesses virtually reformative character; it is Nietzsche's most successful attempt at philosophical communication. Nietzsche positions himself vis-à-vis science as a philosopher, and as a philosopher he opposes art, but at the same time he rejects the past of philosophy and the language of his past. Philosophy no longer exists, but philosophers must continue to exist: They will no longer speak in these concepts about these contents, but they will have to speak in a new way by divesting the survivors, science and art, of their instruments of communication and using them as philosophers. Here, too, an example may be helpful: Consider aphorism 49 on magnanimity. "To me the magnanimous

[. . .] seems to be a human being of the most extreme thirst for revenge, for which a satisfaction is close at hand, and who drinks it so copiously, thoroughly and to the last drop *already in his imagination,* that a tremendously rapid disgust follows this rapid dissipation — he [. . .] forgives his enemy, indeed blesses and honors him" (p. 75). Here the object to be defined is not typical for the philosophical tradition — even though already in Aristotle magnanimity has a complicated relationship with a powerful will — but it is also understood that it is up to the philosopher to occupy himself with this problem. To possess direct knowledge of "great souls" does not of course belong to the experience of the scientist, but the method used by Nietzsche is that of science: In the face of an anomalous human behavioral pattern, such as that of the magnanimous, it becomes a matter of discovering the reason for this anomaly. Certainly this science is "joyful," that is, it shows a preferred interest here as elsewhere in extraordinary individuals and extraordinary behavioral patterns; conversely, the "serious" aspect of science is missing — the abundance of experience and the required industriousness for accumulating it, the research into the average behavioral patterns and the search for norms, the caution and reserve in positing hypotheses. The fragility of this heretofore undescribed balance between science and art, its difficult conquest and simultaneously the impossibility of escaping this opposition, can nonetheless only be properly evaluated when one considers what each newly conquered insight means for Nietzsche in terms of emotion and life experience. If for him sobriety and purity of knowing are more desirable than anything to which his artistic inclination can spur him, why then did he not finish this problem already in *Human, All Too Human?* Decisive for this is Nietzsche's own testimony on the nature of his experience of knowledge: It is always and everywhere associated with agony, fear, and consternation. In his youth, the arduous discipline of philological knowledge was juxtaposed with the ecstasy of musical experience. Then came the period of the *Birth of Tragedy,* and Nietzsche characterized as knowledge, as truth, the disruptive Dionysian intuition of the horror-inducing root of our existence. The conquest of further knowledge followed: history as the making-aware of human errors and horrors, as the disclosure that the past weighs upon us with an irreconcilable sum of blows of fate — and that the study of this past extinguishes life and blunts our creative energy; and science ultimately shrinks that which seems great, relativizes judgments, thwarts consolation.

This for Nietzsche is knowledge; and in his heart this dispenser of suffering is the most powerful demon — so powerful that he now asserts: "*Life as a means to knowledge*" (§324, p. 189). From time to time Nietzsche pursues a new form of knowledge, perhaps in the hope of finding one with softer features. And in doing so, in the end he quite to the contrary stumbles upon the thought of eternal recurrence (§341), upon a truth more terrifying than any other. The past of humanity, composed of sacrilege and fear, is not only irreconcilable and will never yield its place to a future of joy, but it is also destined to recur eternally and remain constantly the same. Thus Nietzsche once again approaches art; he resolves not to completely smother his other calling. He no longer waits to find a truth that does not crush, and as for the joy of knowledge that is more than an ecstatic flash of lightning — this he now dispenses with.

This is not to claim that these considerations might have contributed to making the cheerfulness and the sovereign, utterly weightless hovering of *Joyful Science* more accessible. Nietzsche is a philosopher, already on the basis of the mastery with which he handles abstract concepts and weaves together universalities in unexpected ways: Yet what distinguishes him and reveals his extraordinary artistic talent is the shimmering mutability of the magmatic material from which each of his universalities recomposes itself again and again. And his abstract concepts conceal different content behind the same name at every opportunity.

The Joyful Science appeared in 1887 in a second edition. Nietzsche added the preface, the fifth book, and the "Songs of Prince Vogelfrei." Whereas the concluding book of the first edition, "Sanctus Januarius," achieves that previously indicated expressive zenith of a magical harmony, the later additions no longer succeed in maintaining this extremely sensitive balance. One should compare — as one example among many — aphorism 373, with its grim critique of science, with the earlier aphorism 293 that elegantly and insightfully promotes its appreciation.

Translator's Afterword

Adrian Del Caro

The Joyful Science (*JS*) was published in August 1882, a mere thirteen months after the publication of *Dawn* (*D*), using aphorisms that Nietzsche had originally intended as a continuation of *D*. Mazzino Montinari speaks to the development of *JS* and the singular, momentous thought that preoccupied Nietzsche: "The *Joyful Science* was at first conceived by N as a continuation of *Dawn*. On {25} January 1882 {KGB III:1, 159} he communicated to Peter Gast: 'A few days ago I finished books VI, VII and VIII of "Dawn," and my work on it is done for the time being. For I want to reserve books 9 and 10 for next winter — I am not yet ripe enough for the elemental thoughts I want to present in these concluding books. Among them is one thought that in fact will require 'millennia' to *become* something. Where will I find the courage to utter it!'" (p. 532–33). Books VI, VII, and VIII became books 1–3 of *JS*; a ninth book did not have to wait until the next winter, for as Montinari explains, once Nietzsche met Lou Salomé in April 1882, he resolved to proceed with the publication of *JS* as soon as possible, the fourth and final book of *JS*, at least for the first edition, having been organized from previously written aphorisms in February 1882.[1] So the momentous thought was in fact revealed as part of the overall scope of

---

1. Cf. Montinari's prefatory note to *JS* above, p. 533, and Curt Paul Janz, *Friedrich Nietzsche: Biographie*, 3 vols. (Munich: Carl Hanser Verlag, 1978), 2:105. All citations from Janz will be from the second volume.

JS, even though, as Montinari points out, it makes its appearance only once as aphorism 341 at the conclusion of book 4.

The biographer Curt Paul Janz describes how the thought of eternal recurrence affected Nietzsche personally and how he suppressed it, at least until he found someone with whom to properly share it. "Nietzsche immediately felt the burden that was apportioned to him with this thought. It also remained completely foreign to him, he struggled with it for months to come. But this he had to accomplish on his own, which is why there are still no direct mentions at all in his letters of what is growing inside him, apart from observations that are kept quite general. Only in summer 1882 did he speak to Lou Salomé about it and then only to her."[2] We can infer from Janz's assessment that Montinari was correct in attributing agency to Salomé for Nietzsche's decision to publish *JS.*

As for the other published text in this volume, *Idylls from Messina* (*IM*), Janz explains that some of the poems under this title were begun already in Genoa in March 1882, then revised and supplemented with others in Messina, where he stayed for a few weeks beginning in March; Nietzsche published them in the new monthly periodical *Internationale Monatsschrift* in the June issue, despite his earlier decision to reject the editor's invitation for material.[3] Janz also points out that *IM* represents the only time Nietzsche published his poetry independently, that is, as separate from his philosophical books (107). Later, in 1887, Nietzsche used six of the eight *Idylls* for the second edition of *JS,* whose new content included a preface, a fifth "book," and a lyrical appendix called "Songs of Prince Vogelfrei."

2. Janz, *Friedrich Nietzsche,* 80.

3. Janz suggests that one reason N originally declined to contribute to the monthly was Schmeitzner's anti-Semitism, or at least that of his readers and contributors; pp. 107, 104–5. Cf. also my Afterword in *CW* 16, where I describe N's lawsuit to free his earlier books from the Schmeitzner publishing house. Janz further speculates that N may have chosen Messina in late March, despite the extreme heat further north that had already driven him out of Genoa, for the purpose of "bumping into" Wagner who was living in Palermo and sojourning in Messina (98).

From spring 1881 to July 1882, Nietzsche spent his summers in Sils-Maria, a mountain village in southeastern Switzerland, and the winter in Genoa. From May to July 1881, he stayed in the Swiss town of Recoaro with his friend and disciple Heinrich Köselitz (aka Peter Gast); we can probably count this among Nietzsche's many experiments to find a suitable location for his delicate health (Janz, *Friedrich Nietzsche*, 70–71). In February and March 1882, he hosted a visit in Genoa from his friend Paul Rée, a writer with interests very similar to Nietzsche's, author of *Der Ursprung der moralischen Empfindungen* (*The Origin of Moral Sensations*; 1877), who would soon become his rival over the affections of Lou Salomé (Janz, *Friedrich Nietzsche*, 93). When Genoa became too sultry for him in March 1882, he suddenly booked passage on a freighter to Messina, where he stayed until late April when he joined Rée and Salomé at the home of their friend Malwida von Meysenbug in Rome. For a few weeks in summer 1882, Nietzsche stayed with his sister and mother in their hometown of Naumburg, Germany, where he and his sister prepared the *Pm* of *JS* and sent it to the publisher in installments (cf. 533). This period of his life, spent mostly in Sils-Maria and Genoa, with shorter sojourns in Recoaro, Messina, Rome, and Naumburg, was a relatively happy and extremely productive time, shared with his closest friends, his beloved sister, and for a few months beginning in late April, with Lou Salomé as well. During this period Nietzsche remained close to his friend Franz Overbeck, a professor of Church history at Basel, but they only exchanged letters. In terms of health, Nietzsche suffered especially from July to October 1881 from severe migraines (Janz, *Friedrich Nietzsche*, 75). After 1882 Nietzsche would no longer count Paul Rée among his friends; his impulsive plan to marry Lou Salomé became a disaster; and his relationship with his sister would never be the same owing to her meddling role in the Nietzsche-Salomé affair.

D had already represented a new style for Nietzsche, one influenced by a geographical as well as physical and psychic balance that enabled Nietzsche to write, and this balance of course extends to *JS* because the latter work was originally conceived of as a continuation of *D*. Janz gives us the precise geographical coordinates of Nietzsche's new, successful style and explains how they were leveraged by him: "An impressionistic feature comes into his descriptions, the austere chains of thought are loosened again and again by landscape elements, by landscape picturesque. Here two landscapes predominate as inspiration: mountains and sea" (61–62). Even in Genoa, Nietzsche learned to make the most of his isolation, enhancing his aloof, anonymous existence in the city with extended hikes along the coast (64). By winter of 1881/82, Nietzsche enjoyed "the consciousness of having a task, indeed a mission, namely to proclaim a new philosophy" (108–9). *JS* signals the arrival of this new philosophy, motivated as it is by the thought of the eternal recurrence that Nietzsche first registered in his notebook in August 1881 (cf. 11[141]). He had reached a plateau in terms of productivity, companionship, and vistas to the future; as difficult as the *JS* period was in matters of physical health, this would be the calm before the storm, as Nietzsche's life would become considerably more complicated — his existence would in fact be shattered by what was to come in 1882.

JS leads with "Jokes, Cunning and Revenge: Prelude in German Rhymes," a collection of sixty-three brief lyrical sketches ranging from two to ten lines, each of them numbered and titled. The poems owe their title to an opera libretto published by Goethe in 1790 but never set to music during his lifetime (cf. *JSP* note 1, 539). Nietzsche's friend and disciple Peter Gast, who was a composer, first set this text to music in 1880. The title and subtitle of the prelude therefore signal clearly and somewhat brazenly that Nietzsche's new book lays claim to a rich cultural tradition fed by the ingenuity of Germany's greatest poets, indeed of its acknowledged innovator Johann Wolfgang von Goethe. The book's title is based on the ancient Provençal phrase *gaya scienza*, gay or joyful science, a term used by the troubadours of the twelfth to fourteenth centuries to describe their poetry. In *Ecce Homo* (*EH*) Nietzsche explained that the notion of *gaya scienza* is reminiscent of "that union of *singer, knight* and *free spirit* which raises that wonderful early Provençal culture above all ambivalent cultures" (*EH* "Books" *JS, CW* 9, 276–77). Nietzsche is therefore at his romantic best in launching his book under the banner of romanticism's chief cultural inspiration, the Middle Ages, while *modernizing* the concept of joyful science after the model of Germany's greatest modern poet-scientist, Goethe. A fusion of "singer, knight, and free spirit" informs Nietzsche's view of philosophizing and supplies the energy for his critical investigations — we cannot treat the poetry in which *JS* is encased as though it were merely ornamental.

Yet this tendency to dismiss Nietzsche's poetry has clouded our view of him as a philosopher and a poet. The ancient rivalry between philosophy and poetry is engaged by *JS* not in the jealous, competitive terms established by Plato in the *Republic* but in a playful agonistic spirit in which these two archetypal forces of culture are reconciled in Nietzsche's most balanced, most poised book. In his milestone treatment of Nietzsche's poetry, Phillip Grundlehner argues that there are several reasons for neglecting Nietzsche's poetry, perhaps foremost among them the fact that "[m]ost of his poems are either found as introductions or appendices to his prose works or were written in conjunction with *Zarathustra*."[4] Supposing that most readers approach Nietzsche in the first place for his prose, it is fair to conclude that the lyrical apparatus is frequently discarded or ignored. Or, consider the hermeneutic fate of *Thus Spoke Zarathustra* (*Z*), the most lyrical of all Nietzsche's works — its philosophical content has labored for generations to emerge from the self-imposed lyricality of its style — the brilliance and folly of *Z* are masked, obscured, refracted by the Dionysian lyricality with which Nietzsche infused this book. The lyrical bridge to *JS* must be crossed, however, both because Nietzsche

4. Philip Grundlehner, *The Poetry of Friedrich Nietzsche* (New York: Oxford University Press, 1986), xi.

constructed this bridge as the prelude to the prose and because the title signals an alliance between poetry and philosophy, music and science, play and purpose.

Grundlehner also cites two more important reasons for why Nietzsche's poetry has been neglected; he himself attacked poetry "during all phases of his development,"[5] helping to diminish the regard in which any reader might hold the poems; add to this the tendency of interpreters to view his poetry as "principally a manifestation of his homeless and mentally unstable state."[6] The frequent attacks on poetry and poets I would ascribe to the antiromantic critique that accompanies Nietzsche's career after *The Birth of Tragedy* (*BT*); the fault line that I have designated as "Nietzsche contra Nietzsche" is most apparent when the critical writer Nietzsche struggles with the lyrical writer whom he would condemn as "romantic" and therefore "sick."[7] When these two opposing forces are reconciled or in equilibrium, as they are in *JS,* I argue that Nietzsche is at his romantic best.

Arguing thus for the merit of his poetry is not to seek an equivalency between the poems and the prose, even when they are so conspicuously juxtaposed as in *JS.* For one thing, poetry and prose remain two very different media, the former expressing itself musically, the latter expressing itself cognitively. Nietzsche wants us to engage cognitively with the five prose books of *JS,* but he insists that we immerse ourselves first, and finally, in the musicality of the poetry that frames the book. Nor should we assert that the spirit of lyricality is limited to the poems themselves — the prose is "set up" by the music and sustained by it — not to the greater extent that we observe in *Z,* to be sure, but sufficiently to demonstrate the nuance of a "joyful" science versus the normative view of science that privileges the slow (§231) and the solemn (§327). Finally, we would

5. Grundlehner, *Poetry of Friedrich Nietzsche,* xii.

6. Grundlehner, *Poetry of Friedrich Nietzsche,* xii.

7. Adrian Del Caro, *Nietzsche Contra Nietzsche: Creativity and the Anti-Romantic* (Baton Rouge: Louisiana State University Press, 1989).

err in "only" hearing musicality in the poems; the rhythm of their delivery does not distract from the message; indeed, in some cases, the poems are as charged and pregnant as any of Nietzsche's better aphorisms. The value of Grundlehner's study lies in the philosophical contextualization of the individual poems, most of which are far more profound than they appear. While Grundlehner does not attempt to capture the rhythm, rhyme, and lyricality of the poems, preferring instead to render them as prose, his approach has the advantage of demonstrating how Nietzsche delivered his philosophical message over time in two separate but related registers.

The first poem is appropriately titled "Invitation," in which Nietzsche addresses his readers personally by inviting them not only to break bread *with* him, but more specifically, to sample what he has cooked up. The argument is that partaking will be worth the risk and the food will taste better the more we think about it; these are hallmarks of the aphoristic style that characterize his writing, whereby the thought inoculates and energizes a reader. It is significant that Nietzsche refers to his book as food, inasmuch as his physiological, bodied approach to issues invites holistic engagement, not merely the operation of cognition. The poem's second half refers to the internal process by which Nietzsche generates his ideas. If his diners wish for further helpings or perhaps new dishes, he will revisit his familiar belongings (German *"meine sieben Sachen,"* literally, his seven possessions) and find inspiration in them for seven more creations. The poem has pace, rhythm, a tight rhyme scheme, humility, and a personal touch — readers are told at the outset that this is Nietzsche's fare, he is the chef of what he serves up, and he is apparently an acquired taste. The notion that thoughts or ideas should be nourishing, sustaining, bracing, *tasty*, and tasteful is classic Nietzsche — the feast here is not limited to the eyes.

Section 23 "Interpretation" is motto-like in its brevity, but it, too, sheds light on the special, kinetic relationship Nietzsche wishes to establish with his reader. The verbs with which he puns in line one are *auslegen* (to interpret) and *hineinlegen* (to insert), which I have replaced with "read" and "read into" in order to preserve the meter; admittedly, it is difficult for anyone to interpret himself without reading into himself, since objectivity is lacking. However, Nietzsche is no nihilist in matters of interpretation; if he cannot serve as his own interpreter, his usefulness to others lies in helping them to climb of their own accord, such that on arriving in the higher, brighter sphere, they will find Nietzsche's image there too — ideally as a function of their having interpreted him. This tiny poem resounds with Zarathustrian themes while serving as a metaphor for the kind of philosophical agency Nietzsche embodies (cf. also close cousins §§7, 25, 30, 33, 54).

Book I opens with a powerful, detailed meditation of philosophical historical interest, namely, "The teachers of the purpose of existence," but concludes with a suggestive, polemical sketch on personal happiness, "The craving for suffering" — despite appearances these frames are intimately related and illustrative of a key concern of this work, namely, happiness. Of particular interest is the skill with which Nietzsche unpacks the notion of purpose at the species level, in order to drive home the point that individuals are equally prone and susceptible to, equally shaped and informed by forces whose presence is undeniable yet ambiguous. If we were better equipped to recognize and affirm the forces that govern human existence, he argues, our own personal happiness would more likely rest on authentic grounds, without much of the storm and stress that exhausts us individually when we engage pointless battles.

The singular task of all people, he claims, is "[t]o do what promotes the preservation of the human species" (36). There is no motivation here, only instinct that constitutes "*the essence* of our species and herd." Under the compulsion of this primal force, "[e]ven the most harmful human being is perhaps still the most useful with respect to the preservation of the species," giving rise to the formulation that what is called "evil" is merely part of "the amazing economy of species preservation."

He calls this an "amazing" economy because it includes elements that we are loath to ascribe to economy of any kind, but also because the species proves resourceful in thriving under adverse conditions described as "foolish, wasteful and costly." This unlikely "economy" leading to species preservation governs in all human beings, the base and the refined, "but breaks forth from time to time as reason and passion of the spirit; it then has a brilliant retinue of grounds around it and wants with all its might to make us forget that in its ground it is drive, instinct, folly, groundlessness" (38). It is during an "outbreak" of reason that the powerful, blind drive of species preservation acquires its anthropomorphic trappings: "enter the ethical teacher as the teacher of the purpose of existence; for this he invents a second, different existence and by means of his new mechanism he lifts this old ordinary existence off its old ordinary hinges" (38). This second existence, call it simulacrum, shadow, echo, or teleological double, is the zone in which rational human beings are taught to dwell, with laughter becoming the first casualty — the sacrifice of the sense of humor, of absurdity that ordinarily obtains in nature, is demanded by the new seriousness of the moral teacher, whose priority is maintaining and propounding a "purpose" or meaning of existence. At this point in his opening section of *JS,* Nietzsche's reasoning is strongly reminiscent of the critique of reason in *BT,* as well as the later arguments from *On the Genealogy of Morality* (*GM*) (Third Treatise), in which morality "erupts" occasionally with pathological symptoms that only the priests (read: ethical teachers) can manage and control but can never cure. The problem of living under a "purpose of existence" is fraught: "The human being has gradually become a fantastic animal that has one more condition of existence to fulfill than every other animal: the human being *must* believe from time to time that it knows *why* it exists, its species cannot thrive without a periodic trust in life! Without faith in *reason in life*!" (39). Thus burdened with an existential challenge, humans navigate this "second existence" the best they can, but too often without the healing, flexing benefits of laughter, without what Nietzsche is now calling "joyful science." Our species labors to experience and enjoy happiness, given these strong headwinds in the form of reason, ethics, and purpose of existence.

Nietzsche affords us a closer look at the economy of species preservation and the accompanying problem of happiness under the strain of morality in §4 "What preserves the species." The argument here is reminiscent of *Human, All Too Human* (*HAH*) 224, "Refinement through degeneration," where Nietzsche lays out his famous inoculation theory — namely, a stable community needs occasional inoculation to ward off the natural stupidity that accompanies stable communities over time (cf. *CW* 3, 153–55). Here the emphasis is on evil as the key ingredient of species preservation: "The strongest and evilest minds have so far carried humankind forward the most: again and again they ignited the sleeping passions — all orderly society lulls the passions to sleep" (42). The nature of this "evil" is not metaphysical, not morally determined; rather, "[t]he new, however, is under all circumstances the *evil,* as that which wants to conquer, to throw down the old boundary markers and the old pieties; and only the old is the good!" This important distinction underscores the inevitability of evil while at the same time reinforcing that resisting it is a predictable but unnatural response — not unlike the creation of a "second existence" under the tutelage of ethical teachers. Nietzsche uses the metaphor of continuously planted soil to elaborate his point: "The good human beings of every period are those who dig the old thoughts deep into the ground and bear fruit with them, the plowmen of the spirit. But all land eventually becomes exhausted, and again and again the plowshare of evil must come." He takes issue with the "erroneous teaching of morality that is celebrated especially in England," whereby good is said to advance the species, while evil is said to harm it. Thus Nietzsche's critique of utilitarianism does not dispute the notion of expediency but lays the stress on precisely what should be regarded as expedient: "In truth however the evil drives are expedient, species-preserving and indispensable to exactly the same degree as the good: — only their function is different" (42). The inability to affirm the new would ultimately be lethal to the species, hence in §4 Nietzsche challenges us to reorient ourselves vis-à-vis the good/evil binary, implying that a proper balance of new and old, evil and good, might produce a happier human being than a surfeit of either one.

A similar plea for interrogating the logic and sway of the binary is found in §11 "Consciousness." The biggest quarrel Nietzsche appears to have with consciousness is its novelty and relative frailty compared to ancient, reliable instinct, judging as purely as possible from the standpoint of the organic: "Consciousness is the final and latest development of the organic and consequently also what is least finished and most impotent in it" (47). We take enormous pride in our consciousness, and properly so, insofar as this property distinguishes us from other animals, yet when viewing humankind within the context of the organic, we should be less trusting of consciousness; by treating it as "*the kernel* of human being, its enduring, eternal, ultimate, most original element," we are investing in our least known and least exercised property as if on faith, absent the kind of *awareness* and deliberation that properly defines consciousness: "Because humans have believed themselves to already have consciousness, they have expended little effort to acquire it — and even now the situation is no different!" (48). If the danger of consciousness has only been attenuated by the more powerful instincts, Nietzsche suggests, we must consider a recalibration, or at least, conducting an inventory of what we have incorporated as humans to date, "[t]he task is still an entirely new one, just now dawning on human eyes and still barely discernible, *the task of incorporating knowledge* and making it instinctive — a task that can only be seen by those who have grasped that heretofore only our *errors* have been incorporated and that all our consciousness refers to errors!" (48). This new, indeed inaugural, "incorporation of knowledge" would constitute a reliable improvement over the current anemic state of consciousness — it would place knowledge on a footing with instinct. At the very least, recalibrating our relationship with consciousness promises a future human being more attuned to instinct, more capable of incorporating knowledge (versus merely acquiring it as window dressing), more *conscious* of the force and potential of consciousness. The current imbalance favoring consciousness takes for granted that we have already attained an adequate level of consciousness, whereas according to Nietzsche we have barely begun the process; moreover, our tendency to gloat over consciousness as the crowning human achievement obscures the fact that consciousness is composed of errors.

Evil is the exclusive concern in §19 "Evil," where Nietzsche elaborates on how useful evil is in the strange economy of species preservation. This aphorism expands on §4, using a favorite tree metaphor with which we are asked to imagine how a tall, strong tree could ever grow into the heights without the adversity of "bad weather and storms" (54). The key ingredients to the *greatness* of the tree are adversity and resistance; challenged or beset by these forces, a tree drives its roots deeper and becomes stronger, more resistant. Translated entirely into the human sphere, Nietzsche asks "whether various kinds of hatred, envy, stubbornness, mistrust, harshness, avarice and violence do not belong among the *advancing* conditions without which a major growth even in virtue is scarcely possible." The litany of vices or evils here represents the adversity or resistance that compels the *exceptional* growth of the tree. We could of course imagine a society in which these vices did not exist or in which they were quite mild, barely impactful; but then it would be difficult to account for "great virtue" or "major growth" in virtue — great in comparison to what? Great as a result of having overcome what? The quip that concludes this aphorism of seven lines could serve as a maxim in itself: "The poison from which a weaker nature perishes is strengthening to the strong human — and he doesn't call it poison either."

Compare this maxim with *Twilight of the Idols* (*TI*), "Sayings and Arrows" §8: "*From life's school of war*: What does not kill me makes me stronger" (*CW* 9, 46). The benefit to humankind from resistance and suffering is vintage Nietzsche, a notion that accompanies his writings from *BT* to *TI,* a work of his latest period (autumn/winter 1888).

Neither maxim tells the whole story, of course. What does not kill me may in fact maim or weaken me to the point where my life is wretched, and only a heroic, defiant resolve on my part would render me "stronger," resulting in a "stronger" life in name only. Yet that seems to be at least part of the point in *JS* §19 — the strong man thrives under the effect of what the weaker man considers poison — "and he doesn't call it poison." A familiar lament in Nietzsche is how our moral tradition disregards or disparages natural states, things that we generally ascribe to "evil" and otherwise subject to calumny. Another part of the untold story is precisely the "weaker nature" who does not withstand the adversity of the poisons: Nietzsche has no plan or encouragement for these weaker natures; his focus is on the fostering and survival of the exceptional, the strong, the great. In any case, §19 argues again for embracing the stigmatized, adverse conditions as *favorable to life.* It is often unclear whether the strong in Nietzsche are synonymous with the happy. The individual who embraces the ethos of resistance, suffering, ennoblement, sublimation as illustrated in *JS* would have their fair share of misery, to be sure, yet Nietzsche implies that this "higher" and stronger style of living accords with authentic happiness because it is in balance with nature, because it nurtures itself, authentically and from the grassroots, from all things. This theme will be explored in depth in my analysis of book 4, where Nietzsche lays out the consequences of *amor fati,* or love of fate.

In the critique of consciousness (*JS* §11) Nietzsche concluded that owing to its novelty and unreliability in matters of species preservation, consciousness has thus far contributed to the incorporation of errors and therefore consists mainly of errors.

In §37 "Because of three errors," he lists Europe's major errors and offers one historical figure illustrative of each, as they have motivated the promotion of science in recent centuries. The point is not that science is undeserving of promotion; rather, our reasons for having promoted it are in error. There is merit in exploring how differently we might have developed historically if science had been supported or pursued for different reasons. Newton illustrates how "one hoped best to understand God's goodness and wisdom" (67); here science has clearly played a supporting role to theology. Voltaire, meanwhile, promoted science "because one believed in the absolute utility of knowledge, namely in the innermost bond of morality, knowledge and happiness." Voltaire's brand appears to idealize knowledge just as fervently as Newton's had idealized God. Finally, Spinoza's motivation for promoting science boils down to this: "[O]ne believed that one had and loved in science something selfless, harmless, self-sufficient, truly innocent, in which the evil drives of human beings did not participate at all." Spinoza, Nietzsche adds, "felt himself to be divine" as a knower, and he is by no means the most innocuous of the personifications of the three errors. Consider the fact that Spinoza celebrates precisely those disembodied, nonhuman properties that have been elevated and cultivated at the expense of the instinctive, natural, bodied human being, and one begins to understand why Nietzsche in book 5 (from the year 1887) asserts that modern science is still based on faith in metaphysics (§344). In order for science to have the enlightening, liberating, energizing effect of a *joyful* science, it must serve the needs of species preservation and nourish, rather than diminish, the human dimension otherwise maligned as "the evil drives of human beings." That Nietzsche values science is indisputable, but he also holds it to a higher standard wherein "higher" means more human, more life-affirming, more in keeping with the entire economy of species preservation with its celebration of the closest things. As a force in the service of metaphysics, science is potentially anti-nature; Nietzsche was generally on record in cautioning that morality is anti-nature, so it makes sense that he also remained critical of science's tendency to expunge, rather than sublimate, the natural.

JS §45 "Epicurus" is at the center of three aphorisms that Laurence Lampert discusses in his book *Nietzsche and Modern Times: A Study of Bacon, Descartes, and Nietzsche,* where he makes a good case for Epicurus as "a major element in [Nietzsche's] rethinking of the history of philosophy." As we delve into §45 in the context of happiness that characterizes book 1, we do well to approach it with Lampert's nuanced observation that "Nietzsche experienced the character of Epicurus as marked by happiness," yet Nietzsche claimed to understand Epicurus differently: "Epicurus's happiness did not come from Epicurean *ataraxia,* the indifference to all passions, it came from a passion, from *Wollust* [voluptuousness] grown modest and transformed into the observing eye that watched the sun set on the magnificence of antiquity."[8] The aphorism opens with Nietzsche's confession of how Epicurus resonates with him: "Yes, I am proud to perceive the character of Epicurus differently than perhaps anyone, and to enjoy the happiness of the afternoon of antiquity in everything I hear and read of him" (72). This extremely high praise is not followed by the usual supportive commentary but instead by an image, impressionistic, indulgent, whimsical, yet most revealing in terms of mood:

> I see his eyes gaze upon a broad whitish sea, across shoreline boulders bathed by the sun, while animals large and small play in its light, secure and calm as this light and these very eyes. Such happiness could only have been invented by a constant sufferer, the happiness of an eye before which the sea of existence has become calm and that now cannot see enough of the surface and the multihued, tender, trembling skin of the sea: never before has such a modesty of voluptuousness existed. (72)

8. Lawrence Lampert, *Nietzsche and Modern Times: A Study of Bacon, Descartes, and Nietzsche* (New Haven, CT: Yale University Press, 1993), 423.

The focus of the gaze is a broad sea at first, but then it tightens to display the shoreline, the sunlight on boulders, and animals at play in this light; the play of the animals is "secure and calm as this light and these very eyes," revealing a connectedness between observer and observed, with the light of observation emanating first from the sun, then through Epicurus-Nietzsche. Now the gaze, the animals playing, the sun and sea washing the rocks and the shoreline are all subsumed under happiness, whose author could only be "a constant sufferer." Here is a sample of that incredible *empathy* of which Nietzsche was capable according to Henry Staten, who asks intriguing questions about whom Nietzsche addresses in his writings: "His experimentalism involves his whole self, which is entirely dissolved in the perspective of the moment, and thus ranges freely from the largest and most generous utterances to the meanest and most reactive, as though one voice knew nothing of the others."[9] Staten explains that while Nietzsche consistently criticized pity, he himself praised and cultivated a feeling whereby one is capable "of sharing in the *Urleid,* the primordial suffering of all the world" (153). The kind of pity (*Mitleid,* translated in *CW* as "compassion") that afflicts Nietzsche himself, according to Staten, could be described as *hineinfühlen,* feeling one's way into something, or empathy; *Phantasie,* imagination; or *hineindichten,* creating or writing one's way into something. These expressions would constitute "the deep and genuine version of that which *Mitleid* usually names," and unlike the negative pity or compassion normally condemned by Nietzsche, these alternatives manifested by him are "precisely the sort that feels too immediately and intensely the sufferings of others" (154–55).

Returning now to the impressionistic revelry on Epicurus, we better understand why Nietzsche construes this image of the gazing Epicurus as a sublimation of suffering. The sea is calm here, the gaze and the experience of the observer are entirely at one with the closest things, the surroundings, such

9. Henry Staten, *Nietzsche's Voice* (Ithaca, NY: Cornell University Press 1990), 152.

that the "sea of existence," the life of Epicurus seen through the eyes of Nietzsche, a fellow sufferer, lies calm and voluptuously inviting, voluptuously alluring, but more Platonically voluptuous than erotically so — recall that Nietzsche refers to this as a hitherto unknown "modesty of voluptuousness" and Lampert calls it "*Wollust* [voluptuousness] grown modest and transformed into the observing eye." Indeed, the passion of voluptuousness, normally manifesting in a feeling of erotic arousal, would have to be transformed in order to so appreciate the detail and loveliness of this Apollonian image as it dwells on the surface of the sea: the happiness here is not frenzy, not loss of self, but presence of mind and self in the moment, shared with one's immediate surroundings.

The spiritual equilibrium of *JS* emerges in §45 as a confession of affinity for Epicurus. Keith Ansell-Pearson reminds us that in his middle period, Nietzsche "draws upon [Epicurus's] philosophy as a way of promoting what I would like to call an Epicurean-inspired care of self."[10] Care of self is an apt formulation both because it is commensurate with Epicurus's refined notion of pleasure and because Nietzsche's physical health was a constant challenge to his mental health, or perhaps more accurately, his mental state. It must be remembered that Nietzsche was forced to retire early owing to ill health characterized by migraines, temporary blindness, and gastrointestinal issues; he needed to maintain a highly disciplined and demanding regimen in terms of lighting, temperature, diet, and geography.[11]

At this point a summary of the Epicurean notion of pleasure helps us to see more clearly why Nietzsche turned to Epicurus. Simon Blackburn cautions that Epicurus did not recommend the sensual pleasures but "the pursuit only of pleasures that can be controlled and enjoyed in moderation: pleasures of

10. Keith Ansell-Pearson, "True to the Earth: Nietzsche's Epicurean Care of Self and World," in *Nietzsche's Therapeutic Teaching: For Individuals and Cultures,* ed. Horst Hutter and Eli Friedland (London: Bloomsbury, 2013), 97.

11. Cf. my Translator's Afterword to *CW* 16, 475–77, 486–88, where I discuss factors related to N's health.

friendship, peace, and aesthetic contemplation."[12] While the aim of philosophy is "to live well," this is not synonymous with "the hedonistic trough the word Epicureanism now suggests, after centuries of propaganda against the system" (122). The goal of a pleasant life is attained through the practical wisdom provided by philosophy, and this pleasant life in turn "consists in a preponderance of *katastematic* pleasures, capable of indefinite prolongation, over merely *kinematic* or volatile sensory pleasures. *Katastematic* pleasures are capable of variation but not of increase, so that one who lives longer does not thereby obtain more of them than one who lives less long" (122). Blackburn concludes that *ataraxia* (tranquility or imperturbability) is the highest form of happiness (27), pursued by Epicureans and Stoics alike, and it requires "understanding the limits of life and removal of the fear of death, cultivation of friendships, and the removal of unnecessary desires and false gratifications" (122). The gazing Epicurus of *JS* §45, for whom Nietzsche feels such an affinity and through whom he enjoys the image of the calm sea of existence as the summa of aesthetic contemplation, conforms in many respects with the Epicurean objectives, but we should remain mindful of Lampert's proviso that Nietzsche here is not subscribing to a pure *ataraxia* but instead to a passion, *Wollust* (voluptuousness) "grown modest and transformed" into the gaze.

A sustainable, moderate, peaceful style of happiness suited Nietzsche well in the years that immediately followed his resignation from the University of Basel, and generally speaking *JS* should be seen as the crowning, mature work of the middle period (1878–82). Ansell-Pearson tells us that from Epicurus, Nietzsche "gets the inspiration to give up on what he calls the first and last things, the questions of a theologically inspired metaphysics, and devote attention to the closest things."[13] This observation applies to the entire middle period, then, because

12. Simon Blackburn, *The Oxford Dictionary of Philosophy* (Oxford: Oxford University Press, 1994), 122.

13. Ansell-Pearson, "True to the Earth," 104.

Nietzsche's investigation and celebration of the closest things finds its voice already in *HAH,* and it is the binding thread of all the aphoristic works from 1878 to 1882 (two volumes of *HAH, D, JS*). In the so-called closest things (*die nächsten Dinge*) Nietzsche was able to practice a kind of philosophizing that led to love of fate, which in turn led to the formulation of the eternal recurrence, which is first announced in book 4 of *JS*. I have written extensively on the closest things as they informed Nietzsche's rhetoric of the earth and his ecological propensities.[14] There can be no happiness in Nietzschean terms without a profound respect for and coexistence with the closest things; these "things" in *JS* §45 include everything that forms the image upon which the gazing Epicurus dwells: sea, sunlight, shoreline, rocks, and animals.

A further glimpse into the importance of the closest things is afforded by §55 "The ultimate sense of nobility," which includes rare criticism of nobility as it has been traditionally defined and as Nietzsche apparently embraces it whenever he equates the noble with the strong and the exceptional. He devotes the first part of the aphorism to dispelling baser notions of nobility, including the ability to make sacrifices, following one's passions, and selflessness — all of these, on closer examination, can be achieved by base types, and so they do not pass the nobility test. "Rather, the passion that befalls the noble is something special, without his knowing about this specialness; the use of a rare and singular standard and nearly a craziness; the feeling of heat in things that feel cold to all others; figuring out values for which the scale has not yet been invented; making sacrifices on altars consecrated to an unknown god; bravery without the will to honor; a self-sufficiency that overflows and shares itself with people and things" (78). This list of rare qualities is strikingly reminiscent of the Epicurean project, yet

14. Adrian Del Caro, *Grounding the Nietzsche Rhetoric of Earth* (Berlin: De Gruyter, 2004), cf. 29–34, 104–16, 201–21, 244–54, 352–70, 380–87, 417–31, in particular, but generally throughout as indicated by the entry "closest things" in the index.

throughout his writings generally, and in particular in the chap
ter of *Beyond Good and Evil* (*BGE*) titled "What Is Noble?,"
Nietzsche stresses a more assertive, combative, exploitative
notion of nobility, one that tends to counter the properties o
modern egalitarian herd-values.[15] More will be said about thi
when I discuss the transition from the Epicurean to the Dio
nysian that takes place already, mostly unseen but not unfelt
within the scope of books 1–4 of *JS*.

There is a problem with defining nobility on the basis o
rare qualities and the noble person's ignorance of these very
qualities, as Nietzsche explains in the third and final section o
the aphorism: "But here one should consider that by mean
of this yardstick, everything ordinary, closest and indispens
able, in short, that which most preserves the species and in gen
eral was the *rule* in humankind up till now, has been unfairly
judged and on the whole slandered for the sake of exceptions
To become the advocate of the rule — that could perhaps b
the ultimate form and subtlety in which the sense of nobilit
manifests itself on earth." Observe that what "most preserve
the species," a theme already explored in §4, are precisely th
closest things, everyday indispensable things, all of which
have been unfairly judged in terms of nobility as the resul
of the long-standing bias in favor of the rare. Under the influ
ence of Epicurean philosophy, Nietzsche values the quotidia
because life affirmation, his signature Dionysian issue, is mean
ingless without the affirmation of the everyday, of the quotid
ian, that very human state in which we spend most of our lives
The simple, basic operations of sleeping, waking, hygiene, eat
ing, socializing, observing, learning, working, playing — thes
are all indispensable, and these are "the rule." This particula
aphorism represents a lucid moment in Nietzsche's elaboratio
of the sense of nobility, a generous moment inasmuch as hi
later hardening of the concept of nobility is far more polemi
and scarcely Epicurean.

15. Cf. *CW* 8, 445–51, for my discussion of this chapter of *BGE*.

"The desire for suffering" closes out book 1 as §56, representing the closing frame on the narrative of happiness that weaves its way through the seemingly random topics. The youth of Nietzsche's day "can't endure boredom and themselves," so they use their yearning for suffering to pursue adventures of a sort — they "extract from their suffering a probable grounds for action, for a deed. Neediness is needed!" (78). Next they go about the business of manufacturing needs, distress, and emergencies, indulged all the while in this activity by politicians. Instead of looking inward, Nietzsche observes, they seek external causes for unhappiness, "and their imagination is busy in advance shaping a monster from it, so that later they can fight a monster." This modern quixotic adventure, fueled by ennui, manifests in society at large, in the environment: "[T]hey fill the world with their cries of distress and consequently far too often with *feelings of distress*! They don't know what to do with themselves — and so they paint the unhappiness of others on the wall: they always need others! And time and again other others!" A climate of self-fulfilling doom and gloom characterizes modern youth and society, where individuals manufacture crises in order to feel alive, to experience adventure, to trumpet about the general unhappiness and malaise. To this Nietzsche gives his dissenting opinion in a pithy rejoinder: "Pardon me, my friends, I have dared to paint my *happiness* on the wall."

Contrary to painting witches or the devil on the wall, Nietzsche paints *his own* happiness on the wall, thereby breaking with the perpetuators of unhappiness who pollute their environment with eternally recycling woes. But precisely where, we must ask, did he paint his happiness on the wall, since this entire aphorism treats the unhappiness of modern youth and how it becomes endemic in society? The happiness Nietzsche has painted on the wall, for everyone to see and hear, is book 1 of *JS*, which represents his own happiness and serves as an alternative to the negative loop inspired by a "desire for suffering" that manifests in a futile but loud protest against the distress and victimization of others. Nietzsche demonstrates through his own example that a healthy focus on the self is capable of generating not only personal happiness but also a message worth sharing, one that adds music to the world or puts to music the otherwise unseen and unheard beauty of the world for which Nietzsche wants to show gratitude.

Book 2 presents two seemingly unrelated threads, each representing a specific block or theme, as if in two halves of a whole. Section 57 "To the realists" begins a series of eighteen aphorisms, concluding with §75 "The third sex," that deal explicitly with the theme of woman. Then the aphorisms commenting specifically, lyrically, and critically on issues related to women and the feminine, suddenly cease: §76 "The greatest danger" is a detailed transitional aphorism featuring the binary of reason and madness, and §77 "The animal with a good conscience" serves as the opening section of the second half of book 2, which provides intriguing commentaries on art and certain artists, concluding with §107 "Our ultimate gratitude to art." So the two main themes of this second book of *JS* are woman and art, and stated in these discrete terms, that is, "woman" and "art," they not only appear to be different in content, but Nietzsche also seduces us into thinking they are disparate by packing all the "woman" aphorisms at the front and closing out the second book with all the aphorisms related to art.

On closer examination, however, the two themes have a tendency to converge and share a common conceptual identity or to lose their centers when their singular, "discrete" identity is unpacked and restated. If this assertion sounds like deconstruction, consider that Derrida's *Spurs* makes use of eleven aphorisms from *JS* and, quite famously, one unpublished fragment from the period of *JS*. Derrida must have been struck by the seemingly different themes sailing under a single banner as book 2. His way of packaging Nietzsche's juxtaposition of "woman" and "art" prompted this opening to *Spurs*:

The title for this lecture was to have been *the question of style*.
However — it is woman who will be my subject.
Still, one might wonder whether that doesn't really amount
    to the same thing — or is it to the other.[16]

At this point I am not interested in conflating the subject of
"woman" with the subject of "art," nor do I intend to give a
deconstructive reading of book 2 — but Derrida's observation
regarding style and the confusion he confessed (or teased) by
asking whether style and woman might not be the same are
indeed in the spirit of Nietzsche's arrangement for book 2.
What woman represents to Nietzsche, in one form or another,
provides the energy for the first half ("half" taken more as part,
not equal portion); woman includes creativity, appearance
(semblance), seduction, madness, intoxication — in sum, a
series of properties that Nietzsche had ascribed to art ever since
BT. The second half, with its focus on artists and art, includes
these same properties but adds the significant themes of *healing* and *species preservation*. The entire second book is an interrogation of the binary "illusion versus reality," or appearance
versus reality, and its underlying contribution to *joyful science* is
sounded in the very last sentence of the last aphorism: "And as
long as you are still in any way *ashamed* before yourselves, you
do not yet belong among us!" (116).[17]

The opening aphorism "To the realists" (§57) issues a warn-
ing to realists who feel themselves to be "armed against passion
and fancifulness," whereas they are merely empty and bereft:
"[B]efore you alone reality stands unveiled, and you yourselves

16. Jacques Derrida, *Spurs: Nietzsche's Styles / Éperons: Les Styles de Nietzsche*,
trans. Barbara Harlow (Chicago: University of Chicago Press, 1978), 35–36.
More later on Derrida's *Spurs* when I discuss the unpublished fragments from
the period of *JS*. The aphorisms and fragment in question are: 59, 60, 64, 69,
71, 72, 75, 339, 361, 365, 371, and fr. 12[62].

17. Compare this concluding sentiment, with its embrace of self-
deprecating humor, to the motto of the book: "This house is my own and
here I dwell, / I've never aped nothing from no one / and — laugh at each
master, mark me well, / who at himself has not poked fun."

would probably be the best part of it — oh you beloved images of Sais!" (79). The allusion to Sais circles back to the preface §4, where Nietzsche uses the ancient legend of the statue of Isis to argue for observing the limits of reason: "One should better honor the *modesty* with which nature has hidden herself behind riddles and colorful uncertainties. Perhaps truth is a woman who has grounds for not letting her grounds be seen?" (9). According to the version handed down by Plutarch, "the inscription of the veiled statue of Isis (or perhaps Athena) at the ancient Egyptian city of Sais reads: 'I am all that is, was, and shall be. No mortal has ever lifted my veil.'"[18] In fact, Nietzsche explains, these realists in their "unveiled condition" are still "most passionate and dark creatures," similar to artists in love, still burdened with valuations stemming from "passions and infatuations of earlier centuries"; indeed, their "sobriety still has a secret and ineradicable drunkenness incorporated in it" (79). At the conclusion of §57, Nietzsche reveals where he is positioned on the axis of drunkenness to sobriety: "For us there is no 'reality' — and not for you either, you sober ones — we are by no means as foreign to one another as you think, and maybe our good will to get beyond drunkenness is just as respectable as your belief that you are *incapable* of drunkenness." Realists and artists are both creators, apparently, but the former disavow creativity in favor of claiming absolute apprehension of the world, while the latter seek to move beyond drunkenness (darkness, ignorance, fantasy, fiction, etc.) using good will and creativity.

Woman enters this discussion in the figure of Isis, personified as wisdom, on the one hand, but necessary holder of secrets, on the other. In the preface to *JS*, Nietzsche had personified truth as a woman, something he continues to do in *BGE*. But woman, according to Nietzsche, is practiced in veiling, hence the allusion to veiled Isis and what the goddess represents. The point he makes by using this personification, which was cleverly

18. Douglas Burnham, *The Nietzsche Dictionary* (London: Bloomsbury, 2015), 214. The above is excerpted from Burnham's entry on "mask."

elaborated by Derrida in *Spurs,* is that when men are in an enamored state, their senses prove unreliable in matters of cognition. Stated from the artist's point of view, more positively, when the artist creates out of love or under the inspiration of being enamored, the artist is capable of creating anything — but that creation does not necessarily accord with truth. When Nietzsche asks rhetorically, in §57, "[W]hat is 'reality' to an artist in love" (9), he is invoking a powerful, ineluctable force, one that eclipses "reality" whether it is construed by artists or wooed by reality-seekers — this ineluctable force is the feminine. In this opening aphorism of roughly one page in length, we find several occurrences of the word "love": beloved images, artist in love (twice), infatuations of earlier centuries, love for "reality," ancient "love," old love. It would be difficult to argue that Nietzsche is being critical of love or somehow proposing that we avoid it, inasmuch as love as a passion is a powerful and ineluctable force; in keeping with Nietzsche's overall philosophy that humans need to renaturalize themselves, that they need to continue to sublimate not extirpate their passions, there is every indication that he is urging us to acknowledge the undercurrent of love that informs our creativity as well as our science. I take the message of §57 to be that only an integrated, holistic ontology can strike the balance between reality and appearance, between truth and fiction, between masculine and feminine.

This point Nietzsche states more forcefully and lyrically in §60 "Women and their action at a distance," which at first glance appears to set a tone reminiscent of the gazing Epicurus of §45. Here too, Nietzsche asks us to imagine him at the seaside, and here too the equilibrium will be established by *gazing,* but only after he has liberated his sense of hearing from the din that overwhelms him: "Here I stand in the midst of the blaze of the surf, whose white flames are licking at my feet: — from all sides howling, threatening, screaming, shrilling at me, while in the deepest depths the ancient earth-shaker sings his aria, rumbling like a bellowing bull: he stamps a beat to it, such an earth-shaking beat that the hearts of even these weathered boulder monsters here tremble in their bodies" (81). This is a full-bodied response to the violence of the earth's interaction with the sea, an experience of the terrible sublime that permeates Nietzsche's senses, most notably those of touch and hearing. Observe now that this sea is anything but calm as it was in §45 — this is the unmitigated sea, a dangerous zone of tumult and loss of individuation — until: "Then, suddenly, as if born out of nothing, there appears before the gate of this hellish labyrinth, only a few fathoms away — a great sailing ship gliding silently as a ghost. Oh this ghostly beauty! With what magic does it touch me! What? Has all the calm and taciturnity of the world boarded this ship? Does my very happiness sit in this quiet place, my happier self, my second departed self?" We are now returned to the equilibrium, peace, happiness expressed in the Epicurus aphorism, although we have yet to establish the source of this apparition that *magically touches* Nietzsche, compelling him to gaze at it. He senses that his happier, calmer, "departed" (*verewigt*) self is aboard the ship, enjoying a very different kind of existence, a transitional or middle state between life and death: "Not being dead and yet no longer living either? As a ghostly, quiet, watching, gliding, hovering middle being? Resembling the ship that with its white sails skips over the dark sea like an enormous butterfly! Yes! Skipping *over* existence! That's it! That would be it!" Existence is calm on the surface of the sea, where it can glide and hover, again reminiscent of the sea's enchanting skin in §45.

The gliding, sailing ship that appears to afford Nietzsche the possibility of a calmer existence of course lies *at a distance,* underscored by the statement "All great noise causes us to place our happiness in the quiet and the distance" (82). The final transformation and personification of this distance makes it clear that Nietzsche takes a gendered approach in this aphorism: "When a man stands amidst *his* noise, amidst his surf of projectiles and projects: then he, too, likely sees quiet magical beings gliding past him, whose happiness and seclusion he longs for — *they are women.* He almost thinks that his better self dwells there among the women: in these quiet places even the loudest surf could become deathly silence and life itself a dream about life." The phrase "he almost thinks" is telling and fore-telling, because "deathly silence" and "life itself a dream about life" are ambiguous expressions, reflecting a dawning realization that a man's better self does not, cannot, dwell among women; rather, the interplay between them is and must remain "at a distance," as summarized in the aphorism's last sentence: "The magic and the mightiest effect of women is, to speak the language of philosophers, an effect at a distance, an *actio in distans:* but this requires, first and foremost — *distance*!" The conclusion of this aphorism, with its dispelling of the romantic spell, is typical Nietzschean anti-romantic irony — disruption of a particularly romantic illusion for the purpose of restoring critical distance. The equilibrium or sanity required for a ful-filled life will be found neither in the roaring surf nor among women; yet Nietzsche makes a compelling case that for a man, woman's effect at a distance is key to equilibrium, position-ing the man somewhere between noise and silence, leaving us to quibble over how great or small this distance needs to be. I would stop short of inferring that only a Platonic relationship should obtain between the sexes, since this would disavow the power of love, blunt the effect at a distance, and ensure the dis-continuation of the species.

Perhaps some clarification of the roles played by men and women can be found in §72 "The mothers," where Nietzsche in lauding the female as productive also manages to deliver back-handed compliments and put-downs of the sort shared by most of the aphorisms on woman in book 2. After announcing that animals "think differently about females [*Weibchen*] than humans do" (without explaining how animals think generally), Nietzsche proposes that among animals "the female is consid-ered the productive being" (86). Next the precise relationship of the animal female to her young is described: "Paternal love does not exist among them, but something like love for the children of a lover and habituation to them. In their children females have a satisfaction of their lust to rule, a possession, an occupation, something entirely comprehensible to them with which they can chatter: all of this together is maternal love — it can be compared to the love of an artist for his work." We should not let the anthropomorphizing of the animals in relation to their young obscure the important conclusion of this observation, with which Nietzsche appropriates the productivity of female animals by comparing their controlling, dominating, possessive love with "the love of an artist for his work." In §72 there are actually two appropriations taking place, the first when Nietzsche ascribes human properties and emotions to the animals, the second when he claims the productive operation of womanhood for the male. For next he transitions to human mothers, explaining that pregnancy "has made women milder, more patient, more fearful, more eager to submit; and likewise spiritual pregnancy produces the character of the contemplative ones, which is related to the female character: — these are the male mothers. — Among animals the male sex is considered the beautiful one." Contemplative men are "male mothers," which is to say, they experience "spiritual pregnancy" enabling them to give birth. As if to provide natural evidence for his theory of the male mothers, Nietzsche adds the statement that animals "consider" the male sex to be beautiful, that is, ornamental, pleasing to the eye, suggesting the reverse of the human standard whereby woman is "the beautiful one" but apparently not the productive one.

Given the proximity in §72 of pregnancy, maternal love, and the male contemplator-artist with his "spiritual pregnancy," it is less than surprising that beginning with §77 the remaining aphorisms of book 2 deal with individual artists and art in a variety of forms. We have so far examined aphorisms in which the feminine serves as a creative counter to the barren sobriety of smug realists (§57), as a compelling, enthralling "effect at a distance" for males otherwise doomed to a "hellish labyrinth"[19]

19. Cf. Adrian Del Caro, "Margarete-Ariadne: Faust's Labyrinth," *Goethe Yearbook* 18 (2011): 223–43.

(§60), and finally as a naturally productive force capable of bearing children and inspiring Nietzsche to speak in terms of contemplative, creative "male mothers" (§72). We could regard the first half of book 2 as an interrogation and explication of the male/female binary, with a strong focus on how creativity is dependent not only on two opposing streams but on the mingling of these streams as well. Nietzsche simultaneously draws lines separating the sexes and blurs them, demonstrating that art is a hybrid phenomenon, not unlike the disparate elements that constitute the amazing economy of species preservation. The second half of book 2 delivers a discourse in which art more generally is critiqued in its contemporary manifestations and bolstered on principle for its importance to species preservation.

§86 "On theater" is extremely critical of the modern spectator, who uses theater as a sort of narcotic. Exhausted, worn out, mule-tired and whipped by life, the audience looks for intoxication and emotional highs in the evening: "What would those people know anyway about 'more elevated moods,' if not for intoxicating substances and idealistic lashes of the whip! — and so they have their inspirers in the same way they have their wines" (98). Nietzsche makes it clear that anyone who has experienced "strong and elevated feelings" during the day, including himself, does not seek out these vicarious experiences in the evening's art; the need for such fantasy is among those whose daily lives are a drudgery. The gulf between modern spectators and their art is accentuated in order to highlight its absurdity: "What? We put wings and proud conceits on a mole — before bedtime, before he crawls into his hole? We send him to the theater and put big glasses on his blind and weary eyes? Humans whose life is not a 'plot' but a business deal, sit in front of a stage and watch strange creatures for whom life is more than a deal? 'That's just decency,' you say, 'that's entertaining, that's how culture would have it!'" (98). The mole-men partake of "culture" in order to invigorate themselves and to feel humanly alive, momentarily at least, while men of substance should do otherwise: "Whoever has enough tragedy and comedy in himself will probably prefer to avoid the theater." The issue of the gulf between spectator and spectacle is repeated using two examples: "Whoever is something of a Faust or a Manfred, what does he care about the Fausts and Manfreds of the theater! — whereas it certainly gives him pause *that* such characters are even depicted in theaters. The *strongest* thoughts and passions displayed before those who are not capable of thinking and passion — but of *intoxication*!"

The two heroes cited by Nietzsche present an intriguing case of how incommensurate the modern spectator is with the art he consumes. Both Faust and Manfred are superhumans, for one thing, using Goethe and the German language as a benchmark, and they are both Byronic heroes as well, judging from the standpoint of English Romanticism. Their respective lives and tragedies include profound entanglements with women, contempt for sheep-like humans, Promethean resistance to all powers, and remarkable skill in voicing or expressing their views. These Titans of the stage, so to speak, are juxtaposed with modern theatergoing men, whose sole outcome from consuming such art is intoxication. Clearly Nietzsche regrets that great art is brought down to this level, that it is processed by mole-humans and pressed, mined, for its capacity to intoxicate: "And theater and music as the hashish-smoking and betel-chewing of Europeans! Oh, who can tell us the entire history of narcotics! — It is nearly the history of 'culture,' of so-called higher culture!" The equation of narcotics with culture is unfortunate, but it is a distinguishing feature of Europeans and their history. This aphorism is not entirely gloomy, however, inasmuch as it implies a more uplifting role for art, especially in its citing of *Faust* and *Manfred* as worthy theater, and in the rhetorical question, "Whoever is something of a Faust or a Manfred, what does he care about the Fausts and Manfreds of the theater!" There *is* something of the Faust and Manfred in human beings generally, not merely in men, as Nietzsche's outdated pronouns imply. The question might be phrased as follows: Is there a more productive, bracing, life-affirming role to be played by art than this negative example of theater as intoxication? We know and appreciate that Nietzsche was a sharp critic of modernity and its ills, but we also know he, even more than his artistic predecessors, gave us his own version of "the superhuman."

Book 2 concludes with a detailed aphorism titled "Our ultimate gratitude to art" (§107), and in a manner typical of *JS* it recycles at the end certain key themes that had been sounded in the opening aphorism. A close reading of §107 shows that Nietzsche is keen to restore balance to the binaries that animate us as a species, much more than he is interested in assigning a subordinate role to women, which is all too often the obvious though hasty conclusion taken by too many critics.

The existential service of art is formulated as a strong thesis: "— If we had not given our blessing to art and invented this kind of cult of the untrue: then our insight into the general untruth and mendacity that is now provided to us by science — our insight into delusion and error as a condition of our cognating and sensing existence — would be totally unbearable. *Honesty* would have nausea and suicide in its wake" (116). This stark formulation will be familiar to readers of *BT* (1872), but here art is stripped of the metaphysics and pessimism of that early, Schopenhauer-influenced book and stated in terms of our necessary alliance with knowledge. Once again Nietzsche summons art as the healer: "Now, however, our honesty has a counterforce that helps us to avoid such consequences: art, as the *good* will to appearance" (116). Notice that *good* will is invoked as a means of deploying art against existential despair and in a manner very similar to the conclusion of §57, where Nietzsche spoke to "sober realists" who believe the world to be exactly as they see it: "[M]aybe our good will to get beyond drunkenness is just as respectable as your belief that you are *incapable* of drunkenness" (80). To hear Nietzsche speaking of "good will" is both rare and refreshing; later he reduces will to will to power, denial of free will, and strong or weak will — but here in *JS* good will is a key ingredient because it offers us a way of embracing art as healer without having to embrace anything *absolutely*, like the faith of religion. Nietzsche is aware of the similarity between art and religion, hence the expressions "blessing" and "cult of the untrue" in the opening sentence of §107; he stops short of advocating religious faith as a counter to the nausea produced by scientific honesty, inasmuch as religious faith draws more on denial and less on creativity — humans must grow the flexibility to withstand scientific honesty. Furthermore, as becomes clear later in this aphorism, art is uniquely suited to providing existential flexibility.

The good will to appearance has practical effects: "We do not always block our eyes from rounding off, from composing something to the end: and then it is no longer eternal imperfection that we carry across the river of becoming — then we think we are carrying a *goddess* and are proud and childish in performing this service." If science and its attending honesty demand completion, perfection, and closure, and if we as humans feel deficient in the absence of these ideals, then art gives us license to round off, to complete without perfection, to embrace our flawed, mortal selves. Particularly telling is the metaphor Nietzsche chooses to express this condition of good will to appearance: instead of carrying eternal imperfection across the river of becoming, the human family proudly, childishly, feels as though it were carrying a *goddess* across the river. Once again we have an appeal to the religious impulse, but this impulse is pagan, polytheistic, and most notably, feminine. We recall that §57 invoked the goddess Isis as the personification of creativity, the unconscious, intoxication, and appearance, and here Isis — or actually any female deity — returns to play a vital role in the survival and maintenance of our species. Using the same phrase as in *BT*, Nietzsche states that as "an aesthetic phenomenon" we are able to bear existence and become artworks ourselves; in *BT* he had famously asserted that "only as an *aesthetic phenomenon* is existence and the world eternally *justified*" (chap. 5). Art is the goddess that enables mere human beings to live proudly, childishly or youthfully, hopefully.

But there is more to art than the effect of good will to appearance in terms of species self-esteem. Humans bear their goddess across the river of becoming with pride and yet childishly, an odd combination until we unpack what Nietzsche means by "childish." The child here as later in *Z* "On the Three Transformations" stands for play, innocence, and becoming, it is the regenerative force that Nietzsche ascribes to humans who need to wear the "fool's cap": "[W]e need it for our own sake — we need all exuberant, soaring, dancing, mocking, childish and blissful art in order not to lose that *freedom over things* that our ideal demands of us. It would be a *relapse* for us, especially given our irritable honesty, to become completely embroiled in morality, or even turn into virtuous monsters and scarecrows due to the overly stringent demands we place on ourselves in these matters" (116). We maintain our freedom, our flexibility, and our sustainability as a species by occasionally playing the fool; Nietzsche confers these powers not on the scientist, the moral teacher, or the sage — their effects align with the pressure of nausea-producing honesty; instead, the artist-fool is our saving grace. He concludes book 2 with an invitation: "How could we dispense with art for this, or with the fool? — And as long as you are still in any way *ashamed* of yourselves, you do not yet belong among us!" Earlier I pointed to the symmetry of this conclusion with the lyrical motto of *JS*. Art, here personified as the goddess, contributes to our eternal childishness, encourages us to play, and sustains the nimbleness of mind in the face of withering science. The fool's art, meanwhile, with its healing properties of laughter, humility, and freedom to err, protects us against the dangers of excessive gravity, seriousness, and self-importance. In many respects we can and should be critical of the misogyny that often accompanies Nietzsche's commentaries on women, yet we must also acknowledge the manner in which he argues for a holistic, nonbinary understanding of art in relation to knowledge, wherein the female component is omnipresent. In the *joyful* spirit of *JS* it does not make sense for Nietzsche to condemn women — that would be to submit to absolutism and patriarchy, and it would also impede the vital, sustaining play between forces. Book 2 invites the question of whether Nietzsche is ever as "serious" in his socially offensive remarks about women as the tone and appearance would suggest.

Book 3 is thematic of overcoming, a major concept in the nexus that informs *Z* and the late philosophy in general. The point of departure for this third installment of *JS* is macro in the extreme, namely, how humans will manage their affairs in the absence of God. There are obstacles to overcome, there will be a laborious process of clearing, and in order to break through individually and as a species, we will need to assess precisely where we are in terms of physics as well as physiology. Nietzsche dials up the pressure in book 3, cutting straight to the point with a brief, concise opening aphorism titled "New struggles."

In the variants to this aphorism, the "shadow of God" is not referred to as Buddha's shadow but instead as metaphysics; the variants stress that God's shadow will have to be dealt with for centuries, and the second variant makes an allusion to caves, ostensibly in which the shadow will be shown.[20] Section 108 alludes to the legend of Buddha's shadow in order to sharpen the point that Buddha was dead and yet his "colossal horrific shadow" carries on after his life. "God is dead: but given the way of humanity, there will perhaps be caves for thousands of years in which his shadow will be shown. — And we — we still have to conquer his shadow too!" (117). This first published statement by Nietzsche that "God is dead" dramatizes succinctly the fact that humans and their creations come and go, including God; yet this realization, this "deed" as it is later described in §125 "The madman," is only the beginning: the shadow of God's legacy must also be conquered, and this

---

20. Cf. 14[14] (468) and the two brief variants to *JS* 108 (568n1).

process may require thousands of years. Book 3 signals the start of Nietzsche's Zarathustra period, both because *Z* is premised on the challenge that God is dead and because it offers a parable of how humans must engage the *new struggles* unleashed by this most momentous historical event. New struggles of the magnitude occasioned by the death of God require a new and commensurate apparatus with which to "conquer" the shadow of metaphysics that has shaped our humanity thus far.[21]

In §109 "Let us beware!" Nietzsche issues five major cautions against entrenched ways of thinking that help to spread and perpetuate the shadow of God: (1) we must guard against viewing the world as a living being, an organism, especially since this unduly elevates the organic, that which is "derivative, late, rare, accidental" and found "only on the crust of the earth" (117); (2) we should guard against construing the universe as a machine, insofar as the "overall character of the world . . . is chaos in all eternity," further described as a "music box" that "eternally repeats its tune that must never be called a melody" (a preview of §341, in which eternal recurrence is formally presented); (3) we must "beware of saying there are laws in nature," for there are "only necessities," and the absence of laws renders moot all debate about purpose versus accident; (4) we must avoid claiming that life and death are somehow in opposition, since "[t]he living is only a variety of the dead, and a very rare variety"; (5) finally, Nietzsche cautions against believing that "the world eternally creates new things" and that there are "eternally enduring substances." These five disavowals have at least one thing in common, namely, they address strategies that humans have long used to render the universe comprehensible, predictable, comfortable, or secure — in sum, they represent anthropomorphisms stemming from monotheism. The

21. The presence of Zarathustra-like ideas and commentary is deliberately, strategically muted in bks. 1–4, until it is proclaimed by the final aphorism of bk. 4 that was recycled by N almost verbatim as the opening page of *Z*. The unpublished fragments, however, reveal the true extent to which N had already been placing the ideas of bks. 3 and 4 in the mouth of Zarathustra.

long-term damage of these strategies is stated emphatically in the conclusion: "When will all these shadows of God no longer eclipse us? When will we have totally de-deified nature! When will we be permitted to begin to *naturalize* us as human beings with a pure, newly discovered, newly redeemed nature!" (118). Emerging from God's shadow will require us to de-deify nature and in turn instate ourselves into nature, effectively resulting in a "newly discovered nature." The process will be long and arduous; indeed, it will require a reorientation of human beings toward the earth, under existential conditions that can scarcely be imagined at this early stage.

Enter §125 "The madman," who dramatizes the uncanny, perilous nature of existence in the twilight of God's retreat. Diogenes (ca. 404–323 BCE) was the Greek Cynic philosopher who shined a lantern in the faces of Athenians, claiming to be seeking an honest man; it is this hyperbolic urgency that Nietzsche ascribes to his madman, who runs around the marketplace in broad daylight carrying a lantern, calling out that he seeks God. Section 125 is arguably the most dramatic of all the aphorisms in book 3, both because it compels readers to visualize where they are unaccustomed to visualizing and because its message represents a superlatively negative event — *JS* books 3 and 4 present several scenarios based on superlatives such as holiest, mightiest, remotest, oldest, greatest, most human, favorite, happiest, etc. The enormity of God's death, along with the felt, lived experience of his absence, invites the rhetorical question, "The holiest and mightiest that the world possessed so far, it's bled to death under our knives — who will wipe this blood off us?" (129). The burden on humans is such that they will need to "become gods" in order to appear worthy of their crime: "There has never been a greater deed — and whoever is born after us will belong to a higher history than all history to this day, on account of this deed!" In this aphorism brimming with new metaphors that stretch to convey new dangers and new challenges, Nietzsche dramatizes the insidious nature of God's shadow; the people cannot see, smell, hear, or otherwise feel the death and absence of God; to accuse them of being in denial would be a mere understatement — the shadow is so powerful that it numbs their senses, "*and yet they did it themselves!*" (130).

So much value has been vested in the one God, in monotheism, that humans sleepwalk after the death of God, unable to wake from a terrible dream yet capable of performing mechanical functions. Most of §§114–53 are either overtly critical of religion or focused on the limitations of morality, in keeping with Nietzsche's efforts to illuminate the shadowy existence in which humanity is currently entangled. Section 143 gives us perspective on §125 "The madman," for it straightforwardly argues for the "[g]reatest advantage of polytheism." Nietzsche uses his genealogical method to argue that early, pre-individual humanity was loath to accommodate individuality; if one were to "derive his law, his joys and his rights" from his own ideal, it "surely was regarded as the most monstrous of all human aberrations and as idolatry itself" (137). Polytheism, this "wonderful art and power to create gods," became the mechanism whereby individual ideals could be pursued with relative impunity as long as one blamed a god: "[N]ot I! not I! rather *a god* through me!" Otherwise, the prevailing norm was "'*the* human being' — and every people believed it *possessed* this singular and ultimate norm." Polytheism allowed the proliferation of diverse beings, through which early humans could sublimate the more individualistic drives and urges: "The invention of gods, heroes and superhumans of all kinds, as well as secondary humans and subhumans, of dwarves, fairies, centaurs, satyrs, demons and devils, was invaluable training for justifying the selfishness and self-glorification of the individual." This state of diversity and accommodation of plurality is immediately followed by a strong criticism of monotheism: "Monotheism on the other hand, this rigid consequence of the doctrine of a single normal human being — hence the belief in a normal god beside whom there are only false fairy-tale gods — was perhaps the greatest danger to humankind so far: here it was threatened by that premature stagnation which, as far as we can tell, most other animal species have reached long ago."

Observe that Nietzsche here claims that monotheism was "perhaps the greatest danger to humankind so far," which he amplifies by speculating that all other animals have long since succumbed to stagnation, ostensibly through the same kind of normative rigor that humans inflict on themselves through monotheism. Thus polytheism is credited with nothing less than individual diversity, sublimation of various drives, free-spiritedness and multispiritedness, creativity, and generally open horizons for humans as a species (137–38) — all this should be borne in mind when we consider the grim, apocalyptic picture of the post-God universe inhabited by Nietzsche's madman. An elaboration of the benefits of polytheism is found in §152 "The greatest change," where Nietzsche details how differently ancient humans experienced the most frequent and closest things, inasmuch as everything was animated by belief in dreams, heightened appreciation of the dead, and various gods and demons (141–42). The important point is that humans are more authentic, confident, creative, and affirmative in an environment of their making, especially if a powerful dominant norm can be effectively challenged or subverted.

The various books of *JS* exhibit a pattern whereby the theme or thesis sounded in the first aphorism is echoed by the concluding aphorism, such that a frame is constructed. Another way of spatially describing this arrangement is to speak in terms of a circle, whereby each book completes its circle by embarking from point A and returning to it. Aphorism 108 warns that although God is dead, it will likely take thousands of years before people will be able to liberate themselves from God's shadow. Book 3 concludes with not one aphorism on a related theme but with a series of aphorisms, §§268–75, constructed as a dialogue; each aphorism poses a question that is answered in one terse line, and six of eight use the familiar German pronoun of address, adding a note of intimacy and familiarity. Collectively, these questions and their answers are designed to provide encouragement and hope to individuals who are engaged in the "new struggles" telegraphed by §108. In §268 "What makes one heroic?," we are told "[t]o approach one's highest suffering and one's highest hope at the same time" (161). The overcoming of obstacles — indeed, the overcoming of the self that is emblematic of *Z* — requires the embrace of suffering, not for its own sake but because suffering is endemic to life and Nietzsche exhorts us to life affirmation despite suffering. If suffering can be approached simultaneously as suffering and one's hope, these affirmations and sublimations will serve as a formula for *amor fati.* Section 269 "In what do you believe?" elicits a challenging response: "In this: that the weights of all things must be redetermined" (161). The new benchmark for determining weights, that is, for measuring or assigning value, is the death of God — all things are seen now in a different light; all things are now subject to a new gravity in which the old standards no longer apply. Finally, we recall that the concluding aphorism of book 2 expressed gratitude to art, advocated for the fool's cap, and admonished us to not be ashamed; the concluding aphorism of book 3, §275 "What is the seal of freedom achieved?," asserts: "No longer being ashamed before oneself." Living affirmatively and without shame is itself a new standard, one that echoes the values of joyful science as they are brought to bear on the task of conquering God's shadow. If ever the psyche needed suppleness and flexibility in the face of grave threats, then surely it will require such resilience to maintain its "freedom over things" (§107), which takes on new meaning commensurate with the urgency of new struggles.

While book 3 expressed a heightened sense of urgency for coping with new struggles, laying bare the pitfalls of metaphysics and personifying the enormity of humanity's task in "The madman," book 4 represents the culmination of Nietzsche's strategies for *JS,* inasmuch as it offers both the highest motivation to affirm existence as well as the means to do so. "For the new year" (§276) appropriately enough opens book 4, whose subtitle is "Sanctus Januarius." The previous books had no subtitle, and

we must recall that book 4 was originally the last installment of
JS, with book 5 not added until the second edition of 1887. In
a spirit of renewal symbolized by the miraculous blood of San
Gennaro (Sanctus Januarius), but more irreverently under the
pagan aegis of Janus, the two-faced god who looks backward
and forward simultaneously, Nietzsche offers a philosophical
confession brimming with gratitude and life affirmation.

The Cartesian cogito is re-posited by Nietzsche to place the
stress on living, hence the phrase "I still live; I still think" (162).
This day is special as the first day of a new year, when traditionally we make our new year's resolutions or pledges, but the
implications of this particular day are magnified. Section 276 is
emblematic of all days, all time, for it is the point in time, as it
were, to which Nietzsche returns in §341 "The greatest weight,"
which effectively closes out *JS* with the first published presentation of the thought of eternal recurrence: "[W]ell, so I too
want to say what I wish of myself today and which thought
first entered my heart this year — which thought shall be the
ground, guarantee and sweetness of my entire future life!"
The "thought" or thinking has a direct bearing on Nietzsche's
life, his *heart*; he even refers to it as his future's life's "ground"
and "guarantee." Stated in terms of a challenge, the task for
JS is to formulate and incorporate the thought that has the
greatest impact on living, on existence, such that existence is
rendered most desirable: "I want to learn more and more to
see the necessity in all things as the beautiful: — then I will be
one of those who make things beautiful. *Amor fati:* let that
be my love from now on!" The ability to "see the necessity in
all things as the beautiful" equates to *amor fati*, love of fate, and
Nietzsche pledges himself to this love of fate, explaining that
he will no longer be at war with ugliness and that he will no
longer accuse. If there must be any kind of negation, he adds,
it will be limited to "looking away," because his ultimate goal
is perfect affirmation.

"For the new year," deliberately brief and poignantly upbeat
as it is, nonetheless encapsulates three powerful themes as they

are elaborated in the previous three books. The first theme —
let us call it necessity — challenges humans to learn to affirm
their existence through all things, the closest things as well as
the things we find objectionable about life and wish to banish
with the help of "moral teachers": the economy of species preservation requires the affirmative stance of *amor fati*. Second,
for the theme I would call beauty, as a species we must learn to
embrace the hybrid character of our deepest values, the fact that
the polarity "reality" versus "appearance" cannot be maintained
in the absolute, that categories such as "truth and fiction" and
"male and female" can be constructively blended through art,
yielding a beauty that keeps us mindful and grateful of existence. Third, the theme of affirmation requires a new commitment for the struggle we engage to conquer the shadow of
God; to be a Yes-sayer despite nihilism, suffering, absurdity will
demand a focus as never before on this earth, which assumes its
own new gravity in the absence of God.

So, for example, §283 "Preparatory human beings" sounds a
hopeful note based on signs of a new age that Nietzsche sees
approaching, manlier, more warlike, an age "that above all
will restore honor to courageousness! For it shall pave the way
for an even-higher age and marshal the strength that the new
age will require someday — the age that will carry heroism
into knowledge and *wage wars* for the sake of ideas and their
consequences" (166). The idea of *heroics* was raised at the conclusion of book 3, where it launches the series of personal, Wh-
questions resulting in the seal of freedom achieved through
living without shame. Here in §283 Nietzsche goes into detail
regarding the new heroism, associating it with a heightened
pursuit of knowledge that makes knowledge an existential
imperative. Several key traits will be exemplified by the preparatory human beings: they will be "silent, solitary, resolute;
content and steadfast in invisible activity"; they will possess "an
authentic urge to seek what can be *overcome* in all things"; they
will be gracious in victory and display "cheerfulness, patience,
simplicity and contempt for the great vanities"; they will be

independent and keen in their judgment of victors and "about the contribution of chance to every victory and fame"; they will have "their own festivals, their own workdays, their own periods of mourning"; they will be prepared to command as well as to obey; and overall we can expect "more endangered human beings, more fruitful human beings, happier human beings!" (167). It is at this point that Nietzsche feels himself challenged to formulate how preparatory humans should approach the superlative existence: "[T]he secret to harvesting the greatest fruitfulness and the greatest enjoyment from existence is: *live dangerously!*" "Living dangerously" has become a Nietzschean slogan, a counterintuitive, hyperbolic meme, but we shouldn't have to make a point of distinguishing it from living recklessly or stupidly — the motivation for "living dangerously" has already been provided by book 3.

We face new struggles in our attempt to emerge from the shadow of God, and to pretend that existence has not been threatened by God's death is to sleepwalk; life affirmation will require a new, stronger commitment, a *heroic* resolve. These humans of the future will embody the passion for science and knowledge that Nietzsche described with less fanfare in §123, "Knowledge more than a means," where he tried harder to give a historical framework for the elevation of science. If we deflate some of the rhetoric of §283, the exhortation to "live dangerously" can be stated as a proposition: humans will necessarily lead a more dangerous existence once the news of God's death begins to reach them. As for the gendered, patriarchal lead-in to this famous aphorism, according to which Nietzsche welcomes "all signs that a manlier, a more warlike age is beginning," this, too, might benefit from critical scrutiny. If we agree for the sake of argument that God is dead, then so is patriarchy — phrases like "manly" and "warlike" merely reflect the semantics of the past that Nietzsche is trying to overcome. Nietzsche is definitely critical of modernity in general, and one of modernity's strongest currents has been and continues to be the rise of feminism. The values of honor, courageousness and heroism — indeed, the entire set of virtues that Nietzsche ascribes to preparatory human beings — are not in themselves patriarchal; all humans can embody these virtues and values, and future humans needn't be constrained by the patriarchal bias of past ages, even if Nietzsche continues to be trapped in his own patriarchal semantics.

Much of the rhetorical energy of §283 is maintained in §285 "Excelsior!," where again familiar personal pronouns are used in a series of commandments or prohibitions. This aphorism features a hypothetical "human being of renunciation" (notably, the hypothetical and the personal pronouns will be used again in §341), who is considering a gauntlet of dangers, exposures, and liabilities. Prayer and adoration are forbidden; there can be no standing still before any ultimate power. There will be neither guards nor friends; no view of mountains (no lofty vistas); no avenger or final improver; no reason or love in anything that happens; no finding, only eternal seeking; no ultimate peace, only the eternal recurrence of war and peace: "'— [H]uman being of renunciation, all of this you want to renounce? Who will give you the strength for this? No one has ever had this strength!'" (168). The human being of renunciation sacrifices any source of solace, any condition of final rest or achievement, reminiscent of Goethe's Faust, who dooms himself heroically, titanically, to a life of striving. The prohibitions and privations are enclosed in quotation marks, as if they were commandments, but the extreme difficulty of living in such renunciation is underscored by the speaker; there is no response from the man of renunciation, appropriately enough since the scenario is hypothetical and the commandments function like rhetorical questions. Instead, a parable breaks the silence and concludes the aphorism, shifting from the prosecutorial tension of the speaker to a vision of the future: "— There is a lake that one day forbade itself to run off, and built up a dam where it ran off up till now: since then this lake has risen ever higher. Perhaps that very renunciation will also give us the strength with which to bear renunciation itself; perhaps human beings will rise ever higher at that point where they no longer *flow out* into a god" (168). The litany of human comforts to be renounced here is staggering, but one renunciation in particular is capable of setting our feet on the path to developing heroic renunciation — namely, the renunciation by which I refuse to allow my energies, my own, finite, limited, and precious energies, to flow off and away into a nothing, be it a god, ideal, or other waste of energy. The lake will remain small, at a low level, as long as its waters flow off; by damming itself and by retaining its waters, the lake can only grow higher and deeper.

Renewal of self and species is likewise thematic of §289 "To the ships!" In this aphorism one is reminded again of the "care of self and world" that Ansell-Pearson traces to Nietzsche's appreciation of Epicurean philosophy; in fact, Nietzsche couches this aphorism entirely in terms of philosophy and philosophers. Nietzsche calls for an "overall philosophical justification" of an "individual's manner of living and thinking," whose effect would be like "that of a warming, blessing, fructifying sun that shines for him only" (169). He then enumerates the benefits of this individualized philosophical sun: warmth, fertility, independence, self-sufficiency, richness, generosity, the alchemy of turning evil into good, prevention of the weeds of grief and frustration. At this point in the argument, Nietzsche makes it clear that the philosophy he has in mind is not academic, not esoteric, not even limited to the virtuous and the privileged: "[O]h if only many more new suns like this could be created! Even the evil, even the unhappy, even the exceptional human being should have his philosophy, his good right, his sunshine! What they don't need is compassion!" A self-sustaining, warming sun should also be created for those outside the protection of morality, for those whom morality has consigned to failure and for whom morality has prescribed "compassion." In this plea for inclusiveness we recognize Nietzsche's insistence that humans learn to live within the entire economy of species preservation, which has a place for everyone and everything. These "evil" and "unhappy" ones don't need confessors or forgivers: "Instead, they need a new *justice*! And a new slogan! And new philosophers! The moral earth is round, too! The moral earth has its antipodes, too! The antipodes have their right to existence too! There is yet another world to be discovered — and more than one! To the ships, you philosophers!" (170). Voyages of discovery are not for the timid, but if one were to create a sustaining sun for oneself, by means of a personal philosophical justification of one's way of thinking and living, a new dawn of exploration and discovery could animate our species — it doesn't have to be doom and gloom after the death of God.

The longest "aphorism" of book 4 is §335 "Long live physics!," surpassed in length only by the first aphorism of *JS* and §357 "On the old problem: 'What is German?'" in book 5. The space Nietzsche dedicates to "Long live physics!" does not surprise us when we consider that his alternative formulation for "shadow of God" is "metaphysics" — §335 could have been titled "Down with metaphysics!" but for the fact that Nietzsche strives throughout *JS* to elevate science and the sciences generally, with an occasional lapse in book 5 (published in 1887). In keeping with other positive, encouraging, and inspiring aphorisms, Nietzsche chose this aphorism's title in order to praise rather than condemn. I can only sketch here the values of physics as Nietzsche would like to see them adopted in the struggle to conquer God's shadow, but this should suffice to demonstrate that many different strands of *JS* converge in §335.

This mini-essay on physics opens with a thesis posed as questions: "How many people really understand how to observe? And of the few who understand how — how many observe themselves?" (196). While the skill of observation is key to the sciences, especially the physical sciences, Nietzsche remains critical of humanity's powers of observation generally, and he has the least confidence in our ability to observe ourselves. Our weakness of self-observation becomes apparent whenever questions of morality arise: "But *that* the situation of self-observation is so desperate has no better evidence than the way *almost everyone* speaks about the essence of a moral action, this quick, obliging, convinced, loquacious way, with its look, its smile, its obliging zeal!" People have a tendency to regard themselves as experts in moral matters, and if not experts, at least competent to judge on morality routinely and without delay, as if their judgments or actions were based on close observation and reasoned analysis. However, Nietzsche deconstructs this conceit by pointing out that a process of judging that appears to consist of one act actually consists of three: "[W]hen someone judges '*this is right*,' when he then concludes '*therefore it must happen*!' and now *does* what he recognizes as right and designates to be necessary — then the essence of his action is *moral*!' But, my friend, you're talking here about three actions instead of one" (196). The manner in which the three moral actions of judging, assuming inevitability (righteousness), and executing the deed are laid out is reminiscent of *BGE* 19, in which the *complexity* of willing is broken down into its components, contrary to the tendency even among philosophers to view willing as a simple phenomenon and a given (*CW* 8, 20–22). Several mental steps are taken before one can judge that something is "right," among them: one defers to one's conscience, whereby one disregards intellectual conscience, which Nietzsche obviously respects as a higher authority than the moral conscience; one draws unknowingly on a "prehistory" of "likes, dislikes, experiences and nonexperiences," all of which bias the moral judgment in ways we do not question or explore; we then obey the command of moral conscience, disregarding the fact that obedience here has been conditioned by ulterior motives, blind acceptance of norms, and dedication to duty. Nietzsche spends considerable time critiquing the so-called firmness of one's moral judgments; on closer analysis, this firmness makes a judgment feel as though it were my own: "The *firmness* of your moral judgment could still be proof in fact of your personal wretchedness, of impersonality; your 'moral strength' could have its source in your stubbornness — or in your inability to behold new ideals!" (197).

The Kantian categorical imperative is not spared: "You admire the categorical imperative in yourself? This 'firmness' of your so-called moral judgment? This 'absoluteness' of the feeling 'all must judge as I do in this matter'? Admire your *selfishness* in this instead! And the blindness, pettiness and unpretentiousness of your selfishness!" (198). The categorical imperative is yet another demonstration of the vaunted firmness of one's moral judgment, something that Nietzsche would sooner ascribe to flimsiness of character, lack of character; it is a preposterous idea: "Anyone who still judges 'in this case everyone would have to act like this,' has not yet taken five steps in the direction of self-knowledge: otherwise he would know that the same actions neither exist nor can exist." Up to this point in his argument, Nietzsche has not directly addressed physics and its powers of observation so much as having provided evidence of how mechanically, thoughtlessly, inauthentically we navigate the moral sphere — we act almost reflexively on the flimsiest of data, we trust and default to our drives and biases, and we invoke high-minded imperatives that attest to the firmness of our judgments, while in fact these judgments are not our own. The conclusion of the aphorism, consisting of roughly half a page, lays out the case for adopting the values and practices of physics.

We will be on firmer ground, closer ground, once we extricate ourselves from the ambiguities of morality, a sphere in which we seem to abandon our skills of observation: "Therefore, let's *limit* ourselves to the purification of our opinions and valuations and to the *creation of our own new tablets of goods* ... W]e must be *physicists* in order to be able to be *creators* in this sense — whereas until now all valuations and ideals were built on *ignorance* of physics or in *contradiction* to it. And therefore: Long live physics! And longer yet that which *compels* us to it — our honesty!" (199). There is an unmistakable Zarathustrian tone to this conclusion, with its emphasis on limiting ourselves to achieving what is actually humanly achievable, to excellence in managing and affirming the closest things, to the creation of new values built on a solid foundation using the methods of physics as opposed to those of metaphysics. Indeed, physics has made it possible for humans to push their powers of observation deep into the galaxy, to identify exoplanets, to amass knowledge of the universe and its possible origins, yet when we navigate our own planet, the one that should concern us most, we remain timid, blind, and contemptuous, as if we believed the earth were flat. In §289 "To the ships," Nietzsche placed his hopes in philosophers to launch voyages of discovery; in §335 he suggests an equally transformative role for physicists.

The conclusion of book 4 is as strong in featuring life-affirming aphorisms as was the beginning — §335 "Long live physics!" pleads an excellent case for approaching the conditions of our new gravity in the spirit of physics; §337 "Future 'humaneness'" reveals Nietzsche's vision for a new level of empathy and happiness; §338 "The will to suffer and the compassionate ones" unmasks the hidden dangers of compassion and our addiction to it, in the direction of sharing joy instead of suffering; §339 "*Vita femina*" reprises arguments about the abundant beauty of the closest things, once more comparing the veiled beauty of existence with a woman; §340 "The dying Socrates" sketches a portrait of Socrates at the decisive moment when he chose negation instead of affirmation, arguing that even the highest exemplars of ancient Greece need to be surpassed; §341 "The greatest weight" presents Nietzsche's first detailed revelation of the thought of eternal recurrence, thereby demonstrating an alternative response to that of Socrates; and §342 "*Incipit tragoedia*" (the tragedy begins), the final aphorism of book 4, is actually the opening page of *Z*, Nietzsche's next book indebted to the three fundamental ideas of book 4, namely, the death of God, eternal recurrence, and life-affirmation. "The greatest weight" merits closer analysis in the context of *JS* overall and book 4 in particular.

One thing that emerges clearly from both the content of §341 and its arrangement in book 4 is its continuity with the thought and purpose of *JS*; §341 is not so much a new thought but a radical culmination of thoughts and ideas Nietzsche had floated throughout this book. In my discussion below of the unpublished notes, it will be demonstrated that eternal recurrence dominated Nietzsche's thinking and writing during the *JS* period, but he strategically limited its appearance and presence in *JS*, preferring for a variety of reasons to save it for later elaboration. The superlative in the title is rather typical of the atmosphere constructed by *JS*, in which a heretofore unseen, unfelt, unknown challenge to our species must be communicated rhetorically by means of superlatives, in order to inspire and arouse equally superlative strategies of response. Also familiar is the presentation of §341 as a hypothetical, with Nietzsche using the personal pronoun to address his readers; this sense of intimacy renders the experiment or encounter personal and urgent, foreclosing options for abstract or impersonal disengagement.

The thought of eternal recurrence is initially so devastating, so preposterous, that Nietzsche ascribes its communication to a sneaky demon — even worse, a demon who exploits your lowest, most vulnerable moment. The demon carefully spells out the implications of the thought, ensuring that you understand that *everything* in your life returns eternally — "and there will be nothing new in it, rather every pain and every joy and every thought and sigh and everything unspeakably small and big in your life must recur for you, and everything in the same succession and sequence" (204). Inoculated by this thought at a vulnerable moment and rudely reminded of your frailty, vulnerability, mortality by a demon who contemptuously refers to you as a mere speck of dust, you might understandably panic or despair — after all, you are currently experiencing precisely the kind of moment that you would not wish to recur eternally, such that your normal, predictable response would be an emphatic No! On the other hand, and here Nietzsche's hypothetical pivots using the conjunction "or": "Or have you once experienced a colossal[22] moment

22. Cf. Paul S. Loeb, "The Colossal Moment in Nietzsche's *Gay Science* §341," in *The Nietzschean Mind,* ed. Paul Katsafanas (New York: Routledge, 2018), 427–47. Loeb makes a compelling case for reading *ungeheuer* as "colossal."

where you would answer him: 'you are a god and I've never heard anything more divine!'" (204). Under the optics of a *colossal moment,* a moment so vast and sublime that your retrospective opens up new vistas, opens up an entire outlook, even the demon transforms into a god, and the moment inspires you to speak an emphatic: Yes!

Your response to the thought or idea of eternal recurrence is the key; Nietzsche uses the phrase "if this thought were to gain power over you." The possible responses range from being transformed and perhaps crushed, which seems to equate to the "greatest weight" that would burden you in the midst of each decision you make, to becoming so enamored of life that you actually *crave* the recurrence of all things; there is no middle ground in the response, no room for a tepid indifference or indecision, ostensibly because the thought has "gained power over you." Of course your "transformation" at the hands of this thought can also be affirmative, as opposed to crushing, hence the either/or scenario that Nietzsche uses twice in §341. When we consider the goal Nietzsche sets for himself in §276, the first aphorism of book 4, namely, "I want at some point for once to be only a Yes-sayer!," it becomes apparent that craving nothing more than the eternal recurrence of your life is the ultimate act of affirmation and the ultimate expression of Yes-saying.

The logic or coherence of eternal recurrence was also foreshadowed in §§339 and 340. In §339, Nietzsche alludes to the ancient Greek "prayer" for everything beautiful to return twice and thrice: "Oh, they had a good reason to invoke the gods, for ungodly reality gives us the beautiful not at all or just once! What I mean is, the world is overflowing with beautiful things but nevertheless poor, very poor in beautiful moments and unveilings of these things" (203). Here we see not only the prayer or desire for beauty to return but also Nietzsche's pointed observation that beauty gives itself "not at all or just once." Only eternal recurrence would capture that one instance of beauty eternally; only eternal recurrence can leverage a single "colossal" moment, recollection, experience, or feeling into the eternal affirmation of one's life. Then in §340, where Socrates is praised at first only to be criticized later for looking back on life as if it had been a disease, we have the case of an exemplary human being who chooses the very opposite of eternal affirmation, namely, the condemnation of life. Socrates, like Christians who later practice Christianity as "Platonism of the people,"[23] regards himself as being liberated from life by death; the realm of eternity for Socrates and Christians is Platonic, that is, not of this world, whereas the eternity implied by eternal recurrence is of every facet and detail of your life in *this* world.

Book 5 "We Fearless Ones" was added to *JS* for the second edition of 1887, so that in matters of tone (voice), content, and semantics it is closer to *BGE, GM,* and the copious, sometimes chaotic unpublished notes from the period of *BGE* and *GM.* For a better understanding of book 5 and its immediate philosophical surroundings, one should consult my Translator's Afterword for volume 8 of *CW,* as well as my Translator's Afterword for volume 16; here one will find detailed information about the circumstances around Nietzsche's published and unpublished writings for the years 1886–87. Book 5 must of course be included in any discussion of *JS,* but it would be extremely misleading to allow readers to infer that the last book was cut from the same cloth as the first four. Regarding the integrity of *JS* in its original version of 1882, I had this to say: "In my estimation Nietzsche disrupted the coherence and flow of *The Joyful Science* by adding the fifth book, for the original four books represented an improvement over the earlier aphoristic works in terms of coherence and balance — it also served perfectly as the threshold to *Thus Spoke Zarathustra,* since it featured the aphorisms on the death of God (125) and the eternal recurrence of the same (341), which form the backbone of Zarathustra's doctrine of life affirmation" (*CW* 8, 435–36).

The two major events in Nietzsche's life between 1882 and 1887 were the relationship with Lou Salomé and the writing

---

23. Cf. *BGE* Preface in *CW* 8, 2.

of Z,[24] both events that changed Nietzsche and influenced the voice he would use for his writings. Before I delve into the aphorisms of book 5, in which Nietzsche self-identifies as a new (kind of) philosopher and a Dionysian in the same manner as he does in *BGE,* it will be helpful to recall that his voice was more modest, more limited in the pre-Z works. To be sure, the guiding thoughts of the death of God and eternal recurrence had surfaced already in book 4 of *JS,* but only in a preliminary and tentative form; Nietzsche had not yet accepted for himself nor had he announced his new philosophical *task* in 1882, though he gave intimations throughout *JS* that such a move might be forthcoming. Earlier I quoted Keith Ansell-Pearson regarding what Epicurus meant to Nietzsche at the time of *JS,* and here we should pick up the thread once more. During the middle period, Ansell-Pearson explains, Nietzsche appreciates Epicurus for the ancient philosopher's cultivation of a modest life, his care of the self, and practical philosophical behavior "aimed at the attainment of *eudaemonia [,]* or the flourishing life,"[25] rather than philosophy as a theoretical discourse. We can safely conclude that Nietzsche himself achieved such a balanced, flourishing life and that this enabled him to write *JS* in part as a reflection of that life, as depicted for example in the figure of the gazing Epicurus of §45. But those of us who have written about Nietzsche's "Dionysian" philosophizing have long argued that the emergence of Dionysus in Nietzsche's philosophizing does not reveal itself only in the last chapter of *BGE* but instead that the entire writing and execution of Z was a Dionysian act, the "ultimate Dionysian deed" as Nietzsche would write in *EH.*[26] In this context, it makes sense for Ansell-Pearson to claim that when Dionysus "returns" to Nietzsche's

24. Cf. Adrian Del Caro, "Andreas-Salomé and Nietzsche: New Perspectives," *Seminar* 36, no. 1 (2000): 79–96.

25. Ansell-Pearson, "True to the Earth," 103.

26. Cf. Adrian Del Caro, "Nietzschean Self-Transformation and the Transformation of the Dionysian," in *Nietzsche, Philosophy and the Arts,* ed. Salim Kemal, Ivan Gaskell, and Daniel Conway (Cambridge: Cambridge University Press, 1998), 70–91.

thinking in the late period, the concept of "Dionysian joy" pushes out and eclipses the softer, more gentle and contained aspects of the Epicurean flourishing life.[27]

Section 343 "The significance of our cheerfulness" is a splendid amalgam of earlier *JS* themes as discussed previously in §§108, 125, 283, and 289, together with *BGE* themes infused with the "we" pronoun that characterizes Nietzsche's free spirits and new philosopher companions of the late period. Here he claims in words very similar to those of §125 that the full impact of God's death has not reached us yet, but unlike §125 with its dystopian gloom, the "cheerful" companions of Nietzsche know they have their work cut out for them in terms of undermining the old foundation: "This long profusion and sequence of demolition, destruction, decline, overthrow that now lies ahead: who could guess enough of it today to have to serve as the teacher and foreteller of this monstrous logic of horrors, the prophet of a dimming and a solar eclipse whose like has probably never existed yet on earth?" (207) Bearing in mind that *BGE* was written in part to explain and unpack the more lyrical, cryptic messages of *Z*, we see in §343 an embrace of the challenges that lie ahead: "Indeed, we philosophers and 'free spirits' feel as if we're illuminated by a new dawn at the news that the 'old God is dead'; our heart overflows with gratitude, amazement, presentiment, expectation — finally the horizon seems open again to us, even presupposing it is not bright; finally our ships can put to sea again, put to sea against any danger" (207). "We fearless ones" are synonymous with the free spirits and new philosophers of *BGE*; in §343 Nietzsche makes every effort to touch on prominent *JS* themes, as if to demonstrate continuity with the first four books, yet the mood, voice, and swagger of §343 sound and feel very much like the "prelude to a philosophy of the future."

Nietzsche's advocacy of science throughout the first four books is not without an occasional criticism, but overall the

27. Ansell-Pearson, "True to the Earth," 97. See also Lampert, *Nietzsche and Modern Times,* 136, 423.

message is that science is a powerful tool of enlightenment, embraced by those who will engage the new struggles in the era of the shadow of God. Certainly Giorgio Colli, one of the editors of the German edition of Nietzsche's works, credited him for his strong support of science and made it the centerpiece of his afterword (642–45). Colli drew our attention in particular to §293 as a sample of how Nietzsche treated science in the first four books: "Now with this 'rigor of science' matters stand much as they do with the formality and courtesy of the very best society: — they terrify the uninitiated. But those who are accustomed to it would never live anywhere else but in this bright, transparent, robust, and highly electrified air, in this *manly* air" (173). Contrast this positive, even elitist embrace of science with §373, which Colli regards as "grim criticism": Nietzsche suspects the "faith with which so many materialistic natural scientists are content now, that faith in a world that is supposed to have its equivalent and measure in human thinking, in human value concepts, in a 'world of truth' that one is ultimately capable of figuring out with our little four-square human reason — what?" (251). Faith and truth as represented by scientists may actually be capable of comprehending only the most superficial elements of existence, those immediately available to our senses: "Would it not conversely be quite probable that precisely the most superficial and external aspects of existence — its most apparent qualities, its skin and sensualization — would be grasped first? would perhaps even be the only thing grasped? A 'scientific' world interpretation as you understand it could then still be one of the *most stupid,* that is, most lacking in meaning of all possible interpretations" (251). This is far from the confident, hopeful tone of §335 "Long live physics!," but it is consistent with the second aphorism of book 5, "How we, too, are still pious" (§344), where Nietzsche devotes two full pages to arguing for how science merely mirrors and continues the errors of metaphysics.

The main argument Nietzsche has with science in his late period is its absoluteness, its unconditionality, as seen in this passage: "What do you know from the outset about the character of existence to be able to decide whether there is greater advantage on the side of the unconditionally mistrustful or the unconditionally trusting? But in case both should be necessary, much trust *and* much mistrust: where then is science supposed to acquire its unconditional faith, its underlying conviction that truth is more important than any other thing, even than any other conviction?" (208). Apparently the science that Nietzsche questions here is the one beholden to truth at all costs, because as he completes his thought a moment later: "Precisely this conviction could not have arisen if both truth *and* untruth had constantly proven useful: as is indeed the case." The notion that truth and untruth, good and evil, reality and appearance, are both valuable and effective in the preservation of the species is the foundational idea of book 1 and a sustaining thesis of *JS,* but here in the fifth book Nietzsche prefers to unmask truth rather than highlight the benefits of its pursuit. Consider this portion of the argument, where Nietzsche insists that the character of life consists of semblance, error, deception, dissimulation, blinding, and self-blinding: "'Will to truth' — that could be a hidden will to death. — So the question: why science? leads back to the moral problem: *why morality at all* if life, nature, history are 'immoral'? There is no doubt, the truthful man, in that daring and ultimate sense in which faith in science presupposes him, *thus affirms a different world* from that of life, nature and history; and insofar as he affirms this 'different world,' how it that? must he not then — deny its counterpart, this world, *our* world?" (209) The problem with science as stated here is that it is not necessarily without bias toward life — indeed, that it is possibly a "hidden will to death." We recall that in §1 "The teachers of the purpose of existence," Nietzsche charged that the moral teacher "invents a second, different existence and by means of his new mechanism he lifts this old ordinary existence off its old ordinary hinges" (38). In the context of aphorism §1, Nietzsche prescribed laughter, humor, levity, flexibility in the face of this simulacrum "double" world in which levity is the first casualty. Now in §344 we see a reversal whereby *scientists* are accused of creating this second, double world, for by this time Nietzsche has decided "that even we knowing ones of today, we godless and anti-metaphysical ones also still take *our* fire from the conflagration kindled by an ancient faith that is thousands of years old, that Christian faith that was also the faith of Plato, that God is the truth, that the truth is divine" (209). We are reminded of Colli's words to the effect that book 5 does not successfully maintain the harmony established and reached in book 4; by turning the tables on scientists in such a way that they become almost synonymous with moralists or moral teachers, Nietzsche is dialing up the pressure on philosophy to work as an effective alternative. But the rhetorical equation of morality and science in the long run is counterproductive and certainly not in keeping with the notion and strategies of *joyful science* as it lives out its patently nonabsolutist existence.

And Nietzsche at times in book 5 is lucid about this need to cultivate and maintain a kind of science, a kind of knowledge that any free spirit can be proud of, as seen in §375 "Why we seem like Epicureans." From book 1 we have the image of the gazing Epicurus who gives us an impressionistic portrait of happiness, who serves as the personification of Nietzsche's embrace of the closest things, his overcoming of suffering and its alchemical transformation into golden beauty (§45). Epicurus again inspires Nietzsche to one of his more balanced, more gracious observations in §375, which is part of a cluster of aphorisms treating the interplay between science and morality; his first charge is leveled against dogmatism: "We are cautious, we modern human beings, about ultimate convictions; our mistrust lies in wait for enchantments and deceptions of the conscience that lie in every strong faith, every unconditional Yes and No: how can this be explained?" (253). Even scientists and philosophers are still too capable of unconditional convictions, as demonstrated in §344 with its exposé of the unforeseen consequences of the pursuit of truth, so Nietzsche offers an explanation for why some modern human beings are able to remain cautious and free of ultimate convictions: those who have believed too deeply in the past may have felt burned, for example, and remain wary of believing again — they are referred to as disappointed idealists. On the positive end, Nietzsche praises those who have liberated themselves without subsequently adopting new chains, those who exhibit "the jubilating curiosity of someone who formerly stood in his corner, who was driven to despair by his corner and now revels and raves in the opposite of his corner, in the infinite, in the 'open as such'" (253). The embrace of the open is conceptually the opposite of embracing dogma, and it is practiced by individuals who revel in their liberation from narrow, closed spaces, from painful corners; notably, these celebrants with their "jubilant curiosity" are not averse to question marks or to standing exposed to the open. Nietzsche next invokes Epicurus in describing this jubilant curiosity: "With this, a nearly Epicurean penchant for knowledge develops, which does not want cheaply to let go of the question-mark character of things; likewise an aversion for big moral words and gestures, a taste that rejects all clumsy foursquare oppositions and is consciously proud of its practice in being reserved" (253). The Epicurean penchant for knowledge, it should be recalled, is more practical than the theoretical model of philosophy, resulting in what Ansell-Pearson calls the "care of self and world" displayed by Nietzsche in his middle period. Epicurean knowledge also welcomes question marks, eschews big moral words, rejects clumsy and facile oppositions, and is "consciously proud of its practice in being reserved." Here the pursuit of knowledge is focused, tempered, and validating of oneself in the quest for freedom. As Lampert observes: "Nietzsche's anatomy of this 'jubilant curiosity,' a near synonym of joyous science, describes an almost Epicurean happiness . . . And possessing it brings pride, a particularly Epicurean pride based on self-mastery, mind's mastery of the heart, the mastery on which Epicurus insisted in the face of Plato's concessions to the heart."[28] And lest anyone

---

28. Lampert, *Nietzsche and Modern Times*, 426–27.

underestimate the importance of this juxtaposition of Platonism and Epicureanism, with the former representing dogma and the latter representing the open, Lampert offers this pithy assessment: "Nietzsche's recovery of Epicurus is a key element in his new history of philosophy because it provides another means of access to its all-important themes" (427).

One more important metaphor concludes §375, and Nietzsche uses it to describe the pride that he and his modern peers take in showing reserve, in reserving judgment: "For *this* is what constitutes our pride, this gentle tugging on the reins of our forward-charging urge for certainty, this self-mastery of the rider on his wildest rides: for we still have the same crazy and fiery steeds beneath us, and if we hesitate, then surely danger is least of all what makes us hesitate" (253). The "urge for certainty" is strong, but so is the need, according to Nietzsche, to steer and guide and control this urge, so that the horse one rides does not gallop away wildly, does not dictate one's course, direction, or destination. There is hesitation on the part of the rider who tugs gently at the reins but not because of fear of the unknown and the open but out of respect for the power of the horse and vigilance for maintaining control over it. The Epicurean way of knowing honors the presence of the open and the infinite but does not surrender to it, does not become lost in or to it; indeed, if Epicurean knowing is to serve effectively as a countercurrent to Platonism and the dogmatism it engenders, it must reserve its energies for exploration and affirmation of the closest things, with the earth and our human existence representing not a narrow, closed corner, not a *trap,* but a beloved home whose threshold is always opening to "the open as such."

The "official" last aphorism of book 5 is 382 "The great health," which in *JS* fashion closes the circle begun by §343 with its reiteration of the death of God and a plea to free spirits to set sail with Nietzsche into the open sea. There is an epilogue numbered 383, to be sure, but Nietzsche intends it as a transition to the "Songs of Prince Vogelfrei"; §383 is highly playful, lyrical, musical, a fitting epilogue in which Nietzsche claims to be surrounded by the raucous spirits of his book who will now take over where he leaves off. But §382 "The great health" also returns to the nautical and argonautical aphorisms that Nietzsche uses in abundance to convey heroism, discovery, and particularly the circumnavigation of a new world whose horizons are no longer set in place by God.[29] Nietzsche extends his collective "we" pronoun to "argonauts of the ideal" who will boldly use their new health, who are "dangerously healthy, healthy again and again," to explore a world described as "a yet undiscovered land . . . whose boundaries no one has yet surveyed, something beyond all previous lands and corners of the ideal, a world so superabundant in what is beautiful, strange, questionable, terrible and divine" that they cannot wait to "possess" this world (260). Familiar *JS* themes are the voyages of discovery, living dangerously, experiencing untold beauty, and shifting to a higher plane of human existence. Indeed, it is clear that §382 has a post-*Z* point of departure when Nietzsche describes the ideal of this new human being: "the ideal of a human-superhuman well-being and benevolence, that will often enough appear *inhuman,* for instance, when it shows up next to all previous earthly seriousness, next to every kind of solemnity of gesture, word, tone, look, morality and task looking like their incarnate and involuntary parody" (261). That *JS* again closes on an explicit Zarathustra note, as did book 4, is underscored by the use of the same expression that serves as the Latin title of §342: "*[T]he great seriousness* begins, the real question mark is posed for the first time, the destiny of the soul turns, the clock hand advances, the tragedy *begins . . .*" (261). "The tragedy begins," or *incipit tragoedia,* signals both the beginning of the book *Thus Spoke Zarathustra* as well as the beginning of the new era of affirmative dwelling on the earth as the *meaning* of the earth, namely, as superhumans.

Nietzsche added the *Appendix: Songs of Prince Vogelfrei* in 1887 for the second edition. As Montinari informs us, six of

29. Cf. §§42, 60, 124, 283, 289, 291, 310, 343, 377, 382, as well as poem no. 2 of "Jokes" and "Toward New Seas" in the "Songs."

the eight poems from *Songs* had been published earlier as *Idylls from Messina* in the journal *Internationale Monatsschrift* ("International Monthly") in May of 1882. "They stem from the same extensive mass of poetic experiments of February–April 1882, from which N later constructed his 'Prelude in German Rhymes' for *JS* ('Jokes, Cunning and Revenge')" (604). These poems take up prominent themes from the period of the first edition of *JS:* truth versus fiction (the poet, for better or worse); the north/south dichotomy in cultural terms; love; sea travel; happiness.

"To Goethe" offers Nietzsche's playful take on Goethe's concept of the "Eternal Feminine" (*das Ewig-Weibliche*), which Nietzsche exploits in order to draw attention to how poets are able to seduce their readers into embracing airy ideals and lofty fictions. Goethe's *Faust* conspicuously, and for Nietzsche, suspiciously, ends with the hero's redemption, assisted by the Chorus Mysticus — a host of heavenly Catholic characters, including the blessed Margarete (Gretchen) whom Faust had seduced and who was executed for infanticide. Faust wins his wager with Mephisto by striving unceasingly his whole life long, such that upon his dying, his soul does not get captured by the devil. Instead, Faust's remains are lifted up, and he soars into the heavens, guided by the Penitent Gretchen under the guidance of Mater Gloriosa. The last words of Goethe's masterpiece are spoken by the Chorus Mysticus:

> All that is changeable
> Is but reflected;
> The unattainable
> Here is effected;
> Human discernment
> Here is passed by;
> The Eternal-Feminine
> Draws us on high.[30]

30. Johann Wolfgang von Goethe, *Faust: A Tragedy,* ed. Cyrus Hamlin, trans. Walter Arndt, 2nd ed. (New York: W. W. Norton, 2001), 344.

The redeeming, miraculous cosmic order reflected by these lines, whereby the Eternal Feminine represents both a mystical force that Goethe ascribed to the female principle as well as the human and superhuman forces of love and striving exemplified by Gretchen and Faust, respectively, is gleefully subverted by Nietzsche. There is no such thing as the "ever-enduring" as the alternative to the changeable, to the transitory; the poet merely throws it out as a parable, just as God "the all-blurring" (versus "all-knowing") is a mere poet's fiction. Nietzsche instantiates his own worldview in "To Goethe," sketching a picture of the forces he sees at work in the godless universe. The world-wheel, ceaselessly turning as the circle of eternal recurrence, randomly spawns and spins off goals, and while someone with a grudge or a yearning might call this activity fate or necessity, the fool of Nietzsche's *JS* would more accurately call it play. And as for the bypassing of human discernment and the ultimate lifting up of humans by the Eternal Feminine, Nietzsche's answer is simple: there never was any discernment; it's all play, world-play that blends "truth and tricks," reality and appearance. "The eternally fooling one / Blends *us* — in the mix! . . ." (263). In three terse, clever strophes, Nietzsche deconstructs the Goethean universe and reconstructs his own playfully competing version — if a single poem could embody the ethos and execution of *JS,* that poem would be "To Goethe."

The famous poem "Sils-Maria" memorializes the epiphany of Zarathustra. We know from the unpublished fragment 11[141] that the idea of eternal recurrence occurred to Nietzsche early in August 1881, in the mountains of southern Switzerland at Sils-Maria, "6,000 feet above sea level" (351). As the biographer Curt Paul Janz explains, the basic thoughts of *Z* arise soon thereafter,[31] and in fact we see them interspersed throughout the unpublished notes of this period, but Nietzsche did not yet have "the figure Zarathustra himself," which had to wait until the following winter as he recounts in *EH:* "I spent the winter

31. Janz, *Friedrich Nietzsche,* 79–80.

that followed in the charming, peaceful bay of Rapallo near Genoa, carved out between Chiavari and the foothills of Porto Fino. {. . .} In the mornings, I set off for the heights in a southerly direction along the glorious road to Zoagli, past pines and looking down on the panorama of the sea; in the afternoons, as often as my health permitted, I walked round the whole bay from Santa Margherita right up to Porto Fino. {. . .} On these two pathways the whole of the first book of *Zarathustra* came to me, especially Zarathustra himself, as a type: more correctly, he *overcame me . . .*" ("Books" Z1, *CW* 9, 279–80). The fragment of this poem found among the unpublished notes for summer–autumn 1882 (cf. *CW* 14, 3[3], 92) consists of four lines only, without the concluding couplet naming Zarathustra, and it bears the title "Portofino." Possibly for dramatic effect, but also because in his own mind Nietzsche conflated the epiphany of eternal recurrence with the epiphany of Zarathustra, he named this later Zarathustra poem "Sils-Maria." More on this below when I discuss the concluding rhymed couplet.

Nietzsche is in waiting mode, according to the first line, but not for anything specific.[32] He is literally waiting for nothing (*doch auf Nichts*), and the rest of the strophe consisting of two rhymed couplets describes the intermediary state in which he waits: he is beyond good and evil in moral terms, now enjoying light, now darkness, "all game, / All sea, all midday, all time without aim" (281). There is temporality here, but absent any purpose, and Nietzsche's amoral ontology mingles with play and with the sea, as the experience of eternity. This is a fecund state of becoming, giving birth to the figure named in the concluding lines: "At once then, my friend! One turned into Two — / And Zarathustra strode into my view . . ." (281). Here Grundlehner can help us understand "Sils-Maria" as a poem straddling two geographical locations and two different human beings: "[T]he symbolism of the sea was enhanced appreciably when he met the twenty-one-year-old Lou Salomé

---

32. Grundlehner, *Poetry of Friedrich Nietzsche*, 134–37.

for the first time when he returned after several weeks to Rome from Sicily. In Nietzsche's mind, Lou became a metaphor for a model companion who would accompany him on his ocean journeys of adventure and discovery. It was thus under her influence that he wrote 'Nach neuen Meeren' ('Toward New Seas') and 'Sils-Maria' during the summer of 1882."[33] The confusion about *where* Zarathustra first "appeared" to Nietzsche, that is, whether in Sils-Maria or Portofino/Rapallo, is in part deliberate, because, as mentioned earlier, the thought of eternal recurrence is traceable to Sils-Maria, and eternal recurrence is so closely associated with Zarathustra that it could be said to function as his personification. I think Nietzsche wanted this ambiguity also because two very different forces are at work between Sils-Maria and Rapallo, namely, the mountains and the sea — their marriage, so to speak, produces the offspring Zarathustra, and symbolically, the entire scope of the earth.

The "my friend!" refers to Salomé (*Freundin!*, "lady friend"), to whom Nietzsche tells this story: all at once "One turned into Two" suggests parthenogenesis, as Grundlehner maintains (136), an egg occurring without fertilization. But whether we call this parthenogenesis or palingenesis or simply rebirth, there is suddenly a second out of a first, or two out of one, or new out of old, and we cannot rule out that Salomé herself is the spiritual mother who, with the spiritual father Nietzsche, gives birth to the son Zarathustra.[34] At the very least, Salomé so affected Nietzsche in the period that gave rise to *Z* that we could call her Zarathustra's midwife.

33. Grundlehner, *Poetry of Friedrich Nietzsche*, 122.
34. For the nuances of birth and rebirthing, as well as Salomé's own writings about N as the father of Zarathustra and N's own words about how he came to life after meeting Salomé, see Adrian Del Caro, "Andreas-Salomé and Nietzsche: New Perspectives," note 22 above.

The Unpublished Fragments from the Period of "The Joyful Science" (Spring 1881–Summer 1882)

The notebooks Nietzsche filled with writings from spring 1881 through summer 1882 reveal a fairly remarkable degree of continuity and coherence, despite the fact that for roughly the whole year from spring 1881 to spring 1882, there was no concrete plan for a book called *The Joyful Science*. As Montinari tells us, Nietzsche at the end of January 1882 considered books 6–8 of *D* to be finished; he had published *D* in five books in June of 1881, and these three new sections were supposed to represent a continuation of *D*, just as Nietzsche had kept adding to *HAH*. But *JS* came into being in its own right just a few months later: "Shortly after his acquaintance with Lou von Salomé and during his sojourn in Switzerland with Lou and Rée, N changed his plans, and on 8 May he wrote to his publisher: 'By autumn you will have a manuscript by me: title "The Joyful Science" (with many epigrams and *verses*!!!)'" (533). The relative coherence of the unpublished fragments for *JS* therefore springs from the continuity of this material with the contents of *D*, as well as the existence of one extremely large notebook in particular, M III 1, which contains the first mention of eternal recurrence and many subsequent deliberations inspired by it. In what follows, I have broken the eleven notebooks into six discrete categories. It is worth noting that compared to the unpublished fragments from the period of *BGE* and *GM*, namely, 1886–87, the *JS* notes are briefer, more closely related to one another in theme, and far more uniform both in purpose and voice.

Notebook M III 1 spanning the period from spring to autumn contains fragments 11[1] through 11[348] spread over 160 pages; I will use 11[140] as the cutoff for my first section, because the sheer number of fragments is too large to discuss in one section[35] and because 11[141] is the first mention of eternal recurrence, representing a different and more homogeneous tone for the remaining fragments in this notebook. The prevailing themes of 11[1] through 11[140] are the economy of species preservation,

35. Indeed, M III 1 by itself represents 54 percent of the entire *Nachlaß* of *JS*, based on the pagination of *KSA* 9.

the nature of the organic, evolution-related ideas, the genealogy of morality, critiques of utilitarianism, and the nature of power.

Fragment 11[21] presents a phenomenology of the ego, whereby Nietzsche argues we should abandon this facile concept and replace it with something more accurate: "To describe the history of the *ego-feeling:* and to show how even in altruism this wanting-to-possess is the essential thing" (313). Ego and non-ego are not the proper distinctions, but instead wanting-to-possess, on the one hand, and the appearance of possession, on the other. The manner in which we might achieve this liberation from the erroneous ego concept: "Re-create the ego-feeling! Weaken the personal inclination! Accustom the eye to the reality of things!" (313). At stake here is more than simply rechristening the ego as wanting-to-possess; one must simultaneously stifle the personal inclination while trusting more, investing more, in the reality of things. Nietzsche does not yet have this precise alternative, but he rephrases what he means by it: "Something new has to be created: not *ego* and not *tu* and not *omnes*" (313). The personal pronouns "I" and "thou/you" and the pronoun "everyone" act as a hindrance to the apprehension of things; lessening the filter of the personal will have salutary results: "Seek to become master over *things* and thus satisfy one's wanting-to-possess!" (313). In the relationship between subject and object, which Nietzsche never tires of criticizing as a facile, lazy conceptual shortcut, he would elevate the objects, things generally, and minimize the subject: "**Let** ourselves be **possessed** by things (not by persons) and by the greatest possible scope *of true things*! What *grows* from this remains to be seen: we are *arable land* for things. *Images of existence* should sprout from us: and we should be as this fertility requires us to be" (313). *JS* contains a variety of expressions for affirming things, all the way up to and including the affirmation of everything, namely, *amor fati.* 11[21] represents a fragmentary thought experiment, an attempt to sketch out the implications of submerging the ego and the personal, but one that did not make the cut — the *Nachlaß* for *JS* includes many such notes in which Nietzsche tries to work things out.[36]

Fragment 11[43] is intriguing for its treatment of the concept of natural selection and for the fact that Nietzsche actually uses the word "selection" — which he does not in 11[5], where he uses typical German *Zuchtwahl* (natural selection).[37] Here he takes Herbert Spencer to task for being a glorifier of "selection-expediency": "These glorifiers of selection-expediency (like Spencer) believe they know what *favorable circumstances* of a development are! and fail to reckon *evil* among them! And what would have become of human beings without fear envy greed! They wouldn't exist anymore: and if one thinks of the richest noblest and most fruitful human being, *without* evil — then one is thinking a contradiction" (319). In *JS* §§1 and 4 he had argued for the importance of "evil" as part of the amazing economy of species preservation, while here in 11[43] the same issue is approached from the standpoint of natural selection. If Spencer as well as utilitarians and moralists generally insist on banning the negative drives, instincts, passions from the "favorable circumstances" of natural selection, they are cannibalizing the human being as such and instating a wishful ideal in its place: "[A] beautiful resting humanity would be possible, nourished and blossoming on all sides, but a quite different humanity than *our best one* — for which some things also have to be asserted" (319). Our "best humanity," as Nietzsche calls it, must include those "evil" elements, and toward the conclusion of this fragment he even posits a way of *anticipating* natural selection: "Incidentally, as an individual one could *anticipate* the tremendously slow process of selection, in many respects and temporarily reveal the human being in their goal — my ideal! *Set aside* the unfavorable circumstances by setting *oneself*

<hr/>

36. Cf. also 11[65] for a very similar formulation of the need to see and embrace *things* differently.

37. The 1903 edition of the Thieme-Preusser *Dictionary of the English and German Languages* (Dresden: Verlag von Erwin Haendcke) lists *Zuchtwahl* as the technical term for Darwin's "natural selection" (726).

aside (solitude) *selection* of influences (nature books elevated events) with which to reflect on this! Maintain only benevolent rivals in one's memory!" (319). The different things an individual might do to anticipate natural selection were also suggested in *JS* §283 "Preparatory human beings," where the exhortations to live dangerously are found.

We recall that the subtitle of *D* is "Thoughts on the Presumptions of Morality," and that *JS* was constructed from sections that were supposed to serve as a continuation of *D*. The genealogical method that Nietzsche honed in the aphoristic books of the middle period saw its most successful application in *GM* (1887), where Nietzsche often invokes the rhetoric of pathology to describe "symptoms" of morality that afflict humankind throughout history. In 11[103] we have a precursor of such argumentation, one that is so succinct, so packed with explosive undermining, that it merits inclusion here in its entirety:

> What is morality! A human being, a people has suffered a physiological change, senses this in *communal feeling* and interprets it in the language of its affects and *according to the degree* of its knowledge, without noticing that the seat of the change is in its *physis*. As if someone were hungry and believed they could satisfy it with concepts and customs, with praise and blame! (337)

The physiological change is misconstrued in such a way that a disturbance caused by the body, whether individual or collective, is relegated or isolated to the realm of the mental, where it becomes a moral issue. Of course, the problem cannot be properly treated in this manner, so that the sickness will be prolonged and perpetuated by the "moral physicians" otherwise known as priests. Or compare this even pithier expression, the one-liner that constitutes 11[117]: "Moral judgments are epidemics that have *their time*" (341).

A different, more wide-ranging genealogy and phenomenology is conducted by Nietzsche in 11[134], in which I see early stirrings of the concept of the will to power. This fragment reminiscent of later 14[13] is among those inspired by Nietzsche's reading of Wilhelm Roux's *Der Kampf der Theile im Organismus* ("Struggle of the parts within the organism") (1881; cf. note to 11[128]). The experiment he launches here is stated as follows: "When we translate the properties of the lowest animate beings into our 'reason,' then *moral* drives result" (347). Primitive organisms assimilate their neighbors, converting them into property and nourishment; assimilation leads to appropriation, incorporation, growth, reproduction, exploitation of the weaker (348). Next he focuses on higher organisms, claiming: "Whoever has the most power to reduce others to functions, ends up ruling — but the subordinated have their own subordinates in turn — their ongoing struggles: whose maintenance to a certain degree is the condition of life for the whole. The whole in turn seeks its advantage and finds opponents" (348). Bearing in mind that the experiment here is to translate the activity of the organic into "reason," it is inevitable that digestion will be discussed, along with its attendant or accompanying rational equivalent: "Every body is constantly *excreting*, it separates what is *not* useful to it in the assimilated being: what the human being despises, what causes him disgust, what he calls evil are the *excrements*" (348). So humans regard their despised, disgusting elements as evil, and they excrete their evil just as any organism must be able to excrete in order to maintain itself. The problem, however, is that humans are too quick to decide on what is evil; ignorant "reason," we are told, incorrectly labels as evil those things that are simply obstacles, thereby *mistaking as useless* "that which is hard to gain, hard to conquer hard to incorporate" (348). Evil is not useless; on the contrary, it is of great use in the overall economy of species preservation, but humans must have their excremental outlet, their toilet, so to speak. Now we see Nietzsche's explanation for altruism, sharing, virtue, and even love: "When he '*shares*' with others, is '*unselfish*' — then maybe this is merely the excretion of his *useless* **feces**, which he *mus-*

pass, in order to not suffer from them. He knows that this dung is *useful* to the foreign field and makes himself a *virtue* of his 'generosity.' — 'Love' is a sensation for property or that which we desire as property" (349). A less sentimental interpretation of morality could hardly be imagined; not even Nietzsche's later equation of morality with sickness reaches this blasphemous level of explicitness. When humans of necessity excrete what is useless to them, their excrement, it takes the form of giving or sharing; sharing one's feces in turn is construed by reason as a fertilizing gift to others and elevated to the virtue of generosity.

Fragment 11[141] signals the beginning of Nietzsche's preoccupation with the thought of eternal recurrence, which is referenced over twenty times in the fragments numbering 11[141]–11[348]. Other themes in this second half of M III 1 are the organic, a few draft titles and plans for *Z* and *JS*, the critique of reason, and physics and cosmology. Under the heading "*The Recurrence of the Same.* / Draft." we find five entries for chapters, quite likely preliminary plans for what later became *Z*. The first three are incorporations of basic errors, passions, and knowing; chapter 4 is "The innocent one," and chapter 5 is "The new *weight: the eternal recurrence of the same*" (350). Here Nietzsche poses the question, "What do we do with the *rest* of our life — we who have spent the greatest portion of it in the vastest ignorance? We *teach the teaching* — it is the strongest means of *incorporating* it into ourselves. Our kind of bliss, as teachers of the greatest teaching" (351). Another page and a half are devoted to elaborating on chapter 4 as the "philosophy of indifference," detailing how everything that used to constitute the seriousness of existence must henceforth be approached as if we were children. Indifference will be necessary, otherwise our compassion could topple us: "Indifference has to have affected us deeply and also the pleasure of looking on. Even the misery of future humankind should *not* be of concern to us. But whether *we* still *want to live* is the question: and how!" (352). This fragment of roughly two pages concludes with a final paragraph whose first sentence amounts to instructions to himself: "To consider: the various *sublime states* that I had, as foundations of the various *chapters* and their material" (352). Indeed, in order to serve as the teacher of eternal recurrence, Nietzsche will have to identify these previous "sublime states" and let them set and carry the tone for his planned book.

Fragment 11[148] is highly reminiscent of phrases Nietzsche employed in *Z* when referring to eternal recurrence, and it also contains a few locutions he used in *JS* §341. What is unusual about 11[148] is that it combines cosmological argumentation with the metaphorical language in which eternal recurrence is frequently draped in the published writings. At the outset he writes: "The world of forces sustains no decrease: for otherwise it would have become weak and perished over infinite time. The world of forces sustains no standstill: for otherwise it would have been reached, and the clock of existence would stand still. Therefore the world of forces never arrives at an equilibrium, it never has a moment of rest, its force and its motion are equally great at any time. Whatever state this world *can* ever reach, it must have reached and not once, but countless times" (354). These are the kind of arguments based on physics or cosmology that are rather abundant in the unpublished fragments but rare among the published writings, where Nietzsche preferred to speak of eternal recurrence as he does in the remainder of 11[148]: Your whole life will be turned over again and again like an hourglass; there will be one prodigious moment in between until all the conditions out of which you have developed come together again in the cycle of the world; all suffering, joy, friend and foe — everything will return, the "entire coherence of all things"; the ring in which you are a kernel sparkles again and again: "And in every ring of human existence generally there ⟨is⟩ always one hour when the most powerful thought surfaces first to one, then to many, then to all, the thought of the eternal recurrence of all things — each time for humankind it is the hour of *noon*" (354). Fragment 11[148] represents in one fragment the two major strategies for communicating eternal recurrence, namely, the cognitive approach, whereby its teacher tries to appeal to science, and the metaphorical approach, whereby the teacher speaks in parables about an idea that must be incorporated in order to make sense.

JS §109 "Let us beware!" is the second aphorism of book 3, and therewith the earliest opportunity for Nietzsche to expound on the dangers announced in "New struggles"; after God's death his shadow (read: metaphysics) must also be conquered. Section 109 issues several cautions against adopting views of the world that basically anthropomorphize it, and it closes with an impassioned plea to de-deify nature and renaturalize human beings with the newly liberated nature. Fragments 11[157] and 11[158] represent earlier versions of §109 in which the warnings are focused explicitly on how eternal recurrence should not be misinterpreted or misrepresented, and they use the same refrain, "let us beware," each time to make their point. These fragments illustrate how Nietzsche controlled and suppressed the thought of eternal recurrence in *JS*, releasing it only in small doses, suggestions, and in §341 "The heaviest weight" at the conclusion of book 4. While the published version in *JS* is designed to appeal to readers generally, the fragments, it will be demonstrated, target the teachers of eternal recurrence.

Nietzsche's first concerns in 11[157] are that eternal recurrence will be ascribed a teleology or that it will be dismissed outright as boring or stupid: "Let us beware of attributing any kind of *striving* to this circuit, a goal: or assessing it in keeping with our needs as *boring*, stupid etc. Certainly the highest degree of unreason occurs in it just as well as the opposite: but it should not be measured according to this, rationality or irrationality are *not* predicates for the universe" (357). While he admits that the thought itself may be highly unreasonable or irrational, this criticism is moot, because the opposite could be asserted with equal merit; the point is that "rational" or "irrational" are not proper predicates for speaking of the universe. He likewise cautions against regarding the "law of this circle"

as something that has become, has developed over time; there
was no origin in chaos, no progression to greater harmony then
to circular motion. We should not seek an analogy for eterna
recurrence in the cycles of the stars, in ebb and flow, night and
day, or the seasons. Fragment 11[158] picks up the refrain: "Let
us beware of teaching such a teaching like a sudden religion! It
must seep in slowly, entire generations have to build on it and
become fertile" (358). Here it is plain that Nietzsche tried to
follow his own advice, both by suppressing the communication of eternal recurrence as he did throughout *JS*, then later
as he based *Z* on this founding idea in such a way that he
dramatized the difficulty of adopting eternal recurrence and
effectively teaching it.

Fragments 11[195]–11[197] are drafts for a planned book
titled "Noon and Eternity," dated 26 August 1881. This book's
subtitle was to be: "Hints toward a new life," and Zarathustra
was to be the book's protagonist, judging by the remainder of
11[195]: "Zarathustra, born at Lake Urmi, left his homeland in
his thirtieth year, went to the province of Aria and wrote the
Zend-Avesta in the ten years of his solitude in the mountains"
(372). Fragment 11[196] underscores the symbolic importance
of noon as the transitional, transformative moment that
Nietzsche used to encapsulate eternity; it is written in the mode
of address that Zarathustra uses to communicate with his disciples and brothers. Fragment 11[197] gives a sketch of the different sections or books of the proposed project, aspects of which
are very similar to 11[141] where a book project was planned
under the title "The recurrence of the same." Here in 11[197] four
books or chapters are planned: the first will be written in the
style of the first movement of Beethoven's Ninth Symphony; it
will deal with the dehumanization of nature, feature the bound
Prometheus, and be written "with the cruelty of Κράτος [Kra
tos]" (372). In a different fragment, the "first book" is supposed
to be a eulogy on the death of God (12[21]). The second book
will have a Mephistophelean tone focusing on the incorpora
tion of experience; the third book should feature "The most

sincere and soaring-over-the-heavens writing that will ever be: 'on the *ultimate happiness of the solitary one*'" as the perfect ego. The fourth and final book will be "Dithyrambically comprehensive" and expressive of the ring of eternity — the brief sketch for this particular book or chapter comes closest to what Nietzsche actually achieved in *Z* III, with its conclusion featuring Zarathustra's symbolic marriage with eternity. These plans are very preliminary, and Nietzsche still does not have Zarathustra's role worked out, but they demonstrate the conceptual linkage between eternal recurrence and Zarathustra as its future teacher.

My next segment of fragments includes notebook N V 7, Nietzsche's annotations in his copy of Emerson essays, and notebook M III 5, all of them written in autumn 1881. Here we also find *Z* fragments and plans, the imperative for humans to reclaim nature, as well as a very innocuous, nondescript entry elevated to fame by Jacques Derrida. In 12[23], Nietzsche illustrates the heightened focus on human beings in proportion to the waning of God: "This loneliest of the lonely, the human being, no longer seeks a God, but a *companion*. This will be the *myth-building* drive of the future. He seeks the *friend of human beings*" (425). Once again faced with a superlative challenge in the absence of God, the "loneliest of the lonely, the human being" will predictably cultivate companions and invest his myth-building capacities in this pursuit. This makes good sense in the context of elevating the human while downplaying the divine, and it also happens to mirror the striving of Zarathustra as a protagonist, who more and more learns to seek and rely on companions when he experiences predictable frustrations as a teacher and prophet.

Fragment 12[34] makes explicit mention of Nietzsche's task, namely, "to reclaim all the beauty and sublimity that we have conferred on things real and imagined as the *property and productivity of human beings* and as their most beautiful ornamentation, most beautiful apology" (427). Blended in this task are the notions of *amor fati* and the renaturalization of human beings, such that whatever had previously flowed off in the human condition instead remains with us, validating us as a species as opposed to drifting off into the metaphysical blue (cf. *JS* §285 "Excelsior!"). Everything we admired and worshipped in the past, he explains, was *our* creation: "These are the *poems* and *paintings* of *primitive* humankind, these 'real' nature scenes — back when one did not yet know how else to write and to paint except by *projecting* something into things. And we have received *this inheritance*" (427). Considering how much vital importance Nietzsche ascribes to creativity in the new era, it is fitting that he would reclaim our creative inheritance in the name of human beings, fitting and comforting too, perhaps, insofar as we engage the new struggles not entirely empty-handed after all.

Tucked between 12[61], a terse plea for the invention of a tragic ballet, and 12[63], a deconstruction of cause and effect by demonstrating that the concepts basically rely on the grammatical logic of "I will," we find 12[62], the fragment rendered famous by Derrida in *Spurs,* a mere five words enclosed in quotation marks: "'I have forgotten my umbrella'" (432). The statement enclosed in quotation marks is a non sequitur, it bears no visible relation to any of the fragments or aphorisms surrounding it, and the fact that it is set off by quotation marks makes it even more inscrutable in terms of meaning. We can only speculate as to what Nietzsche meant when he scrawled this line into his notebook — perhaps he had forgotten his umbrella on one of his walks, perhaps he wished to use the sentence to illustrate a point of grammar, or perhaps he penned this line as a figurative expression indicating he had embarked or would embark unprotected into the rain — we will never know. And that is Derrida's point, as he more or less concludes *Spurs* with this assertion: "To whatever lengths one might carry a conscientious interpretation, the hypothesis that the totality of Nietzsche's text, in some monstrous way, might well be of

he type 'I have forgotten my umbrella' cannot be denied."[38] We
know that *JS* was a favorite text of Derrida's and that he drew
on it extensively for his brilliant but frustrating essay. Nietzsche on
balance was a deconstructor, and surely Derrida learned much
from him in terms of technique, but we do not have to embrace
Derrida's conclusion, with its nihilistic equation of Nietzsche's
text with the absurdity of the forgotten umbrella.

Fragment 12[70] shows us how Nietzsche had the example
of Byron's *Manfred* in mind during the gestation phase of *Z*: "I
want to write the whole thing quite personally and as a kind of
Manfred. From human beings I seek *neither 'praise nor compassion nor help'* — on the contrary I want them '*overwhelmed* by
me'" (433). Zarathustra interacts more effectively with nature
than with human beings, not unlike proud but doomed Manfred, and again like Manfred, Zarathustra is a being caught
between worlds. But while Manfred as a striving, titanic,
Byronic hero shares certain stylistic affinities with Zarathustra,
among them his love for making pithy speeches, Nietzsche's
hero is prophetic; he has a teaching, and although he is not
entirely successful in his teaching, he leaves us impressed with
the urgency of his task.

Fragment 13[19] represents yet another strategy to reclaim our
human inheritance and to potentially validate ourselves as the
meaning of the earth, as Nietzsche struggles to express in the preface to *Z*. Greatness must be vested in us, not in deities whom
we worship and before whom we cower, and faith, too, must be
vested in us, for as Nietzsche warns: "How dangerous it is if faith
in the universality of our self is *lacking*!" (463). Embedded in
this fragment is a sentence that Nietzsche would alter for use in the
preface of *Z*, where we read: "Truly, humans are a filthy torrent.[39] It is necessary to be an ocean in order to be able to absorb
a filthy torrent without becoming polluted. / Behold, I teach

<hr />

38. Derrida, *Spurs*, 133.
39. In their translation of *Z* (*CW* 7), Paul S. Loeb and David F. Tinsley note
that "torrent" translates *Strom*, which Grimm's *Deutsches Wörterbuch* indicates
was used in the nineteenth century to describe larger flowing bodies of water.

you the superhumans: they are this ocean in which your great contempt can drown" (*Z* Preface §3). In fragment 13[19] this sentiment is expressed as follows: "We are the ocean into which all rivers of greatness must flow." Several additional expressions of encouragement to future human beings are found among these fragments, such as 14[3] with its plea to put science on a more courageous footing commensurate with the new era, and 14[14], where Nietzsche warns that wherever we still worship today, we worship the shadow of God whom we have pronounced dead. The final two aphorisms in this section, from notebook M III 5, are early versions of *JS* §125 "The madman."

Two notebooks make up the next segment of fragments that are dated autumn 1881 and December–January 1881–82 respectively. These two notebooks, M III 4a and M III 6a, deal mostly with issues of morality and science, with occasional ‹ fragments. Fragment 15[1] opens by bemoaning how we have simplified things and human beings, how we have given our senses a free pass through superficial observation. This fragment reminds us of the sentiment behind *JS* §285 "Long live physics!" as well as §4 "What preserves the species," with its assertion that our so-called evil drives are as necessary as those we label good. In 15[1] scientists are described as just as flawed, just as prone to error as anyone else: "If individual researchers were not one-sidedly prejudiced in favor of their idea, if they did not want to have *their* entertainment, did not fear being disrespected — ‹ they did not mutually keep each other within bounds through envy and suspicion, then *science would lack its just and brave character*" (474). On balance Nietzsche seems resigned to this tendency among scientists to cloak their own failings in morality, for the work they do is solid enough ("These are good senses, this is good thinking at work in science" [474]) and ultimately, as he concludes this fragment, science "sublimates evil into virtues!" (475). Incidentally, Nietzsche used the first sentences of this fragment for §24 of *BGE*, demonstrating that the roots of his best thinking regarding morality and its tenuous relationship with science go back at least as far as *D* and *JS*.

In fragment 15[49] we have a modern ecological discussion of the fate of living things in the Anthropocene. As usual Nietzsche's point of departure is that God is dead, but from the outset he spells out the implications of this proposition: "Up till now God was responsible for every living thing that emerged" (490). If anyone or anything became afflicted with suffering or frailty, it was all in the hands of God, and such unfortunates could look forward to being liberated from our worldly vale of tears. "But as soon as one no longer believes in God and the destiny of human beings in a hereafter, *humans become responsible for all living things* that arise through suffering and are predestined for displeasure in life. 'Thou shalt not kill' — belongs to an order of things where a God disposes over life and death" (490). Here is a statement of human responsibility for stewardship of the earth after the death of God, and the urgency of our stewardship is underscored by the sixth commandment "Thou shalt not kill." The commandment is reasonable enough as an edict from God, and it may even imply that humans bear the responsibility for human and all other life — but absent the hereafter, absent redemption and eternal reward, "Thou shalt not kill" falls entirely on human shoulders. Nietzsche is otherwise fond of repeating that human beings are generally speaking not responsible, that they should not bear guilt, that existence displays the innocence of becoming; fragment 15[49] implicates humans for maintaining the value of all life.

The first fragment of notebook M III 6a reads: "Continuation of '*Dawn*.' / Genoa, January 1882" (16[1], 498). As deep as we are into the fragments of the *JS* period, having sampled thoughts and thought experiments Nietzsche honed into aphorisms for books including *JS, Z, BGE,* and *GM,* here he is in January of 1882 still working on and thinking in terms of the continuation of *D.* Fragment 16[9] offers a reprise of 13[19] above: "'But where then do all the rivers of what is great and greatest in humans ultimately flow? Are they alone in having no ocean?' — Be this ocean: then one exists" (499). Perhaps

one of the lessons of Nietzsche's unpublished fragments is
fecundity, their capacity for not only inspiring and re-inspiring
Nietzsche to new formulations and locutions, but also their
protean durability. At times when reading the fragments, one
gets the impression Nietzsche felt that if he just continued to
write, just continued to follow the veins of ore wherever they
led him, there was no particular need to worry about where one
book ended and another began; the fragments represent a constant source of material that Nietzsche supplemented whenever
his health permitted, and he shaped this material into books
only when the requisite degree of definition manifested itself.
Another lesson of the fragments demonstrated in particular by
those associated with *JS* is that a greater continuity and coherence exists in Nietzsche's thought than is generally understood;
notwithstanding the fact that there is a distinctly post-*Z* phase,
most of Nietzsche's defining ideas and inclinations arise from
the late 1870s and early 1880s, lending weight to the argument
that his "mature thought" is not limited to the post-*Z* period.

Notebook M III 7 contains excerpts that Nietzsche made
of passages from two Emerson essays in particular, namely
"History" and "Self-Reliance." We know which scientific and
scholarly books he was reading during this period, and we
know he "discovered" Spinoza at this time and was quite taken
with his writings. Emerson is another major influence whose
writings Nietzsche regarded as seminal and kindred. Fragment
17[5] traces the creative instinct to what we are able to usefully extract from history, and Emerson states: "[T]here is *only*
biography. Each human being must know *his* entire lesson"
(504). Nietzsche already had from his study of the ancients a
strong sense of the total life as well as the understanding that
philosophy in particular was the life story of the philosopher;
he elaborated these ideas throughout his writings. When
Emerson writes that each human being must know *his* entire
lesson or task, he elevates the importance of the individual
life as a means to achieving a coherent overview or survey of
history: "This wild savage preposterous There and Then must

be done away with and be replaced by the Now and the Here" (505). Whole lives, whole individuals offer perspective, and through them the otherwise cloudy past is replaced by the present, by the moment that Nietzsche elevates both with *amor fati* and with eternal recurrence.

Throughout *JS*, Nietzsche stressed the importance of things in relation to people and the personal — we must live in higher awareness and affirmation of the closest things and of all things. Emerson's formulation of "intellectual nomadism" must have resonated powerfully with Nietzsche: "Intellectual nomadism is the talent of objectivity or the talent of finding feasts for the eyes everywhere. Every human being, every thing is my discovery, my property: the love that animates him for everything *smooths* his brow" (17[13], 506). The objectivity to which Emerson refers here more closely resembles the objectivity of Schopenhauer, whereby the subject-object relationship is suspended or broken down, allowing the subject to experience objectivity because the principle of individuation is dissolved in aesthetic cognition (art). Certainly Nietzsche was capable of similar formulations throughout *Z*, especially in the more lyrical, Dionysian passages expressing love of life.

With the new stress on human beings in the absence of God, a primary task for the species is the de-deification of nature and the associated renaturalizing of humans through the newly liberated nature. When Emerson maintains that "[h]uman beings cannot violate their nature" (17[29], 508), I take this not as a moral commandment but as an observation regarding the natural durability of human beings of character. If we interpret this statement to mean we cannot damage or harm our nature, the implication is that our human nature-character is highly resilient, or stated otherwise, is massive and implacable, like the whole earth itself as opposed to "mere" mountains. Of course we can also read this statement as an affirmation of the power of human nature — contrary to all appearance, we cannot violate our nature, cannot go against it or subvert it. This is strong praise for human beings, a bold statement of what constitutes us. One is reminded of Nietzsche's exhortations to reclaim humanity's inheritance, to consolidate goodness and greatness in particular in human beings.

Fragment 17[33] sounds as if Nietzsche could have written it, with its deep appreciation for the exceptional human being and what he means for humanity at large. "The actions of kings have instructed the world: they act from a broad point of view: they teach through a colossal symbolism the reverence that is due from man to man" (509). Kings on this view are regarded as archetypes or universals, acting not as particular human beings but from a broader viewpoint; ultimately the symbolism of their actions teaches veneration for human beings. Next, Emerson spells out the mechanism whereby kings earn "joyful loyalty" from the people: "There has always been joyful loyalty to the one who moved among them by laws of his own, made his own value scale of humans and things and overturned the existing one, and *represented* the *law in his person*" (509). The specifically Nietzschean dimension of this defense of kings is the act of embodying one's own law, of creating one's own tablet of values — these are traits Nietzsche ascribes to creators and lawgivers generally. To be sure, we do not find outright apologies for kings as such in Nietzsche — but these same "royal" properties of Emerson's kings Nietzsche ascribes to great human beings such as Napoleon, and he frequently includes these properties in his vision of new philosophers. For that matter, Goethe in his healthy, "classical" style also channeled and championed the universal over the particular, and what all three thinkers share is a profound engagement with what Germans call *Naturphilosophie*.

The last segment of fragments spans the period February to summer of 1882. Among these fragments we find drafts for *Z*, lyrical fragments used in *JS*, various titles for what eventually became *JS*, and even Nietzsche's own arrangement of rubrics for the all-important notebook M III 1. Fragment 18[5] reveals a direct link to *JS* via Emerson: "Emerson says, after my heart: To the poet to the philosopher just as to the saint all things are friendly and sacred, all events useful, all days holy, all human beings divine" (512). These words were used as the motto for the first edition of *JS*. Fragments 19[11]–21[1] reveal several book and chapter titles for what eventually became *JS*, demonstrating that Nietzsche entertained the notion of naming the various books of *JS* before he settled on merely assigning numbers to them. In April 1882, Nietzsche met Lou Salomé and embarked on a new period in his life, one defined both by his experience with her and the onset of *Z*.

Index of Persons

Subject Index

IN NINETEEN VOLUMES

Library of Congress Cataloging-in-Publication Data

Names: Nietzsche, Friedrich Wilhelm, 1844–1900, author. | Del Caro, Adrian
    1952– translator, writer of afterword. | Nietzsche, Friedrich Wilhelm, 1844–
    1900. Fröhliche Wissenschaft. English. | Nietzsche, Friedrich Wilhelm
    1844–1900. Idyllen aus Messina. English. | Nietzsche, Friedrich Wilhelm
    1844–1900. Works. English. 1995 ; v. 6.
Title: The joyful science ; Idylls from Messina ; Unpublished fragments from
    the period of The joyful science (spring 1881–summer 1882) / Friedrich
    Nietzsche ; translated, with an afterword, by Adrian Del Caro.
Other titles: Idylls from Messina
Description: Stanford, California : Stanford University Press, 2022. | Series:
    The complete works of Friedrich Nietzsche ; volume 6 | "Translated from
    Friedrich Nietzsche, Samtliche Werke: Kritische Studienausgabe, ed. Gior-
    gio Colli and Mazzino Montinari, in 15 vols. This book corresponds to
    Vol. 3, pp. 333–663, Vol. 9, pp. 441–687, and Vol. 14, pp. 229–277 and 644–
    659." | Includes bibliographical references and indexes.
Identifiers: LCCN 2022005931 | ISBN 9780804728775 (cloth) | ISBN
    9781503632325 (paperback)
Subjects: LCSH: Philosophy.
Classification: LCC B3312.E5 D45 2022 | DDC 170—dc23/eng/20220224
LC record available at https://lccn.loc.gov/2022005931